Communications in Computer and Information Science 1122

Commenced Publication in 2007
Founding and Former Series Editors:
Phoebe Chen, Alfredo Cuzzocrea, Xiaoyong Du, Orhun Kara, Ting Liu,
Krishna M. Sivalingam, Dominik Ślęzak, Takashi Washio, Xiaokang Yang,
and Junsong Yuan

More information about this series at http://www.springer.com/series/7899

Guojun Wang · Abdulmotaleb El Saddik ·
Xuejia Lai · Gregorio Martinez Perez ·
Kim-Kwang Raymond Choo (Eds.)

Smart City
and Informatization

7th International Conference, iSCI 2019
Guangzhou, China, November 12–15, 2019
Proceedings

 Springer

Editors
Guojun Wang (ID)
Guangzhou University
Guangzhou, China

Xuejia Lai (ID)
Shanghai Jiao Tong University
Shanghai, China

Kim-Kwang Raymond Choo (ID)
The University of Texas at San Antonio
San Antonio, TX, USA

Abdulmotaleb El Saddik
University of Ottawa
Ottawa, ON, Canada

Gregorio Martinez Perez (ID)
University of Murcia
Murcia, Spain

ISSN 1865-0929   ISSN 1865-0937 (electronic)
Communications in Computer and Information Science
ISBN 978-981-15-1300-8   ISBN 978-981-15-1301-5 (eBook)
https://doi.org/10.1007/978-981-15-1301-5

This Springer imprint is published by the registered company Springer Nature Singapore Pte Ltd.
The registered company address is: 152 Beach Road, #21-01/04 Gateway East, Singapore 189721, Singapore

Preface

The 7th International Conference on Smart City and Informatization (iSCI 2019) was held in Guangzhou, China, November 12–15, 2019, and was hosted by School of Computer Science, Guangzhou University.

The previous iSCI conference (iSCI 2018) was also held in Guangzhou, China. The iSCI conference series aims to provide a unique platform for multi-disciplinary researchers and teams, industry solution vendors, and government agencies to exchange innovative ideas, challenges, research results, and solutions, as well as share their research project experiences and success stories.

This year, the conference received 139 submissions from many different countries. All submissions were reviewed by at least three experts with relevant subject matter expertise. Based on the recommendations of the reviewers and subsequent discussions of the Program Committee members, 52 papers were selected for oral presentation at the conference and inclusion in this Springer CCIS volume (i.e., an acceptance rate of 37.4%). In addition to the technical presentations, the program included a number of keynote speeches by world-renowned researchers. We are very grateful to the keynote speakers for their time and willingness to share their expertise with the conference attendees. Thank you!

iSCI 2019 was only possible because of the support and dedication of a large number of individuals and organizations worldwide. There is a long list of people who volunteered their time and energy to put together the conference and deserve special thanks. First and foremost, we would like to offer our gratitude to the Steering Committee Chairs, Prof. Guojun Wang from Guangzhou University, China, and Prof. Albert Zomaya from The University of Sydney, Australia, for guiding the entire process of the conference. We are also deeply grateful to all the Program Committee members for their time and efforts in reading, commenting, debating, and finally selecting the papers.

We would like to offer our gratitude to General Chairs, Prof. Guojun Wang, Prof. Zhong Fan, Prof. Md Zakirul Alam Bhuiyan, and Prof. Aniello Castiglione, for their tremendous support and advice in ensuring the success of the conference. Thanks also go to the Program Chairs: Abdulmotaleb El Saddik, Xuejia Lai, and Gregorio Martinez; Workshop Chairs: Richard Hill, Kouichi Sakurai, and Sabu M. Thampi; Local Organizing Committee Chair: Jianer Chen; Publicity Chairs: Carlos Becker Westphall, Scott Fowler, Peter Mueller, and Wenbin Jiang; and Journal Special Issue Chairs: Georgios Kambourakis, Qin Liu, and Tian Wang.

It is worth noting that iSCI 2019 was jointly held with the 5th International Conference on Dependability in Sensor, Cloud, and Big Data Systems and Applications (DependSys 2019), and we encouraged the conference delegates to also participate in the co-located conference in order to obtain the maximize benefit.

Finally, we thank the participants of iSCI 2019 for contributing to the conference and hope that you found the conference to be a stimulating and exciting forum! Hopefully, you also enjoyed the beautiful city of Guangzhou, China!

November 2019

Guojun Wang
Abdulmotaleb El Saddik
Xuejia Lai
Gregorio Martinez
Kim-Kwang Raymond Choo

Organization

General Chairs

Guojun Wang	Guangzhou University, China
Zhong Fan	Keele University, UK
Md Zakirul Alam Bhuiyan	Fordham University, USA
Aniello Castiglione	University of Naples Parthenope, Italy

Program Chairs

Abdulmotaleb El Saddik	University of Ottawa, Canada
Xuejia Lai	Shanghai Jiao Tong University, China
Gregorio Martinez	University of Murcia, Spain

Program Vice Chairs

Track 1: Internet of Things (IoT) and Smart Sensing

Wenjun Jiang	Hunan University, China
Parag Kulkarni	United Arab Emirates University, UAE
Md. Abdur Razzaque	University of Dhaka, Bangladesh

Track 2: Urban Computing and Big Data

Sancheng Peng	Guangdong University of Foreign Studies, China
Konstantinos Kolias	University of Idaho, USA
Rukhsana Afroz Ruby	Shenzhen University, China

Track 3: Sustainable Industry 4.0

Weizhi Meng	Technical University of Denmark, Denmark
Shigeng Zhang	Central South University, China
Sikder M. Kamruzzaman	Ryerson University, Canada

Track 4: Smart Society Informatization Technologies

Fabio Narducci	University of Naples Parthenope, Italy
Yang Liu	Beijing University of Posts and Telecommunications, China
Changqing Luo	Virginia Commonwealth University, USA

Track 5: Cloud/Edge/Fog Computing for Smart City

Jianhua He	Aston University, UK
Wei Chang	Saint Joseph's University, USA

SK Hafizul Islam   Indian Institute of Information Technology Kalyani,
                                    India

Track 6: Applications for Smart City Informatization

Xuxun Liu   South China University of Technology, China
P. Vijayakumar   University College of Engineering Tindivanam, India
Shaohua Wan   Zhongnan University of Economics and Law, China

Program Committee

Track 1: Internet of Things (IoT) and Smart Sensing

Wenjun Jiang (Chair)   Hunan University, China
Parag Kulkarni (Chair)   United Arab Emirates University, UAE
Md. Abdur Razzaque   University of Dhaka, Bangladesh
  (Chair)
Kamran Arshad   Ajman University, UAE
Md. Mahfuz Bosunia   Hankuk University of Foreign Studies, South Korea
Shuhong Chen   Guangzhou University, China
Yinglong Dai   Hunan Normal University, China
Zhiyong Feng   Tianjin University, China
Oana Geman   University of Suceava, Romania
Muhammad Golam Kibria   University of Liberal Arts Bangladesh, Bangladesh
Zhongzhe Gu   Southeast University, China
Hikaru Inooka   Tohoku University, Japan
Takakazu Ishimatsu   Nagasaki University, Japan
Imad Jawhar   Al Maaref University, Lebanon
Yichao Jin   Toshiba Research Europe Ltd, UK
Jien Kato   Ritsumeikan University, Japan
Sy-Yen Kuo   National Taiwan University, Taiwan
Xin Li   Nanjing University of Aeronautics and Astronautics,
                                    China
Pin Liu   Central South University, China
Qin Liu   Hunan University, China
Zhen Liu   Nagasaki Institute of Applied Science, Japan
Entao Luo   Hunan University of Science and Engineering, China
Nazeeruddin Mohammad   PMU, Saudi Arabia
Pouya Ostovari   San Jose State University, USA
Sancheng Peng   Guangdong University of Foreign Studies, China
Tao Peng   Guangzhou University, China
Fang Qi   Central South University, China
Md. Obaidur Rahman   Dhaka University of Engineering and Technology,
                                    Bangladesh
Fuji Ren   Tokushima University, Japan
Xiangshi Ren   Kochi University of Technology, Japan
Chao Song   University of Science and Technology of China, China

Ovcharuk V. N.	Pacific National University, Russia
Can Wang	Griffith University, Australia
Feng Wang	Tokyo University of Technology, Japan
Ning Wang	Rowan University, USA

Track 2: Urban Computing and Big Data

Sancheng Peng (Chair)	Guangdong University of Foreign Studies, China
Konstantinos Kolias (Chair)	University of Idaho, USA
Rukhsana Afroz Ruby (Chair)	Shenzhen University, China
Atiqur Rahman Ahad	Osaka University, Japan
Saqib Ali	Guangzhou University, China
Flora Amato	University Federico II of Naples, Italy
Muhammad Waseem Ashraf	GC University Lahore, Pakistan
Gagangeet Singh Aujla	Chandigarh University, India
Ranbir Singh Batth	Lovely Professional University, India
Giovanni Cozzolino	University Federico II of Naples, Italy
Yinglong Dai	Hunan Normal University, China
Basem M. ElHalawany	Shenzhen University, China
David Freire Obregon	Universidad de Las Palmas de Gran Canaria, Spain
Xing Gao	University of Memphis, USA
Oana Geman	Stefan cel Mare University of Suceava, Romania
Che-Lun Hung	Providence University, Taiwan
Imad Jawhar	Al Maaref University, Lebanon
Sudhan Jha	Kalinga Institute of Industrial Technology, India
Ala Khalifeh	German Jordanian University, Jordan
Guorui Li	Northeastern University, China
Jianwei Niu	Beihang University, China
Cong Wang	Northeastern University, China
Lirong Wang	Soochow University, China
Tian Wang	Huaqiao University, China
Xiaopeng Wei	Dalian University of Technology, China
Jinglong Wu	Okayama University, Japan
Xi Xiao	Tsinghua University, China
Xiaofei Xing	Guangzhou University, China
Wenyin Yang	Foshan University, China
Junmei Yao	Shenzhen University, China
Jianwei Yin	Zhejiang University, China
Yong Yu	Kakoshima University, Japan
Qiang Zhang	Dalian University of Technology, China
Shanjun Zhang	Kanagawa University, Japan
Shaobo Zhang	Hunan University of Science and Technology, China
Congxu Zhu	Central South University, China
Yongpan Zou	Shenzhen University, China

Track 3: Sustainable Industry 4.0

Weizhi Meng (Chair)	Technical University of Denmark, Denmark
Shigeng Zhang (Chair)	Central South University, China
Sikder M. Kamruzzaman (Chair)	Ryerson University, Canada
Marios Anagnostopoulos	Norwegian University of Science and Technology, Norway
Kai By	Zhejiang University, China
Donghoon Kim	Arkansas State University, USA
Gabor Kiss	Obuda University, Hungary
Konstantinos Kolias	University of Idaho, USA
Marjan Kuchaki Rafsanjani	University of Kerman, Iran
Neeraj Kumar	Thapar Institute of Engineering and Technology, India
Raghvendra Kumar	LNCT Group of College, India
Kevin Leach	University of Michigan, USA
Junghee Lee	Korea University, South Korea
Wenjuan Li	City University of Hong Kong, Hong Kong, China
Xin Li	Nanjing University of Aeronautics and Astronautics, China
Yan Li	Singapore Management University, Singapore
Zhongwen Li	Chengdu University, China
Zhuo Li	Beijing Information Science and Technology University, China
Jing Liao	Hunan University of Science and Technology, China
Anyi Liu	Oakland University, USA
Xuan Liu	Hunan University, China
Jiaqing Luo	The University of Michigan, USA
Weizhi Meng	Technical University of Denmark, Denmark
Raffaele Montella	University of Naples Parthenope, Italy
Khan Muhammad	Sejong University, South Korea
Amandeep Nagpal	Lovely Professional University, India
Fabio Narducci	University of Naples Parthenope, Italy
Anand Nayyar	Duytan University, Vietnam
Pouya Ostovari	Temple University, USA
Reza Meimandi Parizi	Kennesaw State University, USA
Sheng-Lung Peng	National Dong Hwa University, Taiwan
Florin Pop	Politehnica University of Bucharest, Romania
Emil Pricop	Petroleum-Gas University of Ploiesti, Romania
Radu Prodan	Klagenfurt University, Austria
Quan Qian	Shanghai University, China
Jun Shao	Zhejiang Gongshang University, China

Track 4: Smart Society Informatization Technologies

Fabio Narducci (Chair)	University of Naples Parthenope, Italy
Yang Liu (Chair)	Beijing University of Posts and Telecommunications, China
Changqing Luo (Chair)	Virginia Commonwealth University, USA
Irfan Ahmed	Virginia Commonwealth University, USA
Flora Amato	University Federico II of Naples, Italy
Silvio Barra	University of Cagliari, Italy
Paola Barra	University of Salerno, Italy
A. M. A. Elman Barshar	Plymouth State University, USA
Carmen Bisogni	University of Salerno, Italy
Jianrui Chen	Shaanxi Normal University, China
Andrea Corriga	University of Cagliari, Italy
Giovanni Cozzolino	University Federico II of Naples, Italy
Fei Hao	Shaanxi Normal University, China
Lazarus Jegatha Deborah	Anna University, India
Raffaele Montella	University of Naples Parthenope, Italy
Vijay Rao	Institute of System Studies and Analysis, India
Debasis Samanta	Indian Institute of Technology, India
Harmanjot Singh Sandhu	Ryerson University, Canada
Kashif Sharif	Beijing Institute of Technology, China
Pradip Sharma	Seoul National University of Science and Technology, South Korea
Vijender Kr. Solanki	CMR Institute of Technology Hyderabad, India
Le Hoang Son	Vietnam National University Hanoi, Vietnam
Chao Song	University of Science and Technology of China, China
Zhiyuan Tan	Napier University, UK
Bing Tang	Hunan University of Science and Technology, China
Muhhamad Imran Tariq	Superior University Lahore, Pakistan
Shahzadi Tayyaba	The University of Lahore, Pakistan
Weitian Tong	Georgia Southern University, USA
Hafiz Gulfam Ahmad Umar	Ghazi University D.G. Khan, Pakistan
Ioan Ungurean	Stefan cel Mare University of Suceava, Romania
Robin Verma	University of Texas at San Antonio, USA
Can Wang	Griffith University, Australia
Ning Wang	Rowan University, USA
Xioliang Wang	Hunan University of Science and Technology, China
Haitao Xu	Arizona State University, USA
Xu Yuan	University of Louisiana at Lafayette, USA

Track 5: Cloud/Edge/Fog Computing for Smart City

Jianhua He (Chair)	Aston University, UK
Wei Chang (Chair)	Saint Joseph's University, USA
SK Hafizul Islam (Chair)	Indian Institute of Information Technology Kalyani, India

Johari Abdullah	Universiti Malaysia Sarawak, Malaysia
Mudassar Ahmad	National Textile University, Pakistan
Hafiz Farooq Ahmad	King Faisal University, Saudi Aribia
Goutham Reddy Alavalapati	Sejong University, South Korea
Mohammed Arif Amin	Higher Colleges of Technology, UAE
Shehzad Ashraf Chaudhry	International Islamic University Islamabad, Pakistan
Jianhua Chen	Wuhan University, China
Chien-Ming Chen	Harbin Institute of Technology, China
Si Chen	West Chester University, USA
Yong Ding	Guilin University of Electronic Technology, China
Christian Esposito	University of Salerno, Italy
Muhammad Faheem	Abdullah Gul University, Turkey
Debashis Giri	Maulana Abul Kalam Azad University of Technology, India
Mohammad Heydari	Shahid Beheshti University, Iran
Marko Holbl	University of Maribor, Slovenia
Zhen Jiang	West Chester University, USA
Marimuthu K.	VIT University, India
Arijit Karati	National Sun Yat-sen University, Taiwan
Xiong Li	Hunan University of Science and Technology, China
Chun-Ta Li	Tainan University of Technology, Taiwan
Dawei Li	Montclair State University, USA
Fagen Li	University of Electronic Science and Technology of China, China
Khalid Mahmood	COMSATS Institute of Information Technology, Pakistan
Tanmoy Maitra	KIIT University, India
Zahid Mehmood	Shanghai Jiao Tong University Shanghai, China
Dhreerendra Mishra	LNMIIT Jaipur, India
Pouya Ostovari	San Jose State University, USA
Raylin Tso	National Chengchi University, Taiwan
Venkatasamy Sureshkumar	PSG College of Technology, India
Ning Wang	Rowan University, USA
Fan Wu	Xiamen Institute of Technology, Huaqiao University, China
Longfei Wu	Fayetteville State University, USA
Zhiqian Xu	Royal Holloway University of London, UK

Track 6: Applications for Smart City Informatization

Xuxun Liu (Chair)	South China University of Technology, China
P. Vijayakumar (Chair)	University College of Engineering Tindivanam, India
Shaohua Wan (Chair)	Zhongnan University of Economics and Law, China
Aniello Castiglione	University of Salerno, Italy
Cheng Guo	Dalian University of Technology, China
Jinguang Han	University of Surrey, UK

Debiao He	Wuhan University, China
Ying Hu	Guangzhou University, China
Sohail Jabbar	National Textile University, Pakistan
Alinani Karim	Hunan University of Science and Technology, China
Hassaan Khaliq	National University of Sciences and Technology, Pakistan
Ahsan Latif	University of Agriculture, Pakistan
Hongbo Li	South China Agricultural University, China
Xiong Li	Hunan University of Science and Technology, China
Weizhi Meng	Technical University of Denmark, Denmark
Gordhan Das Menghwar	Sindh Agriculture University, Pakistan
Mujahid Mohsin	National University of Sciences and Technology, Pakistan
Md Asri Ngadi	Universiti Teknologi Malaysia, Malaysia
Jianbing Ni	University of Waterloo, Canada
Paula Prata	University of Beira Interior, Portugal
Lianyong Qi	Qufu Normal University, China
Samina Rajper	Shah Abdul Latif University, Pakistan
Charnsak Srisawatsakul	Ubon Ratchathani Rajabhat University, Thailand
Zeyu Sun	Luoyang University of Science and Technology, China
Chao Tong	Beihang University, China
Qian-Hong Wu	Beihang University, China
Bing Xiong	Changsha University of Science and Technology, China
Qiuliang Xu	Shandong University, China
Xiaolong Xu	Nanjing University of Science and Technology, China
Tran Viet Xuan Phuong	University of Wollongong, Australia
Liang Xue	University of Waterloo, Canada
Lei Yang	South China University of Technology, China
Fangguo Zhang	Sun Yat-sen University, China
Zijian Zhang	Beijing Institute of Technology, China
Yanqi Zhao	Shaanxi Normal University, China
Yunlei Zhao	Fudan University, China

Workshop Chairs

Richard Hill	University of Huddersfield, UK
Kouichi Sakurai	Kyushu University, Japan
Sabu M. Thampi	Indian Institute of Information Technology and Management - Kerala, India

Local Organizing Committee Chair

Jianer Chen	Guangzhou University, China

Publicity Chairs

Carlos Becker Westphall   Federal University of Santa Catarina, Brazil
Scott Fowler   Linkoping University, Sweden
Peter Mueller   IBM Zurich Research Laboratory, Switzerland
Wenbin Jiang   Huazhong University of Science and Technology, China

Publication Chairs

Tao Peng   Guangzhou University, China
Fang Qi   Central South University, China

Journal Special Issue Chairs

Georgios Kambourakis   University of the Aegean, Greece
Qin Liu   Hunan University, China
Tian Wang   Huaqiao University, China

Registration Chairs

Xiaofei Xing   Guangzhou University, China
Pin Liu   Central South University, China

Conference Secretariat

Wenyin Yang   Foshan University, China

Steering Committee

Guojun Wang (Chair)   Guangzhou University, China
Albert Zomaya (Chair)   The University of Sydney, Australia
Michael Batty   University College London, UK
Md Zakirul Alam Bhuiyan   Fordham University, USA
Azzedine Boukerche   University of Ottawa, Canada
Jianer Chen   Guangzhou University, China
Kim-Kwang Raymond Choo   University of Texas at San Antonio, USA
Zhong Fan   Keele University, UK
Scott Fowler   Linkoping University, Sweden
Geoffrey Fox   Indiana University, USA
Minyi Guo   Shanghai Jiao Tong University, China
Song Guo   The Hong Kong Polytechnic University, Hong Kong, China
Lajos Hanzo   University of Southampton, UK
Richard Hill   University of Huddersfield, UK

Contents

Urban Computing and Big Data

Smart Society Informatization Technologies

Cloud/Edge/Fog Computing for Smart City

Applications for Smart City Informatization

Cyberspace Security

Blockchain and Its Applications

Internet of Things (IoT) and Smart Sensing

Noise Attenuation by Sonic Crystal Window

Hsiao Mun Lee[1,2], Wensheng Luo[3], Long Bin Tan[2], Kian Meng Lim[2], Jinlong Xie[3(✉)], and Heow Pueh Lee[2]

[1] Center for Research on Leading Technology of Special Equipment, School of Mechanical and Electric Engineering, Guangzhou University, 230 Wai Huan Xi Road, Guangzhou 510006, People's Republic of China
[2] Department of Mechanical Engineering, National University of Singapore, 9 Engineering Drive 1, Singapore 117576, Singapore
[3] School of Mechanical and Electric Engineering, Guangzhou University, 230 Wai Huan Xi Road, Guangzhou 510006, People's Republic of China
jlxie@gzhu.edu.cn

Abstract. The main objective of this study is to develop a novel noise attenuation device which can resolve the conflict of noise and ventilation issues faced by conventional glass or louver windows. Therefore, a sonic crystal (SC) window was designed and was tested in a reverberation room. The effects of the jagged flap on the acoustical performance of the SC window were investigated too in the present studies. In the narrow frequency range of 700 Hz to 1400 Hz, the SC window was able to attenuate 4.1 dBA of white noise which accompanied by 40% of wind speed reduction if compared with the case of without window. From the experimental results, we can conclude that the SC window can improve the sustainability of urban environment due to the good balancing of noise mitigation, natural ventilation and daylighting provided by the window.

Keywords: Sonic crystal · Noise attenuation · Urban environment · Natural ventilation · Window

1 Introduction

With the rapid growth of the number of population and technologies, environmental noise becomes one of the primary sources of urban pollution that restricts the quality of the urban living environment. Environmental noise pollution impacts high population density areas by negatively affecting residents daily life such as work, sleep and study. Therefore, the control of environmental noise especially traffic and construction noises have become a critical issue. Effectively attenuation of environmental noise is a complex task and sonic crystal (SC) has been shown to be an efficient way for mitigating environmental noise. SC is defined as periodic distribution of sound scatterers in fluid to inhibit sound transmission by their acoustic band gaps [3]. The destructive Bragg interference is used to explain the phenomenon of band gaps. The distance between adjacent

© Springer Nature Singapore Pte Ltd. 2019
G. Wang et al. (Eds.): iSCI 2019, CCIS 1122, pp. 3–11, 2019.
https://doi.org/10.1007/978-981-15-1301-5_1

scatterers is presented by a lattice constant (α) and is used to determine the center frequency (f_c) of the band gap:

$$f_c = \frac{nc}{2\alpha \sin \theta},$$ (1)

where n is an integer determining the reflection order, c is the speed of sound and θ is the scattering angle.

The noise attenuation ability of SC has been widely studied by researchers over the world. Krynkin et al. [8] studied the performance of the SC noise barrier which composed of infinitely long multi-resonant composite scatterers through experimental and theoretical methods. They claimed that with the use of the resonating elements in the SCs, sound mitigation could be obtained in the low frequency range while at the same time, the SCs still preserving the existence of the Bragg band gap. Sound propagation through a 15 m deep vegetation belt along a road was simulated by Van Renterghem et al. [11] using three-dimensional finite-difference time-domain method. Their results showed that the noise attenuation effect of a vegetation belt could compete with the transmission loss obtained by a classical noise barrier with a height of 1–1.5 m in a non-refracting atmosphere. Sound transmissions through arrays of identical cylinders at filling fractions of 13% and 50% with their axes perpendicular to the ground were studied by Taherzadeh et al. [13] through experimental method. For filling fractions between 13% and 50%, their results showed that the deliberate introduction of perturbations in cylinder location could result in a significantly enhanced broadband transmission loss. Lagarrigue et al. [9] investigated the acoustic transmission coefficient of a resonant SC made of hollow bamboo rods by experimental and theoretical methods. They concluded that a clear transmission band gap could be produced by a SC made from a natural material with some irregularities.

The acoustical performance of a noise reducing device which combined SCs with a conventional noise barrier was evaluated by Koussa et al. [7] using two-dimensional (2D) Boundary Element Method (BEM). They concluded that significant amount of transmission loss could be obtained by the device due to the addition of the SC elements for middle and high frequency ranges of road traffic noise. Some SC acoustic screens formed by cylindrical scatterers embedded in air were designed by Castineira-Ibanez et al. [1] to inhibit the transmission of traffic noise in cities. The acoustic efficiency of artificial cylindrical SC barrier placed near road was studied by Jean and Defrance [6] using 2D BEM approach. They concluded that a 50 m wide barrier could reduce traffic noise by about 10 dB(A) at night, but could also cause an increment in the noise level during day time. Gupta et al. [5] successfully designed a radial SC in polar coordinate based on Webster horn equation where it abled to reduce divergent sound source up to 30 dB. The sound insulation index (SI) of cylindrical SCs arranged in a square lattice according to EN 1793-6 standard was investigated by Morandi et al. [10] using experimental and numerical methods. Significant SI value at the first Bragg band gap and negative value of SI at the second band gap were found in their studies. The performance of a SC acoustic barrier with triangular array of resonant absorbent scatterers was tested by Sanchez-Perez et al. [12]. They claimed that their SC acoustic barrier is a good alternative to the current conventional noise barrier. Cavalieri et al. [2] developed a three-dimensional (3D) locally resonant sonic crystal in order to reduce railway noise. They claimed that the system was able to obtain average IL up to 16.8 dB from 350 Hz to 5000 Hz.

It can be seen that the reported studies on SCs were mostly confined to SC noise barrier while there is no study relates to the implementation of SCs into a household use window. Therefore, the main objective of the current effort is to use experimental methods to investigate the efficiency of a SC window in mitigating noise. In addition, the ventilation performance of the SC window will be investigated too in the present studies. SC window permits noise attenuation while it is fully opened compared to conventional glass or louver windows which need to be fully closed to prevent propagation of noise from outdoor to indoor. Therefore, SC window is more suitable for residential use.

2   Experimental Set-Up

2.1   Noise Measurement

The SC window was tested in between two reverberant rooms. The measuring equipment consisted of a Bruel & Kjaer (B&K) power amplifier (model 2734-A), a Larson Davis Omni-source loudspeaker (model BAS001) and a B&K sound level meter (model 2238) as shown in Fig. 1(a) and (b). White noise was generated by the loudspeaker and the sound level meter was placed at nine different positions as shown in Fig. 2(a). The SC window consisted of eight rows and four columns of hollow rectangular aluminum tubes as shown in Fig. 1(c). Aluminum was selected to fabricate the prototype for ease of fabrication and installation in current stage compared to Perspex. Perspex can be used to fabricate the SC window during the production stage in order to provide natural daylighting in a residential unit due to its transparency characteristic. The distances between the centres of adjacent aluminum tubes were 0.09075 m, 0.0766 m and 0.06535 m which were estimated to produce f_c of 1890 Hz, 2239 Hz and 2624 Hz, respectively, from Eq. 2. Helmholtz resonators were incorporated in the SC window to enhance the noise mitigation in lower frequency region where its slit sizes were 0.003 m, 0.0033 m, and 0.0058 m and 0.0113 m which were estimated to give resonant frequencies (f_r) of 719 Hz, 932 Hz, 1145 Hz and 1325 Hz, respectively, using [4]:

$$f_r = \frac{c}{2\pi} \sqrt{\frac{A}{V(l + 0.9t)}}, \tag{2}$$

where A is the cross-sectional area of the resonator opening, V is the volume of the resonator, l is the length of neck and t is the slit size. These slit sizes were selected in the present studies in order to attenuate the traffic noise which normally centralized at 1000 Hz [13]. Louver blades were attached to the SC window in order to prevent the penetration of water into the room during thunderstorm. In addition, a jagged flap was attached to the edge of the louver blades (see

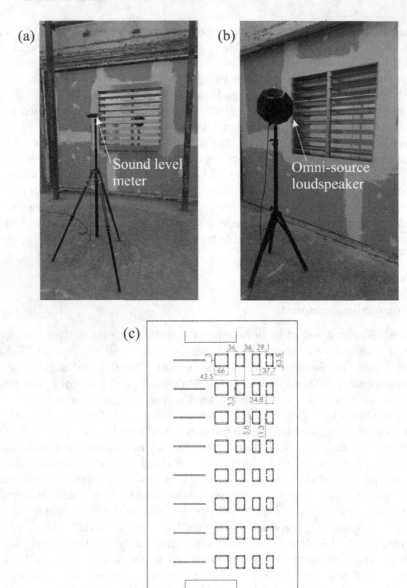

Fig. 1. (a) Sound level meter at the back side of the SC window (b) omni-source loudspeaker at the front side of the SC window (c) geometry of the SC window (side view, units in mm).

Fig. 2(b) and (c)) in order to reduce the strength of possible diffracted noise through the gap in between two rows of SCs.

All data were recorded using sound level meter from 100 Hz to 5000 Hz with interval of 50 Hz and were analysed using M+P VibPilot SO Analyzer. Three

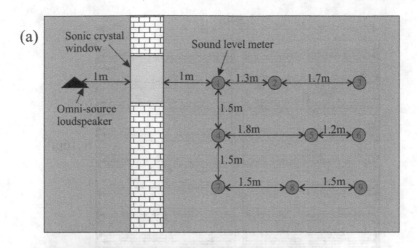

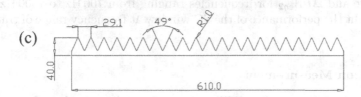

Fig. 2. (a) Schematic diagram of the experimental set-up (top view) (b) louver blade with attached jagged flap (c) dimension of the jagged flap (unit in mm).

samples were recorded and averaged for each data set where the sampling time for each sample is 1 min. Sound pressure levels (SPLs) for all experiments without SC window were also measured in order to obtain the IL which is given by:

$$IL = SPL_{\text{without SC window}} - SPL_{\text{without SC window}}. \tag{3}$$

Equivalent SPL (LA_{eq}) was calculated for each position by taking into account contribution of noise from each frequency which was given by:

$$LA_{eq} = 10 \times log(\sum_{i=1}^{n} t_i 10^{(\frac{SPL_i}{10})}), \tag{4}$$

where t_i is the fraction of the time period that the noise has a sound level of SPL_i. After that, reduction of LA_{eq} (ΔLA_{eq}) was obtained by:

$$\Delta LA_{eq} = LA_{eq(\text{without SC window})} - LA_{eq(\text{with SC window})}. \tag{5}$$

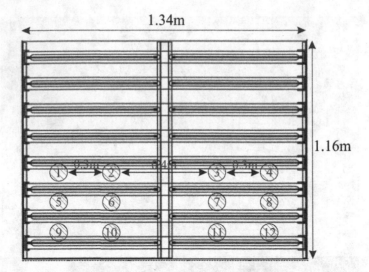

Fig. 3. Positions of anemometer at the back side of the SC window for ventilation measurement.

Two ΔLA_{eq} were calculated for each data set where they were ΔLA_{eq1} for whole frequency range and ΔLA_{eq2} for frequencies ranging from 700 Hz to 1400 Hz in order to highlight the performance of the SC window at frequency range of traffic noise.

2.2 Ventilation Measurement

For ventilation measurement, two ETL 26 in. industrial heavy duty fans were placed at the central and at 0.25 m away from the front side of the SC window. A Lutron (LM-800) anemometer was placed at 12 different positions at the back side of SC window to measure the wind velocity as shown in Fig. 3. Five samples were measured and averaged at each position where the sampling time for each sample is 1 min. Final wind speeds at different opening angles of louver blades (0° means fully opened, 30° and 60°) were obtained by averaging the wind speeds that obtained from twelve different positions. The experiment was repeated for the case of without SC window in order to obtain the amount of wind velocity reduction due to the existence of the window.

3 Results and Discussion

Figure 4 shows the comparison of IL for the SC window with and without jagged flap at different receiver positions when louver blades are fully opened. Only four instead of nine receiver positions are presented here for brevity. Generally, the IL obtained by the SC window with jagged flap is higher than that by without jagged flap at all receiver positions for whole frequency range. This phenomenon

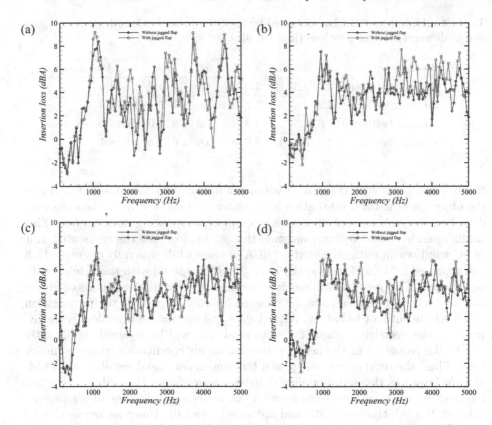

Fig. 4. Comparison of IL for the SC window with and without jagged flap at different receiver positions when louver blades are fully opened. (a) Position 1 (b) position 4 (c) position 6 (d) position 8.

can be explained by the fact where jagged flap is effective in reducing the strength of the noise which diffracts through the gaps in between two rows of SCs. At receiver position 1 for the case of without jagged flap, maximum IL can be found at 1150 Hz which is about 8.4 dBA. This frequency corresponds to the f_r produced by Helmholtz resonators. It can be observed that for frequencies ranging from 100 Hz to 600 Hz at all receiver positions, the IL is negative due to the limitation of the SC window where it is not able to attenuate noise below 719 Hz as lower values of f_c and f_r require bigger space between adjacent SCs and bigger resonator volume, respectively, which are not practical for the design of the SC window. By overall, the SC window without jagged flap obtains 1.6 dBA and 2.0 dBA of noise reduction for whole and narrow frequency ranges, respectively, as shown in Table 1. With the attachment of the jagged flap, the SC window is able to obtain 3.8 dBA and 4.1 dBA of noise reduction for whole and narrow frequency ranges, respectively.

The ventilation measurement results show that the average wind velocity passes through the SC window when the louver blades are fully opened is reduced

Table 1. ΔLA_{eq1} and ΔLA_{eq2} obtained by the SC window with and without jagged flap at different receiver positions (units in dBA).

Position	1	2	3	4	5	6	7	8	9	Average
ΔLA_{eq1} (without)	1.1	1.3	1.8	2.0	1.5	1.5	1.7	1.8	1.8	1.6
ΔLA_{eq1} (with)	4.3	3.8	3.3	3.7	3.1	3.9	4.7	3.4	4.0	3.8
ΔLA_{eq2} (without)	1.6	2.5	1.9	2.3	1.8	1.9	1.8	2.0	2.0	2.0
ΔLA_{eq2} (with)	4.3	5.4	4.0	3.8	4.0	3.6	4.0	3.5	3.9	4.1

by 40% compared with the case of without window. The easiest way to achieve the objective of natural ventilation in a residential unit is to fully open the window, however, this cans conflict with attempting of reducing noise ingress. This conflict can be solved by implementing the SC window into the residential unit as SC window can mitigate about 4.1 dBA of noise while it is fully opened which accompanied by 40% of wind speed reduction if compared with the case of without window. This result is still much better than the conventional glass or louver windows where they need to be fully closed in order to prevent the propagation of noise from outdoor to indoor. With the natural ventilation provided by the SC window, the electricity usage of a residential unit will be reduced significantly due to the reduction of the need for turning on air conditioner during summer time. Thus, the total energy usage of a building is decreased significantly which in turn improves the sustainability of urban environment. In addition, by taking opening angle of louver blades at 0° as reference, velocities of air passing through the SC window at 30° and 60° are 0.7 and 0.4 times as low as that of 0°, respectively.

4   Conclusions

The main objective of this study is to establish an innovative SC window in the form of periodic array of aluminum panels to replace the conventional glass or louver windows. Acoustical and ventilation performances of the SC window were examined in a reverberation room. It is found that the SC window with jagged flap was able to attenuate 4.1 dBA of noise at frequency range of traffic noise when the louver blades were fully opened. The experimental results also showed that the jagged flap was able to reduce the strength of the diffracted noise. When the louver blades were fully opened, the average wind velocity passed through the SC window was reduced by 40% compared with the case of without window. From this study, we can conclude that the SC window can improve the sustainability of urban environment due to the good balancing of noise mitigation, natural ventilation and daylighting provided by the window.

Acknowledgements. This work was supported by Singapore Ministry of National Development and National Research Foundation [L2NICCFP1-2013-8]; National Natural Science Foundation of China [51908142] and Natural Science Foundation of Guangdong Province [2018A030313878].

References

1. Castineira-Ibanez, S., Rubio, C., Vicente Sanchez-Perez, J.: Environmental noise control during its transmission phase to protect buildings. Design model for acoustic barriers based on arrays of isolated scatterers. Build. Environ. **93**(2), 179–185 (2015). https://doi.org/10.1016/j.buildenv.2015.07.002
2. Cavalieri, T., Cebrecos, A., Groby, J.P., Chaufour, C., Romero-Garcia, V.: Three-dimensional multiresonant lossy sonic crystal for broadband acoustic attenuation: application to train noise reduction. Appl. Acoust. **146**, 1–8 (2019). https://doi.org/10.1016/j.apacoust.2018.10.020
3. Dowling, J.: Sonic band-structure in fluids with periodic density variations. J. Acoust. Soc. Am. **91**(5), 2539–2543 (1992). https://doi.org/10.1121/1.402990
4. Everest, F.A., Pohlmann, K.C.: Master Handbook of Acoustics, 5th edn. Mc Graw Hill, New York (2009)
5. Gupta, A., Lim, K.M., Chew, C.H.: Design of radial sonic crystal for sound attenuation from divergent sound source. Wave Motion **55**, 1–9 (2015). https://doi.org/10.1016/j.wavemoti.2015.01.002
6. Jean, P., Defrance, J.: Sound propagation in rows of cylinders of infinite extent: application to sonic crystals and thickets along roads. Acta Acustica United Acustica **101**(3), 474–483 (2015). https://doi.org/10.3813/AAA.918844
7. Koussa, F., Defrance, J., Jean, P., Blanc-Benon, P.: Acoustical efficiency of a sonic crystal assisted noise barrier. Acta Acustica United Acustica **99**(3), 399–409 (2013). https://doi.org/10.3813/AAA.918621
8. Krynkin, A., Umnova, O., Chong, A., Taherzadeh, S., Attenborough, K.: Sonic crystal noise barriers made of resonant elements. In: Proceedings of 20th International Congress on Acoustics, ICA. Sydney, Australia, August 2010
9. Lagarrigue, C., Groby, J.P., Tournat, V.: Sustainable sonic crystal made of resonating bamboo rods. J. Acoust. Soc. Am. **133**(1), 247–254 (2013). https://doi.org/10.1121/1.4769783
10. Morandi, F., Cesaris, S.D., Garai, M.: Experimental evidence of band gaps in periodic structures. In: 10th European Congress and Exposition on Noise Control Engineering Maastricht, pp. 2363–2366. Maastricht, Netherlands (2015)
11. Renterghem, T.V., Botteldooren, D., Verheyen, K.: Road traffic noise shielding by vegetation belts of limited depth. J. Sound Vib. **331**(10), 2404–2425 (2012). https://doi.org/10.1016/j.jsv.2012.01.006
12. Sanchez-Perez, J.V., Michavila, C.R., Garcia-Raffi, L.M., Romero-Garcia, V., Castineira-Ibanez, S.: Noise certification of a sonic crystal acoustic screen designed using a triangular lattice according to the standards en 1793(-1;-2;-3):1997. In: 10th European Congress and Exposition on Noise Control Engineering, pp. 2358–2361. Maastricht, Netherlands (2015)
13. Taherzadeh, S., Bashir, I., Attenborough, K.: Aperiodicity effects on sound transmission through arrays of identical cylinders perpendicular to the ground. J. Acoust. Soc. Am. **132**(4), EL323–EL328 (2012). https://doi.org/10.1121/1.4751991

Cabin Noise of Metro Systems in Various Cities

Heow Pueh Lee[1,2(✉)] ⓘ, Kian Meng Lim[1,2] ⓘ, and Saurabh Garg ⓘ

[1] National University of Singapore, Singapore 117576, Singapore
mpeleehp@nus.edu.sg
[2] National University of Singapore (Suzhou) Research Institute,
Suzhou 215125, Jiangsu, China

Abstract. Metro systems are typically regarded as a means to transport a large number of commuters in a relatively short duration, reduce reliance on cars, and as a means to mitigate traffic congestion, reduced air and noise pollution for a better living environment. Most of the metro systems are either underground in densely populated area to free up the land on the surface for other economic developments or open space for enhancing the quality of life. Some metro systems are also on elevated viaducts especially for the outskirts of cities or in cities for overcoming congested traffic junctions. Noise exposure in metro cabin has become a concern with increased use and extended networks of metro systems as commuters may be exposed to the noise for an extended duration. In this study, the measurement of the cabin noise of various metro systems around the world was carried out using a smartphone with the built in microphones calibrated against a typical type 1 sound level meter using our in-housed developed app. The cabin noise of metro systems for five cities in Asia and Europe was measured on various occasions. The cities are London, Prague, Paris, Singapore and Taipei. We found that the average noise level for all metros were well below 85 dB and therefore traveling on these metro systems for eight hours was not likely to exceed the maximum duration of noise exposure under the National Institute for Occupational Safety and Health (NIOSH) guidelines. We also found that average sound pressure level in dBC was about 6 dB higher when compared to dBA. This indicates the presence of low-frequency components below 200 Hz.

Keywords: Metro systems · Smartphone · Cabin noise

1 Introduction

Metro systems are typically regarded as a means to move a large number of commuters in a relatively short duration, reduce reliance on cars and therefore as a means to mitigate traffic congestion and therefore reduced air and noise pollution for a better living environment. Metro systems in some countries re referred to as subways, U-Bahns or Undergrounds. Most of the metro systems are either underground in densely populated area to free up the land on the ground for other economic developments or open space for enhancing the quality of life. It could also be on elevated tracks in less populated outskirt areas of cities or in densely populated city for avoiding congested roads and traffic junctions. It is also deemed as a means to provide commuters with

© Springer Nature Singapore Pte Ltd. 2019
G. Wang et al. (Eds.): iSCI 2019, CCIS 1122, pp. 12–22, 2019.
https://doi.org/10.1007/978-981-15-1301-5_2

efficient and affordable transportation and even green transportation as the trains can be powered by electricity generated by green energy. The first metro system is the London Underground which was opened as an "underground railway" in 1863 and transformed into an electrified underground line in 1890. A study by Gonzalez-Navarro and Turner [1] found that most subway systems around the world were constructed since the 1970s and '80s. In total, the report identified 7,886 operational subway stations and 10,672 km of subways across 138 cities as of 2010. Commuting by metro is a salient feature in many cities around the world. This trend is likely to continue and even accelerated with the planned construction of metro systems in many smaller cities in China and many developing countries. For example, Xiamen, a city in China with approximately four million population, has its first metro line (line 1) operational in December 2017 with 24 stations and 31.5 km. Another example is Suzhou city with approximately 6.7 million population. It has three lines currently in operation, namely line 1 with 24 stations and 25.7 km, line 2 with 25 stations and 40.4 km and line 4 with 38 stations and 52.8 km. There are another two lines currently under construction, namely line 3 with 31 stations and 45.2 km, and line 5 with 35 stations and 45.1 km. These are just two examples reflecting the heavy investment in metro infrastructures in many developed and developing countries.

A study by Gershon et al. [2] on the New York subway reported that the average noise level measured on the subway platforms was 86 dBA. The maximum levels of 106, 112, and 89 dBA were measured on subway platforms, inside subway cars, and at bus stops, respectively. For the subway car, the mean dBA was found to be 94.5 dBA. They concluded that the noise levels in subway environments had the potential to exceed recommended exposure guidelines from the World Health Organization (WHO) and U. S. Environmental Protection Agency (EPA), given sufficient exposure duration. In fact based on the WHO guideline, the maximum exposure duration for a mean noise level of 94 dB was one hour and for 95 dB was 48 min. The finding implied that a passenger would have exceeded the maximum exposure limit to noise by remaining in the train for more than an hour. This study has highlighted the potential health risk to many commuters on metro systems. This study in 2006 was touted to be the first scientific metro noise assessment in over 30 years, and believed to be one of only two papers published on New York City subway noise; the last one was in the 1930s. There were also reported studies on the annoyance of subway cabin noise on train conductors [3]. The results of sound level meter showed that the mean Leq was 73.0 dBA ±8.7 dBA and the dosimetry mean measured Leq was 82.1 dBA ±6.8 dBA. 80% of conductors were very annoyed or annoyed by noise in their work place. 53.9% of conductors reported that noise affected their work performance and 63.5% reported that noise causes that they lose their concentration. The cabin noise would also affect speech privacy and annoyance. Jeon et al. [4] reported that the annoyance would increase significantly if the background noise, mainly the cabin noise was above 63 dBA. A news report by BBC in 2004 [5] reported that Parts of London Underground were so noisy that they could damage people's hearing. The report cited a study by Professor Deepak Prasher, Head of University College London's Audiology unit, who took the measurements on four Victoria Line journeys. Professor Prasher found that the noise peaked at 118 dBA and found the average level was between 88 and 89 dBA.

There are indeed very limited reported study on the characteristics of cabin noise of metro systems in terms of sound level, let alone the frequency content. The reported studies of the two largest subway systems in the world, namely the New York City metro system and the London Underground have demonstrated the potential health risk of noise exposure inside a metro cabin. Before the invention of smartphone, the common activities on a train or a subway was the reading of magazines or newspapers. The increased use of smartphone in a metro cabin for online chatting, reading and browsing of web content, playing of online games, and voice communication has also resulted in the focus on aural comfort in metro cabins. The present study is motivated by these factors for examining the cabin noise of various metro systems around the world.

2 Methods

In this study, the measurement of the cabin noise of various metro systems around the world was carried out using a smartphone with the built in microphones calibrated using our in-housed developed app. The details of the statistical method that has been used for accurately calibrating a typical smartphone microphone against a reference type 1 microphone can be found in our earlier reported work [6]. We showed that for over 7-hours of environmental noise data, the proposed method has an accuracy of ±0.9 dB for 99.7% of the measurements. This is a significant improvement over the existing reported methods or apps for noise measurement using smartphones. We have developed an Android app named as "*NoiseExplorer*" for measuring Sound Pressure Level (SPL) using smartphones. The app also keeps track of the minimum SPL, the maximum SPL, and the continuous equivalent SPL for the current session in log files. The user can optionally choose to record the audio as uncompressed WAV files. Figure 1 shows the screenshots of the two main screens and settings screen of "*NoiseExplorer*". The user also has the option of capturing the GPS data when the cabin noise is measured. However, the GPS data might be lost when the train is in a tunnel or in areas where GPS coverage is not ideal. The smartphones that have been used for the present study includes Samsung S4, S7 and S8.

Fig. 1. The screenshots of *"NoiseExplorer"*.

The smartphone can be used as a platform for crowd sourcing of in the near future where commuters on various metro systems with their calibrated smartphones could measure and upload the data collected to a server. Crowd sourcing provides a unique opportunity of collecting large amount of data in a short time which is infeasible with a small research team located in one country. With sufficient data, we could then benchmark the cabin noise of many different train systems around the world. The present study is the first step towards such a grand scenario for the future. There is also a potential for the cabin noise to be used for condition monitoring of the metro train systems for preventive maintenance.

3   Results and Discussion

The cabin noise of metro systems for five cities around the world was measured on various occasions. The cities are London, Prague, Paris, Singapore and Taipei. These are metro systems in Asia and Europe. A summary of the number of trips, total duration of sound recorded, the various indicators of sound levels are presented in Table 1 for easy comparison. The variation in cabin noise level could be due to many different factors such as the design of the train, the wheel and track condition, changes in the flow patterns around the train when the train is in a tunnel or on open track, the shape and size of the tunnel, design of elevated viaduct which may affect the train track interaction, train speed, interior designs and materials, train load and many other factors. Some train cabins may not be fully enclosed with open side windows for ventilation. The trains or rolling stocks are usually in different designs and specifications. Some metro lines may run on elevated surface track for part of the journal but underground when it enters into the more densely populated city. An example is the Singapore east-west line where the GPS data is available when the train is on elevated track at the two ends but unavailable when the train is underground for the part within the central business district. LASeq (dBA) is the A-weighted average sound pressure level with slow time response for the whole duration of measurement. LASmax (dBA) is the A-weighted instantaneous maximum sound pressure level. Similarly, LASeq and LASmax (dBC) are defined similarly but using C-frequency weighting. As there are different number of trips, the Max LASeq (dBA) and Max LASeq (dBC) are the maximum value of LASeq and LCSeq, respectively, among all the trips of that city. These values indicate the average SPL for the loudest trip for each city.

Table 1. Comparison of cabin noise of various city metro systems. City 1: London, City 2: Prague, City 3: Paris, City 4, Singapore, City 5, Taipei.

City	No of trips	Duration (h:m:s)	LASeq (dBA)	Max LASeq (dBA)	LASmax (dBA)	LASeq (dBC)	Max LASeq (dBC)	LASmax (dBC)
1	25	00:35:47	82.0	87.4	97.6	89.0	93.2	101.1
2	39	00:46:45	79.9	85.0	92.5	86.4	91.2	97.0
3	27	00:26:00	80.8	89.9	99.6	88.2	94.9	104.5
4	145	03:46:02	79.1	86.4	95.2	84.2	89.4	97.9
5	171	04:32:57	74.6	88.4	100.4	83.4	92.0	99.8

It can be seen from Table 1 that the largest LASmax is for one of the trains in Taipei whereas the largest LCSmax is for one of the trains in Paris. The two of the noisiest trips are from Maison Blanche to Le Kremlin-Bicêtre in Paris on metro line 7 with LASeq of 89.9 dBA and from Zhongshan to Shuanglian in Taipei metro red line with LASeq of 88.4 dBA. The LASeq for all the metro systems are all well below 85 dB. Therefore traveling on any of these metro systems for eight hours is not likely to exceed the maximum duration of noise exposure under the National Institute for Occupational Safety and Health (NIOSH) guidelines. NIOSH has stipulated the maximum exposure duration for different sound pressure level (SPL) in A-weighted measurement. For example, a person can withstand an environment with equivalent noise level at 85 dBA for eight hours, 88 dBA for four hours, 91 dBA for two hours and 94 dBA for an hour. The allowable duration would be reduced by half with every 3 dBA increment in the sound level.

There is significant difference of more than 6 dB between the equivalent value of sound pressure level in dBA and the corresponding value in dBC for all metro systems, indicating a presence of low frequency components of below 200 Hz in all metro systems. Figures 2 and 3 show the spectrogram and average frequency spectrum, respectively, in both dBA and dBC for an underground trip on the Circle line in Singapore. There are two distinct peaks 96 and 144 Hz for the trip.

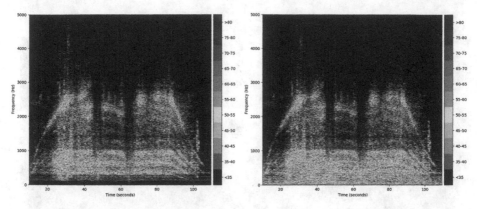

Fig. 2. Spectrogram in dBA (left) and dBC (right) for an underground trip on Circle line in Singapore.

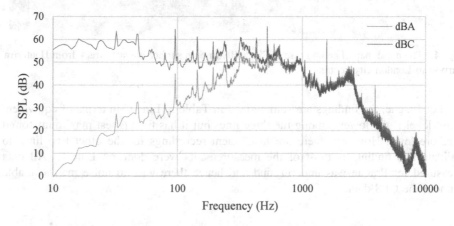

Fig. 3. Average frequency spectrum in dBA and dBC for an underground trip on Circle line in Singapore.

For London, the findings are summarized in Table 2. Piccadilly line which would operate from Heathrow airport to the city was found to be the noisiest among the two lines. The noise map of the Piccadilly line for the portion on surface elevated track with GPS data is shown in Fig. 4. The enlarged map can be accessed via the web link [7]. Most of the measurements were done on Piccadilly Line.

Table 2. Comparison of cabin noise of two metro lines in London underground. Line 1: Piccadilly and Line 2: Jubilee.

Line	No of trips	Duration (h: m:s)	LASeq (dBA)	Max LASeq (dBA)	LASmax (dBA)	LASeq (dBC)	Max LASeq (dBC)	LASmax (dBC)
1	21	00:31:09	82.1	87.4	97.6	87.6	89.9	96.8
2	4	00:04:38	81.8	83.4	88.8	89.2	93.2	101.1

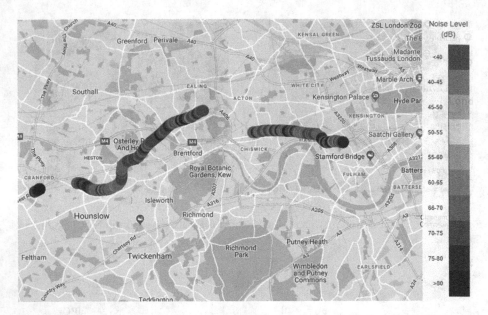

Fig. 4. The noise map of cabin noise in Piccadilly line on surface elevated track from Heathrow Airport to London city centre.

For Prague, the findings are summarized in Table 3. Line C in terms of equivalent noise level is the lowest among the three lines but it has the highest maximum sound pressure level. However, there are insufficient recordings for the other two lines to validate this finding as most of the measurements were done on Line C. All data measured for Prague was underground and hence there was no noise map available without the GPS data.

Table 3. Comparison of cabin noise of three lines in Prague metro system.

Line	No of trips	Duration (h: m:s)	LASeq (dBA)	Max LASeq (dBA)	LASmax (dBA)	LASeq (dBC)	Max LASeq (dBC)	LASmax (dBC)
A	4	00:04:04	80.6	83.9	89.8	88.8	91.2	96.4
B	2	00:02:25	82.8	85.0	90.0	89.1	90.3	94.8
C	33	00:40:16	79.6	84.3	92.5	85.9	89.0	97.0

For Paris, the findings are summarized in Table 4. Line 7 was found to be the noisiest with an equivalent sound pressure level of 85.3 dBA and recorded the highest sound pressure level at 99.6 dBA. The noise map of the metro in Paris for the portion on surface elevated track with GPS data is shown in Fig. 5. The enlarged map can be accessed via the web link [8].

Table 4. Comparison of cabin noise of four lines in Paris metro system.

Line	No of trips	Duration (h: m:s)	LASeq (dBA)	Max LASeq (dBA)	LASmax (dBA)	LASeq (dBC)	Max LASeq (dBC)	LASmax (dBC)
2	7	00:06:01	74.6	80.6	91.3	86.5	88.0	98.0
4	4	00:03:26	73.9	74.7	80.2	82.8	83.6	88.8
5	9	00:08:33	72.7	75.6	86.2	86.0	89.0	98.6
7	7	00:08:00	85.3	89.9	99.6	91.2	94.9	104.5

Fig. 5. The noise map of cabin noise in elevated metro in Paris.

For Singapore, the findings are summarized in Table 5. North South line was found to be the noisiest with an equivalent sound pressure level of 80.9 dBA and recorded the highest sound pressure level at 94.5 dBA. The noise map of the metro in Singapore for the portion on surface elevated track with GPS data is shown in Fig. 6. The enlarged map can be accessed via the web link [9].

Table 5. Comparison of cabin noise of five lines in Singapore metro system. Line 1: Circle, Line 2: Downtown, Line 3: East West, Line 4: North East, Line 5: North South.

Line	No of trips	Duration (h: m:s)	LASeq (dBA)	Max LASeq (dBA)	LASmax (dBA)	LASeq (dBC)	Max LASeq (dBC)	LASmax (dBC)
1	30	00:44:45	79.2	81.8	92.2	83.4	85.9	93.8
2	28	00:39:24	78.1	85.9	95.2	84.9	89.4	97.9
3	32	01:00:42	77.8	84.2	92.0	84.1	86.7	94.8
4	27	00:33:03	78.9	83.2	92.5	85.0	87.8	95.3
5	28	00:48:08	80.9	86.4	94.5	84.0	88.0	96.2

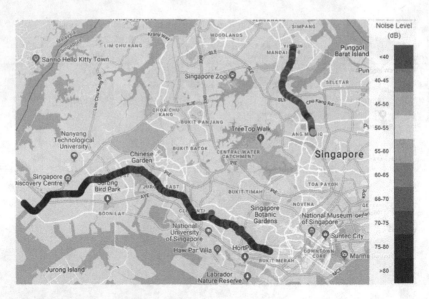

Fig. 6. The noise map of cabin noise in elevated metro in Singapore.

For Taipei, the findings are summarized in Table 6. Green line was found to be the noisiest with an equivalent sound pressure level of 78.6 dBA and Airport line recorded the highest sound pressure level at 100.4 dBA. The noise map of the metro in Taipei is shown in Fig. 7. The enlarged map can be accessed via the web link [10].

Table 6. Comparison of cabin noise of five lines in Taipei metro system. Line 1: Blue, Line 2: Brown, Line 3: Green, Line 4: Red, Line 5 Airport.

Line	No of trips	Duration (h: m:s)	LASeq (dBA)	Max LASeq (dBA)	LASmax (dBA)	LASeq (dBC)	Max LASeq (dBC)	LASmax (dBC)
1	11	00:10:23	77.5	79.3	86.4	83.6	85.3	90.6
2	13	00:17:08	76.9	80.3	84.7	90.2	92.0	98.9
3	13	00:19:26	78.6	86.6	93.3	85.3	90.2	99.8
4	131	03:15:52	73.8	88.4	92.6	81.5	91.4	95.3
5	3	00:30:08	71.5	73.2	100.4	82.7	83.3	99.8

All of the measurements were carried out using calibrated smartphones and except for Taipei and Singapore, the duration of measurement might not be long enough to be representative of the respective noise levels. However, the present work has demonstrated the viability of using smartphones for crowd sourcing of cabin noise of metro systems. If sufficient data can be obtained, the data can be used for condition monitoring of the operating conditions of the rolling stocks. Moreover, if more data is available via crowd sourcing and automated uploading of data to compute server, the data can give the city authority an up-to-date and real-time information of the noise profile of the city.

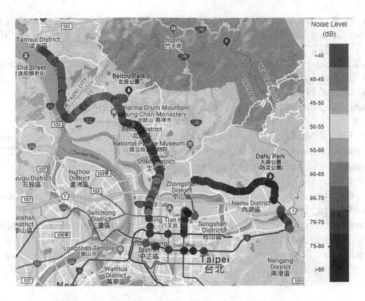

Fig. 7. The noise map of metro cabin noise in Taipei.

4   Conclusions

We have measured and analyzed the cabin noise in metros of five cities in Asia and Europe. The cities are London, Prague, Paris, Singapore and Taipei. The measurement was carried out using a smartphone whose microphone was calibrated against a type 1 microphone. We found that average noise level for all metros were well below 85 dB and therefore traveling on these metro systems for eight hours was not likely to exceed the maximum duration of noise exposure under the National Institute for Occupational Safety and Health (NIOSH) guidelines. We also found that average sound pressure level in dBC was about 6 dB higher when compared to dBA. This indicates the presence of low-frequency components below 200 Hz.

Acknowledgement. The authors would like to acknowledge the financial support by the Singapore Ministry of National Development and National Research Foundation under Land and Livability National Innovation Challenge (L2NIC) Award No. L2NICCFP1-2013-8, and by the Ministry of Education under the Tier 1 Academic Research Grant (R-265-000-639-114).

References

1. Gonzalez-Navarro, M., Turner, M.A.: Subways and urban growth: evidence from earth. J. Urban Econ. **108**, 85–106 (2018)
2. Gershon, R.R.M., Neitzel, R., Barrera, M.A., Akram, M.: Pilot survey of subway and bus stop noise levels. J. Urban Health: Bulletin New York Acad. Med. **83**(5), 802–812 (2006)

3. Hamidi, M., Kavousi, A., Zaheri, S., Hamadani, A., Mirkazemi, R.: Assessment of the noise annoyance among subway train conductors in Tehran. Iran. Noise Health. **16**(70), 77–82 (2014)
4. Jeon, J.Y., Hong, J.Y., Jang, H.S.: Appropriate background noise level regarding speech privacy and annoyance in a train cabin. In: Proceedings of Euronoise 2015, pp. 225–226. Ingenta, Maastricht (2015)
5. BBC News. http://news.bbc.co.uk/2/hi/uk_news/england/london/3895769.stm. Accessed 15 Oct 2019
6. Garg, S., Lim, K.M., Lee, H.P.: An averaging method for accurately calibrating smartphone microphones for environmental noise measurement. Appl. Acoust. **143**, 222–228 (2019)
7. Noise map for Piccadilly line in London. http://worldnoisemap.com/papers/metro/london-metro.html. Accessed 11 May 2019
8. Noise map for Paris metro. http://worldnoisemap.com/papers/metro/paris-metro.html. Accessed 13 May 2019
9. Noise map for Singapore metro. http://worldnoisemap.com/papers/metro/singapore-metro.html. Accessed 13 May 2019
10. Noise map for Taipei metro. http://worldnoisemap.com/papers/metro/taipei-metro.html. Accessed 13 May 2019

A High Throughput MAC Protocol
for Wireless Body Area Networks
in Intensive Care

Amir Javadpour[1] (ID), Guojun Wang[1(✉)] (ID), and Kuan-Ching Li[2] (ID)

[1] School of Computer Science, Guangzhou University,
Guangzhou 510006, China
[2] Department of Computer Science and Information Engineering,
Providence University, Taichung, Taiwan
csgjwang@gzhu.edu.cn

Abstract. Health monitoring systems are one of the fastest-growing industries in the world, as the world's older population grows dramatically at an unprecedented rate. These systems provide an opportunity to share the medical information, medical applications and infrastructures required in a fully automated way accessible everywhere. This paper addresses the need for a protocol in health applications which covers packets collision while considering the balance between transferred information and service quality, as thoroughly examines details of simulating media access control protocols in body area sensor networks based on a combination of pooling and TDMA protocols. Experimental results validate the proposed protocol with high throughput and acceptable delay.

Keywords: IOT monitoring · Wireless Body Area Networks · Intensive care · TaMAC · Vital signs · Internet of Things · Smart sensing

1 Introduction

With the rapid advancement of networking and communications technologies, significant technical innovation makes the usage of wireless sensor networks for everyday life indispensable. Figure 1 illustrates an example of the development of Wireless Body Area Networks (WBAN) in a health care domain, remotely monitoring patients by providing services through Cloud computing, SDN (Software-Defined Network) and IoT (Internet of things) to customers depending on the required information [1–5], sensors are mounted on or inside the body with a narrow range to send and receive information [6–8]. Vital signs of the human body, including respiratory status, heart rate, body temperature, they are collected for central coordinator nodes under unceasing process [4, 5]. In the last two decades, significant advances in the electronics industry and integrated circuits such as designing and manufacturing small and inexpensive sensors, has led to fundamental changes in the provision of medical services. Establishment of low-cost electronic circuits, the feasibility of small and low-power telecommunication and electronic devices, has made it possible to make fundamental

© Springer Nature Singapore Pte Ltd. 2019
G. Wang et al. (Eds.): iSCI 2019, CCIS 1122, pp. 23–34, 2019.
https://doi.org/10.1007/978-981-15-1301-5_3

changes in medicine [10–14] Modern medicine by using new technologies focuses on prevention more than treatment. Continuous monitoring of vital signs, especially in people at high risk of disease, has been possible through the use of information technology [15–18]. Keep the patient's general condition fixed by controlling his vital signs is possible, and the sudden change of symptoms, which includes heart rate and respiration and body temperature, can seriously endanger the health of patients. Diabetes, hypothyroidism, or the presence of other infections in the patients are some reasons for sudden changes in vital signs [19, 20]. Failures in prompt and in-time diagnosis may have irreversible consequences on the patients' health, which is more intense in neonates and older adults. Reducing the required time to measure, store, and ultimately make information available for analysis are other aspects in which WBANs can help. For example, high heart rate, high temperature, and high blood pressure have a direct impact on the nerves (brain) and other body organs where such absence of control may endanger patient's health. Particularly for patients in CCUs (Coronary Care Unit) and ICUs (Intensive Care Unit) as also patients undergoing high-risk surgeries [1], sensor networks body-mounted wireless monitoring systems are used continuously to illustrate a patient's vital signs. One of the most critical issues in WBAN is energy efficiency, where sensor nodes like blood pressure, it is crucial to design an efficient and reliable MAC protocol for WBANs [3, 6, 12]. This paper discusses the design and implementation of the Media Access Control (MAC) layer of WBANs to monitor vital signs.

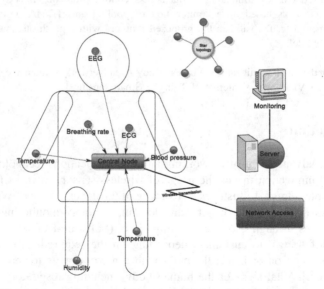

Fig. 1. An example of monitoring vital signs in WBAN network.

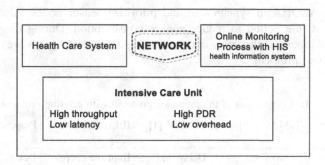

Fig. 2. Healthcare environment and monitoring of vital signs.

As shown in Fig. 2, wireless monitoring systems are used to monitor the vital signs in a therapeutic environment. Interference increases as the number of people serviced in this system augment [21, 22]. For such, the primary goal of this paper is to present a Medium Access Control (MAC) that effectively reduces packet collision in the network as long as the quality of service is satisfied.

2 Related Work

MAC protocols are divided into two categories: competitive and time-based ('contention' and 'scheduled') [23]. In competitive-based protocols, nodes compete with each other to send a packet and collision might occur as a result. Oppositely, each sensor has its time interval and transmits data in that interval in time-based protocols (TDMA) [24, 25]. A TDMA-based MAC protocol cannot cope with the packet collision problem [26], while Medium Fading is possible in TDMA due to synchronicity between transmitter and receiver [1]. Therefore, the IEEE group proposes a unified protocol 802.15.4 for standardization of MAC layer [9], despite this protocol is not useful for WBAN since it cannot support applications with the high data rate.

In [27], a protocol to access media with 0.4-second delay for sending and receiving of the data has been proposed, by using a collection tree to solve delay issue. The protocol uses the MTS (More-To-Send) package mechanism to reduce competition and collisions in the channel. In this mechanism, there is an Idle-Wakeup scheduler that makes it possible to send data over a defined route continuously.

Data prediction is also used to increase activity time interval when several children of the same node have data for transferring, as the major idea in designing such a protocol is a wake-up pattern that can be set up alternately so that packets are sent continuously from the sensor nodes to the central node of the information. In [28], TaMAC (Traffic-adaptive MAC) protocol attempts to optimize energy consumption in

WBAN using ALOHA to synchronize and prioritize sensor nodes. Also, it utilizes competition and Idle period to reduce energy consumption. During the idle period, nodes off should increase the delay in the network. Table 1 compares previous studies with the proposed protocol.

Table 1. Comparison of the proposed protocol with existing protocols.

Issue/idea	TaMAC [28]	IDMAC [1]	IEEE 802.15.04 [29]	Proposed Method
Contribution	Improve energy consumption	Delay and Throughput	Improve energy consumption	Delay, Throughput and reliable
Using TDMA	Yes	Yes	Using tree	Yes
Synchronization problem	Yes	Yes	No	No
Using hardware ID	No	Yes	No	Yes
Pooling	No	No	No	Yes
Probability of not delivering	Yes	Yes	Yes	Yes
Resend	Yes	Yes	no	Yes

3 Proposed Protocol

The proposed protocol is a combination of request and set data in TDMA slots protocols. It is assumed that nodes (patients) send their gathered information into the central station. Figure 3 demonstrates the main idea of this paper for solving synchronization problem and increasing quality of service. The proposed protocol uses a combination of pooling (Aggregation) and TDMA to terminate collision, as it increases the throughput of receiving the packets. The transmitted frame in the proposed method includes header, source, and destination addresses, packet control section, data and error detection. As the processing part of sensor nodes, microcontrollers can change the frame values and put them in active or inactive mode. Header bits are used to synchronize the central node and sensors. The packet control section is activated by a microcontroller with specified data length and ACK settings [1]. In this protocol, data is broadcasted from CentralNode, as depicted in Fig. 1. Next, there is a carrier signal for each node and when the signal is carried, the selected node can send data to CentralNode considering time slot. Then, it waits for receiving an ACK from CentralNode.

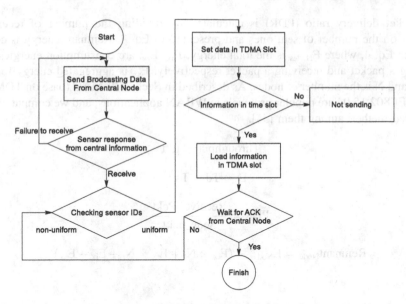

Fig. 3. The flowchart of the proposed method.

4 Simulation and Results

Media Access Layer has been exploited to enhance the reliability and accuracy of online monitoring in WBANs. The network links the IoT to the central node [30, 31], efficiently spreading the information. Due to the lack of proper coordination and synchronization between software and modules to build up real environments with several different modules to full implementation [32], it is not possible to run the proposed method in a real environment, and thus, simulation is considered instead by using NS2 simulator [4, 7, 17, 33, 34], and charts are plotted using MATLAB. It is also assumed that there are propagation delay and errors in the transmission link, and the energy consumption on idle mode is zero. In this simulation, we used a central node for receiving data and other nodes are used as transceiver modules that work with the proposed protocol (Table 2). Based on [35], the throughput of the proposed method is evaluated using the following measurements:

- μ is the number of received bits in t time slots,
- the throughput of the complete network is computed by the average throughput for all nodes,
- D is End-to-end packet delay;
- T_d is delivering time of packets and
- T_s is transmission starting time.

Packet delivery ratio (PDR) is calculated by dividing the number of received packets on the number of sent ones and presented in Eq. 3. Remnant energy is computed in Eq. 4, where E_{Nodes} is the total energy, E_{tx}, E_{rx}, are consumption energies for sending a packet and receiving a packet respectively. E_{sx} is aggregated energy for all nodes and N is the number of nodes. As described in Sect. 2, TaMAC (base on TDMA) and IEEE802.15.04 are popular protocols in WBAN applications; and we compared the proposed method among them [34].

$$Throughput = \mu/t \tag{1}$$

$$D = Td - Ts \tag{2}$$

$$PDR = \frac{Receive\_Pckt}{Sent\_pckt} \tag{3}$$

$$Remnant_{Node} = E_{Nodes} - (E_{tx} \times N_t + E_{rx} \times N_r + E_{ix} + E_{sx}) \tag{4}$$

Table 2. Simulation parameters.

Parameters of NS2 simulation	
Channel type	WirelessChannel
Propagation	TwoRayGround
Network interface type	WirelessPhy
Interface queue type	Queue/DropTail/PriQueue
Antenna	OmniAntenna
Number of nodes	10
Bandwidth	256 Kbps
Radio communication Range	20 m
Collision environment	5 m
Packet length	2–64 byte
Energy transmission	0.60 W
Energy Receiving	0.40 W
Energy Idle	0.35 W
Energy sleeping	0.1 W
Antenna length	1 Cm

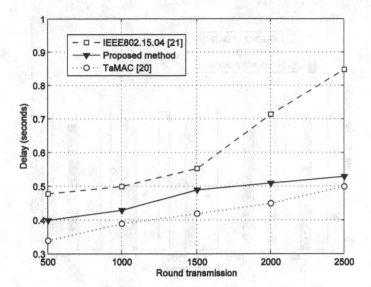

Fig. 4. Analytical and simulated average delay for one node.

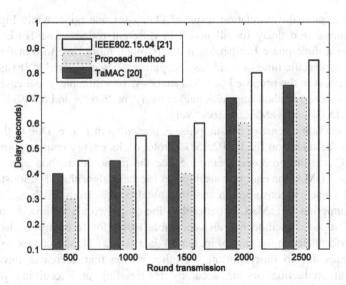

Fig. 5. Analytical and simulated average accumulation delay for all nodes.

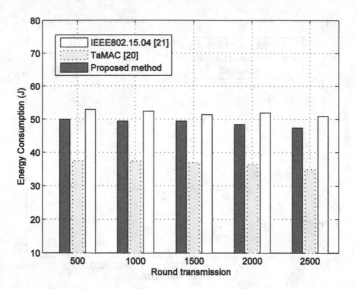

Fig. 6. Analytical and simulated energy consumption in different protocol.

Figure 4 depicts the simulation result of Delay for one node, while Fig. 5 shows average accumulation delay for all nodes in different rounds. The IEEE 802.15.04 protocol uses a three-phase handshake, it needs much more time to transfer a packet, TaMAC uses a specific time slot and has acceptable delay compared to IEEE802.15.04 protocol. Request in the proposed protocol makes it very suitable in the case of packet delay. The proposed method improves packet delay by 26.62% and 6.34% if compared to IEEE802.15.04 and TaMAC, respectively.

The comparison of energy consumption is presented in Fig. 6. Due to the constant activation of the nodes on IEEE 802.15.04 protocol, its energy consumption is higher than TaMAC and the proposed method. Since the proposed method operates on the same basis as TDMA, the energy consumption for these algorithms is almost equal and constant. The energy consumption has improved 5.02% from IEEE 802.15.04 and energy consumption in TaMAC is better than the other two algorithms. As depicted in Fig. 7, the proposed method has an acceptable result for throughput, also showing excellent performance in the case of increased data rate, as TDMA cannot work well at high data rates due to time splitting. Another reason that decreases throughput in TDMA is the reduction on the accuracy for sending and receiving packets by increasing the synchronization speed. A comparison of changing the packet size is presented in Fig. 8 (in 256Kbit/s rate). There is also PDR (packet delivery ratio) with different packet size that is proportional to the throughput, where packet size change and throughput increase are shown in Fig. 9. As overall, evaluations show that the proposed protocol has a higher throughput than the other two protocols.

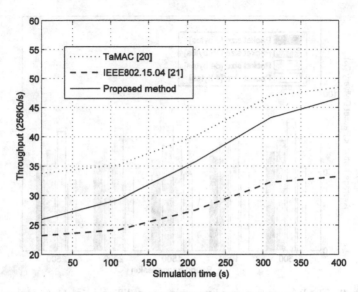

Fig. 7. The throughput of the comparison schemes in different protocols.

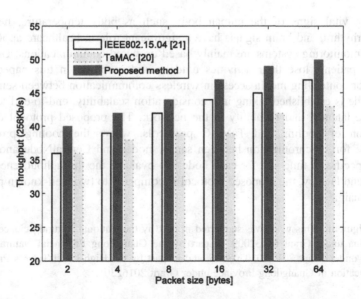

Fig. 8. The throughput against packet size in different protocols.

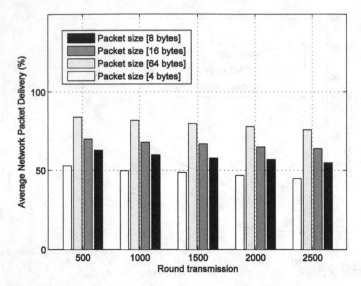

Fig. 9. The PDR against round transmission in different size (4–64 bytes).

5 Conclusions

Monitoring vital signs of the human body such as body temperature, heart rate, breathing rhythm, and brain signals have a significant role in healthcare applications. Available monitoring systems are mainly based on wired communications. Under this condition, patients lose their activities outdoor and mobility. In this paper, a new protocol for controlling media access in wireless communication between sensors and CentralNode is established taking into consideration scalability, end-to-end tolerance, appropriate latency, and reliability in the network. The proposed protocol utilizes a combination of pooling and TaMAC protocols, where the pooling protocol is responsible for synchronization between sensor nodes and CentralNode and TDMA protocol specifies a time slot for each node. To evaluate the throughput, energy consumption and latency, the proposed protocol is compared to two well-known protocols in this domain.

Acknowledgment. This work was supported in part by the National Natural Science Foundation of China under Grant 61632009, in part by the Guangdong Provincial Natural Science Foundation under Grant 2017A030308006, and in part by the High-Level Talents Program of Higher Education in Guangdong Province under Grant 2016ZJ01.

References

1. Javadpour, A., Memarzadeh-Tehran, H., Saghafi, F.: A temperature monitoring system incorporating an array of precision wireless thermometers. In: 2015 International Conference on Smart Sensors and Application (ICSSA), pp. 155–160 (2015)

2. Balampanis, S., Sotiriadis, S., Petrakis, E.: Internet of Things architecture in cloud computing for enhanced living environments. IEEE Cloud Comput. **3**(6), 28–34 (2016)
3. Javadpour, A., Wang, G., Rezaei, S., Chend, S.: Power curtailment in cloud environment utilising load balancing machine allocation. In: 2018 IEEE SmartWorld, Ubiquitous Intelligence Computing, Advanced Trusted Computing, Scalable Computing Communications, Cloud Big Data Computing, Internet of People and Smart City Innovation (SmartWorld/SCALCOM/UIC/ATC/CBDCom/IOP/SCI), pp. 1364–1370 (2018)
4. Javadpour, A.: Improving resources management in network virtualization by utilizing a software-based network. Wirel. Pers. Commun. **106**(2), 505–519 (2019)
5. Javadpour, A.: Providing a way to create balance between reliability and delays in SDN networks by using the appropriate placement of controllers. Wirel. Pers. Commun. (2019)
6. Ali, M., Moungla, H., Younis, M., Mehaoua, A.: IoT-enabled channel selection approach for WBANs. In: 2017 13th International Wireless Communications and Mobile Computing Conference (IWCMC), pp. 1784–1790 (2017)
7. Javadpour, A., Adelpour, N., Wang, G., Peng, T.: Combing fuzzy clustering and PSO algorithms to optimize energy consumption in WSN networks. In: 2018 IEEE SmartWorld, Ubiquitous Intelligence & Computing, Advanced & Trusted Computing, Scalable Computing & Communications, Cloud & Big Data Computing, Internet People Smart City Innovation, pp. 1371–1377 (2018)
8. Zhu, X., Wu, J., Chang, W., Wang, G., Liu, Q.: Authentication of skyline query over road networks. In: Wang, G., Chen, J., Yang, Laurence T. (eds.) SpaCCS 2018. LNCS, vol. 11342, pp. 72–83. Springer, Cham (2018). https://doi.org/10.1007/978-3-030-05345-1_6
9. Bradai, N., Fourati, L.C., Kamoun, L.: Investigation and performance analysis of MAC protocols for WBAN networks. J. Netw. Comput. Appl. **46**, 362–373 (2014)
10. Salayma, M., Al-Dubai, A., Romdhani, I., Nasser, Y.: Reliability and energy efficiency enhancement for emergency-aware wireless body area networks (WBAN). IEEE Trans. Green Commun. Netw. **2**, 804–816 (2018)
11. Wei, Z., Sun, Y., Ji, Y.: Collision analysis of CSMA/CA based MAC protocol for duty cycled WBANs. Wirel. Netw. **23**, 1429–1447 (2016)
12. Ullah, S., et al.: A comprehensive survey of wireless body area networks. J. Med. Syst. **36**(3), 1065–1094 (2012)
13. Filipe, L., Fdez-Riverola, F., Costa, N., Pereira, A.: Wireless body area networks for healthcare applications: protocol stack review. Int. J. Distrib. Sens. Networks **11**(10), 213705 (2015)
14. ur Rahman, H., Wang, G., Chen, J., Jiang, H.: Performance evaluation of hypervisors and the effect of virtual CPU on performance. In: 2018 IEEE SmartWorld, Ubiquitous Intelligence & Computing, Advanced & Trusted Computing, Scalable Computing & Communications, Cloud & Big Data Computing, Internet of People and Smart City Innovation (SmartWorld/SCALCOM/UIC/ATC/CBDCom/IOP/SCI), pp. 772–779 (2018)
15. Javadpour, A., Memarzadeh-Tehran, H.: A wearable medical sensor for provisional healthcare. I: ISPTS 2015 - 2nd International Symposium on Physics and Technology of Sensors Dive Deep Into Sensors, pp. 293–296 (2015)
16. Kang, J., Yoo, S., Oh, D.: Development of a portable embedded patient monitoring system. Int. J. Multimed. Ubiquitous Eng. **8**(6), 141–150 (2013)
17. Javadpour, A., Wang, G., Xing, X.: Managing heterogeneous substrate resources by mapping and visualization based on software-defined network. In: 2018 IEEE International Conference on Parallel Distributed Processing with Applications, Ubiquitous Computing Communications, Big Data Cloud Computing, Social Computing Networking, Sustainable Computing Communications (ISPA/IUCC/BDCloud/SocialCom/SustainCom), pp. 316–321 (2018)

18. Rizvi, S.Q.A., Wang, G., Chen, J.: A service oriented healthcare architecture (SOHA-CC) based on cloud computing. In: Wang, G., Chen, J., Yang, Laurence T. (eds.) SpaCCS 2018. LNCS, vol. 11342, pp. 84–97. Springer, Cham (2018). https://doi.org/10.1007/978-3-030-05345-1_7

19. Catarinucci, L., et al.: An IoT-aware architecture for smart healthcare systems. IEEE IoT J. **2** (6), 515–526 (2015)

20. Javaid, N., Israr, I., Khan, M.A., Javaid, A., Bouk, S.H., Khan, Z.A.: Analyzing medium access techniques in wireless body area network (2013)

21. Ullah, F., Abdullah, A.H., Kaiwartya, O., Kumar, S., Arshad, M.M.: Medium access control (MAC) for wireless body area network (WBAN): superframe structure, multiple access technique, taxonomy, and challenges. Hum.-Centric Comput. Inf. Sci. **7**(1), 34 (2017)

22. Wei, Z., Sun, Y., Ji, Y.: Collision analysis of CSMA/CA based MAC protocol for duty cycled WBANs. Wirel. Netw. **10**, 1–19 (2016)

23. Ullah, S., Shen, B., Riazul Islam, S.M., Khan, P., Saleem, S., Kwak, K.S.: A study of MAC protocols for WBANs. Sensors **10**(1), 128–145 (2010)

24. Khan, Z.A., Rasheed, M.B., Javaid, N., Robertson, B.: Effect of packet inter-arrival time on the energy consumption of beacon enabled MAC protocol for body area networks. Procedia Comput. Sci. **32**, 579–586 (2014)

25. Israr, I., Yaqoob, M.M., Javaid, N., Qasim, U., Khan, Z.A.: Simulation analysis of medium access techniques. In: Proceedings of 2012 7th International Conference on Broadband, Wireless Computing Communication and Applications BWCCA 2012, pp. 602–607 (2012)

26. Rajesh, G.K., Baskaran, K.: A survey on futuristic health care system: WBANs. Procedia Eng. **30**, 889–896 (2012)

27. Latre, B., et al.: A low-delay protocol for multihop wireless body area networks. In: 2007 Fourth Annual International Conference on Mobile and Ubiquitous Systems: Networking & Services (MobiQuitous), pp. 1–8 (2007)

28. Ullah, S., Kwak, K.S.: An ultra low-power and traffic-adaptive medium access control protocol for wireless body area network. J. Med. Syst. **36**(3), 1021–1030 (2012)

29. Kwak, K.-S., Ameen, M.A., Kwak, D., Lee, C., Lee, H.: A study on proposed IEEE 802.15 WBAN MAC protocols. In: 9th International Symposium on Communications and Information Technology ISCIT 2009, pp. 834–840 (2009)

30. Bhanumathi, V., Sangeetha, C.P.: A guide for the selection of routing protocols in WBAN for healthcare applications. Hum.-Centric Comput. Inf. Sci. **7**(1), 24 (2017)

31. Bhuiyan, M.Z.A., Cao, J., Wang, G., Liu, X.: Energy-efficient and fault-tolerant structural health monitoring in wireless sensor networks. In: 2012 IEEE 31st Symposium on Reliable Distributed Systems, pp. 301–310 (2012)

32. Bhuiyan, M.Z.A., Wang, G., Wu, J., Cao, J., Liu, X., Wang, T.: Dependable structural health monitoring using wireless sensor networks. IEEE Trans. Dependable Secur. Comput. **14**(4), 363–376 (2017)

33. Issariyakul, T., Hossain, E.: Introduction to Network Simulator NS2, pp. 1–510. Springer, Berlin (2012). https://doi.org/10.1007/978-1-4614-1406-3

34. Javadpour, A.: An optimize-aware target tracking method combining MAC layer and active nodes in wireless sensor networks. Wirel. Pers. Commun. (2019)

35. Shamshirband, S., Anuar, N.B., Kiah, M., Misra, S.: Anomaly detection using fuzzy Q-learning algorithm. J. Intell. Fuzzy Syst. **11**(8), 5–28 (2014)

FRFP: A Friend Recommendation Method Based on Fine-Grained Preference

Mingmin Shao, Wenjun Jiang$^{(\boxtimes)}$ (iD), and Lei Zhang

College of Computer Science and Electronic Engineering, Hunan University,
Changsha 410082, China
{shaomingmin,jiangwenjun,zhang_lei}@hnu.edu.cn

Abstract. In photography community, users are often asked and encouraged to give relevant tags based on the content of the photos when uploading them. These tags are often fine-grained and can be better used to analyze the user's fine-grained photography preferences for friend recommendation. However, the recommendation faces challenges because the latest related research works rarely pay attention to the user's photography preferences are fine-grained, which leads to poor friend recommendation. Therefore, we try to propose a new Friend Recommendation method by user's Fine-grained Preference (FRFP). Firstly, FRFP method extracts the user's fine-grained photography preference features from the perspective of the fine-grained tag. Then, we use the pagerank algorithm to calculate the importance of the preference feature tag as the score of the user-item scoring matrix, and generate a friend recommendation list through the collaborative filtering algorithm. Finally, we use user activity to weight the users in friend recommendation list, preferentially recommend users with high user activity to target user, and improve the quality of friend recommendation. The experimental results on real-word data show the effectiveness and precision of the proposed method in friend recommendation for photographers.

Keywords: Photography community · Fine-grained preference ·
Social network · Friend recomendation

1 Introduction

1.1 Research Background

In the photography community, photographer can share their photos, communicate and interact with other users, and make friends who have similar photography preferences. For the current popular photography communities, they cannot be able to provide a method to accurately recommend potential friends for photographers with similar photography preferences. Users are encouraged to give relevant tags based on the content of their photos, providing the possibility to analyze their fine-grained photography preferences.

© Springer Nature Singapore Pte Ltd. 2019
G. Wang et al. (Eds.): iSCI 2019, CCIS 1122, pp. 35–48, 2019.
https://doi.org/10.1007/978-981-15-1301-5_4

However, in the recommendation of friends in the photography community, there are the following problems: (1) Users in the photography community have specific photography styles and hobbies, and traditional coarse-grained friend-recommendation methods cannot meet user needs. (2) The number of tags for user photos tends to be large and there is no suitable method for processing the tag data to obtain the user's fine-grained photography preferences. (3) The existing friend-recommendation method has low accuracy and quality, which has little significance in practice.

We are inspired by [25], calculating similarity from users' interest topics to find potential friends with the similar interest in social tagging systems. Because the current photography community contains a huge number of tags, it is a very complicated tag system. However, for the photography community, helping users find friends with similar fine-grained photography preferences can increase user's satisfaction and competitiveness [14]. Therefore, all the work in this paper is based on the following three motivations: (1) Design a suitable method to extract the user's fine-grained photography preferences in the tag system. (2) Calculate the similarity of photography preferences between users, and improve the accuracy of friend-recommendation. (3) When the user preference similarity is close, the user with higher activity is more preferred to be recommended.

In summary, this paper makes the following contributions: (1) We propose a friend recommendation method called FRFP to obtain the user's fine-grained photography preferences through tags. (2) We conduct comprehensive experiments to show that the proposed method significantly improves the accuracy of friend-recommendation. (3) We use user activity to improve the quality of friend recommendations.

The rest of this paper is organized as follows: Sect. 2 discuss related work. Sections 3 and 4 introduce our method and potential friend recommendation. Section 5 shows the analysis and comparison of experimental results. Section 6 summarize this paper and discuss future work.

2   Related Work

Researches about friend recommendation related to our work can divided into two fields: (1) Friend recommendation based on user connections in social networks. (2) Friend recommendation based on similarity of interest preference.

2.1   Friend Recommendation Based on User Connections in Social Networks

Online social networks (OSNs) become a popular tool of meeting people and keeping in touch with friends. OSNs resort to trust evaluation models and algorithms, as to improve service qualities and enhance user experiences. Jiang *et al.* [11,12] propose a modified flow-based trust evaluation scheme GFTrust and address path dependence use network flow, and model trust decay with the leakage associated with each node. The evaluation of a user's social influence is essential for friend recommendation in online social networks (OSNs).

Studying social influence, especially on large-scale social network data, to model and measure the influence between people is very important for friend recommendation in social applications. Wang *et al.* [24] propose a fine-grained feature-based social influence (FBI) evaluation model, which can identify all users' social influences with much less duplication and have a larger influence spread with top-k influential users. Wang *et al.* [23] propose a novel influence evaluation model: the temporal topic influence (TTI) evaluation model, which is a time-aware, content-aware and structure-aware evaluation model. TTI model can calculate users' influences effectively and efficiently, and can distinguish the value of users' social influences.

Based on the user's connection, the friend recommendation problem can be roughly classified into three categories according to the existing algorithms [6, 15]. The classification method mainly uses the features between two nodes, such as the path-based metric Katz or the neighbor-based metric Adamic/Adar. Gong *et al.* [5] predicting the value of friendship by using the SVM model to train the two-classifier for the friendship feature state between users. The fitting method represents the friendship between users and as close as possible to the observed friendship value, for example, using Matrix Factorization to predict the value of an unknown friendship [9,16]. Due to the sparseness of data in open social network, the classification and fitting methods cannot handle the serious data imbalance problems [1]. Thus, the common Bayesian personalized ranking model [20,21] is offen used to solve the imbalance problem effectively.

Zheng *et al.* [28] study the friend recommendation strategy from the perspective of maximizing social influence. For system providers (such as Facebook[1]), the goal is to recommend a fixed number of new friends, so that the user can maximize his/her social influence by making new friends. Huang *et al.* [10] align the user's social relationship network and tag network to generate a possible friend list.

2.2 Friend Recommendation Based on Similarity of Interest Preference

Hannon *et al.* [7] considers user generated content on Twitter[2] and develops a fast algorithm for real-time user-to-user similarity for follower/followee recommendation. It is developed only for text similarity. Xing *et al.* [26] designed an ordinary friend recommendation framework, which can represent user interest in two aspects: context (location, time) and content, and combine domain knowledge to improve recommendation quality.

Huang *et al.* [10] conduct the three-way clustering by users, tags and images to obtain topics that might interest user. Re-recommended the friend recommendation list generated by aligning the user network and the tag network to

---

[1] https://www.facebook.com.
[2] https://www.twitter.com.

optimize the recommendation effect. Hasan *et al.* [8] analyzed the diversification of users in the social network and the dynamism of user interests. At the same time, they measured the frequency of activities completed by users and updated the data set according to the activity. Wu *et al.* [25] proposed a Friend Recommendation algorithm by User similarity Graph (FRUG) to find potential friends with the same interest in social tagging systems.

3   Problem Definition and Preliminary Concepts

In this section, we formulate the problem we address, and provide some preliminary concepts. In the photography community, each user will be given relevant tags based on the content of the photos. However, not all tags are useful and can directly express the user's fine-grained photography preferences, so a large number of tags need to be pre-processed to get tags that can represent fine-grained photography preferences [27].

The FRFP method proposed in this paper processes a large amount of tags to obtain useful tags that can represent the user's fine-grained photography preferences. FRFP mainly includes the following steps (Fig. 1): (1) Perform vectorized representation of user's tags. (2) Use cosine similarity to calculate similarity between word vectors. (3) Cluster tags based on the similarity of word vectors. (4) Extract the high frequency tags and the tags close to each cluster center in same cluster.

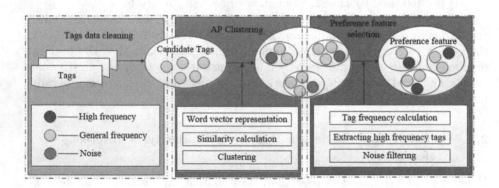

Fig. 1. Fine-grained preference feature selection.

3.1   Problem Definition

Given a set of metadata (U, T, I), U is a set of users, T is a set of user's fine-grained tags and I is a set of user's information. For two different users, u and v in U, we seek to determine how to design an efficient method to extract user's fine-grained preference features, and calculate similarity of u and v. Specifically, how to recommend friends such as v with similar preference for u, and how to combine user's information to improve the quality of friend recommendation simultaneously. Our goal is to design an effective method to extract user's fine-grained preference features from tags system, and improve the precision and quality of friend recommendation based on user's information.

3.2 Preliminary Concepts

In social network-based recommendation system, friend recommendation is the essential part. First, we extract the user's fine-grained preference features. Secondly, the friend list is generated based on users' fine-grained preference similarity. Finally, users' similarity are weighted to generate a final friend recommendation list. The three key concepts of FRFP are as follows:

Definition 1. *In the original tagging system, we first remove the noise tags and get a collection of the candidate tags. Then, we count the frequency of the candidate tags and the tag with a frequency greater than the average frequency is defined as H-tag.*

Definition 2. *After clustering the candidate tags, we define a tag with Euclidean distance to the cluster center less than the average distance of the rest as C-tag.*

3.3 Solution Overview

In the photography community, each user will be given a relevant tag based on the content of the photo. But not all tags are useful and can directly express the user's fine-grained photography preferences, so a large number of tags need to be pre-processed to get tags that can represent fine-grained photography preferences. The FRFP method proposed in this paper processes a large amount of tag data to obtain a tag that can represent the user's fine-grained photography preferences. FRFP mainly includes four tasks are as follows:

Task 1: Word Vector Representation of Fine-Grained Tags. We uses the skip-gram model in the word2vec [17] tool, through the Wikipedia article[3] provided by Matt Mahoney as the English corpus(containing 1 billion characters) for model training. Distribution-representation [18] (200-dimensional word embedding) method is used to obtain the similarity between two words, because it effectively reflects the semantic relationship between two words than traditional one-hot representation. The skip-gram [13] model includes steps are as follows:

Given a sequence of training words $w_1, w_2, ..., w_T$, the objective function of the word vector model is to maximize the average *log* probability.

$$\frac{1}{T} \sum_{t=k}^{T-k} \log p(w_t | w_{t-k}, \cdots, w_{t+k}) \tag{1}$$

where T is the number of training words.

---

[3] http://mattmahoney.net/dc/enwik9.zip.

The prediction task is typically done via a multiclass classifier, such as softmax. There, we have

$$p(w_t|w_{t-k},\cdots,w_{t+k} = \frac{e^{y_{w_t}}}{\sum_i e^{y_i}})\qquad(2)$$

Each of y_i is un-normalized log-probability for each output word i, computed as

$$y = \psi + \vartheta\varphi(w_t|w_{t-k},\cdots,w_{t+k};W)\qquad(3)$$

Where ϑ,ψ are the softmax parameters, W is a word vector matrix, and φ is constructed by a concatenation or average of word vectors extracted from W.

Task 2: Calculate Similarity Between Word Vectors. After word vectorization representation of fine-grained tag, we obtain the similarity between fine-grained tags by calculating the cosine similarity between word vectors. We have

$$\cos(w_i,w_j) = \frac{\sum_{k=1}^{N}(W_i^k \times W_j^k)}{\sqrt{\sum_{k=1}^{N}(W_i^k)^2} \times \sqrt{\sum_{k=1}^{N}(W_j^k)^2}}\qquad(4)$$

Where w_i^k represents the k_{th} dimension of the word vector of the candidate fine-grained tag w_i, N represents the dimension of the vector, w_j^k represents the k_{th} dimension of the word embedding of the candidate fine-grained tags w_j.

Task 3: Tags Clustering Based on Similarity Between Word Vectors. In this paper, the Affinity Propagation (AP) [4] clustering method is used to cluster tags based on similarities of word vectors. The responsibility information and the availability information of similarity data is continuously iteratively updated, until a stable cluster center is generated. The steps of AP clustering algorithm as follows:

Update the responsibility information formula $r_{t+1}(m,n)$ of the $(t+1)_{th}$ iteration.

$$\begin{cases} S(m,n) - \max\limits_{l\neq n}\{a_t(m,l) + r_t(m,l)\}, m \neq n \\ S(m,n) - \max\limits_{l\neq n} S(m,l), m = n \end{cases}\qquad(5)$$

Update the availability information formula $a_{t+1}(m,n)$ of the $(t+1)_{th}$ iteration.

$$\begin{cases} \min\{0, r_{t+1}(n,n) + \sum\limits_{l\neq m,n}\max\{r_{t+1}(l,n),0\}\}, m \neq n \\ \sum\limits_{l\neq n}\max\{r_{t+1}(l,n),0\}, m = n \end{cases}\qquad(6)$$

Where r represents responsibility information, a represents availability information, S is a similarity matrix, and $S(m,n)$ takes a negative Euclidean distance of m and n. When $m = n$, $S(m,n)$ takes the minimum or median of the entire matrix. The larger value of the $S(m,n)$, the greater number of clusters that will eventually be produced. m and n respectively represent two data objects in the same cluster, t represents the number of iterations, $r_{t+1}(m, n)$ represents the responsibility information of the $(t+1)_{th}$ iteration, and $a_{t+1}(m, n)$ represents the availability information of the $(t+1)_{th}$ iteration.

Task 4: Extract User's Fine-Grained Preference Features. In the photography community, H-tag (*Definition* 1) and C-tag (*Definition* 2) often reflect the user's fine-grained photography preferences. A plurality of clusters are formed after clustering candidate tags, and every cluster can represents one aspect of the user's fine-grained photography preferences. First, we delete the unqualified clusters (the number of tags is less than 3), and then select the cluster center tag, H-tag and C-tags in same cluster. Finally, the three kinds of tags are defined as user's fine-grained preference feature.

4   Potential Friend Recommendation

Firstly, we establishe a user-item scoring matrix by processesing the metadata of users and tags. Then, we use the collaborative filtering [2] algorithm to calculate the similarity of fine-grained photography preferences between the target user and other users, and generates a potential friend recommendation list. Finally, we use user activity to weight the users in friend recommendation list, preferentially recommend users with high user activity to target user, and improve the quality of friend recommendation (Fig. 2).

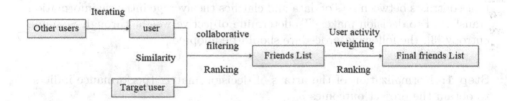

Fig. 2. Potential friend recommendation.

4.1   Calculate User Similarity Based on Preference Features

We use the R to assess the importance of the user's fine-grained photography preference feature tags. The tag frequency and similarity are greater, the larger R will be. In the collaborative-filtering algorithm, we use the value of R as a score in the user-item rating matrix.

The PageRank algorithm [19] is used to calculate the R value of preference feature tag, by the tag frequency and similarity. We define the fine-grained tag i of user u has a R value R_i^u, and all R values satisfy $R_i^u \in (0, 1)$.

In this work, we use jaccard similarity coefficient to evaluate the similarity between user u and v. $J(F^u, F^v)$ is defined as follows:

$$J(F^u, F^v) = \frac{|F^u \cap F^v|}{|F^u \cup F^v|} \tag{7}$$

where F^u and F^v are N-dimensional vectors consisting of 0 and 1, N represents the number of different tags for all users. For example, $F^u = (1, 0, 1, ..., 0, 1)$, 1 means that the tag is included, and 0 means that the tag is not included. We sort the users in descending order according to the similarities and generate a friend list.

4.2 Filtering Friends Recommendation List Based on User Activity

In photography community, we need to use user's information to extract more attractive features, which often play an important role in friend recommendations. In this paper, we select the number of photos, fans and pageviews as features to assess the user's activity.

We define $\lambda_1, \lambda_2, \lambda_3$ as the weight of photos, fans and pageviews. Entropy concept has been widely employed in social and physical sciences, and we use Entropy Weight Method (EWM) to determine the value of $\lambda_1, \lambda_2, \lambda_3$. A mathematical theory of communication was proposed by Shannon. Entropy evaluates the expected information content of a certain message. Entropy concept in information theory can be considered as a criterion for the degree of uncertainty represented by a discrete probability distribution. Entropy idea can be effectively employed in the process of decision making, because it measures existent contrasts between sets of data and clarifies the average intrinsic information transferred to decision maker. To determine objective weight through Shannon entropy [3], the following procedure should be adopted.

Step 1: Normalization of the arrays of decision matrix (performance indices) to obtain the project outcomes p_{ij}:

$$Y_{ij} = \frac{X_{ij} - \min(X_i)}{\max(X_i) - \min(X_i)} \tag{8}$$

$$p_{ij} = Y_{ij} / \sum_{i=1}^{N} Y_{ij} \tag{9}$$

Step 2: Computation of the entropy measure of project outcomes using the following equation:

$$E_j = -\ln(n)^{-1} \sum_{i=1}^{N} p_{ij} \ln p_{ij} \tag{10}$$

Step 3: Defining the objective weight based on the entropy concept:

$$\lambda_i = \frac{1 - E_i}{k - \sum E_i} \tag{11}$$

We define A_u as the activity of the user u, and the greater number of user's photos, fans, and pageviews, the greater activity of user will be. When the users' fine-grained preference similarities are close, the user with high activity is preferentially recommended as friend of the target user. We normalize the number of photos, fans and pageviews of all users. $A_u \in (0, 1)$ is defined as follows:

$$A_u = \lambda_1 \times \frac{w_u}{w_m} + \lambda_2 \times \frac{f_u}{f_m} + \lambda_3 \times \frac{p_u}{p_m} \tag{12}$$

Where w_u, f_u and p_u are the number of photos, fans and pageviews respectively of user u. w_m, f_m and p_m are the maximum number of photos, fans and pageviews respectively. In which, $\lambda_1 + \lambda_2 + \lambda_3 = 1$, $\lambda_1 \in (0, 1)$, $\lambda_2 \in (0, 1)$, $\lambda_3 \in (0, 1)$.

The preference feature similarities of potential friend recommendation list are multiplied by the user activity, and the result are defined as Rec-coefficient. We sort Rec-coefficient in descending order according to the size, and the top-k users are selected as the final friend recommendation list.

Table 1. Dataset statistics.

User	2,170
Photos	17,087
Tags	53,438 tags from 17,087 photos

5 Experimental Evaluation

5.1 Dataset

The dataset (Table 1) of this paper is mainly from the data of one of the world's largest photography communities, Flickr[4]. The dataset mainly include tags and user's information such as id, the number of pageview, fan and photo. In this work, we focus on analyzing the 2170 users' fine-grained preferences features through tags and recommending potential friends with similar fine-grained preferences for the target user.

Tagging systems can provide users effective ways to collaboratively annotate and organize items with their own tags. However, the flexibility of annotation brings with large numbers of redundant tags. It is a very difficult task to find

---

[4] https://secure.flickr.com/.

Table 2. Candidate tags.

mountains	alps	italy	mood	moody	fantasy
sunset	wilderness	adventure	peaks	bled	sunrise
lake	fog	austria	mountain	castle	river
photographer	frozen	ridge	scenery	landscape	scenic
tree	dawn	heritage	clouds	travel	reflection
water	sky	storm	summer	outdoors	nature

users' interest exactly and recommend proper friends to users in social tagging systems. Therefore, we need to pre-process the tag data to get the candidate tag set: (1) Delete all the fine-grained tags whose frequency of the tag is less than 2. (2) Delete fine-grained tags with misspellings. (3) Convert all uppercase letters to lowercase letters. (4) Delete tags that cannot be vectorized.

Table 3. Metrics

Homogeneity	Completeness	V-measure	Mutual information	Silhouette coefficient
0.902	0.346	0.500	0.338	0.490

5.2 Case Study for AP Clustering

We select the target user id is 29507649@N02 for a case to analyze. After pre-processing the target user's tags, the set of candidate tags is shown in Table 2. In this work, the Affinity Propagation (AP) clustering method is used to cluster the candidate tags and get three clusters are shown in Table 4. We calculate the distance between the cluster center and other tags in the same cluster by the Euclidean distance (Fig. 3). The metrics are given to evaluate AP clustering, and the clustering effect is shown in the Table 3.

5.3 Evaluation Methodology

We use several reference methods to show the advantage of our proposed method in friend recommendation. (1) Random tag similarity. (2) On-Line Collaborative Filtering(OLCF) [22]. (3) Friend Recommendation algorithm by User similarity Graph (FRUG) [25]. At the same time, we use Precision and Recall to evaluate the performance of the method.

Precision is defined as follows:

$$Precision = \frac{\sum\limits_{u \in U} |R(u) \cap T(u)|}{\sum\limits_{u \in U} |R(u)|} \qquad (13)$$

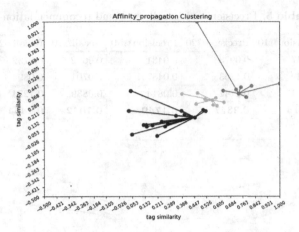

Fig. 3. Candidate tags for AP clustering.

Recall is defined as follows:

$$Recall = \frac{\sum\limits_{u \in U} |R(u) \cap T(u)|}{\sum\limits_{u \in U} |T(u)|} \tag{14}$$

where U is a set of all users. $R(u)$ is the list of potential friends whom recommended to user u by the algorithm. $T(u)$ is the list of friends in test data.

Table 4. Tags distribution after clustering

Cluster center	Candidate tags
scenic	fog, castle, scenery, landscape, tree, heritage, clouds, sky, storm
lake	river, mountains, ridge, wilderness, peaks, alps
sunset	italy, mood, moody, fantasy, adventure, bled, sunrise, austria, photographer, frozen, dawn, water, travel, reflection, summer, outdoors, nature

Experimental results are shown in Table 5. The performance measured in terms of precision and recall. The number of potential friends recommended to the target user is 10, 20 and 50 respectively. We can see Similarity have poor performance, and FRFP is better than the other three methods.

To further validate the performance of FRFP, the number of potential friends is validated in more details. N is the number of potential friends recommended to target user. In our experiments, the value of $N \in [5, 50]$. The results in terms of precision and recall in Top-N are shown in Fig. 4, we can see that FRFP is still better than other three methods.

Table 5. Precision and Recall on friend recommendation

Method	Precision@10	Precision@20	Precision@50	Recall@10	Recall@20	Recall@50
Similarity	0.1037	0.0973	0.0431	0.0612	0.0732	0.1045
OLCF	0.1689	0.1263	0.04871	0.0701	0.0894	0.1438
FRUG	0.2034	0.1747	0.0814	0.0839	0.1274	0.1843
FRFP	**0.2714**	**0.2347**	**0.1749**	**0.1042**	**0.1464**	**0.2147**

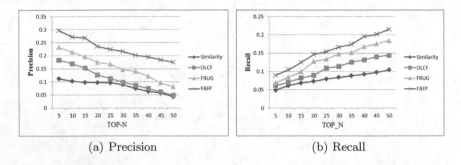

(a) Precision   (b) Recall

Fig. 4. Comparison of methods in precision and recall

6 Conclusion

In this paper, a personalized friend recommendation method called FRFP is proposed based on user fine-grained preferences feature tag in photography community. In tagging system, the value of R as a score in the user-item rating matrix to calculate the similarity of users' fine-grained preference. We also use Au to weight the friend recommendation list, and improve the quality of friend recommendations. However, due to the user's cold start problem in the photography community, and the user's photography preferences will change over time. For example, user uploaded new photos. Therefore, we need to deal with the above problems in the future work, and further study the hybrid recommendation system.

Acknowledgment. This research was supported by NSFC grant 61632009 and Outstanding Young Talents Training Program in Hunan University 531118040173.

References

1. Mislove, A., Marcon, M., Gummadi, K., Druschel, P., Bhattacharjee, B.: Measurement and analysis of online social networks. Association for Computing Machinery (ACM) (2007)
2. Badrul, S., George, K., Joseph, K., John, R.: Item-based collaborative filtering recommendation algorithms. In: Proceedings of ACM World Wide Web Conference (2001)
3. Hwang, C.-L., Paul, Y.K.: Multiple attribute decision making. Methods and applications. A state-of-the-art survey (1981)

4. Frey, B.J., Dueck, D.: Clustering by passing messages between data points. Science **315**(5814), 972–976 (2007)
5. Gong, N.Z.: Jointly predicting links and inferring attributes using a social-attribute network (SAN). Computer Science (2011)
6. Han, S., Xu, Y.: Friend recommendation of microblog in classification framework: using multiple social behavior features. In: International Conference on Behavior (2015)
7. Hannon, J., Bennett, M., Smyth, B.: Recommending twitter users to follow using content and collaborative filtering approaches. In: Recommender Systems, pp. 199–206 (2010)
8. Hasan, M.M., Shaon, N.H., Marouf, A.A., Hasan, Md.K., Khan, Md.M.: Friend recommendation framework for social networking sites using user's online behavior. In: International Conference on Computer and Information Technology (2015)
9. He, C., Li, H., Xiang, F., Yong, T., Jia, Z.: A topic community-based method for friend recommendation in online social networks via joint nonnegative matrix factorization. In: Third International Conference on Advanced Cloud and Big Data (2016)
10. Huang, S., Zhang, J., Lu, S., Hua, X.S.: Social friend recommendation based on network correlation and feature co-clustering (2015)
11. Jiang, W., Jie, W., Feng, L., Wang, G., Zheng, H.: Trust evaluation in online social networks using generalized network flow. IEEE Trans. Comput. **65**(3), 952–963 (2016)
12. Jiang, W., Wang, G., Bhuiyan, M.Z.A., Wu, J.: Understanding graph-based trust evaluation in online social networks: methodologies and challenges. ACM Comput. Surv. **49**(1), 1–35 (2016)
13. Le, Q.V., Mikolov, T.: Distributed representations of sentences and documents. In: International Conference on International Conference on Machine Learning (2014)
14. Li, M., Jiang, W., Li, K.: Recommendation systems in real applications: algorithm and parallel architecture. In: Wang, G., Ray, I., Alcaraz Calero, J.M., Thampi, S.M. (eds.) SpaCCS 2016. LNCS, vol. 10066, pp. 45–58. Springer, Cham (2016). https://doi.org/10.1007/978-3-319-49148-6_5
15. Li, Z., Fang, X., Sheng, O.: A survey of link recommendation for social networks: methods, theoretical foundations, and future research directions. Social Science Electronic Publishing (2015)
16. Menon, A.K., Elkan, C.: Link prediction via matrix factorization. In: Gunopulos, D., Hofmann, T., Malerba, D., Vazirgiannis, M. (eds.) ECML PKDD 2011. LNCS (LNAI), vol. 6912, pp. 437–452. Springer, Heidelberg (2011). https://doi.org/10.1007/978-3-642-23783-6_28
17. Mikolov, T., Chen, K., Corrado, G., Dean, J.: Distributed representations of sentences and documents (2016)
18. Mikolov, T., Sutskever, I., Chen, K., Corrado, G., Dean, J.: Distributed representations of words and phrases and their compositionality (2013)
19. Page, L., Brin, S., Motwani, R., Winograd, T.: Bringing order to the web. The pagerank citation ranking (1999)
20. Qiu, S., Cheng, J., Yuan, T., Leng, C., Lu, H.: Item group based pairwise preference learning for personalized ranking, pp. 1219–1222 (2014)
21. Rendle, S., Freudenthaler, C., Gantner, Z., Schmidt-Thieme, L.: BPR: Bayesian personalized ranking from implicit feedback. In: Conference on Uncertainty in Artificial Intelligence (2009)
22. Rendle, S., Schmidt-Thieme, L.: Onlineupdating regularized kernel matrix factorization models for large-scale recommender systems (2008)

23. Wang, F., Li, J., Jiang, W., Wang, G.: Temporal topic-based multi-dimensional social influence evaluation in online social networks. Wirel. Pers. Commun. **95**(3), 2143–2171 (2017)
24. Wang, G., Jiang, W., Wu, J., Xiong, Z.: Fine-grained feature-based social influence evaluation in online social networks. IEEE Trans. Parall. Distrib. Syst. **25**(9), 2286–2296 (2014)
25. Wu, B.-X., Xiao, J., Chen, J.-M.: Friend recommendation by user similarity graph based on interest in social tagging systems. In: Huang, D.-S., Han, K. (eds.) ICIC 2015. LNCS (LNAI), vol. 9227, pp. 375–386. Springer, Cham (2015). https://doi.org/10.1007/978-3-319-22053-6_41
26. Xing, X.: Potential friend recommendation in online social network. In: IEEE/ACM International Conference on Green Computing and Communications and International Conference on Cyber (2010)
27. Xu, Y., Zeng, Q., Wang, G., Zhang, C., Ren, J., Zhang, Y.: A privacy-preserving attribute-based access control scheme, pp. 361–370 (2018)
28. Zheng, H., Jie, W.: Friend recommendation in online social networks: perspective of social influence maximization. In: 2017 26th International Conference on Computer Communication and Networks (ICCCN) (2017)

Band Segmentation and Detection of DNA by Using Fast Fuzzy C-mean and Neuro Adaptive Fuzzy Inference System

Muhammad Arif[1], Guojun Wang[1(✉)] (iD), Valentina Emilia Balas[2] (iD), and Shuhong Chen[1]

[1] School of Computer Science, Guangzhou University, Guangzhou 510006, Guangdong, China
arifmuhammad36@hotmail.com, csgjwang@gmail.com, shuhongchen@gzhu.edu.cn
[2] Aurel Vlaicu University of Arad, Arad, Romania
balas@drbalas.ro

Abstract. Currently, band segmentation is used in medical science, because it helps the scientist to detect and calculate the band and line respectively. Segmentation is very important in medical images, because it provides the clinical assistance to physician. Such as, the DNA images are used to detect and segment the bands and line and calculate the local minima and maxima. For segmentation, we use Fast Fuzzy C-Mean Clustering (FFCM). FFCM is a clustering method that allows a piece of data to be in two or more clusters. Clustering involves the task of dividing the data points into homogeneous classes or the clusters, so that items in the same class are as equitable as possible and the items in the different classes are different. Our results indicate that our proposed method effectively detects the band and counts the lines.

Keywords: DNA · Band · Segmentation · Clustering · ANFIS · Detection

1 Introduction

In this article, the most important issues and methods identified by the advanced image investigation of DNA images will tend to segment specific DNA images. Such segmentation is critical in an image, for example, DNA images are used to distinguish and segment groups and lines and to draw neighbourhood minimum and maximum values [10,28]. Image segmentation is the way in which an image is divided into areas, such as the colors and the objects [1,17,19,29]. These areas are a set of pixels and have some important data about the objects [5,15,16,23]. The result of image segmentation is that the image becomes more important, more obvious and easier to analyse [2,20] proper fragmentation of results can be very helpful in checking, predicting, and deciding. Use branches in various areas, similar to traffic development, vehicle development, safety and protection

© Springer Nature Singapore Pte Ltd. 2019
G. Wang et al. (Eds.): iSCI 2019, CCIS 1122, pp. 49–59, 2019.
https://doi.org/10.1007/978-981-15-1301-5_5

projections [3, 4, 6–8, 21]. For the purpose of segmentation, we utilized the FFCM, it is a method for aggregating, which gives one-bit information the location of at least two groups. Grouping involves focusing the partition information in the same category or grouping, with the goal of things in a similar class compared to things that are prudent, things in each category are different from what is expected in this case. Grouping can also be thought of as an information pressure in which a large number of tests are converted to a few representing models or clusters [13]. Depending on the information and application, you can use a variety of closely related metrics to classify areas, where the formation of similar metrics control groups [9, 14, 22].

Some of the qualitative examples that can be used for comparability measures include separation, networking and power [24]. In non-fluffy or hard grouping, the information is isolated into new bundles, where each reference point has a position of only one cluster [12]. In a fluffy aggregation, the information focus can have a location with multiple groups, and associated with each focus is the participation comment, which shows how much information is focused in multiple clusters [12]. Nevertheless, one of the main advantages of FFCM is that it does not take into account any spatial data in the image settings, which makes it very sensitive to noise and other imaging artifacts [30].

We created a FFCM restricted space system to increase fuzzy clustering results. We also change the FFCM target function by using spatial punctuation in the membership function, which is the result of a duplicate algorithm that, have the much similarity with the original FCM clustering and agrees for the estimation of spatial member-ship function to be smooth. Later, we applied the Adaptive-Neuro-Fuzzy-Inference-System (ANFIS) to classify and identify the lines of DNA images.

2   Materials and Methods

2.1   Fast Fuzzy C-mean Clustering

In the past decades, the division of medical images has been used. Neural networks (NN), self organizing schemes (SOM), unsustainable frameworks and the section are emergent, medical image dividing methods [26]. Among the available methods for categorizing medical imagery, fuzzy clusters have the extra applications in comparisons with the other clustering techniques, as they can retain much knowledge about the actual image by using fuzzy memberships [31]. The FCM method was implemented in the 1970s and after that it have many variations [32]. The FCM allocates C-membership privileges per pixel. Though, updating the membership function matrix with the cn member is a time overriding method [18]. In the FCM, the centroids are reorganized by the fuzzy membership that requires a lot of time. To decrease the time and the amount of calculations in the FFCM, we allocate the hard membership functions to the pixels for updating the cluster centres at every repeat step [27]. Nevertheless, division is a fuzzy method, by implementing a strict membership function, the new updated algorithm for updating the centroids is suggested as follows:

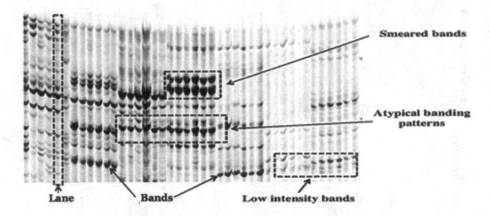

Fig. 1. Sample DNA image with lanes and band patterns

Step1: For the p-dimensionally input the data, rearrange u_{ij} to $d_1 d_2$ matrix; where the d_1, d_2 are the input dimensions.

Step2: Set the original fuzzy membership function as u^*_{ij} and the label the matrix as $L = L^1, L^2, L^c$; where the L^k is label matrix of kth cluster in current iteration.

Step3: Set all the data point, which are the corresponded to L^k label matrix as the I^K.

Step4: Define the $I^k = I^k_1, I^k_2, \ldots, I^k_{nck}$ for kth cluster, where the $-nc_k$ are the number of the data points in the kth cluster.

Step5: Updating the centroid of the kth cluster by the equation given below:
$v^*_k = (\sum_{j=1}^{nck} I^j_k)/ - nc_k.$

The new updated fuzzy membership functions, and after that we compute the cost function.

We used the FFCM method to implement a precision segmentation technique for detecting the DNA bands. In Figs. 1, and 2, we show the sample DNA image with lanes and the graph of the intensity of the sample DNA image. Three attributes of DNA are known as line width, gap detection, and line extraction. Segmentation plays an important role in determining the characteristics mentioned, which helps to classify and measure band and division detection [25]. In our method, the division mentions to the precise determination of the division of a DNA image.

In the Fig. 3, we show the color segmentation of the DNA image, we apply the FFCM with 3 clusters. The Fig. 4(a, b, c), represents the 3 membership map function the clustering steps on DNA sample case. At the subsequent step to decrease the FFCM result dimensions, we utilize the ANFIS for the detection and classification of the bands.

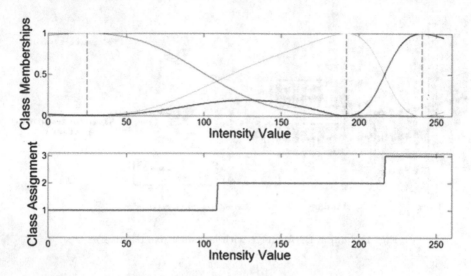

Fig. 2. Sample DNA case intensity graph

Fig. 3. Color segmented abnormal case

2.2 Adaptive Neuro Fuzzy Inference System (ANFIS)

The ANFIS is an influential builder that links the ability of NN and the fuzzy systems [11]. This approach makes utilizations of the conditions based on 'if and else' in the decision making process. A set of these conditions is known as the fuzzy rules [16]. ANFIS can also be utilized as the basis for constructing a group of the rules with the assistance of the membership functions that can generate the necessary couples of inputs and outputs. After that, these memberships function turn into inputs and output data. ANFIS is about getting the Fuzzy Inference System (FIS) based on a set of the inputs and the output data that it creates with its backward algorithm. FIS has three implications:

(1) The rule of law.
(2) The database.
(3) The procedure of reasoning.

The first module covers a set of fuzzy rules, the second part elaborate the membership functions in each fuzzy rules. Finally, the third module performs the

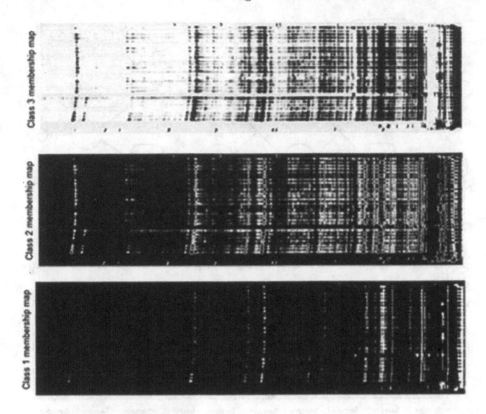

Fig. 4. Clustering steps on sample DNA image (a) shows class 1 membership map, (b) shows class 2 membership map, (c) shows class 3 membership map.

deduction method using the facts given to achieve the result [16]. Information, methods, and procedures are collected from multiple sources and combined into this scheme. These schemes have the social ability of obvious areas to learn from and acquaint themselves with dissimilar environments. Supports the adaptation of these schemes from the NN. In this research, the fuzzy logical toolbox in the MATLAB is utilized in all phases of the training to evaluate FIS. As shown in Fig. 5, there are the five layers in the ANFIS framework. In our proposed method, we utilized the first order sugeno model with the two inputs and the fuzzy IF-THEN rules of the takagi and the Sugeno type:

$$\text{if } x \text{ is } A \text{ and } y \text{ is } C \text{ then } f_1 = p_1 x + q_1 y + r_1$$

The first layer contains the MFs input function, which is considered as input 1, 2. This layer is accountable for displaying input value to the subsequent layer. Now each node is compatible with the node function $O = \mu_{AB}(x)$ and $O = \mu_{CD}(x)$, where as the $\mu_{AB}(x)$ and $\mu_{CD}(x)$ are the MFs. In this research, angular MFs are considered at a maximum of 1 and at least 0.

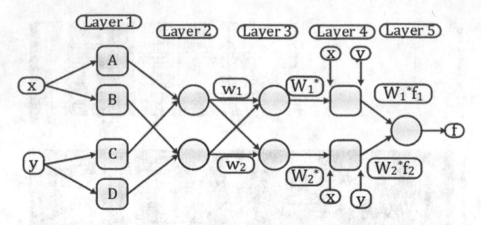

Fig. 5. ANFIS architecture

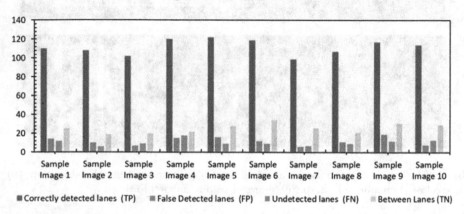

■ Correctly detected lanes (TP)   ■ False Detected lanes (FP)   ■ Undetected lanes (FN)   ■ Between Lanes (TN)

Fig. 6. Shows TN, FN, FP, TP, on ten sample images

$$\mu(x) = bell(x; a_i, b_i, c_i, d_i) = 1/(1 + [((x - c_i)/a_i)^2]^{b_i}).$$
$$a_i, b_i, c_i, d_i,$$

Theses set of variables are assumed as a parameters. While x and y are node inputs that represent a combination of two parameters that affect the detection of the bands ans lanes. The 2nd layer is responsible for checking the weights of every MF. The input value of the 1st layer and the function as MF correspond to the fuzzy sets of input variables. Unlike the 1st layer, every node in the 2nd layer is non-consistent. The 2nd layer multiplies the acknowledged signals and forward the product the same way as,

$$w_i = \mu_{AB}(x) * \mu_{CD}(y).$$

Output at each node describes the firing strength of the fuzzy rule. The 3rd layer is quantified as the layer of rules. In layer the every node performs

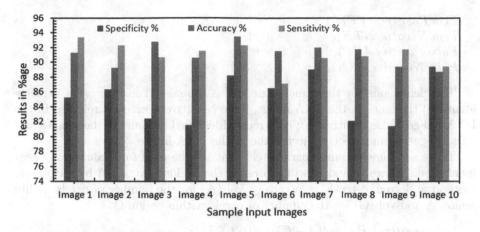

Fig. 7. Shows the specificity, accuracy and sensitivity on ten sample images

a prerequisite corresponding of the fuzzy rules, which means they calculate the activation level of each rule and the number of layers correspondent to the number of the fuzzy rules. Each node in layer is non well-suited and computes the normal weight and the ratio of the firing power of the rule to the total firing forces of all the rules, where the,

$$w_i^* = w_i/(w_1 + w_2), i = 1, 2.$$

The outputs of this layer appear to be normal firing power. The 4th layer is known as the de-fuzzification layer. It is the responsibility of providing the output values that result from inference of rules. Here each node is compatible with the node function as,

$$O_i^4 = w_i^* x f = w_i^*(p_i x + q_i y + r_i)$$

where p_i, q_i, r a set of the constraints, that are defined as the resulting constraints. The 5th layer is known as output layer, and it collects all the input data that is from layer 4, also falsifies the results of the fuzzy classification into binary. This layer contains a non-consistent node that calculates the generic output as the sum of the input signal.

$$O_i^5 = \sum_i w_i^* x f = (\sum_i w_i f)/(\sum_i w_i)$$

3 Evaluation

To understand the performance of the developed system, we need to evaluate the method in terms of measures. In this area, there are common measures to evaluate the proposed system that are,

$TruePositives(TP),$
$TrueNegatives(TN),$
$FalsePositives(FP),$
$FalseNegatives(FN).$

The definitions for these measures are as follows. True Positive: Correctly identified the lanes in the DNA image, True Negative: Correctly rejected in the DNA image, False Positive FP: incorrectly identified the lane in the images and False Negative: incorrectly rejected the in the DNA image.

There are some common parameters that will be used for evaluation of segmentation. Where A and G will represent the regions extracted by automatic method and ground truth, respectively, vol (A) for the number of pixels within region A and vol (G) for the number of pixels within region G.

$False positive FP = vol(A - G)/vol(G),$
$False negative FN = vol(G - A)/vol(G),$
$True positive TP = vol(A - G)/vol(A),$
$True negative TN = vol(A - G)/vol(A).$

For calculating the difference ratio between ground truth and segmented region we will use matching ratio. Evaluation for classification and identification of lanes. There are some common parameters like sensitivity, specificity, accuracy are used for evaluation of classification and identification. These parameters are defined as follows,

$Sensitivity(also known as recall rate) = (TP/TP + FP) * 100$
$Specificity = (TN/TN + FP) * 100$
$Accuracy = (TP + TN/TP + TN + FP + FN) * 100$

4   Results

We segment the DNA images and detect the lanes with 3 membership classes and after that applying FFCM and ANFIS for calculating the local minima and maxima and for gap detection between the lines because after applying fuzzy c-mean the information is divided into clusters and it is easy for us to calculate the local as well as the global minima and maxima. The average image intensity of the DNA image of each individual will be referred to as the severity profile and will display the data of the relevant DNA image. For each valley in the intensity distribution, the algorithm is used to estimate its local minimum correct position.

The horizontal lines (called "line levels") that pass from both sides of the valley are located in the lower part of the image. Calculate and record the midpoint between points that were stolen from the horizon. Then, the horizontal surface moves to the largest local neighbour, and the centre point between the storage point and the line level is again calculated and recorded.

The method repeats to the level of the line starting from the largest and largest local area of the valley. Finally, a linear regression is performed on the line level values for each valley. The starting point of the regression line and the relevant sea area is at least the correct range, and the centre line of the relevant sea in the strength specification. In our computations, the detection rate of the training network is explained as,

Recognition rate = correctly identified lanes/total counted lanes.

We are currently using the ANFIS network to discuss the results of the correct channel identification based on the defined detection rate. We started the training procedure with just 10 sample images. ANFIS $X1, X2, X3, ..., X10$ has 10 input vector. These input vectors are obtained after division. After the training procedure, topological knowledge is stored for a set of the support points for ten inputs in only 25 neuron activators of the NN. We analysed several gel images using the trained NN and the results are presented in the Fig. 6. We select the some sample images for testing our method, it is clearly seen that our method count the lanes very efficiently.

First of all, we calculate the TP, TN, FP, FN of some sample images, and we used these calculations to compute the sensitivity, specificity, accuracy, the calculations are shown in Fig. 6. There are some common parameters like sensitivity, specificity, accuracy are used for evaluation of classification and identification. The results of sensitivity, specificity, accuracy are presented in Fig. 7.

5   Conclusion

We segment the DNA images and detect the lanes with 3 membership classes and after that applying fast fuzzy c-mean clustering and ANFIS for calculating the local minima and maxima. After, applying fuzzy c-mean the information is divided into clusters and it is easy for us to calculate the local as well as the global minima and maxima. The average image intensity of the DNA image of each individual will be referred to as the severity profile and will display the data of the relevant DNA image. We select the some sample images for testing our method, it is clearly seen that our method count the lanes very efficiently.

Acknowledgments. This work was supported in part by the National Natural Science Foundation of China under Grant 61632009, in part by the Guangdong Provincial Natural Science Foundation under Grant 2017A030308006, and in part by the High-Level Talents Program of Higher Education in Guangdong Province under Grant 2016ZJ01.

References

1. Arif, M., Abdullah, N.A., Phalianakote, S.K., Ramli, N., Elahi, M.: Maximizing information of multimodality brain image fusion using curvelet transform with genetic algorithm. In: 2014 International Conference on Computer Assisted System in Health, pp. 45–51. IEEE (2014)
2. Arif, M., Alam, K.A., Hussain, M.: Application of data mining using artificial neural network: survey. Int. J. Database Theory Appl. **8**(1), 245–270 (2015)
3. Arif, M., Mahmood, T.: Cloud computing and its environmental effects. Int. J. Grid Distrib. Comput. **8**(1), 279–286 (2015)

4. Arif, M., Shakeel, H.: Virtualization security: analysis and open challenges. Int. J. Hybrid Inf. Technol. **8**(2), 237–246 (2015)
5. Arif, M., Wang, G.: Fast curvelet transform through genetic algorithm for multi-modal medical image fusion. Soft Comput. 1–22 (2019)
6. Arif, M., Wang, G., Balas, V.E.: Secure VANETs: trusted communication scheme between vehicles and infrastructure based on fog computing. Stud. Inform. Control **27**(2), 235–246 (2018)
7. Arif, M., Wang, G., Chen, S.: Deep learning with non-parametric regression model for traffic flow prediction. In: 2018 IEEE 16th International Conference on Dependable, Autonomic and Secure Computing, 16th International Conference on Pervasive Intelligence and Computing, 4th International Conference on Big Data Intelligence and Computing and Cyber Science and Technology Congress (DASC/PiCom/DataCom/CyberSciTech), pp. 681–688. IEEE (2018)
8. Arif, M., Wang, G., Peng, T.: Track me if you can? Query based dual location privacy in VANETs for V2V and V2I. In: 2018 17th IEEE International Conference on Trust, Security and Privacy in Computing and Communications/12th IEEE International Conference on Big Data Science And Engineering (TrustCom/BigDataSE), pp. 1091–1096. IEEE (2018)
9. Arif, M., Wang, G., Wang, T., Peng, T.: SDN-based secure VANETs communication with fog computing. In: Wang, G., Chen, J., Yang, L.T. (eds.) SpaCCS 2018. LNCS, vol. 11342, pp. 46–59. Springer, Cham (2018). https://doi.org/10.1007/978-3-030-05345-1_4
10. Bajcsy, P.: An overview of DNA microarray grid alignment and foreground separation approaches. EURASIP J. Adv. Signal Process. **2006**(1), 080163 (2006)
11. Belaout, A., Krim, F., Mellit, A., Talbi, B., Arabi, A.: Multiclass adaptive neuro-fuzzy classifier and feature selection techniques for photovoltaic array fault detection and classification. Renew. Energy **127**, 548–558 (2018)
12. Binesh, N., Rezghi, M.: Fuzzy clustering in community detection based on nonnegative matrix factorization with two novel evaluation criteria. Appl. Soft Comput. **69**, 689–703 (2018)
13. Couso, I., Borgelt, C., Hullermeier, E., Kruse, R.: Fuzzy sets in data analysis: from statistical foundations to machine learning. IEEE Comput. Intell. Mag. **14**(1), 31–44 (2019)
14. Geman, O., Chiuchisan, I., Ungurean, I., Hagan, M., Arif, M.: Ubiquitous healthcare system based on the sensors network and android internet of things gateway. In: 2018 IEEE SmartWorld, Ubiquitous Intelligence & Computing, Advanced & Trusted Computing, Scalable Computing & Communications, Cloud & Big Data Computing, Internet of People and Smart City Innovation (SmartWorld/SCALCOM/UIC/ATC/CBDCom/IOP/SCI), pp. 1390–1395. IEEE (2018)
15. Javaid, Q., Arif, M., Awan, D., Shah, M.: Efficient facial expression detection by using the adaptive-neuro-fuzzy-inference-system and the bezier curve. Sindh Univ. Res. J.-SURJ (Sci. Ser.) **48**(3) (2016)
16. Javaid, Q., Arif, M., Talpur, S.: Segmentation and classification of calcification and hemorrhage in the brain using fuzzy c-mean and adaptive neuro-fuzzy inference system. Quaid-e-Awam Univ. Res. J. Eng. Sci. Technol. **15**(1), 50–63 (2016)
17. Javaid, Q., Arif, M., Shah, M.A., Nadeem, M., et al.: A hybrid technique for denoising multi-modality medical images by employing cuckoo's search with curvelet transform. Mehran Univ. Res. J. Eng. Technol. **37**(1), 29 (2018)
18. Mikaeil, R., Haghshenas, S.S., Haghshenas, S.S., Ataei, M.: Performance prediction of circular saw machine using imperialist competitive algorithm and fuzzy clustering technique. Neural Comput. Appl. **29**(6), 283–292 (2018)

19. Muhammad, A., Guojun, W.: Segmentation of calcification and brain hemorrhage with midline detection. In: 2017 IEEE International Symposium on Parallel and Distributed Processing with Applications and 2017 IEEE International Conference on Ubiquitous Computing and Communications (ISPA/IUCC), pp. 1082–1090. IEEE (2017)

20. Oktay, O., et al.: Anatomically constrained neural networks (ACNNS): application to cardiac image enhancement and segmentation. IEEE Trans. Med. Imaging **37**(2), 384–395 (2017)

21. Petković, D., Arif, M., Shamshirband, S., Bani-Hani, E.H., Kiakojoori, D.: Sensorless estimation of wind speed by soft computing methodologies: a comparative study. Informatica **26**(3), 493–508 (2015)

22. ur Rahman, H., Azzedin, F., Shawahna, A., Sajjad, F., Abdulrahman, A.S.: Performance evaluation of VDI environment. In: 2016 Sixth International Conference on Innovative Computing Technology (INTECH), pp. 104–109. IEEE (2016)

23. ur Rahman, H., Wang, G., Chen, J., Jiang, H.: Performance evaluation of hypervisors and the effect of virtual CPU on performance. In: 2018 IEEE SmartWorld, Ubiquitous Intelligence & Computing, Advanced & Trusted Computing, Scalable Computing & Communications, Cloud & Big Data Computing, Internet of People and Smart City Innovation (SmartWorld/SCALCOM/UIC/ATC/CBDCom/IOP/SCI), pp. 772–779. IEEE (2018)

24. Rizvi, S.Q.A., Wang, G., Chen, J.: A service oriented healthcare architecture (SOHA-CC) based on cloud computing. In: Wang, G., Chen, J., Yang, L.T. (eds.) SpaCCS 2018. LNCS, vol. 11342, pp. 84–97. Springer, Cham (2018). https://doi.org/10.1007/978-3-030-05345-1_7

25. Sharif, M., Khan, M.A., Iqbal, Z., Azam, M.F., Lali, M.I.U., Javed, M.Y.: Detection and classification of citrus diseases in agriculture based on optimized weighted segmentation and feature selection. Comput. Electron. Agric. **150**, 220–234 (2018)

26. Tripathi, S., Anand, R., Fernandez, E.: A review of brain MR image segmentation techniques. In: Proceedings of International Conference on Recent Innovations in Applied Science, Engineering & Technology, pp. 16–17 (2018)

27. Yang, M.S., Nataliani, Y.: A feature-reduction fuzzy clustering algorithm based on feature-weighted entropy. IEEE Trans. Fuzzy Syst. **26**(2), 817–835 (2017)

28. Yang, Y.H., Buckley, M.J., Dudoit, S., Speed, T.P.: Comparison of methods for image analysis on cDNA microarray data. J. Comput. Graph. Stat. **11**(1), 108–136 (2002)

29. Yazdi, M., Bouwmans, T.: New trends on moving object detection in video images captured by a moving camera: a survey. Comput. Sci. Rev. **28**, 157–177 (2018)

30. Zhang, H., Bruzzone, L., Shi, W., Hao, M., Wang, Y.: Enhanced spatially constrained remotely sensed imagery classification using a fuzzy local double neighborhood information c-means clustering algorithm. IEEE J. Sel. Top. Appl. Earth Obs. Remote Sens. **11**(8), 2896–2910 (2018)

31. Zhang, Y., Bai, X., Fan, R., Wang, Z.: Deviation-sparse fuzzy c-means with neighbor information constraint. IEEE Trans. Fuzzy Syst. **27**(1), 185–199 (2018)

32. Zhu, Y.P., Li, P.: Survey on the image segmentation algorithms. In: Qu, Z., Lin, J. (eds.) Proceedings of the International Field Exploration and Development Conference 2017. SSGG, pp. 475–488. Springer, Singapore (2019). https://doi.org/10.1007/978-981-10-7560-5_43

A Management Platform for Citizen's Data Protection Regulation

Alberto Huertas Celdrán[1]([✉]) [iD], Manuel Gil Pérez[2] [iD], Izidor Mlakar[3] [iD],
Jose M. Alcaraz Calero[4] [iD], Félix J. García Clemente[2] [iD],
and Gregorio Martínez Pérez[2] [iD]

[1] Waterford Institute of Technology, Waterford, Ireland
ahuertas@tssg.org
[2] University of Murcia, Murcia, Spain
{mgilperez,fgarcia,gregorio}@um.es
[3] University of Maribor, Maribor, Slovenia
izidor.mlakar@amis.net
[4] University of the West of Scotland, Paisley, Scotland
jose.alcaraz-calero@uws.ac.uk

Abstract. The evolution of information and communications technology, and particularly the Internet of Things as the basis for the setting up of the Smart Cities, are provoking a worldwide revolution in terms of data protection management. A clear example of this shift can be seen in the European Union which is adapting the regulation to meet current society requirements, although similar initiatives are being undertaken by the rest of continents. However, existing data regulation and management solutions offer isolated tools that cover particular rights and laws and are actually not conceived to be integrated with libraries widely used by organizations to implement data management processes. To cover the previous gap, we propose a novel platform which is geared toward the protection of citizen's sensitive data according to their data protection preferences and the rights provided by current data protection regulation laws. Finally, we present a case study to demonstrate how our platform manages data anonymization, protecting a private citizen's right.

Keywords: Personalized data protection · Management platform · Data protection policies · EU GDPR

1 Introduction

Information and Communications Technology (ICT) has become a critical tool to support the need of all aspects of the modern digital society. In last 20 years, ICT has had a profound impact on personal data processing. The explosion of Big Data, the Internet of Things (IoT), and consequently the Smart Cities are provoking a worldwide revolution in terms of sensitive data generation, management, and exchange [1]. The Smart Cities paradigm is being highly influenced

© Springer Nature Singapore Pte Ltd. 2019
G. Wang et al. (Eds.): iSCI 2019, CCIS 1122, pp. 60–72, 2019.
https://doi.org/10.1007/978-981-15-1301-5_6

by having to manage citizen's data securely, preserving their rights and privacy in all the domains made up by the Smart Cities such as Smart Transportation, Smart Homes, Smart Industry, Smart Offices, and Smart Health, just to name a few. In these environments, data emerges in different size, shape, and format that needs to be protected, such as sensitive data for citizens (photos, videos, text, location data where they are and what they are doing in their position, private data registered in their Electronic Health Records, etc.) as well as data collected from sensors situated around the Smart City to ensure operational functions [2]. This explosion is influencing governments around the world to create new data protection regulations to face with the new cyber scenario. A clear example of this shift can be seen in the European Union (EU), which is adapting its regulation to meet society data protection requirements.

From May 2018, a new and single data regulation, entitled *General Data Protection Regulation* (GDPR) [3], has come into effect in the EU to support data protection of EU citizens (*data subjects*). Among the key aspects in this regulation, some of the most relevant are:

- the definition of a global and single territorial scope, which is the biggest change with respect to previous regulation erected in 1995;
- the law applies to all organizations processing sensitive data of the different EU citizens, regardless of the organization location;
- EU citizens have the control over their sensitive data;
- the breach of EU GDPR can be fined up to 4% of annual global turnover or €20 million; and
- organizations will no longer be able to use legal statements not fully understood by citizens due to their difficulty and length.

Moreover, EU GDPR establishes several important rights and obligations for the EU citizens such as consent and revocation, right to erasure, data portability, and data breach notifications, among others.

The implementation of a new data protection regulation introduces organizational, technical, and infrastructural challenges for all organizations. In this context, existing general-purpose software tools have successfully demonstrated, but in an isolated way, so as to provide risk management [4], software and system assurance [5], and data protection [6]. Other solutions go a step further by providing general and integrated platforms focused on managing specific rights and obligations of particular laws. However, despite the benefits offered by the existing solutions, they provide isolated tools that just cover a reduced number of rights and laws, missing a comprehensive solution to most of them. Furthermore, an important number of such solutions are conceived to be integrated with marginal or proprietary tools, instead of well-known libraries and processes widely considered by organizations. In this context, the challenge of creating a general and integrated management platform to assist citizens and organizations in the accomplishment of the data protection regulation is still open. Data protection is an even greater challenge in a Smart City ecosystem, where resource-constrained devices (that sensors and users can use) with limited processing and battery power need to interact with data management processes [7].

With that goal in mind, the main contributions of this article are:

- The design of an innovative management platform focused on protecting the citizen's sensitive data according to their preferences and the rights provided by data protection regulation laws. The proposed solution supplies organizations with security mechanisms to allow meeting data protection requirements of citizens and laws. Additionally, the proposed platform lets citizens define in a user-friendly way their data protection rights and preferences in terms of anonymization, scope and retention, consent and revocation, right to erasure, and portability, among others.
- The formal definition of policies that cover citizen's rights according to the most important data protection regulation laws. To this end, our proposed solution allows citizens to decide and control in real time *what* pieces of sensitive data can be processed by others, *which* organizations can manage such data, in which geographical location (*where*) organizations can store and manage sensitive data, *when* and for *how long* organizations can process sensitive data, and *how* data must be managed by organizations.
- A case study that demonstrates how the proposed management platform can manage citizen's rights according to the EU protection regulation laws. This case study shows how we provide anonymization when collected data is used by a single organization.

Although the latest case study focuses on the EU GDPR data protection laws, it is worth mentioning that our platform could be extended, through policies, to other regulation laws applied by other countries and continents. As clearly stated in the comprehensive review presented in [8], anonymization is a data protection right that has not only been recognized in the EU GDPR, but has also been enacted by Brazil in its General Data Protection Law (Law No. 13,709/2018) [9] and by China in its Personal Information Security Specification [10,11], which has been recently revised in February 2019.

The remainder of the paper is structured as follows. Section 2 discusses some related works focused on current data protection regulation technologies and solutions. Section 3 shows the components making up the proposed management platform, which allows citizens to control the privacy of their sensitive data according to current data protection regulations. Section 4 shows a case study where a citizen's right is managed according to the EU GDPR, in particular the anonymization of citizen's sensitive data for use by a given service provider. Finally, conclusions and future work are drawn in Sect. 5.

2   Related Work

The International Association of Privacy Professionals (IAPP) has released the "2018 Privacy Tech Vendor Report" [12], in which a complete list of software tools belonging to more than 200 companies from the private corporate sector is presented. This report classifies those products in 10 big categories regarding their privacy management software: activity monitoring, assessment manager, consent management, data discovery, data mapping, pseudonymity, enterprise communications, incident response, privacy information manager, and website scanning. However, none of these companies (over 200) provide software tools that meet EU GDPR requirements and cover all of the above categories.

Listed in the report, the Baycloud Consent Platform [13] provides a privacy-related software that properly complies with the forthcoming ePrivacy Regulation [14] and the GDPR in Europe. The Baycloud platform is a privacy-aware software solution, which is provided by privately a held company. This fact means that it is for sale to customers who wishes to manage their personal data. Nymity [15] is another platform focused on covering the accountability principle, which includes an accountability roadmap for demonstrable EU GDPR compliance as well as a number of policies, procedures, and guidelines for processing sensitive data according to the EU GDPR. It provides a free GDPR compliance toolkit, being an extension of its Privacy Management Accountability Framework for GDPR compliance. The authors of [17] propose a decentralized ridesharing architecture which gives the opportunity to shift from centralized platforms to decentralized ones. Digital communications in the propose solution are specifically designed to preserve data privacy and avoid any form of centralization. OneTrust [16] offers a cross-jurisdictional privacy management software to help organizations to be compliant with the EU GDPR. It is used by over 1,500 organizations globally and the platform provides solutions for accountability and consent management, incident and breach management, and website scanning, among others.

On the other hand, AuraPortal GDPR [18] ensures that employees process data in compliance with the regulation. AuraPortal GDPR includes features that cover the spectrum of needs for any type of company such as retention periods, explicit consent, records, diligence, data breach communication, data processors, and register and reports.

Finally, OpenGDPR [19] is an open-source GDPR compliance framework that provides an operational platform, which includes audit and migration tools as well as the expected support for the management of the right to be forgotten. For its implementation, the community of people behind OpenGDPR states that it will use open source tools, although they make no reference to which open source tools they will use.

In conclusion, this section has shown that there is no existing platform in the state of the art providing an interoperable tool that cover the main pillars of current data protection regulation laws such as data erasure, scope & retention, consent & revocation, portability, and anonymization. This fact could lead to more challenging law enforcement in environments with users and heterogeneous IoT devices, particularly on the Smart City ecosystem.

3   The Data Protection Platform

This section presents a platform that provides worldwide organizations with a set of mechanisms to deal with citizen's sensitive data according to their rights and the existing data protection laws. Organizations integrating our platform into their management processes are considered as honest and trusted, meaning that they do not intend to modify or fake the platform mechanisms and communications. The other main goal is to allow citizens to define their preferences regarding the following data protection rights in a user-friendly way:

- *Data Erasure*. Citizen's sensitive data must be eliminated and destroyed after the expiration date.
- *Scope & Retention*. Sensitive data cannot be processed with a different goal than allowed.
- *Consent & Revocation*. Citizens must be asked for consents when organizations need to manage new pieces of their sensitive data. In addition, revocations of consents must be available.
- *Portability*. Data sharing between different organizations must be carried out in compliance to the current regulation and the citizen's preferences.
- *Anonymization*. Relevant pieces of citizen's sensitive data must be anonymous when they decide it.

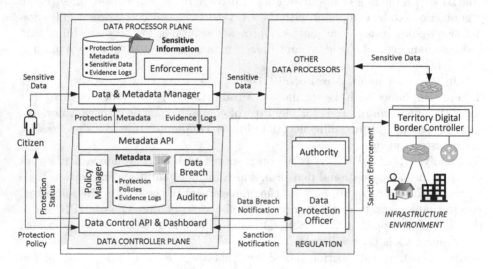

Fig. 1. Management platform for data protection. The Data Controller Plane allows citizens to define their data protection preferences; organizations managing citizen's sensitive data according to their preferences is achieved by the Data Processor Plane; Regulation guarantees that management processes follow existing regulations; and the Infrastructure Environment enables the communication between the previous elements.

To achieve the aforementioned two goals, our management platform defines four main actors: (i) *Citizen*, person consuming services that manage sensitive data; (ii) *Data Controller*, organization allowing citizens to define and control their rights according to the existing data protection regulation laws; (iii) *Data*

Processor, organization providing citizens with services that use sensitive data; and (iv) *Data Protection Officer*, authorities responsible for ensuring that organizations follow citizen's rights and data protection regulation laws.

Figure 1 depicts how the previous four actors are considered by the proposed management platform.

3.1 Data Controller Plane

The Data Controller Plane allows *Citizens* to specify how organizations should manage their *Sensitive Data* according to the existing data protection regulation laws. The plane components work with data *Protection Policies* and *Metadata* (non-sensitive data) as well as provide the required mechanisms to check out the data management processes through an *Auditor*. Every organization compliant with data regulation laws is considered as Data Controller and should integrate this plane into its management processes.

In this control plane, the *Data Control API & Dashboard* component is the entry point for Citizens and *Regulation* authorities. This component reflects two main goals. First, it allows different Citizens to establish their data protection requirements, which must be accommodated by any organization processing such sensitive data. To this end, Citizens can create, modify, and delete policies that indicate their data protection requirements. Secondly, the other goal is to notify Regulation authorities of possible *Data Breaches* by data management processes and receive notifications about the sanctions and actions taken to address the breaches (e.g. restriction of given services of organizations that had violated citizen's rights). Sanctions are applied by the Regulation authorities and Citizens can check their status thanks to this component.

A relevant component of this plane is the *Policy Manager*, which is in charge of managing and evaluating the data Protection Policies defined by Citizens. Policies denote different rights such as scope, erasure, anonymization, portability, and consent of sensitive data in a flexible and dynamic way. Using policies, Citizens can personalize how their Sensitive Data must be treated, which organizations (acting as given Data Processors) have access to that data, how much time organizations can use and store the data, what locations are allowed to store and manage such data, etc.

The policies of the proposed platform are composed of the following elements: *Type* is the kind of policy; *Maker* is the citizen whose data is being managed by the policy; *Target* is the organization managing citizen's sensitive data; *Location* (optional) is the geographic allocation in which the result of the policy will be applied; and *Result* sets the data protection right that organizations must accomplish when managing the citizen's sensitive data.

$$Type \wedge Maker \wedge Target \wedge [Location] \rightarrow Result$$

After finishing the policy definition process, policies are stored in an internal database. This latter not only maintains data Protection Policies, but also *Evidence Logs* generated by the Data Processor Plane (explained in Sect. 3.2).

The next component in Fig. 1 is the *Metadata API*, an interface with two main goals: (i) supply organizations that are managing sensitive data (i.e. Data Processors) with the *Protection Metadata* –policy results– information indicating what data protection requirements must be accomplished; and (ii) receive specific Evidence Logs for further analysis of the data management process performed by Data Processors.

Once such Evidence Logs are received and stored by the Data Controller, the Auditor analyzes them according to the data protection requirements that are indicated by Citizen's policies. The data protection platform considers the data erasure, scope & retention, consent & revocation, portability, and anonymization of citizen's rights, as detailed at the beginning of this section. After performing the auditing process, the Data Breach component checks any violation of the Citizen's rights and, if so, if it requires to notify the Regulation authorities.

3.2   Data Processor Plane

The Data Processor Plane in Fig. 1 allows organizations to manage the Citizen's Sensitive Data according to particular Citizen's data protection requirements and in accordance with the existing regulations. Any organization, regardless of its location, which stores or manages citizen's sensitive data is considered as Data Processor and should integrate this plane in its data management processes.

Citizens interact with the *Data & Metadata Manager* component (see Fig. 1) to insert and manage their Sensitive Data, which must be managed according to the data Protection Policies defined by Citizens in the Data Controller Plane. The results (or Protection Metadata) of Citizen's data regulation policies are received by the Data & Metadata Manager, which provides the Data Controller Plane with Evidence Logs that shape the management processes of organizations as Data Processors. Finally, the *Enforcement* component is focused on protecting Citizen's Sensitive Data according to their data protection rights. To this end, the Enforcement has different modules ensuring data erasure, scope & retention, consent & revocation, portability, and anonymization rights. All actions taken by the previous modules are recorded and stored by the Enforcement as Evidence Logs for further analysis, stored in an internal database and shared through the Data & Metadata Manager with the Data Controller Plane.

3.3   Regulation and Infrastructure Environment

The Regulation context is managed by authorities, therefore, it is independent of our platform. This contains the agencies or *Authorities* that oversee governing and regulating the data protection laws of each country. These authorities could have several *Data Protection Officers*, responsible for ensuring data protection strategies, regulating the compliance of management processes with current law requirements, and enforcing sanctions to organizations (Data Processors).

Sanctions according to regulation are decided later (off-line) as non-automatic evaluation processes, and are notified to the Data Controller Plane and enforced by Data Protection Officers directly over the *Infrastructure Environment*. This infrastructure refers to the networking and equipment required to enable the exchange of data and metadata between organizations distributed around the world. Every single country has a *Territory Digital Border Controller* in charge of controlling and enforcing the countermeasures required by its Authorities when data protection requirements are not accomplished by a given Data Processor. An example of its functionality could be to restrict network communications of a given Data Processor when it has violated any citizen's right.

3.4   Data Model

The proposed solution defines a data model to formally represent the relationships and functionality of its main actors. Figure 2 depicts how we manage *Sensitive Data* of *Citizens*, either *Personal Data* of Citizens or information belonging to *Data Processors* (e.g. *Contextual Data* and *Provider Data*). On the other hand, the data model shows how *Data Controllers* protect Citizen's Sensitive Data and audit the *Evidence Logs* generated by the Data Processors when they manage Sensitive Data. Furthermore, Data Controllers report to the corresponding *Data Protection Officer* in case of data breaches, which regulates data management processes to comply with the law requirements demanded by their authorities, and, if necessary, enforces the appropriate sanctions due to law violations.

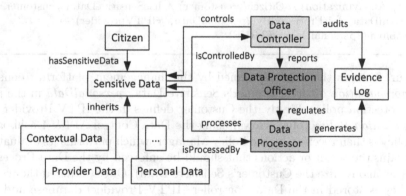

Fig. 2. Data model for the data protection platform.

4   A Case Study: Anonymizing Sensitive Data Under the EU GDPR

This section presents a case study to demonstrate how the proposed management platform allows citizens, organizations processing sensitive data, and authorities to deal with the regulations defined by current data protection regulation laws.

Internet Protocol Television (IPTV) is one of the killer applications for Internet consumers. One of the main opportunities for IPTV providers is to improve customer's experience by offering personalized recommendations about audiovisual content according to the customer's gender, age, status, and behavior (e.g. likes, searches, or watched content). Data involved in personalization must be regarded as sensitive, and the heterogeneous pieces of data must be managed according to the current data protection regulation laws. To this end, our proposal enables the management of customer's sensitive data according to the data protection policies defined by users themselves and the current EU GDPR data protection laws. This case study shows how a EU citizen, who is customer of an IPTV Provider, indicates her data protection requirements in terms of anonymizing her personal data before being managed and stored by the IPTV Provider. In this case study, the Data Controller and the Data Processor are the same entity located in the same legislation territory.

The IPTV Provider is acting as Data Processor when it manages the sensitive data of its customers, and as Data Controller when it allows customers to establish their personalized data protection policies. The customer (Citizen in Fig. 1) of the IPTV Provider defines the *anonymization policy* detailed below, which opens only anonymized personal data fragments to the IPTV Provider. It is worth pointing out that the data managed by the data protection policies is represented in the data model shown in Fig. 2.

Type(#Anonymization) ∧ Citizen(#customer) ∧ hasSensitiveData(#customer, ?personalData) ∧ isProcessedBy(?personalData, #IPTVprovider) → hasAnonym(?personalData, #TRUE)

Figure 3 shows the steps performed by the management platform to enable the *Anonymization* of the Customer's Sensitive Data –*personalData* in the previous protection policy. Firstly, the Customer defines in the IPTV Provider the *Anonymization Policy* (blue arrows) using the Data Control API & Dashboard. The policy is then received by the Policy Manager, which performs its evaluation and obtains the result or actions that should be enforced by the Data Processor Plane (i.e. anonymize the Customer's Sensitive Data). Once obtained the result, the policy is stored in the Data Controller (IPTV Provider) database and the result is sent to the Data Processor Plane as *Anonymization Metadata*.

From the Data Processor standpoint, the IPTV Provider receives the data protection action as Anonymization Metadata through the Data & Metadata Manager component and stores it in its database. Once the Customer's data protection requirements have been established, the green arrows of Fig. 3 show when the Customer provides the IPTV Provider with Sensitive Data and checks if the requirements are accomplished by the IPTV Provider. The Sensitive Data enters through the Data & Metadata Manager, and the *Anonymization* module of the Enforcement component applies the mechanisms required to anonymize the Customer's Sensitive Data. Additional to this process, this module generates

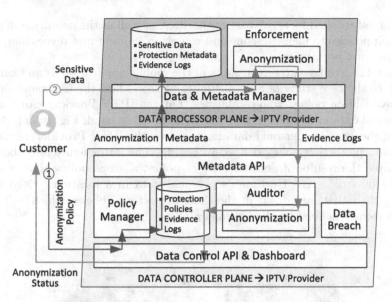

Fig. 3. Case study where the IPTV Provider acts as both Data Controller and Data Processor and the Customer defines an Anonymization policy.

an Evidence Log modeling both the data management and the anonymization processes. Both types of data (the anonymized Customer's Sensitive Data and the Evidence Log) are stored in the Data Processor database and the Evidence Log is sent to the Data Controller for auditing purposes.

As final step, the Auditor module audits and validates if the anonymization requirement was accomplished during the data management life-cycle. Once the auditing process is finished, the Evidence Log and its result can be seen by the Customer through the Data Control API & Dashboard.

4.1 Data Controller Deployment

The Data Controller API & Dashboard allows citizens to manage their data protection requirements in a user-friendly way, and check if their data is being processed according to their preferences and the existing regulation laws. In this context, we designed a mobile application that interacts with the Data Control API & Dashboard (explained in Sect. 3), which provides citizens with the following functions in real time:

- Definition and management of data protection policies to allow citizens to establish their data protection preferences and restrictions.
- Provision of auditing information regarding citizen's sensitive (personal) data stored and managed by organizations acting as Data Processors.

Additional operations may also be carried out through the mobile application such as, among others, the notification of data breach information and enforced sanctions, established by regulatory authorities, as well as the definition of other protection policies to manage scope and retention, consent and revocation, right to erasure, and portability.

Figure 4 illustrates two screen shots of the mobile application as an example, oriented to the case study of Sect. 4. Figure 4a shows how the Customer defines an anonymization policy, who establishes that the IPTV Provider can manage her personal data in an anonymized way. On the other hand, Fig. 4b depicts the status of the sensitive personal data managed by the IPTV Provider, according to the data protection policy defined in Fig. 4a. The latter figure also shows as an example the results of another type of policy, a *scope* policy that is being breached by storing the Customer's personal data in a location (without the consent) than that laid down in the data protection policies which will have been previously defined by the Customer.

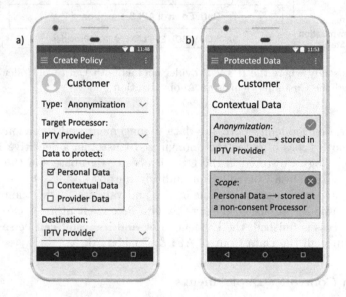

Fig. 4. How a Customer (citizen) can manage with the proposed platform her data protection rights through a mobile application: (a) defining the anonymization policy, as detailed in the previous policy type #Anonymization; and (b) checking the status of her anonymized personal data managed by the IPTV Provider.

5   Conclusion and Future Work

We have presented a data protection management platform, which is focused on protecting the citizen's sensitive data according to their preferences and the existing data protection regulation laws. Our solution supplies organizations with security mechanisms to allow meeting data protection requirements of citizens and laws. Citizens are capable of defining in a user-friendly fashion what pieces of sensitive data can be processed, what organizations can manage them, where organizations can store such sensitive data, how long organizations can process such data, and how data must be managed by organizations. Finally, a case study has also been introduced to demonstrate how the proposed platform can manage data anonymization, protecting a private citizen's right, also presenting a mobile application that citizens can utilize to define data protection policies and check sensitive data status.

As next steps of research and as proof of concept, we plan to implement the planes making up the data protection platform and make it publicly available for organizations interested in managing sensitive data from citizens. Another future step to improve the usability of our solution is to provide citizens with privacy-preserving policies, generated by default, and allow those citizens to adapt or modify the policies according to their preferences.

Acknowledgment. This work has been partially supported by the Irish Research Council, under the government of Ireland post-doc fellowship (grant code GOIPD/2018/466); and by a post-doctoral INCIBE grant within the "Ayudas para la Excelencia de los Equipos de Investigación Avanzada en Ciberseguridad" Program, with code INCIBEI-2015-27352.

References

1. Wachter, S.: Normative challenges of identification in the Internet of Things: privacy, profiling, discrimination, and the GDPR. Comput. Law Secur. Rev. **34**(3), 436–449 (2018)
2. Government of India: DataSmart Cities: Empowering Cities through Data. Smart Cities Mission-Ministry of Housing and Urban Affairs, December 2018. https://smartnet.niua.org/data-smart-cities
3. Official Journal of the European Union: General Data Protection Regulation (GDPR). EU Regulation 2016/679, April 2016. http://data.europa.eu/eli/reg/2016/679/oj
4. The European H2020-ICT MUSA Project: Multi-cloud Secure Applications (2015–2017). http://musa-project.eu
5. Eclipse Foundation Inc.: OpenCert, June 2019. https://www.polarsys.org/projects/polarsys.opencert
6. Mai, P.X., et al.: Modeling security and privacy requirements: a use case-driven approach. Inf. Softw. Technol. **100**, 165–182 (2018)
7. Lucic, D., Boban, M., Mileta, D.: An impact of general data protection regulation on a smart city concept. In: 41st International Convention on Information and Communication Technology, Electronics and Microelectronics, pp. 390–394, May 2018
8. Determann, L., Gupta, C.: Indian Personal Data Protection Act, 2018: Draft Bill and Its History, Compared to EU GDPR and California Privacy Law. UC Berkeley Public Law Research Paper, pp. 1–27 (2019)
9. Brazilian Federal Senate: General Data Protection Law No. 13,709/2018, August 2018. http://portaldaprivacidade.com.br/wp-content/uploads/2018/08/LGPD-english-version.pdf

10. Greenleaf, G.: China's Personal Information Standard: The Long March to a Privacy Law (2018). http://www.dgcs-research.net/a/Opinion/2018/0306/122.html
11. China's National Information Security Standardization Technical Committee: Personal Information Security Specification (drafted version), February 2019. https://www.tc260.org.cn/upload/2019-02-01/1549013548750042566.pdf
12. International Association of Privacy Professionals (IAPP): 2018 Privacy Tech Vendor Report vol 2.4e (2018). https://iapp.org/media/pdf/resource_center/2018-Privacy-Tech-Vendor-Report.pdf
13. Baycloud Systems Ltd.: Baycloud Consent Platform: Consent Makes the Law. http://www.baycloud.com/#CookieQ
14. European Commission: Proposal for an ePrivacy Regulation, June 2019. https://ec.europa.eu/digital-single-market/proposal-eprivacy-regulation
15. Nymity Inc.: Nymity' GDPR Toolkit for Demonstrable GDPR Compliance. http://info.nymity.com/gdpr-compliance-toolkit
16. OneTrust, LLC: The Leading Privacy Management Software Platform. http://onetrust.com
17. Semenko, Y., Saucez, D.: Distributed privacy preserving platform for ridesharing services. In: Wang, G., Feng, J., Bhuiyan, M.Z.A., Lu, R. (eds.) SpaCCS 2019. LNCS, vol. 11611, pp. 1–14. Springer, Cham (2019). https://doi.org/10.1007/978-3-030-24907-6_1
18. AuraPortal GDPR: A Global Business Process Management (BPM) Software Leader. https://www.auraportal.com
19. The OpenGDPR Project: Open-Source Initiative to Protect Consumers' Privacy and Data Rights (2017). https://www.opengdpr.org

Securing Smart Offices Through an Intelligent and Multi-device Continuous Authentication System

Pedro Miguel Sánchez Sánchez[1]([✉])(iD), Alberto Huertas Celdrán[2](iD),
Lorenzo Fernández Maimó[3](iD), Gregorio Martínez Pérez[1](iD),
and Guojun Wang[4](iD)

[1] Department of Information and Communications Engineering,
University of Murcia, 30100 Murcia, Spain
{pedromiguel.sanchez,gregorio}@um.es
[2] Telecommunication Software and Systems Group,
Waterford Institute of Technology, Waterford X91 P20H, Ireland
ahuertas@tssg.org
[3] Department of Computer Engineering, University of Murcia, 30100 Murcia, Spain
lfmaimo@um.es
[4] School of Computer Science, Guangzhou University, Guangzhou 510006, China
csgjwang@gzhu.edu.cn

Abstract. Smart Offices promise the improvement of working conditions in terms of efficiency, productivity and facility. However, new cybersecurity challenges arise associated with the new capabilities of Smart Cities. One of the key challenges is the utilisation of continuous and non-invasive authentication mechanisms since traditional authentication methods have important limitations. Thus, to cover these limitations, the main contribution of this paper is the design and deployment of a continuous and intelligent authentication architecture oriented to Smart Offices. The architecture is oriented to the cloud computing paradigm and considers Machine Learning techniques to authenticate users according to their behaviours. Some experiments demonstrated the suitability of the proposed solution when recognising and authenticating different users using a classification algorithm.

Keywords: Smart office · IoT devices · Continuous authentication · Behaviour patterns · Machine learning · Classification

1 Introduction

Recent advances of technology and computing paradigms such as 5G networks, the Internet of Things (IoT) or Big Data have made the vision of Smart Cities closer to the reality than ever [1]. Smart cities promise the improvement of persons' daily life from different perspectives like, for example, transport optimisation, energy saving, or working conditions. In this context, traditional offices are

G. Wang et al. (Eds.): iSCI 2019, CCIS 1122, pp. 73–85, 2019.
https://doi.org/10.1007/978-981-15-1301-5_7

evolving to smart places where IoT devices like sensors, smart objects, tablets, smartphones, or computers allow employees to work better, faster and smarter.

Such interconnected and heterogeneous environment opens the door to new cybersecurity challenges. As an example, attack vectors affecting one or more IoT devices of a Smart Office can provoke the disruption of a given service, a malicious control of devices, or a chain attack to get a privilege upgrade and access to sensitive information. To keep these devices and services secure, the most applied mechanisms are the maintenance of the software up-to-date; the use of security mechanisms such as antivirus, firewalls, or intrusion detection/prevention systems (IDS/IPS); and the use of authentication mechanisms to control the access. Regarding authentication mechanisms, the focus of this work, traditional systems relay on passwords or PINs. However, both can be stolen or forgotten. Moreover, these authentication methods do not check the user identity once the device is unlocked. Alternative solutions based on biometric features, like fingerprint or face recognition, were proposed to mitigate the previous drawbacks. However, they have other limitations like dirty fingers for fingerprint or low light scenarios in facial recognition. In addition, they do not authenticate the user in a continuous way, and they are intrusive affecting the user's interaction with the device.

In this context, continuous authentication systems [2] emerged with the goal of addressing the previous limitations. They aim to identify the owner of a device in a permanent and non-intrusive fashion. Compared to traditional mechanisms, continuous authentication improves both the level of security and the user's quality of experience (QoE) during the user's interaction. These systems model the users' behaviour in a particular device to later measure how similar is the current behaviour compared to the well-known. The fact of having the user permanently authenticated, and not from time to time, contributes to providing a higher level of security and confidence compared to traditional methods. Additionally, continuous authentication systems minimise the use of credentials during authentication processes [3].

Notwithstanding the important benefits provided by continuous authentication systems, their performance and integration in new environments such as Smart Offices also mean open challenges that still require additional efforts. Among them, we highlight the following challenges:

- The acquisition and processing of several dimensions and features provided by heterogeneous IoT devices to create rich behaviour patterns. This is one of the most critical aspects to reach great accuracy during the authentication process.
- The generation of relevant datasets modelling the behaviour of different users interacting with IoT devices.
- The selection of features and machine learning (ML) algorithms associated with the Smart Office scenario.
- The design of a global architecture able to integrate data coming from many devices to provide a global and real-time continuous authentication system for Smart environments.

With the goal of improving the previous challenges and the security of Smart Offices, the main contribution of this paper is the design and implementation of an intelligent and automatic architecture able to authenticate continuously users located at Smart Offices. The proposed architecture is oriented to the cloud computing paradigm and creates behavioural profiles according to the interaction of users with the devices of Smart Offices. After that, ML-based techniques, based on classification [4], are used to identify and authenticate the users. Once authenticated, the proposed architecture communicates with the IoT devices to allow users to perform particular task without requiring additional authentication processes. Finally, a pool of experiments with real users utilising mobile devices and personal computers, showed favourable results in terms of accuracy during the authentication process.

The remainder of the paper is structured as follows. Section 2 discusses some related work from the academia and industry focused on continuous authentication for IoT environments as well as in computer and mobile devices. Section 3 shows the design details of the proposed architecture. Section 4 explains the implementation details of the proposed architecture in a Smart Office created as Proof of Concept. Section 5 discusses the performed experiments carried out to demonstrate its suitability. Finally, conclusions and future work are drawn in Sect. 6.

2 Related Work

This section reviews the existing continuous authentication systems found in the literature. Different approaches enabling continuous authentication in the IoT, desktop and mobile devices are analysed.

2.1 Continuous Authentication in Mobile Devices

Focused on mobile devices, Jorquera Valero et al. [5] presented an adaptive continuous authentication system which monitors the app usage and mobile sensors (gyroscope and accelerometer). The performed experiments showed a recall of 92% and a precision of 77% during the authentication process. The authors used ML to detect anomalies in the users' behaviours and the adaptability of the system came through dynamic changes in the training dataset. In addition, authors also tested the resilience of the system to adversarial attacks. Another proposal was presented by Bo et al. in [6], where they focused on identifying users through typing patterns and biometric behaviour. Specifically, the authors acquired data such as rotation, vibration, or pressure by considering touchscreens and sensors of mobile devices. Once the data was collected, they used semi-supervised learning techniques to classify the profile according to the user's behaviour. Another relevant work was presented by Patel et al. in [7]. In this article, the authors performed an interesting analysis about the different dimensions and ML algorithms that can be used in continuous authentication systems. The analysed dimensions were facial recognition, gestures, applications and location. The main conclusion of the authors was that the fact of merging data belonging to different dimensions allows obtaining better results in terms of accuracy and error rate. Finally, Ehatisham-ul-Haq et al. [8] presented a solution based on the use of the device sensors (accelerometer, gyroscope, and magnetometer). Based on the users' habits, the authors inferred different positions where the device could be located (pocket, at waist height, in the upper arm, and on the wrist). After performing several tests, they concluded that the SVM (Support Vector Machine) algorithm is not appropriate for mobile devices due to its high computational consumption.

2.2   Continuous Authentication in Computers

In the literature, different continuous authentication solutions have been proposed by using computers and desktop devices. In this sense, Deutschmann and Lindholm [9] identified the person using the dimensions of the keyboard, the mouse and the use of applications. In their work, authors collect data from different users and perform a training phase in which user profiles are created. After the training phase, different classifiers are used to filter and sort the data in different categories. The results of this solution show that incorrect users are detected in 18 s using the keyboard, in 2.4 min using a mouse and 1.5 s in the exchange of applications. Another work is proposed by Lex Fridman et al. [3], where they consider the keyboard and mouse to authenticate users. This work performs a mapping of the keys pressed with the application in the foreground. The proposed system uses a Naive Bayes classifier for mouse movements and keystroke dynamics, and SVM for the user stylometry. That is, authors propose a binary decision fusion architecture. With the complete dataset authors got a False Acceptance Rate (FAR) of 0.004 and a False Rejection Rate (FRR) of 0.01 after 30 s of interaction with the device. After 5 min, metrics decrease to 0.001 and 0.002 respectively.

On the other hand, the solution presented by Aljohani et al. [10] uses an Artificial Immune System (AIS) to authenticate users continuously. AIS is an intelligent computational system that is inspired by the procedures and principles of the Biological Immune System (BIS) [11]. The authors use the AIS Negative Selection (NS) algorithm on their generated dataset, which contains data on keyboard and mouse dimensions. In this sense, after a period of initialisation through NS, they analyse blocks of keyboard and mouse interactions. Through an experiment with 24 users, the proposed system achieved an average accuracy of 97.053%, being the lowest accuracy achieved 96.6% and the highest 97.74%. Finally, Mondal and Bours [12] proposed a continuous authentication system which uses both keystroke and mouse dynamics to authenticate the user. Authors collected data from 53 users in uncontrolled conditions using a data collection software and then tested their system on the gathered data. The experiments tested many ML classification algorithms to finally develop a trust model based on a threshold established on a dynamic score. This score is based on the user behaviour classification results.

2.3   Continuous Authentication in IoT Environments

In this classification, the most related to the scope of this work, two solutions have been detected in the literature. Ashibani et al. [13] proposed a continuous authentication framework for Smart Homes. This solution uses different contextual information sources like user context (GPS location, logs, calendar, etc.), device context (location, browser, OS, applications, etc), network context (IP address, ping, connection speed, etc.), and environmental context, gathered from IoT devices distributed over the home. However, compared to our proposal this solution does not takes into account the behaviour of the same user with different devices. In addition, the solution proposed by Nespoli et al. [14] is based on the usage of ontologies and policies for authentication and authorisation. It uses IoT devices to obtain information about the scenario status that can be used to model the user and allow him to access, or continue using, certain services. However, this solution is strongly dependent on the deployment context, thus requiring extensive training to correctly model the users' behaviour.

As can be seen, there are different continuous authentication proposals using different devices and getting good performance during the authentication process. However, the existing solutions do not combine the behavioural information obtained from different devices, which is applied by our proposal to authenticate the same user in many devices at the same time.

3   Architecture Proposal

This section describes the design of the proposed continuous authentication architecture oriented to the cloud computing paradigm. Figure 1 shows the modular architecture enabling the inclusion or modification of new functionality, if it is required.

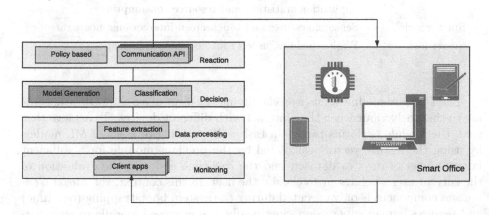

Fig. 1. Design of the continuous authentication architecture for Smart Offices.

- The *Monitoring* module acquires in real time the data generated by the devices of the Smart Office.
- The *Data processing* module filters, aggregates, and manages the previous data to generate relevant features making up the users' behavioural profiles.
- The *Decision* module generates the ML models to classify users according to their behaviour.
- The *Reaction* module establishes different sensitivity levels to authenticate users considering the output of the previous modules. Furthermore, it provides the interfaces to enable a global authentication mechanism in the Smart Office.

From bottom to up, the *Monitoring* module is able to gather data generated by devices of the Smart Office when they are used by users. As an example, Table 1 gives an overview of the main dimensions that can be monitored in a Smart Office.

The *Data processing* module periodically receives raw behavioural data from the previous module. The Feature extraction component is in charge of filtering, aggregating and processing the behavioural raw data to calculate relevant features that model the user's behaviour. This aggregation is also carried out periodically by considering the raw data obtained during a given period of time called time window. This time window is established by the architecture administrator.

Table 1. Possible monitored dimensions on user's devices.

Device type	Dimensions
Mobile device	Sensors, gestures and touchscreen interactions, application statistics, and typing patterns
Desktop computer	Mouse events, keyboard events, typing patterns, application statistics, and resource consumption
Smartwatch	Sensors, gestures and touchscreen interactions, heart rate
Smart-lock	Work schedules, user's routines, lock/unlock speed

The *Decision* module focuses on classifying the users of a Smart Office according to their behaviour when they interact with different devices. To achieve that goal, the module performs two main tasks: the training of a set of ML models by using the feature vectors calculated by the previous module for a sufficient large number of days as dataset, and the real-time and periodic evaluation of the current user's behaviour to classify the user. In this context, the *Model Generation* component is only executed during the system bootstrapping (one time) and requires human supervision. Specifically, the proposed module receives feature vectors and trains a set of ML algorithms to classify users based on their behaviour. This component also performs a training/validation process, which allows the administrator to select the model with the best performance for each

IoT device. Once the previous processes have been performed, the *Classification* component evaluates in real time and periodically the trained models fed with the feature vectors of the current user (provided also by the Feature extraction component), giving as output an authentication score per device.

Finally, the *Reaction* module combines the output of the different ML models to authenticate the user. In addition, it enables a global and non-invasive authentication system in the Smart Office and improves the security of devices when impersonation attacks are executed. To achieve the previous goals, the *Policy-based* component uses rules, predefined by the system administrator, to indicate the user' authentication level and proper reaction actions like for example, locking a particular IoT device, or loging in a user without requiring additional credentials. In this way, critical devices in the Smart Office could be reactive to stricter rules, while devices without sensitive information may have more permissive ones. The reaction module also creates and maintains log files where the different evaluation results and reaction decisions are stored for analysis purposes. To conclude, the *Communication API* component sends the authentication or mitigation actions to the devices of the Smart Office when it is required.

4   Architecture Deployment in a Smart Office

This section shows the details and the added value of deploying the proposed architecture in a realistic scenario. As proof of concept, we have designed a Smart Office, where five users interact with smartphones, tablets, laptops and IoT devices. This interaction allows our solution to authenticate the previous users enabling a global authentication system in the Smart Office. It means that, according to the behaviour of a given user when he/she interacts with one or more devices, he/she will be able to use (or not) other devices without requiring additional authentication mechanisms. In contrast, when some unauthorised user is detected, our solution will lock or shut down automatically the device or devices. All those devices are connected wirelessly to the Internet through the Smart Office network. In addition, the Smart Office has a cloud computing platform to host the Data processing, Decision and Reaction modules making up the proposed architecture. Below we provide the implementation details of our architecture.

4.1   Client Applications

To monitor the users' behaviours, the Smart Office devices with enough computational capabilities host an application that implements the *Client apps* of the Monitoring module. In the case of resource-constrained devices, the Client app is hosted by a third-party or proxy. This application periodically recollects data generated through the user's interaction. The duration periods are indicated in Data Processing module by the architecture administrator. As proof of concept, we have implemented client applications for two devices: personal computers and mobile devices (smartphones and tablets).

Personal Computers. We have designed and implemented a client application to monitor mouse and keyboard events as well as applications and resource usage statistics. Since sensitive data is managed and to preserve the users' privacy, the application aggregates and processes the raw data in time windows, previously defined by the Smart Office administrator, extracting statistical data from the user's actions. Among the considered data, which has a total length of 18,000 fields (most of them due to fact that several values have been computed for all the combinations of two alphanumerical keys), we highlight the values shown in Table 2 due to their capacity to characterise user behaviour. Regarding the implementation, we have implemented the application for Windows, since it is the most used operating system (OS) on desktop computers [15]. Specifically, we have used Python to implement this application, the py2exe [16] tool to generate an executable that is installed on user devices, the pynput [17] library to monitor the mouse and keyboard events, and psutil [18] and pywin32 [19] libraries to monitor the consumption of resources and use of applications respectively. Finally, after retrieving the events during a time window, they are pre-processed and sent to the Data Processing module using a REST API.

Table 2. Data monitored in personal computers.

Dimension	Value
Time	- Time stamp (milliseconds since 1 Jan 1970)
Keyboard	- Number of pressed keys
	- Proportion of erase keys
	- Mean and standard deviation of the time elapsed between two consecutive keystrokes
	- Number of written words
Mouse	- Mean and standard deviation of the time spent clicking on each of the mouse buttons (left, right and center) and double clicking on the left button
	- Mean speed of mouse in each direction
	- Histogram of the distance of movements
Application usage and resource consumption	- Identifier of the current and previous application
	- Average number of applications kept opened during the time window
	- Number of changes between applications
	- Mean and deviation of CPU and RAM usage percentage

Mobile Devices. The client application for mobile devices has been designed and implemented for smartphones and tablets. In this case, the selected dimension is the application usage statistics. Specifically, the monitored data is shown by Table 3. The previous functionality has been implemented in Android, since it is the most used OS on mobile devices [15]. Specifically, the application is compatible from Android 5.0 (API 21) and uses Android.app.usage class [20] to gather the information about the application usage statistics. To keep a low resource consumption we used Android.app.AlarmManager [20]. Finally, we used a REST API to send the data to the Data Processing module and receive the duration of the data acquisition window.

Table 3. Data monitored in mobile devices.

Dimension	Value
Application usage statistics	- Number of apps and number of different apps opened for the last day and the last minute
	- App most times used and number of times used in the last minute. The same for the last day
	- Last and next-to-last apps used
	- Application most frequently used just before the currently active application
	- Bytes sent and received during the last minute

4.2 Cloud Computing Platform

The Data processing, Decision, and Reaction modules have been implemented in a cloud platform hosted by the Smart Office. These modules require large storage and processing capabilities, as they are in charge of processing and storing the data generated by the devices of the Smart Office.

The Data processing module provides a REST API to receive data from the Client applications. The received data is processed following the next steps to obtain a set of datasets, one per IoT device:

1. Process and aggregate the raw data in time windows of 1 min (configurable) to generate features vectors of different users.
2. Label the features vectors with the owner ID.
3. Use the one hot encoding technique to replace textual fields with values that the ML algorithm can understand.
4. Filter features that have a value of 0 for all vectors.

Once having the datasets with the features vectors, the Decision module uses a Random Forest as classification algorithm to identify and authenticate the different users. In this sense, we use the implementation of Random Forest provided by Scikit-learn [22], which is able to classify users in a computational order lower than other solutions [21]. In addition, the most important libraries used by this module are Scikit-learn to train and execute the ML models, and pandas [23] to manipulate and process data. Thus, a Random Forest model is generated for each type of IoT device by training the algorithm with the data of the different monitored users. After that, periodically, the Classification component evaluates the feature vectors generated by a user in a time window with the different Random Forest models to get the probabilities of being each one of the trained users for each IoT device.

Finally, the Reaction component is implemented in Python and uses rules that consider the probabilities provided by Classification component (one value per model associated with a given device). The rules are defined by the system administrator and their consequent is the user's authentication level. This authentication level can be calculated considering one or more models (belonging to different devices). Below we provide several rules, as an example of possible rule set to calculate the authentication levels:

- Level 1: The user is classified correctly and the difference with the probability of belonging to other classes (users) is high. This situation reflects normality and that the user who is using the device is the usual.
- Level 2: The user is classified correctly, but there are other users evaluated with a similar probability (± 0.10). This situation also reflects normality but with a greater uncertainty, so that at this level some functionality of the device could be blocked, such as having administrator privileges in some applications or closing sensitive applications.
- Level 3: The user is not classified correctly, but the user class has a probability close to the selected class (± 0.10). This situation is indicative that the person using the equipment may be someone else and not its owner. At this level it is decided to send an email to the user notifying that a possible anomalous situation may be occurring.
- Level 4: The user is not classified correctly and the probability assigned to the user to whom the device belongs is very low compared to the probability assigned to the selected class. In this case the device will be blocked directly and an email sent to the owner.

Moreover, the Reaction module implements a REST API to communicate with the different devices of the Smart Office. This API sends to the Smart Office devices the level of user authentication and the actions to be performed.

5   Experiments

This section demonstrates the viability and performance of the proposed architecture. For that, we have monitored the behaviour of five volunteers interacting with their personal computers, laptops, smartphones and tablets for two weeks. In this scenario, the goal of the performed experiments is to measure the precision of our continuous authentication system.

As indicated in Sect. 4 we used Random Forest to generate the models. In this context, we generated two ML models, one shaping the behaviour of the five users when they interact with personal computers, and another when they use their mobile devices. We used Random Forest because its output can be interpreted as the probability of belonging to each one of the trained classes (users in this case). These probabilities tell us how similar is the behaviour of the current user compared to the behaviour of each of the five users present in the models.

Once selected the features and the classification algorithm (see Sect. 4), we performed the experiment to calculate the performance to classify the behaviours of the five users. Figure 2 shows the results obtained when classifying the users' behaviours in personal computer and Fig. 3 shows the results obtained when considering mobile devices. In both figures, the user's identifier is represented on the X axis.

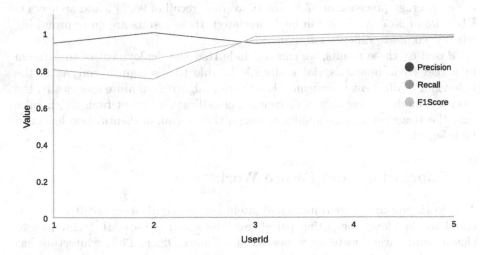

Fig. 2. Classification of users according to their behaviour in personal computers.

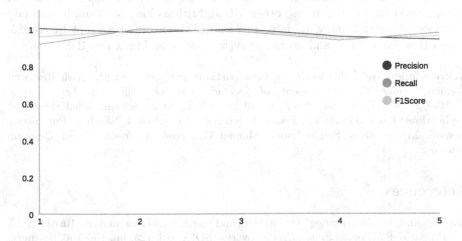

Fig. 3. Classification of users according to their behaviour in mobile devices.

The metrics used to measure the experiment results are: Precision, which is the ratio between the elements classified as belonging to a class and those that really belong to it; Recall, which is the ratio between the number of elements that belong to a class and the number of elements that have been classified as belonging to that class; and F1-Score, which gives a single score combining precision and recall. It is calculated as $(2 \times precision \times recall)/(precision + recall)$.

Thus, for classification on personal computers, the obtained results are an average precision of 96.32%, an average recall of 90.00% and an average F1-Score of 92.70%. Meanwhile, the results for the classification in mobile devices are an average precision of 97.43%m an average recall of 96.20% and an average F1-Score of 96.76%. As it can be appreciated, these results are quite promising when it comes to differentiating users.

Based on these results, we can conclude that the deployment of the system in a real environment is viable since it is able to distinguish and verify the behaviour of different users using classification algorithms. More specifically, the Decision module is capable of throwing a classification output from which rules that the Reaction module applies to assign the user an authentication level can be inferred.

6   Conclusions and Future Work

This work proposes a continuous and intelligent authentication architecture oriented to the cloud computing paradigm. The solution uses ML techniques to classify and authenticate users located in a Smart Office. The architecture has been implemented and validated in a smart office created as a proof of concept. Finally, a pool of experiments demonstrated the suitability of the solution when recognising and authenticating different users using classification algorithms.

As future work, we plan to validate our solution with a higher number of users. Moreover, we plan to use other ML algorithms like for example anomaly detection systems. Finally, we intend to extend the proof of concept by considering other IoT devices and operating systems such as Linux and iOS.

Acknowledgment. This work has been partially supported by the Irish Research Council, under the government of Ireland post-doc fellowship (grant code GOIPD/2018/466). Special thanks to all those voluntaries who installed the client applications: Oscar Fernández, Pedro A. Sánchez, Francisco J. Sánchez, Pantaleone Nespoli, Mattia Zago, Sergio López, Manuel Gil, José M. Jorquera and Gregorio Martínez.

References

1. Suzuki, L.R.: Smart cities IoT: enablers and technology road map. In: Rassia, S.T., Pardalos, P.M. (eds.) Smart City Networks. SOIA, vol. 125, pp. 167–190. Springer, Cham (2017). https://doi.org/10.1007/978-3-319-61313-0_10

2. Almalki, S., Chatterjee, P., Roy, K.: Continuous authentication using mouse clickstream data analysis. In: Wang, G., Feng, J., Bhuiyan, M.Z.A., Lu, R. (eds.) SpaCCS 2019. LNCS, vol. 11637, pp. 76–85. Springer, Cham (2019). https://doi.org/10.1007/978-3-030-24900-7_6

3. Fridman, L., et al.: Multi-modal decision fusion for continuous authentication. Comput. Electr. Eng. **41**, 142–156 (2015)

4. Montgomery, M., Chatterjee, P., Jenkins, J., Roy, K.: Touch analysis: an empirical evaluation of machine learning classification algorithms on touch data. In: Wang, G., Feng, J., Bhuiyan, M.Z.A., Lu, R. (eds.) SpaCCS 2019. LNCS, vol. 11611, pp. 147–156. Springer, Cham (2019). https://doi.org/10.1007/978-3-030-24907-6_12

5. Jorquera Valero, J.M., et al.: Improving the security and QoE in mobile devices through an intelligent and adaptive continuous authentication system. Sensors **18**, 3769 (2018)

6. Bo, C., Zhang, L., Li, X.: SilentSense: Silent User Identification via Dynamics of Touch and Movement Behavioral Biometrics. CoRR, pp. 187–190 (2013)

7. Patel, V.M., Chellappa, R., Chandra, D., Barbello, B.: Continuous User Authentication on Mobile Devices: Recent progress and remaining challenges. IEEE Signal Process. Mag. **33**, 49–61 (2016)

8. Ehatisham-ul Haq, M., et al.: Authentication of smartphone users based on activity recognition and mobile sensing. Sensors **17**, 2043 (2017)

9. Deutschmann, I., Lindholm, J.: Behavioral biometrics for DARPA's active authentication program. In: International Conference of the BIOSIG Special Interest Group (BIOSIG). Darmstadt, vol. 2013, pp. 1–8 (2013)

10. Aljohani, O., Aljohani, N., Bours, P., Alsolami, F.: Continuous authentication on PCs using artificial immune system. In: 2018 1st International Conference on Computer Applications & Information Security (ICCAIS). https://doi.org/10.1109/cais.2018.8442022

11. Dasgupta, D.: An Overview of Artificial Immune Systems and Their Applications. Springer, Heidelberg (1999). https://doi.org/10.1007/978-3-642-59901-9

12. Mondal, S., Bours, P.: A study on continuous authentication using a combination of keystroke and mouse biometrics. Neurocomputing **230**, 1–22 (2017). https://doi.org/10.1016/j.neucom.2016.11.031. ISSN 0925-2312

13. Ashibani, Y., Kauling, D., Mahmoud, Q.H.: Design and implementation of a contextual-based continuous authentication framework for smart homes. Appl. Syst. Innov. **2**, 4 (2019)

14. Nespoli, P., et al.: PALOT: profiling and authenticating users leveraging internet of things. Sensors **19**, 2832 (2019)

15. Operating System Market Share. Stat Counter. http://gs.statcounter.com/os-market-share/. Accessed 23 June 2019

16. Python to exe, Python Library. http://www.py2exe.org/. Accessed 22 June 2019

17. pynput, Python Library. https://pypi.org/project/pynput/. Accessed 22 June 2019

18. psutil, Python Library. https://pypi.org/project/psutil/. Accessed 22 June 2019

19. pywin32, Python Library. https://pypi.org/project/pywin32/. Accessed 22 June 2019

20. Android Developers, Android Library. https://developer.android.com. Accessed 26 June 2019

21. Caruana, R., Niculescu-Mizil, A.: An empirical comparison of supervised learning algorithms. In: Proceedings of the 23rd International Conference on Machine Learning - ICML 2006. https://doi.org/10.1145/1143844.1143865

22. Scikit-learn: Machine Learning in Python, Python Library. https://scikit-learn.org/stable/. Accessed 19 June 2019

23. Python Data Analysis Library, Python Library. https://pandas.pydata.org/. Accessed 23 June 2019

Data Center Job Scheduling Algorithm Based on Temperature Prediction

Weiguo Wu[✉], Zhuang Hu, Simin Wang, Yixuan Xu,
and Yifei Kang

Faculty of Electronic and Information Engineering, Xi'an Jiaotong University,
Xi'an 710049, Shaanxi, China
wgwu@mail.xjtu.edu.cn

Abstract. Improved energy efficiency of data center is in hotspot. Prevailing data center energy-conservation measures are intended for computing devices, but ignoring the potential energy savings from cooling equipment whose energy consumption accounts for about 40% of the total energy consumption of data center. In addition cooling equipment is often set to an excessively low temperature to ensure the thermal safety of the data center, resulting in energy waste. In this paper, we propose a neural network-based distributed temperature prediction algorithm including an inter-server joint modeling framework based on the thermal locality principle, which significantly reduces the training time of the temperature prediction model and make the proposed algorithm be easily extended to large data centers. Furthermore, we propose a job scheduling algorithm based on the proposed temperature prediction algorithm. The job scheduling algorithm monitors the server inlet temperature in real time and controls the load of each server using feedback control. It guarantees that thermal reliability of servers and attempts to avoid the creation of a hot point. It selects the best job scheduling strategy based on the result of the temperature prediction algorithm. The two proposed algorithms are evaluated on a small data center. Our results show that the average prediction error of the proposed temperature prediction algorithm is only 0.28 °C in a 10-min predicted field of view. The proposed job scheduling algorithm can achieve approximately 10% cooling energy consumption compared with the load balancing algorithm while ensuring the thermal reliability of the data center.

Keywords: Data center job scheduling · Energy consumption of data center · Temperature prediction · Machine learning · Neural network

1   Introduction

The scale of worldwide data centers has grown significantly with the rapid development of mobile internet. According to the China Information and Communication Research Institute, the number of servers in China's data centers reached 1.66 million by the end of 2017. The rapid development of data centers has also resulted in high energy consumption. According to research, the power consumption of data centers

© Springer Nature Singapore Pte Ltd. 2019
G. Wang et al. (Eds.): iSCI 2019, CCIS 1122, pp. 86–104, 2019.
https://doi.org/10.1007/978-981-15-1301-5_8

exceeded 100 billion kWh in 2015, and the annual electricity consumption exceeded 1.5% of the total amount of electricity. The cost of cooling equipment accounts for approximately 45% of all energy costs. Therefore, it is important to solve the problem of excessive energy consumption caused by the inefficient operation of cooling equipment such as computer room air conditioners (CRAC). Due to the lack of transparency in data center operations, refrigeration equipment must be set to an excessively low temperature to reduce the risk of hot spots, which result in excessive energy consumption. The non-computing energy consumption of more than 85% data centers accounts for more than 40% of total energy consumption.

The traditional method of conserving energy involves the reduction of the computing energy consumption of server nodes. Many underlying energy-saving technologies are used, such as processor voltage frequency adjustment. Job scheduling is also an important component. Selected algorithms move virtual machines into one physical machine to shut down the idle physical machine and thus achieve energy saving purposes. These approaches have resulted in good energy-saving effects, but they do not consider the energy consumption of refrigeration equipment. In fact, the energy consumption of refrigeration equipment accounts for a non-negligible proportion of the overall energy consumption of the data center. Therefore, energy conservation based on cooling equipment is highly important. We summarize the reasons for the high cooling energy consumption of the data center as follows:

1. Refrigeration equipment must strictly control the temperature of the data center within a reasonable range. The power density of server clusters in the data center has been growing rapidly due to the increased power consumption of its hardware components, reduced form factor and tighter packaging [1, 2]. High power density causes high temperatures, and high data center temperatures can seriously affect device reliability. The experience data from the Little Blue Penguin Cluster show that for every 10-degree increase in temperature, the failure rate of the device is doubled [3]. Studies have shown that more than 23% of data center downtime is due to self-protection shutdown caused by server overheating. To ensure that the equipment operates at a normal temperature, the cooling equipment is often simply set to an excessively low a temperature, and thus excessive cooling energy is consumed.
2. The data center temperature distribution is uneven. From a spatial point of view, the temperature of the data center is unevenly distributed at different nodes and different locations due to the hardware layout, load distribution, and other factors. From a temporal point of view, the external environment of the data center varies periodically due to natural phenomena. The internal computing resource utilization of the data center changes as the user task load changes. Therefore, the spatial and temporal fluctuations of temperature distribution in the data center require excessive cooling of the refrigeration equipment because it is necessary to ensure that the equipment remains reliable and safe, even in the most dangerous situations.

The above two reasons are based on a lack of temperature perception during data center operation, resulting in reduced server reliability and waste of energy consumption. Therefore, we propose a neural network-based distributed temperature prediction algorithm. Because minimizing the peak temperature of servers is equivalent to minimizing the cooling energy consumption [4], we propose a temperature-aware job scheduling algorithm based on the temperature prediction algorithm, which can reduce hot spots and improve cooling efficiency through reasonable allocation of jobs. Our work increases the efficiency of the cooling equipment and reduces the cooling energy consumption while ensuring safe and stable operation of the data center.

2 Related Work

2.1 Temperature Prediction Algorithm

Two main categories of data center temperature prediction algorithms are currently available. The first category is the thermodynamic-based algorithm that uses the basic thermodynamic laws and data center layouts to derive thermodynamic models at different locations within the data center [5]. Tang et al. simplified the computational fluid dynamics (CFD) model of a data center using a matrix to represent the influence coefficient of each cabinet temperature on the server inlet temperature [6]. This approach increases the speed of temperature prediction but sacrifice accuracy. Heath et al. simulated the temperature distribution of the server based on simplified thermodynamic laws, CPU temperature, utilization, and airflow velocity [7]. Li et al. proposed a simplified temperature model based on thermodynamics. The parameters of the model are obtained by machine learning [8]. However, the thermodynamic-based temperature prediction model relies on certain assumptions on the aerodynamics of a specific data center layout. The model is fixed and not suitable for different data centers.

The second category is the data-driven algorithm based on machine learning or data mining methods. Yu et al. proposed a new model that combined the cloud model and RBF neural network to predict the inlet temperature of servers [9]. Moore et al. proposed a model based on artificial neural networks to learn and predict the temperature distribution of the data center under a static workload distribution [10]. This method relies on the steady-state thermal model, which is not suitable when the workload distribution of the servers changes dynamically. Chen J et al. proposed a real-time linear prediction algorithm based on simulated temperature distribution using CFD and temperature sensor measurements. The existing data-driven approaches do not consider that temperature changes are time-dependent, and the temperature change trend is highly important for temperature prediction. The existing model has an insufficient ability to process time series temperature data, leading to defects in temperature prediction.

Aiming at the above two problems, we propose a data-driven real-time temperature prediction model based on an artificial neural network trained by time series data. To achieve scalability and avoid the poor real-time performance caused by an excessive model, we build the model based on the principle of thermal locality, i.e., the temperature surrounding the server is primarily affected by its neighboring servers.

The model can be distributed among servers because of thermal locality. Each server has its own prediction model, and each server trains the model with its own data, data from neighboring servers and temperature sensor measurements from its surroundings. Thus, the complexity of the proposed model does not increase as the size of the data center increases, and the algorithm can be theoretically extended to large data centers.

2.2 Temperature-Aware Job Scheduling Algorithm

The basic concept of the temperature-aware data center job scheduling algorithm balances the temperature of each server and prevents the occurrence of hotspots, resulting in reduced cooling requirements and achievement of energy savings. Because the temperature distribution of the data center is more uniform, the cooling efficiency of the data center is higher. The uniform outlet profile algorithms are proposed according to this principle [11, 12]. The goal of these algorithms are to make the outlet temperature of the servers in the data center more uniform. The minimized heat recirculation algorithm [13] aims to ensure that the servers that have more heat recirculation produce less heat. The algorithm allocates the power budget according to the factor of heat recirculation to reduce the total heat recirculation in the data center. This power-oriented job scheduling algorithm is not practical because power is not a variable that the administrator can directly control [14]. In addition, it is possible that the server with a large heat recirculation factor has a larger power budget than other servers but might have a lower actual power because the power budget is only a server power cap. The lowest inlet temperature algorithm monitors all servers and distributes the load to the server with the lowest inlet temperature at each time. The temperature-aware job scheduling algorithms mentioned above either focus on minimizing cooling energy consumption or minimizing calculation energy consumption. These methods are intuitive and simple.

Some researchers have proposed job scheduling algorithm in order to save energy consumption of servers and cooling equipment. Paper [15] presents a scheduling approach that combines energy efficiency and network awareness. Paper [16] formulates a novel mixed-integer linear mathematical model to achieve effective machine selection, job sequencing, and machine off-on decision making, for the purpose of saving energy. Paper [17] proposes a coordinated cooling-aware job placement and cooling management algorithm. However, these methods only take into account the current operation placement and cooling status, ignoring the cooling hysteresis problem.

These algorithms all suffer from lag problems, i.e., they are based on the temperature feedback mechanism, and insensitivity to the temperature change trend causes delay of the control. We propose a temperature-aware job scheduling algorithm based on the proposed temperature prediction algorithm. The proposed job scheduling algorithm avoids the delay of control by distributing the tasks with future temperature information.

3 Distributed Temperature Prediction Algorithm Based on a Neural Network

3.1 Temperature Prediction with Time-Series Data

Large-scale data centers typically contain tens of thousands of servers, multiple CRAC units, and fans, and these devices cause complex thermal interactions and network effects, making precision temperatures prediction more difficult. Temperature prediction in data centers can be divided into conditional temperature prediction and sequential temperature prediction [18].

Conditional temperature prediction considers the conditions and the surrounding environment of the node. The proposed conditional temperature prediction approach takes the largest energy consumption of tasks on the current node queue, the average energy consumption of all tasks, and the maximum and minimum values of the neighboring node temperatures of the most recent period as the input of the neural network, and the output is the peak temperature of the node under certain conditions [19].

Sequential temperature prediction builds a model based on historical data to predict the temperature of the nodes after a period of time [20]. The training data are extracted from the historical data of the data center. The main inputs are the current node load, the current node temperature, and the surrounding factors that might affect the node temperature. The output is the inlet temperature after a period of time. This method can also be updated with new data and predicted in real time as the data center runs.

For a typical data center, the number of tasks changes periodically with time, and the change in the task amount is the main cause of temperature changes. In addition, heat generation and heat dissipation are gradual processes in the closed computer room environment, which is an important reason for us to select temperature prediction with time-series data.

3.2 Joint Modeling Framework

Large-scale data centers have large spatial scales and mostly use inter-partition job scheduling management mechanisms. The unified modeling method results in poor performance of temperature prediction. We propose a joint modeling framework in which each server itself models a temperature prediction model and predicts its own temperature.

The joint modeling framework takes advantage of the physical properties of heat generation and propagation, i.e., heat is locally diffused following a thermodynamic model. Although the model parameters might vary greatly depending on the rack height, server location, server type, on/off status, etc., the model structure remains the same. Another advantage of the joint modeling framework is that model learning and prediction is distributed. Each server uses its own data to learn neural network models and make predictions. No data dependency exists among servers, and this lack of dependency is highly suitable for distributed computing.

Many factors affect the server inlet temperature. The first factor is the state of the server itself, including server CPU utilization and CPU fan speed as well as the air flow rate and the temperature at the CRAC vents. In addition, the temperature at various points near the server inlet also affects the server inlet temperature. Generally, the temperature at one point is primarily affected by the heat source that is closest to it and is less affected by heat sources that are far away. Therefore, we assume that the inlet temperature of a server is only affected by the close servers and ignore the impact of other servers. In Sect. 5, we verify the extent to which the inlet temperature of the server is affected by nearby servers. We build the joint modeling frame-work with the current server and the two server inlet temperatures adjacent to it, according to the verified results. This assumption is in line with the laws of physics and simplifies the problem. The relationships among servers are shown in Fig. 1.

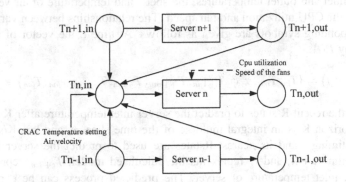

Fig. 1. Factors affecting the server node inlet temperature

In summary, server n uses its own inlet and outlet temperatures; the inlet and outlet temperatures (n − 1 and n + 1), air velocity, and temperature at the CRAC vents of its neighbors; and its own CPU utilization and fan speed to build a model and calculate the inlet temperature after a period of time.

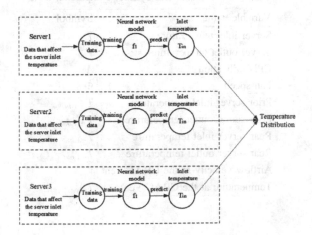

Fig. 2. Joint modeling framework

The final joint modeling framework is shown in Fig. 2. Each server node trains its own neural network model with actual operational data, ultimately building the temperature distribution across the data center.

3.3   Construction of Neural Networks

Generation of data is the first step in training a neural network. Table 1 lists the variable names that must be used and their corresponding symbols. We collect data from the data center as it runs and use that data to generate a data set. We collect data in a period time s, and these data are the factors that primarily affect the server inlet temperature, including the server inlet and outlet temperatures, the neighboring (n − 1 and n + 1) inlet and outlet temperatures, the speed and temperature of air vents of the CRAC, and the CPU utilization and fan speed. The relationships between variables and their corresponding symbols are given as follows. At time t, the vector of all data is expressed by $P(t)$.

$$P(t) = \left(T_{in}, T_{out}, \alpha, \varphi, T_{+1,in}, T_{+1,out}, T_{-1,in}, T_{-1,out}, v_{fan}, T_{fan}\right).$$

We use the recent R states to predict the server inlet temperature after K time. The predicted horizon K is an integral multiple of the time slices s, and k = K/s. In other words, the timing t and its nearest Rstates are used to predict the server inlet temperature at time t + k, and f_k represents the calculated model, $T_{t+k,in}$ represents the timing $t+k$ inlet temperature of server. The predicted process can be expressed as $T_{t+k,in} = f_k(P(t-R+1), P(t-R+2), \cdots, P(t-1), P(t))$. The input and output of the f_k function form the input and output of the required data set. Thus, $<(P(t-R+1), P(t-R+2), \cdots, P(t-1), P(t)), T_{t+k,in}>$ represent a data pair, and $<(P(t-R+2), P(t-R+3), \cdots, P(t), P(t+1)), T_{t+k+1,in}>$ also constitute a data pair.

Table 1. Variable name and symbol comparison table

Variable name	Symbol
Server inlet temperature	T_{in}
Server outlet temperature	T_{out}
CPU utilization	A
Fan speed	Φ
Prior server inlet temperature	$T_{+1,in}$
Prior server outlet temperature	$T_{+1,out}$
Rear server inlet temperature	$T_{-1,in}$
Rear server outlet temperature	$T_{-1,out}$
Airflow velocity at the CRAC vent	v_{fan}
Temperature at the CRAC vent	T_{fan}

The second step of training is to determine the structure of the neural network. This paper uses the three-layer BP neural network structure. The input layers are located in the front, the output layers are located in the rear, and the hidden layers are situated in the middle. The number of neurons in the input layer is equal to the number of input parameters of the data set. The number of input parameters is 10R ($R \in N_+$), and thus the number of input layer neurons is 10R. The number of neurons in the hidden layer is set to 20.

In the hidden layer, every neuron i accepts N_i inputs from the upper layer, and for each input x_a, we apply weighting factor $W_{i,a}$ and use the sum of the weighted inputs as the input value of its activation function g. The result of this function y_i is passed to the next layer neurons. The activation function $g(x)$ uses the sigmoid function.

$$y_i = g\left(\sum_{a=0}^{N_i} W_{i,a} * x_a\right) \tag{1}$$

We use the back propagation algorithm to train the neural networks. The iterative training process continues until the MSE reaches a user-defined minimum threshold or until the training process performs the specified number of iterations.

4 Job Scheduling Algorithm Based on Temperature Prediction

4.1 Introduction of Job Scheduling Algorithm

First, we propose a job scheduling method based on feedback control and subsequently introduce the temperature prediction based on this method. As shown in Fig. 3, the algorithm is based on the LVS (Linux Virtual Server) load balancer and two daemons. Every server has one temperature daemon (known as tempd), and a load control daemon is also present on the load balancer (known as ctrld). Tempd wakes up periodically (once per minute in our experiments) and measures the server inlet

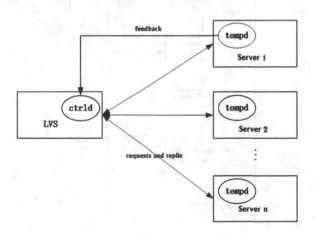

Fig. 3. System framework

temperatures. Tempd is also responsible for triggering and deactivating thermal reactions and sending feedback to ctrld. Ctrld uses the tempd feedback to configure the load balancer.

The tempd daemon monitors the server inlet temperature, and we define three thresholds for this variable: low (T_l), high (T_h), and alert (T_v). For the servers, when tempd detects that the server inlet temperature is higher than T_h, it means that the server inlet temperature is too high, the temperature needs to be reduced, and the thermal reaction is triggered. At this time, tempd sends a message to ctrld, which adjusts the load on the balancer supply server based on this message, consequently reducing the server inlet temperature. The daemon communication and load adjustments are periodically run (once per minute in our experiments) until the component temperature is below T_h. When the temperature is less than T_l, the tempd command ctrld removes restrictions on the server load because the server is sufficiently cool and the hot emergency has been eliminated. For temperatures between T_l and T_h, the load distribution is not adjusted because no communication occurs between the daemons. In general, the regulation strategy is simple. When the temperature is higher than T_h,

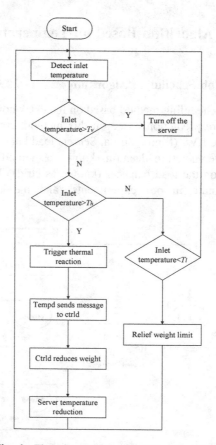

Fig. 4. Flowchart of job scheduling algorithm

regulation is started. When the temperature is lower than T_l, regulation is turned off. In the middle of T_h and T_l, the temperature stays the same. The flowchart of the algorithm is shown in Fig. 4.

The server will shut down only when the server inlet temperature exceeds the alert temperature T_v. This threshold indicates the maximum temperature that the server can reach, and the reliability of server might be reduced if the temperature exceeds T_v. Thus T_h should be set to less than T_v, e.g., 2 °C, depending on how quickly the temperature rises during the observation period.

Although we have applied measures to prevent the server inlet temperature from reaching the warning temperature, the temperature might not be effectively controlled in an emergency. For example, assuming that the entrance of the server is completely blocked, the temperature continues to rise even if all the workload of this server has been migrated. Thus no matter how effective the thermal management system is, it occasionally must shut down the server in such an extreme emergency.

Specifically, the information sent by tempd is the output of the PD (proportional and derivative) feedback controller. The output of the PD feedback controller is calculated as follows:

$$\text{output} = \max(k_p(T_{curr} - T_h) + k_d(T_{curr} - T_{last}), 0)$$

where k_p and k_d are gain constants, and T_{curr} and T_{last} are the current and last measured temperatures. The purpose of feedback control is to reduce the temperature to below T_h. In addition, because $T_{curr} - T_{last}$ might be negative, the output might be negative. When output < 0, we let output $= 0$.

The LVS adjust its request distribution by setting the weight of the hot server based on the output. the weight reduces to the current weight divided by output plus 1.

In addition, when the entire system load increases, the actual load allocated to the hot server might increase even if the weight is reduced. To solve this problem, we limit the number of connection requests sent to the servers whose inlet temperature exceeds T_h during the current time interval (one minute in our experiment). The current interval request does not exceed the number of requests from the previous interval. In this manner, the load assigned to the hot server does not increase under any circumstances. Specifically, we use the variable C_{hot} to record the number of connection requests processed by each server during the time interval before triggering of the thermal reaction and the variable C_{curr} to record the cumulative number of connection requests that the load balancer has assigned to this hot server during the current time interval. When $C_{curr} \geq C_{hot}$, the load balancer does not assign any connection requests to this hot server.

4.2   Job Scheduling Algorithm Based on Temperature Prediction

1. Feedback control in these strategies relies on careful adjustment of the gain constant, which can be tricky and time consuming;

2. For different types of emergencies, the gain constants might need to be adjusted differently;
3. The reaction intensity is related to the temperature threshold and the monitoring interval of the thermal management system. For example, T_h is usually set lower than T_v, e.g., 2 °C lower, depending on how quickly the temperature is expected to rise between observations. However, a weak response to an emergency might cause the temperature immediately below T_h to increase by more than $T_v - T_h$ during an observation interval, thus forcing the server to shut down.

The three points mentioned above are a problem of confusing response strength. The effect of lowering the temperature of the hot server is not good if reaction is too weak. If the reaction is too strong, the performance of the server is degraded. Therefore, we have improved this method by combining this method with the temperature prediction algorithm described in the previous chapter and selecting the optimal reaction intensity using the temperature prediction algorithm.

As mentioned earlier, the load control daemon ctrld determines the response strength based on the value of output, i.e., it adjusts the load weight of the hot server to 1/(output + 1) the current weight. We define three thermal reactions, r_1, r_2 and r_3, i.e., the weak, medium and strong reactions, and the reaction intensity increases in turn. The values of r_1, r_2 and r_3 are described as follows. More predefined thermal reactions are possible, and in theory, the more definitions, the better. However, we only define three, because three are sufficient to verify our thinking. We use the prediction to decide which reaction should be used.

$$r_1 = \frac{1}{\text{output} + 1}$$

$$r_2 = \frac{1}{3(\text{output} + 1)}$$

$$r_3 = \frac{1}{5(\text{output} + 1)}$$

The basic principle followed by the reaction selection algorithm is preferential selection of a reaction that has little effect on performance, i.e., a weaker reaction, and if a weaker reaction does not satisfy the need to lower the temperature, a stronger reaction is selected. For each of the predefined thermal reactions, the temperature distribution prediction algorithm is used to predict the inlet temperature of the thermal server for a period of time (in our experiment, five minutes). We assume that the predicted temperatures corresponding to r_1, r_2 and r_3 are t_1, t_2 and t_3, respectively. The algorithm used to select the response is shown in Algorithm 1.

Algorithm 1. Thermal reaction selection algorithm pseudo-code

```
Algorithm: Thermal response selection algorithm
Input: Predefined three thermal reactions
Output: Optimal thermal response selected
```

```
1:   function SelectReaction(r1, r2, r3)
2:      t1 = ForecastTemp(r1)
4:      t2 = ForecastTemp(r2)
5:      t3 = ForecastTemp(r3)
6:      /* tv is alert temperature */
7:      if t1 < tv then
8:         return r1
9:      else if t2 < tv then
10:        return r2
11:     else
12:        return r3
13:     end if
14: end function
```

5   Experiment and Analysis

5.1   Results of the Temperature Prediction Experiment

We experimented on a small test platform. The test platform consists of 15 servers (model: Dell PowerEdge 850) placed in a single rack. The rack is placed in a small room and insulated by a foam board. Above the rack is an exhaust port for excluding hot air from the room. The air conditioner is placed outside the room, and the air conditioner is connected to the air intake of the room floor, sending cold air directly to the front of the rack; this outcome is consistent with the cooling airflow of the popular raised floor cooling design. A wireless temperature sensor (model: TelosB Mote TPR2420CA) is placed at the entrance and exit of each server. A temperature sensor and airflow speed sensor (Model: DegreeC F333) are placed at the floor air inlet to monitor the air conditioning airflow and flow rate.

The experiment in this article collected 25 h of operational data from the test data center. The time interval between collected data was 5 s. The model was trained using 21 h of data, and the remaining 4 h of data used in testing. Data were collected in the event of a dynamic change in the server load.

First, we verify and determine the specific number of neighbouring servers that are used to build the federated modeling framework. We take one of the servers as an example. Figure 5 shows a comparison of the root mean square error (RMSE) values of the current and neighbouring server numbers and the predicted results when we build the joint prediction framework. Based on the comprehensive consideration of RMSE and modeling time, we determined that the joint modeling framework used the temperature and running data of the current server and the two adjacent servers.

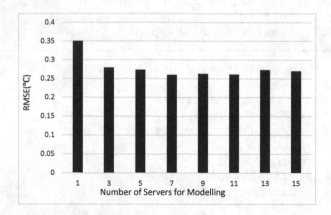

Fig. 5. Effect of the number of selected units on the RMSE of prediction results

ThermoCast [9] is selected for comparison to prove the effectiveness of the proposed temperature prediction algorithm. ThermoCast builds a temperature prediction model based on simplified thermodynamic laws and uses machine learning to obtain model parameters. ThermoCast is designed for data centers with floor air supply. So it's suitable for our test platform-. Our proposed temperature predictions algorithm is not only applicable to data centers with floor air supply but also to data centers with lateral air supply because the algorithm is a data-driven model which is not related to the layout of data center directly.

The parameters of the prediction model are set to R = 1 and K = 600 s. The temperature distribution after 10 min is predicted. Figures 6 and 7 show the predicted results of server 3 and server 8 respectively as examples. Each of figure contains two pictures of (a) and (b), where (a) is the prediction result of the algorithm proposed in this paper, and (b) is the prediction result of ThermoCast algorithm. It can be clearly observed from the figure that the proposed prediction algorithm of this paper can more accurately predict the server inlet temperature, and the error is smaller than that of the ThermoCast algorithm (the closer two lines are to each other, the smaller is the prediction error). Specifically, the root mean square error of the proposed prediction algorithm is 0.28 °C, and the root mean square error of ThermoCast is 0.33 °C. Therefore, the prediction algorithm proposed in this paper is more accurate compared with the ThermoCast algorithm.

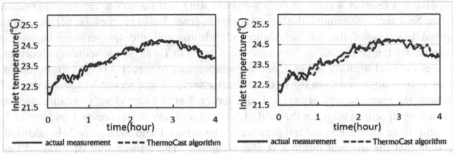

(a) Prediction results of the proposed algorithm (b) Prediction results of ThermoCast algorithm

Fig. 6. Prediction results of server 3

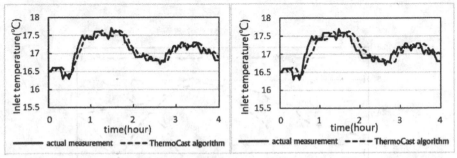

(a) Prediction results of the proposed algorithm (b) Prediction results of ThermoCast algorithm

Fig. 7. Prediction results of server 8

5.2 Results of Job Scheduling Experiment

Our job scheduling algorithm is evaluated on a single-layer web server cluster. The cluster consists of four Apache HTTP servers behind a LVS load balancer. The Apache HTTP server and LVS run on a wave NF5280M2 server with two 2.4 GHz to strong E5620 processors and 16 gigabytes of memory. We use httperf [21] to generate the HTTP load to test our job scheduling algorithm

We set the three parameters of the job scheduling algorithm to the formula (2).

$$\begin{cases} T_l = 23(^\circ C) \\ T_h = 25(^\circ C) \\ T_v = 27(^\circ C) \end{cases} \tag{2}$$

First, we observe how the proposed job scheduling algorithm based on temperature prediction manages the server temperature in experiments. Figure 8 shows a graph of server inlet temperature versus time under the control of the proposed job scheduling algorithm. It can be observed that near the 17th minute, the inlet temperature of server 4 reaches T_h first. When T_h is reached, the thermal reaction is triggered, and the inlet temperature of server 4 starts to decrease, indicating that the job scheduling algorithm works. Near the 19th minute, the temperature of server 3 also reaches T_h, triggering the thermal reaction of the job scheduling algorithm, and the temperature begins to decrease. By the 26th minute, the temperature drops to T_l, the job scheduling algorithm releases the load limit on server 3, and the temperature of server 3 begins to rise again. It can also be observed from the figure that after server 4 and server 3 trigger a thermal reaction, the temperatures of server 1 and server 2 start to accelerate because the job scheduling algorithm migrates the load of server 4 and server 3 to server 1 and server 2, resulting in an increase in the temperature of the server 1 and the server 2. In addition, we note that the thermal reaction is also triggered. The temperature of server 4 and server 3 decrease at different rates, and the inlet temperature of server 3 decreases more quickly because the thermal response triggered by server 3 is greater than the strength of server 4, which is the function of the thermal reaction selection algorithm. These phenomena are consistent with the setting of the algorithm.

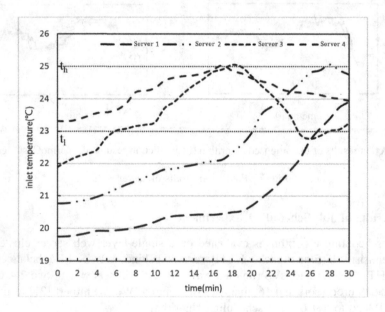

Fig. 8. Server inlet temperature result for the proposed algorithm

This experiment proves that the proposed job scheduling algorithm can effectively manage the inlet temperature of the server and avoid creation of hot spots.

Another experiment is carried out to observe the effect of the temperature prediction-based job scheduling algorithm in reducing cooling energy consumption, and we compare the results with the other two methods. The following gives a brief introduction to the two methods.

1. Load balancing based on minimum connection. This approach is a traditional job scheduling strategy without consideration of the temperature factors. The load balancer uses LVS, and the algorithm uses minimum connection scheduling.
2. Job scheduling algorithm based on model predictive control(MPC) [22]. This approach uses DVFS (Dynamic Voltage and Frequency Scaling) to adjust the CPU frequency of the servers to control the servers' temperature. The algorithm controls the CPU frequency of each server at the next moment according to the current information and ensures that the inlet temperature of each server is controlled within a prescribed threshold.

The temperature set point of the cooling equipment is mainly determined by the maximum inlet temperature of all servers in the data center because the cooling equipment must ensure that the hottest server can also operate stably. Therefore, the smaller the maximum inlet temperature, the higher the efficiency of the cooling equipment and the greater the energy savings. Therefore, we evaluate the effect of three algorithms on reducing the energy consumption of cooling equipment through the maximum inlet temperature.

As shown in Fig. 9, the four line graphs in the figure are curves formed by the maximum inlet temperature of the three methods varying with time. It can be observed from the figure that the proposed job scheduling algorithm in this paper can control the maximum inlet temperature below 25 °C. the maximum inlet temperature of the proposed job scheduling algorithm is lower than that of the other two methods at most of time. The average maximum inlet temperatures for the three methods over a 30-min period were 24.3 °C, 25.2 °C, and 24.6 °C, respectively. The average maximum inlet temperature of the proposed job scheduling algorithm is 0.9 °C lower than that of the load balancing algorithm based on minimum connection and 0.3 °C lower than that of the job scheduling algorithm based on MPC. It can be estimated that the cooling energy consumption can be reduced by 10% compared with the load balancing algorithm based on minimum connection through method proposed in literature [4].

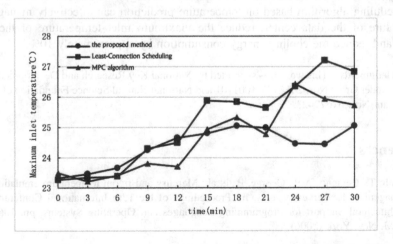

Fig. 9. Comparison of the maximum inlet temperatures obtained by the three methods

6 Summary

Data center management faces two pressures currently. First, the energy consumption cost of the data center is notably high, and cooling energy consumption accounts for a large proportion of the total energy consumption. Therefore, the data center must reduce the cooling energy consumption. Second, the density of the computing devices in data center is increasing. A rack might contain hundreds of computing cores, generating a large amount of heat. If the heat dissipation is not timely, it can affect the safe operation of the entire data center. Reduction of the cooling energy consumption under the premise of ensuring safe and stable operation of the data center has become an urgent problem to be solved.

To solve this problem, this paper focuses on the data center job scheduling algorithm to minimize the energy consumption of the cooling equipment while ensuring the data center thermal safety. We first propose a temperature prediction algorithm based on neural network. The algorithm can accurately predict the temperature of the data center. Based on the temperature prediction algorithm, we propose a job scheduling algorithm, which can manage the heat by adjusting the workload of the node.

Specifically, the data center temperature prediction algorithm is based on the neural network. According to the local characteristics of heat propagation in the data center, a joint prediction framework is proposed to solve the scalability problem of the temperature prediction model in a large-scale data center.

Furthermore, a data center job scheduling algorithm based on temperature prediction is proposed. The algorithm can effectively reduce the hot spots in the data center and ensure the thermal security requirements of the data center.

The proposed temperature prediction algorithm and job scheduling algorithm were evaluated on a small data center. The temperature prediction algorithm can accurately predict the server inlet temperature under a dynamic load. The average prediction error under the 10-min prediction field is only 0.28 °C. Moreover, the proposed joint modeling framework in temperature prediction algorithm can effectively reduce the training time of the model and facilitate expansion to large data centers. The data center job scheduling algorithm based on temperature prediction can effectively manage the temperature of the data center, reduce the maximum inlet temperature of the data center, and reduce the cooling energy consumption by approximately 10%.

Acknowledgments. This work was supported by National Key Research and Development Plan of China under Grant Nos. 2017YFB1001701 and National Natural Science Foundation of China under Grant Nos. 61672423.

References

1. Heath, T., Centeno, A.P., George, P., et al.: Mercury and freon: temperature emulation and management for server systems. In: Proceedings of the 12th International Conference on Architectural Support for Programming Languages and Operating Systems, pp. 106–116. ACM, New York (2006)

2. Skadron, K., Abdelzaher, T., Stan, M.R.: Control-theoretic techniques and thermal-RC modeling for accurate and localized dynamic thermal management. In: Proceedings Eighth International Symposium on High Performance Computer Architecture, pp. 17–28. IEEE, Cambridge (2002)

3. Hsu, C.H., Feng, W.C., Archuleta, J.S.: Towards efficient supercomputing: a quest for the right metric. In: 19th IEEE International Parallel and Distributed Processing Symposium, pp. 99–110. IEEE, Denver (2005)

4. Tang, Q., Gupta, S.K.S., Varsamopoulos, G.: Thermal-aware task scheduling for data centers through minimizing heat recirculation. In: 2007 IEEE International Conference on Cluster Computing, pp. 129–138. IEEE, Austin (2007)

5. Li, X., Jiang, X.H., Wu, C.H., et al.: Thermal management of green data center. Chin. J. Comput. 38(10), 1976–1996 (2015)

6. Tang, Q., Mukherjee, T., Gupta, S.K.S., et al.: Sensor-based fast thermal evaluation model for energy efficient high-performance datacenters. In: 4th International Conference on Intelligent Sensing and Information Processing, pp. 203–208. IEEE, Bangalore (2006)

7. Heath, T., Centeno, A.P., George, P., et al.: Mercury and freon: temperature emulation and management for server systems. In: 12th International Conference on Architectural Support for Programming Languages and Operating Systems, pp. 106–116. ACM, New York (2006)

8. Li, L., Liang, C.-J.M., Liu, J., et al.: ThermoCast: a cyber-physical forecasting model for datacenters. In: 17th ACM SIGKDD International Conference on Knowledge Discovery and Data Mining, pp. 1370–1378. ACM, New York (2011)

9. Yu, Y., Sun, W.C., Zhang, B.B., et al.: Temperature prediction based on cloud model and RBF in data center. J. Shenyang Ligong Univ. 32(4), 9–14 (2013)

10. Moore, J, Chase, J.S., Ranganathan, P.: Weatherman: automated, online and predictive thermal mapping and management for data centers. In: 2006 IEEE International Conference on Autonomic Computing, pp. 155–164. IEEE, Dublin (2006)

11. Vanderster, D.C., Baniasadi, A., Dimopoulos, N.J.: Exploiting task temperature profiling in temperature-aware task scheduling for computational clusters. In: Choi, L., Paek, Y., Cho, S. (eds.) ACSAC 2007. LNCS, vol. 4697, pp. 175–185. Springer, Heidelberg (2007). https://doi.org/10.1007/978-3-540-74309-5_18

12. Varsamopoulos, G., Banerjee, A., Gupta, S.K.S.: Energy efficiency of thermal-aware job scheduling algorithms under various cooling models. In: Ranka, S., et al. (eds.) IC3 2009. CCIS, vol. 40, pp. 568–580. Springer, Heidelberg (2009). https://doi.org/10.1007/978-3-642-03547-0_54

13. Moore, J., Chase, J., Ranganathan, P., et al.: Making scheduling "Cool": temperature-aware workload placement in data centers. In: Proceedings of the Annual Conference on USENIX Annual Technical Conference, p. 5. USENIX Association, Berkeley (2005)

14. Tang, Q., Gupta, S.K.S., Stanzione, D., et al.: Thermal-aware task scheduling to minimize energy usage of blade server based datacenters. In: 2nd IEEE International Symposium on Dependable, Autonomic and Secure Computing, Indianapolis, IN, USA, pp. 195–202 (2006)

15. Moore, J., Chase, J., Farkas, K., et al.: Data center workload monitoring, analysis, and emulation. In: 8th Workshop on Computer Architecture Evaluation using Commercial Workloads, pp. 1–8. IEEE, New York (2005)

16. Wang, L., von Laszewski, G., Huang, F., et al.: Task scheduling with ANN-based temperature prediction in a data center: a simulation-based study. Eng. Comput. 27(4), 381–391 (2011)

17. Zhang, S., Chatha, K.S.: Approximation algorithm for the temperature-aware scheduling problem. In: 2007 IEEE/ACM International Conference on Computer-Aided Design, pp. 281–288. IEEE/ACM, San Jose (2007)

18. Kliazovich, D., Bouvry, P., Khan, S.U.: DENS: data center energy-efficient network-aware scheduling. Cluster Comput. **16**(1), 65–75 (2013)
19. Zhang, L., Tang, Q., Wu, Z., et al.: Mathematical modeling and evolutionary generation of rule sets for energy-efficient flexible job shops. Energy **138**(1), 210–227 (2017)
20. Banerjee, A., Mukherjee, T., Varsamopoulos, G., et al.: Integrating cooling awareness with thermal aware workload placement for HPC data centers. Sustain. Comput. Inform. Syst. **1**(2), 134–150 (2011)
21. The httperf HTTP load generator. https://github.com/httperf/httperf. Accessed 28 June 2019
22. Zhao, X.G., Hu, Q.P., Ding, L., et al.: Energy-saving scheduling algorithm for data center based on model predictive control. J. Softw. **28**(2), 429–441 (2017)

Transfer Learning for Facial Attributes Prediction and Clustering

Luca Anzalone[2], Paola Barra[2], Silvio Barra[1](✉), Fabio Narducci[3],
and Michele Nappi[2]

[1] Department of Mathematics and Computer Science, University of Cagliari,
Cagliari, Italy
`silvio.barra@unica.it`
[2] Department of Computer Science,University of Salerno, Salerno, Italy
`{pbarra,mnappi}@unisa.it`,
`l.anzalone2@studenti.unisa.it`
[3] Department of Science and Technology, University of Naples "Parthenope",
Naples, Italy
`fabio.narducci@uniparthenope.it`

Abstract. Notwithstanding the enhancement obtained in the last decade researches, the recognition of facial attributes is still today a trend. Besides the mere face recognition, the singular face features, like mouth, nose and hair, are considered as soft biometrics; these can be useful for human identification in cases the face is partially occluded, and only some regions are visible. In this paper we propose a model generated by transfer learning approach for the recognition of the face attributes. Also, an unsupervised clustering model is described, which is in charge of dividing and grouping faces based on their characteristics. Furthermore, we show how clusters can be evaluated by a compact summary of them, and how Deep Learning models should be properly trained for attribute prediction tasks.

Keywords: Attribute clustering · k-means · Face attributes · Transfer learning · Cluster summary

1 Introduction

Recognizing and grouping facial attributes is a very important task since it may result very useful in different applications, like verification and identification. Notwithstanding, this task becomes very challenging in the cases in which the subject is not collaborative, or not aware that he is being acquired. This usually happens in environments like smart cities, sensitive places, like banks and airports [5], but also for smart devices applications [6,7] and learning platforms [8], which aims at granting the identity of the user [4]. In fact, whereas in collaborative scenarios many face variations, like illumination and pose, can be eliminated or greatly reduced, in an unconstrained ones, even the detection of the face becomes a very challenging activity.

© Springer Nature Singapore Pte Ltd. 2019
G. Wang et al. (Eds.): iSCI 2019, CCIS 1122, pp. 105–117, 2019.
https://doi.org/10.1007/978-981-15-1301-5_9

Common face variations encountered in face-related tasks are the so-called PIE-issues, following explained:

- **Occlusions**: objects like hats, eyeglasses and scarfs tent to cover relevant regions of the face, eventually hiding the underneath features;
- **Pose**: the pose is probably one of the most challenging issue to address, since the face results deformed and the some of the features may be hidden;
- **Illumination**: high or low degrees of brightness may create noise. on the face;
- **Expressions**: occur when a change in expression alters the face features, thus reducing the change of a correct analysis.

In most cases, a face captured in unconstrained environments needs to be normalized before being further analyzed.

Some approaches for pose estimation are based on a mixture of trees model [28], while other are able to detect even occlusions by performing landmarks estimation [1,3]; at the state of the art, the most effective and robust approaches rely on training based methods like convolutional neural networks (CNNs) [14, 17,27].

The approach here proposed relies on CNNs. In this way the model can learn robust features (compared to hand-made features like HOG, Haar, LBP), allowing it to infer facial attributes.

When dealing with smartcities, it may result very useful to apply face recognition based on a collection of soft biometrics, like the single facial features are. This is particularly true in the cases in which the normal pose of a subject may not permit an exhaustive capturing of the whole face. In this paper, a clustering and a recognition approach is faced [16], basing on the estimation of the facial features, in order to be used in a following operation of recognition. In particular, the main contributions of this paper are the following:

1. A model heavily based on the Transfer Learning approach, that estimates facial attributes; along with some training insights.
2. According to the detected attributes, we evaluate different clustering methods in order to discover and visualize the best grouping technique.

The paper is organized as follows: in Sect. 2, the state of the art in attribute prediction, clustering methods and transfer learning topics is presented. Section 3 presents the proposed approach and the results are organized in the Sect. 4. Section 5 concludes the paper.

2   Related Works

Although the recognition of face characteristics and the related grouping using Clustering techniques have been extensively analyzed in the literature, the clustering of facial images is a less discussed topic. In this section, the related works in the topics of the face attribute prediction and the clustering methods are shown.

2.1 Attribute Prediction

In [14], the authors proposed an approach for face attribute prediction, by training. A model composed by two Convolutional Neural Networks: LNet and ANet; each of them pre-trained in a different way: the former on massive categories of general objects (for face localization), and the latter on large number of facial identities for attribute prediction. Then, either are trained and fine-tuned jointly with attributes tags.

Pre-training ANet on face identity allows the model to manage complex face variations thanks to the learnt face features.

Another possible way to deal with this problem is to learn a discriminative face representation. Researches in [13,21], proposed a mode synthesising a face into a compact representation, called face embedding, that, being properly trained, is able to take apart faces belonging to the same subject (identity).

During the training process, the model implicitly learns enough features to distinguish face identities (the embeddings related to the same identity will lie on the same hyperplane). However the resulting face embedding is hard to interpret because it hides the learnt facial features, consequently losing any relations among attributes.

Thus, the embedding-based approaches are extremely good at maximizing the performance of a single feature; in this case the feature is the face identity. Indeed these are one of the most effective way of performing accurate face recognition tasks (which are based on a single high-level concept: identity).

2.2 Clustering Methods

For the proposed approach, three clustering techniques have been compared: K-means, Agglomerative Clustering, and DBSCAN.

The K-Means algorithm [2] clusters data by trying to separate samples in n groups of equal variance, minimising the inertia criterion (the average squared distance between points in the same cluster). This algorithm requires the number of clusters to be specified as an input parameter. It scales well to large number of samples and has been used across a large range of applicative domains.

The Agglomerative Clustering approach falls within the Hierarchical clustering family. Hierarchical methods works by building nested clusters, obtained through merging or splitting underneath clusters. This nesting process stops when a single cluster is constructed; so the hierarchy of clusters is usually represented as a tree or dendrogram.

Differently from the other two, the DBSCAN algorithm is able to discover clusters of arbitrary shape; so, it doesn't require the number of clusters as input parameter. Moreover, DBSCAN is designed to require a minimal knowledge of the domain data, together with a good efficiency on large databases.

Otto et al. [15] faced the problem of clustering millions of faces into thousands clusters of related identities. They proposed an approximate Rank-Order clustering algorithm that performs better than popular clustering algorithms (k-Means and Spectral) by achieving a better accuracy and run-time complexity.

Finally, among the various works analyzed, another interesting evaluation was carried out on the work done by Rosebrock [18]. In this case an algorithm has been developed which extracts an array of 128 real numbers from each face and creates clusters with these data.

Each cluster contains a set of faces with similar facial features. Obviously, using a clustering approach based on DBSCAN, the number of the created clusters depends on the algorithm, which is structured to return an optimal number of clusters.

Even in this case it doesn't fit our needs perfectly, as another goal that has been set is the possibility of independently choosing the number of clusters to be displayed.

2.3   Transfer Learning

As the research goes further, the complexity of the ML tasks increases. The resulting model architectures becomes even bigger too, and slower to train. This aspect is particularly verified for Convolutional Neural Networks [11], which require a huge amount of data and computational power.

Thanks to the ImageNet classification challenge [19], many effective models have been trained (like the groundbreaking AlexNet [11]). It turned out that models like VGG [22], InceptionNet [23], and ResNet [9] are very good for solving general ML tasks.

Thus, the Transfer Learning [12] techniques allows to recycle a model architecture in order to perform a different task from the one it was developed for.

In this work, this technique is exploited to fine-tune our model.

3   Our Approach

In this section, more details are given about the proposed detection-clustering pipeline.

Basically, the entire workflow consists of three parts:

- **Attributes inference**: in which we fine-tune a pre-trained model on 37 facial attributes taken from the CelebA [14] dataset.
- **Attributes clustering**: the labels predicted by the proposed model are given as input to a commonly available clustering algorithm (such as K-Means) which computes the grouping of the input faces according to a criterion of closeness.
- **Visualization and analysis**: by simply computing the occurrences of the attributes (of the given clusters), it is shown that these are enough to evaluate quantitatively the accuracy of the resulting clustering. Moreover, we provide an even more concise way to graphically evaluate clusters.

3.1   The CelebA Dataset

All experiments and studies have been conducted on the CelebA dataset [25]. Unlike other datasets of faces (like LFW [10]), CelebA is a large-scale face attributes dataset with more than 200 K celebrity images, each with 40 attribute annotations.

This dataset is very challenging and, at the same time, appealing since it contains face-images covering a large amount of pose, expression, age, and occlusion variations.

We found out that CelebA has heavily imbalanced attributes (Fig. 1): more than a third of attributes are extremely rare (with frequencies below 10%), and only a couple of them are very common (by occurring more than 70% of the times).

This unbalance has pointed out the weaknesses of widely adopted loss functions, when training a model on rare-occurring instances.

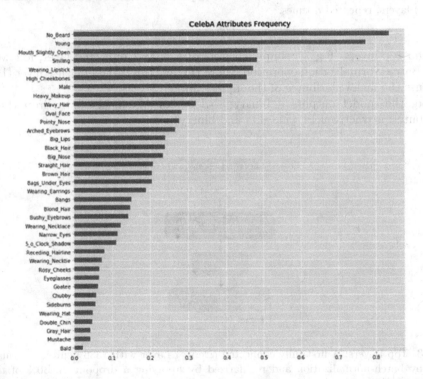

Fig. 1. Frequencies of CelebA attributes: the chart clearly shows the discrepancy about the occurrence of the attributes.

3.2   The Fine-Tuning of the Model

We employ the Transfer Learning approach to fine-tune our model architecture, in order to achieve a faster training convergence.

Our baseline model is represented by the MobileNetV2 [20] architecture, but without the top classification layers (Fig. 2).

Input	Operator	t	c	n	s
$224^2 \times 3$	conv2d	-	32	1	2
$112^2 \times 32$	bottleneck	1	16	1	1
$112^2 \times 16$	bottleneck	6	24	2	2
$56^2 \times 24$	bottleneck	6	32	3	2
$28^2 \times 32$	bottleneck	6	64	4	2
$14^2 \times 64$	bottleneck	6	96	3	1
$14^2 \times 96$	bottleneck	6	160	3	2
$7^2 \times 160$	bottleneck	6	320	1	1
$7^2 \times 320$	conv2d 1x1	-	1280	1	1
$7^2 \times 1280$	avgpool 7x7	-	-	1	-
$1 \times 1 \times 1280$	conv2d 1x1	-	k		-

Fig. 2. MobileNetV2: Each line describes a sequence of 1 or more identical (modulo stride) layers, repeated n times.

Our top layers (Fig. 3), simply consists of a Fully Connected layer, followed by a Batch Normalization operation before the final multi-label Dense layer that outputs the facial attributes of the input sample.

So, the model outputs a binary 37-d vector (we decided to drop three attributes: attractiveness, pale skin and blurry).

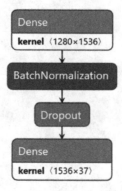

Fig. 3. Top Layers: A first fully-connected (Dense) Layer with 1536 neurons, normalized by batch-normalization and regularized by applying a dropout on 30% of the connections. The last dense layer outputs the labels for every attribute (thus, requires 37 neurons *sigmoid*-activated).

In order to let the model generalize better, a Data Augmentation technique has been used. This method consists of augmenting the training images by applying some random modifications to them. In particular we apply the following augmentations:

- Rotation: the image is rotated by a maximum of 20°.
- Shift: a translation (shift) on either width and height is applied, with a factor of 0.2.
- Shear: a random distortion is applied with an effect of 0.2.
- Zoom: the image is magnified by a maximum of 20% of their total dimension.
- Flipping: only horizontal flipping is applied to images.

In this way the number of training instances can be effectively increased: the model will see slightly different training samples during each epoch.

The common loss function like mean absolute error (MAE) and mean squared error (MSE), when used as the training objective, fails completely in their aim.

These kind of loss function are not suitable for sparse binary multi-labeled data, when the position of a single bit is informative: different vectors but with the same amount of 1s (e.g. [0, 0, 1, 0] and [1, 0, 0, 0], versus [0, 0, 1, 0] and [0, 1, 0, 0]), produces the exactly same loss.

Training a model with these loss function leads to a completely dumb model: it predicts an array of 0's for whatever input instance regarding the belonging attributes. This scenario gets even worse when we deal with rare (in this case sparse) features.

The following example is provided for sake of clarity: if the model needs to predict whether a face belongs to a young person or not, and that feature is 1 for only 5% of the instances, a prediction of 0 (for every test instance) results in an accuracy of 95%. But the truth is that the model has not properly learned the feature.

For this reason, only relying on accuracy results may be misleading. In fact, we double-check the accuracy of our model with: qualitative results, and misprediction ratio.

Finally, a good loss function should understand the difference between two samples. Cosine Proximity is the loss function used for this purpose, and reported in the Eq. 1

$$L = -\frac{\mathbf{y} \cdot \hat{\mathbf{y}}}{\|\mathbf{y}\|_2 \cdot \|\hat{\mathbf{y}}\|_2} = -\frac{\sum_{i=1}^{n} y^{(i)} \cdot \hat{y}^{(i)}}{\sqrt{\sum_{i=1}^{n}(y^{(i)})2} \cdot \sqrt{\sum_{i=1}^{n} \hat{y}^{(i)}2}} \tag{1}$$

where $\mathbf{y} = (y^{(1)}, y^{(2)}, \ldots, y^{(n)}) \in \mathbf{R}^n$ and $\hat{\mathbf{y}} = (\hat{y}^{(1)}, \hat{y}^{(2)}, \ldots, \hat{y}^{(n)}) \in \mathbf{R}^n$.

This function treats a binary array as a vector in a multidimensional space. The differences (or similarities) between the true and predicted labels are expressed as the arccos of the angle between them. When two vectors are orthogonal (there's a 90° angle between them), means that they are completely different (the loss value is at its maximum). Instead, when two vectors overlap (the angle is 0°), they result the same (the loss value is at its minimum). The training process with cosine proximity is effective: it allows the model to effectively learn patterns, used to infer the facial attributes.

In (Table 1) the facial attributes recognition results are shown, along with the comparison against the LNet + ANet model proposed in [25].

Table 1. Performance comparison of attribute prediction models

	5 Shadow	Arched Eyebrows	Bags Under Eyes	Bald	Bangs	Big Lips	Big Nose	Black Hair	Blond Hair	Brown Hair	Bushy Eyebrows	Chubby	Double Chin	Eyeglasses	Goatee	Gray Hair	Heavy Makeup	High Cheekbones	Male
Our model	95	81	85	99	96	71	84	90	96	89	92	96	96	99	97	98	91	87	98
LNets+ANet	91	79	79	98	95	68	78	88	95	80	90	91	92	99	95	97	90	87	98

	Mouth Slightly Open	Mustache	Narrow Eyes	No Beard	Oval Face	Pointy Nose	Receding Hairline	Rosy Checks	Sideburns	Smiling	Straight Hair	Wavy Hair	Wearing Earrings	Wearing Hat	Wearing Lipstick	Wearing Necklace	Wearing Necktie	Young	**Average**
Our model	94	97	87	96	76	76	93	95	98	93	83	82	90	99	91	88	97	88	**91**
LNets+ANet	92	95	81	95	66	72	89	90	96	92	73	80	82	99	93	71	93	87	**87**

4   Experimental Results

As anticipated in the previous section, the dataset which has been used is CelebA dataset: for the training phase, it has been divided in three partitions: *training, validation,* and *testing*; according to the partitioning suggested by the CelebA authors. For training, the model has been fed with the entire training partition (160 k samples resized to 224×224 and augmented) and validate each epoch on 20 k of samples (validation-set). The model has been trained with a batch size of 64 images (mainly due to resource limitation), and let the AdaDelta [26] optimizer minimize the cosine proximity loss function. The AdaDelta optimizer has been selected since it requires less hyperparameter-tuning. Moreover, AdaDelta has a few interesting features:

- It's able to adapt the learning rate according to a moving window of gradient updates, preventing to stop learning after many iterations.
- It converges faster: thanks to the adaptive learning, it's able to accelerate when the direction is promising and to slow down when the loss starts to get worse.

4.1   Clustering

The clustering approach is probably the richest contribution of the paper, since it allows to group the faces, according to the facial features of each of them;

in unconstrained environment, the possibility to associate an identity to a face, even if partially occluded is a big benefit, mainly in sensitive areas. Thank to the cluster syntetization, it is possible to group faces with the same features, so to simplify potential identikit recognition, very useful in forensics. The steps which characterize the here proposed clustering approach are the following:

– Choosing the number of clusters (no fixed values);
– Eventually, selecting a subset of the available attributes;
– Graphically visualizing the resulting clustering;
– Synthesizing a cluster into one face, which is the cluster's *eigenface*.

So, the target of the clustering method is to group together instances having similar attributes.

According to these requirements, it has been evaluated the goodness of different clustering algorithms by computing the *silhouette score* of each clustering. Furthermore, we give graphical insights by: attributes-occurrence plot, and the cluster's eigenface.

Considering that DBSCAN discovers the optimal number of clusters (for a given set of data), for a fair evaluation, we tested the performance of all the methods on the same number of clusters (the one discovered by DBSCAN), in order to analyze which one is the best (Fig. 4).

Subsequently, the performances of both K-Means and Agglomerative Clustering on a variable number of clusters has been compared with those of DBSCAN (Fig. 4).

In particular, as regards Agglomerative Clustering, various input parameters are analyzed in order to optimize performance. In fact, it processes by merging clusters together according to a linkage criteria:

– **Ward** minimizes the sum of squared differences within all clusters. It is a variance-minimizing approach and in this sense is similar to the K-Means objective function but tackled with an agglomerative hierarchical approach.
– **Maximum or complete linkage** minimizes the maximum distance between observations of pairs of clusters.
– **Average linkage** minimizes the average of the distances between all observations of pairs of clusters.
– **Single linkage** minimizes the distance between the closest observations of pairs of clusters.

Also, the linkage criteria determines the metric used for the merge strategy: The latter can be euclidean, 11, 12, manhattan, or cosine. If linkage is ward, only euclidean is accepted.

The best combination of metric and linkage criteria is "complete" and "manhattan", but despite this choice, the algorithm's performance is still inferior to that of K-Means. Agglomerative Clustering reaches a silhouette score of 0.73, while K-Means achieves a value of 0.83.

Despite the better performances of DBSCAN, with a silhouette score of 0.87, we have decided to use K-means, since, as can be evaluated from the charts, it proves to be the best among the algorithms that allow you to choose the number of clusters.

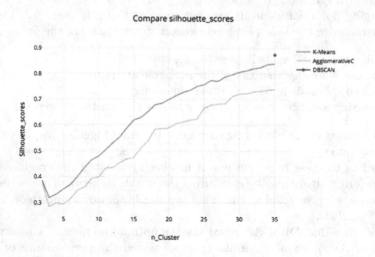

Fig. 4. Comparison of clustering algorithms: as we can see K-Means performs always better than Agglomerative Clustering.

More in details, the K-Means algorithm divides a set of N samples X into K disjointed clusters C, each described by the mean μ_j of the samples in the cluster. The means are commonly called the cluster centroids; they are not, in general, points from X, although they live in the same space.

The K-Means algorithm aims at choosing centroids which minimize the inertia, or within-cluster sum-of-squares criterion:

$$\sum_{i=0}^{n} \min_{\mu_j \in C}(||x_i - \mu_j||^2) \tag{2}$$

Following the clustering process, the results obtained by each cluster are analyzed, both in terms of characteristics and in terms of the corresponding eigenface.

The eigenfaces are computed (by standard dimensionality reduction methods, like PCA) in order to obtain an exhaustive and meaningful representation of each cluster.

Hand-checking the attributes of the faces in a given cluster is tidy and error-prone, especially for clusters with a large amount of faces.

Regarding this, here two simple ways to summarize a cluster are shown:

1. By simply showing the chart of occurrences of the facial attributes within a given cluster, it is possible to understand the frequency of each attributes.
   With a chart like the one in Fig. 5, it is possible to determine which are the noisy attributes (those with low occurrence) and which are the prominent

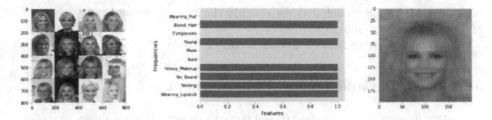

Fig. 5. Clustering results: the cluster (left), the attributes-occurence chart (middle), and the cluster's eigenface (right).

attributes (those with a very high occurrence); as regards the first, these outlier attributes are some sort of mistakes, made by the model and/or by the clustering method;

2. An Eigenface can be seen as a cluster representation, being representative and compact (it results in a single image).

   From a given cluster its eigenface is generated, by simply performing Principal Component Analysis (PCA) [24] on vectors obtained by flattening the images belonging to that cluster.

   The resulting eigenface is a face characterized by the prominent attributes of the given cluster. So, by simply observing the cluster eigenface is possible to determine what are the relevant attributes of that cluster.

In order to further improve the clustering process, a weight criterion is adopted in relation to the most frequent characteristics, or alternatively, to the less frequent characteristics (Fig. 6).

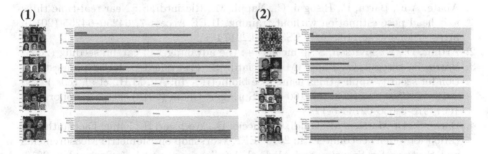

Fig. 6. 1. Clusters without weights 2. Clusters with weights

Thanks to this expedient, it is possible to drastically reduce the quantity of features that are only partially present within the cluster. The chart shown, in fact, describes the results following this operation.

Before focusing on the MobileNetV2 architecture, we have tried different model architectures even with 10x more parameters (our model has only 4.3 M of parameters); each model achieves roughly the same accuracy, but at the cost of a much slower training.

Our model achieves 90.95% testing accuracy (table

5   Conclusion and Future Enhancements

Biometric Recognition in unconstrained scenario is not always an easy practice; the light conditions, the pose and eventual occlusions, do not allow an accurate detection, with the consequent activity of subject recognition which results very challenging. Also, a precise recognition in such scenarios is not constantly ensured, and the guide of an operator is often needed for recognizing a subject and associating an identity to a face. In such cases, relying on soft biometrics, like facial features taken singularly, is an interesting and even more realistic decision. From this point of view, in this work it has been proposed a framework for facial features recognition by means of MobileNet-like convolutional neural network, and face clustering based on K-means and Eigenface for centroid definition. The results show that the recognition accuracy is higher than the net proposed by [25] and also the clustering return very interesting results. Qualitative and quantitative results have been proposed, also showing the advantages of the k-means with respect to DBSCAN and Agglomerative Clustering techniques.

Acknowledgment. A special thank goes to the students Luca Anzalone, Marialuisa Trere and Simone Faiella for having conducted the experiments and proposed the model.

References

1. Abate, A.F., Barra, P., Bisogni, C., Nappi, M., Ricciardi, S.: Near real-time three axis head pose estimation without training. IEEE Access **7**, 64256–64265 (2019). https://doi.org/10.1109/ACCESS.2019.2917451
2. Arthur, D., Vassilvitskii, S.: k-means++: the advantages of careful seeding (2006)
3. Barra, P., Bisogni, C., Nappi, M., Ricciardi, S.: Fast quadtree-based pose estimation for security applications using face biometrics. In: Au, M.H., et al. (eds.) NSS 2018. LNCS, vol. 11058, pp. 160–173. Springer, Cham (2018). https://doi.org/10.1007/978-3-030-02744-5_12
4. Barra, S., De Marsico, M., Galdi, C., Riccio, D., Wechsler, H.: Fame: Face authentication for mobile encounter. In: 2013 IEEE Workshop on Biometric Measurements and Systems for Security and Medical Applications, pp. 1–7, September 2013. https://doi.org/10.1109/BIOMS.2013.6656140
5. Barra, S., Castiglione, A., Narducci, F., Marsico, M.D., Nappi, M.: Biometric data on the edge for secure, smart and user tailored access to cloud services. Future Gener. Comput. Syst. (2019). https://doi.org/10.1016/j.future.2019.06.019
6. Fenu, G., Marras, M.: Leveraging continuous multi-modal authentication for access control in mobile cloud environments. In: Battiato, S., Farinella, G.M., Leo, M., Gallo, G. (eds.) ICIAP 2017. LNCS, vol. 10590, pp. 331–342. Springer, Cham (2017). https://doi.org/10.1007/978-3-319-70742-6_31

7. Fenu, G., Marras, M.: Controlling user access to cloud-connected mobile applications by means of biometrics. IEEE Cloud Comput. **5**(4), 47–57 (2018). https://doi.org/10.1109/MCC.2018.043221014

8. Fenu, G., Marras, M., Meles, M.: A learning analytics tool for usability assessment in moodle environments. J. E-Learn. Knowl. Soc. **13**(3), 23–34 (2017). https://doi.org/10.20368/1971-8829/1388

9. He, K., Zhang, X., Ren, S., Sun, J.: Deep residual learning for image recognition (2015)

10. Huang, G.B., Mattar, M., Berg, T., Learned-Miller, E.: Labeled faces in the wild: a database forstudying face recognition in unconstrained environments (2008)

11. Krizhevsky, A., Sutskever, I., Hinton, G.E.: ImageNet classification with deep convolutional neural networks. University of Toronto (2012)

12. Link: http://cs231n.github.io/transfer-learning/#tf

13. Liu, W., Wen, Y., Yu, Z., Li, M., Raj, B., Song, L.: Sphereface: Deep hypersphere embedding for face recognition. Carnegie Mellon University and Sun Yat-Sen University, Georgia Institute of Technology (2017)

14. Liu, Z., Luo, P., Wang, X., Tang, X.: Large-scale celebfaces attributes (celebA) dataset. The Chinese University of Hong Kong, Multimedia Laboratory (2015)

15. Otto, C., Wang, D., Jain, K.: Clustering millions of faces by identity

16. Raina, R., Battle, A., Lee, H., Packer, B., Ng, A.Y.: Self-taught learning: transfer learning from unlabeled data. In: Proceedings of the 24th International Conference on Machine Learning, pp. 759–766. ACM (2007)

17. Ranjan, R., Patel, V.M., Chellappa, R.: Hyperface: a deep multi-task learning framework for face detection, landmark localization, pose estimation, and gender recognition. IEEE (2017)

18. Rosebrock, A.: Face clustering with Python (2018)

19. Russakovsky, O., et al.: ImageNet large scale visual recognition challenge (2015)

20. Sandler, M., Howard, A., Zhu, M., Zhmoginov, A., Chen, L.C.: MobileNetV2: Inverted residuals and linear bottlenecks. In: Proceedings of the IEEE Conference on Computer Vision and Pattern Recognition, pp. 4510–4520 (2018)

21. Schroff, F., Kalenichenko, D., Philbin, J.: Facenet: A unified embedding for face recognition and clustering

22. Simonyan, K., Zisserman, A.: Very deep convolutional networks for large-scale image recognition (2015)

23. Szegedy, C., et al.: Going deeper with convolutions (2014)

24. Wold, S., Esbensen, K., Geladi, P.: Principal component analysis (1987)

25. Yang, S., Luo, P., Loy, C.C., Tang, X.: From facial parts responses to face detection: a deep learning approach. In: The IEEE International Conference on Computer Vision (ICCV), December 2015

26. Zeiler, M.D.: ADADELTA: an adaptive learning rate method. arXiv preprint arXiv:1212.5701 (2012)

27. Zhang, K., Zhang, Z., Li, Z., Qiao, Y.: Joint face detection and alignment using multitask cascaded convolutional networks. IEEE Sig. Process. Lett. **23**(10), 1499–1503 (2016). https://doi.org/10.1109/LSP.2016.2603342

28. Zhu, X., Ramann, D.: Face detection, pose estimation, and landmark localization in the wild

Identification of Plant Leaf Diseases Based on Inception V3 Transfer Learning and Fine-Tuning

Zhenping Qiang[1] (ID), Libo He[2] (ID), and Fei Dai[1]([⊠]) (ID)

[1] College of Big Data and Intelligent Engineering,
Southwest Forestry University, Kunming 650224, China
daifei@swfu.edu.cn
[2] Information Security College,
Yunnan Police College, Kunming 650223, China

Abstract. Crop disease is a major factor currently to jeopardize agricultural production activities. In recent years, with the great success of deep learning technology in the field of image classification and image recognition, and with the convenient acquisition of crop leaf images, it is possible to automatically identify crop disease through deep learning based on plant leaf disease images. This paper mainly completed the research and analysis of leaf disease identification of agricultural plants based on Inception-V3 neural network model transfer learning and fine-tuning. A large number of model accuracy tests are carried out by training neural networks with different parameters. When the network parameter Batch is set to 100 and the learning rate is set to 0.01, the training precision and test precision of the network reach the maximum. Its training precision rate for crop disease image recognition in the PlantVillage DataSet is 95.8%, and the precision rate on the test set is as high as 93%, and far exceeding the accuracy of manual recognition. This fully proves that the deep learning model based on Inception-V3 neural network can effectively distinguish crop disease.

Keywords: Crop disease identification · Inception V3 · Transfer learning · Fine-tuning · Deep learning

1 Introduction

Crop disease is one of the most serious hazards in agricultural production. It causes significant losses to the agricultural economy every year because of its characteristics of many types, wide range of influences and frequent large-scale outbreak [1]. The most common diseases in agricultural production activities are the following types: powdery mildew, wheat rust, cotton aphid, rice sheath blight, rice blast, wheat scab, etc. These agricultural diseases have caused extremely significant losses to agricultural economic activities. Therefore, the identification of crop disease has become an urgent problem to be solved in agricultural production [2].

Traditional crop disease diagnosis generally requires professional plant protection personnel to identify it. For agricultural growers, especially in the early stages of crop

© Springer Nature Singapore Pte Ltd. 2019
G. Wang et al. (Eds.): iSCI 2019, CCIS 1122, pp. 118–127, 2019.
https://doi.org/10.1007/978-981-15-1301-5_10

disease, there is generally no ability to identify it. This will lead to the lag of obtaining disease information in the production process, which will seriously affects the accuracy of disease prediction.

In recent years, on the one hand, with the development of science and technology, and with the improvement of people's living standards, all families have multimedia acquisition equipment for taking videos and photos, which can easily obtain pictures of crop diseases and process them. This provides the basic conditions for automatic identification of crop diseases through image processing technology. On the other hand, with the widespread application of computer image processing technology in many fields, especially the rapid development of deep learning technology in recent years has achieved great success in the field of image recognition, it makes it is possible to identify agricultural diseases through deep learning methods [3, 4].

Crop disease diagnosis based on image processing technology has been extensively studied in recent years [5]. In general, it includes detection methods using image segmentation technology [6–8], detection methods based on feature extraction [9–11], and methods based on recognition technology [12–15]. Although these methods can automatically identify plant diseases, on the one hand, they are vulnerable to the influence of light, color and noise, on the other hand, because the images of various diseases are different, the shapes are different and the rules of outbreaks are different. Because of these factors, the recognition accuracy of these methods is not high enough to meet the needs of practical application.

In recent years, the effect of deep learning in the field of image classification has become better and better [16]. Especially since 2014, the deep learning models such as GoogLeNet [17–21], VGGNet [22], ResNets [23] and SENet [24] have made the image recognition accuracy by using convolutional neural networks increase continuously and rapidly. The ability of computers to classify images has begun to transcend the ability of human image classification. At present, the Inception series convolutional neural network developed by Google has a Top-5 recognition error rate of 3.05% or less in ImageNet Large-Scale Visual Recognition Challenge. Identify the accuracy that is far from possible. This is the accuracy rate that humans are far from impossible to achieve for image recognition. Therefore, the image recognition of agricultural diseases through deep learning methods can almost completely replace the diagnosis of traditional agricultural diseases [4]. On the one hand, such methods can improve the accuracy of recognition, and on the other hand, these methods can increase the efficiency of agricultural production. Hence, the identification of agricultural diseases based on deep learning technology has become a hot research topic.

This paper is to study the method based on deep learning techniques for identifying plant diseases through plant leaf images. The related theory based on deep learning image recognition will be briefly introduced in Sect. 2. The data set and image pre-processing work used in this experiment will be introduced in Sect. 3. In Sect. 4, based on transfer learning technology we will propose a plant leaf disease identification method based on Inception V3. We will compare the plant leaf disease identification method based on classical machine learning with the method based on deep learning and validate the proposed method based on Inception V3 in Sect. 5. Finally, a summary and conclusions will be given in Sect. 6.

2 Related Theory

The essential of recognizing plant leaf diseases by using computer vision technology is image classification. Presently, For the classification problem, the existing classical machine learning methods include linear regression, decision tree, naive Bayes and KNN and so on. And the basis of the image classification method based on the deep learning framework is the convolutional neural network.

Convolutional neural network (CNN) is a feed-forward neural network [25] and it has excellent performance in the field of image classification. By using CNN to classify image, the first thing is to extract the features of the input image through the convolution layer, and then reduce the dimension of the extracted features through the pooling layer to reduce the computational load, which greatly reduces the computational load of the whole neural network and improves the performance of the network. The convolutional neural network model was first proposed by Professor Yann LeCun and used in Handwritten Data Set (MINST). A typical convolutional neural network is usually composed by a convolutional layer, Relu layer, pooling layer, fully-connected layer, and activation functions. The function of each layer is as follow:

Convolutional layer: The convolutional layer is consists of several convolution units and its function is to extract the features of the input image.

ReLU layer: The ReLU layer refers to use the Rectified Linear Units (ReLU) in the activation Function of Neural Networks.

Pooling layer: The main function of the pooling layer is to reduce the dimension of the features extracted from the input image through the convolution layer and to reduce the computational complexity of the neural network.

Fully-connected layer: The function of Fully-connected layer is to transform the local features extracted from the upper layer into global features, which effectively improves the accuracy of classification.

Using this framework, classic classified convolutional networks include: AlexNet [26], VGGNet [22], GoogLeNet [17–21], ResNet [23], SENet [24] and so on.

Christian Szegedy et al. in Google introduced Google LeNet in 2015. Google LeNet has 22 layers of depth, but the parameter size is only 1/12 of AlexNet [26], and it is the winner of the 2014 ILSVRC14 competition in ImageNet. It's core idea is to replace full connection, even partial connection with sparse connection. A deep sparse network can be simplified layer by layer, and its expressive ability has not been significantly weakened because it retains the statistical properties of the network. A Inception structure is proposed in Google LeNet, which is a big advancement in deep learning network design. Google LeNet includes five versions: Inception V1, Inception V2, Inception V3, Inception V4 and Xception. Inception V3 adds factorization and Batch Normalization basis on V2, which can not only accelerate calculation, but also decompose one convolution into two convolutions, which further increases the depth of the network and increases the non-linearity of the network. So Inception V3 has good performance in image classification. And in this paper we propose a method of plant leaf disease identification based on Inception V3 transfer learning and fine-tuning.

3   Data Set and Preprocessing

Because there are few kinds of data sets in agricultural disease images, this paper mainly uses the PlantVillage data set collected by the University of Pennsylvania to validate the model. PlantVillage is a research and development unit of Penn State that empowers smallholder farmers and seeks to lift them out of poverty using cheap, affordable technology to reduce yield losses to plant diseases and pests [27].

The PlantVillage data set has a large number of agricultural diseases images which collected by a research institute affiliated to the University of Pennsylvania. The PlantVillage data set has a total of 38 agricultural diseases in 14 economic crops (apples, blueberries, cherries, etc.). The data set includes a total of 54305 images with resolution of 256 × 256 pixels. Compare to other small data sets of agricultural diseases, PlantVillage data sets have abundant and many kinds of agricultural diseases pictures. Furthermore the resolution of all agricultural diseases pictures in PlantVillage data sets is 256 × 256, which is easy to use in experiments. The Fig. 1 is a set of actual data set images.

(a) apple scab   (b) apple black rot   (c) cedar apple rust   (d) healthy (apple)

(e) Cercospora leaf spot   (f) Common corn rust   (g) healthy (corn)   (h) northern leaf blight

Fig. 1. Examples of various plant diseases in the PlantVillage data set

For different deep learning networks, image preprocessing mainly includes two parts, one is image filtering, the other is data set preparation depending on different deep learning platforms.

For Inception V3 transfer learning and fine-tuning network, it is necessary to transform the original image with 256 × 256 resolution into 299*299, and divide the data set into training set and test set (the ratio is 8:2). Furthermore, we use TensorFlow to implement the proposed method, and the image file needs to be transformed into a TFRecord file (the suffix is .tfrecord). The .tfrecord format file is the official dataset format recommended by Google, and the .tfrecord format file is binary. Therefore, the . tfrecord format file is not as easy to understand as other types of file formats, but the advantage of .tfrecord files over other format files is that they can make better use of memory and can be moved easily.

4 Plant Leaf Diseases Recognition Based on Inception V3 Network Transfer Learning

The Inception series of convolutional neural networks is a series of neural networks that cannot be ignored in the history of convolutional neural networks. Most neural networks only deepen the depth of the network by increasing the convolutional layer to get better performance before the emergence of Inception neural network. Inception neural network has changed this strategy. The Inception module proposed by Inception Neural Network uses different sizes of filters and maximum pooling to reduce the dimension of the data. This has the advantage of obtaining richer features with significantly reduced computation and fewer parameters. Inception V3 uses the asymmetric method to decompose a large-scale convolution kernel into a small-scale convolution kernel, which is to decompose a 3×3 convolution kernel into two convolution kernels (1×3, 3×1), and to reduce network parameters while maintaining network performance. By using asymmetric decomposition, the depth of the neural network can be deepened and the nonlinearity of the network can be improved. The corresponding Inception V3 basic module is shown in Fig. 2:

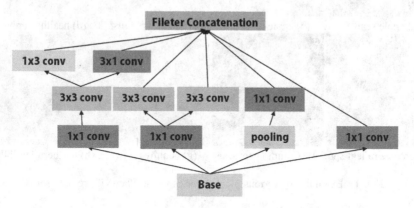

Fig. 2. The basic module in Inception V3.

where 'Base' is previous layer, 'pooling' is pooling layer, 'Filter Concatenation' is to link the input feature maps by depth.

Traditionally, convolutional neural networks use pooling operations to reduce the mesh size of the feature map generally. To avoid bottlenecks, we need to extend the activation dimension of the network activation before applying maximum pooling or average pooling. The convolutional neural networks use the two methods shown in

Fig. 3 to solve this problem, but the method Fig. 3(left) will cause a characteristic representation bottleneck problem, resulting in poor representation of the network, and the computational complexity of the method Fig. 3(right) is three times to the method Fig. 3(left). In Inception V3, a module that reduces the size of the mesh and expands the filters is proposed. This module solves the problem of feature representation and reduces the amount of calculation, as shown in Fig. 4.

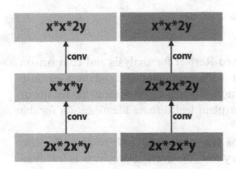

Fig. 3. The Traditional way to reduce feature size

Fig. 4. The way to reduce feature size in Inception module

Table 1. Framework information of the proposed method.

Type	Input size	Patch size/stride or remarks
conv	299*299*3	3*3/2
conv	149*149*32	3*3/1
conv padded	147*147*32	3*3/1
pool	147*147*64	3*3/2
conv	73*73*64	3*3/1
conv	71*71*80	3*3/2
conv	35*35*192	3*3/1
3 X Inception	35*35*288	Inception module (Fig. 2)
5 X Inception	17*17*768	Inception module (Fig. 2)
pool	8*8*2048	8*8
linear	1*1*2048	logits
softmax	1*1*1000	classifier
Fully-connected layer	1*1*38	1*1
Fully-connected layer	1*1*38	1*1
Fully-connected layer	1*1*38	1*1

In this paper, transfer learning is used to the classified Inception V3 network trained on ImageNet, which enables the network to have the ability to classify and identify plant leaf diseases. The specific work mainly consists of two parts. The first part is to freeze all the base_model layers of the trained Inception V3 network, that is, these layers are not involved in the training during the training phase of the transfer learning. The second part is to build a three-layer fully connected neural network layer from the bottleneck node to classify the features learned from the front. Since there are 38 plant diseases in the PlantVillage data set, the output classification number is set to 38. Using the Softmax function, the recognition results of the images can be obtained from the 38 objects output from the convolutional neural network according to the output value. The framework information of the proposed neural network is shown in Table 1.

5   Results

We selected the KNN method and the fine-tuned ResNet for analysis and comparison in order to analyze the effect of traditional machine learning methods and deep learning based methods on plant leaf diseases identification. Figures 5 and 6 show the results of KNN method and ResNet networks method for plant leaf disease identification for the PlantVillage data set, respectively.

When using traditional machine algorithms (for example KNN) to classify plant leaf image diseases, the training precision is very low, the average precision is less than 60%, and the highest precision is 85%. And as the number of iterations increases, the method does not converge very well. This shows that the model based on deep learning can accurately identify plant leaf disease images with high probability, and it also shows that it is feasible to use convolutional neural networks to predict crop disease images.

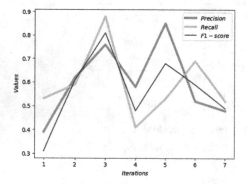 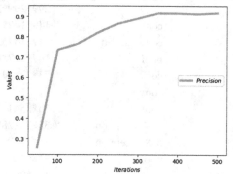

Fig. 5. The recognition results of KNN method

Fig. 6. The recognition results of fine-tuned ResNet method

Further, based on the Inception V3 transfer learning and fine-tuning method, the plant leaf disease recognition of the PlantVillage data set is analyzed in detail. In this experiment, 12 sets of different neural network parameters were used to train the Inception-V3-based transfer learning model on the PlantVillage dataset, and the precision of the different trained models were compared in the PlantVillage test dataset. In the experiment, the batch is set to 64, 100 and 128, the learning rate is set to 0.01, 0, 001 and 0.0001. The training precision results comparison are shown in Fig. 7.

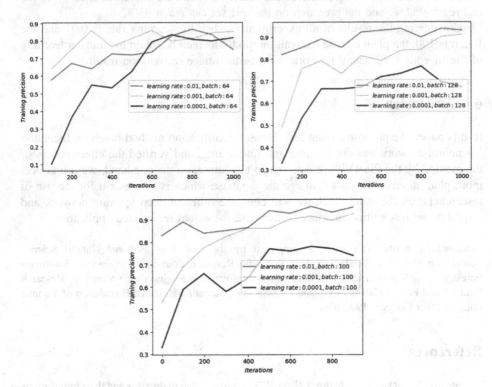

Fig. 7. The training precision results comparison of different parameters set on the Inception V3 transfer learning and fine-tuning method.

For the network trained by different parameters, Fig. 8 shows the precision on the test set.

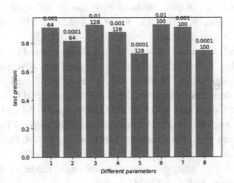

Fig. 8. The test precision results comparison of different parameters set on the Inception V3 transfer learning and fine-tuning method.

By comparing the results of the 12 sets of experiments, the model achieved the best results when the Batch is set to 100 and the learning rate is set to 0.01. When training to the 100th round, its training precision can reach 82%, and the highest training precision can reach 95.8%, and the precision on the test set can reach 93%.

Considering the results of all experiments, when the learning rate is 0.01 and the Batch is 100, the plant disease recognition model learned based on the transfer learning of the Inception V3 neural network has a better image recognition result.

6   Conclusion

In this paper, we propose a plant leaf disease identification method based on Inception V3 neural network transfer learning and fine-tuning, and verified the effectiveness of the method by the PlantVillage data set. In the future, on the one hand, we can collect more plant disease images to enlarge the database which is convenient for the use of researchers; on the other hand, we will compare different deep learning network and providing an recognition interface to facilitate the actual recognized application.

Acknowledgements. This work is supported by the project of National Natural Science Foundation of China (11603016), Key Scientific Research Foundation Project of Southwest Forestry University (111827), Kunming Forestry Information Engineering Technology Research Center Fund Project (2015FBI06), and the project of Scientific Research Foundation of Yunnan Police Officer College (19A010).

References

1. Savary, S., Ficke, A., Aubertot, J.N., et al.: Crop losses due to diseases and their implications for global food production losses and food security. Food Secur. **4**(4), 519–537 (2012)
2. Barbedo, J.G.A.: A review on the main challenges in automatic plant disease identification based on visible range images. Biosyst. Eng. **144**, 52–60 (2016)
3. Mohanty, S.P., Hughes, D.P., Salathé, M.: Using deep learning for image-based plant disease detection. Front. Plant Sci. **7**, 1419 (2016)
4. Kaur, S., Pandey, S., Goel, S.: Plants disease identification and classification through leaf images: a survey. Archiv. Comput. Methods Eng. **26**(2), 507–530 (2019)
5. Martinelli, F., Scalenghe, R., Davino, S., et al.: Advanced methods of plant disease detection. A review. Agron. Sustain. Dev. **35**(1), 1–25 (2015)
6. Jadhav, S.B., Patil, S.B.: Grading of soybean leaf disease based on segmented image using k-means clustering. Int. J. Adv. Res. Electr. Commun. Eng. **4**(6), 1816–1822 (2015)
7. Rangel, B.M., Fernández, M.A., Murillo, J.C., et al.: KNN-based image segmentation for grapevine potassium deficiency diagnosis. In: IEEE International Conference on Electronics, Communications and Computers (CONIELECOMP), pp. 48–53 (2016)
8. Zhang, X., Li, D., Yang, W., et al.: A fast segmentation method for high-resolution color images of foreign fibers in cotton. Comput. Electron. Agric. **78**(1), 71–79 (2011)
9. Oberti, R., Marchi, M., Tirelli, P., et al.: Automatic detection of powdery mildew on grapevine leaves by image analysis: optimal view-angle range to increase the sensitivity. Comput. Electron. Agric. **104**, 1–8 (2014)

10. Phadikar, S., Sil, J., Das, A.K.: Rice diseases classification using feature selection and rule generation techniques. Comput. Electron. Agric. **90**(90), 76–85 (2013)
11. Gharge, S., Singh, P.: Image processing for soybean disease classification and severity estimation. In: Shetty, N., Prasad, N., Nalini, N. (eds.) Emerging Research in Computing, Information, Communication and Applications, pp. 493–500. Springer, New Delhi (2016). https://doi.org/10.1007/978-81-322-2553-9_44
12. Asfarian, A., Herdiyeni, Y., Rauf, A., et al.: Paddy diseases identification with texture analysis using fractal descriptors based on fourier spectrum. In: The International Conference on Computer, Control, Informatics and Its Applications, IC3INA 2013. IEEE (2013)
13. Wang, L., Dong, F., Guo, Q., et al.: Improved rotational kernel transformation directional feature for recognition of wheat stripe rust and powdery mildew. In: IEEE 7th International Conference on Image and Signal Processing CISP, Dalian, pp. 286–291 (2014)
14. Sanyal, P., Patel, S.C.: Pattern recognition method to detect two diseases in rice plants. J. Photogr. Sci. **56**(6), 319–325 (2013)
15. Pires, R.D.L., Goncalves, D.N., Oruê, J.P.M., et al.: Local descriptors for soybean disease recognition. Comput. Electron. Agric. **125**, 48–55 (2016)
16. Al-Saffar, A.A.M., Tao, H., Talab, M.A.: Review of deep convolution neural network in image classification. In: 2017 International Conference on Radar, Antenna, Microwave, Electronics, and Telecommunications (ICRAMET). IEEE (2018)
17. Szegedy, C., Liu, W., Jia, Y., et al.: Going deeper with convolutions. In: 2015 IEEE Conference on Computer Vision and Pattern Recognition (CVPR) (2015)
18. Ullah, K.R., Xiaosong, Z., Rajesh, K.: Analysis of ResNet and GoogleNet models for malware detection. J. Comput. Virol. Hacking Tech. **15**, 29–37 (2018)
19. Szegedy, C., Vanhoucke, V., Ioffe, S., et al.: Rethinking the inception architecture for computer vision. In: 2016 IEEE Conference on Computer Vision and Pattern Recognition (CVPR), pp. 2818–2826 (2016)
20. Szegedy, C., Ioffe, S., Vanhoucke, V.: Inception-v4, Inception-ResNet and the impact of residual connections on learning. arXiv preprint arXiv:1602.07261v1 (2016)
21. Chollet, F.: Xception: deep learning with depthwise separable convolutions. In: 2017 IEEE Conference on Computer Vision and Pattern Recognition (CVPR). IEEE (2017)
22. Simonyan, K., Zisserman, A.: Very deep convolutional networks for large-scale image recognition. arXiv preprint arXiv:1409.1556 (2014)
23. Targ, S., Almeida, D., Lyman, K.: ResNet in ResNet: generalizing residual architectures. arXiv preprint arXiv:1603.08029 (2016)
24. Jie, H., Li, S., Albanie, S., et al.: Squeeze-and-excitation networks. arXiv preprint arXiv: 1709.01507 (2017)
25. Lecun, Y., Bottou, L., Bengio, Y., et al.: Gradient-based learning applied to document recognition. Proc. IEEE **86**(11), 2278–2324 (1998)
26. Krizhevsky, A., Sutskever, I., Hinton, G.E.: ImageNet classification with deep convolutional neural networks. Adv. Neural Inf. Process. **25**(2), 1097–1105 (2012)
27. PlantVillage. https://plantvillage.psu.edu/. Accessed 20 Sept 2019

Edge Computing-Enabled Resource Provisioning for Video Surveillance in Internet of Vehicles

Xiaolong Xu[1,2], Qi Wu[1], Chengxun He[1], Shaohua Wan[3], Lianyong Qi[4(✉)], and Hao Wang[5]

[1] School of Computer and Software,
Nanjing University of Information Science and Technology, Nanjing, China
[2] Jiangsu Collaborative Innovation Center of Atmospheric Environment
and Equipment Technology (CICAEET),
Nanjing University of Information Science and Technology, Nanjing, China
[3] School of Information and Safety Engineering,
Zhongnan University of Economics and Law, Wuhan, China
[4] School of Information Science and Engineering,
Qufu Normal University, Rizhao, China
lianyongqi@gmail.com
[5] Department of Computer Science,
Norwegian University of Science and Technology, 2815 Gjøvik, Norway

Abstract. As a novel technology, Internet of Vehicles (IoV) is employed to gather real-time traffic information for drivers from sensors and video surveillance devices with image processing, circumstances analysis and events recognition. In spite of multiple advantages of IoV, preprocessing the huge data may demand abundant computation resources for video surveillance devices. Migrating tasks to remote servers for performing is efficient to solve this problem, but it needs high network bandwidth, which causes traffic congestion and delay. Edge computing has capability to enhance processing performance, which complements video surveillance device and addresses numerous shortcomings. Nevertheless, edge computing for video surveillance remains a challenge to achieve low-latency and load balance through limited amount of edge servers. To handle this challenge, an Edge computing-enabled Resource Provisioning Method (ERPM) for Video Surveillance in IoV is proposed in this paper. Technically, SPEA2 (improving the Strength Pare to Evolutionary Algorithm) is picked to solve the multi-objective optimization problem aiming at minimizing the time consumption and optimizing load balance. Finally, experimental simulation for Evolution algorithm demonstrate the appropriation and efficiency of ERPM.

Keywords: Internet of Vehicles · Edge computing · Resource allocation · Video surveillance

© Springer Nature Singapore Pte Ltd. 2019
G. Wang et al. (Eds.): iSCI 2019, CCIS 1122, pp. 128–140, 2019.
https://doi.org/10.1007/978-981-15-1301-5_11

1   Introduction

From the past few years, with the development of communication and networking technologies, e.g., wireless sensor networks, 5G communication networks and short-range wireless communication, the Internet of Things (IoT) is evolving to a paradigm that achieves special prominence to the interconnection of physical objects and human inhabitant [1, 2]. As an emerging technology of IoT, Internet of Vehicles (IoV) consists of vehicles, intelligent mobile cameras, sensors, actuators and applications through internet, which has significant affects in smart city [3]. IoT technology enables devices to collect and analyze the traffic information that comprises position, driving status and road condition from the sensors of the vehicles and video surveillance devices. The majority of traffic information about traffic condition is gathered from video surveillance devices, and preprocessed in video surveillance systems, which supports for image processing, traffic condition analysis and events recognition. Then, video surveillance systems have crucial impact in IoV.

Meanwhile, the proliferation of video surveillance equipment has been a fundamental device deployed in public places, such as shopping centers, streets, schools, city facilities, and home. In 2012, approximately 8 million surveillance devices worldwide were connected to the Internet and the number is expected to grow to 170 million in 2021 [4]. To preprocess the massive amounts of all-day-operating video data at the camera nodes (e.g., extracting features), video surveillance devices demands abundant local computation resources. Whereas in reality, these devices cannot sustain the huge work, and then migrate the tasks to the remote servers to release the pressure, which the migration needs high network bandwidth and lead to significant delay [5]. Obviously, the paradigms cannot satisfy the requirement of real-time video processing and analyzing tasks.

Recently, as an emerging technique of distributed computing for the preprocessing video data, edge computing enables video surveillance devices to reduce the transmission delay [6]. Video surveillance devices deploy edge node with computing, storage, and network connectivity through switches, routers, embedded equipment, electronic facilities. By supporting the edge computing, the communication and computation capabilities of video surveillance systems can be utilized to deal with the computing tasks that include video compressing, preprocessing and analyzing through short-range wireless communications [7]. However, the transmission of a mass volume of video data may lead to congestions and delays due to limited network bandwidth. In this paper, in order to improve the processing capability of monitoring terminals, we present a brand new smart resource allocation for video surveillance system in edge computing. Taking traffic monitoring as an instance of work, the proposed edge computing based surveillance system is able to obtain the video data information for traffic condition in real-time, and offload the real-time data to cloud computing center [8]. The captured data been analyzed and filtered by edge servers firstly that mitigate simultaneously the workload of the transmit network and the cloud data center [9, 10].

The main contributions of this paper are summarized as:

- Analyze the details of process of tasks computing for Video Surveillance in Internet of Vehicles with Edge Computing enabled.
- Formulate the resource provisioning problem as a multi-objective optimization problem to optimize the time consumption and load balance of ENs (Edge Nodes).
- Adopt an method named ERPM by employing SPEA2 (Improving the strength pare to evolutionary algorithm) with simulation experimental to solve the objective problem we proposed.

The remainder of this paper is organized as follows. In the next Section, system model and problem formulation is discussed. Furthermore, an edge computing-enabled resource provisioning method for video surveillance in internet of vehicles is provisioned in Sect. 3. Experimental evaluation is presented in Sect. 4. After that, we present related work in Sect. 5. Finally, conclusion and future works are drawn in Sect. 6.

2   Related Work

The technical aspects and potential benefits of edge computing have been researched extensively in the recent literature. The video surveillance system in edge computing can be leveraged to improve the performance of processing tasks from monitoring terminals [11,12]. An efficient resource-allocation tactics and a real-time video packet scheduler are presented in [13] that formulates an effective real-time video uplink framework to enhance utility, boost transfer efficiency, and stabilize image quality. Reference [14] employs Deep Learning (DL) algorithms to study a Distributed Intelligent Video Surveillance (DIVS) system which migrates computing workloads from the network center to edges to reduce tremendous network communication overheads and provide low-latency and precise video analysis solutions. In [4], Puvvadi et al. explored a new protocol to drastically weaken the delay to execute computing tasks (e.g., cryptographic mechanisms) and increase the supported bit rate compared with the baseline, while providing desirable security features.

The smart edge computing for video surveillance devices is proposed to provision the computation and allocate resources for the execution of computation tasks. However, when employing the edge servers to accommodate the computing tasks, the scarce computing capability of edge servers should be prioritized. In other words, the supplies of joint running computing tasks on edge server must be prevented. In this situation, the computing tasks should be properly distributed to various edge servers for execution. The trade-off between limited bandwidth and resource allocation in edge computing framework is investigated in [4] where the authors exploit an framework for cooperative video processing to send back a few video features to remote servers through nearby edge nodes while delivering original video would lead to bandwidth starvation.

In [15], Xu et al. emploied Non-dominated Sorting Genetic Algorithm II (NSGA-II) to accomplish multi-objective optimization to shorten the offloading time of the computing tasks and reduce the energy consumption of the edge computing nodes. Different from the existing work (NSGA-II), our design target is to exploit an appropriate and efficient way through SPEA2 to allocate resources via edge nodes, which deploys legitimately edge nodes and ensures high edge resource utilization [16,17].

3   System Model and Problem Formulation

In this section, we present a system framework for video surveillance at traffic road in edge computing. In the monitoring spot, there is M smart video surveillance equipment, denoted as $R = \{r_1, r_2, \cdots, r_M\}$, along the roadside. The smart video surveillance equipment consist of monitoring terminals, APs and edge servers. In this framework, monitoring terminals transmit video datum through APs. The acquiring video datum accesses edge servers to processing. Edge servers have powerful computing ability that can execute complicated computing tasks, and the cost of servers stays at a relatively high level; thus, it is unreasonable to deploy one edge server on every control rod. Then, there are W edge servers, denoted as $S = \{s_1, s_2, \cdots, s_W\}$ $(W < M)$ and each edge server consists of L virtual machine (VM) instances, denoted as $V = \{v_1, v_2, \cdots, v_L\}$. Suppose the capacity of edge server equates to the amount of VM instances in corresponding edge server. Then, the capacity of the m-th $(m = \{1, 2, \cdots, M\})$ server s_M can bear the number of VM which is denoted as a_M. Assume $v_{w,l}$ represents the l-th $(l = \{1, 2, \cdots, L\})$ VM in the s_w $(w = \{1, 2, \cdots, W\})$. Assume that there are J computing tasks running on the edge servers, denoted as $T = \{t_1, t_2, \cdots, t_J\}$, and $t_{m,j}$ represents the j-th computing task in the m-th video surveillance equipment.

3.1   Time Consumption Model

The time consumption consists of four parts, i.e., the time of migration between adjacent access points, the computing time in corresponding edge server, feedback time and the offloading time from edge servers to cloud center. To better support for advanced functions of video surveillance equipment, we aim to minimize the time consumption.

When the video data generated by monitoring terminals without edge server access the nearby edge servers, the process will have the time of migration, which is calculated by

$$g_m^n = \sum_{j=1}^{J} q_m^n \frac{f_{m,j}}{\alpha} \tag{1}$$

where α is the data transmission rate between APs, q_m^n is a binary variable to judge whether the j-th computing task in the m-th video surveillance equipment is transmitted from s_m to s_n, which is defined by

$$q_m^n = \begin{cases} 1, & t_{m,j} \text{ is transmitted from } s_m \text{ to } s_n, \\ 0, & \text{otherwise.} \end{cases} \tag{2}$$

The computing time of r_m is to be determined by the number of VM instances in edge server, the length of computing task and the processing performance of each VM instances. Accordingly, the task length is denoted as F_m, and the processing performance of each VM is denoted as p. The computing time is calculated by

$$h_m = \sum_{j=1}^{J} \frac{F_m}{a_m \cdot p} z_{m,j} \tag{3}$$

where $z_{m,j}$ judges whether $t_{m,j}$ has been transmitted, i.e. each video surveillance equipment obtains amount of computing tasks that process in the local or nearby edge nodes, which is defined by

$$z_{m,j} = \begin{cases} 0, & t_{m,j} \text{ has been transmitted,} \\ 1, & \text{otherwise.} \end{cases} \tag{4}$$

The edge nodes that handle the executing task from nearby nodes should return the results to the original node, which generate the feedback time. The feedback time of r_m is calculated by

$$b_m = \sum_{j=1}^{J} q_m^n \frac{f_{m,back}}{\alpha} \tag{5}$$

where $f_{m,back}$ is the data size of returned results.

The processed video data (e.g. extracting feature) that only have small volume will offloading from the network edge to center. The offloading time of rm is calculated by

$$o_m = \frac{f_{m,output}}{\beta} + \frac{f_{m,output}}{\gamma} \tag{6}$$

where $f_{m,output}$ is the data size of the acquiring results for computing r_m, β is the data transmission rate from edge servers to base stations, γ is the data transmission rate from base stations to cloud data center.

The total time consumption for calculate all computing task is measured by

$$TC = \sum_{m=1}^{M} (g_m + h_m + b_m + o_m) \tag{7}$$

3.2 Load Balance Analysis

The resource utilization is a crucial element to evaluate the computing ability of the edge servers. The aim of this paper is improving the average resource utilization.

To ensure successful transmission for multiple functions of monitoring terminals, the resource allocation of VM on data links should be balanced. Therefore, the resource utilization of sw can be represented by

$$U_w = \frac{1}{a_w} \sum_{j=1}^{J} \sum_{l=1}^{a_w} qv_{j,l} \tag{8}$$

where $qv_{j,l}$ judges whether t_j occupied v_l in the s_w.

$$qv_{j,l} = \begin{cases} 1, & \text{if } t_j \text{ occupied } v_{w,l}, \\ 0, & \text{otherwise.} \end{cases} \tag{9}$$

Based on the number of servers which are occupied, we can calculate the average resource usage of edge servers. The number of occupied servers is defined by

$$OS = \sum_{w=1}^{W} qs_w \tag{10}$$

The average resource utilization of all edge servers is calculated by

$$U = \frac{1}{OS} \cdot \sum_{w=1}^{W} U_w \tag{11}$$

where qs_w judges whether s_w is occupied

$$qs_w = \begin{cases} 1, & \text{if } s_w \text{ is occupied,} \\ 0, & \text{otherwise.} \end{cases} \tag{12}$$

The load balance variance of s_w is calculated by

$$B_w = \frac{1}{(U_w - U)^2} \tag{13}$$

The average load balance variance of all edge servers is calculated by

$$B = \frac{1}{OS} \cdot \sum_{w=1}^{W} B_w \cdot qs_w \tag{14}$$

3.3   Problem Formulation

In this paper, we aim to achieve the goal of minimizing the time consumption presented in (7) and obtaining load balance in (14). The formalized problem is given as

$$\min (TC), \tag{15}$$

$$\min (B), \tag{16}$$

$$s.t. \quad 0 \le \sum_{w=1}^{W} qs_w \le M \tag{17}$$

4 An Edge Computing-Enabled Resource Provisioning Method for Video Surveillance in Internet of Vehicles

In summary, the goal of this paper is willing to solve this multi-objective optimization problem with minimizing the time consumption and optimizing load balance of video surveillance system in Internet of Vehicles at the same time. Compared with common genetic algorithms (GA) and evolutionary algorithms (EA), SPEA2, the method we choose eventually, with its superior performance and better robustness, is widely used in dealing with this kinds of problems to obtain a number of optimal strategies. Then the following job is to select the optimal solutions by using Simple Additive Weighting (SAW) and Multiple Criteria Decision Marking (MCDM) methods.

4.1 Encoding

In this chapter, the computing tasks in ENs are encoded firstly. In the GA, the value of the decision variable, i.e., the strategies for resource provisioning, are represented through gene. Ultimately a set of genes converge to a chromosome which represents optimal solution of the multi-object problem.

4.2 Fitness Functions and Constraints

The fitness functions in GA, which are used as decision criterion to evaluate the pros and cons of each individual. In this paper, the fitness functions include two different categories: the time consumption and the load balance of edge serverswhich represented respectively by (8) and (14). As is shown in (15), the design purpose of the method is to optimize the average resource utilization of edge servers and reduce the time consumption of computing tasks at the same time. Furthermore, the constraints are demonstrating in (16).

4.3 Initialization

In the initialization operation, the related parameters should be determined at first, which including the size of population SP, the probability of crossover PC, the probability of mutation PM, the number of iterations T and the size of archive SA. Each chromosome in GA represents the resource provisioning strategies in the population set which denoted $US^i = (US_1, US_2, US_3, \cdots, US_j)$ and US^i represents the i-th chromosome.

4.4 Selection

In the selection operation of SPEA2 algorithm, individuals who has more desirable fitness are selected from the current evolutionary group and placed into the mating pool. Hence the crossover and the mutation operation will select individuals from the mating pool only to generate a better population.

4.5 Crossover and Mutation

In the crossover operation of SPEA2 algorithm, two different parental chromosomes are combined to generate new chromosomes with better performance. In the first place, a crossover point in the parental chromosomes is picked in the crossover operation, then on both sides of this point, two genes are interchanged. Eventually, two new chromosomes are created around this point.

Mutation operation of SPEA2 algorithm takes place when the premature convergence emerges due to the descendant chromosome performs no longer more outstanding than their last generation but still not approach the satisfactory optimal solution. This vital operation is utilized to ensure the diversity of different individual and the equal mutation probability of each gene.

4.6 Optimal Strategy Selection by Using SAW and MCDM

The resource provisioning method this paper is dedicated to achieving a dynamic tradeoff between the two intent objective function E.g. time consumption and load balance in this paper. Meanwhile, both the time consumption and the load balance which given by the target problem of this paper are negative criteria. In other words, if the execution time of computing tasks getting longer, the result turns into more undesirable. Consequently, when the objective problem demands normalizing resource-scheduling indicator, which is the performance of time consumption and average resource utilization, that where SAW and MCDM take place. The load balance value is denoted as $LB = (LB^i, 1 \leq i \leq I)$, and the time consumption value is denoted as $\text{TC} = (TC^i, 1 \leq i \leq I)$. The chosen result is calculated by

$$OLB_{i,j} = \begin{cases} \frac{LB^{\max} - LB^{i,j}}{LB^{\max} - LB^{\min}} , LB^{\max} - LB^{\min} \neq 0, \\ 1 \qquad\qquad , LB^{\max} - LB^{\min} = 0. \end{cases} \tag{18}$$

$$OTC_{i,j} = \begin{cases} \frac{TC^{\max} - TC^{i,j}}{TC^{\max} - TC^{\min}} , TC^{\max} - TC^{\min} \neq 0, \\ 1 \qquad\qquad , TC^{\max} - TC^{\min} = 0. \end{cases} \tag{19}$$

where LB^{max}, LB^{min}, TC^{max} and TC^{min} represent the maximum value of load balance, the minimum value of load balance, the maximum value of time consumption and the minimum value of time consumption, respectively. Eventually, we calculate the utility value by

$$OR_i = OLB_{i,j} \cdot tl + OTC_{i,j} \cdot tw, \tag{20}$$

where tl, tw represent the weight of the load balance and the time consumption, respectively.

4.7   Method Review

The final destination of objective question of this paper is to optimize the average load balance and the time consumption of all computing tasks deployed in edge servers. Due to the resource provisioning problem is a multi-objective optimization problem essentially, with its excellent performance we select SPEA2 algorithm to solve our target problem finally by means of comparing it with other GA. Above all, the objective problem is encoded. Then we proposed all of the fitness functions and the constraints to prepare for use. Furthermore, via implementing the environmental selection operation, chromosomes with more desirable performance of fitness are picked from their evolutionary group into the mating pool. Shortly afterwards, the crossover operation and the mutation operation is carried out to against the premature convergence and generate new individuals with more outstanding descendants. Eventually, normalization processing of resource utilization and time consumption is carried out by ways of SAW and MCDM methods.

Algorithm 1. computing the optimal strategy by using SPEA2

Require: T
Ensure: OR
 1: **for** $i = 1$ *to* I **do**
 2:     t=1
 3:     **while** $t \leq T$ **do**
 4:         Calculate the total time consumption TC by $(1) - (7)$
 5:         Calculate the average load balance variance LB by $(8) - (14)$
 6:         Environmental selection to ensure the amount of OR
 7:         Crossover and mutation operations to ensure the offspring
 8:         t=t+1
 9:     **end while**
10:     Evaluate utility value with SAW and MCDM method by (18)(19)
11:     select the optimal solution by (20)
12: **end for**
13: **return** OR

In summary, we proposed the procedure of obtaining the optimal strategy, the T represents the number of iterations and the OR represents the best strategy in the Algorithm 1.

5   Experimental Evaluation

5.1   Comparison of Employed ENs

With more ENs is employed, the time consumption and the load balance are affected soon. As an important parameter, the number of employed ENs must be taken into consideration. What's more, with the increase of the computing tasks, the more ENs will be employed. Figure 1 illustrates the number of ENs employed by the different resource provisioning methods. Apparently, the method ERPM occupied less ENs in dealing with same amount of computing tasks.

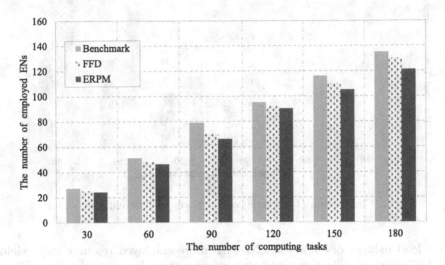

Fig. 1. Comparison of the number of employed ENs by different task scales.

5.2 Comparison of Time Consumption

After all computing tasks of processed and transmitted, the total time consumption is definitely achieved. The number of the time consumption has great importance in the whole computing tasks. Figure 2 shows the comparison of total time consumption of the ENs by using Benchmark, FFD and ERPM at different scales of computing tasks. The time consumption is calculated according to the executing process, the tasks migration and the offloading data. The value of time consumption is compared in Fig. 2. It shows that the method ERPM has better performance at time consumption, that is to say, our proposed method ERPM based on SPEA2 wastes fewer time than the other methods.

5.3 Comparison of Load Balance

The load balance is a criterion to evaluate the resource utilization of ENs. It aims to optimize resource use, minimize response time, maximize throughput, and avoid overload of any single resource. Load balance improves the distribution of workloads across multiple computing resources In the method we proposed in this paper, six datasets of load balance are used to assess the pros and cons of our method. Figure 3 illustrates the comparison of the load balance of the ENs by using Benchmark, FFD and our ERPM at different scales of computing tasks.

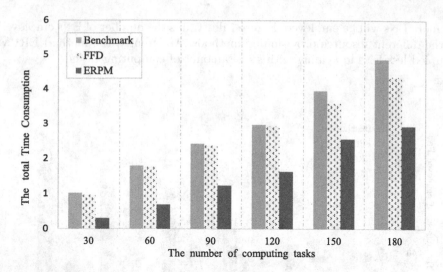

Fig. 2. Comparison of the time consumption by different task scales.

Fewer load balance of employed ENs with more employed resource units yield a higher resource utilization and better performance. It is intuitive from Fig. 3 that the method ERPM we proposed achieves better load balance than the other two offloading methods, which means to some extent, our method ERPM could reduce the overload or underload of ENs.

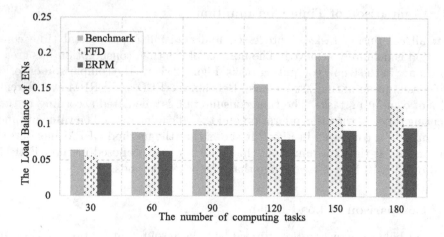

Fig. 3. Comparison of the load balance of the ENs by different scales.

6 Conclusion

As a significant technology of information age, great influence is generated by video surveillance in Internet of Vehicles, not to mention other aspects of everyone's life in our land. Hence it is extremely urgent and important to optimize the time consumption and the load balance of all the ENs for edge computing-enabled resource provisioning for Video Surveillance in Internet of Vehicles. A better tasks computation offloading method is proposed and practiced in our paper. With its more desirable performance and the nature of offloading problem the SPEA2 algorithm is picked to achieve our goal. At the beginning, we analyze the details of process of tasks computing, then we formulate the problem as a multi-objective optimization problem. finally, we select an Evolution algorithm with simulation experimental to solve the objective problem we proposed.

In the future work, we are going to complicate our problem to adopt to the real world better and keep improve our algorithm with experiment.

Acknowledgment. This research is supported by the National Science Foundation of China under grant no. 61702277 and 61872219.

References

1. Atzori, L., Iera, A., Morabito, G.: The internet of things: a survey. Comput. Netw. **54**(15), 2787–2805 (2010)
2. Xu, Z., et al.: An IoT-oriented offloading method with privacy preservation for cloudlet-enabled wireless metropolitan area networks. Sensors **18**(9), 3030 (2018)
3. Kumar, N., Rodrigues, J.J., Chilamkurti, N.: Bayesian coalition game as-a-service for content distribution in internet of vehicles. IEEE Internet Things J. **1**(6), 544–555 (2014)
4. Puvvadi, U.L., Di Benedetto, K., Patil, A., Kang, K.D., Park, Y.: Cost-effective security support in real-time video surveillance. IEEE Trans. Ind. Inform. **11**(6), 1457–1465 (2015)
5. Long, C., Cao, Y.: Edge computing framework for cooperative video processing in multimedia IoT systems. IEEE Trans. Multimedia **20**(5), 1126–1139 (2018)
6. Lopez, P., et al.: Edge-centric computing: vision and challenges. ACMSIGCOMM Comput. Commun. Rev. **45**(5), 37–42 (2015)
7. Eriksson, E., Dán, G.: Predictive distributed visual analysis for video in wireless sensor networks. IEEE Trans. Mob. Comput. **15**(7), 1743–1756 (2016)
8. Zhang, J., et al.: Hybrid computation offloading for smart home automation in mobile cloud computing. Pers. Ubiquitous Comput. **22**(1), 121–134 (2018)
9. Zhang, J., Qi, L., Yuan, Y., Xu, X., Dou, W.: A workflow scheduling method for cloudlet management in mobile cloud. In: 2018 IEEE SmartWorld. https://doi.org/10.1109/SmartWorld.2018.00167
10. Shi, W., Cao, J., Zhang, Q., Li, Y., Xu, L.: Edge computing: vision and challenges. IEEE Internet Things J. **3**(5), 637–646 (2016)
11. Qi, L., Chen, Y., Yuan, Y., Fu, S., Zhang, X., Xu, X.: A QoS-aware virtual machine scheduling method for energy conservation in cloud-based cyber-physical systems. World Wide Web J. (2019). https://doi.org/10.1007/s11280-019-00684-y

12. Qi, L., et al.: Finding all you need: web APIs recommendation in web of things through keywords search. IEEE Trans. Comput. Soc. Syst. (2019). https://doi.org/10.1109/TCSS.2019.2906925
13. Wu, P.-H., Huang, C.-W., Hwang, J.-N.: Video-quality-driven resource allocation for real-time surveillance video uplinking over OFDMA-based wireless networks. IEEE Trans. Veh. Technol. **64**(7), 3233–3246 (2015)
14. Chen, J., Li, K.: Distributed deep learning model for intelligent video surveillance systems with edge computing. IEEE Trans. Ind. Inform. https://doi.org/10.1109/TII.2019.2909473
15. Xu, X., et al.: An energy-aware computation offloading method for smart edge computing in wireless metropolitan area networks. J. Netw. Comput. Appl. **133**, 75–85 (2019)
16. Al-Nadwi, M.M.K., Refat, N., Zaman, N., Rahman, M.A., Bhuiyan, M.Z.A., Razali, R.B.: Cloud enabled *e*-glossary system: a smart campus perspective. In: Wang, G., Chen, J., Yang, L.T. (eds.) SpaCCS 2018. LNCS, vol. 11342, pp. 251–260. Springer, Cham (2018). https://doi.org/10.1007/978-3-030-05345-1_21
17. Yang, J., Wang, H., Wang, Z., Long, J., Du, B.: BDCP: a framework for big data copyright protection based on digital watermarking. In: Wang, G., Chen, J., Yang, L.T. (eds.) SpaCCS 2018. LNCS, vol. 11342, pp. 351–360. Springer, Cham (2018). https://doi.org/10.1007/978-3-030-05345-1_30

The Optimization of Network Performance Evaluation Method for Virtual Desktop QoE Based on SPICE

Weimin Li[1], Jinfang Sheng[2(✉)], Yikang Yan[2], Shaobo Zhang[3], Xingyu Deng[1], and Wenxiu Huang[1]

[1] School of Information, Science and Technology, Hunan University of Humanities, Loudi 417000, China
weiminli@csu.edu.cn, xinyudeng.ivy@gmail.com, xiuhuang0329@foxmail.com
[2] School of Computer Science and Engineering, Central South University, Changsha 410083, China
jfsheng@csu.edu.cn, yyaq117@gmail.com
[3] School of Computer Science and Engineering, Hunan University of Science and Technology, Xiangtan 411201, China
shaobozhang@hnust.edu.cn

Abstract. The evaluation of user experience of virtual desktop service, which aims to make the results obtained through the evaluation method as close as possible to the user's real feelings, has been widely concerned. At present, the mainstream evaluation methods based on client and network capture packet have the deficiency that the collection of relevant performance indicators is not objective and real, especially in network performance. This paper proposes a network performance evaluation and optimization solution for the virtual desktop service based on the open source desktop transport protocol SPICE. It takes the real feeling of the client user as the benchmark, and considers the clock synchronization between client and server. Then, on the basis of deeply understanding the internal principle of SPICE protocol, the network performance test data packet is integrated into it, and the time stamp of the data packet that is sent and received, and the packet loss situation is recorded. The experimental results show that the network performance indicators obtained by the optimization method is closer to the real application scenario.

Keywords: Virtual desktop · QoE · Performance evaluation · SPICE · Network performance

1 Introduction

With the wide attention of virtualization technology in the industry, many remote desktops are integrated with virtualization technology to run the remote desktop environment in the virtual machine hosted on the server, gradually forming the virtual desktop technology. One of the key technologies involved in

© Springer Nature Singapore Pte Ltd. 2019
G. Wang et al. (Eds.): iSCI 2019, CCIS 1122, pp. 141–151, 2019.
https://doi.org/10.1007/978-981-15-1301-5_12

the implementation of virtual desktop is Virtual Desktop Infrastructure (VDI), which hosts users' desktop operating system in a virtual machine on a remote server, and each virtual machine is scheduled to run under the management and control of hypervisor. Users can access their desktop systems through virtual desktop transfer protocols by using a variety of devices anytime and anywhere [6]. Therefore, the virtual desktop transfer protocol is the core of the VDI solution. Using the virtual desktop transfer protocol, the client sends user data, such as key, mouse, keyboard, peripherals, etc., to the server, and then returns the corresponding generated graphical output data to the client [8].

At present, there are three major VDI solutions: Citrix, Microsoft and VMware. However, due to commercial interests, the technology involved is often relatively closed. Red Hat has came up with a set of open virtual desktop solutions, which includes three components: KVM (Kernel-based Virtual Machine) based hypervisor, SPICE protocol, virtualized desktop management platform. SPICE adopts unique layered architecture, classified compression and self-adaptive processing technology of graphics, which can support multimedia desktop experience including audio and video transmission. SPICE has the advantages of low transmission bandwidth, good graphics display quality, high security, and its open source features, making it become a research focus in academia [2, 4, 5].

The Quality of User Experience (QoE), which mainly involves two aspects: QoE improvement and QoE evaluation, is always the most critical requirement of virtual desktop. This paper focuses on the optimization of network performance evaluation methods for virtual desktop QoE based on SPICE. Virtual desktop service is an application mode with rich media and high degree of interaction with users. Therefore, the QoE is a comprehensive process of objective performance and subjective feeling. In terms of objective performance, the most critical factor affecting the QoE is the low response time of the service [1]. The main factors affecting service response time are the speed at which the server responds to the client request and the speed of processing and the transmission rate of the data and instructions in the network. Among them, the impact of network transmission on service response time is the most critical [9]. Therefore, a basic work of network transmission performance evaluation is how to accurately test and obtain objective network performance indicators.

The virtual desktop network performance evaluation method can be classified into three categories: server-based evaluation, client-based evaluation, and network-based. The most accurate method is measurement solution based on clients, since the real user experience is what the user feels when using the service on the client device. However, such methods usually need to go deep into the internal principles of the desktop transport protocol, and integrate the performance evaluation mechanism into the transport protocol, which often requires intrusive modification for the protocol. Although these methods are more difficult and specialized as well as weak generality, the QoE evaluation of a specific virtual desktop service is very valuable because of their highest accuracy and objectivity. To this end, this paper proposes a client-based network performance indicator evaluation and optimization method for the SPICE-based virtual desktop platform. The network performance test packet is integrated into the SPICE protocol and periodically sent to the server from the client. Then the time when the client sends and receives the packet is marked, and the packet loss situation is recorded. The experimental results verify that the network performance index test of this method is more accurate and objective than the common method with network packet capture.

2 Related Works

The QoE evaluation of cloud desktop services involves many objective factors and even subjective factors. This adds complexity to the QoE evaluation benchmarks and methods of cloud desktop services. Different cloud service models have their own application characteristics. Terefore, the factor or indicator of their QoE evaluation tend to be different. For instance, with regard to cloud storage service, the most important factor affecting QoE is usually the network bandwidth, and for the cloud desktop service, the network delay has the greatest impact on its QoE [1]. The authors in [9] ran different applications in the VNC-based remote desktop system, and the method of packet tracking simulation is used to obtain the RTT (Round-Trip Time) between sending a request from the user and returning the corresponding screen update. The main finding of this paper was that the more interactive the application is, the more sensitive its service response time is to network latency. In [3], the authors compared the bandwidth and latency consumption of several remote desktop systems in LAN and WAN environments. The test technique adopted was a set of slow-motion benchmarking methods [10], which inserts a delay between two screen updates on the client side. This method ensured that the client displayed all visualization components in the same time sequence, thus greatly improving the accuracy and repeatability of the test. Instead of relying on manual benchmarks, the authors in [6] adopted the experimental method based on real user conversation, where the power consumption and network utilization of mobile terminal devices was obtained with different remote access protocols and application types. Furthermore, the availability and user experience of remote desktop services in a mobile cloud computing environment were analyzed. The authors in [7] designed a quantitative experimental approach to compare resource usage and response time for Windows 8 and Windows 10 as virtual desktop operating systems. The authors in [67] changed the parameters of the network in a controlled experimental environment, such as packet loss rate, jitter and delay

From the above related works, we can see that researchers are trying to quantitatively evaluate QoE by testing some objective indicators. The key link is how to accurately test the objective indicators, and the essence of the problem is whether the QoE test method is objective and true. However, most of the current solutions run the benchmark tools on the virtual desktop server, which can only reflect the performance of the virtual machine when running programs, and can not objectively reflect the performance of the client image display update. Meanwhile, if the test tool runs on the client side, the results will be more objective and accurate, but the difficulty of implementation could be greatly increased, because it needs to fully understand the internal principles of the client and desktop transport protocol in order to invade the test tool, especially in the face of virtual desktop solutions without open source, this method is basically not available. Another widely used test scenario is to use network monitoring packet capture to test certain actions (such as browsing a web page) to evaluate the response time when the client sends the request to receive the response. This method can be closer to the real test requirements, however, is still an overgeneralization, because the user's real experience is actually determined by the client image update display, and in many cases, high refresh rate will result in a large number of packet loss, At this point, the method can not truly represent the user's experience. To sum up, it is of great practical significance to design a feasible evaluation method for SPICE virtual desktop service based on open source, which can more objectively and truly reflect the quality of user experience.

3   The Design of Test Platform

This paper intends to design a test solution for the network performance of SPICE-based virtual desktop service QoE, which will make some key indicators and data more objective and accurate, and the QoE evaluation result is closer to the user's real experience. In order to achieve this goal, according to the service characteristics of the virtual desktop, the following issues should be considered:

(1) The experience of the virtual desktop user should reflect the real feeling of the user when using the client. The image data generated and sent by the server may not be completely displayed and updated on the client device. Therefore, the method which measures the corresponding network performance indicators based on the client is the closest to the user's real experience;

(2) The access and use of virtual desktop is a real-time process. The real-time parsing of image transmission would lead to more performance consumption and seriously affect user experience. On the other hand, The way to record and play back user operations by creating a synthetic test benchmark or script is not based on the user's real input, and is separated from the user's real interaction scenario;

(3) The most critical factor of QoE for virtual desktop services is the response time. For a user, a real user experience quality process should be the response time from sending the user request to receiving the corresponding desktop display. If this time interval can be objectively tested, it can truly reflect the user's QoE;

(4) When using the client device as the test benchmark and using the transmitted data packets as the research object, it is necessary to deeply understand the principle of the virtual desktop, especially the related mechanism of the desktop transfer protocol, and then invasively modify the code (open source software only), which is a relatively difficult work.

Based on the above analysis, the QoE network performance measurement platform for virtual desktop service based on SPICE consists of router, NTP (Network Time Protocol) server, SPICE client, SPICE server and virtual machine cluster based on transparent desktop, as shown in Fig. 1.

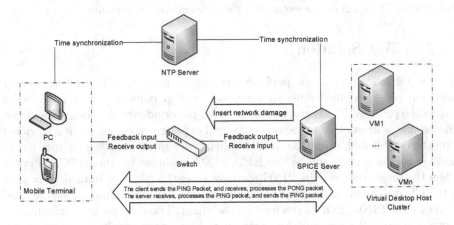

Fig. 1. The architecture of network performance indicator test platform

NTP server: NTP is a computer time synchronization protocol. It synchronizes time from the server or clock source, and provides high precision time correction (standard deviation is less than 1 millisecond in LAN environment). In this experiment, the time synchronization takes the C/S mode to periodically pull and correct time from the server based on the LAN environment. If have better conditions, users can use PTP (Precision Time Synchronization Protocol) server to achieve higher precision and reach time synchronization at the nanosecond level. If there are better conditions, users can use the PTP (Precision Time Synchronization Protocol) server to achieve higher precision (nanosecond level) time synchronization.

SPICE client: It is an application modified and customized based on the desktop version of Remote Viewer. In addition to the original functions of sending mouse/keyboard input and rendering output images to the server, it adds the application-level functions of sending and processing PONG data packets by self-defined PING data packets, which is used to evaluate RTT in the network monitoring environment of SPICE applications.

SPICE server: A high-performance Linux computer based on KVM and Qemu, which virtualizes several VM instances in the background while inserting controllable network damage (delay, packet loss, and jitter) into the outlet flow through TC (a traffic controller in Linux) and Netem (a network simulation module in Linux kernel).

Data acquisition first requires an excellent console output. The SPICE framework is based on extensions on the Glib and GNOME libraries, which uses the spice_logger to set the environment variable SPICE_DEBUG_LEVEL or

G_MESSAGES_DEBUG to control the log output level. Secondly, the server manages the virtual resources of KVM and QEMU through Libvirt (VMM-like mechanism), and collects detailed resources of the virtual machine according to related APIs. Finally, the performance and configuration of the NTP server determines the time error of the experimental environment composed of multiple computers. The smaller the error, the more accurate the measured data.

4   The Test Solution

The most challenging of all performance status metrics is the network-layer collection scheme, which aims to accurately test a request packet from being sent to the processed and returned RTT. This paper adopts the client-based test scheme that is most close to the objective real experience. As shown in Algorithm 1, on the established Main Channel, the client periodically sends a custom PING message to the server (unlike the RED_PING initiated by the SPICE server). When the server receives the PING message from the client, it immediately goes to the client. The client responds to a PONG message, and finally analyzes and processes the PING/PONG received by the client. The data packets transmitted between spice protocols must be encapsulated into packets which can be parsed by SPICE protocol before they can be transmitted on the specified channel.

Algorithm 1. The network performance indicator collection on the SPICE client

---

Input:
   interval: packet interval;
   count: the number of consecutive packets;
   timeout: timeout coefficient;
Output:
   result: the log file of network performance during acquisition;
   Begin the loop;
   Step1: According to the input parameter count, the client continuously sends PING packets with the count quantity;
   Step2: Whenever the server receives the PING packet, it will immediately feedback PONG to the client;
   Step3: Calculate the unilateral delay based on the accuracy of the NTP server;
   Step4: Every time the client receives PONG packet, calculate the round delay RTT (if timeout does not receive the PONG packet corresponding to the last PING packet, the packet is lost);
   Step5: The client continues sending according to the input interval;
   Step6: End the loop when meeting user needs;
   Step7: Calculate the overall packet loss rate, delay and jitter of the process;
   return the log file result that saves the data;

The client-initiated custom PING package and the server-side feedback PONG package are designed in detail as follows:

(1) Message format. When transferring PING/PONG packets between SPICE protocols, they must be encapsulated as packets parsed by the SPICE protocol before they can be transmitted over a specified channel. After SPICE initializes the main channel, all transmission packets must remain in a uniform message format for next transmission and parsing. SPICE supports both the SpiceData and the SiceMiniData message formats, where SpiceMiniData is a reduced version of SpiceData, and SiceMiniDataHeader is the header of its message. There are only three fields: type, size and data. In order to merge PING/PONG packets into the SPICE protocol, and considering the performance impact, the less packet Header header and optional message content, the better. Thus, the resulting PING/PONG message format is shown in Fig. 2. The serial is the serial number that corresponds to the self-incrementing of the transmission channel and type is the corresponding channel type. The size represents the size of the main data of the PING/PONG Message message, which plays the role of sliding window and preventing the network from sticking packets. The data represents the principal part of the PING/PONG message, as described in the segment message format description.

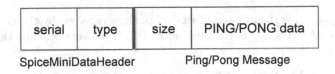

| serial | type | size | PING/PONG data |

SpiceMiniDataHeader   Ping/Pong Message

Fig. 2. The message format of PING/PONG

(2) Segment message format description. The primary purpose of sending PING/PONG packets is to measure client-to-server network performance, meaning that packets need to be on top of communication capabilities that does not affect the original SPICE protocol. Simplify the contents of the packet as much as possible. The PING packet contains two fields, ID and Time, and ID uses UINT32 to represent the self-increasing sequence number of PING, which is different from the serial attribute of the channel global autoaddition in Header. Time uses UINT64 to represent the client local timestamp at the time the packet was sent. The PONG packet also contains two fields, ID and Time, and ID uses UINT32 to represent and respond to the serial number of the PING packet. Time uses UINT64 to indicate when the PING packet was received, as shown in Fig. 3. The timestamp uses the get_monotonic_time function. Get_monotonic_time function is a function in glib that calculates time by querying the system clock. It is fast and accurate at the microsecond level, and is not affected by NTP time correction, regress, and synchronization, and the time be measured more accurately.

(3) Computing method. It is assumed that a complete in the process of transmitting PING and responding to a PONG message, the time that the client sends the PING packet with the sequence number 1 is a t_1. When the server

Fig. 3. The message format of PING/PONG data

receives the PING packet with serial number 1 and responds to PONG, the local time is t_2. When the client receives the PONG packet with serial number 1 again, the local time is t_3. The time delay can be calculated as follows.

The client-to-server unilateral delay:

$$delay = t_2 - t_1,$$

The round trip delay from client to server:

$$RTT = t_3 - t_1,$$

The packet loss rate:

$$loss = PKG_{accepted}/PKG_{total},$$

where $PKG_{accepted}$ is the number of PONG packets received by the client during the process, and PKG_{total} is the number of PING packets sent for the process.

Table 1. The configuration for experiment platform.

Device	Hardware	OS and software
Server	CPU:Intel(R) Core i7-6700k @4.0 GHz	CentOS 7
	MEM:32G	QEMU+KVM
	DISK:2T	SPICE Server
VMs	CPU:Logical host*2	Windows 7
	MEM:4G	Google Chrome
	DISK:20G	
Client	CPU:Intel(R) Core i5-3470@3.20 GHz	Windows 10
	MEM:8G	Customized Remote Viewer
	DISK:500G	
Switch	H3C S5024P	

5   Experimental Verification

After the design of the above experimental solution is completed, the test platform is further implemented, and the specific software and hardware configurations of the test environment are shown in Table 1. The experimental test environment consists of a server and multiple PCs, as well as a network switch. The server builds the virtual environment and SPICE server with KVM+QEMU on CentOS 7, which runs multiple Windows 7 virtual machines at the same time, and uses the TC and Netem to control network delay, network bandwidth, and packet loss rate to simulate various network conditions. The PC runs the SPICE client (Remote Viewer) that has modified the source code.

In order to verify the validity of the proposed QoE evaluation and optimization scheme for cloud services based on SPICE, and to verify that the network layer data acquisition method based on modifying SPICE client is more accurate, a 5-minute test was carried out in this chapter. To get close to the real situation, perform short-term random operations on commonly used applications during this period, and use the same recording script to play back mouse and keyboard input events. Compare the results with ATKKPING, an enhanced network testing software. On the one hand, TC/Netem is used to control the packet loss rate between 0 and 10%, and the change step size is 1%. The experiment was repeated for 10 times and the average value was calculated. After modification, the packet loss rate detected by SPICE client was compared with that detected by ATKKPING, as shown in Fig. 4. The modified SPICE packet loss rate is slightly lower than that measured by ATKKPING, because in practice not only SPICE packets are discarded, but also packets from other applications are included. Therefore, the optimized measurement method is closer to the real requirement of SPICE application.

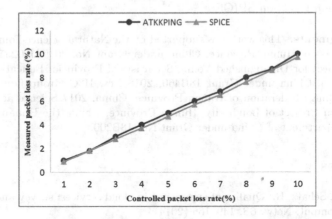

Fig. 4. The comparison of packet loss rate

On the other hand, we use the TC control delay between 0 ms and 200 ms, to send the packet and response time delay is tested, the repeat 10 times, and the average results as shown in Table 2. The time delay measured by sending the PING packet through the client is very close to that of ATKKPING, and the time delay measured by ATKKPING is slightly smaller. The reasons are as follows: (1) due to the system works at the network layer above the PING command, by sending the ICMP directly with IP communications, custom PING package at the transport layer, communicate with the server host via TCP; (2) a custom PING packet needs to be sent with the SPICE message protocol, which is slightly complicated.

Table 2. The delay comparison between custom SPICE-PING package and ATKKPING.

	Deday (ms)				
	0	10	50	100	200
SPICE-PING	0.283	10.306	50.286	100.278	200.282
ATKKPING	0.267	10.263	50.265	100.257	200.263

6   Conclusion

This paper took the virtual desktop service based on SPICE as the research object. By deeply understanding the principle of SPICE protocol, a method of QoE network performance evaluation based on client user experience was proposed. The performance indicators obtained by this method were more objective and real, which provided a more accurate and real data basis for virtual desktop QoE evaluation based on SPICE.

Acknowledgments. This work was supported by the Natural Science Foundation for Young Scientists of Hunan Province, China under Grant No. 2019JJ50285, Scientific Research Project for Distinguished Young Scientists of Provincial Education Department of Hunan, China under Grant 18B460, 2018 New H3C Group Foundation for Internet of Things Federation of Hunan Province, China, 2017 Science and Technology Innovation Project of Loudi city, Hunan Province, China, the Hunan Provincial Education Department of China under Grant No. 18B200.

References

1. Casas, P., Schatz, R.: Quality of experience in cloud services: survey and measurements. Comput. Netw. **68**, 149–165 (2014)
2. Celesti, A., Mulfari, D., Fazio, M., Villari, M., Puliafito, A.: Improving desktop as a service in openstack. In: 2016 IEEE Symposium on Computers and Communication (ISCC), pp. 281–288. IEEE (2016)
3. Lai, A.M., Nieh, J.: On the performance of wide-area thin-client computing. Acm Trans. Comput. Syst. **24**(2), 175–209 (2006)
4. Lan, Y., Xu, H.: Research on technology of desktop virtualization based on spice protocol and its improvement solutions. Front. Comput. Sci. **8**(6), 885–892 (2014)
5. Li, W., Wang, B., Yu, J., Zhu, C., Xiao, S., Sheng, J.: The optimization of transparent-desktop service mechanism based on spice. Concurr. Comput.: Pract. Exp. **28**(18), 4543–4556 (2016)

6. Lin, Y., Kämäräinen, T., Francesco, M.D., Ylä-Jääski, A.: Performance evaluation of remote display access for mobile cloud computing. Comput. Commun. **72**, 17–25 (2015)
7. Nakhai, P.H., Anuar, N.B.: Performance evaluation of virtual desktop operating systems in virtual desktop infrastructure. In: 2017 IEEE Conference on Application, Information and Network Security (AINS), pp. 105–110. IEEE (2017)
8. Tian, G., Shenoy, P., Ramakrishnan, K.K., Gopalakrishnan, V.: Latency-aware virtual desktops optimization in distributed clouds. Multimed. Syst. **24**(1), 1–22 (2017)
9. Tolia, N., Andersen, D.G., Satyanarayanan, M.: Quantifying interactive user experience on thin clients. IEEE Comput. **39**(3), 46–52 (2006)
10. Yang, S.J., Nieh, J., Novik, N.: Measuring thin-client performance using slow-motion benchmarking. Acm Trans. Comput. Syst. **21**(1), 87–115 (2003)

Trustworthy Data Collection for Cyber Systems: A Taxonomy and Future Directions

Hafiz ur Rahman[1], Guojun Wang[1](✉) (iD), Md Zakirul Alam Bhuiyan[2],
and Jianer Chen[1]

[1] School of Computer Science, Guangzhou University, Guangzhou 510006, China
hafiz_rahman@e.gzhu.edu.cn, csgjwang@gmail.com, jianer@gzhu.edu.cn
[2] Department of Computer and Information Sciences, Fordham University,
New York, NY 10458, USA
mbhuiyan3@fordham.edu

Abstract. Due to technology limitation and environmental influence (i.e., equipment faults, noises, clutter, interferences, and security attacks), the sensor data collected by Cyber-Physical System (CPS) is inherently noisy and may trigger many false alarms. These false or misleading data can lead to wrong decisions. Therefore, data trustworthiness (i.e., the data is free from error, up to date, and originate from a reputable source) is always preferred. However, it often has high cost and challenges to identify fault, noise, cyber-attack, and real-world facts, especially in heterogeneous and complex IoT environment. In this article, we briefly review the current developments and research trend in this research area. We highlighted all the challenges and potential solutions for the trustworthy data collections in CPS and propose a taxonomy for data trustworthiness in CPS. Taxonomy aims to describe different aspects of research in this field. Furthermore, it will help researchers as a reference point for the design of data reliability and data trustworthiness evaluation methods. Based on the observations, future directions are also suggested.

Keywords: Trustworthy data · Taxonomy · Cyber-Physical System · Internet of Things

1 Introduction

Internet of Things (IoT) can integrate physical objects with the virtual world (i.e., smart devices, sensors, computers, etc.) for various operations. According to Cisco reports that 50 billion objects and accessories will be connected to the Internet by 2020. These figures will exceed the number of people on earth [1]. This prediction suggests that the Internet of things will be a considerable part of the lives of people. Moreover, IoT has a broad prospect and is commonly used in the fields of traffic management, health care, education, weather forecasting,

© Springer Nature Singapore Pte Ltd. 2019
G. Wang et al. (Eds.): iSCI 2019, CCIS 1122, pp. 152–164, 2019.
https://doi.org/10.1007/978-981-15-1301-5_13

supply chain, and so on [2–6]. It can make people's lives more comfortable and smarter by using intelligent objects to work together.

Nevertheless, IoT sensors are generally deployed to monitor and measure different attributes of the environment. These sensors sense and generate a substantial amount of data that will be used in future for decision and policy-making [7–9]. Nonetheless, deployed sensors are vulnerable to damage in rough environments. It is challenging to differentiate meaningful and significant data from trusted data with a considerable quantity of noisy data. Current approaches for measuring data trustworthiness are generally meant for web and traditional sensor network. These methods are less suited to IoT and Cyber Physical System (CPS) since IoT and CPS has inherently different nature than other paradigms or domains.

According to a recent report that a huge amount of sensor network data was affected by data failures [10]. About 60%, 50%, and 25% of the data items were faulty and erroneous in the great duck island, macroscope project, and Berkeley lab experiments, respectively. Due to technology limitation and environmental influence (e.g., equipment faults, noises, clutter, and security attack), the sensor data collected by CPS is inherently noisy and may trigger many false alarms [14–16]. These false or misleading data can lead to wrong decisions and ultimately results in wastage of resources, time, and could be risking of human life. Therefore, it is highly desirable to acquire and shift meaningful information/data from a large volume of noisy data. As a motivation, we need accurate and reliable data for trustworthy cyber systems before to invest cost and time for processing, storing, and transmitting of unsecured and untrustworthy data. However, the trustworthiness of the data is versatile and it is hard to identify Fault, Noise, Cyberattack, and Time/real-world facts [8,9,17]. Moreover, data trustworthiness is a difficult problem which often depends on the semantics of the application domain. Besides, current solutions for assuring data trustworthiness are typically meant and apply for traditional WSN and Internet/Web applications. These methods are less favorable to IoT and CPS applications. For ensuring data trustworthiness require articulated solutions by combining different approaches and techniques.

In this work, we briefly review the latest achievements in this regard. We highlighted all the challenges and potential solutions for the trustworthy data collections in IoT/CPS environment and propose a taxonomy for data trustworthiness in IoT/CPS. The objective of the taxonomy is to characterize the various facets of research in this field. Other researchers can use our taxonomy as a reference point in designing their data trustworthiness evaluation techniques.

The rest of the paper is organized as follows. Section 2 provides an overview of the data characteristics of IoT/CPS and IoT architecture. Section 3 describes the need for data trustworthiness and its different challenges. We present the taxonomy of the data trustworthiness in IoT/CPS Sect. 4 and draw conclusions and further research directions in Sect. 5.

2　IoT Data Characteristics

Typically, the IoT system consists of three layers: a physical awareness layer that observes and measures the physical environment, a network layer that sends and processes collected data, and an application layer that provides situational awareness information service, as shown in Fig. 1.

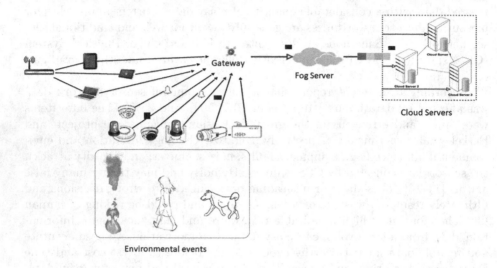

Fig. 1. Generalized IoT system

The interconnected "things" such as sensors or mobile devices monitors and collects different types of environmental event (e.g., sleep habits, fitness levels, humidity, temperature, movement positions, pressure, etc.). These data or events can be further aggregated, fused, processed, and disclose to derive useful information for smart services. All IoT-related smart services, no matter how diverse they may be, follow these five basic steps at all times: (1) Sense; (2) Transmit; (3) Store; (4) Analyze; (5) Act. Therefore, many characteristics are associated with the data in IoT/CPS [7,12,13]. These characteristics are given for the sake to apply an appropriate method according to the nature of IoT/CPS. Following is a brief summary of these features:

Immense Dimension: A standard IoT/CPS involves a large number of sensors, and each sensor produces data most of the time. A control method is needed to treat the enormous dataset and estimate/judge the signals with significant accuracy.

Noisy Data: Multiple deployment practices have confirmed that unpredictable and noisy data are the main concerns for IoT/CPS applications. The noise and errors in the sensor data can be associated with the vulnerability of the environment, in which the sensor is used in a defenseless manner and makes the sensor to failure/defect.

Diverges of Sensors: An IoT/CPS system has moderate repetitions in data. For instance, infrequently a sensor does not work accurately, but others can still produce reliable data. In such a situation, different values for the same event are generated, and the observer does not identify the true state/vale, the system requires to conclude the trustworthy data from the contradictory data.

Uncertainty of Objects: Due to hardware limitations (e.g., computational and battery power, memory constrain, etc.), the sensors cannot present comprehensive information about intrusion victims. The IoT/CPS system need to infer and integrate data from different sensors and generate a piece of complete information about an event.

Vulnerability to Malicious Attacks: Sensors are also vulnerable to malicious attacks, which can lead to incorrect data. The system needs to identified and distinguished malicious attacks form data faults/error.

3   The Need for Data Trustworthiness and Challenges

There may be a dilemma if untrustworthy or compromised data are received at the time of the acquisition; and we apply several robust security algorithms to process, store, and transfer the data; and finally, we make decisions for numerous CPS applications. As a result, decisions made in a cyber-system based on the collected data may be meaningless/untrustworthy, i.e., we may process the compromised data, we may transmit the compromised data, we may encrypt the compromised data, or we may store the compromised data. Therefore, we need trustworthy data for trustworthy cyber systems before to invest cost and time for processing, storing, and transmitting of unsecured and untrustworthy data. Data trustworthiness is defined as the possibility to ascertain/'make sure of' the correctness of the data provided by the data source or in its simplest form means the probability that the data is correct [14,19]. Specifically, the aim of data trustworthiness methods is to ensure: The data is free from errors; Up to date; and Originates from reputable sources. However, there are different challenges to achieve trustworthy Data for trustworthy CPS. Some challenges are:

1. Ensuring data trustworthiness is a complex issue which generally depends on the semantics of the purpose domain.
2. The trustworthiness of the data is versatile, and it is hard to identify fault, noise, cyberattack, and time/real-world facts.

3. How to identify the compromised data once the data reaches high-end storage?
4. How to ensure the trustworthiness of a cyber-system in which data with integrity problem (e.g., System Integrity, Data Integrity, Security Attacks, Fault Occurrences) is already processed and ready for decision-making?
5. In which stage the data is altered and become untrustworthy (i.e., at the acquisition, after the acquisition, at the transmission, during transmission, after transmission, or before aggregation)?

Currently, there is no comprehensive approach to the problem of high assurance data trustworthiness for trustworthy IoT and cyber systems. Complete data trustworthiness requires an articulate solution by combining different approaches/techniques. Therefore, before to invest time and cost, we need to highlight all the challenges and potential solutions for trustworthy data collections. Also, a framework/solution for computing data trustworthiness in IoT is required.

4 Data Trustworthiness Taxonomy for IoT/CPS

Figure 2 depicts the data trustworthiness taxonomy for IoT/CPS. The objective of the taxonomy is to portray the different viewpoints of research in these fields. With the taxonomy, other researchers can use our taxonomy as a reference point in designing their data trustworthiness evaluation techniques. Explanations for each item in the classification are outlined below.

4.1 Data Provider

Data provider indicates who produce the data. It can be a direct human, or it can be a sensor in the embedded device. In a people-centered situation or the social environment, the trustworthiness of the data is estimated based on friendship, loyalty, cultural communication, etc. For device-based, data trustworthiness can be assessed by the reliability of the sensors and measuring the data correlation among sensors in the area [8,18,19].

4.2 Data Processing

Data processing refers to the period when the data are processed for computing the trustworthiness. Data processing applies to the time when the data are treated for measuring for data trustworthiness. Real-time, near real-time, and batch processing are three different choices for data trustworthiness. Real-time data processing mean that the data is processed instantly at the root node for the time-sensitive application. Real-time data processing allows on the spot detection of data fault and immediate decision making. In batch processing, a defined amount of data is firstly received, then the computation for data trustworthiness are performed [18,19].

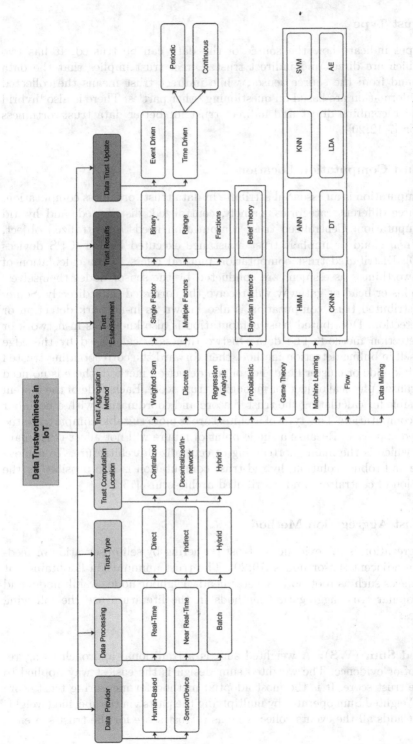

Fig. 2. Data trustworthinesses taxonomy for Internet of Things (IoT) and Cyber-Physical System (CPS)

4.3   Trust Type

Trust types indicate how the source of the data can be trusted. It has two kinds, which are direct and indirect trust. Direct trust implies that the data is first hand from the source sensor; while indirect trust means the collected data or information are based on questioning other parties. There is also 'hybrid trust' which combine direct and indirect trust for better data trustworthiness estimation [7,12,20].

4.4   Trust Computation Location

Trust computation is an essential attribute in data trustworthiness computation. It has three different categories, namely, centralized, distributed, and hybrid trust computation. Centralized trust computation needs a centralized object, either a real cloud or implicit trust assistance executed by IoT/CPS devices [10,11,20]. Distributed trust computation method refers to the calculation of the trustworthiness assessment are conducted by the sensor nodes themselves, and the cluster head or gateway will receive the corrected data directly. Sometimes Distributed trust computation is also known as in-network detection or online detection. Distributed trust computation is also known as in-network or online detection method. The data trustworthiness is calculated by the edge sensor itself in online detection method, then forward the corresponding trusted data to sink node or cluster head. For online detection method, there is no need of a centralized physical object for managing trust score. Each node of the system is responsible for calculating the trusted score and coordinating with a neighbor for trust computation. This type of architecture is more suitable compared to the centralized approach. Because a single point of failure will not affect trust management which is the main shortcoming of centralized architecture. To achieve a reliable and robust solution, hybrid trust computation is also possible by the combination of centralized and distributed architecture [13,18].

4.5   Trust Aggregation Method

Trust aggregation is the evidence of trust gathering by self-observation or feedback from adjacent sensor nodes [19,20]. The trust ammunition is obtained at various places such as root node, cluster head, neighbor node, a sink node, and so on. Popular trust aggregation methods in the literature use the following techniques:

Weighted Sum (WS): A weighted sum is a traditional approach to aggregate proof or evidence. The weighted sum design is the easiest way applied to aggregate trust score. It is the most adopted method for measuring trust score [18,21]. Weighted Sum operates by multiplying the parts via the specified weight. Finally, it adds all the events collectively as a trust score for the trust score.

Discrete Models: This method used human's common wisdom or knowledge instead of utilizing any actual computational paradigm to estimate the level of trustworthiness of an item. For instance, a heuristic-based strategy can be used to determine the trust score [11, 20].

Regression Analysis (RA): Regression analysis is a way of aggregating trust scores by examining the associations among data. It is a statistical technique for measuring the correlations amongst variables. It can also be applied to predict the relationships between trust and variables portraying the node behavior [4, 25, 26]. A score is calculated based on an estimate of the relationship between the trust factor and a group of other variables that affect trust.

Probabilistic Models: Probability models take the probability of the appearance of an event rather than the value of direct discrete input. Although, several algorithms estimate probability as a measure of inferring trust score. Bayesian Reasoning (BI) and Belief Theory (BT) are the most popular probability models for trust computing. Bayesian reasoning (BI) is a widespread trust computing method because it is easy and has a sound statistical foundation [2, 22]. Belief Theory is a General Framework for Uncertain Reasoning and Probability. It is also known as Evidence Theory or Dempster Shafer Theory (DST) [23]. It produces a way to use Dempster's rules to aggregate and trust scores from different evidence.

Game Theory (GT): Game theory involves obtaining decisions between two or more decision-makers involved in a particular competition. It can also be used when competition rules predicted conclusively [5].

Machine Learning (ML): Machine learning techniques can be applied to interpret and estimate the ultimate behavior of objects in the IoT/CPS based system on analyzing their antecedent activities. Popular machine learning algorithms to gain the dynamic behavior of an entity are Hidden Markov Model (HMM), Artificial Neural Network (ANN), K-Nearest Neighbors Algorithm (KNN), Support-vector machine (SVM), Compressed kNN (CKNN), Linear Decision Tree (DT), Discriminate Analysis (LDA), Auto-encoder (AE), and so on [24, 27, 28]

Flow Dynamic (FD): In Flow Dynamic (FD) model, trust is computed in an iterative manner taking into account the long chain of transitivity within objects. Calculation of trust score regards the views of distinct entities in the system. The incoming and outgoing streams on the object are used to update the trust score of that item [29, 30].

Graph Theory Model: Graph Theory Models: To measure the degree of trust for an object, Centrality and Distance are frequently practiced in Graph Theory. Centrality outlines the consequence of an object by estimating in-degree and out-degree while Distance between two items describes connectivity between them. Eigen Trust is the most popular method in graph-based trust estimation [29, 30].

Fuzzy Logic (FL): Fuzzy logic is a method of multivalued logic. It deals with approximation rather than fixed and exact reasoning. FL has values from 0 to 1 for trust score aggregation. In addition, FL implements different rules for reasoning with fuzzy criteria [20, 34].

Data Mining: Data Mining methods have been used in various forms to assess trust, especially for the analysis of large data, such as privacy protection based on multi-level trust, which identifies trust, distrust, and privacy. In addition, it analyzes trust relationships in a big volume of data on social networking applications such as Facebook and Twitter. It also evaluates trust behavior pattern of objects based on a statistical method called logit regression [24, 28].

4.6 Trust Establishment

Trust establishment refers to how ultimately trust scores derive from multiple attributes. There are two aspects to trust-building, namely, single trust and multi-trust. Single trust means that only one trust attribute is considered when calculating the overall trust score. In contrast, multiple trust factors are used by multi-trust institutions in calculating the overall trust value of data. Most existing works use a multi-trust attribute in the calculation of trust scores and choose two attributes such as communication, node awareness, power, and node honesty on average [9, 19].

4.7 Trust Results

Trust results/decision is an element of data trustworthiness computation, which involves how to describe the result to the requester [11, 18] Trust results also called "Trust formation" which relates to how to form a global trust from multiple trust attributes. The trust result is applied to express the trustiness status of a node and data. There are three ways to describe a result as binary, fractional, or a series/range of values. Binary means that the result or data can only exist in two types: trusted or distrusted. As a result, only trusted data can be selected for further processing in the binary decision. For Range, this means that the calculated data trustworthiness value can fall within any possible confidence Range. This is a bit like the Richter scale, in which more than two options are used to determine trust values. Fraction trust output gives more flexible trust values to the user or requester or the application layer. Fractional trust output provides more flexible trust values for the user, requester, or application layer. For instance, from -1 to $+1$ ranges of fraction values, where a trust score from

−1 to −0.3, −0.3 to +0.4, and 0.4 to 1, indicates untrustworthy, uncertain, and a trustworthy, respectively [12,32].

4.8 Update and Maintenance

The ultimate stage of data trustworthiness taxonomy is the preservation of trustworthiness of things in the system. In order to maintain the recent behavior of an entity/node, its trust score and data must be updated and maintained regularly [18,19]. Especially in dynamic situations, the behavior of devices/objects in the Internet of things is not immutable throughout time. Therefore, the trust score for nodes and data needs to be updated periodically [31]. If the updated period is very long, then we cannot interpret the current state of nodes and data accurately. Generally, there are two scenarios for trust update and maintenance, namely, event-driven and time-driven [33,35]. In the event-driven approach, trust for the device can be updated when an event is encountered. While in a time-driven design, evidence such as self-observation or recommendation for an entity and data are regularly collected, and trust is updated using trust aggregation methods.

5   Conclusions and Future Directions

We need trustworthy data for trustworthy cyber systems before to invest cost and time for processing, storing, and transmitting of unsecured and untrustworthy data. Various relevant techniques have been suggested that can be applied as constructing blocks for data trustworthiness in IoT/CPS application. Based on the literature, it can be concluded that the research on the data trustworthiness in IoT/CPS domain is still in its infancy and limited work has been done so far. Due to the dynamic and complex IoT environment, data trustworthiness [e.g., the data is free from error, up to date, and originate from reputable source] is always preferable. However, assuring data trustworthiness is not an effortless task to identify fault, noise, cyber-attack, and real-world facts. Therefore, more works are required since data trustworthiness is prevalent in IoT to ensure efficient and accurate decision-making. Consequently, more work needs to be done for useful and accurate decision. The following are some directions for future practices in assessing and computing the reliability of IoT and CPS data:

(a) Much of the work to date has focused on the reliability of data based on human data estimation or quantification. More considerable attention should also be placed to the data trustworthiness of sensor-based data in a dynamic and complex IoT/CPS environment.
(b) Majority of the work to date has taken into account the continuity of near real-time processing of the Internet of things. Attention should be paid to calculate the reliability of the data in real-time. In addition, due to the resource-constrained nature of the sensor, such a technique is required to compute trust scores in a short period without storing them as historical data for a long time.

(c) The use of a direct and indirect trust is not sufficient for an independent assessment of trust. An effective hybrid trust model should be built, which contains attributes of direct and indirect trust.

(d) For trust computing methods, distributed methods are more feasible because they do not need to wait for trust reports from centralized locations and only send real data and discard the faulty data. It can also solve the high data transmission and latency problems. Therefore, higher emphasis should be given to distributed and hybrid (i.e., which contains attributes of centralized and distributed) trust computing methods.

(e) For trust aggregation, Weighted Sum, Bayesian Reasoning, Belief Theory, and Regression Analysis are most commonly used for simple implementations, but they cannot correctly and precisely ascertain trust values. A more efficient work should be done further consideration such as machine learning, fuzzy logic, and data mining techniques to solve all these limitations. More efficient work, such as machine learning, fuzzy logic, and data mining techniques, should be done to address all these limitations. For example, machine learning algorithms can be used for trust aggregation and event detection at different layers of IoT, such as sensor (node) level, edge (sink node) level, and the cloud level.

(f) It is highly recommended that machine learning techniques make decisions faster in a distributed network or at the sensor level. However, taking a faster decision without the need for a centralized entity (e.g., cloud) still presents different challenges.

(g) It is recommended to develop a system that can distinguish data faults, noise, and cyberattacks during the data life cycle (e.g., during data collection, data transmission, and cloud data storage).

Acknowledgments. This work was supported in part by the National Natural Science Foundation of China under Grant 61632009 and 61872097, in part by the Guangdong Provincial Natural Science Foundation under Grant 2017A030308006, and in part by the High-Level Talents Program of Higher Education in Guangdong Province under Grant 2016ZJ01.

References

1. Cisco: Internet of Things (IoT) - Cisco IoT Product Portfolio - Cisco. http://www.cisco.com/c/en/us/solutions/internet-ofthings/iot-products.html. Accessed 23 May 2019
2. Bao, F., Chen, I.-R.: Dynamic trust management for internet of things applications. In: Proceedings of International Workshop on Self-aware Internet of Things, pp. 1–6, September 2012
3. Aggarwal, C.C., Ashish, N., Sheth, A.: The Internet of Things: a survey from the data-centric perspective. In: Aggarwal, C. (ed.) Managing and Mining Sensor Data. Springer, Boston, MA (2013). https://doi.org/10.1007/978-1-4614-6309-2_12
4. Wang, Y., Lu, Y.C., Chen, I.R., Cho, J.H., Swami, A.: LogitTrust: a logit regression-based trust model for mobile ad hoc networks. In: 6th ASE International Conference on Privacy, Security, Risk and Trust, Boston, MA, December 2014

5. Lim, H.-S., Ghinita, G., Bertino, E., Kantarcioglu, M.: A gametheoretic approach for high-assurance of data trustworthiness in sensor networks. In: 2012 IEEE 28th International Conference on Data (2012)
6. Li, M., Jiang, W., Li, K.: Recommendation systems in real applications: algorithm and parallel architecture. In: Wang, G., Ray, I., Alcaraz Calero, J., Thampi, S. (eds.) SpaCCS 2016. LNCS, vol. 10066, pp. 45–58. Springer, Cham (2016). https://doi.org/10.1007/978-3-319-49148-6_5
7. Karkouch, A., Mousannif, H., Al Moatassime, H., Noel, T.: Data quality in internet of things: a state-of-the-art survey. J. Netw. Comput. Appl. **73**, 57–81 (2016)
8. Bhuiyan, M.Z.A., Wu, J.: Trustworthy and protected data collection for event detection using networked sensing systems. In: 2016 IEEE 37th Sarnoff Symposium. IEEE (2016)
9. Bhuiyan, M.Z.A., Wang, G., Choo, K.-K.R.: Secured data collection for a cloud-enabled structural health monitoring system. In: 2016 IEEE 18th International Conference on High Performance Computing and Communications; IEEE 14th International Conference on Smart City; IEEE 2nd International Conference on Data Science and Systems (HPCC/SmartCity/DSS). IEEE (2016)
10. Saied, Y.B., Olivereau, A., Zeghlache, D., Laurent, M.: Trust management system design for the Internet of Things: a context-aware and multi-service approach. Comput. Secur. **39**, 351–365 (2014)
11. Hui-hui, D., Ya-jun, G., Zhong-qiang, Y., Hao, C.: A wireless sensor networks based on multi-angle trust of node. In: International Forum on Information Technology and Applications, 2009. IFITA-2009, vol. 1, pp. 28–31 (2009)
12. Sathe, S., Papaioannou, T.G., Jeung, H., Aberer, K.: A survey of model-based sensor data acquisition and management. In: Aggarwal, C. (ed.) Managing and Mining Sensor Data. Springer, Boston (2013). https://doi.org/10.1007/978-1-4614-6309-2_2
13. Javed, N., Wolf, T.: Automated sensor verification using outlier detection in the Internet of Things. In: 2012 32nd International Conference on Distributed Computing Systems Workshops (ICDCSW), pp. 291–296 (2012)
14. Bao, F., Chen, I.R.: Dynamic trust management for the Internet of Things applications. In: International Workshop on Self-Aware Internet of Things, San Jose, USA, September 2012
15. Elahi, H., Wang, G., Li, X.: Smartphone bloatware: an overlooked privacy problem. In: Wang, G., Atiquzzaman, M., Yan, Z., Choo, K.-K.R. (eds.) SpaCCS 2017. LNCS, vol. 10656, pp. 169–185. Springer, Cham (2017). https://doi.org/10.1007/978-3-319-72389-1_15
16. Makhdoom, I., et al.: Anatomy of threats to the Internet of Things. In: IEEE Communications Surveys and Tutorials, vol. 21, no. 2, pp. 1636–1675 (2018)
17. Arif, M., Wang, G., Wang, T., Peng, T.: SDN-based secure VANETs communication with fog computing. In: Wang, G., Chen, J., Yang, L. (eds.) SpaCCS 2018. LNCS, vol. 11342. Springer, Cham (2018). https://doi.org/10.1007/978-3-030-05345-1_4
18. Haron, N., Jaafar, J., Aziz, I.A., Hassan, M.H., Shapiai, M. I.: Data trustworthiness in Internet of Things: a taxonomy and future directions. In 2017 IEEE Conference on Big Data and Analytics (ICBDA), Kuching, pp. 25–30 (2017)
19. Tang, L.A., et al.: Trustworthiness analysis of sensor data in cyber-physical systems. J. Comput. Syst. Sci. **79**(3), 383–401 (2013)
20. Guo, J., Chen, R.: A classification of trust computation models for service-oriented internet of things systems. In: IEEE International Conference on Services Computing (SCC), vol. 2015, pp. 324–331 (2015)

21. Pouryazdan, M., Kantarci, B., Soyata, T., Foschini, L., Song, H.: Quantifying user reputation scores, data trustworthiness, and user incentives in mobile crowd-sensing. IEEE Access **5**, 1382–1397 (2017)

22. Chen, I.-R., Bao, F., Guo, J.: Trust-based service management for social Internet of Things systems. IEEE Trans. Dependable Secure Comput. **13**(6), 684–696 (2015)

23. Josang, A.: A logic for uncertain probabilities. Int. J. Uncertainty Fuzziness Knowl.-Based Syst. **9**(3), 279–311 (2001)

24. Anjum, B., Rajangam, M., Perros, H., Fan, W.: Filtering Unfair Users: A Hidden Markov Model Approach. SciTePress, Setúbal (2015)

25. ur Rahman, H., Azzedin, F., Shawahna, A., Sajjad, F., Abdulrahman, A.S.: Performance evaluation of vdi environment. In 2016 Sixth International Conference on Innovative Computing Technology (INTECH), pp. 104–109. IEEE, August 2016

26. ur Rahman, H., Wang, G., Chen, J., Jiang, H.: Performance evaluation of hypervisors and the effect of virtual CPU on Performance. In: 2018 IEEE SmartWorld, Ubiquitous Intelligence & Computing, Advanced & Trusted Computing, Scalable Computing & Communications, Cloud & Big Data Computing, Internet of People and Smart City Innovation (SmartWorld/SCALCOM/UIC/ATC/CBDCom/IOP/SCI), pp. 772–779. IEEE, October 2018

27. Zong, B., Xu, F., Jiao, J., Lv, J.: A broker-assisting trust and reputation system based on artficial neural network. In: IEEE International Conference on Systems, Man and Cybernetics (SMC), pp. 4710–4715, October 2009

28. Liu, X., Datta, A., Lim, E.P.: Computational Trust Models and Machine Learning. CRC Press, Boca Raton (2014)

29. Page, L., Brin, S., Motwani, R., Winograd, T.: The pagerank citation ranking: bringing order to the web. Technical report, Stanford Digital Library Technologies Project (1998)

30. Kamvar, S.D., Schlosser, M.T., Molina, H.G.: The EigenTrust algorithm for reputation management in P2P networks. In: Proceedings of the 12th International World Wide Web Conference, Budapest, May 2003

31. Carbone, M., Nielsen, M., Sassone, V.: A formal model for trust in dynamic networks. In: Proceedings of International Conference on Software Engineering and Formal Methods (SEFM 2003), Brisbane, September 2003

32. Dhulipala, V.S., Karthik, N., Chandrasekaran, R.M.: A novel heuristic approach based trust worthy architecture for wireless sensor networks. Wireless Personal Commun. **70**(1), 189–205 (2013)

33. Bertino, E.: Data trustworthiness—approaches and research challenges. In: Garcia-Alfaro, J., et al. (eds.) DPM/QASA/SETOP -2014. LNCS, vol. 8872, pp. 17–25. Springer, Cham (2015). https://doi.org/10.1007/978-3-319-17016-9_2

34. Khan, M.F., Wang, G., Bhuiyan, M.Z.A.: Wi-Fi frequency selection concept for effective coverage in collapsed structures. Fut. Gener. Comput.Syst. **97**, 409–424 (2019)

35. Han, G., Jiang, J., Shu, L., Niu, J., Chao, H.-C.: Management and applications of trust in wireless sensor networks: a survey. J. Comput. Syst. Sci. **80**(3), 602–617 (2014)

Urban Computing and Big Data

Optimization of Score-Level Biometric Data Fusion by Constraint Construction Training

Andrea F. Abate[1], Carmen Bisogni[1(✉)], Aniello Castiglione[2], Riccardo Distasi[1], and Alfredo Petrosino[2]

[1] Department of Computer Science, University of Salerno, 84084 Fisciano, Italy
{andaba,cbisogni,ricdis}@unisa.it
[2] Department of Science and Technology, University of Naples Parthenope, 80133 Naples, Italy
castiglione@ieee.org, alfredo.petrosino@uniparthenope.it

Abstract. This paper illustrates a multibiometric method to optimize the fusion of multiple biometries at the score level. The fused score is a linear combination of the individual scores. As a consequence, well-known traditional linear optimization techniques become suitable to determine the constants to be used in the linear combination. The proposed method uses training to optimize the constants. After experimenting with dummy datasets, a fresh multi-biometric dataset of infrared images has been prepared. The data has been subject to extra distortion and occlusions, and then used to train first the individual biometric systems, based on GoogleNet CNNs, and then the fusion engine. Results obtained through the proposed method have an accuracy over 90% in the best configuration. The system at present performs user verification, but an extension to identification can be obtained by reworking the constraints in the optimization problem. A sketch of such extension is provided.

Keywords: Multibiometric · Score-level fusion · Optimization · Training · IR · Fingerprint · Face biometric · Ear biometric · CNN

1 Introduction

One of the issues with biometric systems is obtaining as much resistance to spoofing as possible, because impostors can gain undue advantage by impersonating the legitimate user [1]. A well known example of possible spoofing is the fingerprint vulnerability found in several mobile devices [2]. If users tie their bank account to their fingerprint, the 'undue advantage' becomes access to the victim's funds.

One possible way to make biometric systems more robust is to use multiple biometries—be them different traits or the same trait as captured by different physical sensors. Multibiometric systems have been attracting research interest approximately since 2009 [3,4]. Such systems consider more than one biometric

© Springer Nature Singapore Pte Ltd. 2019
G. Wang et al. (Eds.): iSCI 2019, CCIS 1122, pp. 167–179, 2019.
https://doi.org/10.1007/978-981-15-1301-5_14

trait, while single biometry systems just use one. The multiple traits considered by a multibiometric system might also consist in the same trait acquired by different devices. Of course, once we decide to use multiple traits for increased robustness, we are left with the problem of how to actually merge the different pieces of data. Section 2 discusses the fusion strategies adopted in other methods, while the proposed system is detailed in Sect. 3. Section 4 describes the results obtained from experiments performed to assess the effectiveness of the system. Finally, Sect. 5 contains a few concluding remarks.

2   Background

When designing a multibiometric system, an important aspect is the order and the way in which biometric inputs are processed.

The main topologies for fusion are the following.

– Serial or cascade mode, in which one biometry at a time is examined;
– Parallel mode, in which biometries are examined simultaneously;
– Hierarchical mode, in which the classifier has a tree-like structure.

More information about biometric data fusion, including a more detailed taxonomy, can be found in [5].

At least as important as the topology is the point in the workflow where fusion is performed. As shown in Fig. 1, there are two broad categories: fusion before matching and fusion after matching—see [6] for more.

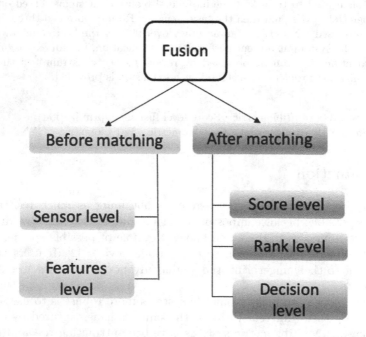

Fig. 1. Fusion before or after matching.

2.1   Fusion Before Matching

Fusion before matching may be performed at the level of sensors or features. When done at the sensor level, the fusion procedure merges data from various sensors, most often about the same biometric trait. This approach is not too common, although it does got used in some hybrid systems [7]. In these cases, there is often competition with other approaches in order to improve the Equal Error Rate (EER). EER is one of the main indicators of robustness in biometric systems: the value where the rate of false positives equals the rate of false negatives.

When fusion is done at the level of features, different features are extracted via different techniques. They are then processed in order to produce a new feature array. Examples of this approach using neural networks can be found in [8,9]. In [8], there are network types: one is fully connected and the other bilinear. The system generates a shared representation from which a cancelable template is obtained. This helps select a set of discriminating features. The work described in [9] focuses on multibiometric system for autenticating mobile users. Three frameworks are discussed: (a) early fusion, where deep feature representation from pretrained CNN models are concatenated and fused using machine learning classifiers; (b) an intermediate multi-biometric fusion with layers of a CNN being merged, and (c) a late fusion, where the output of the various CNN models are probabilities, eventually fused by the product rule.

2.2   Fusion After Matching

Fusion after matching can be carried out at the score level, rank level or decision level.

Decision level fusion is the latest possible stage. After feature extraction, matching and recognition, each biometric subsystem gives a response as to the authenticity of the subject. The final decision combines the individual response, usually by means of logical or Boolean operators.

The most common contemporary use of decision level fusion is in cryptosystems. Typical examples are multibiometric cryptosystems that manage cloud uploads subject to multibiometric authentication [10], or crypto key generation that uses multiple biometrics with decision level fusion [11]. The key, in turn, is used to protect access to biometric templates.

Rank level fusion means the classifiers rank the classes, with higher rank implying a better match, and the rankings are combined to obtain the final rank. These techniques can be refined in several ways. For instance, a hierarchy of levels can be created, and the processing steps can be arranged in series and in parallel. See [12] for such a system and for an overview of rank level fusion in general.

Score level fusion is what is being used in the present work. With score level fusion, different algorithms produce individual scores, possibly based on different biometric traits. These scores are combined to obtain the final score, which determines the final decision. Score level fusion methods can be divided into three main categories: density based, transformation based, and classifier based.

The individual scores can be fused by a simple sum, as in [13], but a generally more effective way to combine them is a weighted sum, as seen in [14] and [15]. Determining the weights is the next conceptual issue. The weights are based on the score's reliability in [14].

The fusion techniques used in score level fusion are the most diverse found in fusion. The present paper addresses one possible way to determine the score coefficients in a way than can be called optimal.

3   The Method

In this model, each biometric system provides an accuracy score between 0 and 1. The actual origin of the individual scores is immaterial for the discussion. They could be derived from neural networks, as has been the case for our experiments, or other methods. What matters is that we have available a quantity of labeled data where we know if the subject is genuine or an impostor.

One of the key point of the presented method is the use of more than one biometric classifier but only one final decision function as the fusion of the classifiers. Each biometric classifier is trained on genuine and impostor subjects, labels the letters and distinguishing one subject from another. The final decision function will work properly to distinguish genuine from impostors regardless of who the subject is, understanding and weighing biometric classifiers reliability. Due to this peculiar configuration, in the fusion process, we will use one classifier in total instead of one for each subject.

Let n be the number of biometric recognizers, and m the number of labeled samples. We arrange the scores into an $m \times n$ matrix A of values between 0 and 1. Each row contains the n biometric scores of a subject, while each column contains a specific biometric score for all m subjects.

Let G be the binary array of m labels, so that $g_i = 0$ if the i-th subject is an impostor and $g_i = 1$ if the i-th subject is genuine.

$$A = \begin{bmatrix} a_{11} & a_{12} & \dots & a_{1n} \\ \vdots & \vdots & \ddots & \vdots \\ a_{m1} & a_{m2} & \dots & a_{mn} \end{bmatrix} ; \quad G = \begin{bmatrix} g_1 \\ \vdots \\ g_m \end{bmatrix} . \tag{1}$$

Let us consider the following control function:

$$f_i(x_1, x_2, \dots, x_n) = x_1 a_{i1} + x_2 a_{i2} + \dots + x_n a_{in}, \tag{2}$$

that is, a linear combination of scores, where $a_{i1}, a_{i2}, \dots, a_{in}$ are the biometric scores of the i-th subject and $x_1, x_2, \dots, x_n$ are the the the constants we need to determine in order to have the function in (2) actually discriminate between genuine and impostor subjects. We impose the following conditions:

1. In order to represent scores as percentages, $f_i(\cdots)$ should have values between 0 and 1.

2. In order to detect genuine subjects, $f_i(\cdots)$ should be greater than 0.5 if the scores $a_{i1}, a_{i2}, \ldots, a_{in}$ come from a genuine subject.
3. In order to detect impostor subjects, $f_i(\cdots)$ should be smaller than 0.5 if the scores $a_{i1}, a_{i2}, \ldots, a_{in}$ come from an impostor subject.

From Condition 1, we have

$$f_i(x_1, x_2, \ldots, x_n) > 0, \quad 1 \leq i \leq m \tag{3}$$

and

$$f_i(x_1, x_2, \ldots, x_n) < 1, \quad 1 \leq i \leq m. \tag{4}$$

From the second condition, we have

$$f_i(x_1, x_2, \ldots, x_n) > 0.5 \text{ iff } g_i = 1. \tag{5}$$

From the third condition, we have

$$f_i(x_1, x_2, \ldots, x_n) < 0.5 \text{ iff } g_i = 0. \tag{6}$$

To turn this into a linear optimization problem, we have to define an objective function to minimize and rewrite constraints in the canonical form $Ax \leq B$.

The objective function does not matter much: since we are just interested in one of the n-uples $(x_1, x_2, \ldots, x_n)$, it is not important that the n-uple actually minimizes a specific function. Therefore, we will choose a simple linear function as our dummy objective:

$$\min \sum_{1 \leq i \leq m} x_i. \tag{7}$$

In order to obtain constraints of the form $Ax \leq B$, we have to multiply Eqs. (3) and (5) by -1. If the number of genuine subjects in our sample is p, Eqs. (3) and (4) will give us m inequalities each, while Eqs. (5) and (6) will give us p and $m - p$ inequalities respectively, for a total of $3m$ constraints.

Rather than the simplex algorithm, which finds an optimal solution by traversing the edges between vertices on a polyhedral set, we chose the interior point method that moves through the interior of the feasible region. This is because the interior point method is preferable when the number of constraints is much larger than the number of variables.

The optimization algorithm chosen automatically searches for non negative values of x_i and tolerate few violation of constraints (5) and (6), up to 5% of constraints, in order to obtain solution anyway.

It is clear that solutions like $x = [0\ 0\ 1]$, $x = [0\ 1\ 0]$ and $x = [0\ 0\ 1]$ of the optimization function, in the case of three biometric traits, will never be taken under consideration in our method, even if a biometric trait outperfom the other two. This is because we want to obtain a system that, fusing three biometric traits outperform the best biometric classifier used. What we have just said is confirmed by experiments set out in Sect. 4. We never obtained solutions as above in our experiments and the fusion system outperform the better biometric classification algorithm chosen.

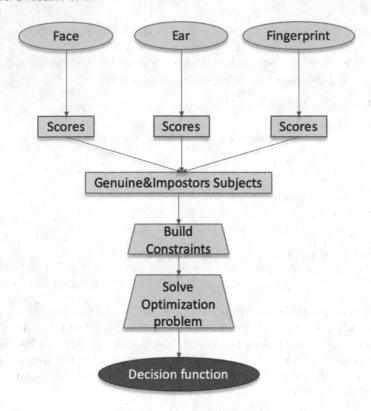

Fig. 2. Workflow of the proposed method.

The workflow of the method is depicted in Fig. 2.

The proposed method, and in particular the training set as it has been built, is suitable for verification. That is, merely verifying the identity of a subject. The system is not suited to identification, that is, recognizing who the subject is. Indeed, the array of labels G in Eq. (1) only contains 1 for genuine and 0 for impostor. When subjects have to be recognized by the system, each individual biometric systems will provide a recognition score, and our control function, trained on genuine and impostor scores from all the subjects, will check the subject's identity. The training is only focused on learning the optimal coefficients for fusion. The only relevant answer the system provides is whether a given set of scores belongs to a genuine or impostor subject.

The system can be extended into performing identification. This will require redefining the constraints by changing the labels in the array G. One possible way to do that would be defining a new control function $f'()$ with a larger range, depending on the number of subjects in the database. As an intuitive explanation, imagine two genuine subjects with id's a and b, and an impostor class with id x. The constraints could be reformulated as follows:

$$f_i'(x_1, x_2, \ldots, x_n) > 0 \text{ iff } b_i = a \tag{8}$$
$$f_i'(x_1, x_2, \ldots, x_n) < 1 \text{ iff } b_i = a \tag{9}$$

$$f_i'(x_1, x_2, \ldots, x_n) > 1 \text{ iff } b_i = b \tag{10}$$
$$f_i'(x_1, x_2, \ldots, x_n) < 2 \text{ iff } b_i = b \tag{11}$$

$$f_i'(x_1, x_2, \ldots, x_n) > 2 \text{ iff } b_i = x \tag{12}$$

The constraints in (3) would stay the same, and the constraints in (4) could be disregarded altogether. If the number of impostor samples is p, there will be m total inequalities for (8), (10) and (12), $m - p$ total inequalities for (9) and (11), and m inequalities for (3), totaling $3m - p$ inequalities. The control function $f'()$ will assume values in the first, the second or the last range depending on the subjects to which the biometric traits belong.

4   Experiments

At first, we did not have enough real scores and ground truth data to estimate the parameters for a specific multibiometric system, so in the preliminary design stage, we proceeded with randomly generated scores and ground truth. After a working proof of concept, we built an infrared dataset with three biometric traits: face, ear, fingerprint. Our choice of traits was motivated by previous experience with similar datasets in both the context of data fusion and of single trait biometry [16, 17].

4.1   The IR-FEF Dataset

A dataset of infrared images of faces, ears and fingerprints (IR-FEF for InfraRed Face-Ear-Fingerprint) has been built using two devices. For face and ear images, an infrared IP camera has been used in conditions of very low light. The fingerprints were acquired by a 4000B scanner by DigitalPersona U.are.U. There were 15 unique subjects, but 20 images were acquired for each biometry, totaling 3000 images. In the case of face and ear, the subjects were asked to vary their pose allowing 3 degrees of freedom for head rotation. The fingerprint scans were varied by systematically changing the angle of their index finger on the sensor's surface.

An example of the three biometries obtained by this procedure is shown in Fig. 3. The image dataset has also been converted into a feature dataset, so it can be distributed while maintaining the subjects' privacy.

We used IR images instead of RGB in order to simulate a more competitive light condition widely used in security and video surveillance. However, we found the images to be too "clean" to approximate real life forensic use. Therefore, we

Fig. 3. Example from the multibiometric dataset IR-FEF.

Fig. 4. Example of filter effects: clear image vs. motioned image

added some noise to the images and processed them with blur and motion filters. An example of such treatment can be seen in Fig. 4.

As for the fingerprints scans, they were processed by superimposing some random partial occlusions, as depicted in Fig. 5

Fig. 5. Example of occlusions in fingerprints: clear vs. occluded fingerprint scan

In order to train the new fusion method, we needed individual scores for the single biometric traits; that is, we needed 3 trained single biometry systems. Our choice fell on GoogleNet, so we adapted 3 networks to our data by transfer learning.

After running the networks, the input data for our system—namely the scores obtained from the GoogleNet networks—were used for training and testing the fusion method. As groundtruth we used the ID of each subject from 1 to 15 and the ID 0 for impostors scores obtained combining biometric trait of different subject. And then we binarize this data by assigning 1 to genuine scores from 1 to 15 and remaining 0 for impostors.

4.2   Results

We are interested in a feasible solution of the optimization problem. Feasible solutions are generally more than one, e.g. two or more. This mean that it is possible to obtain different accuracy value in different experiments with the same settings due to this property. It is for this reason that we perform the method 10 time with the same partition in training set and testing set and we display in Table 1 the mean accuracy and time obtained. It is important to emphasise that to have a more generically result we randomize the training set and test set at each experiment. As an example, the mean value of accuracy with a fixed number of training sample, is the result of different random partition of the dataset with the same number of training sample.

The accuracy, as usual, is the percentage of genuine and impostors properly classified. We used the formula:

$$acc_{test} = \frac{(N_{test} - Err) * 100}{N_{test}} \tag{13}$$

where N_{test} is the number of samples in the testing set and Err is the number of errors committed by the system. In other words, Err is the sum of genuine subjects misclassified as impostor and impostor subjects misclassified as genuine, namely false negative and false positive, respectively.

Table 1. Results with different training partition.

Training samples	Test samples	Mean accuracy in %	Mean time in seconds
50	2823	99.5360	0.1953
100	2773	99.6538	0.5212
150	2723	99.6940	0.8873
200	**2673**	**99.3004**	**0.0839**
250	2623	98.8944	0.0645
300	2573	98.6203	0.0755
350	2523	98.1490	0.0901
400	2473	98.6090	0.1088
450	2423	98.3203	0.1124
500	2373	98.4576	0.1359

As we can appreciate from Table 1 the mean accuracy increase until 150 training samples, together with computational mean time. For 200 training samples accuracy slowly decreases and time quickly decreases and increase from 250 onwards. It is for this reason that we find the better configuration at 200 training samples, 2673 test samples with a mean accuracy of 99.3 and a mean time of 0.08.

In Table 2 we compare these results with the accuracy of the single biometric methods, as mentioned above, performing transfer learning on the GoogleNet. It is clear that the combination of these three biometric traits through the proposed method outperform each single biometric system. Furthermore the computational time to obtain the decision function or, in other words, the weights, is more than acceptable.

Table 2. Accuracy of each biometric trait through GoogleNet compared to the proposed method.

Biometric trait	Accuracy in %
Face	93
Fingerprint	64
Ear	89
Proposed method	**99.3**

Experiments has been performed on a MacBook Air, with a 2.2 GHz Intel Core i7 Processor and a Graphic Card Intel HD Graphics 6000 1536 MB.

In Sect. 3 we said that the threshold selected to build the constraints is 0.5. However, for the sake of completeness, we tested the method also with other threshold between 0.3 and 0.7 as can be seen in Table 3. The threshold 0.5 results being the better to reach high accuracy with the better configuration of 200 training samples. We repeat the experiments ten times for each threshold, as in previous experiments.

Table 3. Accuracy of different thresholds.

Threshold	Mean accuracy in %
0.3	93.92
0.4	98.68
0.5	**99.3**
0.6	98.94
0.7	99.21

This is a just work in progress at the moment, but the strong points are already evident:

- The training is extremely fast: less than a tenth of a second for 200 scores triplets.
- High reliable verification, over 99%.
- Remarkable robustness: these results were obtained with images that had been distorted and clipped.
- Low hardware requirements: computation has been purposely performed by second tier computer.

About the last point—low requirements, it is due to the linear formulation of the problem. The training phase is a linear programming problem, while testing is a simple matter of m additions and m multiplications. In this instance, $m = 3$, and the addition of more biometric traits is entirely possible, at the expense of a slightly harder training phase. Given the extremely quick training times, this does not appear to be a significant hindrance.

Evaluating the experiments, a few points that can be improved emerged along in an overall positive context.

- The system as it is only performs verification; not identification. However, it is possible to extend it to deal with identification, as sketched in the previous section. This will require additional work. Which is already under way.
- The dataset is based on 15 real persons only. However, for each person several photos and sensor readings were taken, so we made up a toy database of nearly 3000 individuals.
- Testing was limited to a single dataset, since in this initial phase it was only meant to assess the viability of the method; not to perfect it.

Neither of these negative points offers conceptual or practical difficulties, and indeed they are being worked upon already. Hopefully, more general results will follow.

5   Conclusions and Future Work

The presented method show a possible way to implement score-level fusion in multibiometric system. Actually, this method may be applied in each context in which we have scores to combine. The high accuracy reached encourage further research.

Can the system be modified to perform identification? It would take some work. First, the labels in G should be changed from zeros and ones to the ID codes of the subjects in the database. A single ID could be attributed to all impostors. The matrix A can remain unchanged. Then, the constraints would have to be redefined by expanding the range of the control function.

A larger dataset would also be appropriate for proper system validation. Furthermore, other optimization functions can bring interesting results. Instead of standard linear programming, we may use linear programming relaxation or try constraint separation. It is also possible to experiment with some heuristics.

References

1. Hosseini, S.: Fingerprint vulnerability: a survey. In: IEEE, 2018 4th International Conference on Web Research (ICWR). https://doi.org/10.1109/ICWR.2018.8387240
2. Galbally, J., Marcel, S., Fierrez, J.: Biometric antispoofing methods: a survey in face recognition. IEEE Access. 2, 1530–1552 (2014). https://doi.org/10.1109/ACCESS.2014.2381273
3. De Marsico, M., Distasi, R., Nappi, M., Riccio, D.: Fractal indexing in multimodal biometric contexts. In: Kocarev, L., Galias, Z., Lian, S. (eds.) Intelligent Computing Based on Chaos. Studies in Computational Intelligence, vol. 184. Springer, Heidelberg (2009). https://doi.org/10.1007/978-3-540-95972-4_5
4. De Marsico, M., Distasi, R., Nappi, M., Riccio, D.: Multiple traits for people identification: face, ear and fingerprints. In: Sencar, H.T., Kocarev, L., Galias, Z., Lian, S. (eds.) Intelligent Multimedia Analysis for Security Applications. Studies in Computational Intelligence, vol. 282, pp. 79–98. Springer, Heidelberg (2010). https://doi.org/10.1007/978-3-642-11756-5_4
5. Singh, S.A.: Review on multibiometrics: classifications, normalization and fusion levels. In: IEEE, 2018 International Conference on Advances in Computing and Communication Engineering (ICACCE). https://doi.org/10.1109/ICACCE.2018.8441727
6. Jaafar, H., Ramli, D.A.: A review of multibiometric system with fusion strategies and weighting factor. Int. J. Comput. Sci. Eng. (IJCSE) 2(4), 158–165 (2013)
7. Imran, M., Rao, A., Kumar, G.H.: A new hybrid approach for information fusion in multibiometric systems. In: IEEE, 2011 Third National Conference on Computer Vision, Pattern Recognition, Image Processing and Graphics. https://doi.org/10.1109/NCVPRIPG.2011.57
8. Talreja, V., Valenti, M.C., Nasrabadi, N.M.: Multibiometric secure system based on deep learning. In: 2017 IEEE Global Conference on Signal and Information Processing (GlobalSIP). https://doi.org/10.1109/GlobalSIP.2017.8308652
9. Rattani, A., Reddy, N., Derakhshani, R.: Multi-biometric convolutional neural networks for mobile user authentication. In: 2018 IEEE International Symposium on Technologies for Homeland Security (HST). https://doi.org/10.1109/THS.2018.8574173
10. Nair, V.S., Reshmypriya, G.N., Rubeena, M.M., Fasila, K.A.: Multibiometric cryptosystem based on decision level fusion for file uploading in cloud. In: IEEE, 2017 International Conference on Recent Advances in Electronics and Communication Technology (ICRAECT). https://doi.org/10.1109/ICRAECT.2017.19
11. Li, C., Hu, J., Pieprzyk, J., Susilo, W.: A new biocryptosystem-oriented security analysis framework and implementation of multibiometric cryptosystems based on decision level fusion. IEEE Trans. Inf. Forensics Secur. 10(6), 1193–1206 (2015). https://doi.org/10.1109/TIFS.2015.2402593
12. Sharma, R., Das, S., Joshi, P.: Rank level fusion in multibiometric systems. In: IEEE, 2015 Fifth National Conference on Computer Vision, Pattern Recognition, Image Processing and Graphics (NCVPRIPG). https://doi.org/10.1109/NCVPRIPG.2015.7489952
13. Kadri, F., Meraoumia, A., Bendjenna, H., Chitroub, S.: Palmprint & iris for a multibiometric authentication scheme using Log-Gabor filter response. In: IEEE, 2016 International Conference on Information Technology for Organizations Development (IT4OD). https://doi.org/10.1109/IT4OD.2016.7479287

14. Kabir, W., Ahmad, M.O., Swamy, M.N.S.: Score reliability based weighting technique for score-level fusion in multi-biometric systems. In: 2016 IEEE Winter Conference on Applications of Computer Vision (WACV). https://doi.org/10.1109/WACV.2016.7477580

15. Patil, A.P., Bhalke, D.G.: Fusion of fingerprint, palmprint and iris for person identification. In: IEEE, 2016 International Conference on Automatic Control and Dynamic Optimization Techniques (ICACDOT). https://doi.org/10.1109/ICACDOT.2016.7877730

16. Abate, A.F., Nappi, M., Riccio, D., De Marsico, M.: Face, ear and fingerprint: designing multibiometric architectures. In: 14th International Conference on Image Analysis and Processing (ICIAP 2007) (2007)

17. Abate, A.F., Nappi, M., Ricciardi, S.: Smartphone enabled person authentication based on ear biometrics and arm gesture. In: 2016 IEEE International Conference on Systems, Man, and Cybernetics (SMC) (2016)

Dynamic Online Course Recommendation Based on Course Network and User Network

Xixi Yang and Wenjun Jiang[✉][iD]

College of Computer Science and Electronic Engineering, Hunan University,
Changsha 410082, China
{yangxixi,jiangwenjun}@hnu.edu.cn

Abstract. E-learning attracts much attentions and gains sustainable development in recent years. Course recommendation tries to recommend proper courses to users from a large number of online courses. Existing works usually focus on improving the accuracy, neglecting to match the recommended course with user's knowledge level. It results in a high enrollment rate but low grades, indicating poor learning results. Moreover, course recommendation also faces the challenges of sparse user-rating matrix and sparse social learning network. In this paper, we try to recommend courses that are fit to user's knowledge level. To this end, we (1) propose to construct social learning network, for which we first build the user network and the course network, and combine them together; (2) explore the social learning network to extend the user-rating matrix by HITS algorithm, so as to overcome the sparsity challenge; (3) sort the recommendation list to meet user's knowledge level, exploiting the course network. Experiments in a real e-learning dataset show that our model performs well in online course recommendation, and the learning results are better, validating the effectiveness of considering user's knowledge level.

Keywords: User network · Course network · User-rating matrix · User's knowledge level · Dynamic course recommendation

1 Introduction

E-learning has been well developed all over the world. Take MOOCs (Massive Open Online Courses) for example, 2012 has been regarded as the year of MOOCs [25]. In China, Xuetangx [3], Chinese University MOOC [2], NETEASE open class [1] have millions of learners. Foreign MOOCs website like Coursera, Edx and Udacity have been welcomed all over the world. What's more, the quantity of users and courses in the web site we have mentioned above gain a continual growth. But the numerous course in E-learning website makes it difficult for users to choose, which makes online course recommendation necessary [22].

Existing course recommendation methods can be divided into three types: (1) CF (collaborative filtering)-based recommendation; (2) content based

G. Wang et al. (Eds.): iSCI 2019, CCIS 1122, pp. 180–196, 2019.
https://doi.org/10.1007/978-981-15-1301-5_15

recommendation which includes course concept or course relation; (3) hybrid approach which in includes machine learning, LDA (latent dirichlet allocation) and others.

Apart from all the achievements in online course recommendation. There are also some problems in online course recommendation that need further exploration. Among all MOOCs web site in China, only Chinese University MOOC provides user with rating module. And the rating matrix in Chinese MOOC is sparse and most of them reach almost or exact full five score. Existing E-learning course recommendation ignore the importance of recommending user with suitable course considering user's knowledge level. At the same time, in E-learning, course recommendation researches about user network, course network and their combination have ignored.

In this paper, we intend to recommend courses which suit for user's knowledge level and overcome the sparse of user-rating matrix. We build a user-course bipartite graph with user network and make use of HITS algorithm [20] to generate user-rating matrix. We further generate candidate course sequence by user based collaborative filtering [30] and sort it with the help of course network. Thus, we make use of user network, course network and their combination to overcome the sparse of user-rating matrix and recommend users with appropriate courses which suit for their knowledge level.

Our contributions in E-learning course recommendation are listed as follows:

(1) We first put forward the concept of user network and course network in social learning network. We develop a new method to build user network and course network. With a fully consideration of the relation between course and user. We apply the social learning network formed by them in recommendation to gain a proper recommendation for user.
(2) We use HITS algorithm to calculate user's rating score. In this way overcome the sparse of user-rating matrix in E-learning web sites.
(3) We put forward a novel metric about the result of course recommendation: learning result. And we design experiments to verify that the course list gained by our algorithm is more suitable for user's knowledge level and thus gain a better learning result.

2   Related Work

2.1   CF-Based Recommendation

To overcome sparse of user-course matrix problem, [24] uses L0 regularization, while [21] take advantage of two-stage user based collaborative filtering, and [10] combine CF with a clustering mechanism-Artificial Immune Network Theory. Attribute level recommend is used in [32] with previously defined course attribute. By using similarity with senior students [12] recommend top t optional courses with the highest predicted scores. Similar to [9,12] make recommendation based on the subsequency graph formed by senior students and use algorithm to discover the most optimal transition from course to course. Also in [8], the bias of different kinds of algorithm is explored which include NP, SCF, MF and LTR.

2.2   Content Based Recommendation

With the help of user log, course prerequisite relationship and user demographic information [18] proposed a content based recommend framework. The course prerequisite relationship in [18] is isolated, while in [26,27] the course prerequisite relationship is chained with three kind of from: AND, OR and AND-OR form and consider different goal. Apart from course prerequisite relationship, [14] take the field student attempted currently into consideration and use RNN to achieve it's goal. [19] uses questionnaire to invest the relation between motivation and behavior. Also in [11,23] query user interests directly to gain user interests and use methods to study user interests further.

2.3   Hybrid Approach

As a class topic extraction model LDA, [7] is used in [5] to generate user topic model based on user profile, and match them with course syllabus. Inspired by data mining process, [4] verify the usefulness of clustering, association rule mining and their combine. [33] also uses association rule mining, but utilize big data platform. [6] uses association rule too, but add user ratings. While in [28] neural network is used and evaluate the suitableness. Some work make use of social network for trust evaluation [15,17,31] and then conduct recommendation [16] by the result of trust evaluation. By use user network, [13] make email recommendation.

3   Problem Definition

3.1   System Settings and Concepts

We make use of user network and course network to recommend a proper course that fits for user's knowledge level. User network refers to a net formed by user activities. In user network, node represents user, and edge between nodes means the user node edge connected once enrolled in a same course. Course network is constructed based on course relation, and the relation is depending on user enroll order. We measure user's knowledge level about a certain course. Root set is current user node. Extension set is sub network formed by root set, the nodes connect with root set and the edges between them in user-course bipartite graph. User-course bipartite graph includes user net. Relevance score is the metric of how tightly two courses related. And learning result is the mean value of Weighted-score. The notations used in this paper are listed in Table 1.

3.2   Course Recommendation Problem

Given the users learning histories, our course recommendation problem tries to recommend proper courses that are suitable for users. In this paper, we will construct user network and course network, and try to recommend proper courses that can match user's knowledge level.

Table 1. Symbols

Notation	Explanation
Input U	$U = \{u_1, u_2, u_3, ..., u_n\}$ is all users in our data set
Input C_{u_i}	$C_{u_i} = [c_{u_i}^1, c_{u_i}^2, c_{u_i}^3, ..., c_{u_i}^s]$ is user u_i's history course set ordered by time
Input C	All courses in our dataset
U_{c_p}	All users who learn course c_p
$t_{u u_p}$	Time when user enroll course c_p
α	The lower limit of relevance score
$\vec{u_i}$	Course vector of user u_i
$c_{u_i}^r$	$c_{u_i}^r \subseteq C_{u_i}$. Course user u_i have learned
μ	The knowledge level target course required
c_x	Course user need to learn before taking target course
$p_{f_{u_i}^{m\prime}}$	Order of course $f_{u_i}^{m\prime}$ in recommend list
F	$F = [f_{u_i}^1, f_{u_i}^2, f_{u_i}^3, ..., f_{u_i}^m, ..., f_{u_i}^k]$, candidate course set
Output F'	$F' = [f_{u_i}^1, f_{u_i}^2, f_{u_i}^3, ..., (f_{u_i}^m)', ..., f_{u_i}^k]$. Finally recommend sequence. $(f_{u_i}^m)' = f_{u_i}^m$ or c_x

4 CRBN: Courses Recommendation Based on User and Course Network

We propose a recommendation framework as shown in Fig. 1. It has three steps: (1) Construct user network and course network. We construct a user network based on user historical activity and build a course network based on course relation. (2) Generate candidate course list. We use HITS algorithm to generate user-rating matrix and use user based collaborative filtering to generate a sequence of candidate course for user. (3) Course rearrange and recommendation. We rearrange user candidate sequence with the help of course network to match users with knowledge level course required and dynamically recommend it to user.

4.1 Construct User Network and Course Network

We make use of user enrollment information to construct user network and course network.

Because E-learning website lacks a list of user's friend information or pay attention to follow and be followed information, E-learning researches pay less attention to the user network. But learning is a social behavior, in which users realize the dissemination of information. After register a course, users will post opinions, answer questions, ask questions, or express their concerns through thumb up or thumb down in forum. Therefore, users exchanges information

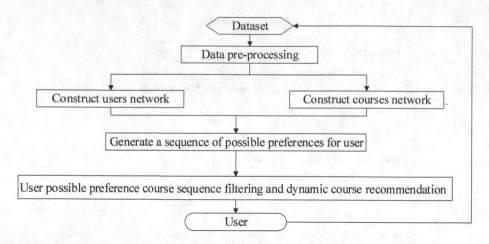

Fig. 1. Recommendation framework

in the forum. At the same time, all users who have registered this course share information provided by this course. Thence, there is a user network formed by flow of information. User net reflects the exchange and share of information among users in social learning web site.

Construct User Network. We build a user network based on user registration records, taking the user id as a node. Establish a two-way directed edge between users who have studied the same course to build user network. A fully connected sub graph is formed between all registered users for the same course.

Construct Course Network. In course recommendation field, some studies consider the relationship of course, such as [18,26,27], but the exploration of the course prerequisite relationship in these papers are chained or discontinuous. Base on the fact that when users involve in a certain new field, most users will register foundation and less difficult courses in the early time. So our paper uses the order of user registration sequence to calculate the relevance score of course. The relevance score indicates how tightly the knowledge is connected between two courses. Relevance score can be calculate as Eq. (1) shown.

$$S(c_p, c_q) = \frac{\sum_{u \subseteq U_{c_p} \cap U_{c_q}} t_{u_{c_p}} < t_{u_{c_q}}}{U_{c_p} \cap U_{c_q}} \tag{1}$$

$S(c_p, c_q)$ represents the relevance score, when course c_p serve as course c_q pre-related course. U_{c_p} means the user set enrolled course c_p. U_{c_q} means the user set enrolled course c_q. $t_{u_{c_p}}$ represents the time when user u enrolled course c_p. $t_{u_{c_q}}$ represents the time when user u enrolled course c_q. The numerator indicates number of users who registered c_p before c_q, and the denominator indicates number of all users registered courses c_p and c_q. We define the two related nodes connected by directed edges, the outbound node is the pre-related courses of the inbound nodes, and the inbound node is the post-related courses of the outbound nodes. The weight value represents the relevance score.

$$S(c_p, c_q) = \begin{cases} S(c_p, c_q), & S(c_p, c_q) \geq \alpha \\ 0, & S(c_p, c_q) < \alpha \end{cases} \tag{2}$$

Equation (1) is able to calculate the relevance scores for all courses, and we set the relevance scores less than a certain threshold α to zero according to Eq. (2), without directed edge between corresponding course pairs. For the course pair that satisfies Eq. (2), we define course c_p as the pre-related course of the course c_q, and the equivalently course c_q is the post-related course of the course c_p. The value of α is learned from the data set, and α needs to satisfy: $\alpha > 0.5$. This is because according to the calculation Eq. (1): $S(c_p, c_q) + S(c_q, c_p) = 1$. If $\alpha <= 0.5$, then $S(c_p, c_q)$ and $S(c_p, c_p)$ both satisfy Eq. (2), so that the course c_p is the pre-related course of the course c_q and the course c_q is the pre-related course of the course c_p too. This contradict with itself which is impossible.

The relevance score $S(c_p, c_q)$ between some courses is relatively small. This indicates that the course c_p is registered as a small probability or random event before the course c_q, thus does not mean that the course c_p is pre-related course for c_q. When $S(c_p, c_q)$ is very small, it means that $S(c_q, c_p)$ is large, so course c_j is the pre-related course of course c_p. When $S(c_p, c_q)$ is around 0.5, it is considered that the courses c_p and c_q is not related.

As illustration we shown in Fig. 2. In case(1), there is 70% users both select course c_p and c_p select c_p before c_p, the relevance score $S(c_p, c_q)$ is 0.7, and the relevance score $S(c_q, c_p)$ is 0.3. $0.3 < 0.5$, so in course net there is no edge pointed form c_q to c_p. c_p is the pre-related course of c_q and c_q is the post-related course of c_p. In case(2), users who choose c_q before c_p or choose c_p before c_q is evenly separate. So $S(c_p, c_q) = S(c_q, c_p) = 0.5$, and there is no relation between them, no edge between corresponding course node in course network. In case(3), although $S(c_p, c_q)$ is small, $S(c_q, c_p)$ is bigger than 0.5, so there is a directed edge from c_p to c_p in course net, and the weight of the edge is equal to relevance score $S(c_q, c_p)$, which is 0.9.

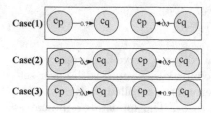

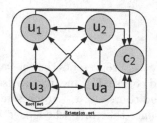

Fig. 2. Relation between two courses   **Fig. 3.** The base of u_3

4.2   Generate Candidate Courses Based on HITS Algorithm

In this paper, HITS algorithm [20] is used to generate user-rating matrix, then apply user based collaborative filtering [30] to generate a candidate course list for user. We extend user network to generate user-course bipartite graph by creating a directed edge from user node to course node which user has learned.

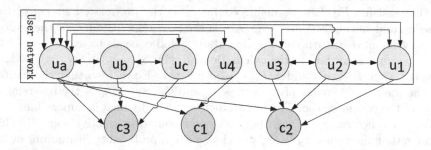

Fig. 4. User-course bipartite graph with user network

We generate user ratings by HITS algorithm. The Authority and Hub value of node is calculated in Eq. (3). After a series of calculations until A and H is converged, and implement Authority of course node as user rating. We set different user node as the Root set, and gain the rating matrix of user according to our method.

$$\begin{cases} A = \sum H \\ H = \sum A \end{cases} \tag{3}$$

The base of u_3 is shown in Fig. 3. The node u_3 is the Root set, and all the nodes connected to the u_3 are defined as Extension set to form the base. In Fig. 3, all the nodes connect to u_3 would gain a value of Authority. We only keep the value of course node. The Authority of all nodes after normalization is u_1: 0.1875, u_2: 0.1875, u_3: 0.1875, c_2: 0.25, u_i: 0.1875, and u_3 rates course c_1, c_2, c_3 as: 0, 0.25, 0. Thus the rating vector of u_3 is $(0, 0.25, 0)$. Figure 4 is an example of user-course bipartite graph. We use the cosine similarity of the user-course matrix to calculate the user similarity, as follows:

$$Similarity(u_i, u_j) = cos(u_i, u_j) = \frac{\overrightarrow{u_i} \times \overrightarrow{u_j}}{|\overrightarrow{u_i}| \cdot |\overrightarrow{u_j}|} \tag{4}$$

$\overrightarrow{u_j}$ and $\overrightarrow{u_j}$ are the course vector of user u_i and u_j. The recommendation is based on a user-based collaborative filtering algorithm to generate a sequence of candidate course F.

4.3   Measuring User's Knowledge Level

This paper proposes to make a selective recommendation based on user's knowledge level about course. The user's knowledge level of the course, which is not yet learned but interested depend on the weight of edge in course network from already-learned course to the target course. We calculate user u_i's knowledge level about candidate course $f_{u_i}^m$ in the candidate course sequence F as $K(f_{u_i}^m)$:

$$K(f_{u_i}^m) = \sum_i^s weight(c_{u_i}^r, f_{u_i}^m) \tag{5}$$

$f_{u_i}^m \subseteq F$, $c_{u_i}^r \subseteq C_{u_i}$ and $weight(c_{u_i}^r, f_{u_i}^m)$ means the weight of edge in course net from $c_{u_i}^r$ to $f_{u_i}^m$. Screening F based on user's knowledge level:

$$f_{u_i}^{m\prime} = \begin{cases} f_{u_i}^m, & K(f_{u_i}^m) \geq \mu \\ c_x, max_{c_x \nsubseteq C_{u_i}} weight(c_x, f_{u_i}^m), & K(f_{u_i}^m) < \mu \end{cases} \tag{6}$$

Where μ is the threshold of knowledge level course required. $c_x \nsubseteq C_{u_i}$ means that c_x is not in the history course set C_{u_i} of user u_i.

If $K(f_{u_i}^m) \geq \mu$, we say that user's knowledge level satisfy the require of course $f_{u_i}^m$, then we keep $f_{u_i}^m$ as related course and keep the order of it. Otherwise we consider user's knowledge level doesn't meet course $f_{u_i}^m$'s requirement. Then we need to switch it with the pre-related course c_x of course $f_{u_i}^m$, and exclude c_x from the course set user has learned. Also we make sure that in the course net the weight of edge between c_x and $f_{u_i}^m$ is maximum among all the pre-related course of course $f_{u_i}^m$ user u_i has not learned. By this way, we can recommend the most related pre-related course of course $f_{u_i}^m$ enable user make a good perpetration for course $f_{u_i}^m$. The value of μ represents the knowledge level about the course user needs to master before taking the course.

4.4   Learning Result and Precision Evaluation

We use learning result and MRR to evaluate the performance of our method. For course $f_{u_i}^{m\prime}$ in the user u_i's recommendation sequence, calculate Weighted-score as Eq. (7):

$$Weighted - score(f_{u_i}^{m\prime}) = \frac{score(f_{u_i}^{m\prime})}{p_{f_{u_i}^{m\prime}}} \tag{7}$$

Where $p_{f_{u_i}^{m'}}$ is the position of the course $f_{u_i}^{m'}$ in the recommendation sequence, if $f_{u_i}^{m'}$ is the first place, then $p = 1$. $score(f_{u_i}^{m'})$ is the score user u_i finally gain in course $f_{u_i}^{m'}$. Learning result is the mean value of Weighted-score. E.g. user learned course order is: [b, e, f], the score of them is: [98, 23, 62] and our recommend list is $[a, b, c, d, e, f]$. Then the $Weighted\_score$ of these courses is: $\frac{98}{2}$, $\frac{23}{5}$, $\frac{62}{6}$. And learning result is the mean value of $Weighted\_score$ about course user have learned. In the example above user's learning result is: $\frac{1}{3}(\frac{98}{2} + \frac{23}{5} + \frac{62}{6})$. MRR (Mean Reciprocal Rank) is calculated in the same way but numerator is 1.

4.5   Dynamical Course Recommendation

Based on CRBN we proposed in Sect. 4. We can conduct one round of recommendation as in Algorithm 1. And after recommend F' to user, change user historical course set C_{u_i} based on user action and begin another round recommendation. By this way we can dynamically recommend course to user C_{u_i}. In Algorithm 1, Lines 2–6 generate user network; Lines 7–10 generate course network; Lines 11–14 calculate user-rating matrix and similarity and Lines 15–23 generate candidate recommend sequence and rearrange the list based on user's knowledge level. The time complexity of our algorithm is $O(n^2)$, n is the number of users.

Algorithm 1. Recommendation process

1: Input u_i historical learning course set $C_{u_i} = \{c_{u_i}^1, c_{u_i}^2, c_{u_i}^3, \ldots, c_{u_i}^c\}$ and score u_i
    finally gained $score(c_{u_i}^k)$
2: **for** each $u_i \in U = \{u_1, u_2, ..., u_n\}$ **do**
3:    add user node u_i to user network G_u;
4:    **for** each node $u_j \in G_u \& j \neq i$ **do**
5:      **if** $C_{u_i} \bigcup C_{u_j} \neq \phi$ **then**
6:        create a two-way edge between node C_{u_i} and node C_{u_j} in G_u
7: **for all** $c \in C$ which include all course **do**
8:    calculate $S(c_p, c_q)$ for each course pairs in C
9:    **if** $S(c_p, c_q) > \alpha$ **then**
10:     set a directed edge from node c_p to node c_q in G_c
11: **for** each user node $u_i \in G_u$ **do**
12:    set u_i as root set, apply our method to create base of u_i and use $a_k = (A^T.A)a_{k-1}$
    to get user u_i's rating vector
13: **for all** user in user-course matrix **do**
14:    $Similarity(u_i, u_j) = cos(u_i, u_j)$
15: **for** $u_i \in U$ **do**
16:    CF recommendation result user u_i:$F = [f_{u_i}^1, f_{u_i}^2, f_{u_i}^3, \ldots, f_{u_i}^k]$
17:    **for** $f_{u_i}^m \in F$ **do**
18:      **if** $K(f_{u_i}^m) <= \mu$ **then**
19:        replace $f_{u_i}^m$ with c_x
20:    gain F' by 17-19
21:    recommend F' to user u_i

---

5   Experiments

5.1   Data Set

This article uses the data set from [29] in Xuetangx 2013–2014. After filter out entrusted data such as test users and courses, information of data-set is shown in Table 2. Data distribution is shown in Fig. 5(a) is the distribution of course number user have enrolled, Fig. 5(b) is the distribution of register user number of course. They are both consistent with the long tail distribution. Figure 5(c) and (d) show the score distribution of users who satisfy or not satisfy course requirement before learn the course. In Fig. 5(c) and (d), the mean value of score is 6.43 VS 4.52, certificate rate is 5.4% VS 4.1% and the zero point rate is 77.4% VS 80.2%. It indicates that users reach the knowledge level required by course before taking the course would gain a higher score, as well as higher pass rate and lower drop out rate.

Table 2. Data set statistics

Records	Users	Courses	Duration	Cores
533,871	225,451	132	8/22/2013–10/1/2014	18,218

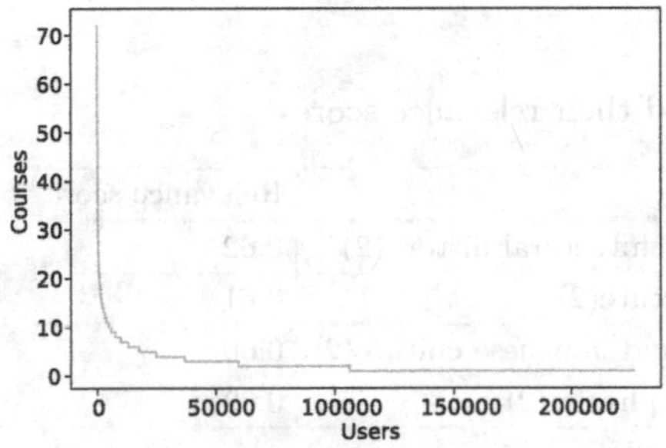

(a) Course distribution

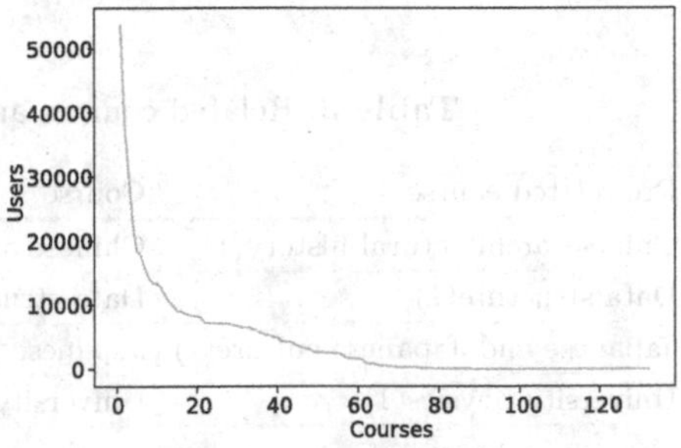

(b) User distribution

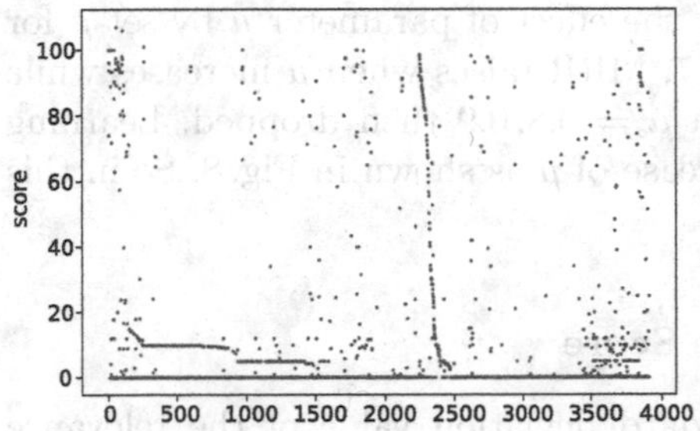

(c) Score distribution of user who satisfy knowledge level

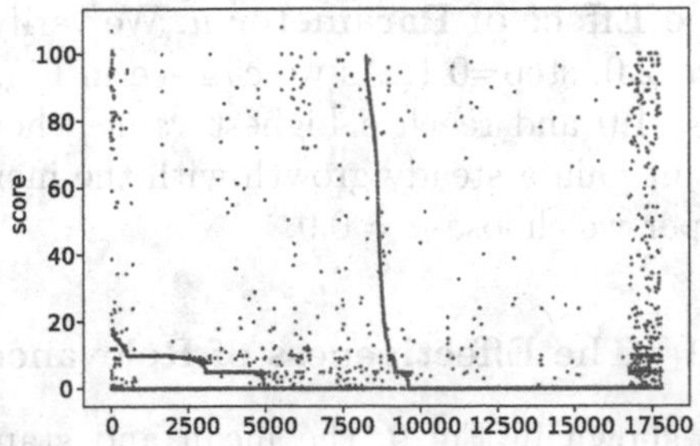

(d) Score distribution of user who not satisfy knowledge level

Fig. 5. Data distribution

5.2   The Effect of Parameters α and μ

The Effect of Parameter α. Course relationship between some course pairs can be known from course name. Table 3 list some already known course relationship and the relevance scores calculated according to our formula. In Table 3, the weight of edge from first column to the second column is biggest among all edge pointed to second column in course net, except for University Physical(1) and University Physics(2). The relevance score of University Physics is not in line with expectations due to the duration of the course University Physics(2) is only 3 months, and the duration of other courses is mostly around one year.

Omit the last line in Table 3, the minimum relevance score for these known course pairs is 0.6. The relation between pairs of courses in the Table 3 is strongly related. There are also exist some courses relation are weaker. To capture the weak correlation between courses, we set $0.5 < \alpha < 0.6$. When the data set changes, the upper limit of α may change, but as we explained in Sect. 3.1, the lower limit of α must be greater than 0.5.

As we have mentioned above, the threshold α need to satisfy $0.5 < \alpha < 0.6$. So we vary α from (0.5,0.6], step=0.01, and we use the value of learning result with HITS algorithm to evaluate the value of α. As it's shown in Fig. 6, learning result without course net keep the same when α changes. But learning result with course net changes when α changes, and we gain a maximum value of learning result when $\alpha = 0.51$. Thus in this paper we set $\alpha = 0.51$.

Table 3. Related courses and their relevance scores.

Pre-related course	Course	Relevance score
Chinese architectural history(1)	Chinese architectural history(2)	0.62
Data structure(1)	Data structure(2)	0.61
Japanese and Japanese culture(1)	Japanese and Japanese culture(2)	0.60
University physics(1)	University physics(2)	0.09

The Effect of Parameter μ. We verify the effect of parameter μ by set μ for 0 to 2.0, step=0.1. As we can see in Fig. 7, MRR raises when μ increases while $\mu < 1.0$ and reach a highest value when $\mu = 0.8, 0.9$ then dropped. Learning result gain a steady growth with the increase of μ as shown in Fig. 8. So in this paper we choose $\mu = 0.9$.

5.3   The Effectiveness of Relevance Score

As shown in Fig. 9, the mean and standard deviation value of the relevance scores for the course in course network are normally distributed. To validate the effectiveness of relevance score, we choose the TOP 10% of mean and standard deviation values of relevance scores shown in Tables 4 and 5.

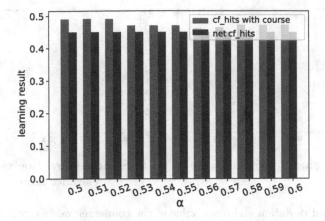

Fig. 6. Learning result change with α.

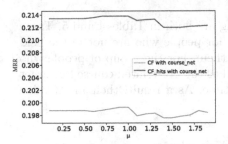

Fig. 7. MRR change with μ.   **Fig. 8.** Learning result change with μ.

TOP 10% Mean Value. Top 10% mean value. Courses in Table 4 are that with TOP 10% mean value. In Table 3 there are some basic, easy understand courses that can be learned by different people with various profession. Thus it can be learned before any course by the masses. Other pre-related course (e.g., in Table 3) also gain high relevance scores and they can be the pre-related course for most course.

TOP 10% Standard Deviation Value. Table 5 shows the TOP 10% standard deviation value for courses. The courses in Table 4 are professional course. These courses are limited in applicability, but highly targeted, as a pre-related course for some courses is irreplaceable and necessary. But for most course there is no correlation. Which results in the value distribution of the relevance scores is relatively discrete. So the standard deviation is high.

Course Included in TOP 10% Mean Value Course List and TOP 10% Standard Deviation Value Course List. Overview of Tsinghua Department, Introduction to Computational Thinking and Data Science and Introduction to

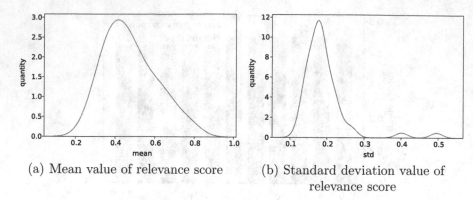

(a) Mean value of relevance score   (b) Standard deviation value of
                                           relevance score

Fig. 9. Standard deviation and mean value of the course relevance scores distribution in the course network.

Computer Science and Python Programming are both in Tables 4 and 5. These courses are basic courses, but it is not easy for people who are not in the field thus only certain groups of people will like them. For the group of people who need or like them, they are indispensable and as the pre-related course for target course or goal they need to learn at early time. As a result, their mean value and standard deviation value are both large.

Table 4. TOP10% mean value.

Course	Mean value	Standard deviation
Overview of Tsinghua Department	**0.782**	0.401
Introduction to Computational Thinking and Data Science	**0.775**	0.266
Introduction to Computer Science and Python Programming	**0.725**	0.263
Molecular biology and principle technology	**0.7**	0.226
English Writing Guide - Getting Started with Writing	**0.663**	0.182

5.4   Recommendation Result Comparison

We show the result of our method and the baseline in Figs. 10 and 11, which shows the effectiveness of our approach. Comparing (a) and (b) in Fig. 10, it can be seen that after use the user-rating matrix calculated by the HITS algorithm, the recommendation result becomes better. Taking MRR as evaluation metric, the recommendation result without course network is increased by 9.0%, and that with course network is increased by 8.8%. Moreover the convergence is faster,

Table 5. TOP10% standard deviation value.

Course	Mean value	Standard deviation
Linux Operating System Analysis	0.56	**0.496**
Overview of Tsinghua Department	0.782	**0.401**
Introduction to Computational Thinking and Data Science	0.775	**0.266**
Introduction to Computer Science and Python Programming	0.725	**0.263**
Document management and information analysis	0.626	**0.238**

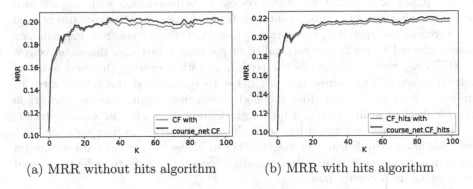

(a) MRR without hits algorithm   (b) MRR with hits algorithm

Fig. 10. Recommendation result of MRR. The abscissa K is user's TOP K neighbors.

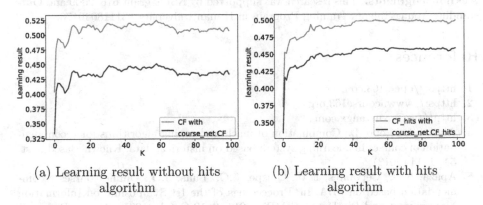

(a) Learning result without hits algorithm   (b) Learning result with hits algorithm

Fig. 11. Recommendation result of learning result. The abscissa K is user's TOP K neighbors.

and it is more stable after convergence. Converging faster means that we can choose a smaller K when we making a TOP K similar user selection, reducing the amount of calculation. Comparing Figs. 10(a) and 11(a), Figs. 10(b) and 11(b), it can be seen that, whether the HITS algorithm is used or not, learning result with the course network is better than that of without the course network. In summary, there are several benefits of using the HITS algorithm to generate a user-rating matrix: converge faster, more stable, and better learning result, which indicates the robustness of our method. What's more, in terms of MRR and learning result, when the course network is incorporated, although MRR drops a little, the learning result improves a lot. In Fig. 10(a) and 11(a), MRR drop 1.5% but the learning result gains a 17% improvement; In Figs. 10(b) and 11(b), it is 1.4% drop VS 9% improvement.

6   Conclusion

In this paper, we conduct a suitable course recommendation with the aid of a social learning network, which combines user network. HITS algorithm is used to overcome the sparsity of user-rating matrix. Different contrast experiments are conducted to verify the rationality of parameter settings, the effectiveness of HITS algorithm to improve the recommendation results, the reasonable of relevance score. The course network helps to recommend the right course to users, which can be seen from the higher learning result. We use the grade represents the learning result. A higher grade indicating a better learning result.

In future work, we would like to explore user relation in user network. The information on the E-learning website is rich. These behavioral data are useful for course recommendation. We are also interested to verify the effectiveness of our method in different data sets.

Acknowledgments. This research was supported by NSFC grant 61632009 and Outstanding Young Talents Training Program in Hunan University 531118040173.

References

1. https://open.163.com
2. https://www.icourse163.org
3. http://www.xuetangx.com
4. Aher, S.B., Lobo, L.: Combination of machine learning algorithms for recommendation of courses in e-learning system based on historical data. Knowl.-Based Syst. **51**, 1–14 (2013)
5. Apaza, R.G., Cervantes, E.V., Quispe, L.C., Luna, J.O.: Online courses recommendation based on LDA. In: Proceedings of the 1st Symposium on Information Management and Big Data - SIMBig 2014, 8–10 October 2014, Cusco, Peru, pp. 42–48 (2014)
6. Bendakir, N., Aïmeur, E.: Using association rules for course recommendation. In: Proceedings of the AAAI Workshop on Educational Data Mining, vol. 3, pp. 1–10 (2006)
7. Blei, D.M., Ng, A.Y., Jordan, M.I.: Latent dirichlet allocation. In: Advances in Neural Information Processing Systems 14 [Neural Information Processing Systems: Natural and Synthetic, NIPS 2001, 3–8 December 2001, Vancouver, British Columbia, Canada], pp. 601–608 (2001)

8. Boratto, L., Fenu, G., Marras, M.: The effect of algorithmic bias on recommender systems for massive open online courses. In: Azzopardi, L., Stein, B., Fuhr, N., Mayr, P., Hauff, C., Hiemstra, D. (eds.) ECIR 2019. LNCS, vol. 11437, pp. 457–472. Springer, Cham (2019). https://doi.org/10.1007/978-3-030-15712-8_30

9. Bridges, C., Jared, J., Weissmann, J., Montanez-Garay, A., Spencer, J.C., Brinton, C.G.: Course recommendation as graphical analysis. In: 52nd Annual Conference on Information Sciences and Systems, CISS 2018, 21–23 March 2018, Princeton, NJ, USA, pp. 1–6 (2018)

10. Chang, P.C., Lin, C.H., Chen, M.H.: A hybrid course recommendation system by integrating collaborative filtering and artificial immune systems. Algorithms **9**(3), 47 (2016)

11. Gulzar, Z., Leema, A.A.: Course recommendation based on query classification approach. IJWLTT **13**(3), 69–83 (2018)

12. Huang, L., Wang, C., Chao, H., Lai, J., Yu, P.S.: A score prediction approach for optional course recommendation via cross-user-domain collaborative filtering. IEEE Access **7**, 19550–19563 (2019)

13. Jiang, F., Tang, M., Tran, Q.A.: User preference-based spamming detection with coupled behavioral analysis. In: Wang, G., Ray, I., Alcaraz Calero, J.M., Thampi, S.M. (eds.) SpaCCS 2016. LNCS, vol. 10066, pp. 466–477. Springer, Cham (2016). https://doi.org/10.1007/978-3-319-49148-6_38

14. Jiang, W., Pardos, Z.A., Wei, Q.: Goal-based course recommendation. CoRR abs/1812.10078 (2018)

15. Jiang, W., Jie, W., Feng, L., Wang, G., Zheng, H.: Trust evaluation in online social networks using generalized network flow. IEEE Trans. Comput. **65**(3), 952–963 (2016)

16. Jiang, W., Jie, W., Wang, G.: On selecting recommenders for trust evaluation in online social networks. ACM Trans. Internet Technol. **15**(4), 1–21 (2015)

17. Jiang, W., Wang, G.: Swtrust: generating trusted graph for trust evaluation in online social networks. In: IEEE International Conference on Trust (2012)

18. Jing, X., Tang, J.: Guess you like: course recommendation in MOOCs. In: Proceedings of the International Conference on Web Intelligence, pp. 783–789. ACM (2017)

19. Kizilcec, R.F., Schneider, E.: Motivation as a lens to understand online learners: toward data-driven design with the OLEI scale. ACM Trans. Comput.-Hum. Interact. **22**(2), 6:1–6:24 (2015)

20. Kleinberg, J.M.: Hubs, authorities, and communities. ACM Comput. Surv. (CSUR) **31**(4es), 5 (1999)

21. Lee, E.L., Kuo, T.T., Lin, S.D.: A collaborative filtering-based two stage model with item dependency for course recommendation. In: 2017 IEEE International Conference on Data Science and Advanced Analytics (DSAA), pp. 496–503. IEEE (2017)

22. Li, M., Jiang, W., Li, K.: Recommendation systems in real applications: algorithm and parallel architecture. In: Wang, G., Ray, I., Alcaraz Calero, J.M., Thampi, S.M. (eds.) SpaCCS 2016. LNCS, vol. 10066, pp. 45–58. Springer, Cham (2016). https://doi.org/10.1007/978-3-319-49148-6_5

23. Li, X., Wang, T., Wang, H., Tang, J.: Understanding user interests acquisition in personalized online course recommendation. In: U, L.H., Xie, H. (eds.) APWeb-WAIM 2018. LNCS, vol. 11268, pp. 230–242. Springer, Cham (2018). https://doi.org/10.1007/978-3-030-01298-4_20

24. Lin, J., Pu, H., Li, Y., Lian, J.: Sparse linear method based top-n course recommendation system with expert knowledge and L_0 regularization. In: Zu, Q., Hu, B. (eds.) HCC 2017. LNCS, vol. 10745, pp. 130–138. Springer, Cham (2018). https://doi.org/10.1007/978-3-319-74521-3_15

25. Pappano, L.: The year of the MOOC. New York Times **2**(12), 2012 (2012). http://www.nytimes.com/2012/11/04/education/edlife/massive-open-online-courses-are-multiplying-at-a-rapid-pace.html

26. Parameswaran, A., Venetis, P., Garcia-Molina, H.: Recommendation systems with complex constraints: a course recommendation perspective. ACM Trans. Inf. Syst. (TOIS) **29**(4), 20 (2011)

27. Parameswaran, A.G., Garcia-Molina, H., Ullman, J.D.: Evaluating, combining and generalizing recommendations with prerequisites. In: Proceedings of the 19th ACM International Conference on Information and Knowledge Management, pp. 919–928. ACM (2010)

28. Pardos, Z.A., Fan, Z., Jiang, W.: Connectionist recommendation in the wild: on the utility and scrutability of neural networks for personalized course guidance. User Modeling User-Adapted Interact. **29**(2), 487–525 (2019)

29. Qiu, J., et al.: Modeling and predicting learning behavior in MOOCs. In: Proceedings of the Ninth ACM International Conference on Web Search and Data Mining, 22–25 February 2016, San Francisco, CA, USA, pp. 93–102 (2016)

30. Schafer, J.B., Frankowski, D., Herlocker, J., Sen, S.: Collaborative filtering recommender systems. In: Brusilovsky, P., Kobsa, A., Nejdl, W. (eds.) The Adaptive Web. LNCS, vol. 4321, pp. 291–324. Springer, Heidelberg (2007). https://doi.org/10.1007/978-3-540-72079-9_9

31. Wang, G., Jiang, W., Wu, J., Xiong, Z.: Fine-grained feature-based social influence evaluation in online social networks. IEEE Trans. Parallel Distrib. Syst. **25**(9), 2286–2296 (2014)

32. Wang, Y., Liang, B., Ji, W., Wang, S., Chen, Y.: A weighted multi-attribute method for personalized recommendation in MOOCs. In: Proceedings of the 2nd International Conference on Crowd Science and Engineering, pp. 44–49. ACM (2017)

33. Zhang, H., Huang, T., Lv, Z., Liu, S., Zhou, Z.: MCRS: a course recommendation system for MOOCs. Multimedia Tools Appl. **77**(6), 7051–7069 (2018)

Context-Aware Personalized POI Sequence Recommendation

Jing Chen and Wenjun Jiang$^{(\boxtimes)}$ (iD)

College of Computer Science and Electronic Engineering, Hunan University,
Changsha 410082, China
{jessicachan,jiangwenjun}@hnu.edu.cn

Abstract. The Point Of Interest (POI) sequence recommendation
applies to scenarios like itinerary and travel route planning which belongs
to the class of NP-hard problem. What's more, the external environment like the weather, time can affect the user's check-in behavior such
as people prefer to check-in in ice cream shop when the temperature
is higher. We propose an algorithm to solve these problems that called
Context-Aware Personalized POI sequence Recommendation based on
reinforcement learning (CAPR for short). First, we model the users
dynamic preferences that incorporate contextual information associated
with the users' sequence of check-ins. Then we use the Monte Carlo
Tree Search algorithm to select the user-satisfied POI in different environments. What's more, we can get the context-aware personalized POI
sequence under the specified time limit. Finally, we test the proposed
algorithm using an open source dataset. The experimental results show
that the weather and time context can improve the accuracy of the recommendation. Our algorithm can improve the effectiveness of travel recommendations.

Keywords: Context-aware · Reinforcement learning · POI sequence ·
Recommendation · Personality

1 Introduction

The latest data shows that the tourism industry has gradually developed into
the world's largest emerging industry [23]. With the rapid development of information technology and the improvement of people's living standards, more and
more people tend to check-ins on location-based social networking platforms
(LBSN), such as Weeplaces, Foursquare and so on. They can share information
and experience with the POI in LBSN. And the massive check-in data can better
recommend personalized itineraries and optimal travel routes for users.

It is a complex task to recommend the POI sequence due to the following
reasons: (1) The POI sequence recommendation needs to compute all permu-
tations from many POIs of a city, which is an NP-hard problem [3]. (2) Daily
trip and travel need to consider various contextual information, such as different time, weather and friends, which will affect the user' check-in behavior. (3)

© Springer Nature Singapore Pte Ltd. 2019
G. Wang et al. (Eds.): iSCI 2019, CCIS 1122, pp. 197–210, 2019.
https://doi.org/10.1007/978-981-15-1301-5_16

The recommended POI sequence needs to consider the user's interest and the popularity of the POI in different scenarios.

In the existing itinerary and travel route recommendation researches, they most only consider the impact of space (distance), time and social relationships, without considering the impact of weather on POI sequence recommendations. In real life, the weather, time [11,13,14], and social relationships [12,28] are important factors affecting users' behavior. The importance of weather on individual POI recommendations is described in [26].

There are some researches on the impact of weather and time on user check-in behavior. Xu et al. [30] count the number of times on POIs in different weather. And they recommend the POI with high check-in frequency for the user in this weather. It can't improve the user's serendipity. Manotumruksa et al. [2,22] consider the impact of time on venue and itinerary recommendation in many ways, but they don't consider other contexts.

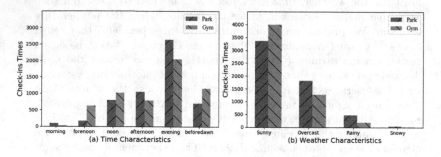

Fig. 1. The popularity of Park and Gym in different time and weather

We conduct some data analysis like Fig. 1. Figure 1(a) shows that park is more popular than gym in forenoon, gym is more popular in the evening. In Fig. 1(b), Users tend to visit parks on cloudy and snowy days, while on rainy days they tend to exercise. When we recommend the POI sequence, we should consider the context information. They are important factors affecting the users' check-in.

In our work, we propose a context-aware personalized POI sequence recommendation system based on reinforcement learning. Our model considers the impact of weather and other contexts on user check-in, modeling context-aware user interests and POI popularity. Our model uses the reinforcement learning algorithm to recommend the most satisfactory POI for a user in different environments (different weather and time). Until reached the travel time budget, a personalized POI sequence is recommended to the target user.

- We identify a novel problem that the weather and time can influence the POI sequence recommendation.
- Through capturing the different check-ins behavior with different context information, we model the POI popularity and implemented weather and time-aware user collaborative filtering algorithms to model user interest.

- We firstly apply the Monte Carlo tree search algorithm to the context-aware personalized POI sequence recommendation scenario. And we propose CAPR algorithm that can recommend the user satisfactory a POI sequence considering the weather and time.
- We evaluate the effectiveness of our algorithm using weeplaces dataset.

2   Related Work

Due to POI sequence recommendation can reduce the process of active search and provide users with the plan they like, many recommenders have studied it from various aspects.

POI Sequence Recommendation: Recommendation systems are popular in academia [18,19]. Among them, the POI recommendation has been studied by many researchers. The POI sequence recommendation is to recommend a series of POIs to the user, which are applied to the user's daily travel and travel scenarios. [7] is one of the earlier research on travel recommendation, which is based on Orientation Problem (references) (determining start and end locations), and recommended to users most popular travel route. Chen et al. [6] propose a probabilistic model to implement travel route recommendations. [5, 20, 29] are a combination of personalized travel recommendation scenarios, such as recommending comfortable travel routes to users by sensing traffic conditions [5]; perceiving locations for crowded periods as well as the queuing time in the theme park [20]. Zhang et al. [32] used feature-centric collaborative filtering to predict the preference (rating) of POIs that users have not visited. Considering the POI opening and closing time (the availability of POI) under actual conditions, recommending a set of POIs to users; Ge et al. [10] proposed a cost-conscious travel recommendation system that can recommend users. A travel route that suits your travel expenses.

Context-Aware Recommender Systems: Abowd et al. defined context as 'any information useful to characterize the situation of an entity (e.g., a user or an item) that can affect the way users interact with systems' [1]. Contextual information includes natural environment(weather), time, relationship environment (social), space (distance of distance), activities, etc. [11,17,27] validated the accuracy of recommending with the assist of context in the territory of music, movies and so on. At the first time, [31] proposed the timeaware POI recommendation. Importantly, they explained that most users tend to visit different POI at different times. Trattner et al. [26] proved that different weather conditions, including temperature, rainfall intensity, humidity and so on, can affect the popularity of POI and the users' interest with a lot of data analysis. Shi et al. [25] presented the concept of local exploration and local trajectories to capture the geographical influence from the distance between every pair of locations visited by the same user.

Context-Aware POI Sequence Recommendation: Context-aware. POI sequence recommendation: Xu et al. [30] made use of the context(season) given in his travel histories in other cities to obtain the topic distribution, and then recommended the personality travel POIs for the user based on collaborative filtering algorithm. [21,30] both simply applied the weather(season) to filter the travel histories, gaining the users' interest at this season. Debnath et al. [8] presented an Apriori-based travel route generation algorithm which proposed time influences the users' preference. The deep learning model is used for context-aware travel recommendations in [22]. [2] presented the capability of RNNs to incorporate context (eg., temporal, categorical and spatial) while he couldn't combine the weather. Manotumruksa et al. [22] realized itinerary recommendation based on attention mechanism, they also combined the context such as temporal and spatial.

The current research work mainly focuses on temporal information to assist the POI sequence recommendation yet. Our work realized context-aware personality POI sequence recommendation based on reinforcement learning. Our system can make optimal decisions (choosing the optimal POI under the current state) under different conditions (different weather, time and social) and recommend a popular and user-interested POI sequence.

3   Problem Definintion

3.1   System Settings and Concepts

In this section, we define some terms used in this paper. Then we present the problem statement of POI sequence recommendation.

In our paper, a single user in the dataset is represented by the letter u, and let $U : \{u_1, u_2, \ldots, u_n\}$ be a set of n users. We use p_i to express POI, and $P : \{p_1, p_2, \ldots, p_n\}$ express all POIs.

We mainly analyse the impact of several weather features on user check-in, like sunny, overcast, rainy and snowy. According to the Wikipedia, the time of a day is divided into six main time intervals, like morning, forenoon, noon, afternoon, evening and early morning. In the code, we use letter w_t to express the weather and T_t to express the time intervals.

Definition 1: POI sequence

For a single user u, the user's historical check-in records imply the user's travel record. We define his check-ins history as an ordered sequence, $S_u : \{I_1, I_2, \ldots, I_n\}$, where I_i is a check-ins activity and is represented as $I_i : \{p_i, t_{p_i}^a, w_t, T_t\}$ indicating the POI $(p_i)$of the check-in in the weather of w_t , arrival time $t_{p_i}^a$ to p_i, and the belongs to time section (T_t). As in earlier studies [7], the travel sequence can be split into small subsequences if the interval between two consecutive visits to POI is more than 8 h. We quoted this interval division.

Definition 2: Travel Time

Travel time is the average of the travel time between two POIs. We compute travel time using distance divided by the average speed. We use $travel_{p_i,p_j}$ to indicate travel time. The distance was estimated using the Haversine formula [24] and the walk speed was 5 km/h [4].

Definition 3: Duration Time

Duration time means the time that the user stayed at the POI. Duration time is calculated by $\left(t^a_{p_{i+1}} - t^a_{p_i} - \text{travel}\,(p_i, p_{i+1}) \right)$.

3.2 Problem

Our personalized POI sequence recommendation is similar to the Orienteering Problem [29]. Given the starting and ending POI, and the time budget for completing the POI sequence, we recommend a contextualized personalized POI sequence for the target user. The objective function is summarized as follows:

$$\max \left(\sum_{i=1}^{P-1} \sum_{j-2}^{P} x\,(i, j, c_t) * (\text{Int}_u\,(p, c_t) + \text{pop}(p, c_t)) \right). \tag{1}$$

where $\text{Int}_u\,(p, c_t)$ indicates the user's interest on POI p under the context and $\text{pop}(p, c_t)$ indicates the POI's popularity under the context which will be introduced in Sects. 4.2 and 4.3. The value of the function $x(i, j, c_t)$ is 1 if p_i to p_j exist in the user history check-in records, otherwise 0.

Our objective function is designed to maximize user satisfaction while considering dynamic changes in time and changes in weather.

3.3 Solution Overveiw

Figure 2 shows the main framework of our work. It consists of three steps: (1) Context-aware POI popularity modeling. The value of POI popularity is the number of times that all users have checked in different contexts (different weather and time). (2) Context-aware user interest modeling. We extend the user-based collaborative filtering model to model the user's interest preferences based on the user's check-in records in different weather and time. (3) CAPR algorithm recommendation. Under the premise of maximizing the objective function, the CAPR algorithm can recommend a POI sequence that is satisfactory to the user.

4   Context-Aware Personalized POI Sequence Recommendation Based on Reinforcement Learning

4.1   Context-Aware POI Popularity Modeling

We consider the popularity of all users in different time intervals and different weather characteristics and get the context-aware POI popularity. Suppose p is a POI, c_t is the context (the weather and time interval) and $\text{Vis}\,(p, c_t)$ is the number of the POI visit in different c_t. The popularity of a POI denoted as $Pop\,(p, c_t)$ and can be calculated as follows:

$$\text{Pop}\,(p, c_t) = \frac{\text{Vis}\,(p, c_t)}{\max\,(\text{Vis}\,(p, c_t))} \tag{2}$$

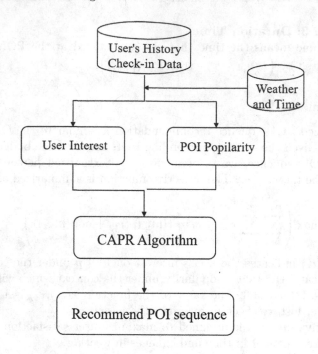

Fig. 2. Solution overview

When the weather and time information is not considered, we normalize the number of visits by all users in the POI as the POI popularity. This section serves as a comparative experiment to test the advantages of adding contextual information when recommending.

4.2   Context-Aware User Interest Modeling

Through the user's history check-in records, we can get the user's interest score on the visited POI (The more times you check in the POI, the more users like it). Our recommendation system also considers the social relationship of the target user, and models user's interest that the user may like but has not visited. Therefore, we extend the user-based collaborative filtering model to get the user's interest value for unvisited POIs.

First, we create a user-POI scoring matrix from historical check-in records. Taking into account weather and time information, we use different user-POI scoring matrices for different contexts. In Eq. (3), $R_{u,p}^{c_t}$ is the interest value of user u on POI p in specific weather and time,

$$R_{u,p}^{c_t} = \frac{Vis_{u,p}^{c_t}}{\max\left(Vis_{u,p}^{c_t}\right)} \tag{3}$$

Where $Vis_{u,p}^{c_t}$ indicates the number of times check-ins on POI p of the user u under the condition weather and time interval.

We use the context-based user-POI scoring matrix as the input of the user-based collaborative filtering model, and the user's interest rating for the unvisited POI is calculated as follows:

$$R_{u,p^*}^{c_t} = \frac{\sum_{u' \in U} W^{c_t} * R_{u,p}^{c_t}}{\sum_{u' \in U} W_{u,u}^{c_t}} \tag{4}$$

Where p^* indicates the POI which user didn't visited and we use $W_{u,u'}^{c_t}$ to represent the similarity between users and users in different weather and time. $W_{u,u'}^{c_t}$ defined by Eq. (5).

$$W_{u,u'}^{c_t} = \frac{\sum_{p \in P} v_{u,p}^{c_t} * v_{u',p}^{c_t}}{\sqrt{\sum_{p \in P} v_{u,p}^{c_t^2}} * \sqrt{\sum_{p \in P} v_{u',p}^{c_t^2}}} \tag{5}$$

Based on the extended collaborative filtering model, we define user interest as:

$$Int_u(p, c_t) = R_{u,p}^{c_t} \tag{6}$$

4.3 Monte Carlo Tree Search and POI Sequence Recommendation

We apply the Monte Carlo Tree Search (MCTS) algorithm for recommending a personalized POI sequence.

MCTS is a heuristic search algorithm used in some decision-making processes. The most striking is the use of the game AlphaGo. A prime example is the Fuego-an open-source framework for board games and Go engine based on the Monte Carlo Tree Search, which is also used in other board games, instant video games, and uncertainty games. [20] first applied him to the theme park's itinerary recommendation; our article first used Monte Carlo Tree Search as the main algorithm for context-aware personalized POI sequence recommendation. The Monte Carlo Tree Search consists of four main parts: (1) Selection; (2) Expansion; (3) Simulation; (4) Backpropagation.

Step 1: Selection. The essence of the Monte Carlo Tree Search algorithm is to select the child nodes in each state. The board game starts from the root node and selects successive child nodes down to the leaf nodes. Choosing a node algorithm can make the game tree develop in the optimal direction. The main difficulty in selecting sub-nodes is to maintain some balance between exploit and exploration. The first formula for balanced use and exploration in games is called UCT (Upper Confidence Bound 1 applied to trees) proposed by Jobé Sebishwari [15], its main principle is shown in Eq. (7).

$$UCT_p^{c_t} = \frac{totalreward_{p_j}}{visitcount_{p_j}} + 2C\sqrt{\frac{2\ln(visitcount_{p_i})}{visitcount_{p_j}}} \tag{7}$$

Our recommended model also uses UCT algorithm. We select the POI that the user is satisfied with according to the current weather conditions and time.

Step 2: Expansion. In the game, unless the winning or losing of either party causes the game to end at L, create one or more child nodes and select one of the nodes.

Step 3: Simulation. Starting from node C, the game is played with a random strategy, also known as playout or rollout, to get a winning or losing result. The winning reward is 1 otherwise 0.

Our POI sequence recommendation selects the POI from each state and gets the bonus score for the POI in each state. Our reward score is shown as follows:

$$Reward = (\text{Int}_u \, (p_i, c_t) + \text{Pop} \, (p_i, c_t)) \tag{8}$$

Step 4: Backpropgation. This part mainly uses the result of random games to update the node information from the child node C to the root node path, including the number of visits and rewards.

Similarly, our POI sequence recommendation also backtracks, adding 1 to all POIs selected, and the reward value is backtracked to the root of the search tree based on the user's interest and the popularity of the POI.

4.4   CAPR Algorithm

Our context-aware personalized POI sequence recommendation extends the Monte Carlo Tree Search algorithm which is based on a reinforcement learning model and a simulation strategy [9]. As shown in Fig. 3, different weather conditions and time intervals are equivalent to different states in the reinforcement learning environment, abbreviated St. We get the distribution of rewards in the current state through user interest and POI popularity model, and then select the best action based on the reward. The optimal action corresponding to our recommendation algorithm is to select the POI that is most satisfactory to the user in the current environment. Finally, within the time budget, the algorithm recommends to the user a personalized POI sequence that perceives the context. And next, we mainly describe the details of the context-aware personalized POI sequence recommendation algorithm.

The input of CAPR algorithm includes the starting POI and time, the ending POI, and the total time spent on user demand. After N iteration experiments, CAPR algorithm can return the user a personalized POI sequence.

We initialize two similar trees (T_{visit} and T_{reward}) with the root node as the starting POI p_1. These two trees can record the number of visits and rewards of nodes during the iteration process. In Algorithm 1 (line 15), c_{t_i} and the two similar trees as the input of the selection node algorithm.

Algorithm 1 (line 6–31) embodies the four steps of the MCST. (1) Algorithm 1 (line 16–17) is the Selection and Expansion. Equation (7) shows the principle of Selection and Expansion. To select the best node under the current environment we set c to $1/\sqrt{2}$ which Kocsis and Szepesv [16] has proved to be the best value as satisfies Hoeffding's inequality. After selecting the node, Algorithm 1 (line 14–18) estimate the time overhead, update the current context, and continue

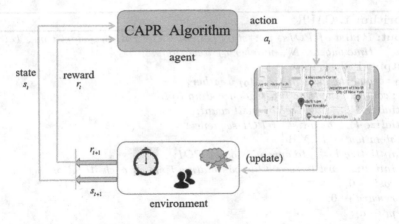

Fig. 3. CAPR algorithm architecture

to select nodes until the total time budget is reached. (2) Algorithm 1 (line 19–21) shows the Simulation step. It calculates the node' reward after each node selection. It use the user interest (line 19) and POI popularity models (line 20) in Sects. 3.2 and 3.3 to get the reward value of the node. (3) Algorithm 1 (line 25–27) shows the Backpropgation, BackpropC (line 25) updates the T_{visit} tree in this iteration. If the algorithm recommended the ending poi in this iteration is p_n, it will update the T_{reward} tree.

Algorithm 1 returns the recommended POI sequence whose rewards is the biggest.

5 Experiment and Evaluation

5.1 Dataset

We use the weeplaces dataset to do experiments. The Weeplaces[1] dataset does not contain weather data, so we use API[2] to crawl the weather data of a city in New York, and climbed the POI' Weather characteristics (sunny, overcast, rainy, snowy), temperature and humidity. The city's New York check-in record contains 863,800 data, 4,476 users, and 16,100 POIs.

Table 1. Description of the dataset

Weeplaces dataset			
No. of check-ins	No. of users	No. of POIs	No. of years
7658368	15709	971309	2002–2012

---

[1] https://www.yongliu.org/datasets/.
[2] https://api.darksky.net/forecast/.

Algorithm 1. CAPR

Input: P : *list of POIs*, p_1 : *start_poi*, p_n : *end_poi*, t_0 : *start time*, B : *time bugets*, N : *number of iterations*.

Output: POI sequence

1   W_{t0} : *crawl the current time(t_0) weather*;
2   T_{t0} : *compute the time intervals accoding to t_0*;
3   *initialize T_{visit} as a tree of visit count*;
4   *initialize P_{list} as a list of POI sequence*;
5 **for** *iteration* $\leftarrow$ *1...N* **do**
6   *initialize P_{temp} to append choosed POI*;
7   *initialize cost to record the cumulative time of each iteration*;
8     $cost \leftarrow 0$;
9     $reward \leftarrow 0$;
10     $p_i \leftarrow a_1$;
11     $p_j \leftarrow \phi$;
12     $t_i \leftarrow t_0$;
13   **while** $cost < B$ **do**
14       $c_{t_i} \leftarrow$ *Get the context based on the current time(t_i)*;
15       $p_j \leftarrow selectNode(P_i, c_{t_i}, T_{visit}, T_{reward})$;
16   *Append p_j to P_{temp}*;
17       $cost \leftarrow cost + tra_{p_i,p_j} + dva_{p_j}$;
18       $Int \leftarrow IntModel(c_{t_i}, u, p_j)$;
19       $Pop \leftarrow PopModel(c_{t_i}, p_j)$;
20       $reward \leftarrow reward + (Int_u + Pop_u)$;
21       $t_i \leftarrow cost + t_0$;
22       $p_i \leftarrow p_j$;
23   **end**
24     $BackPropC(I_{temp}, T_{visit})$;
25   **if** $(p_j = p_n)$ **then**
26       $BackPropR(P_{temp}, T_{reward}, reward)$;
27   *Append P_{temp} to P_{list}*;
28   **end**
29 **end**
30 **return** best POI sequence I from P_{list}

For each user, we use the top ninety percent of the sequence number as training data and the last ten percent used as test data.

5.2   Metrics

To verify the accuracy and effectiveness of the algorithm, we adopted the following evaluation indicators (Table 1).

Precision(Pre): we defined the test poi sequence sample as P_t, and the recommended POI sequence as P_r. And calculate the precision by $Pre = \frac{P_r \cap P_t}{P_r}$

Recall(Rec): The indicator Rec measures the recall rate of the recommended sequence which is calculated by $Rec = \frac{P_t \cap P_r}{P_t}$

F score(F1): F1 is defined as the harmonic mean of the accuracy and recall, as follows:

$$F1 = 2\frac{\text{Pre} * \text{Rec}}{\text{Pre} + \text{Rec}} \tag{9}$$

5.3 Baselines

To verify the accuracy of our proposed model, we use a user-based collaborative filtering algorithm and Popularity recommendation algorithm for comparison. What's more, our work considers the context information such as weather. In order to verify that the weather can improve the accuracy of the recommendation algorithm, we use the following baselines to compare.

UCF (User-based Collaborative Filtering algorithm): We used the congtext-aware user-based collaborative filtering algorithm to get top-k POIs. We take the ranked topk POIs and add them to the starting POI until reaching the time budget, getting the POI sequence.

TAPR (Time-Aware POI sequence Recommendation): Unlike CAPR algorithm, we only use time context instead of weather and time together. This algorithm is mainly to verify the impact of weather on the user's check-in behavior.

PR (POI sequence recommendation): We model the user's interest and POI popularity without contexts and the other part is similar to the CAPR algorithm.

POP (POPularity): This algorithm only considers the popularity of POI. It satisfies the time budget and recommends the user's top k popular POIs.

5.4 Evaluation and Reslut

Our algorithm uses the user's real POI sequence as a test sample and the length of POI sequence is more than 3.

As can be seen from Table 2, the CAPR model out-performs all baselines across weelplaces dataset. We compared the CAPR algorithm with the TAPR algorithm which improved the precision by 3%, the recall rate by 10%, and the F1 score by 5%. The result shows the weather can effect the users' check-in. And the comparison between CAPR algorithm and PR algorithm can be seen that the precision improved by 10%, the recall rate improved by 20%, and the F1 score improved by 16%. The results show that the context-aware recommendation algorithm can improve the accuracy. What's more, our algorithm out-performs PR algorithm and UCF algorithm which improved the precision by 24–35%, the recall rate by 19–37%, and the F1 score by 22–46%.

Many experiments have shown that the optimal number of iterations N is 1000. Moreover, the POI sequence recommended by our algorithm tends to converge to the end. We took an average of 5 h to run test samples of all users. The more iterations, the more time it takes. The spatial complexity of our algorithm exits in storaging the node when using the Monte Carlo search tree model. The complexity of the space depends on the number of nodes.

Table 2. Performance comparison by three evaluation metrics.

Algorithm	Precision	Recall	F1-Measure
POP	0.3528	0.2525	0.2089
UCF	0.4586	0.4352	0.4466
PR	0.5823	0.4371	0.5020
TAPR	0.6796	0.5214	0.5900
CAPR	**0.7073**	**0.6221**	**0.6619**

6   Conclusion

In this paper, we propose CAPR algorithm that can be applied to scenarios such as trip planning and travel route recommendations. Our algorithm takes into account the impact of weather and time on user travel and it can recommend a context-aware personalized POI sequence, which maximizes user satisfaction.

In the future, we will discuss these problems as follows: (1) cold start problem. (2) In our work, we only consider the situation of walking, and in the future, we will consider different travel tools (bicycles, cars, etc.) according to different user needs. (3) we will consider the other context informations like the local classic POI.

Acknowledgments. This research was supported by NSFC grant 61632009 and Outstanding Young Talents Training Program in Hunan University 531118040173.

References

1. Abowd, G.D., Dey, A.K., Brown, P.J., Davies, N., Smith, M., Steggles, P.: Towards a better understanding of context and context-awareness. In: Gellersen, H.-W. (ed.) HUC 1999. LNCS, vol. 1707, pp. 304–307. Springer, Heidelberg (1999). https://doi.org/10.1007/3-540-48157-5_29
2. Baral, R., Iyengar, S., Li, T., Balakrishnan, N.: Close: contextualized location sequence recommender. In: Proceedings of the 12th ACM Conference on Recommender Systems, pp. 470–474. ACM (2018)
3. Bienstock, D., Goemans, M.X., Simchi-Levi, D., Williamson, D.: A note on the prize collecting traveling salesman problem. Math. Program. **59**(1–3), 413–420 (1993)
4. Browning, R.C., Baker, E.A., Herron, J.A., Kram, R.: Effects of obesity and sex on the energetic cost and preferred speed of walking. J. Appl. Physiol. **100**(2), 390–398 (2006)
5. Chen, C., Zhang, D., Guo, B., Ma, X., Pan, G., Wu, Z.: Tripplanner: personalized trip planning leveraging heterogeneous crowdsourced digital footprints. IEEE Trans. Intell. Transp. Syst. **16**(3), 1259–1273 (2014)

6. Chen, D., Ong, C.S., Xie, L.: Learning points and routes to recommend trajectories. In: Proceedings of the 25th ACM International on Conference on Information and Knowledge Management, pp. 2227–2232. ACM (2016)
7. De Choudhury, M., Feldman, M., Amer-Yahia, S., Golbandi, N., Lempel, R., Yu, C.: Automatic construction of travel itineraries using social breadcrumbs. In: Proceedings of the 21st ACM Conference on Hypertext and Hypermedia, pp. 35–44. ACM (2010)
8. Debnath, M., Tripathi, P.K., Biswas, A.K., Elmasri, R.: Preference aware travel route recommendation with temporal influence. In: Proceedings of the 2nd ACM SIGSPATIAL Workshop on Recommendations for Location-Based Services and Social Networks, p. 2. ACM (2018)
9. Enzenberger, M., Muller, M., Arneson, B., Segal, R.: Fuego-an open-source framework for board games and Go engine based on Monte Carlo tree search. IEEE Trans. Comput. Intell. AI Games 2(4), 259–270 (2010)
10. Ge, Y., Liu, Q., Xiong, H., Tuzhilin, A., Chen, J.: Cost-aware travel tour recommendation. In: Proceedings of the 17th ACM SIGKDD International Conference on Knowledge Discovery and Data Mining, pp. 983–991. ACM (2011)
11. He, L., Wu, F.: A time-context-based collaborative filtering algorithm. In: 2009 IEEE International Conference on Granular Computing, pp. 209–213. IEEE (2009)
12. Jiang, W., Wu, J., Wang, G.: On selecting recommenders for trust evaluation in online social networks. ACM Trans. Internet Technol. (TOIT) 15(4), 14 (2015)
13. Jiang, W., Wu, J., Wang, G., Zheng, H.: Fluidrating: a time-evolving rating scheme in trust-based recommendation systems using fluid dynamics. In: IEEE INFOCOM 2014-IEEE Conference on Computer Communications, pp. 1707–1715. IEEE (2014)
14. Jiang, W., Wu, J., Wang, G., Zheng, H.: Forming opinions via trusted friends: time-evolving rating prediction using fluid dynamics. IEEE Trans. Comput. 65(4), 1211–1224 (2015)
15. Kocsis, L., Szepesvári, C.: Bandit based Monte-Carlo planning. In: Fürnkranz, J., Scheffer, T., Spiliopoulou, M. (eds.) ECML 2006. LNCS (LNAI), vol. 4212, pp. 282–293. Springer, Heidelberg (2006). https://doi.org/10.1007/11871842_29
16. Kocsis, L., Szepesvári, C., Willemson, J.: Improved Monte-Carlo search. University of Tartu, Estonia, Technical report 1 (2006)
17. Lee, W.P., Lee, K.H.: Making smartphone service recommendations by predicting users' intentions: a context-aware approach. Inf. Sci. 277, 21–35 (2014)
18. Li, J., Deng, H., Jiang, W.: Secure vibration control of flexible arms based on operators' behaviors. In: Wang, G., Atiquzzaman, M., Yan, Z., Choo, K.-K.R. (eds.) SpaCCS 2017. LNCS, vol. 10656, pp. 420–431. Springer, Cham (2017). https://doi.org/10.1007/978-3-319-72389-1_34
19. Li, M., Jiang, W., Li, K.: Recommendation systems in real applications: algorithm and parallel architecture. In: Wang, G., Ray, I., Alcaraz Calero, J.M., Thampi, S.M. (eds.) SpaCCS 2016. LNCS, vol. 10066, pp. 45–58. Springer, Cham (2016). https://doi.org/10.1007/978-3-319-49148-6_5
20. Lim, K.H., Chan, J., Karunasekera, S., Leckie, C.: Personalized itinerary recommendation with queuing time awareness. In: Proceedings of the 40th International ACM SIGIR Conference on Research and Development in Information Retrieval, pp. 325–334. ACM (2017)
21. Majid, A., Chen, L., Mirza, H.T., Hussain, I., Chen, G.: A system for mining interesting tourist locations and travel sequences from public geo-tagged photos. Data Knowl. Eng. 95, 66–86 (2015)

22. Manotumruksa, J., Macdonald, C., Ounis, I.: A contextual attention recurrent architecture for context-aware venue recommendation. In: The 41st International ACM SIGIR Conference on Research & Development in Information Retrieval, pp. 555–564. ACM (2018)
23. Peters, M., Frehse, J., Buhalis, D., et al.: The importance of lifestyle entrepreneurship: a conceptual study of the tourism industry (2009)
24. Robusto, C.C.: The Cosine-Haversine formula. Am. Math. Monthly 64(1), 38–40 (1957)
25. Shi, Y., Jiang, W.: Point-of-interest recommendations: capturing the geographical influence from local trajectories. In: 2017 IEEE International Symposium on Parallel and Distributed Processing with Applications and 2017 IEEE International Conference on Ubiquitous Computing and Communications (ISPA/IUCC), pp. 1122–1129. IEEE (2017)
26. Trattner, C., Oberegger, A., Eberhard, L., Parra, D., Marinho, L.B., et al.: Understanding the impact of weather for POI recommendations. In: RecTour@ RecSys, pp. 16–23 (2016)
27. Villegas, N.M., Müller, H.A.: Managing dynamic context to optimize smart interactions and services. In: Chignell, M., Cordy, J., Ng, J., Yesha, Y. (eds.) The Smart Internet. LNCS, vol. 6400, pp. 289–318. Springer, Heidelberg (2010). https://doi.org/10.1007/978-3-642-16599-3_18
28. Wang, G., Jiang, W., Wu, J., Xiong, Z.: Fine-grained feature-based social influence evaluation in online social networks. IEEE Trans. Parallel Distrib. Syst. 25(9), 2286–2296 (2013)
29. Wang, X., Leckie, C., Chan, J., Lim, K.H., Vaithianathan, T.: Improving personalized trip recommendation by avoiding crowds. In: Proceedings of the 25th ACM International on Conference on Information and Knowledge Management, pp. 25–34. ACM (2016)
30. Xu, Z., Chen, L., Chen, G.: Topic based context-aware travel recommendation method exploiting geotagged photos. Neurocomputing 155, 99–107 (2015)
31. Yuan, Q., Cong, G., Ma, Z., Sun, A., Thalmann, N.M.: Time-aware point-of-interest recommendation. In: Proceedings of the 36th International ACM SIGIR Conference on Research and Development in Information Retrieval, pp. 363–372. ACM (2013)
32. Zhang, C., Liang, H., Wang, K., Sun, J.: Personalized trip recommendation with POI availability and uncertain traveling time. In: Proceedings of the 24th ACM International on Conference on Information and Knowledge Management, pp. 911–920. ACM (2015)

Effect on the Demand and Stock Returns: Cross-Sectional of Big Data and Time-Series Analysis

Amelec Viloria[1]([⊠]), Indira Meñaca Guerrero[2],
Hugo Martínez Caraballo[2], Nelson Orellano Llinas[3], Lesbia Valero[4],
Hugo Hernández Palma[4], Edwin Caño Otero[4],
and Omar Bonerge Pineda Lezama[5]

[1] Universidad de la Costa, St. 58 #66, Barranquilla, Atlántico, Colombia
aviloria7@cuc.edu.co
[2] Universidad Simón Bolívar, Barranquilla, Colombia
{indira.menaca,hugo.martinez}@unisimonbolivar.edu.co
[3] Corporación Universitaria Minuto de Dios – UNIMINUTO,
Barranquilla, Colombia
nelson.orellano@uniminuto.edu
[4] Corporación Universitaria Latinoamericana, Barranquilla, Colombia
{lvalero,hhernandez,ecano}@ul.edu.co
[5] Universidad Tecnológica Centroamericana (UNITEC),
San Pedro Sula, Honduras
omarpineda@unitec.edu

Abstract. For reducing the degree of uncertainty caused by constant change in the environment, large, medium or small, private or public organizations must support their decisions in something more than experience or intuition; they must be supported by the development of accurate and reliable forecasts in order to meet the needs in the organization planning tasks. This case study presents a growing company dedicated to the storage of perishable products and incorporates time series forecasting techniques to estimate the volume of storage to foresee the requirements of additional facilities, personnel and materials needed for product mobility.

Keywords: Warehousing · Cold chain · Forecasts · Time series · Perishable products

1 Introduction

Warehousing is a fundamental part in the development of both supply chain strategies and logistics. In this sense, [1, 2] mention that warehouses are involved in the different stages of the supply chain, as well as in the different internal processes of the companies, through the procurement, material handling, and the storage or securing of products. In this way, "the design of the chambers must guarantee the quality of the product for offering a proper customer service that satisfy thermal requirements and accessibility to the product in the chambers to achieve the readiness of orders and their fast dispatch" [3–6].

© Springer Nature Singapore Pte Ltd. 2019
G. Wang et al. (Eds.): iSCI 2019, CCIS 1122, pp. 211–220, 2019.
https://doi.org/10.1007/978-981-15-1301-5_17

However, "in our environment, the sizing of future storage needs is not adequately supported by accurate data and forecasts. On the contrary, simplifications are often made based on personal assumptions and perceptions, which leads to over-dimensioning or little space available in the short term, consequently generating higher operating costs" [7, 8]. Therefore, there is a number of initiatives to address uncertainty and improved performance in the supply chain and accuracy of forecasting, where the main idea is that decision-makers work throughout the chain to determine inventory and replenishment strategies through the recovery and analysis of historical data, known as time series, which provides coordination with forecasts [9–12].

Given the above, it should be borne in mind that "the objective of a forecast is to enable decisions about the future and to provide an estimate of the risk involved in the decision" [13, 14]. Thus, the importance of a forecast derives from the fact that inaccuracies cannot be separated from reality, causing all organizations to operate in an environment of uncertainty. For this reason, in order to reduce the risk of making managerial or operational decisions and to be able to model what will happen in the future, as well as to qualify this perception of uncertainty, it is important to make use of all available information from the present and the past, and not only to rely on assumptions in order to avoid bad decisions. It must also be considered that decision-making models are attached to reality of the company and not to that of the environment, since a rational belief is not necessarily a true belief [15, 16].

Therefore, "the primary consideration in the choice of a forecasting method is that the results should facilitate the decision-making process of the organization" [17, 18]. In this sense, the forecasts applied to the storage demand allow to efficiently determine both the size of the warehouse and the interior design of a new facility, or in existing facilities, to develop an improvement plan in the interior design that supports the expected growth, thus allowing anticipating the needs of customers or consumers, focusing on increasing profits with a high level of service. Specifically, "short term prediction is used to plan the operation of the system, while long term prediction is usually used as an input in decisions to expand generation capacity and the distribution system" [19–22].

Given the importance of products storage for developing regions, such as Latin American countries [23, 24], this paper focuses on the use and application of time series forecasting techniques, through the analysis of past information, allowing the selection of the forecasting tool in order to estimate the volume of income and expenditures of perishable food products in cold stores in a Mexican company. These forecasts seek to assess the volume of income and expenditure mobility in perishable products, validating the capacity at which the chamber works and identifying whether additional facilities are needed to handle the growing demand, as well as guidance to decision-makers on the staffing requirements and resources needed for better mobility of products [25, 26].

2 Method

The forecasts made through the use of these techniques show the premise that the tendency given will be kept, which helps obtain quite precise forecasts in the short term. These techniques include the simple moving average, weighted moving average, exponential softening, exponential softening adjusted to the tendency, multiplicative seasonal method and time series with seasonal and tendency influences, among others. Causal methods, on the other hand, assume that the factor to be predicted exhibits a cause-effect relationship with one or more independent variables. The purpose of causal models is to describe the form of relationship between variables and use it to predict future values of the dependent variable. Among the most commonly used causal methods are regression and econometric techniques [27–30].

In the present case study applies quantitative forecasting techniques based on the analysis of historical data on the behavior of income and expenses of perishable products in a cold store, divided into 52 periods (weeks), corresponding to historical data provided by a company of perishable products, which present a growing linear trend (as shown in Fig. 1).

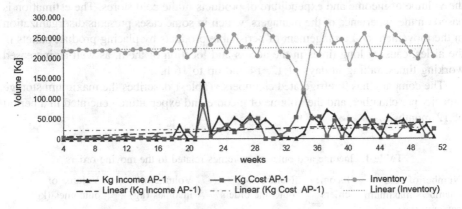

Fig. 1. Incomes and outcomes of the AP-1 product of chamber 2

From the analysis, the following time series techniques are applied in order to produce a comparative statement and identify the technique that provides the best result: simple moving average, weighted moving average, exponential smoothing and adjusted exponential smoothing [31, 32].

In this case study, the data considered for the forecasting techniques are: for the moving average, n = 3; for the weighted moving average, its weighting factor was C_i = 20% for the most distant period; 30% for the intermediate period and 50% for the most recent period, which is consistent with the assumptions of [33, 34], who point out that the most recent periods soften the fluctuations. On the other hand, for the exponential smoothing technique, it was 0.1, 0.2 and 0.3; and for the adjusted exponential smoothing, smoothing constants of both 0.1, 0.2, 0.3 were considered, considering the selection of these constants as precision criteria, impulse response and noise damping capacity [35–38].

3 Results

This section studies a company dedicated to controlled temperature storage, refrigeration services, freezing, cold maquila, specialized distribution service and dry storage, mainly focused on the storage of perishable food products in 9 cold rooms. In the controlled temperatures, the one required by the client is provided, fast freezing to temperatures of up to −40 °C, and conservation of the product to temperatures of −18 ° C to −25 °C. Through cold maquila, added value is generated through the service requested by the client, control and follow-up of the client's inventory, verification point and sanitary certification center.

The products stored in the cold rooms are mainly classified into families of dairy products, meats and juices. In the process of controlling inventories in the storage of cold stores, the company does not use quantitative support methodologies to estimate the volume of income and expenditure of products in the cold stores. The estimation is based on the experience of the managers, which in some cases presents disorganization in the movement and arrangement of perishable products by placing product pallets in the aisles, causing long times in the access and location of them, as well as increased working times, falling in days of 12, 14 and up to 16 h.

The company has 9 refrigerated chambers. Table 1 describes the maximum storage capacity per chamber, and the volume of income and expenditure generated in a period of 12 months.

Table 1. Income and outcome volumes related to the moving orders

Number of cold chambers maximum capacity (kg)		Income orders	Number of outcome orders	Volume of incomes (kg)	Volume of outcomes (kg)
0	889.000	45	175	137,752	141,357
1	2,330,000	4	10	10,915	7,521
2	1,960,000	689	6.453	5,987,819	6,354,946
3	1,076,000	131	1.780	1,365,434	1,187,331
4	1,687,000	47	995	587,435	682,029
5	575,000	3	17	6,339	11,485
6	0	0	0	0	0
7	4,685,000	4	68	31,751	48,357
8	3,987,000	3	14	20,244	14,521

Tables 2 and 3 show the results obtained from the 4 forecasting techniques applied, represented in Sect. 2, for the movement volumes of products AP-1 and NE-2 of cold store No. 2. Initially, Table 2 illustrates the forecast of product entry volume AP-1 for weeks 53 to 56. Thus, for week 53, 11,987 kg are predicted through the technique of weighted moving averages, observing that this is the smallest predicted volume. By means of the adjusted exponential smoothing technique, a volume with the highest value represented by 82,982 kg is presented, and with the technique of weighted moving averages, the smallest error is presented comparatively with the other 3 techniques applied, being 0.99, and the DMA related to this value is 17,852 kg, which implies an overestimated tendency of the forecast.

In other words, the forecast will be positive or increasing based on historical data. Additionally, it is identified that, for weeks 53, 54 and 55, the lowest error is represented by the technique of weighted moving averages. In this way, it is identified that the data obtained from the forecast of the volume of income of the product AP-1 with the technique of weighted moving averages are the most acceptable to consider for the mobility planning.

Table 2. Income forecast for the product AP-1 of the chamber N° 2

Technique	Week incomes	53 (kg)	Error DMA ST	Week incomes	54 (kg)	Error DMA ST	Week incomes	55 (kg)	Error DMA ST	Week incomes	56 (kg)	Error DMA ST
Moving averages	15,785	17,147	1.37	9,853	17,861	1.75	11,378	16,784	1.79	12,781	16,852	1.44
Weighed moving averages	11,987	17,852	0.99	9,741	15,783	0.97	9,945	16,255	1.81	10,654	16,476	1.83
Exponential smoothing	18,452	15,698	4.42	18,698	14,141	4.13	18,756	14,454	4.60	19,251	14,952	4.38
Adjusted exponential smoothing	82,982	20,785	1.65	83,458	20,754	18.92	85,574	19,657	20.44	87,426	19,497	19.97

Table 3. Outcome forecast for the product AP-1 of the chamber N° 2

Technique	Week incomes	53 (kg)	Error DMA ST	Week incomes	54 (kg)	Error DMA ST	Week incomes	55 (kg)	Error DMA ST	Week incomes	56 (kg)	Error DMA ST
Moving averages	12.123	16.856	0,40	15.122	16.852	0,48	12.354	15.147	0,42	13.469	15.140	0,48
Weighed moving averages	13.478	16.685	0,49	13.856	16.741	0,47	13.421	15.685	0,48	13.741	15.983	0,44
Exponential smoothing	18.685	14.421	3,78	18.652	14.958	3,14	18.987	13.483	3,873	18.985	13.251	3,94
Adjusted exponential smoothing	50.785	15.147	0,14	51.998	15.878	0,145	52.723	15.981	0,198	54.456	14.147	0,152

Table 3 shows the forecasts of expenditures of the AP-1 product. Unlike the income, in which the technique with the lowest error identified is the weighted moving averages technique; in the expenses, the smallest error is presented in the adjusted exponential smoothing technique, with a value of 0.14. This technique foresees that the kilograms of output of the product AP-1 for the aforementioned periods are 50,785, 51,998, 52,723, and 54,456 kg, respectively. Given the above, it is identified that the forecasts obtained from week 53 to week 56 represent an increase of 3.4% average.

Besides, it is identified that, as the periods to forecast increase, the error also grows, indicating that the forecast may be less accurate to increase the forecast periods.

Figures 2 and 3 illustrate a comparison between the forecasts of the income volume of and outcome of products AP-1 and NE-2 from weeks 53 to 56 versus the volume of weeks 1 to 4. Initially, Fig. 2 graphically shows the forecasts of weeks 53 to 56 of product AP1. The prognosis for this product estimates an average income of 11,000 kg. On the other hand, the forecast of expenditures estimates around 53,000 kg per period, which means an average increase of 44,000 kg compared to the same period of the previous year. It should be noted that the behavior of the expenditures of this product in its analogous period, that is, in weeks 1–4, has a notorious fall in weeks 3 and 4, maintaining the level of the inventory in 3,600 kg approximately, and presenting the highest income in week 4 with 16,145.3 kg; behavior that is different from the predicted for weeks 55 and 56.

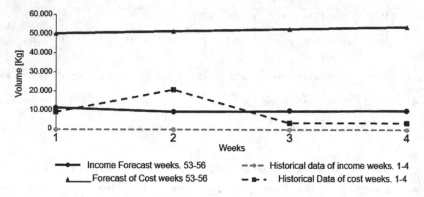

Fig. 2. Comparison between the forecasts of income and outcome volumes of product AP-1.

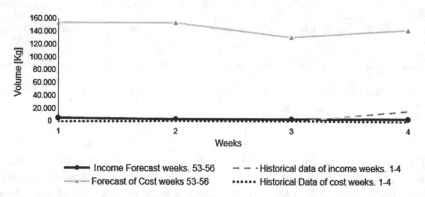

Fig. 3. Comparison between the forecasts of income and outcome volumes of product NE-2

Figure 3 shows NE-2 product forecasts. As can be noted, the predicted incomes for weeks 53–56 are very similar to those for weeks 1–4, with an average income variation of 520 kg between each week. However, the predicted expenditures (outcomes) have a very different behavior to those obtained in the first 4 periods, being predicted a volume of expenditures between 155,000 and 147,000 kg, where the largest expenditure will be demanded in week 2, with a volume of 145,775 kg, and the smallest volume demanded is displayed in week 3, with 145,271 kg.

From the results obtained, it is estimated, for the analyzed period, an income average volume of product AP-1 of 10 tons (ton), and an average outcome of this same product of 52 ton, which means that the outcomes exceed the income by 82.3%. In the case of the product NE-2 the forecast is an average income of 4.35 ton and an average outcome of 157.2 ton, representing an output of the product of 98.4% with respect to income. Summarizing, in both products are predicted expenditures higher than income. In addition, it was identified an increase of 43.4 ton of the product AP-1, with respect to the historical data in the same period. On the other hand, in the product NE-2 there is an average increase of 146.7 ton.

4   Conclusions

The analysis of obtained results allows to plan actions and strategies that satisfy the demand for analyzed products, as well as the tools and personnel required for their storage and mobility of the products. In particular, it is highlighted that for the 4 periods of study, the volumes of outcome of the selected products are higher than the volumes of income, with an average of 184,600 kg of product. This shortage represents 99.6% of products. From the results obtained, it is possible to highlight the behavior of one of the products, the AP-1, which contrasts with the historical data analyzed since the movement in the outcome until the first 18 weeks is almost null and, later, from week 19, shows an increasing tendency of expenditure.

Regarding the NE-2 product, an average growth of 146,450 kg is estimated in the outflow, with respect to income, for the 4 periods of analysis. This situation, together with the behavior at the end of the study period, in which the inventory was almost null, foresee a shortage of NE-2 product in the chamber, so that the shortage of both products represents a decrease in the total inventory volume of almost 11% of product in the chamber. In other words, it is predicted that the total capacity of the chamber will be occupied at 64% of the total volume. This forecast allows to know an estimate and make decisions regarding the resources required in personnel, vehicles, materials, tools, etc., as well as the elaboration of the annual, monthly, weekly storage and mobility plan. As part of the benefits in the results obtained from the application of forecasting techniques, it stands out that they allow to know the capacity to which they work allowing to design new strategies to enter new products, in order to use to the maximum capacity of the cold room.

The development of this research demonstrates the usefulness of forecasts for decision making in several areas and the planning of activities in storage companies and mobility of perishable products. As a consequence, the uncertainty in the operations is minimized and a more detailed planning of the processes is allowed. Therefore, the planning and management of inventories, or movements of product volumes in the perishable goods warehouse can be done in a more efficient and reliable way. As future work, it is intended to use forecasts as an analysis tool for various strategies in which resource management plays a fundamental role.

These strategies should take into account various characteristics of the products, such as dimensions, weights, product rotation, expiration dates, as well as the characteristics of their perishable properties. Additionally, the strategies will take into account these characteristics to propose a new lay-out of the chambers, which allows the zoning for the reception, accommodation and exit of perishable products from the different cold rooms, considering the assignment of personnel and forklifts required for product mobility, assignment of cold room, accommodation and identification of products in the racks, which seeks to minimize the accommodation time of the products or maximize the cost of storage.

References

1. Torres, M.: Pronósticos, una herramienta clave para la planeación de las empresas. Instituto Tecnológico de Sonora [consultado 12 Ene 2016]. Disponible en (2011). http://itson.mx/publicaciones/pacioli/Documents/no71/47a. pronósticos, una herramienta clave para la planeación de las empresas.pdf
2. Velázquez, J.D., Dyner, R.I., Souza, R.C.: Políticas para la integración del juicio experto y los pronósticos estadísticos en el marco organizacional. Estudios Gerenciales 99(22), 131–150 (2006)
3. Velázquez, J., Franco, C., García, H.: Un modelo no lineal para la predicción de la demanda mensual de electricidad en Colombia. Estudios Gerenciales 25(112), 37–54 (2009)
4. Vidal, C.J., Londono, J.C., Contreras, F.: Aplicación de los modelos de inventario en una cadena de abastecimiento de productos de consumo masivo con una bodega y N Puntos de venta. Ingeniería y Competitividad 6(1), 35–52 (2004)
5. Alonso, J., Arcila, A.: Empleo del comportamiento estacional para mejorar el pronóstico de un commodity: el caso del mercado internacional de azúcar. Estudios Gerenciales 29(129), 406–415 (2013)
6. Arango, M., Adame, W., Zapata, C.: Gestión cadena de abastecimiento—logística con indicadores bajo incertidumbre, caso aplicado sector panificador Palmira. Ciencia e Ingeniería Neogranadina 20(1), 97–115 (2010)
7. Arrendondo, F., Vázquez, J.: Un modelo de análisis racional para la toma de decisiones gerenciales, desde la perspectiva elsteriana. Cuadernos de Administración 26(46), 135–158 (2013)
8. Medina, S.: Las cadenas de frío y eltransporte refrigerado en México. Comercio Exterior, 59(12), 1010–1017 (2009)
9. Medina, J., Ortegón, E.: Manual de prospectiva y decisión estratégica. Naciones Unidas, CEPAL, ILPES, Santiago de Chile (2006)
10. Munoz, A.: Metodología para el dimensionamiento de almacenes basado en la estimación de la demanda para el sector cosmético. Universidad Militar Nueva Granada [consultado 14 Ene 2016]. Disponible en (2014). http://repository.unimilitar.edu.co/bitstream/10654/12624/1/ART%C3%8DCULO%20FINAL.pdf
11. Pindyck, S., Rubinfeld, L.: Econometría, modelos y pronósticos: pronósticos con un modelo de regresión de una sola ecuación, 4th edn. McGraw Hill, México (2001)
12. Izquierdo, N.V., Lezama, O.B.P., Dorta, R.G., Viloria, A., Deras, I., Hernández-Fernández, L.: Fuzzy logic applied to the performance evaluation. honduran coffee sector case. In: Tan,

Y., Shi, Y., Tang, Q. (eds.) ICSI 2018. LNCS, vol. 10942, pp. 164–173. Springer, Cham (2018). https://doi.org/10.1007/978-3-319-93818-9_16

13. Pineda Lezama, O., Gómez Dorta, R.: Techniques of multivariate statistical analysis: an application for the Honduran banking sector. innovare. J. Sci. Technol. **5**(2), 61–75 (2017)
14. Fogarty, D., Blackstone, J., Hoffmann, T.: Administración de la producción e inventarios, 2. a edn. México (2014)
15. Patria. Gallego, G., Toktay, L.: All-or-nothing ordering. Under a capacity constrain and forecast of stationary demand (2003) [consultado 13 Oct 2015]. Disponible en: https://pdfs. semanticscholar.org/81ef/e6d84d9fc4414d3685bf018fc4ff35d46ed4.pdf
16. Gutiérrez, V., Vidal, C.: Modelos de gestión de inventarios en cadenas de abastecimiento: revisión de la literatura. Revista Facultad Ingeniería Universidad de Antioquia **43**, 134–149 (2008)
17. Hanke, J.E., Wichern, D.W.: Pronósticos en los negocios, 8.a edn. Pearson Educación, México (2006)
18. López, C.: Manual para la preparación y venta de frutas y hortalizas: del campo al mercado. Boletín de servicios agrícolas de la FAO **151**, 49–50 (2003)
19. Masini, J., Vázquez, F.: Compendio de modelos cuantitativos de pronósticos (2014). [consultado 20 Dic 2015]. Disponible en: https://books.google.com.mx/books?id= fnLcBQAAQBAJ&printsec=frontcover&hl=es#v=onepage&q=los%20metodos%20&f= false
20. Toro, E.M., Mejia, D.A., Salazar, H.: Pronóstico de ventas usando redes neuronales. Scientia et technica **10**(26), 25–30 (2004)
21. Villada, F., Muñoz, N., García, E.: Aplicación de las Redes Neuronales al Pronóstico de Precios en Mercado de Valores, Información tecnológica **23**(4), 11–20 (2012)
22. Wen, Q., Mu, W., Sun, L., Hua, S., Zhou, Z.: Daily sales forecasting for grapes by support vector machine. In: International Conference on Computer and Computing Technologies in Agriculture, pp. 351–360 (2013)
23. Wu, Q., Yan, H.S., Yang, H.B.: A forecasting model based support vector machine and particle swarm optimization. In: 2008 Workshop on Power Electronics and Intelligent Transportation System, pp. 218–222 (2008)
24. Ballou, R.H.: Logística, 5.a edn. Administración de la cadena de suministro. Pearson Educación, México (2004)
25. Corres, A., Esteban, A., García, J., Zarate, C.: Análisis de series temporales. Ingeniería Ind. **8** (1), 21–33 (2009)
26. Erossa, V.: Proyectos de inversión en ingeniería: su metodología. Limusa, México (2004)
27. Rahman, M.A., Islam, M.Z.: A hybrid clustering technique combining a novel genetic algorithm with K-Means. Knowl. Based Syst. **71**, 345–365 (2014). https://doi.org/10.1016/j. knosys.2014.08.011
28. Amelec, V.: Increased efficiency in a company of development of technological solutions in the areas commercial and of consultancy. Adv. Sci. Lett. **21**(5), 1406–1408 (2015)
29. Amelec, V.: Validation of strategies to reduce exhausted shelf products in a pharmaceutical chain. Adv. Sci. Lett. **21**(5), 1403–1405 (2015)
30. Varela, I.N., Cabrera, H.R., Lopez, C.G., Viloria, A., Gaitán, A.M., Henry, M.A.: Methodology for the reduction and integration of data in the performance measurement of industries cement plants. In: Tan, Y., Shi, Y., Tang, Q. (eds.) Data Mining and Big Data. LNCS, vol. 10943, pp. 33–42. Springer, Cham (2018). https://doi.org/10.1007/978-3-319-93803-5_4

31. Lis-Gutiérrez, M., Gaitán-Angulo, M., Balaguera, M.I., Viloria, A., Santander-Abril, J.E.: Use of the industrial property system for new creations in Colombia: a departmental analysis (2000–2016). In: Tan, Y., Shi, Y., Tang, Q. (eds.) Data Mining and Big Data. LNCS, vol. 10943, pp. 786–796. Springer, Cham (2018). https://doi.org/10.1007/978-3-319-93803-5_74
32. Pickrahn, I., et al.: Contamination incidents in the pre-analytical phase of forensic DNA analysis in Austria—Statistics of 17 years. Forensic Sci. Int. Genet. **31**, 12–18 (2017). https://doi.org/10.1016/j.fsigen.2017.07.012
33. Isasi, P., Galván, I.: Redes de Neuronas Artificiales. Un enfoque Práctico. Pearson, London (2004). ISBN 8420540250
34. Kulkarni, S., Haidar, I.: Forecasting model for crude oil price using artificial neural networks and commodity future prices. Int. J. Comput. Sci. Inf. Secur. **2**(1), 81–89 (2009)
35. Mazón, J.N., Trujillo, J., Serrano, M., Piattini, M.: Designing data warehouses: from business requirement analysis to multidimensional modeling. In: Proceedings of the 1st International Workshop on Requirements Engineering for Business Need and IT Alignment. Paris, France (2005)
36. Viloria, A., Lis-Gutierrez, J.P., Gaitán-Angulo, M., Godoy, A.R.M., Moreno, G.C., Kamatkar, S.J.: Methodology for the design of a student pattern recognition tool to facilitate the teaching - learning process through knowledge data discovery (big data). In: Tan, Y., Shi, Y., Tang, Q. (eds.) Data Mining and Big Data. LNCS, vol. 10943, pp. 670–679. Springer, Cham (2018). https://doi.org/10.1007/978-3-319-93803-5_63
37. Barrios-Hernández, K.D.C., Contreras-Salinas, J.A., Olivero-Vega, E.: La Gestión por Procesos en las Pymes de Barranquilla: Factor Diferenciador de la Competitividad Organizacional. Información tecnológica **30**(2), 103–114 (2019)
38. Atsalakis, G.S., Valavanis, K.P.: Surveying stock market forecasting techniques – Part II: Soft computing methods. Expert Syst. Appl. **36**(3, Part 2), 5932–5941 (2009)

Optimization of Factors that Influence the "Settlement" of the Concrete in Mixer Transport

Alexander Parody[1(✉)], Abel Ávila[2], Mercedes Gaitán[3],
Marjorie Galofre[2], María Wilches[2], Leila Ramírez[4], Dionicio Neira[5],
and Jesús Silva[6]

[1] Universidad Libre Barranquilla, Barranquilla, Colombia
alexandere.parodym@unilibre.edu.co
[2] Universidad Autónoma del Caribe, Barranquilla, Colombia
abel_avila24@hotmail.com.co,
{mgalofre,mwilches}@uac.edu.co
[3] Corporación Universitaria Empresarial de Salamanca – CUES,
Barranquilla, Colombia
m_gaitan689@cues.edu.co
[4] Universidad Libre Bogotá, Bogota, Colombia
leylan.ramirezc@unilibre.edu.co
[5] Universidad de la Costa (CUC), Calle 58 # 55-66, Atlantico,
Barranquilla, Colombia
dneiral@cuc.edu.co
[6] Universidad Peruana de Ciencias Aplicadas, Lima, Peru
jesussilva@gmail.com

Abstract. The research seeks to determine the relationship of the settlement as a parameter of the quality of the concrete, with the volume and pressure of the manometer of the concrete mixer truck, by means of a multiple linear regression model in a concrete manufacturing company. A regression model was generated where the variables volume of the mixer and pressure turned out to be statistically significant (p value < 0.05), the linear correlation coefficient was 72.4% which speaks well of the level of relationship between the independent variables and the dependent variable, in addition the average forecast error was 0.0000003 following the model residuals a normal distribution, p value of the Kolmogorov-Smirnov test was 0.5913, therefore the model has good behavior at the time to correctly forecast the value of the settlement. The model will allow an approximate estimation of the settlement behavior.

Keywords: Settlement · Concrete · Quality · Customer satisfaction · Regression model

© Springer Nature Singapore Pte Ltd. 2019
G. Wang et al. (Eds.): iSCI 2019, CCIS 1122, pp. 221–230, 2019.
https://doi.org/10.1007/978-981-15-1301-5_18

1 Introduction

The settlement is a very important variable in the assessment of the quality of it, since it is the measure of consistency of the concrete. That is, it measures the ease of concrete for molding, pushing and smoothing. The settlement is measured in magnitude of distance and the standards expressed in units of inches and/or millimeters. The greater the settlement, the more fluidity and manageability the concrete will have.

The companies that manufacture concrete have been presenting inconveniences with the measurement of settlement in the hydraulic concrete at the time of the start of civil works, which in many cases affects the programming of the activities because the concrete does not meet the specifications of quality required for the settlement of the concrete, which forces to reprocess said concrete.

It is an obligation for companies and/or organizations to provide material or immaterial products, goods or quality services that meet their needs and expectations. To achieve this, a set of interrelated or intertwined activities is needed, acting in a synergistic way that receive certain inputs (inputs) and that are transformed into outputs (outputs) or into a product. The latter will be the quality characteristics or response variables, which reflect the results obtained in the process. The effectiveness of the process lies in the values of these variables [1].

The type of concrete is determined by the size of the settlement. Once you have direct contact with the client, the first specification that refers is the value of the measure, as this is stipulated in the regulations in force governing the production and quality of the concrete. Once the concrete is produced in the hoppers and poured into the trucks through the dosing machines, it has to be strictly verified if it complies with the specification limits set out in the regulations.

Therefore, the variable of settlement quality must be controlled so that it meets the specifications of the clients and requirements according to national and international regulations. This parameter is measured through an assay called Cono Abrams. However, there is a stipulated sampling plan that limits the test to all trucks leaving the plant to put the product on site.

A second measurement option is carried out by means of a pressure gauge that measures the hydraulic pressure (PSI) exerted by the load of the concrete on the truck's pot when it is turned to its opposition. This device does not measure settlement in real terms, but is taken as a reference measure according to the type of concrete design. The company does not have an instruction or characterization card that provides the vehicle operator or laboratory technician with an accurate measurement that relates the settlement and pressure of the manometer.

The worker has always taken the measurements according to their experience, sometimes even the value demanded is not reliable because it is not always the same, so it is important that there may be other variables that explain such behavior and that not yet they are identified the manometer is an instrument that measures the pressure of gases or fluids contained in a certain closed container, whatever it may be [2].

For this reason, there is no certainty of the numerical value of the pressure for this type of container and material, that is, the mixer truck and concrete. In addition, it was found that the supplier, manufacturer of the mixer trucks, does not provide any instructions or tables that relate both variables, only provides the manual for use and calibration of said device.

For all the above, it is important to establish a relationship between settlement and pressure in order to provide more accurate, reliable and rapid information that corrects the failures that are occurring in the measurement method and thus continue to generate cost overruns for return, rework of material and compensation to customers. Not to mention the damage to the organization's image.

2 Methodology

Initially, a descriptive statistical analysis was carried out to determine which variables theoretically could influence the behavior of the settlement, followed by the guidelines given by the American Concrete Institute ACI to carry out the measurements to the runs established for the research project taking into account the variables initially identified in the descriptive phase, finally a multivariate statistical analysis is generated by means of a regression model that allows to generate a settlement estimation model based on parameters that can be measured in mixer trucks and thus prevent noncon-formities in the settlement.

American Concrete Institute ACI, through its standards ACI 301 and ACI 318, establishes the requirements and/or specifications of the clients in relation to the tests. This body advises to make the settlement measure both in the laboratory and at the point of placement in the work or delivery point [3]. ASTM C 172 provides for the collection of representative samples of fresh concrete at the project site or when tests to determine the quality of fresh concrete are required. Sampling is constituted in stationary mixers, pavers, mixer trucks and other equipment with or without agitation that is used to transport mixed plant. The indications to be taken into account in this standard during the experimental part of the project are mentioned below [4].

2.1 Use of the Abrahams Cone Method for the Measurement of the Settlement

2.1.1 Summary of the Method

Take a sample of fresh concrete and see yourself in a conical trunk mold while it is compacted by a rod. The mold rises allowing the concrete to settle. The difference between the initial position and the displaced position of the upper surface of the concrete, is known as settlement. The measurements should be taken in the center of the upper face. The value of the resulting settlement will be that which should be included in the report.

2.1.2 Apparatus

– Mold

The sample must be made in a mold resistant to the attack of the cement paste. The minimum metal size must be No. 16 (BWG); If the mold has been made by the embossing process, no point on the wall should have a thickness of less than

1.14 mm. The mold should have the shape of the lateral surface of a cone trunk of 203 mm ± 3.0 mm in diameter at the larger base, 102 mm ± 3.0 mm in diameter from the base less and 305 mm ± 3.0 mm in height. The bases must be open, parallel to each other and perpendicular to the axis of the cone. The mold should be provided with handles and devices to hold it with the feet, as indicated in Fig. 1. The mold can be manufactured with or without seams. When a seam is required, this should be done as shown in Fig. 1. The inside of the mold should be free of dents and be relatively smooth, without protrusions, such as protruding rivets. A mold attached to a base can be accepted instead of the one illustrated, provided that the arrangement of the fasteners allows its removal without movement of the mold.

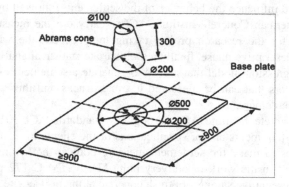

Fig. 1. Model of cone of abrams (units of measure in mm)

- **Compactor rod**

  It must be steel, cylindrical, smooth, 16 mm in diameter and with a length of approximately 600 mm; The compactor end must be hemispherical with a diameter of 16 mm.

2.1.3 Sample

The concrete sample from which the specimens are obtained must represent the total of the batch and must be obtained in accordance with NTC 454.

2.1.4 Procedure

The procedure is shown below:

I. The mold is moistened and placed on a rigid, flat, moist and non-absorbent horizontal surface. It is held firmly with the feet and filled with the concrete sample in three layers, each one of approximately one third of the mold volume. Note 1. One third of the mold volume corresponds to a depth of 67 mm; two thirds of the volume, to one of 155 mm.

II. Each layer should be compacted with 25 strokes of the rod, evenly distributed over its cross section. For the bottom layer it is necessary to slightly tilt the rod giving approximately half of the blows near the perimeter and advancing with vertical blows in a spiral, towards the center. The bottom layer should be compacted throughout its thickness; each of the intermediate and upper layers must be compacted throughout their respective thickness, so that the rod penetrates slightly into the immediately lower layer.

III. When filling the top layer, concrete must be stacked on the mold before compacting. If in doing so, it sits below the upper edge, concrete must be added so that there is an additional amount on the mold at all times. After compaction, the last layer should be smoothed flush with the surface of the concrete using the compactor rod. Immediately remove the mold, lifting it carefully in a vertical direction.

The mold is lifted at a distance of 300 mm for 5 ± 2 s, by a uniform upward movement without producing lateral or torsional movement to the concrete.

The complete operation, from the moment the mold is filled until it is removed, must be carried out without interruption for a maximum time of 2 min, 30 s.

IV. Immediately the settlement is measured, determining the vertical difference between the upper part of the mold and the displaced center of the upper surface of the sample.

If a pronounced collapse or a detachment of the concrete towards one side of the sample occurs, the test should be rejected and the determination made on another portion of the sample.

Note 2. If two consecutive tests on a concrete sample show failure or shearing of a concrete portion, it probably lacks the plasticity and cohesion necessary for the settlement test to be applicable.

2.1.5 Report

The settlement must be recorded in millimeters, with an approximation of 5 mm, and is determined as follows: Settlement = 305 - height in millimeters after the concrete has settled.

2.1.6 Accuracy and Bias

– **Accuracy**

Interlaboratory test methods. No interlaboratory test program has been carried out for this test method. Because it has not been possible to provide equivalent concretes at different test sites, free of errors from sources other than settlement measurements, it would not be significant to establish multilaboratory accuracy.

– **Bias**

No bias has been established for this test method because the settlement is defined only in terms of this test method.

Sampling

1. The time lapse between obtaining the first portion and the final portion of the composite sample should not exceed 1 min.

2. Transport the individual samples to the place where the fresh concrete tests will be conducted or where the test specimens will be molded. The samples should be combined and mixed again with a shovel as little as necessary to ensure uniformity and compliance with the maximum time limits specified in the next step.
3. Begin the settling tests, temperature and air content of the 5 min after obtaining the final portion of the composite sample. In an expeditious manner obtain and use the sample and protect the sample from the sun, wind and other sources of rapid evaporation, and from contamination.

The ASTM C 143 standard establishes the method of determining the settlement of hydraulic concrete, both in the laboratory and in the field. The most relevant for the present project in said measurement in the taking of samples, the norm establishes the following [5]:

- Equipment for settlement
    Cone Abrams
    Lower diameter: 200 mm
    Diameter top 100 mm
    Height 300 mm
    Minimum thickness 1.5 mm, 1.15 mm embossed
- Compactor bar
    Smooth steel bar with hemispherical tip
    Diameter 5/8″ (16 mm) × 24″ (600 mm)
- Measure instrument
    Rigid metal rule (Wincha)
    Long ≥ 12, divisions of ¼″ (5 mm)

The acceptance criteria of the settlement in the concrete expressed by the ASTM C 143 standard are shown below (Table 1):

Table 1. Criterion of average values of settlement measurement

Rate of settlement	Tolerance
0 a 1,25'	±0,75' [20 mm]
1,50' a 3,5'	±1,00' [25 mm]
3,75'>	±1,50' [40 mm]

The ASTM C 94 standard establishes the specifications on ready-mix concrete when the settling tolerances are as fixed or nominal requirement, or are designated by the buyer [6] as reflected below (Table 2):

Table 2. Tolerances for fixed or nominal settlement

Specified settlement of:	Tolerance
2 in. (50 mm) smaller	±½ in. (15 mm)
Between 2 in. and 4 in. (50 mm to 100 mm)	±1 in. (25 mm)
More than 4 in. * (100 mm)	1½ in. (40 mm)

*More than 4 inches (100 mm) is tolerated ± 1 ½ inches (40 mm) if a medium or high range water reducing admixture (plasticizer or fluidizer) is dosed, as long as there is no segregation that affects the durability and strength of the concrete.

3 Results

After carrying out a descriptive analysis of the possible predictive variables of the settlement behavior, it was determined that the variables: Volume, Pressure and Sand Type, could be used as useful parameters to predict the value of the settlement in the mixer truck.

Once the data is collected during the sampling, we proceed to find the model that best explains the behavior of the settlement variable from the volume and pressure, with the help of the software STATGRAPHICS version 16 (Tables 3 and 4):

Table 3. Analysis of variance for SETTLEMENT

Source	Sum of squares	df	Middle square	Reason-F	Value-P
Model	121,3	2	60,63	23,88	0,0000
Residue	289,4	114	2,539		
Total (corrected)	410,7	116			

Table 4. Sum of squares type III

Source	Sum of squares	df	Middle Square	Reason-F	Value-P
VOLUME	34,61	1	34,61	13,63	0,0003
PRESSURE	113,6	1	113,6	44,74	0,0000
Residue	289,4	114	2,539		
Total (corrected)	410,7	116			

Correlation Coefficient = 72, 46%

According to [7–9] this correlation coefficient value would be given by virtue of a high correlation between the variables involved. The regression model generated is a model of lineal regression multiple where the significance test exposed in the sum of squares type III evaluate differences between the average values of settlement to different values of the independent variables, where the null hypothesis expose that the coefficient that accompanies the variable of the model is equal to zero and the alternative hypothesis expose that this coefficient is different to zero which means this variable has significant influence in the behavior of the settlement. The variables with significant influence were the volume and pressing, also these two variables explain the 72.46% of the variability in the behavior of the settlement (Table 5).

Table 5. Confidence limits 95.0% for the estimated coefficients (SETTLEMENT)

Parameter	Error				
	Estimated	Standard	Lower limit	Upper limit	V.I.F.
CONSTANT	10,98	0,8772	9,245	12,72	
VOLUME	0,3359	0,09097	0,1557	0,5161	1,102
PRESSURE	−0,004601	0,0006879	−0,005964	−0,003238	1,102

$$SETTLEMENT = 10,98 + 0,3359 * VOLUME - 0,004601 * PRESSURE$$

Starting from the model we can conclude that the settlement is directly proportional to the volume because the coefficient that accompanies to the variable in the model is significant (0.3359), instead the pressure has a contrary effect over the settlement, they are inversely proportional because the coefficient is negative (−0.004601). To test the predictive capacity of the model, the residuals (forecast errors) were generated for the model, calculating the average value and performing a normality test (Table 6 and Fig. 2).

Table 6. Kolmogorov-Smirnov test

	Normal
DMAS	0,06444
DMENOS	0,07131
DN	0,07131
Value-P	0,5913

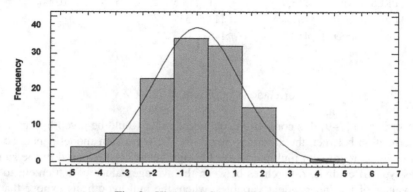

Fig. 2. Histogram for model residuals

Mean of errors = 0.0000003

To corroborate the suitability of the model [10], the waste graphs were generated (residuals vs independent variables, residuals vs predicted settlement, residuals vs row number), and no type of correlation was presented.

The objective of the graphic analysis of the residuals is to determine if there is any factor associated with the model that can affect the prediction capacity from the influence on the forecast errors, in the presented graphs it can be noticed that the behavior of the waste is not seen affected neither by the independent variables, nor the position of the data nor by the predicted value of the settlement. Therefore, the model proved to be reliable enough to estimate the settlement value of the concrete [11–16].

4 Conclusions

The volume and pressure variables of the concrete in the mixer truck have been shown to be sufficient to explain in a very approximate way the behavior of the concrete settlement, allowing from the moment in which the concrete is placed in the truck to know if it has the conditions of quality that the client requests, generating a consistent improvement of the process by decreasing the returns due to the non - conformity in the mechanical properties of the concrete, this also reduces the rework which helps to optimize the process.

Acknowledgment. Acknowledgment to the Universidad Autonoma del Caribe and Universidad Libre Seccional Barranquilla, especially to its research group GIDE, for making possible the realization of this research of interest in the cement industry.

References

1. Gutiérrez, H., De la Vara, R.: Control estadístico de calidad y Seis sigma, 2ª ed. McGraw Hill Companies Inc., México D.F. (2009)
2. Mott, L.R.: Mecánica de fluidos, 6ª ed. Pearson Education, Atlacomulco (2006)
3. American Concrete Institute ACI - seccional colombiana. (14 de Marzo de 2013). ACI 301: Especificaciones del concreto estructural, I. Santana, ed. ACI publicaciones técnicas(24), 1–21 (2013)
4. American Society for Testing Materials. ASTM C 172: Práctica normalizada para el muestreo de concreto fresco recién mezclado. West Conshohocken. ASTM International Committee Standards, USA (2008)
5. American Society for Testing and Materials. ASTM C 94: Especificación estándar para concreto premezclado. West Conshohocken, ASTM International Committe Standards, USA (2007)
6. American Society for Testing Materials. ASTM C 143: Método de ensayo estándar para la determinación del reventimiento en el concreto a base de cemento hidráulico. West Conshohocken. ASTM International Committe on Standards, USA (2005)
7. Ibañez Plana, M., Rosell Polo, J.R., Rosell Urrutia, J.I.: Energías Renovables Tecnología Solar, Ediciones Mundi-Prensa (2011)

8. Meena, S., Meena, Ch.S., Bajpai, V.K.: Thermal performance of flatplate collector: an experimental study. Int. J. Eng. Res. Appl. 1–4 (2014)
9. Madhukeshwara, N., Prakash, E.S.: An investigation on the performance characteristics of solar flat plate collector with different selective surface coatings. Int. J. Energy Environ. **3**, 99–108 (2012)
10. Krishnaiah, K., Shahabudeen, P.: Applied Design of Experiments and Taguchi Methods. PHI Learning Private Limited (2012)
11. Roy, R.K.: Design of Experiments Using Taguchi Approach (16 Steps to Product and Process Improvements), 1st edn. Wiley (2001)
12. Cetin, M.H., Ozcelik, B., Kuram, E., Demirbas, E.: Evaluation of vegetable based cuttings fluids with extreme pressure and cutting parameters in turning of AISI 304L by Taguchi method. J. Cleaner Prod. **19**, 2049–2056 (2011)
13. Castillo Ramirez, M., Viloria, A., Parody Muñoz, A., Posso, H.: Application of multiple linear regression models in the identification of factors affecting the results of the chelsea football team, pp. 45–52 (2017)
14. Viloria, A.: Commercial strategies providers pharmaceutical chains for logistics cost reduction. Indian J. Sci. Technol. **8**(1), 1–6 (2016)
15. Amelec, V.: Increased efficiency in a company of development of technological solutions in the areas commercial and of consultancy. Adv. Sci. Lett. **21**(5), 1406–1408 (2015)
16. Amelec, V., Carmen, V.: Design of a model of evaluation of productivity for microfinance institutions. Adv. Sci. Lett. **21**(5), 1529–1533 (2015)

Smart Society Informatization Technologies

Educational Psychology in Latin America: With Linear Hierarchical Models

Jesús Silva[1][✉], Darwin Solano[2], Claudia Fernández[2], Ligia Romero[2], Nataly Orellano Llinás[3], Ana María Negrete Sepúlveda[4], Luz Estela Leon Coronado[3], and Rosio Barrios González[3]

[1] Universidad Peruana de Ciencias Aplicadas, Lima, Peru
jesussilvaUPC@gmail.com
[2] Universidad de la Costa, St. 58 #66, Barranquilla, Atlántico, Colombia
{dsolano1, cfernand10, lromero11}@cuc.edu.co
[3] Corporación Universitaria Minuto de Dios – UNIMINUTO,
Barranquilla, Colombia
nataly.orellano@uniminuto.edu,
luzleoncoronado@gmail.com, rosiobarriosgo@hotmail.com
[4] Universidad Cooperativa de Colombia campus Montería, Montería, Colombia
ana.negrette@campusucc.edu.co

Abstract. Research in clinical psychology, since its inception, has been aimed at analyzing, predicting and explaining the effect of treatments, by studying the change of patients in the course of them. To study the effects of therapy, research based on quantitative analysis models has historically used classical methods of parametric statistics, such as Pearson correlations, least squares regressions Student's T-Tests and Variance Analysis (ANOVA). Hierarchical linear models (HLMs) represent a fundamental statistical strategy for research in psychotherapy, as they allow to overcome dependence on the observations usually presented in your data. The objective of this work is to present a guide to understanding, applying and reporting HLMs to study the effects of psychotherapy.

Keywords: Hierarchical linear models · Growth curve models · Multilevel models · Psychotherapy

1 Introduction

The data used in clinical psychology research is usually nested. This means that they are grouped into hierarchical structures that have different levels, which would make the presence of correlations between observations belonging to the same grouping level [1] expected. To illustrate the phenomenon of data nesting that usually occurs in clinical psychology, let's imagine a study aimed at analyzing change levels in a sample of 100 patients who were exposed to 20 sessions of a treatment and who completed a measure of clinical severity, at the beginning of therapy (t1), mid-treatment (t2) and at the end of 20 sessions (t3) [2]. In this case, it is expected that a patient's scores at the time t1 correlate with their own scores at the time t2 and t3; In this way, we will say

© Springer Nature Singapore Pte Ltd. 2019
G. Wang et al. (Eds.): iSCI 2019, CCIS 1122, pp. 233–242, 2019.
https://doi.org/10.1007/978-981-15-1301-5_19

that repeated measures of the severity instrument are nested within patients [3]. Similarly, the patients who make up this hypothetical sample could be treated by a smaller number of therapists (for example, ten therapists who have each treated ten patients of the total sample). As patients are grouped (i.e. nested) within a set of therapists, correlations are also expected in observations present at this level [4].

The use of classical statistical methods against a violation of the assumption of independence of observations can lead to significant biases in the analysis, such as an inflation of the probability of making a Type error [5]. Hierarchical linear models (HLMs, [6]) emerged in the context of educational psychology as an alternative strategy for estimating regression parameters based on data that are nested and organized in a structure defied, dealing with the problems of dependence on observations. These methods, in addition to overcoming the limitation of observation dependence, have additional implications for clinical psychology research, as they allow (i) a robust estimate of patients' exchange rates the effects of (ii) disaggregate sources of variation at different levels of the structure (intra-patient or in-patient effects, effects between patients and effects between therapists), (iii) include predictors at each level of the organization (variables that have repeated measurements, patient characteristics, therapist characteristics, etc.) [7, 8].

While at the international level HLM models have had several recent applications in the context of research in psychotherapy [9, 10], currently considering the leading statistical analyses in the field of studies in clinical psychology, its application in the Latin American region has been much more limited. This may be due to the fact that performing these analyses requires a very sophisticated and specific statistical and technical knowledge, which is not widely disseminated in the region through training courses or publications explaining these models in Spanish [11].

In this context, the objective of this work is to make a comprehensive presentation of HLM models to carry out research in clinical psychology, facilitating their application in studies in this area of knowledge. To illustrate the application of these models and explain how to interpret their results, a clinical sample from a psychotherapy center will be used, which will be explained in detail later. We seek that this work helps to increase the knowledge and dissemination of HLM models among researchers in the Latin American region, providing a valuable technical resource to robustly analyze the data of research in psychotherapy, establish their effects and identify associated predictors.

2   Description of the Database Used

As previously stated, in order to illustrate how HLM models are applied and reported to investigate the effects of psychotherapy, we will rely on a database of a clinic in Colombia. This institution aimed at providing mental health treatment services, built in conjunction with a research team, a short questionnaire to evaluate the evolution of the general well-being of the patient, called the Treatment Evolution System (SET), they systematically send their patients, after each session, to monitor their progress (See [12]).

The SET consists of four items rated on a scale of 1 to 10, which explore the degree of patient well-being in different areas of life (individual, relational, behavioral and global). The four scores of the items are added in a general welfare index that will be our dependent variable in our exemplification of the models. In this work we will use the results obtained during the first four treatment sessions. The questionnaire was sent to a total of 2151 patients treated by 198 therapists in the period from April 7, 2017 to December 20, 2018.

Of these patients, only 1754 completed set at least once. Because HLMs allow for the analysis of cases with missing data, all those participants who completed at least one of the repeated measures of the dependent variable were included in the analyses [13, 14]. In summary, this database has four repeated measures of the questionnaire that analyzes well-being (level 1 of analysis) in 1754 patients (level 2 of analysis) treated by 154 therapists (level 3 of analysis). In addition to the questionnaire, patients completed an extra item, aimed at exploring "To what extent have you made progress on the reason for consultation so far?", with a scale of 4 points from 1 ("nothing") to 4 ("much").

This additional item, along with the gender of the participants, were used as examples of predictors in the models. It should be noted that the patients included in the sample used to exemplify the analyses had a wide diagnostic variability (anxiety disorders, mood disorders, adaptive disorders, eating disorders, among others) which was not registered for this study or included in the analyses. In addition, in all cases the treatment was a non-manualized approach based on short problem-solving therapy [15] which characterizes the centre from which the without an alternative treatment or control group, to study the differential effect of the approach [16].

3 Statistical Software to Apply HLM Models

A wide variety of softwares are currently available to fit HLM models. There is a specific program to run these analyses that is called HLM and is based on the assembly of the equations of the model [17]. This software [18] allows to estimate the effect of predictors in each of the levels, from their inclusion in the multilevel equation of the model being adjusted. While the program has a paid license, it has a student version that can be downloaded for free. Another alternative to run these models, highly recommended, is the open access program R. Such program has a package called "lme4" [19] which includes the lmer() function, which allows a high degree of flexibility in adjusting HLM models.

4 Identifying the HLM Model that Best Fits the Data

When performing an HLM analysis, the first step is to adjust different unconditional models (without any predictors) with different number of levels, to see which of them best fits the data. This requires determining from which level of information grouping a significant variation among participants begins to be observed [20]. Subsequently, once the number of levels of the model has been identified, models will be adjusted over time as the sole predictor, introducing different possible paths (more specifically linear and quadratic), again to see which one best describes the data obtained. Because in the database we will use, we expect three sources of variation (intra-patient effects, effects between patients and effects between therapists), we must first run an unconditional three-tier model [12] to analyses the variability around to the estimated constant, which in this case will represent the levels of patient well-being during the first four sessions [2].

The lack of significant variability around that mean would imply that it is not necessary to include random effects at that level and, therefore, that the level can be excluded. In order to establish whether there is significant variability at the top level of grouping (the level of the effects of therapists), being appropriate to use a three-tier model, there are two complementary methods. One of the strategies is to identify the percentage of variance of the dependent variable, explained by the third grouping level, by calculating ICCs. To calculate these coefficients, it is taken at the variance observed at level 3 (A) and divided by the sum of the variance at level 1 (x2), level 2 (a) and level 3 (a) [13].

Based on the variance components of the three-tier unconditional model, adjusted to the clinical data used, the ICC formula in this case would be: .004 [.30/ (.31 + 61.11 + 24.87)]. To facilitate the compression of the coefficient, the BCI can be multiplied by 100 and interpreted as a percentage of variance explained by level 3 (i.e. by the effect of therapists). In this case the effect of therapists in this sample explains the .31% (ICC .0031) of the variance of well-being in patients. The effect of a level is considered significant when it explains at least 1.1% of the variance in the dependent variable. Otherwise, as in the analyses carried out, it is concluded that there is no significant effect of therapists on the well-being of patients, so the third level of the model should be removed.

The second method for analyzing the adequacy of adjusting a three-tier model is to see if the random effects of level 3 (u0) are significant, suggesting a relevant variation among patients of different therapists, in their degree of Welfare. The lack of significant variation among therapists in their patients' average scores would mean that there is no need to include a third level in the model. In the sample used in this study, consistent with the results of the BCI, no significant variation was observed between therapists in the well-being scores of their patients, u00 = .56, $\chi2$ (144) = 143.12, p = .459.

Because both low BCI values and the lack of significant variation between therapists suggest not adjusting a three-tier model, then a two-tier model should be run, excluding the level of variability from therapists. This adjusts an unconditional two-tier model (without any predictor), which tells of repeated welfare measures (level 1) grouped in patients (level 2). By adjusting this unconditional two-tier model, it was found that 33% of the variance of the welfare score is explained by differences between patients (ICC .31). In turn, a significant variation was observed around the mean of the patient's welfare scores, r0 = 5.43, $\chi2(1754)$ = 2176.14, p < .001. These two indicators suggest retaining the two-tier model as the base model for analysis. Subsequently, it is necessary to identify which paths best describe the change in the welfare variable over time. In this way, a linear model and then a quadratic model were adjusted.

To select the most appropriate model based on the data, the model comparison test is used to determine whether the inclusion of new terms improves the percentage of variance explained by the models. This test based on the chi square statistic uses both information on the variability of the model and the number of parameters to be estimated. A significant result in this test implies that the inclusion of new parameters improves the percentage of variance explained by the model.

Using this procedure we first compare a two-tier unconditional model with a two-tier linear model including the time variable in weeks as the only predictor at level 1. By performing this analysis on the clinical database used, the result showed that the inclusion of the linear term significantly improved the fit of the model, $\chi2(3) = 37.50$, $p < .001$. Next we compare the linear model with a two-level quadratic model. This quadratic model has as predictors time in weeks (linear term) and time in weeks raised squared (quadratic term). However, the model comparison test determined that the inclusion of the new quadratic term did not significantly improve the percentage of variance explained by the model, $\chi2(4) = 3.33$, $p > .50$. Therefore, the comparison of all models suggests that the model that best fits the data (final model of the analysis) is a two-tier linear model, with time in weeks as the only predictor. The results of the different fitted models can be found in Table 1.

Table 1. Summary of models adjusted based on the clinical database used

Fixed Effects	Three-Level Model			Two-Level Model		
	Coefficient	EE	Component of Variance	Coefficient	EE	Component of Variance
Unconditional model						
Constant	23.58***	.31	.33	22.14***	.21	26.32***
Linear Model						
Constant				23.60***	.35	36.56***
Weeks				.812***	.16	3.17**
Quadratic Model						
Constant				23.85***	.39	36.53***
Weeks				.51	.51	15.45
Weeks squared				-.13	.17	1.78*
Conditional models with changes in query reason as a level 1 predictor						
Constant				22.87***	.35	26.14***
Weeks				.31	.17	3.63**
Reason				2.85***	.21	6.50**
Gendered conditional models as a level 2 predictor						
Constant				24.89***	.35	36.47***
Weeks				.87***	.17	3.25**
Effect of the gender on Constant				.30	.72	
Effect of the gender in weeks				.30	.34	

Note. EE - Standard Error, Weeks - Change in weeks, Reason - Changes in relation to the query reason, *** p < .001, ** p < .01, * p < .05.

5   Interpretation of Linear Model Parameters (Time as Sole Predictor)

The results of the model show that on average the patients had an average of 24.60 at the end of the session 4 ($\beta00 = 23.60$; in a theoretical range of 0 a 44), and an average increase of .84 units of well-being ($\beta10 = .84$) session-to-session. The appropriate way to report these results is to present the parameter coefficients, the standard error (EE), the confidence interval (CI), the t-test statistic, and the p-value of significance (in that order). All these elements appear in the results of the different statistical programs that allow to estimate hierarchical linear models (HLM, R, etc.), with the exception of ICs, which programs such as HLM do not report it. In this case, the intervals can be calculated from the formula: Coefficient $\pm$ EE $*$ 1.96.

Therefore, for the average welfare scores at the end of session 4, the results are presented as follows: $\beta00 = 23.60$, EE $= .35$, CI95 [22.94, 24.36], t(1754) = 68.871, p < .001. While, for the average weekly change in well-being the results are presented in this way: $\beta10 = .84$, EE $= .16$, CI95 [.53, 11.23], t(1754) = 5.853, p < .001. For the constant significance test, the null hypothesis is that the wellness scores in session 4 are equal to 0. Whereas for the linear term ($\beta00$) the null hypothesis of the contrast is that the session-to-session change in the well-being is equal to 0. Therefore, the results show that patients have a level of well-being greater than 0 at the end of session 4 (something that from a conceptual point of view is not conceptually relevant in this case but could have it in other analyses) and that patients had a significant improvement between sessions during the first four meetings with their therapists.

6   Adjusting Conditional Models

In addition to the models that allow us to estimate values of the dependent variable and its evolution over time, one of the most relevant applications of the HLM models lies in the possibility of including predictors in each of the organizational levels of the analyzing its effect on the dependent variable, by adjusting conditional models. As an example, we adjust two conditional linear models, of two levels each. In the first model, the perception of changes relative to the query reason was included as a level 1 predictor. Because this variable has repeated measures at the same times as the dependent variable, it represents a temporary covariate in the model. To facilitate the interpretation of the parameters, we focus this predictor from its sample mean. Then, we adjust a model including the patient gender (encoded as Female 1, Male, 0) as a predictor of level 2. In this case, the strategy used to include the gender as a predictor is the same one that would be used to study the effects of a treatment compared to a control group or two different diagnostic groups.

6.1   Reporting and Interpreting Conditional Models with Level 1 Predictors

The results of the models show a significant effect of improvement in relation to the reason for consultation on the patient's levels of well-being, $\beta10 = 2.42$, EE $= .22$,

CI95 [1.74, 2.31], t(1153) = 10.681, p < .001. The results of the effect of the predictors are interpreted in terms of increment units in the dependent variable, starting with the increase of a unit in the predictor. Therefore, these findings show that a unit of increase in improvement scores associated with the reason for consultation was related to a 2.22 unit increase in patient welfare scores. A significant effect on the randomized component r1 was observed, implying that patients varied significantly around the mean effect of improvement in relation to the reason for consultation on the welfare of the subjects, r1 = 2.87, $\chi2(326) = 416.02$, p = .005. This result suggests the possibility of including predictors (at level 2) to explain the variability of that effect. Finally, the inclusion of the predictor significantly improved the fit of the model, $\chi2(3) = 150.78$, p < .001, so it is recommended to retain this conditional model.

6.2 Reporting and Interpreting Conditional Models with Level 2 Predictors

The results of the conditional models with the gender as a predictor at level 2, show that this variable does not have a significant effect on the levels of well-being of patients at the end of session 4 (the constant), $\beta01 = .28$, EE = .75, CI95 [−1.11, 1.77], t (1754) = .444, p = .71, or on its exchange rate (linear slope), $\beta11 = .29$, EE = .43, CI95 [−.38, .94], t(1754) = .891, p = .39. Again, in these models the coefficients are interpreted in terms of the number of increment/decrease units in the constant ($\beta01$) and the linear slope ($\beta11$), from a unit of increase in the predictor. Because the predictor in this case is a dichotomous variable (gender), the coefficient represents the difference between the reference group, encoded as 1 (female gender) and the other condition encoded as 0 (male gender).

Thus, in session 4 female had on average a higher level of well-being .30 units compared to that of male people ($\beta01 = .33$) and also a higher .30-unit increase in their session-to-session change at levels of welfare ratio ($\beta11 = .29$). Random terms show that patients varied significantly around the average gender effect on welfare scores in session 4, r1 = 1.72, $\chi2(778) = 842.01$, p < .001, and on their change session-to-session, $\chi2(4) = 153.94$, p < .001, and on their change session-to-session, $\chi2(2) = .96$, p > .50. This implies that other predictors can be included in the model for patient well-being levels at the end of session 4 and their change session-to-session.

6.3 Calculating Effect Sizes for Conditional Models

By observing a significant effect, it is possible to estimate measures of effect size, in terms of proportion of variance explained in the result variable from the predictor, by computating Pseudo R2 coefficients. These coefficients are calculated by comparing the difference between the variance of the unconditional model and that of the conditional model, divided by the variance of the unconditional model [13]. Therefore, Pseudo R^2 (Unconditional Model Variance − Conditional Model Variance)/Unconditional Model Variance. Pseudo R^2 coefficients can be transformed to percentage of variance explained by the predictor, from multiplying their values by 100. For the conditional model, with the improvement relative to the query reason as a predictor at level 1, we calculate Pseudo R^2 based on the level 1 variance of that model and the model (replacing the unconditional).

In this case the linear model was used because the predictor of the conditional model was included above that change estimation model (without any other predictors than time). The calculation, then, was as follows: Pseudo R^2 .074 [(56.71 − 52.42)/56.71]. The result suggests, therefore, that improvements in relation to the reason for consultation account for 8% of the variance of well-being scores in patients. For the conditional model with the patient gender included as a level 2 predictor, we calculated Pseudo R^2 coefficients for both constant as for linear slope, using the variance components of both elements.

Pseudo R^2 of the constant .002 [(37.82 − 35.47)/37.82]. Pseudo R^2 of the linear slope .0069 [(3.11 − 3.19)/3.11]. This result implies that the gender of the patients explains only the .2% of the variance of their well-being at the end of session 4 (constant) and .8% of the variance in the weekly exchange rate (linear slope). Although we have presented the calculation of both effect sizes for illustrative purposes, if the hypothesis tests corresponding to the coefficients do not yield statistically significant results, from a theoretical point of view it would have no value calculate these effect size measurements.

7 Conclusions

Complementing previous efforts made in the international literature [1, 3, 10, 13, 18], this work attempts to highlight the value of HLM models as a statistical resource of fundamental importance for psychotherapy studies aimed at determining their effects and explaining them by predictors of different nature. These models, first of all, allow to deal with the ubiquitous nesting of data in the field of research in psychotherapy. Second, they facilitate a robust estimate of patient change, the main focus of clinical psychology studies, analyzing both average trajectories in a sample and individual patterns of evolution.

Third, they provide the ability to include predictors, at different levels of data organization, to explain the variance of the change. Finally, they allow us to determine the contribution of the figure of the therapist to the improvement of patients. While internationally, in recent years there has been a number of researches that applied these models for research in psychotherapy, few examples of their application have been found in Argentine and/or Latin American authors, and the few exceptions have been published in English-speaking journals [12]. Being able to realize and understand these models requires a high degree of technical knowledge in such analyses, which for many students and researchers in psychotherapy in the region remains inaccessible, due to the lack of application guides and interpretation of these models in Spanish.

With this work we have tried to present a guide to perform, understand and report models of HLM analysis, facilitating its application and trying to amplify its reach to potential researchers in the area. The possibility of generalizing the use of these models to research in psychotherapy will represent a valuable contribution to both research and practice in the Latin American region. By overcoming the limitations of classic parametric methods, further dissemination of these models has the potential to improve the quality of analyses for studies in psychotherapy. This would not only have methodological implications in terms of the soundness of the results (and their possible impact on the academic field), but could also impact at the practice level, starting with the creation of a more robust and close knowledge to the clinic, with cultural validity for the Latin American region, which will help to improve the processes and results of the therapies, making patients get a better profit from them.

References

1. Bates, D., Mäechler, M., Bolker, B., Walker, S.: Fitting linear mixed-effects models using lme4. J. Stat. Softw. **67**(1), 1–48 (2015). https://doi.org/10.18637/jss.v067.i01
2. Behn, A.J., Errázuriz, P.A., Cottin, M., Fischer, C.: Change in symptomatic burden and life satisfaction during short-term psychotherapy: focusing on the role of family income. Counselling Psychother. Res. **18**(2), 133–142 (2017). https://doi.org/10.1002/capr.12158
3. Gómez Penedo, J.M., Constantino, M.J., Coyne, A., Westra, H., Antony, M.: Markers for context-responsiveness: client baseline interpersonal problems moderate the efficacy of two psychotherapies for generalized anxiety disorder. J. Consult. Clin. Psychol. **85**(10), 1000–1011 (2017). https://doi.org/10.1037/ccp0000233
4. Gómez Penedo, J.M., Juan, S., Manubens, R.T., Roussos, A.: The study of change in psychotherapy: conceptual challenges and problems of empirical research. Yearbook Psychol. Res. **24**, 15–24 (2018)
5. Hayes, A.F.: Introduction to Mediation, Moderation, and Conditional Process Analysis: A Regression-Based Approach. Guilford Publications, New York (2017)
6. Bucci, N., et al.: Factor analysis of the psychosocial risk assessment instrument. In: Tan, Y., Shi, Y., Tang, Q. (eds.) DMBD 2018. LNCS, vol. 10943, pp. 149–158. Springer, Cham (2018). https://doi.org/10.1007/978-3-319-93803-5_14
7. Gaitán-Angulo, M., Viloria, A., Abril, J.E.S.: Hierarchical ascending classification: an application to contraband apprehensions in colombia (2015–2016). In: Tan, Y., Shi, Y., Tang, Q. (eds.) DMBD 2018. LNCS, vol. 10943, pp. 168–178. Springer, Heidelberg (2018). https://doi.org/10.1007/978-3-319-93803-5_16
8. Viloria, A., Lezama, O.B.P.: An intelligent approach for the design and development of a personalized system of knowledge representation. Procedia Comput. Sci. **151**, 1225–1230 (2019)
9. Viloria, A., Lis-Gutiérrez, J.P., Gaitán-Angulo, M., Godoy, A.R.M., Moreno, G.C., Kamatkar, S.J.: Methodology for the design of a student pattern recognition tool to facilitate the teaching - learning process through knowledge data discovery (big data). In: Tan, Y., Shi, Y., Tang, Q. (eds.) DMBD 2018. LNCS, vol. 10943, pp. 670–679. Springer, Cham (2018). https://doi.org/10.1007/978-3-319-93803-5_63
10. Viloria, A., et al.: Determination of dimensionality of the psychosocial risk assessment of internal, individual, double presence and external factors in work environments. In: Tan, Y., Shi, Y., Tang, Q. (eds.) DMBD 2018. LNCS, vol. 10943, pp. 304–313. Springer, Cham (2018). https://doi.org/10.1007/978-3-319-93803-5_29
11. Wang, J., Xie, H., Fisher, J.H.: Multilevel Models: Applications Using SAS. De Gruyter, Berlin (2012)
12. Areas, M., Roussos, A., Hirsch, H., Hirsch, P., Becerra, P., Gómez Penedo, J.M.: Evaluation of a research device oriented to practice in the development of a feedback system in psychotherapy. Argentine J. Psychol. Clinic **27**(2), 229–249 (2018)

13. Westra, H.A., Constantino, M.J., Antony, M.M.: Integrating motivational interviewing with cognitive-behavioral therapy for severe generalized anxiety disorder: an allegiance controlled randomized clinical trial. J. Consult. Clin. Psychol. **84**(9), 768–782 (2016). https://doi.org/10.1037/ccp0000098

14. Zilcha-Mano, S., Errázuriz, P.: One size does not fit all: examining heterogeneity and identifying moderators of the alliance–outcome association. J. Counseling Psychol. **62**(4), 579–591 (2015). https://doi.org/10.1037/cou0000103

15. Hox, J., Maas, C.: Multilevel analysis. In: Encyclopedia of Social Measurement, vol. 2, pp. 785–793 (2005). https://doi.org/10.1016/b0-12-369398-5/00560-0

16. Mellado, A., et al.: Disentangling the change-alliance relationship: observational assessment of the therapeutic alliance during change and stuck episodes. Psychotherapy Res. **27**(5), 595–607 (2017). https://doi.org/10.1080/10503307.2016.1147657

17. Ogles, B.M.: Measuring change in psychotherapy research. In: Lambert, M.J. (ed.) Bergin and Garfields's Handbook of Psychotherapy and Behavior Change, pp. 134–166. Wiley, New Jersey (2013)

18. Raudenbush, S.W., Bryk, A.S.: Hierarchical Linear Models: Applications and Data Analysis Methods, 2nd edn. Sage, Thousand Oaks (2002)

19. Raudenbush, S.W., Bryk, A.S., Cheong, Y.F., Congdon, R.T., du Toit, M.: HLM7: Hierarchical Linear and Nonlinear Modeling. Scientific Software International, Chicago (2011)

20. Skrondal, A., Rabe-Hesketh, S.: Generalized Latent Variable Modeling. Chapman & Hall/CRC, Boca Raton (2004)

Modeling and Simulating for the Treatment of Subjectivity in the Process of Choosing Personnel Using Fuzzy Logic

Noel Varela Izquierdo[1], Mercedes Gaitan[2],
Omar Bonerge Pineda Lezama[3], Nelson Alberto Lizardo Zelaya[3],
Jesus Silva[4(✉)], Roberto Rene Moreno Garcia[5],
and Rafael Gomez Dorta[6]

[1] Universidad de la Costa (CUC), Calle 58 # 55-66,
Atlantico, Baranquilla, Colombia
nvarela2@cuc.edu.co
[2] Corporación Universitaria Empresarial de Salamanca – CUES,
Barranquilla, Colombia
m_gaitan689@cues.edu.co
[3] Universidad Tecnologica Centroamericana (UNITEC),
San Pedro Sula, Honduras
{omarpineda, nelson.lizardo}@unitec.edu
[4] Universidad Peruana de Ciencias Aplicdas, Lima, Peru
jesussilvaUPC@gmail.com
[5] Universidad de Oriente, Santiago de Cuba, Cuba
rrmg@uo.edu.cu
[6] Becamo, Villanueva, Honduras
rafaelluciano@yahoo.es

Abstract. Every day organizations pay more attention to Human Resources Management, because the human factor is preponderant in the results of it. One of the important policies is the Selection of Personnel, these are needed for their decision-making results, which in many organizations is done in a subjective manner and which brings consequences not very favorable to them. Taking this problem into account, it is decided to design and apply procedures and tools of fuzzy mathematics to reduce subjectivity and uncertainty in decision-making, creating work algorithms for this policy that includes multifactorial weights and analysis with measurement indicators that they allow tangible and reliable results. In this case of personnel selection, eight candidates were taken into account and by applying a diffuse evaluation system, the candidate with the highest rating of 98% was chosen. This indicates that subjectivity was reduced when choosing the best evaluated candidate.

Keywords: Personnel selection · Fuzzy mathematics · Diffuse evaluation system

G. Wang et al. (Eds.): iSCI 2019, CCIS 1122, pp. 243–252, 2019.
https://doi.org/10.1007/978-981-15-1301-5_20

1 Introduction

The human capital models (HCM) [1] focus their objectives on improving organizational results, but from the perspective of human resources, where the selection of personnel plays an important role in it. In this regard, research related to the evaluation by competences [2], evaluation by graphic scales [3], and personnel selection [4, 5] stand out.

The personnel selection process includes complex and inaccurate information, evaluating different criteria to make the decision to choose the best candidate. Several authors [4, 6] use multicriteria methods to deal with the problem of personnel selection. Others like [7, 8] state that the multicriteria techniques most used in the literature are the AHP (analytic hierarchy process) and TOPSIS (Technique for order of preference by similarity to ideal solution), ANP (analytic network process) and expert systems.

In any case by their nature, the schemes used for the selection of personnel are subject to certain levels of subjectivity and are presented as a succession of stages, in which the candidates that are considered less suitable are successively eliminated, at the same time, it is tried to capture the qualities that those most suitable for carrying out the tasks that define the job have.

For the treatment of subjectivity and uncertainty, [9] developed Fuzzy Logic models, this can be applied to take into account subjective factors in personnel selection, reducing uncertainty, which facilitates decision making and makes it more effective.

The purpose of this work is to develop a model of application of diffuse mathematics to the selection of personnel for the treatment of its subjectivity, in which they will propose:

(a) A new flexible selection framework: in which the evaluators will be able to express their opinions through information valued in different domains of expression (numerical, interval, linguistic) depending on the nature of the indicator or technique used and the knowledge on it of the evaluator.
(b) A diffuse model of personnel selection: capable of handling the non-homogeneous information of the previous evaluation framework and of handling the uncertainty of the information provided by the evaluators.

2 Methodology

This section shows an analysis of the tendencies, methods and fundamental techniques that are used for the selection of personnel, uses of diffuse mathematics in the same and the methodology used for this research.

2.1 Fuzzy Logic Methodology

Multivariate fuzzy logic allows in practical ways to address problems as they occur in the real world. It originates from the fuzzy set theory proposed by [9], which represents a generalization of the classical set theory and applies to categories that can take any value of truthfulness within a set of values that fluctuate between the absolute truth and total falsehood. The foundation of fuzzy sets is the fact that the building elements of human reasoning are not numbers but linguistic labels; thus fuzzy logic emulates these characteristics and makes use of approximate data to find precise solutions.

The theory of fuzzy sets has been developed to try to solve problems in which the description of activities and observations are inaccurate, vague or uncertain.

By applying fuzzy sets, it is intended to describe inaccurate concepts mathematically, or in other words the theory of fuzzy sets attempts to model all these phenomena present in real life and that cannot be accurately evaluated. Another application of this theory is in situations where specific data are not available for a statistical analysis with sufficient reliability.

For a better understanding, in Fig. 1 shows the basic elements of a diffuse set graphically described.

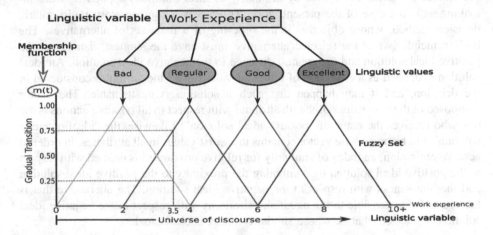

Fig. 1. Graphical representation of a fuzzy set

The basic concepts of a diffuse set and its component elements are presented below [9].

Diffuse set: A fuzzy set is given by A = {(x, μ_A (x)) :x∈U} (1), where μ_A (x) is the membership function for the set of all elements x in U.

Speech universe: It is the range of values that the elements that have the property expressed by the linguistic variable can take.

Diffuse number: It is that number that is assigned to the variables within the discourse universe.

Linguistic variable: It is a variable defined by a word or a sentence that is said by the person.

Diffuse variable: Those variables that define the speech universe of the linguistic variable.

Degree of belonging: It is that function that has its corresponding value within the zero and one interval.

Diffuse subset: It is a class of objects with continuous degrees of belonging. Said subset is characterized by a membership function that assigns each object a degree of membership within the zero and one interval.

Membership function: It is that application that associates to each element of a diffuse subset the degree to which the associated linguistic value belongs. The membership function can have different forms, the best known are: triangular, trapezoidal, Gaussian and bell.

On the other hand, in the field of human resources, fuzzy logic has been applied to the selection of personnel by [8, 10] develop the principles of the TOPSIS method (Technique for Order Preference by Similarity to Ideal Solution) applied to decision-making as is the case of the present work. TOPSIS is a compensatory multi-criteria decision method, whose objective is the ordering of a finite set of alternatives. The basic principle is that the selected alternative must have the shortest distance to the positive ideal solution and the greatest distance to the negative ideal solution. An ideal solution is defined as a collection of scores or values in all the attributes considered in the decision, and it may happen that such a solution is unattainable. The vector composed of the best values of the jth attribute with respect to all possible actions is the one who receives the name of "positive ideal solution"; Likewise, the "ideal negative solution" will be one whose vector contains the worst values in all attributes. In order to achieve ordination, an index of similarity (or relative proximity) is defined with respect to the positive ideal solution by combining the proximity to the positive ideal solution and the remoteness with respect to the negative ideal solution. The alternative that is located as far as possible to the maximum similarity with respect to the negative ideal solution is selected, that is, whose similarity index is closer to 1.

2.2 Staff Selection

Other authors such as [6, 11] present a concrete proposal for the incorporation of fuzzy logic in the final process of personnel selection, that is, in decision making, giving specific values to the traits evaluated. [8, 12] on the other hand, carried out a proposal in which they integrate the diffuse logic of [9], but they do so by including it in a multicriteria model in which They also consider the 2-tuple linguistic representation model and the technique for order preference by similarity to ideal solution (TOPSIS), a technique for multi-criteria decision making.

On the subject of Personnel Selection using fuzzy logic the most prominent articles are shown in the following Table 1:

Table 1. Research in personal selection with fuzzy approach

Author	Article
Alliger et al. [13]	"Fuzzy sets and personnel selection: discussion and an application"
Durson and Karsak [12]	"A fuzzy MCDM approach for personnel selection"
Canos, Casasus, Crespo, Lara and Perez [11]	"Personnel selection based on fuzzy methods"
Belezentis et al. [6]	"Personnel selection based on computing with words and fuzzy MULTIMOORA"
Özdaban and Özkan [18]	"A case study on evaluating personnel and jobs jointly with fuzzy distances"
Kelemenis and Askounis [10]	"A new TOPSIS-based multi criteria approach to personnel selection"

The applications presented in the articles by [11–18], clearly show a role in the personnel selection process with the specific assignment of values to each desired skill in the candidate. This allows a decision based exclusively on quantifiable results. The elimination of vagueness, inaccuracy and ambiguity in the personnel selection process is essential for these authors, who find the model useful and feasible, even to keep pace with contemporary efficiency requirements.

2.3 Practical Cases

For the practical application of the tool the personnel selection was chosen [11], in this methodology some adjustments were made in correspondence with the application of diffuse mathematics. In addition, the methodology of the graphic scales presented by [19] was taken into consideration.

2.3.1 Methodology for Personnel Selection
Figure 2 shows the procedure for the selection of personnel.

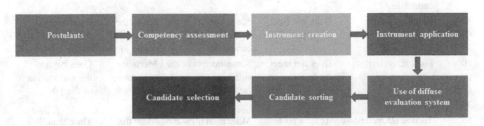

Fig. 2. Procedure for personnel selection

The sequence of stages of this procedure covers the stages of recruitment and selection of personnel, where the measuring instruments are defined for each candidate, and all the results are processed based on an analysis with diffuse logic, the system allows an objective evaluation of each candidate for the final selection in each place.

3   Results of the Application

Next, the application of the procedure for the selection of personnel in 7 stages described in Fig. 2.

Stage 1: To show the results of the model, a personnel selection process in a fuel trading company was taken as a reference, starting from 8 applicants to be selected in the work areas in the dispatch and store track.

Stage 2 and 3: Table 2 shows the assessment in competence and creation of the instrument for each position, the measurement scales and the tests that are performed on all candidates, subdivided into different techniques (Psychometric tests, Interviews and Knowledge tests), the specific importance weight of each technique, as well as its qualitative evaluation (Bad, Regular, Good, Excellent).

Table 2. Graphic scale for personnel selection.

Weight	Evaluation techniques	Quantitative evaluation			
		Bad	Regular	Good	Excellent
30%	Psychometric test				
35	Personality test	At least 60%	More than 60% and at least 75%	More than 75% and at least 90%	More than 90%
35	IQ test	At least 60%	More than 60% and at least 75%	More than 75% and at least 90%	More than 90%
30	Values test	Not according to the values of the profile	Some factors don't fit the profile	According to the profile	Goes beyond the profile
40%	Interview to candidates				
30	Initial interview	Does not meet the expectation	Some doubts in the suitability of the candidate	Meets the expectation of the job	Goes beyond the expectation of the job
70	Final interview	Does not meet the expectation	Some doubts in the suitability of the candidate	Meets the expectation of the job	Goes beyond the expectation of the job
30%	Knowledge test				
50	Technical/Operational	At least 60%	More than 60% and at least 80%	More than 80% and at least 90%	More than 90%
50	Computer skills	At least 60%	More than 60% and at least 80%	More than 80% and at least 90%	More than 90%

Stage 4 and 5: Once you define the scale and the techniques to be used and following the proposed methodology, proceed to its application (See Figs. 3 and 4) evaluating the behavior of each employee before each defined technique.

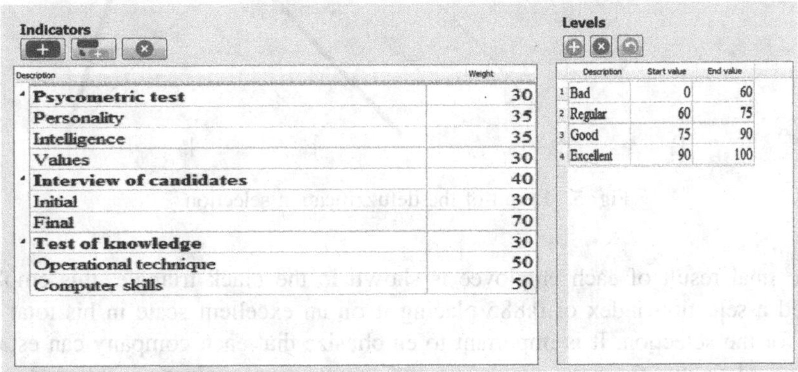
Indicators
Description
Weight
Psycometric test 30
Personality 35
Intelligence 35
Values 30
Interview of candidates 40
Initial 30
Final 70
Test of knowledge 30
Operational technique 50
Computer skills 50
Levels
Description Start value End value
1 Bad 0 60
2 Regular 60 75
3 Good 75 90
4 Excellent 90 100

Fig. 3. Specific levels and weights determined for the evaluation of candidates

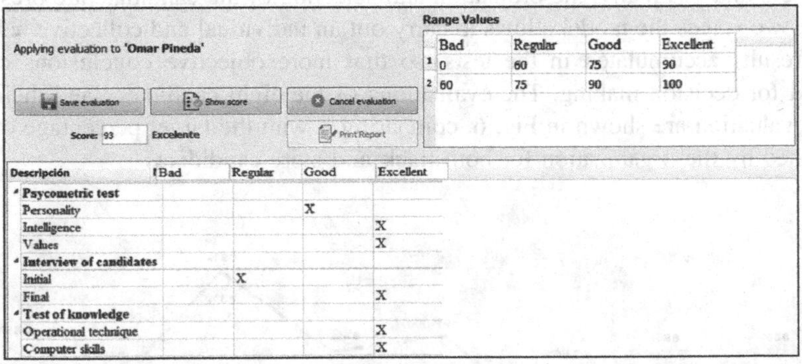
Applying evaluation to 'Omar Pineda'
Save evaluation
Show score
Cancel evaluation
Print Report
Score: 93
Excelente
Range Values
Bad Regular Good Excellent
1 0 60 75 90
2 60 75 90 100
Descripción Bad Regular Good Excellent
Psycometric test
Personality X
Intelligence X
Values X
Interview of candidates
Initial X
Final X
Test of knowledge
Operational technique X
Computer skills X

Fig. 4. Evaluation system of each candidate according to defined techniques

When applying the diffuse evaluation model to the previous graphic scale, the evaluator defines for each technique, the qualitative evaluation obtained by each candidate, this evaluation assumes a diffuse triangular number that is multiplied by the specific weight of each technique, obtaining a diffuse global result. Subsequently, the defuzzification process is carried out using the centroid method, [20–22] where each candidate obtains a qualitative evaluation (Bad, Regular, Good, Excellent) and a quantified evaluation after defuzzification that moves between 0 and 1 (See Fig. 5), this value allows an analysis of their results and comparative behavior both individually and collectively with their area and organization.

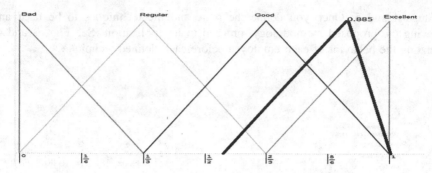

Fig. 5. Result of the defuzzification selection

The final result of each employee is shown in the black triangle, this employee obtained a selection index of 0.885 placing it on an excellent scale in his total evaluation for the selection. It is important to emphasize that each company can establish the standard values for each qualitative and quantitative evaluation obtained, which means that it designs and establishes the policy of evaluation of its results and assigns it in the defuzzification rules.

Stage 6 and 7: Finally, the ordination and selection of the candidate are presented; in these two stages the model allows to carry out an individual and collective behavior of the results accumulated in the tests, so that more objective conclusions can be obtained for decision making. The evaluations of the eight candidates and their individual evaluation are shown in Fig. 6, comparing it with the target percentage of 85% established by the organization for both track and store candidates.

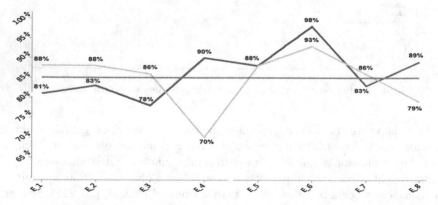

Fig. 6. Result of the eight evaluations of the track and store candidates.

Once the results have been analyzed and taking into account Fig. 6, it is shown that the candidates with the best score for both track and store are number 6 with a score of 98%

and 93% respectively. With this information, the company must make the final decision of whether or not to hire the candidates, but demonstrates that the technique helps the decision making process and, above all, minimizes the subjectivity of the same.

4 Conclusions

The implementation of a mathematical model based on fuzzy logic for the personnel selection process, provides greater objectivity and provides a solid basis for justification on the results obtained to support the decisions to be made.

The selection of personnel in companies, is a process of subjective selection in the fundamentals, which must reduce emotionality and personal reasoning through validated instruments and flexible selection techniques that can increase reliability and allow a prediction as closely as possible to conditions and characteristics that are in accordance with the company.

The diffuse evaluation system for personnel selection provides concrete and tangible data. In addition, it allows to observe the results in graphical form which provides simplicity, convenience, speed and efficiency in the analysis of the information for the selection of the best candidate.

References

1. Cuesta, A.: Tecnología de Gestión de Recursos Humanos (Tercera Edición). La Habana, Editorial Félix Varela (2010). ISBN 9789590713415
2. Gallego, M.: Gestión humana basada en competencias contribución efectiva al logro de los objetivos organizacionales. Revista universidad EAFIT 36(119), 63–71 (2012)
3. Varela, N., Fernández, D., Pineda, O., Viloria, A.: Selection of the best regression model to explain the variables that influence labor accident case electrical company. J. Eng. Appl. Sci. 12, 2956–2962 (2017)
4. Zhang, S., Liu, S.: A GRA based intuitionistic fuzzy multicriteria group decision making method for personnel selection. Expert Syst. Appl. 38(9), 11401–11405 (2011)
5. Domínguez, L.A.P., Iniesta, A.A., Alcaraz, J.L.G., Rosales, D.J.V.: Análisis Dimensional Difuso Intuicionista para la Selección de. Practitioner 1, 9 (2015)
6. Baležentis, A., Baležentis, T., Brauers, W.K.M.: Personnel selection based on computing with words and fuzzy MULTIMOORA. Expert Syst. Appl. 39, 7961–7967 (2012)
7. Chai, J., Liu, J.N.K., Ngai, E.W.T.: Application of decision-making techniques in supplier selection: a systematic review of literature. Expert Syst. Appl. 40, 3872–3885 (2013)
8. Afshari, A.R., Yusuff, R.M., Derayatifar, A.R.: Linguistic extension of fuzzy integral for group personnel selection problem. Arabian J. Sci. Eng. 38(10), 2901–2910 (2013)
9. Zadeh, L.A.: Fuzzy sets. Inf. Control 8, 338–353 (1965)
10. Kelemenis, A., Askounis, D.: A new TOPSIS-based multicriteria approach to personnel selection. Expert Syst. Appl. 37(7), 4999–5008 (2010)
11. Canós, L., Casasús, T., Crespo, E., Lara, T., Pérez, J.: Personnel selection based on fuzzy methods. Revista de Matemática: Teoría y Aplicaciones 18(1), 177–192 (2011)
12. Dursun, M., Karsak, E.E.: A fuzzy MCDM approach for personnel selection. Expert Syst. Appl. 37(6), 4324–4330 (2010)

13. Alliger, G.M., Feinzig, S.L., Janak, E.: Fuzzy sets and personnel selection: discussion and an application. J. Occup. Organ. Psychol. **66**, 163–169 (1993)
14. Licata, I.: General system theory, like-quantum semantics and fuzzy sets. In: Minati, G., Abram, M. (eds.) System of Emergence, Research and Development, pp. 724–734. Springer, New York (2006). https://doi.org/10.1007/0-387-28898-8_52
15. Zadeh, L.A.: Toward a perception-based theory of probabilistic reasoning with imprecise probabilities. J. Stat. Plan. Inference **105**, 233–264 (2002)
16. Kabak, M., Burmaoglu, S., Kazancoglu, Y.: A fuzzy hibrid MCDM approach for professional selection. Expert Syst. Appl. **39**, 3516–3525 (2012)
17. Zadeh, L.A.: Toward extended fuzzy logic. A first step. Fuzzy Sets Syst. **160**, 3175–3181 (2009)
18. Özdaban, I., Özkan, C.: A case study on evaluating personnel and jobs jointly with fuzzy distances. Int. J. Ind. Eng. **18**(4), 169–179 (2011)
19. Izquierdo, N.V., Viloria, A., Lezama, O.B.P., Gaitán-Angulo, M., Herrera, H.H.: Performance evaluation by means of fuzzy mathematics. The case of a clinical laboratory. J. Control Theory Appl. (2016). ISSN 0974-5572
20. Izquierdo, N.V., Lezama, O.B.P., Dorta, R.G., Viloria, A., Deras, I., Hernández-Fernández, L.: Fuzzy logic applied to the performance evaluation. Honduran coffee sector case. In: Tan, Y., Shi, Y., Tang, Q. (eds.) ICSI 2018. LNCS, vol. 10942, pp. 164–173. Springer, Cham (2018). https://doi.org/10.1007/978-3-319-93818-9_16
21. Viloria, A.: Commercial strategies providers pharmaceutical chains for logistics cost reduction. Indian J. Sci. Technol. **8**(1), 1–6 (2016)
22. Viloria, A., Wichez, M., Acuna, N.: Turnover increased Massive Consumer Products through the Implementation of Design Standards based on the Buyer. Indian J. Sci. Technol. **9**(46), 35–42 (2016)

A Consortium Blockchain-Based Model for Data Sharing in Internet of Vehicles

Qifan Wang[1], Lei Zhou[1], Zhe Tang[1], and Guojun Wang[2](✉) iD

[1] School of Computer Science and Engineering, Central South University,
Changsha 410083, China
[2] School of Computer Science, Guangzhou University, Guangzhou 510006, China
csgjwang@gmail.com

Abstract. Internet of Vehicles (IoV) provides a broad range of services of data exchange of traffic information to improve the effectiveness of smart vehicles. However, the security issues in Internet of Vehicles are multifaceted: data theft, message tampering and forgery, etc., which results in possibilities of incorrect data sharing. To address above issues, we proposed an efficient blockchain-based data sharing model. In this paper, we leverage the consortium blockchain and enhanced Diffie-Hellman algorithm to build a trust decentralized verifying mechanism, which is designed to secure the data sharing process in IoV. To improve the performance, we optimize the consensus mechanism on our blockchain-based system by decreasing the consensus delay without affecting the correctness of consensus verifying. The security analysis and simulation experiments show that our model meets security requirements and the overhead from our system is acceptable for IoV.

Keywords: Internet of Vehicles · Consortium blockchain · Access policy · PBFT Algorithm · Diffie-Hellman key agreement algorithm

1 Introduction

In recent decades, the widely deployed Internet of Vehicles (IoV) [1] represents a tend of developing smart transportation, because the Intelligent Transportation System (ITS) is playing an increasingly significant role in improving the efficiency of transportation systems. ITS introduces information technology to the transportation infrastructures and aims to improve road safety and traffic efficiency. Since the IoV is a core component of ITS, it develops a new type of self-organizing network consisting of mobile vehicles with sensing, computing, storage and wireless communication capabilities and basic communication facilities on the road [2]. With IoV, it becomes possible to control the whole process of transportation in an intelligent way, to effectively improve traffic safety and facilitate user driving, and also to provide an effective platform for daily transportation or value-added services such as travel and entertainment etc.

© Springer Nature Singapore Pte Ltd. 2019
G. Wang et al. (Eds.): iSCI 2019, CCIS 1122, pp. 253–267, 2019.
https://doi.org/10.1007/978-981-15-1301-5_21

There are two main communication modes, that is, vehicle-to-vehicle (V2V) and vehicle-to-roadside units (V2R), respectively, in the traditional IoV architecture. Various of communication mechanisms can be adopted in each model to achieve better performance in different IoV scenarios. However, the main issue in IoV is still about the security. In IoV service scenario, vehicles are constantly moving, which leads to a complex communication environment. There are many security risks involved in the communication process, such as: message tampering, forged identity, message stealing, etc. In recent years, many researchers address those IoV security issues by using identity authentication, information integrity monitoring and other checking approaches [3]. Those secure IoV architecture [4] is divided into four layers: the first layer is the central management organization, which is the certificate authority (CAs), and the second layer is composed of a series of security domains, responsible for managing the encryption-related information. The third layer consists of RSUs (Roadside Units), which are built on the road by following certain rules, and the forth layer is the vehicle nodes. However, all the above mechanisms could be susceptible to some attacks, such as: the single point of failure [5], data lost, data tampering, etc., and all of them would lead to information leakage, traffic accidents, or other untrusted data sharing problems. In this paper, we proposed a consortium blockchain-based model for data sharing in IoV, and the traditional information transmission mode in IoV is optimized through the data encryption, access policy matching, time stamp and the improved consensus algorithm. Our contributions can be generalized as follows:

- We developed a secure data sharing system based on consortium blockchain, which becomes the core part of distributed vehicle networking communication architecture, and adopted symmetric encryption and Diffie-Hellman key agreement algorithm.
- We optimized the consensus algorithm for our model, which can efficiently improve the consensus efficiency. In addition, we improved the consensus system effectiveness by introducing the access control policy.
- We evaluated the security advantages in our model, and the result of simulation experiment is acceptable for data sharing in IoV.

The remainder of this paper is organized as follows. In Sect. 2, we briefly discuss the related work. Section 3 contains the architecture of data sharing model in IoV. Then we present the detailed design of our model in Sect. 4. In Sect. 5, we give the security analysis and conduct the performance evaluation for our model through the simulation experiment. Finally, we come into our conclusion in Sect. 6.

2   Related Work

IoV faces many opportunities and challenges, many researchers have tried to solve the security problems mentioned in former section in IoV. Zeadally [6] proposed to patch a time-stamp when the vehicle sends messages to others, and the receiver can detect anti-replay attack by checking the consistency of time-stamp. Varshney [7] proposed to add a digital signature in sharing data. When the vehicle sends messages to others, the message is signed by using the private key held by the vehicle, and the receivers use the sender's public key to verify the signature, which can ensure the non-repudiation of the information. But all above approach has a significant problem that key or signature used in a centralized sever, which may lost its power after attacking.

In recent years, blockchain, a decentralized distributed database which generates lots of blocks that store transaction record, has gradually been regarded as an significant technique that can be used in IoV. In order to solve the problem of single point failure, Li [8] proposed an anonymous authentication mechanism, called "CreditCoin", to check the entry of malicious nodes in the Ad-hoc network. In addition, it was created based on the blockchain technology to effectively protect the privacy of users and ensure the security of communication between vehicle nodes. Zhang [9] proposed a scheme about secure data sharing and storage based on a consortium blockchain, it guarantees that the data stored in the RSU is safety in tamper-proof device. Meanwhile, smart contracts are used to limit the triggering conditions for preselected nodes when transmitting and storing data. But these schemes can't solve many problems in IoV.

Blockchain is managed and maintained by all of the participating computational nodes, even part of nodes become untrusted, the entire system should still work. Although the blockchain brings many possibilities for the IoV, the issues of efficiency in consensus mechanism need to be resolved. Thus, Castro and Liskov proposed Practical Byzantine Fault Tolerance (PBFT) [10], which reduced the complexity of the Byzantine protocol from exponential to polynomial, made it possible to apply the Byzantine protocol in distributed systems. Gan et al. [11] proposed an improved practical Byzantine fault-tolerant consensus algorithm, they optimized PBFT's consensus process to improve consensus efficiency and improved the method of PBFT's master node selection. Consensus verified by a few important nodes will significantly reduce the number of messages broadcast in the network. In the digital currency-based applications, the weights can also correspond to the user's currency, thus achieving a consensus mechanism which is similar to the proof of stake (PoS) [12]. A problem that cannot be ignored in the consensus mechanism is sybil attack [13] caused by the free entry and exit of nodes. The consensus based on the proof mechanism is usually applied to the public chain which allows the free access of nodes, and the PoW mechanism is used by Bitcoin and Ethereum. The consensus based on voting mechanism is generally applied to the consortium blockchain authorized by the node.

3   System Model

In our work, the goal of secure model is to build a trust data sharing system in IoV. We predefine a reasonable scenario: A city is divided into several regions according to the partition of urban transportation system, i.e., business center, airport, railway station, as shown in Fig. 1. Each region can be regarded as a

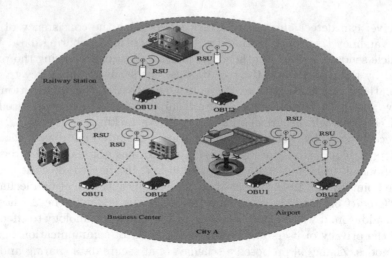

Fig. 1. System architecture diagram.

vehicle convergence zone and some main facilities are selected as RSU. In each specific alliance member, a retail store, a gas station, a toll station, or a transportation station can be selected as the RSU. The RSU periodically broadcasts road condition information at regular intervals based on actual conditions. The general content includes: time, location, and traffic conditions in the coverage area.

In our model, each zone comprises multiple RSUs and OBUs (Onboard Units), as a alliance member of the whole IoV system. The size of each part depends on the local scenario, for example, business center is a region where has a larger daily traffic flow, and the size should be greater in order to access more RSU and OBU nodes. Meanwhile, to maintain a stable IoV network, we assumed a reasonable communication range for each node in consortium. Depending on the capability of existing IoV wireless technology [14], the wireless communication range is about 1KM in normal conditions. Therefore, in our model, with a radius of 1KM, one RSU can be deployed every 2KM to achieve full coverage.

OBU, represents the vehicle in the consortium blockchain network. OBU sends and receives the message from other nodes. To ensure a trust communication, we leverage the consensus mechanism and optimize Diffie-Hellman algorithm to protect the data. In addition, we adopt access control policy to reduce the overhead. The OBU who requests information can leverage their attributes to match others' access policy.

RSU, refers to the fixed building in network, which possesses a greater storage and computational capicity. RSU collects private information including the position and speed of vehicles from sensors, monitors the running status of the vehicle who passes through the range covered by RSU. Meanwhile, RSU is a roadside unit node which is capable of storing and forwarding information, and taking part in the consensus process as an accounting node in the consortium blockchain. To improve the communication's efficiency and reduce the overhead, RSU is also designed to store the encrypted messages.

After the system initialization, the workflow in this model is designed as follows:

- First, we assume OBU1 is the data provider, and it has the information requested by OBU2.
- Second, OBU2 broadcasts its attribute set and request to other nodes. Other nodes will check the attribute set using their self-defined access control policy when they receive message sent by OBU2. In this model, we make the assumption that OBU1 receives the attribute set sent by OBU2.
- Third, as long as OBU1 matches the request from OBU2, OBU1 will sent cryptography parameters to OBU2 and encrypt the message using the symmetric key. Meanwhile, a transaction between OBU1 and OBU2 is initiated and the related block will be sent to blockchain. Once the transaction succeed, OBU1 sends the ciphertext to the nearby RSU.
- Last, after verifying the transaction block, the RSU then send the corresponding ciphertext to OBU2. OBU2 decrypts the ciphertext with the symmetric key to get the data.

In whole system, the main challenges include the security of information transfer, message tampering and efficiency issues. We adopt consortium blockchain to solve the problem of tampering and over centralization by leveraging this decentralized architecture. We leverage symmetric encryption and DH key agreement algorithm to ensure the security of the messages and keys. We also adopt access control policy and improve PBFT algorithm to enhance the system efficiency. Moreover, we will make detailed description in the following sections about the implementation of the system.

4   System Design

Since it has different situations in real transportation environment, we select a typical scenario as the Fig. 2 shown. The vehicle node OBU2, traveling in the urban area of the city A, try to collects real-time traffic information of the current vehicle node, including: speed, direction, location, road congestion index and other information, such as, information about the car park. Then we will implement each phase based on the above application.

4.1   Data Sharing Phase in IoV

We assume OBU2 traveling on the road request to get real-time traffic information about the car park. Thus, OBU2 broadcasts in the network to find a OBU which hold its needed data. We leverage the consortium blockchain to process the data sharing transaction which ensure the contents without tampering. Once the transaction about information requested by OBU2 is verified, it will be stored in the block. In addition, the content of the data will be encrypted before transmission. Using the Diffie-Hellman key agreement algorithm [15], OBU2 and the message sender can obtain a key through the session. We demonstrate the model with simple DH algorithm, but it may be attacked by the man-in-the-middle attack (MITM), however, this can be solved by using some enhanced DH algorithm [16,17] which is out of our goal. The detailed steps are as follows:

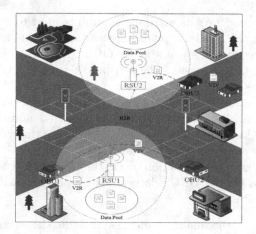

Fig. 2. Business center for data sharing.

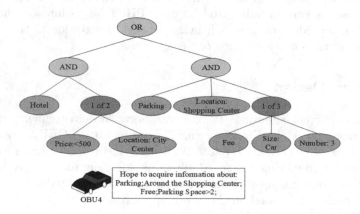

Fig. 3. Access policy tree

Initialization: We define public parameters p and g, and g should satisfy: $2 \leq g \leq p - 1$, those two parameters p, g are open to whole network nodes. The broadcast request $br = <p, g, S>$ including: the prime number p and integer g, where g is the generator of p, OBU2's attribute set $S = \{Parking; Shoppingcenter; S'\}$, $S' = \{Free; ParkingSpace > 2\}$.

Attribute Matching: The nodes nearby the OBU2 will receive the request from OBU2, here we refer the existing routing mechanism. We assume that OBU1 has the corresponding information requested by OBU2 and the attribute set S in the OBU2's request matches the access policy tree defined by OBU1. Once successfully matching, the match is successful, as shown in the Fig. 3, the values of the first two leaf nodes in the right subtree in the access policy tree $\{Parking; Location : ShoppingCenter\}$ satisfy the first two attributes in S, $\{ParkingSpace = 3\}$, satisfying the last one in S. For '1 of 2' or '1 of 3', it represents a successful match as long as an attribute in S matches one of the two or three leaf nodes. Therefore, the attribute matches successfully.

Key Agreement: Then, OBU2 produces a private random number A, A satisfies $1 \leq A \leq p - 1$. Meanwhile, it calculates $Y_a = g^A \mod p$ and sends this value to OBU1. In same workflow, OBU1 chooses a private random number B, which is required $1 \leq B \leq p - 1$ and calculates $Y_b = g^B \mod p$ and sends it to OBU2. At the same time, the data known by OBU1 are p, g, B, Y_a, and OBU1 obtains the negotiation key K_b by calculating $K_b = (Y_a)^B \mod p$. Meanwhile, OBU2 receives the corresponding information sent by OBU1 and obtains the key K_a by calculating $K_a = (Y_b)^A \mod p$. According to the algorithm, $K_a = K_b$. This result can be verified as follows: For OBU2: $K_a = (Y_b)^A \mod p = (g^B \mod p)^A \mod p = g^{(B \times A)} \mod p$. For OBU1: $K_b = (Y_a)^B \mod p = (g^A \mod p)^B \mod p = g^{(A \times B)} \mod p$.

Data Sharing: The message m sent by OBU1 is encrypted by the symmetric key K to get the ciphertext c, and the time-stamp t is attached to get $< c, t >$ and then sent to the nearby RSU where stored and maintained by RSU. OBU1 uses the negotiation key Y_b to encrypt the symmetric key K, and get the encrypted file c_key. OBU1 then sends c_key and index information about the RSU where stored the ciphertext c to OBU2.

OBU2 can get the symmetric key K by decrypting c_key with K_a. Then OBU2 initiates a transaction, the transaction structure includes a version number v, a transaction input tx_in, an output tx_out, and a lock time $locktime$. After the transaction parties OBU1 and OBU2 confirm this transaction, the related transaction information is sent to the accounting node for a consensus. Only if the consensus is successful, the RSU storing ciphertext c will allow OBU2 to obtain this ciphertext after the transaction is completed. Among them, the RSU confirms whether the transaction is successful by querying whether a block in the blockchain contains this transaction. RSU can verify the existence of the transaction in the block in a short time by utilizing the Merkle root in the block header and Bloom Filter [18].

However, the above mechanism works on the vehicle nodes which are in same region's group (nodes in same group can communicate each other without message forwarding). Considering the data sharing between different group's nodes, the message should be forward by one of RSUs. We assume that there is an OBU3 traveling in the surrounding area of airport, as shown in Fig. 1, it first launches the information requirement related to business center. OBU3 then queries the block record on the consortium blockchain to find the transaction record which match the requirement by querying the information abstract. To remove the invalid or outdated data, it filtrates the useless block by calculating the timestamp. After that OBU3 finds a matching transaction record successfully (We assumed the related information comes from OBU1), then OBU3 and OBU1 exchange a secret key, and OBU3 initiates the transaction. Since OBU3 and OBU1 are in different groups without directly communication channel. This can be solved by leveraging the powerful node, RSU, to forward the session message, and the routing algorithm can choose the existing ad-hoc routing approaches [19].

4.2   Consensus Phase

In the data sharing phase, the consortium blockchain verify the correctness of the data transaction between OBU1 and OBU2. The verifying process works in whole accounting nodes, which selected from all of the OBUs and RSUs through PBFT voting mechanism. When the verification is successful, the corresponding block will be generated to record the transaction information about OBU2 and OBU1. However, the traditional PBFT algorithm cannot satisfy the actual IoV scenario due to the long delay of consensus computing. In this section, we propose an efficient practical byzantine fault-tolerant algorithm (EPBFT). Among those accounting nodes, the consensus process of the primary node leader is in a view v, and v is a consecutive numbered integer in each view. Among them, there are the following roles: requester, primary node, and replica node. The three role functions are as follows:

Requester: After the transaction originator OBU2 initiates the transaction, the transaction and the signatures are sent to the network. If the node receiving the information is not the accounting node, the message is broadcast to other nodes; otherwise, the signature should be verified and message will be written to the cache when the signature is correct. The request format is $<REQUEST, t, trans, Sig>$, where t is the time stamp to unique the request which promise the valid information applying. The $trans$ represents the transaction, Sig represents the OBU2's signature on this transaction.

Primary Node: In this paper, the primary node is mainly responsible for receiving transactions, and after a period of time, the received transaction generates a block. The primary node is a node selected from the accounting nodes participating in the consensus, and also serves as the private key generation center, and the other replica nodes act as the signer group. A block is generated when a certain amount of transaction $trans$ is stored in the primary node's cache or after a certain time interval Δt.

Replica Node: Replica node is mainly responsible for picking up messages sent from primary node and other replica nodes, executing some corresponding verifications, finally sending the consensus result back to the requester.

A collection of all nodes is represented by R, and each copy in the collection can be represented by an integer from 0 to $|R| - 1$. The ideal number of nodes in the collection is: $|R| = 3f + 1$. f is the maximum number of failed nodes, $|R|$ is the number of nodes. Although more nodes can be deployed, this will only reduce system performance and will not help the consensus process.

View Change: Considering the height h of the current block and the view number v, the selection of the primary node number p is determined by the following formula: $p = (h-v) mod N$. When the primary node fails, the consensus request is not initiated within Δt time after the consensus starts, or the primary node is suspected from the node, the view change will be initiated and the view will be switched, then the primary node is replaced. The specific process is as follows:

- When the replica node finds that the primary node is invalid or suspects that the primary node is a malicious node, it broadcast a message about view change to other nodes in the cluster. The format of the message is $<view - change, V_{old}, V_{new}, h, p, \Delta t, S_i>$, V_{new} represents the new view number, S_i represents the node that initiated the view change.
- The other replica nodes will verify that V_{old} is the same as the current view number when they receive the message about view change. Then they compute the formula: $V_{new} = V_{old} + 1$. Replica nodes will check whether the primary node is invalid. If the primary node is valid and the proposal sent by the primary node is not considered to be problematic, the message about view change will be ignored; if the verification is passed, they will broadcast view change confirmation message, $<view - change - confirmation, V_{old}, V_{new}, h, p, \Delta t, S_i>$.

When the replica node receives the confirmation values from $2f + 1$ replica nodes, then it will start to enter the primary node re-voting phase, and obtains a new primary node according to the steps above.

In the application scenario of IoV, the transaction originator OBU2 is located in a region with many nodes, including RSUs and OBUs. For OBUs, it is a mobile node that appears in various areas according to the user's own driving intentions. Information owned by nodes may lag behind other nodes due to personal reasons or failure of some nodes themselves. Based on the dynamic check mechanism, the Δt_{check} is used as the time interval, and the replica node backs up the data including v, h, pre_hash. After the backup data is verified, it can be saved to the same state.

The transaction originator OBU2 initiates a transaction, signs the transaction with its own private key, and broadcasts it to other nodes in the network. If the accounting node receives the transaction, it verifies whether the transaction is legal. If it is legal, the transaction will be recorded in the cache; if other non-accounting nodes receive the information about the transaction, they only need to broadcast to other nodes. Thus, the specific steps of this algorithm are as follows:

- **Consensus Request Phase:** After Δt time or the primary node p stored a number of transactions, the message is broadcasted to other accounting nodes participating in the sharing process. The format of the message is $<<consensus - request, v, h, p, d, \sigma_p>, block>$, v represents the view number, h is the height of the current block, p is the current primary node number, *block* is the block information propagated by the primary node, d is the summary of the block, and σp is the signature generated by the primary node p using the ECDSA signature algorithm to verify the integrity of the information.

- **Consensus Confirmation Phase:** After receiving the consensus request sent by the primary node, the replica node $Node_i, i \in 0, 1, \cdots, N-1$, participating in the verification, sends a consensus confirmation message to the other node. A confirmation message is broadcast to other nodes than itself, and messages generated during the consensus request phase and the consensus confirmation phase are written to the message log. The format of the message is $<consensus - confirm, v, h, d, Node_i, \sigma_i, Result>$, *Result* represents the result of the verification about the signature. If the result is 1, it means the signature verification is successful; otherwise, it means the signature is invalid. The flag for completion of the consensus confirmation phase is to receive $2f + 1$ acknowledgment messages from different replica nodes, and then issue the *block* from the primary node.

After the rest of the nodes confirm that the current round of consensus computing is completed, the nodes delete the transactions recorded in their own cache and start a new round of consensus.

5   Security Analysis and Evaluation

In this section, we evaluate our system about the security and performance. Through simulate the system, the experimental result compares to previous proposed approaches to show the improvement of our new model.

5.1   Security Analysis

Security is a very serious issue that need to be addressed in IoV application. Incorrect vehicle information can cause some extremely terrible accidents and threaten driver's lives. Due to the importance of users' privacy, users is not willing to share all of their traveling information, including locations, directions, destination etc., with others [20]. Since there are some traditional attacks in IoV [21,22], we summarize some of them into follow aspects as follows:

Confidentiality Attacks: Eavesdropping [23] is an simple attack targeting confidentiality by sniffing transmitted communication messages and eventually intercepting passwords, etc.

Integrity Attacks: This type of attack contains some typical features, which including message spoofing and tampering, timing attack, etc. The worse situation may cause an accident and threaten users' lives. Messages shared in V2V and V2I communications can be tampered with and influence user's judge in the real-time traffic. Attackers may add delay between packets which causes a reception behind the time and finally, traffic congestion or even accidents.

Privacy Attacks: For example, the vehicle can be tracked and their privacy about location will be leaked. Sybil attack, mentioned in the section of related work, represents that a malicious vehicle sends wrong numerous messages to other vehicles with different fabricated identities. And the messages transmitted in IoV may be theft by other attackers, what's worse, they can get some important information and even influence the whole system.

Our model enable to against these attacks to promise a security data sharing in IoV through following aspects:

Decentralization: By leveraging the consortium blockchain, nodes in network no need to trust other nodes in generally. Attacks on those traditional data sharing severs will affect whole data sharing process. Fortunately, server in blockchain does not depend on the trusted third-party entity but verified by whole consortium nodes. Meanwhile, times-stamp in the message help us defend timing attack. This decentralized storage system has good scalability and reliability.

Data Security: We adopt Diffie-Hellman key agreement algorithm. It generate a couple secure and private key at both sides, the DH key is privacy, but data can be secure encrypted and decrypted by each other without leaking the cryptography information. It can be proved by the following example: We assume that Eve, who is a attacker, hacked the relevant information, including p, g, Y_a, Y_b. Even in this case, Eve is hard to crack the key K_a or K_b. In fact, if p is large prime number, it's extremely hard for Eve to get A according to the following formula: $g^A \mod p = Y_a$. The time complexity of the most efficient algorithm for calculating this problem is $O(\sqrt{p})$, so the difficulty in solving the problem in computing ensures the security of the Diffie-Hellman algorithm. Meanwhile, we adopt some improved schemes to address the MITM attack which is mentioned in Sect. 4.1.

Fault Tolerance: Our model proposed the EPBFT consensus mechanism to ensure the system working normally, even 33% of the RSUs or OBUs in the entire system are compromised. According to the EPBFT algorithm, if there are f invalid RSU nodes in the whole network and the total number of nodes satisfies $n \geq 3f + 1$, our proposed system can defend against the security attacks initiated by invalid RSU nodes. It ensure that the final consensus result are not changed based on this proof.

5.2 Performance Evaluation

After we analyzed the requirements of IoV data sharing system, for example, Scalable, Lightweight, Key security, etc., shown in Table 1. Our system meets most of the requirements and reach an acceptable performance. Also, comparing to other existing approaches, our mechanism shows more advantages as the follows.

In this paper, we leverage the consortium blockchain as the key mechanism to construct a decentralize system for IoV data sharing with trust trading parters. Meanwhile, the suitable access policy matching mechanism help the whole system reduce the generation of unnecessary blocks. The improved EPBFT algorithm in this paper makes some improvements based on the traditional PBFT algorithm, and simplifies the algorithm steps to make it suitable for the vehicle networking scenario. Improving the primary node selection and view change

Table 1. Evaluation between our scheme and other schemes

	Azees et al.'s scheme [24]	Liu et al.'s scheme [25]	Dorri et al.'s scheme [26]	Our scheme
Decentralization	NO	YES	YES	YES
Traceable	NO	YES	YES	YES
Scalable	NO	NO	YES	YES
Lightweight	NO	NO	YES	YES
Key security	NO	NO	NO	YES
Low overhead and high efficiency	YES	NO	NO	YES

methods in the algorithm to prevent malicious nodes from leading the consensus process. Through the data synchronization and verification methods, the reliability of each node is guaranteed. It is better than other algorithms in their schemes.

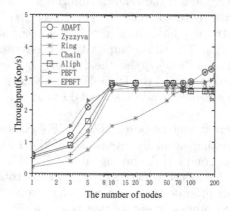

Fig. 4. The comparison of throughput for consensus algorithms

We evaluated the system throughput and delay. Throughput generally refers to the number of transactions processed by the system per unit time. The throughput indicates the ability of the system to withstand the data loading, transactions applying, processing and answering. Due to the difficulties of deploying experimental nodes in real-world IoV scenarios, we conducted simulation experiments to simulate the performance of improved consensus algorithm. The results are reported in Figs. 4 and 5. We can see that our scheme is better than other schemes in the simulated experimental environment. We refer to Bahsoun's scheme [27], to test the performance of our model by assessing the throughput and the delay when changing the number of nodes. The number of nodes in the Fig. 4 refers to the number of nodes that send transaction requests. In the traditional PBFT algorithm, the client sends a request to the master node. In the improved PBFT algorithm, we set the vehicle node to broadcast transaction

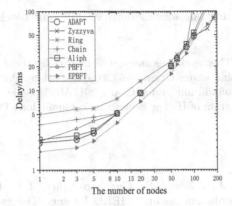

Fig. 5. The comparison of delay for consensus algorithms

records to the whole network. This mechanism is more suitable for P2P networks. When the number of nodes requested is small, the throughput of several schemes in the figure increases with the number of nodes, and the throughput of several schemes is improved. Our scheme has a certain improvement compared with the schemes such as Ring; As the number of nodes continues to increase, the throughput may even decrease. In Fig. 5, as the number of nodes sending transaction records increases, the consensus delay also increases rapidly. Therefore, sending too many nodes will affect the performance of the system. In summary, our scheme has higher throughput than other schemes when the number of nodes is constant.

6 Conclusion

In this paper, we present a secure data sharing system for IoV by leveraging the consortium blockchain. Since the blockchain technology is continuously developed and improved, it provides an effectively mechanism against the data tampering and is applicable to the vehicle data transferring. In our system, we built a secure traffic data sharing model in IoV system. Consortium blockchain in IoV is well matched the different zone in city, and proposed a local trusted data verifying mechanism. In addition, to solve the privacy of data when it is exchanged in whole network, we proposed the corresponding key agreement algorithm for IoV data encrypted/decrypted. Since performance is the key issue of blockchain, we developed the modified EPBFT algorithm, it decreased the consensus delay, and only useful blocks are created in chain, which significantly reduce the overhead during the process of the data transaction in IoV. Simulation result shows that our model performs a secure application and the performance has been greatly improved and compared with the exiting consortium blockchain scenarios. Future researches should focus on the cross-chain technology that are common in the research of blockchain and attempts should be made to apply it to the IoV system to solve the cross-chain transactions between different blockchains in different cities.

Acknowledgments. This work was supported in part by the National Natural Science Foundation of China under Grant 61632009, in part by the Guangdong Provincial Natural Science Foundation under Grant 2017A030308006, and in part by the High-Level Talents Program of Higher Education in Guangdong Province under Grant 2016ZJ01.

References

1. Contreras-Castillo, J., Zeadally, S., Guerrero-Ibañez, J.A.: Internet of vehicles: architecture, protocols, and security. IEEE Internet Things J. **5**(5), 3701–3709 (2017)
2. Wang, Q., Duan, G., Luo, E., Wang, G.: Research on internet of vehicles' privacy protection based on tamper-proof with ciphertext. In: Wang, G., Atiquzzaman, M., Yan, Z., Choo, K.-K.R. (eds.) SpaCCS 2017. LNCS, vol. 10656, pp. 42–55. Springer, Cham (2017). https://doi.org/10.1007/978-3-319-72389-1_4
3. Huang, X., Xu, C., Wang, P., Liu, H.: LNSC: a security model for electric vehicle and charging pile management based on blockchain ecosystem. IEEE Access **6**, 13565–13574 (2018)
4. Kang, J., Yu, R., Huang, X., Zhang, Y.: Privacy-preserved pseudonym scheme for fog computing supported internet of vehicles. IEEE Trans. Intell. Transp. Syst. **19**(8), 2627–2637 (2017)
5. Li, Y., Qi, F., Tang, Z.: Traceable and complete fine-grained revocable multi-authority attribute-based encryption scheme in social network. In: Wang, G., Atiquzzaman, M., Yan, Z., Choo, K.-K.R. (eds.) SpaCCS 2017. LNCS, vol. 10656, pp. 87–92. Springer, Cham (2017). https://doi.org/10.1007/978-3-319-72389-1_8
6. Zeadally, S., Hunt, R., Chen, Y.S., Irwin, A., Hassan, A.: Vehicular ad hoc networks (VANETS): status, results, and challenges. Telecommun. Syst. **50**(4), 217–241 (2012)
7. Varshney, N., Roy, T., Chaudhary, N.: Security protocol for VANET by using digital certification to provide security with low bandwidth. In: 2014 International Conference on Communication and Signal Processing, pp. 768–772. IEEE (2014)
8. Li, L., et al.: CreditCoin: a privacy-preserving blockchain-based incentive announcement network for communications of smart vehicles. IEEE Trans. Intell. Transp. Syst. **19**(7), 2204–2220 (2018)
9. Zhang, X., Chen, X.: Data security sharing and storage based on a consortium blockchain in a vehicular adhoc network. IEEE Access **7**, 58241–58254 (2019)
10. Castro, M., Liskov, B., et al.: Practical byzantine fault tolerance. In: OSDI, vol. 99, pp. 173–186 (1999)
11. Gan, J., Li, Q., Chen, Z., Zhang, C.: Improvement of blockchain practical Byzantine fault tolerance consensus algorithm. J. Comput. Appl. **39**(7), 2148–2155 (2019)
12. Kiayias, A., Russell, A., David, B., Oliynykov, R.: Ouroboros: a provably secure proof-of-stake blockchain protocol. In: Katz, J., Shacham, H. (eds.) CRYPTO 2017. LNCS, vol. 10401, pp. 357–388. Springer, Cham (2017). https://doi.org/10.1007/978-3-319-63688-7_12
13. Lin, J., Li, M., Yang, D., Xue, G., Tang, J.: Sybil-proof incentive mechanisms for crowdsensing. In: IEEE INFOCOM 2017-IEEE Conference on Computer Communications, pp. 1–9. IEEE (2017)

14. Huang, W., Li, P., Zhang, T.: RSUs placement based on vehicular social mobility in VANETs. In: 2018 13th IEEE Conference on Industrial Electronics and Applications (ICIEA), pp. 1255–1260. IEEE (2018)
15. Bresson, E., Chevassut, O., Pointcheval, D., Quisquater, J.J.: Provably authenticated group Diffie-Hellman key exchange. In: Proceedings of the 8th ACM Conference on Computer and Communications Security, pp. 255–264. ACM (2001)
16. Johnston, A.M., Gemmell, P.S.: Authenticated key exchange provably secure against the man-in-the-middle attack. J. Cryptol. **15**(2), 139–148 (2002)
17. Gennaro, R.: Multi-trapdoor commitments and their applications to proofs of knowledge secure under concurrent man-in-the-middle attacks. In: Franklin, M. (ed.) CRYPTO 2004. LNCS, vol. 3152, pp. 220–236. Springer, Heidelberg (2004). https://doi.org/10.1007/978-3-540-28628-8_14
18. Guan, Z., et al.: Privacy-preserving and efficient aggregation based on blockchain for power grid communications in smart communities. IEEE Commun. Mag. **56**(7), 82–88 (2018)
19. Royer, E.M., Toh, C.K.: A review of current routing protocols for ad hoc mobile wireless networks. IEEE Pers. Commun. **6**(2), 46–55 (1999)
20. Samad, A., Alam, S., Mohammed, S., Bhukhari, M.: Internet of vehicles (IoV) requirements, attacks and countermeasures. In: Proceedings of 12th INDIACom; INDIACom-2018; 5th International Conference on "Computing for Sustainable Global Development" IEEE Conference, New Delhi (2018)
21. Sun, Y., et al.: Security and privacy in the internet of vehicles. In: 2015 International Conference on Identification, Information, and Knowledge in the Internet of Things (IIKI), pp. 116–121. IEEE (2015)
22. Abassi, R.: Vanet security and forensics: challenges and opportunities. Wiley Interdiscip. Rev.: Forensic Sci. **1**(2), e1324 (2019)
23. Zeng, Y., Zhang, R.: Wireless information surveillance via proactive eavesdropping with spoofing relay. IEEE J. Sel. Top. Sig. Process. **10**(8), 1449–1461 (2016)
24. Azees, M., Vijayakumar, P., Deboarh, L.J.: EAAP: efficient anonymous authentication with conditional privacy-preserving scheme for vehicular ad hoc networks. IEEE Trans. Intell. Transp. Syst. **18**(9), 2467–2476 (2017)
25. Liu, H., Zhang, Y., Yang, T.: Blockchain-enabled security in electric vehicles cloud and edge computing. IEEE Netw. **32**(3), 78–83 (2018)
26. Dorri, A., Steger, M., Kanhere, S.S., Jurdak, R.: Blockchain: a distributed solution to automotive security and privacy. IEEE Commun. Mag. **55**(12), 119–125 (2017)
27. Bahsoun, J.P., Guerraoui, R., Shoker, A.: Making BFT protocols really adaptive. In: 2015 IEEE International Parallel and Distributed Processing Symposium, pp. 904–913. IEEE (2015)

Semantic Knowledge Based Graph Model in Smart Cities

Saqib Ali[1,2], Guojun Wang[1(✉)], Komal Fatima[2], and Pin Liu[3]

[1] School of Computer Science, Guangzhou University,
Guangzhou 510006, China
{saqibali,csgjwang}@gzhu.edu.cn
[2] Department of Computer Science, University of Agriculture,
Faisalabad 38000, Pakistan
{saqib,2014ag5719}@uaf.edu.pk
[3] School of Computer Science and Engineering, Central South University,
Changsha 410083, China
jiandanglp@csu.edu.cn

Abstract. In smart cities, pervasive IoT devices generate an elephantine amount of multi-source heterogeneous data. The semantics helps to explore such complex datasets and drive towards higher-level insights. Later, these high-level insights are transformed to develop interlinks and associations among diverse sources of the data which leads towards knowledge discovery in a smart city. This discovery when combines with the domain knowledge using ontology-based approaches develop concepts and perceptions which initiate decision making in complex environments. However, the ontology-based approaches come up with certain limitations including an incapability to transform semi-structured data into useful knowledge, issues in handling inconsistent data, and inability to process large-scale, multi-source, and complex data of smart cities. Therefore, in this paper, we proposed a Semantic Knowledge Based Graph (SKBG) model as a solution to overcomes these limitations. The SKBG model is particularly customized to a smart city environment and purely utilizes knowledge-based graphs to incorporate any type of domain knowledge by combining diversify domains as a unit. As a result, the model works fine with diverse domain knowledge, automatically classify heterogeneous data by using machine learning techniques, handle large knowledge databases and support intelligent semantic search algorithms in smart cities. Finally, the results are summarized in the form of a knowledge graph which gives a comprehensive insight into the data.

Keywords: Smart cities · Semantic Knowledge Based Graph model · Semantic data mining · Ontology-based approaches · Linked data

1 Introduction

In smart cities, highly innovative technologies and services are emerging which produce an elephantine amount of interlinked heterogeneous data [6]. This big

© Springer Nature Singapore Pte Ltd. 2019
G. Wang et al. (Eds.): iSCI 2019, CCIS 1122, pp. 268–278, 2019.
https://doi.org/10.1007/978-981-15-1301-5_22

data in smart cities is quite challenging to harvest it timely and to get useful data patterns due to its volume, velocity, and variety [4]. However, it creates great opportunities for data analytics in the field of semantic data mining and knowledge discovery. In semantic data mining, we process on the semantics of the data by in cooperating the domain knowledge [19,21]. Further, the domain knowledge is supplemented with particular semantics which helps to analyze the relationships between document set and terms resides in the document set to highlight new domain concepts and insights.

Normally, when semantic data mining is applied to widespread contextual data of smart cities, we practice formal ontologies for processing semantics and are known as ontology-based approaches [17,18]. The principal step of these ontology-based approaches is data preprocessing. The preprocessing phase helps to find out the semantic gaps and missing data between the entities or actors of the smart cities [20]. Further, it instruments vital procedures of cleanness, normalization, integration, transformation, extraction, and feature selection to explicitly specify the concepts and patterns that support domain knowledge which helps to take rightful decisions in smart cities [9,30].

There is no doubt* that ontology-based approaches provide a set of techniques for data modeling, defining features and concepts of formal semantics [16]. However, the ontology-based approaches come up with certain limitations. One such limitation is its inability to transform semi-structured data into useful knowledge [12]. Second, there are limited techniques for exploring knowledge in ontology-based approaches. Third, sometimes it allows inconsistent data to be loaded into a database with traditional data processing techniques [1]. Finally, the scarcity of robust algorithms and techniques to process large-scale, complex and heterogeneous data of smart cities using the full strength of the ontologies [14,23].

Multiple methodologies exist in literature to overcome the limitations of ontology-based approaches and data preprocessing. For example, semantic annotations, filter and multivariate methods for feature selection and different taxonomies for better classification [9,13]. Particularly, the semantic annotations proposed a technique to deal with semi-structured data. For this purpose, a semantic search algorithm is used to bring out meaning in the semantic data and annotate the semi-structured data [15]. Similarly, many featured based models are also proposed to classify, extract and select right terms for building search models in the smart cities [24]. However, these algorithms do not fulfill the requirements of handling the diverse amount of high-speed data in smart cities [10].

In this paper, we proposed a Semantic Knowledge Based Graph (SKBG) model as a solution which overcomes the basic limitations of conventional ontology-based approaches as discussed earlier. The proposed SKGB model is particularly customized to a smart city environment which works seamlessly upon semantics by using knowledge-based graph. Our SKBG model interlinks heterogeneous data, find meaning, concepts, and patterns of the data in smart cities. The model purely utilizes knowledge-based graphs to incorporate any type of domain knowledge by combining diversify domains as a unit. In particular, it combines three terms i.e., text mining, machine learning, and knowledge-based graph to search out semantics, interlinking them by finding relationships among them, discover unique patterns in data and representation of information. As a result, the model works fine with diverse domain knowledge, automatically classify heterogeneous data, handle large knowledge databases and support intelligent semantic search algorithms by using machine learning techniques in smart cities.

The main contributions of this paper are summarized as follows.

- First of all, the limitations of ontology-based approaches and data preprocessing in semantic data mining regarding smart cities are thoroughly analyzed.
- Secondly, we propose SKBG model for semantic data mining using knowledge-based graphs for complex and heterogeneous data from the diverse origins in the smart cities.
- Finally, the key features of the proposed model are explained and analyzed to have a better insight into the model concerning the challenges features of the smart cities.

The remaining of the paper is organized as follows. Section 2 describes the related work. Section 3 gives a brief description of ontology-based approaches and data preprocessing regarding smart cities. Section 4 describes the proposed model. Section 5 comprises of features of SKBG model in smart cities. Section 6 provides the future work. Finally, Sect. 7 concludes the paper.

2   Related Work

Current ontology-based approaches and data preprocessing techniques generally work on structured and unstructured data. Many researchers have surveyed semantic data mining, data preprocessing, and ontology-based approaches in smart cities [7,15]. Additionally, the researchers have combined different approaches of ontology and preprocessing to overcome their limitations [21]. However, these ontology-based approaches mainly concentrate on handling data of the single type and used classical algorithms for classification, clustering, feature selection and decision making in smart cities [9,19].

The researchers also tried to improve these approaches by improving rules i.e., association rule mining which was first introduced for prioritizing and rectifying different variants of k means algorithms applied to a group data [2]. However, these algorithms only cover similar data sets. Afterward, fuzzy sets were introduced to cover the diverse data sets [25,27]. Later, it was suggested that these fuzzy sets also need revisions as they failed to cover every combination of the data. There were chances that these fuzzy sets miss out, not all, but some semantic of the data sets [8]. Similarly, semantic annotations were applied separately to handle semi-structured data [11,22]. Many similar techniques were also introduced to improve the data preprocessing in data mining for better normalization of the data [3].

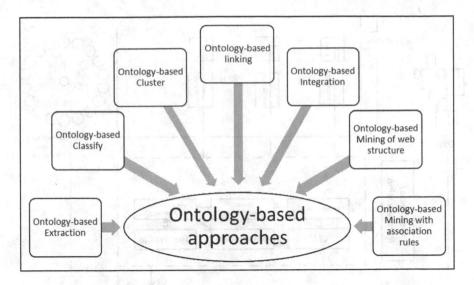

Fig. 1. Ontology-based approaches in semantic data mining

In smart cities, some featured based approaches focused on feature selection steps for better prediction and decisions making [5]. However, these techniques are used to handle data separately with different perspectives. At present, the semantic data mining in smart cities is facing diverse challenges where only specific domain knowledge is not enough and one type of content cannot be processed separately [6,14]. Therefore, there is a need for an intelligent system to resolve large and complex conflicts in semantic data mining [26]. Further, better representation formats for better understanding of domain knowledge are the key requirements of the smart cities [19]. Thus, in order to resolve these challenges, we proposed a Semantic Knowledge Based Graph model as a solution to mine concepts and patterns from complex heterogeneous data originating from the diverse sources of the smart city.

3 Formal Semantic Mining with Ontologies and Preprocessing

In smart cities, semantic data mining usually combines several stages by including ontologies for conceptualization and content management [28]. Ontology-based approaches are comprised of extraction, classification, mining with association rules, clustering, finding links, mining of web structure, integration and recommending systems as shown in Fig. 1. These steps focus on the semantics of the content. However, when these steps are applied to a data commencing from a smart city domain, knowledge extraction becomes complex and time-consuming [12,30].

Similarly, data preprocessing when specifically focuses on semantics and in finding relations in these semantics with similar meanings to interlink them with

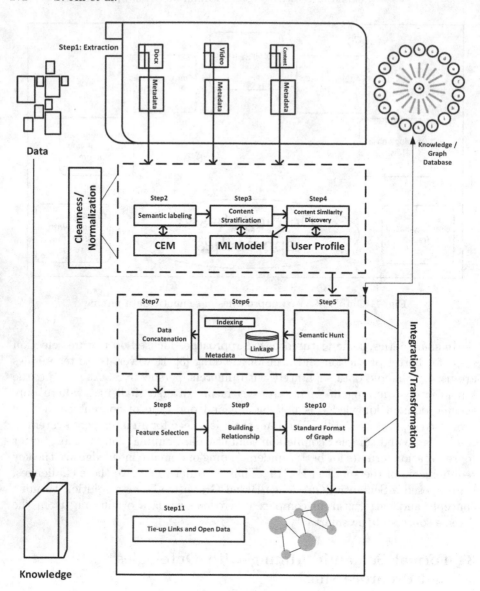

Fig. 2. Semantic Knowledge Based Graph model

one another; requires available domain knowledge. Further, it applies traditional techniques like the cleanness of data by using regression for smoothing noise, inconsistencies and semantic gaps. Also, data is classified by labeling through binning and then finally integrate them to transform into something processable. However, to undertake these tasks on the data originating from the smart cities is quite complicated and challenging [15,29].

4 Proposed Model: Semantic Knowledge Based Graph (SKBG)

In this section, we proposed a Semantic Knowledge Based Graph model as a solution to above-mentioned limitations in conventional ontology-based approaches and preprocessing data in smart cities. The model helps in transforming knowledge discovery practices. It integrates the semantic mining in diverse and tedious data catalogs of smart cities via fusing structured, unstructured and semi-structured data intelligently. As a result, information retrieval becomes very swift and effective. Further, the model effectively handles, manages and interlinks the semantics of the contents by discovering new and unique patterns during the knowledge discovery phase in smart cities.

4.1 Work Flow of Semantic Knowledge Based Graph Model

Following are the key steps of the proposed SKBG model with the objective to work seamlessly upon semantics in a smart city environment by using knowledge-based graphs. This is carried out by interlinks heterogeneous data, finding meanings, concepts, and patterns of the complex data. Moreover, the steps help to overcome the basic limitations of conventional ontology-based approaches in the smart city.

Step 1: Extraction. In the first step, extraction is performed to excavate and mine all kind of smart city data available in any format. The data can be structured (tables), semi-structured (Emails, CSV, TSV, XML or docx) and unstructured (audios, videos, images). The step is highlighted in Fig. 2.

Step 2: Semantic Labeling. During this step, excavated data is tagged with some useful and authentic semantic names. We used CEM (Concept Elicitation Mode) which helps in finding and making correct tagging as shown in Fig. 2. As a result, documents are checked out from top to bottom. Text is analyzed to mine the concepts, keywords, and topics form the content. Finally, semantic labeling helps in generating relationships between them.

Step 3: Content Stratification. In this step of our model, smart word stratification is used for grouping or classifying the content using artificial intelligence and core machine learning (supervised and unsupervised) algorithms as shown in Fig. 2. The machine learning makes the content classification process quite robust and impulsive as compared to static approaches.

Step 4: Content Similarity Discovery. In this step, the model checks the documents correspondence with similar documents and separate them. This step will figure out, how much one content data is similar to other content data? Further, the similarity index set the path for the linking of the data originating from the diverse source of a smart city. To get better experience, more enhanced graphs of different user's history and profiles are used to find out the content similarity in a smart city as shown in Fig. 2.

Step 5: Semantic Hunt. In this step, semantics of search results are analyzed as user search different and relevant words to get their desired results. Afterwards, the outcomes are linked to get better semantics in a specific domain.

Step 6: Link to Reference Data. In this step contents are linked to the reference data which is available in the knowledge database of the semantics. Two-way approaches are used for establishing the links. First, by adding reference data to the knowledge database. Second, by indexing the existed data known as meta-data as shown in step 6 of the Fig. 2. Later, both approaches help to tack back the original data.

Step 7: Data Concatenation. This step is similar to integration step in the traditional ontology-based approaches of data processing. However, it has an edge on traditional approaches as it merges both external and internal data more actively and efficiently. Semantics that are relevant to a specific domain are integrated as unit during this step.

Step 8: Features Selection. In this step, datasets after integrating semantics as a unit are analyzed extensively. As a result, some key features and attributes are mined on which knowledge graphs are established. Further, decisions are carried out regarding the combination of these features to improve the semantics of the data.

Step 9: Building Relationship. In this step after selecting unique features in the datasets, need arises to discover the unique relationships that exist among them. Therefore, by analyzing them in different dimensions' unique relationships are apprehended among the selected features.

Step 10: Standard Format of Graph. During this step, a related and standard framework is selected that represents the precise meanings in the semantic data. Further, a framework is conceived which helps to visualize the actual relationship in the semantic data.

Step 11: Tie-Up Links in Open Data. Finally, in this step, we merge two things. One is the links which are the diverse data combinations. Second is the open data which refers to the data which is free and handy to everyone. Graphical representation of knowledge is also generated for visualization as shown in Fig. 2.

Semantic Knowledge Based Graph model works with a systematic procedure and use knowledge/graph database of semantics. Our model helps to mine every type of data initiating from different sources available in the smart cities. The model employs machine learning algorithms for better classification and feature selection of the data. It helps to search relevant semantics for a specific problem and find links in them. Later, the model combines them with specific patterns which reside in them. Finally, the model shows the output in a graphical form. Hence, the Semantic Knowledge Based Graph model completely process raw data in parallel to discover and gain useful knowledge in an environment like a smart city.

5   Features of Semantic Knowledge Based Graph Model

The ontology-based approaches when applied to multi-source complex datasets (e.g., data originating from the smart cities) requires a preprocessing stage to be carried out separately. However, in our proposed SKBG model there is no need to perform the preprocessing of the data separately. All the steps in the

Table 1. Correspondence of SKBG model and preprocessing steps

No.	SKBG model steps	Preprocessing steps
1	Extraction	Nil
2	Semantic Labeling	Cleanness of data/Normalization
3	Content Stratification	Cleanness of data/Normalization
4	Content Similarity Discovery	Cleanness of data/Normalization
5	Semantic Hunt or Search	Integration and transformation
6	Linkage to Reference Data	Integration and transformation
7	Data Concatenation	Integration and transformation
8	Selection of indications or Features	Integration and transformation
9	Building Relationship	Integration and transformation
10	Settle on Standard Format of Graph	Integration and transformation
11	Tie-up links and open data	Nil

proposed model are integrated well enough to perform their specific task individually without linking or merging the data. Therefore, our SKBG model can be a pioneer for more advance knowledge discovery and data visualization in smart cities. The correspondence of SKBG model and preprocessing steps are summarized in Table 1.

Finally, Our proposed SKBG model provides a conceptual framework which mines multi-source raw data and interconnects them without having any kind of specific domain knowledge. The model is equipped with machine learning algorithms which provide persistent learning, data refining, and process monitoring as a continuous process in knowledge discovery. Further, it also connects the additional knowledge from people and different domains of the smart cities to get the diverse illustration of the data.

6   Future Work

As future work, we will evaluate our model by conducting experiments on structured, semi-structured, and unstructured datasets typically originating from a smart city domain. Also, we will define semantic labeling and semantic indexing more precisely in a smart city environment to symbolize information related to the user' s interest.

7   Conclusion

In this paper, we thoroughly analyzed the limitations of traditional ontology-based approaches and data preprocessing. Ontology-based approaches and data preprocessing are traditional ways of handling data in smart cities. However, only a single type of data can be extracted with these approaches whereas we have heterogeneous multi-source type data in smart cities. To overcome these limitations, we proposed a Semantic Knowledge Based Graph (SKBG) model. The model works with a systematic procedure and instrument a multi-source knowledge/graph database of semantics for knowledge discovery. Further, the model provides persistent learning by employing machine learning algorithms for better classification and feature selection. It searches relevant semantics for a specific problem in a smart city and interlinks them graphically for generating patterns and relationships in data. Finally, the results are summarized in the form of a knowledge graph which gives a complete insight into the data.

Acknowledgments. This work was supported in part by the National Natural Science Foundation of China under Grant 61632009, in part by the Guangdong Provincial Natural Science Foundation under Grant 2017A030308006, and in part by the High-Level Talents Program of Higher Education in Guangdong Province under Grant 2016ZJ01.

References

1. Ali, A., Qadir, J., Rasool, R.U., Sathiaseelan, A., Zwitter, A., Crowcroft, J.: Big data for development: applications and techniques. Big Data Anal. **1**(1), 2 (2016). https://doi.org/10.1186/s41044-016-0002-4
2. Altaf, W., Shahbaz, M., Guergachi, A.: Applications of association rule mining in health informatics: a survey. Artif. Intell. Rev. **47**(3), 313–340 (2017). https://doi.org/10.1007/s10462-016-9483-9
3. Bandaru, S., Ng, A.H., Deb, K.: Data mining methods for knowledge discovery in multi-objective optimization: part a - survey. Expert Syst. Appl. **70**, 139–159 (2017). https://doi.org/10.1016/j.eswa.2016.10.015
4. Consoli, S., et al.: Producing linked data for smart cities: the case of catania. Big Data Res. **7**, 1–15 (2017). https://doi.org/10.1016/j.bdr.2016.10.001
5. d'Aquin, M., Davies, J., Motta, E.: Smart cities' data: challenges and opportunities for semantic technologies. IEEE Internet Comput. **19**(6), 66–70 (2015). https://doi.org/10.1109/MIC.2015.130
6. González-Vidal, A., Jiménez, F., Gómez-Skarmeta, A.F.: A methodology for energy multivariate time series forecasting in smart buildings based on feature selection. Energy Build. **196**, 71–82 (2019). https://doi.org/10.1016/j.enbuild.2019.05.021
7. Gyrard, A., Zimmermann, A., Sheth, A.: Building IoT-based applications for smart cities: how can ontology catalogs help? IEEE Internet Things J. **5**(5), 3978–3990 (2018). https://doi.org/10.1109/JIOT.2018.2854278
8. Huang, Y., Li, T., Luo, C., Fujita, H., Horng, S.J.: Matrix-based dynamic updating rough fuzzy approximations for data mining. Knowl.-Based Syst. **119**, 273–283 (2017). https://doi.org/10.1016/j.knosys.2016.12.015
9. Kaur, N., Aggarwal, H.: Query based approach for referrer field analysis of log data using web mining techniques for ontology improvement. Int. J. Inf. Technol. **10**(1), 99–110 (2018). https://doi.org/10.1007/s41870-017-0063-2
10. Lau, B.P.L., et al.: A survey of data fusion in smart city applications. Inf. Fusion **52**, 357–374 (2019). https://doi.org/10.1016/j.inffus.2019.05.004
11. Lepri, B., Antonelli, F., Pianesi, F., Pentland, A.: Making big data work: smart, sustainable, and safe cities. EPJ Data Sci. **4**(1), 16 (2015). https://doi.org/10.1140/epjds/s13688-015-0050-4

12. Li, J., et al.: Feature selection: a data perspective. ACM Comput. Surv. **50**(6), 94:1–94:45 (2017). https://doi.org/10.1145/3136625

13. Lin, H., Liu, G., Yan, Z.: Detection of application-layer tunnels with rules and machine learning. In: Wang, G., Feng, J., Bhuiyan, M.Z.A., Lu, R. (eds.) SpaCCS 2019. LNCS, vol. 11611, pp. 441–455. Springer, Cham (2019). https://doi.org/10.1007/978-3-030-24907-6_33

14. Moustaka, V., Vakali, A., Anthopoulos, L.G.: A systematic review for smart city data analytics. ACM Comput. Surv. **51**(5), 103:1–103:41 (2018). https://doi.org/10.1145/3239566

15. Pouyanfar, S., Yang, Y., Chen, S.C., Shyu, M.L., Iyengar, S.S.: Multimedia big data analytics: a survey. ACM Comput. Surv. **51**(1), 10:1–10:34 (2018). https://doi.org/10.1145/3150226

16. Ravi, K., Ravi, V.: A survey on opinion mining and sentiment analysis: tasks, approaches and applications. Knowl.-Based Syst. **89**, 14–46 (2015). https://doi.org/10.1016/j.knosys.2015.06.015

17. Rettinger, A., Lösch, U., Tresp, V., d'Amato, C., Fanizzi, N.: Mining the semantic web. Data Min. Knowl. Discov. **24**(3), 613–662 (2012). https://doi.org/10.1007/s10618-012-0253-2

18. Ristoski, P., Paulheim, H.: Semantic web in data mining and knowledge discovery: a comprehensive survey. J. Web Semant. **36**, 1–22 (2016). https://doi.org/10.1016/j.websem.2016.01.001

19. Saggi, M.K., Jain, S.: A survey towards an integration of big data analytics to big insights for value-creation. Inf. Process. Manag. **54**(5), 758–790 (2018). https://doi.org/10.1016/j.ipm.2018.01.010

20. Shvaiko, P., Euzenat, J.: Ontology matching: state of the art and future challenges. IEEE Trans. Knowl. Data Eng. **25**(1), 158–176 (2013). https://doi.org/10.1109/TKDE.2011.253

21. Sànchez, D., Batet, M., Isern, D., Valls, A.: Ontology-based semantic similarity: a new feature-based approach. Expert Syst. Appl. **39**(9), 7718–7728 (2012). https://doi.org/10.1016/j.eswa.2012.01.082

22. Ullah, F., Habib, M.A., Farhan, M., Khalid, S., Durrani, M.Y., Jabbar, S.: Semantic interoperability for big-data in heterogeneous iot infrastructure for healthcare. Sustain. Cities Soc. **34**, 90–96 (2017). https://doi.org/10.1016/j.scs.2017.06.010

23. Vaduva, C., Georgescu, F.A., Datcu, M.: Understanding heterogeneous eo datasets: a framework for semantic representations. IEEE Access **6**, 11184–11202 (2018). https://doi.org/10.1109/ACCESS.2018.2801032

24. Wang, H., Xu, Z., Fujita, H., Liu, S.: Towards felicitous decision making: an overview on challenges and trends of big data. Inf. Sci. **367–368**, 747–765 (2016). https://doi.org/10.1016/j.ins.2016.07.007

25. Wang, H., Xu, Z., Pedrycz, W.: An overview on the roles of fuzzy set techniques in big data processing: trends, challenges and opportunities. Knowl.-Based Syst. **118**, 15–30 (2017). https://doi.org/10.1016/j.knosys.2016.11.008

26. Witten, I.H., Frank, E., Hall, M.A., Pal, C.J.: Data Mining: Practical Machine Learning Tools and Techniques. Morgan Kaufmann, Burlington (2016)

27. Xu, Y., Gao, W., Zeng, Q., Wang, G., Ren, J., Zhang, Y.: FABAC: a flexible fuzzy attribute-based access control mechanism. In: Wang, G., Atiquzzaman, M., Yan, Z., Choo, K.-K.R. (eds.) SpaCCS 2017. LNCS, vol. 10656, pp. 332–343. Springer, Cham (2017). https://doi.org/10.1007/978-3-319-72389-1_27

28. Xue, X., Liu, S.: Matching sensor ontologies through compact evolutionary tabu search algorithm. In: Wang, G., Chen, J., Yang, L.T. (eds.) SpaCCS 2018. LNCS,

vol. 11342, pp. 115–124. Springer, Cham (2018). https://doi.org/10.1007/978-3-030-05345-1_9

29. Zhang, Q., Yang, L.T., Chen, Z., Li, P.: A survey on deep learning for big data. Inf. Fusion **42**, 146–157 (2018). https://doi.org/10.1016/j.inffus.2017.10.006

30. Zhang, S., Boukamp, F., Teizer, J.: Ontology-based semantic modeling of construction safety knowledge: towards automated safety planning for job hazard analysis (JHA). Autom. Constr. **52**, 29–41 (2015). https://doi.org/10.1016/j.autcon.2015.02.005

A Multi-layer Security Model for 5G-Enabled Industrial Internet of Things

Hussain Al-Aqrabi[1](✉) ⓘ, Anju P. Johnson[1] ⓘ, Richard Hill[1] ⓘ, Phil Lane[1] ⓘ, and Lu Liu[2]

[1] School of Computing and Engineering, University of Huddersfield, Huddersfield, UK
{h.al-aqrabi,a.johnson,r.hil,p.lane}@hud.ac.uk
[2] Department of Informatics, University of Leicester, Leicester, UK
l.liu@leicester.ac.uk

Abstract. This article considers the need for secure communications between Industrial Internet of Things (IIoT) devices that operate in 5G-enabled environments. 5G networks enable greater data throughput and lower latency, which presents new opportunities for the secure authentication of business transactions between IoT hardware. We propose an approach to developing a flexible and secure model for IIoT components in 5G environments. Using the National Institute of Standards and Technology (NIST) seven layer model of cloud computing, in conjunction with Physically Unclonable Function (PUF) hardware provided via FPGAs, we demonstrate algorithms that replicate common authorisation challenges in 5G enabled IoT scenarios.

Keywords: Internet of Things · 5G · Security · Physical Unclonable Functions · Analytics

1 Introduction

Adopting emerging business models that can exploit the potential of Internet of Things (and Industrial Internet of Things) devices, is tempered by valid security and privacy concerns [1]. Industrial users in particular recognise that a significant proportion of the value that they generate is directly linked to the ownership and continued development of Intellectual Property (IP). Any breach of security that might threaten the exclusivity of IP presents a considerable risk to the underlying business model of an enterprise [2].

Whilst cloud computing is an example of how technologies and operating models can come together to offer new capabilities for businesses [5], there are still cases of organisations being threatened by new risks which are attributed explicitly to the adoption of flexible, often multi-tenanted cloud services [7].

5G infrastructure promises new opportunities for closer integration of physical devices which is particularly suited to IIoT for the following reasons:

© Springer Nature Singapore Pte Ltd. 2019
G. Wang et al. (Eds.): iSCI 2019, CCIS 1122, pp. 279–292, 2019.
https://doi.org/10.1007/978-981-15-1301-5_23

- *Greater data throughput* facilitates the exchange of data between devices, which supports the introduction of meta data to support robust transactions to establish trust between devices;
- *Lower power requirement* permits the extended use of sensing and computational devices in remote settings;
- *Reduced network latency* improves response times and has the potential to improve the rigour of security protocols, without harming the user experience of the system.

The use of millimetre band for 5G is a key enabler of the improved network performance [6], albeit at a loss of transmission distance. While the higher throughput frequency band provides some physical security [22,23], this cannot be relied upon. A malicious insider stood next to machinery could relay data outside [12–15,18]. Being highly complex and heterogeneous, IoT also faces significant security and privacy threats. The protection of privacy in the IoT setting is more susceptible than in the traditional Information and communications technology (ICT) network due to a large number of vector attacks on IoT organisations [16,17].

Therefore, we need to be able to develop a scalable security architecture that can robustly marshall the appropriate authentications for various parties, whilst being tolerant of the dynamic nature of how IIoT devices can flexibly interact.

This article describes how a cloud approach has been used to inform the design of a security model for the following reasons. First, cloud architectures directly support dynamic demands through elasticity [10,11], and promote the harmonisation of disparate technologies through abstraction. Second, there is a mature architectural reference model provided by NIST [9], and this is universally adopted. Third, cloud systems exhibit shared characteristics with IIoT systems, in that there are multiple parties that need to collaborate [5] and cooperate through the secure sharing of data and resources, generally using a service-based approach.

Prior work [2–5] has explored the particular case of multi-party authentication in cloud based architectures, for the provision of enterprise Business Intelligence systems [4,7]. We have developed and extended this work to support the development of specific use cases where the availability of 5G network infrastructure can enable new business possibilities through enhanced performance. To enable these possibilities, we have augmented a cloud-based architecture to include hardware with Physically-Unclonable Functions (PUF).

PUFs are resistant to spoofing attacks, which is important for situations where it is necessary to rapidly authenticate a party, or multiple parties, to establish trusted communications. The provision of analytics services from manufacturing plant is a use case that we have considered, where there is a need for the secure exchange of raw data, as well as processed results, between IIoT components and the organisation's enterprise system.

This work has considered probable attack vectors upon such a system, to assist in the design of an effective multi-layer security model. In doing so, we have developed algorithms to allow authentication using PUFs, to enable secure access to cloud-based applications. As such, we consider the emerging scenario whereby IIoT devices are being attached and embedded within manufacturing plants to facilitate new levels of secure coordination, control, knowledge exchange, and ultimately, the protection of Intellectual Property provided by fundamental business operations.

The remainder of this article is organised as follows. In Sect. 2, we describe multi-layer security models. Section 3 describes a multi-layer approach to connectivity using Physical Unclonable Functions (PUF). In Sect. 4, we provide experimental results to establish the effectiveness of the design. Finally, we conclude in Sect. 5.

2   Multi-layer Security Model

A key challenge of managing network connectivity in a densely-equipped environment such as a smart factory, is the identification and marshalling of different attack vectors. Using a fundamental principle of cloud computing - resource abstraction - we have elected to construct a security model that separates a number of checkpoints across multiple layers. Again, the convenience of the cloud computing model has inspired us to consider each of the layers as a discrete cloud which will contain myriad hardware resources such as servers, storage arrays, FPGA devices and suchlike. As such, system designers are free to focus optimisation efforts on each cloud as a separate entity to ensure that operating overheads are kept within acceptable timeframes [21].

Figure 1 illustrates the overall security model architecture. We have continued with the use case of a typical enterprise system that contains analytics functionality for the purposes of supporting strategic and operational business decision-making.

As such, our model has been tested in a cloud environment where individual users are tenants within a multi-tenant scenario. Since the model allows for resource abstraction, users making requests for access to the enterprise system can do so via Virtual Machines, remote systems, and directly via hardware devices such as IIoT components. For the purposes of modelling within Fig. 1, each user or IIoT device is represented as an eventual tenant of the multi-cloud enterprise system.

All external requests are initially marshalled by firewalls that hold authentication data for each of the prospective tenants. This metadata contains access controls for the functionality that has already been authorised for each individual tenant. As the first line of defence, a lack of requisite authentication data will prohibit a user from successfully connecting to the system.

After basic authentication has been verified, there is a Tenant Metadata layer, which holds the rule-based controls to indicate which aspect of the enterprise system can be accessed by each authorised tenant of the system. This might refer to specific repositories, or reporting for example. In the case of IIoT devices providing data for analytics processing, this is likely to include not only the appending of data to a repository, but also the controlled access to other data

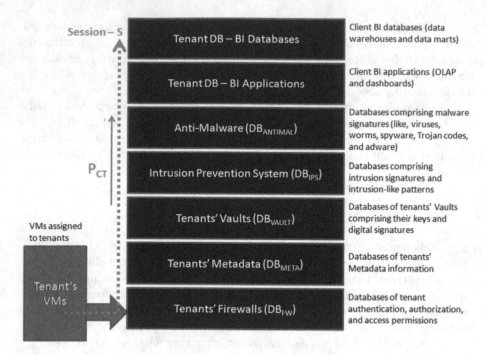

Fig. 1. Layered security model [3] for an organisational enterprise system inspired by NIST [8].

sources that may be fused and aggregated to with the process data, in order to provide enhanced analytics services.

It is necessary to establish a trustworthy connection and this is achieved through the use of PKI. Public Key certificates are retained within a Digital Vault, within its own layer of the model, and this provides a further level upon which a tenant (user) session can be authorised or eliminated.

Layer four provides a deeper level of protection for instances where malicious attackers have successfully penetrated the first three layers. While the previous layers' controls are sufficient to protect against many threats, they do not protect against a malicious insider who will already have suitable credentials to gain access to the system so far. The Intrusion Prevention System contains logic to identify patterns and strange behaviour, in order to conclude the session of a user who is engaging in threatening behaviour.

Layer four is bolstered by an anti-malware protection layer. More surreptitious activity, such as concealed executable code, can create havoc when deployed further into the enterprise system. Layer five maintains a log of such activity, as well as a repository of threats that have been identified.

The applications layer cloud contains the enterprise functionality that is of interest to the business users. By the time a user has arrived at this layer, basic authentication, session authentication via PKI, intrusion detection and antimalware checks have already been made, with opportunities at each layer to terminate a session. Within the application layer, there is still the need for role-based permission control, so that data of differing sensitivity can be accessed by the appropriate authority.

Aside from enterprise applications, there is a need for a particular type of user to have access to enterprise repositories, either directly via APIs, or through querying and reporting interfaces, typically delivered through a web portal. Layer seven provides for such access, and similar to the preceding layers, abstracts the functionality into a cloud for additional protection.

2.1 NIST Seven Layer Model

The security model can be mapped to the NIST seven layer model of cloud computing [8] as follows. Tenant users, which can be either VMs or hardware devices, are resident in NIST layers 1–3.

Each session is usually marshalled to layer 6 (if the destination is a Software-as-a-Service, SaaS, application) through a series of authentication and verification steps contained within the fourth and fifth layers. Access to layer 7 is reserved for API interfaces to applications that are likely to be hosted on premises, and are usually unique to the organisation.

Using cloud nomenclature, the firewall is an example of Infrastructure-as-a-Service (IaaS) and subsequent controls are Platform-as-a-Service (PaaS) with the exception perhaps of level 6 which may be SaaS.

2.2 Session Workflow

As described above, the security model maps to the IaaS and PaaS layers of the NIST model for cloud architecture [8].

The instantiation of a new session by a prospective IIoT tenant user, results in session IDs being assigned in layers two and three. This is followed by access identification provided from within layer four. It is after this stage that packet inspection is the fundamental activity for each of the sessions that have progressed thus far.

The initial DB_{META} and DB_{VAULT} layers enable IIoT requests to be verified, prior to packet inspection for each session to be performed using DB_{IPS} and $DB_{ANTIMAL}$. In the context of the NIST model, DB_{IPS} and DB_{META} map directly to PaaS functions. In contrast DB_{FW} is regarded as IaaS in the model.

If there is a SaaS instance at layer six, there will be additional authentication applied for each user, though at this stage, a considerable amount of verification has taken place already. However, this authentication check is to enforce enterprise system role-based permissions, for organisational data protection, such as the subset of staff who require access to confidential payroll information.

3   Multi-layer Connectivity Model Using PUF

So far, our security model accomodates requests from users for access to services (typically analytics) in an industrial setting. We are primarily concerned with user requests emanating from hardware IIoT devices which are either embedded or retro-fitted to manufacturing plant.

Such devices may be represented by FPGA units, that include storage and computational resource that can be used to process data at the edge of enterprise networks. This functionality has a great deal of potential for industrial use cases if the data collected and processed locally, can be combined with additional enterprise data in real-time. The low-latency characteristics of 5G networks are thus attractive solutions to such challenges.

The multi layer model allows for elasticity in the system, which can tolerate not only an increase in processing volume, but also an increase in the total volume of transactions in response to an increase in the number of IIoT devices that are communicating with the system.

We now consider the approach taken to introduce an IIoT component that itself has design features that increase the level of trust between devices, through the use of Physically-Unclonable Functions (PUF).

The first protocol to consider is the process by which a new user is enabled to access an IIoT node, after being introduced to the system by an existing user.

There exist K verification layers in the model. For every genuine client IIoT device (FPGA in this example), there exists a PUF in each layer of our security model (we consider a $K = 7$ layer cloud model). The PUF is used for authentication and is unique to each genuine client. The cloud management unit generates a combined PUF model (M_A) (mathematical) which is transferred through a secure communication channel.

The model is represented as an obfuscated bitstream which is downloadable and implementable on the client FPGA. An authorisation request of U_A is handled by the management plane, which sends q challenge bits CH_p, each of length n and a random number $rand$ to U_A.

U_A applies the challenge bits on the mathematical model and generates the responses for each layer. There exist K responses for a single challenge string. Hence a total of $K.q$ responses are generated, which are jumbled using a pre-agreed shuffling scheme with a random number $rand$.

The shuffled string of responses, encoded using a pre-agreed encoding scheme $E(.)$ is sent to the security model for verification. The encoded responses are decoded using the decoding scheme $D(.)$ and are reordered by the management layer and are provided to the K layers for verification.

At each security layer, the original challenge bits are applied to the respective PUFs in the cloud and the received model responses are compared with the physical PUFs. Upon successful authentication at all K layers, U_A is declared to be trustworthy. We consider a strong arbiter PUF with > 10 constituent XOR-PUFs to resist any machine learning attacks [22, 28, 29].

3.1   Multi-layer Hierarchical Packet Inspection Using PUF

Central to the overall secure connectivity model is the use of multi-layer hierarchical packet inspection. Each IIoT client FPGA must satisfy some standards to qualify as a valid recipient of the cloud service.

Algorithm 1. Multi-layered connectivity model using PUF: Client is an existing User

---

Objective:

(a) The seven layer cloud model consisting of FPGA clouds verifies the identity of a client FPGA (U_A) who is requesting access.
(b) The cloud model provides application access for the genuine client (U_i).

Prerequisites:

(a) An n-bit input, 1-bit output XOR PUF P_1 is reconfigured in all layers of the $Cloud - FPGA$. There exists a PUF for every authenticated user. PUF P_{ij} represents the identity of the user i in the cloud layer j.
(b) A combined mathematical model M_i representing all the K PUFs in the cloud layers, resides with each user U_i.
(c) $Cloud - FPGA$ and user U_i have agreed on a fixed encoding scheme $E()$ and a decoding scheme $D(.)$, such that for any binary string x, $E(.)$ and $D(.)$ are injective, $X = E(x)$ and $D(X) = x$.
(d) $Cloud - FPGA$ and user U_i have agreed on a shuffling scheme $Y = S(X, rand)$, and $S'(Y, rand) = X$ where $rand$ is a random number.

Input:

$S, P_{CT}, DB_{FW}, DB_{META}, DB_{VAULT}, DB_{IPS}, DB_{ANTIMAL}$

(a) Tenant session: S
(b) Contents of session packets: P_{CT}
(c) Contents of FW: DB_{FW}
(d) Contents of $TENANT_{META} : DB_{META}$
(e) Contents of $TENANT_{VAULT} : DB_{VAULT}$
(f) Contents of $IPS : DB_{IPS}$
(g) Contents of $ANTIMALWARE : DB_{ANTIMAL}$
    Note: DB_j represents content DB of layer j

Each FPGA requires a Dynamic Partial Reconfiguration (DPR) capability and dynamic partitions in the FPGA fabric to promote analysis by the cloud service. We use (PUF) in addition to the existing verification to ensure security. Each of the cloud layer FPGAs contains PUFs representing each client. We assume that amn IIoT client contains a mathematical model of the PUF which is downloaded as an obfuscated bitstream to the client FPGA using DPR. A strong PUF which cannot be cloned using machine learning strategies is of paramount importance to ensure the overall security of this model.

The client FPGA sends PUF responses of the mathematical model to the multi-layer cloud model for verification. Side channel parameters are collected by the malware detection layer by downloading an obfuscated bitstream on the

---

Algorithm 1 continued. Output:
A value in variable S to show that the application access is granted ($S = 1$) or denied ($S = 0$).
Steps:

1. Initialize $S = 1$, $E = 1$
2. U_i to management plane MP: request access to application A
3. MP to U_i: MP sends a random number $rand$ and a set of challenges CH_p consisting of q challenge bits each of length 'n'.
4. U_i calculates the following:
   - $Rim_{p,j} = Mi(CH_{p,j})$, $p = 1 \ldots q$, $j = 1 \ldots K$
   - $Rim = \{Rim_{p,j}, 1 \leq p \leq q, 1 \leq j \leq K\}$
   - $CA_i = S\Big(E(Rim), rand\Big)$
5. U_i to MP: certificate CA_i
6. **foreach** layer j **do**
   (a) Initialize $Mem = 0$, $Match = 0$
   (b) **If** ($E = 1$)
       (a) $MP : Rim_{p,j} = S'\Big(D(CA_i), rand\Big)$
       (b) MP to $Cloud - C_i$: Set of challenges CH_p and $Rim_{p,j}$
       (c) $Cloud - C_j$ calculates the following
           - $Rif_{p,j} = Pi(CH_{p,j})$, $p = 1 \ldots q$, $j = 1 \ldots K$
           - $N_{ij} = (1 - \frac{\sum_{(p=1)}^{q}(R_{imp} \oplus R_{ifp})}{q})$
           - **if** $Nij \geq 0.99$ $Mem = 1$
       (d) **if** ($P_{CT} \in DB_j$, $| DB_j \in \{DB_{FW}, DB_{META}, DB_{VAULT}\}$ AND $P_{CT} \notin DB_j$, $| DB_j \in \{DB_{IPS}, DB_{ANTIMAL}\}$); $Match = 1$
       (e) **if** (Mem && $Match$), $E = 1$; proceed to next higher layer
       (f) **else** Exit; set $E = 0$, $S = 0$; DenyTenantAccess()
7. **if** $S = 1$; AuthoriseTenantAccess()

---

client FPGA. This is to ensure that the IIoT client FPGAs do not produce any parameter variations following infected hardware trojans [23].

This fingerprint measured in terms of side-channel parameters is a means of identifying and preventing attack by hardware trojan horses in the device. Multiple side channel parameters are collected using dynamic partial reconfiguration.

The bitstreams are erased using another DPR following successful collection of samples. The cloud directly collects samples to avoid the client from manipulating the parameters.

3.2   Algorithm Design

Any user requesting access to an application is described in Algorithm 1. Each item in the sequence represents the various checks that are enacted through the multi-layer security model. We have provided for extensibility through this design, in that should an enterprise require additional security layers to be augmented, such controls can be implemented using the basic premise of abstraction to marshall and control the findings of any stage of packet inspection.

Algorithm 2. Multi-layered connectivity model using PUF: New client

Objective:

(a) The seven layer cloud model consisting of FPGA clouds verifies the identity of a new client FPGA (U_B) who is requesting access.
(b) The cloud model provides application access for the genuine client (U_B).

Prerequisites:

(a) New client $ClientU_B$, requesting application access is known to an existing client U_A as a genuine applicant
(b) $Cloud-FPGAs$ have built-in controllers to facilitate secure dynamic partial reconfiguration.
(c) $Client-FPGA$ has built-in controllers to facilitate secure dynamic partial reconfiguration initiated by the cloud.
(d) The $Cloud-FPGA$ fabric is divided into two parts, a) static fabric and b) dynamic fabric. Static fabric consists of hardware configurations which existed before deployment. The dynamic fabric of the $Cloud-FPGA$ is dedicated to configure additional security primitives (mostly PUFs) for any genuine clients using secure dynamic partial reconfiguration.
(e) The $client-FPGA$ fabric is divided into two parts, a) static fabric and b) dynamic fabric. Static fabric consists of hardware configurations which existed before deployment. The $Client-FPGA$ has secure remote DPR controllers in the static partition facilitating configuration of PUF mathematical model in the dynamic fabric, via an obfuscated bitstream.

Input:

$P_{CT}, DB_{FW}, DB_{META}, DB_{VAULT}, DB_{IPS}, DB_{ANTIMAL}$ of $UserU_A$

(a) Tenant session: S
(b) Contents of session packets: P_{CT}
(c) Contents of FW: DB_{FW}
(d) Contents of $TENANT_{META} : DB_{META}$
(e) Contents of $TENANT_{VAULT} : DB_{VAULT}$
(f) Contents of $IPS : DB_{IPS}$
(g) Contents of $ANTIMALWARE : DB_{ANTIMAL}$
    Note: DB_j represents content DB of layer j

Output:

A value in Flag to show a successful dynamic partial reconfiguration ($Flag = 1$) or denied ($Flag = 0$).

Steps:

1. Initialize $V = 1$, $E = 1$, $Flag = 0$
2. U_B requests U_A, for an introduction to access application A
3. U_A to MP: request introduction of U_B to cloud layers C_j
4. MP to U_A: MP sends a random number $rand$ and a set of challenges CH_p consisting of q challenge bits each of length 'n'.
5. U_A calculates the following:
   - $RAm_{p,j} = MA(CH_{p,j})$, $p = 1 \ldots q$, $j = 1 \ldots K$
   - $RAm = \{RAm_{p,j}, 1 \le p \le q, 1 \le j \le K \}$
   - $CA_A = S\left(E(RAm), rand\right)$
6. U_A to MP: certificate CA_A
7. **foreach** layer j **do**
   (a) Initialize $Mem = 0$, $Match = 0$
   (b) **If** $(E = 1)$
      (a) $MP : RAm_{p,j} = S'\left(D(CA_A), rand\right)$
      (b) MP to $Cloud - C_j$: Set of challenges CH_p and $RAm_{p,j}$
      (c) $Cloud - C_i$ calculates the following
         - $RAf_{p,j} = PA(CH_{p,j})$, $p = 1 \ldots q$, $j = 1 \ldots K$
         - $N_{Aj} = (1 - \frac{\sum_{(p=1)}^{q}(R_{Amp} \oplus R_{Afp})}{q})$
         - if $NAj \ge 0.99$ $Mem = 1$
      (d) **if** $(P_{CT} \in DB_j, | DB_j \in \{DB_{FW}, DB_{META}, DB_{VAULT}\}$ AND $P_{CT} \notin DB_j, | DB_j \in \{DB_{IPS}, DB_{ANTIMAL}\}$); $Match = 1$
      (e) **if** $(Mem \, \&\& \, Match)$, $E = 1$; proceed to next higher layer
      (f) **else** Exit; set $E = 0$, $Flag = 0$
8. **if** $V = 1$; Verified introducing client
   (a) **foreach** layer j **do**
      (a) $Cloud - FPGA$, C_j initiates DPR and configures a new PUF $P_{B,j}$, PUF $P_{B,j}$ represents the identity of the U_B in the cloud layer j
      (b) C_j to MP PUF modeling parameters $param_j$
   (b) MP generates a combined Mathematical model M_B of all PUFs $P_{B,j}$ in the cloud layers
   (c) MP generates obfuscated bitstreams of PUF mathematical model M_B
   (d) MP initiates remote dynamic partial reconfiguration of PUF M_B in the dynamic partition of the $client - FPGA$ U_B
   (e) $Flag = 1$ and exit; follow protocol-1. U_B is same as any other existing client.

One example that is particularly pertinent to manufacturing enterprises arises through developments in thinking around Industry 4.0 or *smart manufacturing*. These movements advocate the sharing of resources and services in a horizontal fashion, cutting across industrial sectors to facilitate new levels of collaboration. This thinking is driven by new capabilities in analytics, and the control and feedback of Cyber Physical Systems (CPS). In such cases, orgainsations that choose to embrace the sharing of services, and indeed exploit the possibilities of packaging existing functionality into services to share, will require the ability to be able to extend the security model so that satisfactory security inspections are in place.

Algorithm 1 thus describes an arrangement where a set of challenge bits are sent to the client and the cloud layers. The management unit responds with a set of q challenges, each of size r.

For every user, the management unit maintains a database of challenges that have been previously used for PUF-based authentication, and disregards every challenge that has expired.

However, for challenge set size of q in each authentication attempt, with each challenge being r-bit, the probability of repeated challenges occurring (represented as the "Failure Probability") is almost zero with a typical value of $q = 1000$ and $r = 64$ [21]. Each IIoT client generates model responses and sends them to the cloud security layers for verification.

Cloud layers then generate responses using the physical PUF. Both responses are checked for a match of at least 99%. Following a successful match, the content of the packet is analysed by the cloud before proceeding to the next cloud layer in the security model.

Algorithm 2 represents the steps for introducing a new IIoT client to the application. In this case, an existing IIoT client introduces a new IIoT client by sharing its model responses.

On successful authentication of the existing client, the model generates a new PUF in the dynamic part of the cloud FPGA fabric. A combined mathematical model of the PUFs is downloaded to the client FPGA (as before) using an obfuscated bitstream following a DPR process. Again, the security model assumes that a secure DPR process is followed to retain system integrity. The new cloud client then utilises Algorithm 1 to provide access to the application layer.

4   Hardware Implementation

The basic XOR PUF architecture consisting of 64 challenge bits and 10 parallel arbiters is implemented on an FPGA to compute the design expense in a cloud architecture. Nexys 4 DDR board with Artix-7 FPGA [25] (device xc7a100t, package csg324, speed -1) from Xilinx is used for implementation.

The architecture is designed in Verilog Hardware Description Language (HDL) following the flow in Xilinx ISE 14.7 design suite [24]. Xilinx power analysis tool [26] and Chipscop-Pro [27] are used for testing and analysis.

Table 1 reports the implementation cost in terms of resources consumed, total on-chip power (using vector-less activity propagation) and the configuration bitstream size.

Results show that the XOR PUF is realissable with reduced resources and occupies only 8% of the device slices. This figure is negligible for large FPGAs deployed in clouds and data centers.

From Table 1, it is evident that the required bitstream size for adding a reconfigurable PUF is relatively small. The Internal Configuration Assess Port

(ICAP) of the targeted FPGA board is designed to run in 8 bit configuration at a clock frequency of 100 MHz. Hence DPR for the required PUF file is performed in the order of micro-seconds.

Table 1. Implementation overhead

Hardware consumption*	Slice	Slice Reg	LUTs
	1291	10	1282
Power consumption		0.082 W	
Bitstream size		3737 KB	

*Note: The design does not contain any LUTRAMs, BRAMs/FIFOs, DSPs or buffers

5 Conclusions

We have described the extension of a prior work on multi-layer cloud security models [3] to include hardware devices with PUF capability. Using experience of cloud architectures and myriad attack vectors upon Virtual Machines in multi-tenant cloud systems, we describe a PUF-based system that demonstrates an ability to marshall not only external adversarial attacks, but also internal attacks, which are particularly of relevance to industrial organisations.

The use of cloud-inspired abstraction layers leads to an architecture where a wide range of surreptitious activity can be quarantined to resist a multitude of attack vectors. Multiple layers of packet inspection ensures that determined adversaries, who may employ a number of methods simultaneously, can be halted.

Security is provided beyond firewalls by compromising further attacks and therefore establishing a trail of evidence of the potential multitude of exploit attempts. An IPS layer prevents one level of exploit, and is shored-up by an anti-malware layer that detects other forms of compromise such as trojans.

A key advantage of this approach is the inherent flexibility and scalability that is brought about by the cloud-inspired layering and containerisation of security functions. The continued expansion and accessibility of IIoT hardware, together with ever-stronger business cases for embedding analytics functions into industrial organisations, means that extensible, flexible architectures are required to take full advantage of high speed networks and increased numbers of IIoT devices. We have proposed the use of hardware security primitives such as PUFs to ensure security within the model. This is strengthened by monitoring of the side channel parameters of client IIoT devices to provide additional security from hardware trojans. The robustness of the implementation relies upon this integration of both software and hardware technologies to ensure security in cloud computing in the IIoT revolution.

References

1. Alrawais, A., Alhothaily, A., Hu, C., Cheng, X.: Fog computing for the Internet of Things: security and privacy issues. IEEE Internet Comput. **21**(2), 34–42 (2017)
2. Al-Aqrabi, H., Liu, L., Xu, J., Hill, R., Antonopoulos, N., Zhan, Y.: Investigation of IT security and compliance challenges in security-as-a-service for cloud computing. In: Proceedings of 15th IEEE International Symposium on ISORC 2012, Shenzhen, China, 11–13 April, pp. 124–129. IEEE (2012)
3. Al Aqrabi, H., Liu, L., Hill, R., Antonopoulos, N.: A multi-layer hierarchical inter-cloud connectivity model for sequential packet inspection of tenant sessions accessing BI as a service. In: Proceedings of 6th International Symposium on (CSS) and IEEE 11th International Conference on (ESS), France, Paris, 20–22 March, pp. 137–144. IEEE (2014)
4. Al-Aqrabi, H., Liu, L., Hill, R., Antonopoulos, N.: Cloud BI: future of business intelligence in the Cloud. J. Comput. Syst. Sci. **81**, 85–96 (2015)
5. Al-Aqrabi, H., Hill, R.: Dynamic multiparty authentication of data analytics services within cloud environments. In: 20th IEEE International Conference on High Performance Computing and Communications, HPCC-2018, 28-30 Exeter (2018)
6. AlAlawi, K., Al-Aqrabi, H.: Quality of service evaluation of VoIP over wireless networks. In: 2015 IEEE 8th GCC Conference and Exhibition (GCCCE), pp. 1–6 (2015)
7. Panian, Z.: How to make business intelligence actionable through service-oriented architectures. WSEAS Trans. Bus. Econ. **5**(5), 210–221 (2008)
8. NIST: US Government Cloud Computing Technology Roadmap. Special Publication 500-293. Cloud Computing Program, National Institute of Standards and Technology (NIST), US Department of Commerce, pp. 13–78 (2011)
9. Mell, P., Grance, T.: The NIST definition of cloud computing, Computer Security Division, Information Technology Laboratory, NIST (2011)
10. Demchenko, Y., Ngo, C., de Laat, C., Lopez, D.R., Morales, A., García-Espín, J.A.: Security infrastructure for dynamically provisioned cloud infrastructure services. In: Pearson, S., Yee, G. (eds.) Privacy and Security for Cloud Computing. CCN, pp. 167–210. Springer, London (2013). https://doi.org/10.1007/978-1-4471-4189-1_5
11. Carvalho, M.: SECaaS-security as a service. ISSA J. 20–24 (2011)
12. Luo, S., et al.: Virtualization security for Cloud computing service. In: Proceedings of 4th International Symposium on Cloud and Service Computing, Hong Kong, 12–14 December 2011, pp. 174–179. IEEE (2011)
13. Semenko, Y., Saucez, D.: Distributed privacy preserving platform for ridesharing services. In: Wang, G., Feng, J., Bhuiyan, M.Z.A., Lu, R. (eds.) SpaCCS 2019. LNCS, vol. 11611, pp. 1–14. Springer, Cham (2019). https://doi.org/10.1007/978-3-030-24907-6_1
14. Kumar, N., DuPree, L.: Protection and privacy of information assets in the cloud. In: Halpert, B. (ed.) Auditing Cloud Computing: A Security and Privacy Guide. Wiley, New York (2011)
15. Pearson, S.: Taking account of privacy when designing cloud computing services. In: Proceedings of International Symposium on Software Engineering Challenges of Cloud Computing, Vancouver, Canada, 23 May 2009, pp. 1–9. IEEE (2009)
16. Roman, R., Najera, P., Lopez, J.: Securing the internet of things. Computer **44**(9), 51–58 (2011)

17. Li, J., Zhang, Y., Chen, Y.F., Nagaraja, K.: A mobile phone based WSN infrastructure for IoT over future internet architecture. In: Proceedings of IEEE International Conference on Cyber, Physical and Social Green Computing and Communications (GreenCom), pp. 426–433 (2013)
18. Diaz-Sanchez, D., et al.: Media gateway: bringing privacy to private multimedia cloud connections. Telecommun. Syst. **2013**, 1–16 (2013)
19. Pervez, Z., Khattak, A.M., Lee, S., Lee, Y.: SAPDS: self-healing attribute-based privacy aware data sharing in Cloud. J. Supercomput. **62**, 431–460 (2012)
20. Chadwick, D.W., Fatema, K.: A privacy preserving authorisation system for the Cloud. J. Comput. Syst. Sci. **78**, 1359–1373 (2012)
21. Johnson, A.P., Chakraborty, R., Mukhopadhyay, D.: A PUF-enabled secure architecture for FPGA-based IoT applications. IEEE Trans. Multi-Scale Comput. Syst. **1**(2), 110–122 (2015)
22. Tobisch, J., Becker, G.T.: On the scaling of machine learning attacks on PUFs with application to noise bifurcation. In: Mangard, S., Schaumont, P. (eds.) RFIDSec 2015. LNCS, vol. 9440, pp. 17–31. Springer, Cham (2015). https://doi.org/10.1007/978-3-319-24837-0_2
23. Seetharam, N., et al.: Hardware Trojan detection by multiple-parameter side-channel analysis. IEEE Trans. Comput. **62**(11), 2183–2195 (2012)
24. ISE Design Suite Overview, Xilinx Inc. https://www.xilinx.com/support/documentation/sw_manuals/xilinx11/ise_c_overview.htm. Accessed 21 May 2019
25. Digilent Nexys 4 Artix-7 FPGA Trainer Board, Xilinx Inc. https://www.xilinx.com/products/boards-and-kits/1-3yznp5.html. Accessed 21 May 2019
26. Xilinx Power Estimator User Guide, Xilinx Inc. (2018). https://www.xilinx.com/support/documentation/sw_manuals/xilinx2018_3/ug440-xilinx-power-estimator.pdf. Accessed 21 May 2019
27. ChipScope Pro Software and Cores, Xilinx Inc. (2012). https://www.xilinx.com/support/documentation/sw_manuals/xilinx14_7/chipscope_pro_sw_cores_ug029.pdf. Accessed 21 May 2019
28. Pappu, R., Recht, B., Taylor, J., Gershenfeld, N.: Physical one-way functions. Science **297**(5589), 2026–2030 (2002). https://doi.org/10.1126/science.1074376. Bibcode:2002Sci...297.2026P. hdl:1721.1/45499. PMID 12242435
29. Gassend, B., Clarke, D., van Dijk, M., Devadas, S.: Silicon physical random functions. In: Proceedings of the Computer and Communications Security Conference, November 2002

Cloud/Edge/Fog Computing for Smart City

Securing Smart Healthcare Systems from Vulnerability Exploitation

Gemini George[1,2] and Sabu M. Thampi[1(✉)]

[1] Center for Research and Innovation in Cyber Threat Resilience,
Indian Institute of Information Technology and Management-Kerala,
Thiruvananthapuram 695581, India
{gemini.res15,sabu.thampi}@iiitmk.ac.in
[2] Cochin University of Science and Technology, Kochi 682022, India

Abstract. The capabilities of the IoT to track entities, measure and analyze vital information captured by sensors, and to transmit data over a fleet of devices, has convincingly placed it best suited toward the realization of the future-ready smart hospitals and healthcare applications. Real time sensing and monitoring of vital signs of patients, efficient scheduling of medical procedures, effective tracking of scarce resources, and optimized supply chain management of drugs and medical devices help not only to significantly improve the quality of health services but also to lower healthcare costs. However, bringing the healthcare systems under the IoT network poses huge security challenges. Once the devices controlling the life supporting equipments are under attack, the damages are beyond imagination. The vulnerabilities in the IoT-based devices can pose serious threats to the IoT healthcare systems. In this work, we propose a graphical modeling of possible attacks through exploitation of such vulnerabilities. The proposed model helps to foresee the possible attack paths exist in a network and to design suitable defense mechanisms. We also propose strategies for improving the security of the IoT-assisted networks.

Keywords: Vulnerability analysis · IoT Network · IoT Healthcare · Risk assessment · Risk mitigation

1 Introduction

Health metrics of population are fundamental pointers to the progress of any country. Hence efficient, easily accessible and low-cost healthcare facilities are of essential priority to any progressive government. A well oiled health machinery should be capable of addressing the challenges such as aging population, life-style related diseases, organ transplants, epidemic diseases, rising accidents, and disasters. The changing dynamics of the new and re-emerging diseases together with the wider needs of diverse patients, make the art of healthcare design challenging. The complex nature of these requirements critically demands faster integration

© Springer Nature Singapore Pte Ltd. 2019
G. Wang et al. (Eds.): iSCI 2019, CCIS 1122, pp. 295–308, 2019.
https://doi.org/10.1007/978-981-15-1301-5_24

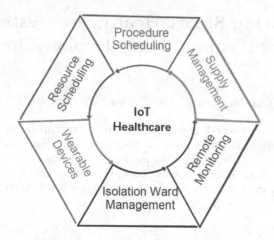

Fig. 1. Smart IoT controlled healthcare verticals

of the technological advancements to the healthcare industry for proper scaling, quality and to lower costs.

The IoT characteristics such as easiness in deployment, openness of the system, accessibility to sensors and actuators, analytics of gathered data, wireless connectivity, ability to operate in constrained environments and remote access has placed it in such an advantageous position that industries find it hard to resist or deny. Rather, industries are competing for the faster adaptation of the IoT to benefit from its tremendous advantages, and are dynamically re-organizing to optimize the operations by leveraging the IoT features.

The healthcare industry is also at the inflection point in embracing the IoT technology and is re-configuring for radical changes in the domains as shown in Fig. 1. Wearable IoT devices such as smart watches, wrist bands and chip implants help the doctors in the remote monitoring of the patients. This results in a better trade-off between the capacity limitations of hospitals and the need for continuous monitoring of parameters of patients. The remote access feature of the IoT system together with the capability to operate in resource constraint environments can lead to significant improvements in facilitating rural healthcare services. Management of isolation wards for patients with spreading epidemics by the IoT devices and systems, not only effectively restricts the spreading of such deadly diseases, but also safeguards the doctors and hospital assistants from being affected. The IoT analytics on historical medical readings of patients can provide significant insights in the diagnosis process and can be effectively used for early detection and prevention of diseases. With efficient scheduling of medical procedures and effective management of resources, the IoT-based healthcare systems envisage a quality healthcare at significantly lower costs.

An example of a smart IoT-enabled hospital network is shown in Fig. 2. Tele-medicine enables patients to consult doctors remotely for the purpose of diagnosis, treatment, follow-up and to seek a second opinion, without being

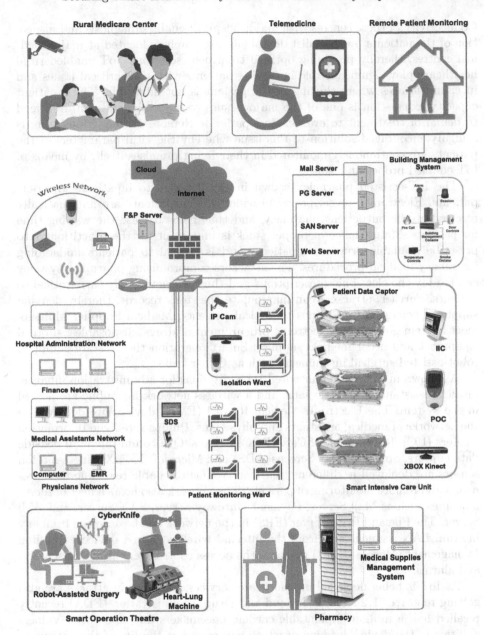

Fig. 2. An example IoT-enabled hospital network

subjected to the stresses of travel, waiting and chances of exposure to infectious environments. Mobile applications are available to enable these facilities. Rural healthcare facilitates the doctors in major hospitals to serve the people at rural areas and challenging terrains through primary health centres and clinics.

Connectivity of these centres with major hospitals enables diagnosis and inspection of the patients by specialist doctors and researchers located at major medical centres, thereby providing optimal treatment solutions. IoT enabled rural healthcare play significant role in serving patients with time-critical issues and in circumstances where shifting of the patient is not advisable. The inpatient capacity exhaustion is one of the major issues of hospitals, and can even lead to denial of treatment to even critical patients. Remote Patient Monitoring is a highly encouraged solution to this issue whereby the vital parameters of the patients are continuously monitored in their living premises itself, by means of IoT enabled probes and sensors.

The IoT-assisted pharmacy shown in Fig. 2 caters to inpatients and outpatients. Electronics prescriptions provided for outpatients are automatically received at the outpatient pharmacy, and thus helps to ease the waiting time for patients. Maintenance of proper stock is important for the practitioners to prescribe available drugs to inpatients and is critical to patients undergoing emergency medical procedures. The attackers compromising pharmacy systems can modify the electronic prescriptions and thus can potentially turn critical to patients. Further, attackers can manipulate the stock records, thereby denying supply of emergency medicines to critical patients. Medical Supplier Management System governs the electronic procurement of drugs, disposables, surgical equipment and other medical supplies. Smart operation theatres are equipped robot-assisted surgical instruments such as Cyber-knife.

As shown in Fig. 2 the four wired LAN divisions for administration, finance, medical assistants and physicians, and a wireless network for public are hosted in the system. The Electronic Medical Record (EMR) devices are deployed in the networks of medical assistants and physicians. Philips Intellivue Information Centers (IIC), Roche Point of Care (POC) devices, Qualcomm Life vital bedside data-captors, Smart Display Screens (SDS) and Microsoft XBOX Kinect motion sensors are deployed in different treatment rooms to enable real time measurements and remote monitoring of patients. The network also hosts a fleet of server machines such as Mail Server, Payment Gateway Server, SAN Server, and Web Server. The File and Print Server (FPS) in the network can be accessed from any internal LAN segment and from the internal wireless shared devices. Building Management Console (BMC) manages the access controls, environment sensors, and alarms.

As IoT is being deployed in healthcare services, huge rise in attacks are also getting reported [1, 2]. The U.S. Food and Drug Administration (FDA) recently recalled half a million implantable cardiac pacemakers due to security vulnerabilities in the device, hacking of which can even put the life of the patient in hostility. The FDA also issued warning to hospitals to discontinue the use of infusion pumps from medical device maker Hospira, due to security flaws that can lead to remote attackers taking control of the device. The list of such medical recalls are available in [3]. Pacific Alliance Medical Center at Los Angeles witnessed an attack that compromised the protected health information of 266,123 patients [4]. The rise in the attacks on the IoT-based healthcare services demands more investigations in the security related challenges of the system and deployment of stronger defense mechanisms to secure the present Internet of 'insecure' healthcare systems.

Many studies emphasized the lack of proper upgrades or patches for numerous vulnerabilities in the constrained IoT devices [5,6] and the associated security issues. However, not many works have investigated solution for these security issues in the IoT networks. This leaves a huge scope for research in this domain and motivates us to study the issues that arises in the IoT-assisted network due to the existing vulnerability flaws and to propose strategies for risk mitigation. The following describes the novelty and contributions of this work:

- A graphical model to analyze the security impact due to the relations among vulnerability exploits in the IoT-based network is presented.
- The severity of vulnerabilities are quantified to conduct the risk assessment at the devices in the network.
- A priority-based strategy to truncate potential attack paths which provide easy paths for attackers to reach the target devices is presented. Further, a strategy for the selective priority-based removal of vulnerabilities that pose severe threat to the system is discussed.

The proposed techniques are discussed in the context of an IoT-enabled healthcare network. The remaining sections are organized as follows. The important works related to our discussions are presented in Sect. 2. The graphical model is introduced in Sect. 3. Major algorithms for priority-based strategies for risk mitigation are discussed in Sects. 4 and 5. Simulation results are discussed in Sect. 6. The work is concluded in Sect. 7.

2   Related Works

The process of integration of the IoT with the healthcare has attracted significant research interest. A survey of IoT related solutions for healthcare services and applications is presented in [7]. Chiuchisan et al. detailed the benefits of IoT-assisted healthcare services [8]. The work also presented the case study of a smart Intensive Care Unit which monitors the patients and the environmental parameters, and alerts medical assistants in the rise of emergency situations. Yang et al. proposed an intelligent home-based IoT platform referred to as *iHome Health-IoT* which consisted of three sub-units namely *iMedBox, iMedPack,* and *Bio-Patch* [9]. The iMedBox serves as a health service point, iMedPack deals with dispensing the medicines and the Bio-Patch module monitors the vital signs of the patients. Doukas et al. proposed the management of data generated by pervasive healthcare devices with the help of cloud computing infrastructure [10]. A cooperative IoT environment for monitoring the health parameters of rural people is proposed in [11].

Catarinucci et al. presented a smart hospital network exploiting the benefits of RFID, Wireless Sensor Networks (WSN) and IoT [12]. The proposed network is equipped with real time acquisition of physiological parameters from patients with the help of 6LoWPAN nodes. The system also tracks patients and medical devices using the RFID technology. Zhang et al. proposed a tiered architecture for WSN-based healthcare systems focusing on ubiquitous computing [13]. An IoT-enabled system for emergency health related services is proposed in [14].

The challenges in adopting IoT in the health sector is discussed in [15,16]. Gope et al. performed a study on the security and privacy issues in IoT-based Body Sensor Network (BSN) [17]. Anil C. et al. [18] discussed various potential attacks toward the healthcare networks due to the vulnerabilities existing in the IoT-based medical devices. Yu et al. [6] presented a vulnerability-based security architecture *IoTSec* while adopting IoT devices into different industrial applications. Simpson et al. [19] presented the security problems due to the numerous vulnerabilities detected in various IoT devices, for home-based applications.

A graph-based visualization for the vulnerability-based attacks in IoT network is proposed in [20]. Further, a target specific security structure is proposed [21] for evaluating the threat level at each of the target resources. A vulnerability-based security evaluation tool *C-SEC* for cyber physical systems is proposed in [22] for industrial networks. [23] presented *CAULDRON*, a vulnerability visualization tool. *CyGraph* [24] is another graphical tool for visualizing vulnerability relations and the attack paths inside networks. Risk reduction strategies are proposed in [5] to defend vulnerability-based attacks in industrial IoT applications. A target isolation algorithm [25] has been introduced to isolate critical targets from attack initiators.

However, most of the related works discussed above focus on the vulnerability-based security issues and do not discuss solutions for these issues. Though some other works propose attack path visualizations tools for domain specific applications such as home-IoT, they can not be adopted to healthcare applications. This motivates us to propose a graph-based security modeling for vulnerability-based attacks in generic IoT-assisted applications and to suggest risk mitigation strategies.

3   Modeling of Network Risk Assessment Graph

This section discusses the graph modeling to represent the vulnerability-based security relations associated with the underlying network.

Definition 1. *The Network Risk Assessment Graph (NRAG) is a directed graph given by $NRAG = (V, E, L)$ where,*

- *V is a subset of Vulnerability Space. The vulnerability space is the set of all Vulnerability Instances in the network. A vulnerability instance is of the form (v, d) where v denote the vulnerability exists in a device d. A vulnerability instance can be a security weakness in any of the software, security holes in the device configurations, or some improper network configurations in any of the network devices. V represents the set of all such vulnerability instances for which the Penetration Test results in a TRUE value. The penetration test for a vulnerability associated with a device gives a TRUE value only if the vulnerability in a device can be exploited by an attacker to attack the system.*

- E is the set of edges that represents the relation among the vulnerability instances in the network. The edges are of the form $((v_i, d_j), (v_x, d_y))$ and represent the possibility of exploitation of the vulnerability v_x in the device d_y by an attacker who already has compromised the device d_j through the vulnerability v_i in the device.
- L is the set of likelihood values defined on E. L on $((v_i, d_j), (v_x, d_y))$ represents the chance of successful exploitation of the vulnerability v_x in the device d_y by an attacker who already has compromised the device d_j through the vulnerability v_i in the device.

The likelihood values are derived from the Common Vulnerability Scoring System (CVSS) [26]. The quantification of severity of vulnerabilities in the network enables risk assessment at different medical devices.

4 Priority-Based Algorithm for Hop-Based Termination of the Attack Paths

Attackers prefer to choose the paths with low hop-lengths to reach their targets. Hence, the removal of the low hop paths can meaningfully contribute to the safety of the network. The proposed procedure is implemented in two steps.

Algorithm 1. Algorithm for finding the attack paths and hop-lengths

---

Input: A $NRAG$, a table T for storing the attack path details.
Output: A table T of the attack paths toward end node denoted by end_node and the parameters associated with each path.

1: Set $T = \phi$
2: Set $step = \phi$
3: **function** PF($NRAG, end\_node, temp, step, Path, T$)
4:     **for** each node x adjacent to $temp$ **do**
5:         $Path[step] := temp$
6:         **if** $x = end\_node$ **then**
7:             $P[++step] := x$
8:             $hop\_length := step$
9:             Add path in P and hop_length to the table T.
10:            return;
11:        **end if**
12:        PF($NRAG, end\_node, x, step + 1, Path, T$)
13:    **end for**
14: **end function**

The procedure starts with the construction of a table T to store the attack paths. The table contains entries for the starting node, ending node, path number, path and the hop-length of the path. It then follows a strategy to remove the attack paths with low hop lengths.

Algorithm 2. Priority-based algorithm for hop-based removal of attack paths

Input: $NRAG$, a table T for storing the path details, and a parameter μ representing maximum permissible paths to be removed.

Output: A sub-graph $NRAG'$ of $NRAG$ with some of the attack paths removed.

1: Set $T = \phi$
2: Set $step = \phi$
3: $Number\_path = \phi$
4: Set $V(NRAG') = V(NRAG)$
5: Set $E(NRAG') = E(NRAG)$
6: Call $PF(NRAG, end\_node, temp, step, Path, T)$ with $temp$ as the $start\_node$.
7: Sort T in ascending order of hop_length
8: **for** each path P in T **do**
9:     **if** $Number\_path <= \mu$ **then**
10:        $Number\_path = Number\_path + 1$
11:        Remove the edges in P from $NRAG'$
12:    **end if**
13: **end for**
14: Return

The procedure for the construction of the table T is given in Algorithm 1. To find the attack paths from a starting node denoted by $start\_node$ to an end node denoted by end_node, the algorithm PF(abbreviation of Path Finder) is to be invoked with $temp$ set as the $start\_node$. The scaling issues of the graph are resolved by endorsing the monotonicity assumption [27] in $NRAG$. The directed acyclic nature of the $NRAG$ guarantees the termination of the algorithm. As PF is a back tracking algorithm, its complexity is given by $O(hq)$, where q denotes the number of paths between the $start\_node$ and the end_node and h denotes the hop-length of the longest path.

The priority-based algorithm for the removal of attack paths on the basis of hop-length is described in Algorithm 2. It starts with a call to PF for constructing the table T which is sorted in the ascending order of the hop-length. Further, paths are removed till the number of such path reaches the permissible value μ. The complexity of the algorithm is $O(q^2)$ excluding that of PF, where q is the number of paths.

5 Identification and Removal of Strongly Connected Vulnerabilities in the Healthcare Network

Attacks propagate in the network by chaining the relations among the vulnerabilities. These relations are represented as edges in the $NRAG$. The vulnerabilities with more number of relations correspond to nodes with higher degrees and are referred to as Strongly Connected Nodes (SCNs) in the $NRAG$. Such nodes provide more attacking paths. Hence, identification and removal of such strongly connected vulnerabilities from the IoT healthcare network will reduce the propagation space for the attackers and thus contribute to significant improvement in securing the system. This problem can be mapped as the identification and removal of the SCNs in the $NRAG$. However, healing of the vulnerabilities is cost incurring and hence, if the security administrator has the provision to remove a fixed number of vulnerabilities, it is logical to remove the SCNs according to their strength so as to optimize the overall security. Let this fixed number be denoted as μ. In view of the above, we propose algorithms for identification and removal of SCNs in $NRAG$.

Algorithm 3. Algorithm for identification of SCNs in the network

---

Input: A $NRAG$, a table T for storing the connectivity strength of each node in the $NRAG$.
Output: A table T with the connectivity strength of the nodes in the $NRAG$.

```
1: function SCNFINDER(NRAG, T)
2:     Add the node number of each node to the table T.
3:     for i:=0 to n-1 do
4:         con_in = 0;
5:         con_out = 0;
6:         for j:=0 to n-1 do
7:             con_in = con_in + NRAG[j][i];
8:             con_out = con_out + NRAG[i][j];
9:         end for
10:        con_strength := con_in + con_out;
11:        Add con_strength to the second field of the i^th row of T.
12:    end for
13:    Return T
14: end function
```

Algorithm 3 describes the procedure for finding the SCNs in the network. It renames n nodes of $NRAG$ from 1 to n. The total number of relations that a node has, is referred to as the connectivity strength. The algorithm provides a table T as its output that contains the connectivity strength of each node in the $NRAG$. The complexity of the algorithm is $O(n^2)$.

The priority-based strategy for removal of SCNs is described in Algorithm 4. It starts with a call to the function $SCNFINDER$ on the $NRAG$ to create the table T containing the node identifiers and corresponding connectivity strengths. It then sorts the table in the decreasing order of the connectivity strength. The algorithm proceeds with deleting row entries from the table T on a priority basis such that the rows of the nodes with higher connectivity strengths are removed first. The procedure terminates while the number of nodes removed reaches the permissible number μ. It is easy to see that the complexity of the algorithm is $O(n^2)$.

Algorithm 4. Priority-based algorithm for removal of SCNs

Input: A $NRAG$, a Table T for storing node identifiers and associated connectivity strength $con\_strength$

Output: A Table T with the node identifiers and associated connectivity strength of SCNs which are to be removed.

1: Call SCNFINDER($NRAG, T$)
2: Sort T in descending order of $con\_strength$
3: $Number\_removed = \phi$
4: **for** each node in T with $con\_strength$ **do**
5:    **if** $Number\_removed <= \mu$ **then**
6:        $Number\_removed = Number\_removed + 1$
7:        Remove the corresponding row from table T
8:    **end if**
9: **end for**
10: Return

6   Results and Discussions

Attackers obtaining control over datacaptors and Intellivue Information Centers (IIC) described in the example network described in Fig. 2 can lead to disastrous consequences. Some of the possible attack scenarios among the many identified in the attack graph shown are detailed as follow.

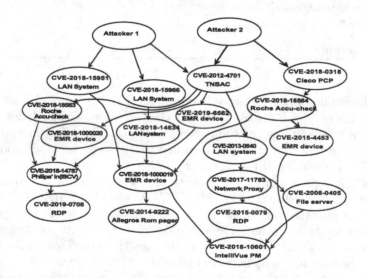

Fig. 3. NRAG for the example network in Fig. 2

The external attacker denoted as attacker 1 initiates the attack with exploitation CVE-2012-4701 in Tridium Niagara framework which is a smart building management software, which allows remote attacker to read sensitive information and arbitrary code execution. The attacker proceeds with exploiting CVE-2019-6562 in the Philips Tasy EMR software and edits the user inputs before it is placed to output. The attacker can then penetrate into very sensitive information by exploiting CVE-2018-14787 in Philips' IntelliSpace Cardiovascular (ISCV). The attacker further proceeds to the Microsoft flaw referred to as Blue keeper CVE-2019-0708 in the file servers and can control critical devices such as Cyberknife through RDP protocol. In another possible attack, the attacker 1 starts the penetration from an Adobe reader vulnerability CVE-2018-15966 present in the medical assistant system, and then escalates the privilege through the privilege escalation vulnerability CVE-2018-14634 in the Linux kernel. Further, the attacker exploits the vulnerabilities CVE-2015-4453 and CVE-2018-1000019 in the EMR device from which it can control the data-captor through exploitation of CVE-2014-9222.

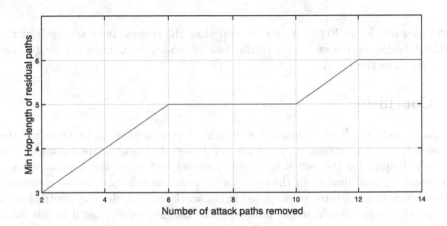

Fig. 4. Effect of removal of attack paths on residual hop-length

Another attack scenario is possible in which attacker designated as attacker 2 exploits a security bypass vulnerability CVE-2018-0318 in the software functionality of a Cisco networking device. The attacker further exploits CVE-2018-18564 in the Point-of-Care testing device Roche Accu-Chek Inform ll. By this, the attacker can exploit the vulnerabilities CVE-2015-4453 and CVE-2018-1000019 of the EMR device, and advances to the data-captor device and the Philips' IntelliVue Patient and Avalon Fetal Monitors by exploiting the vulnerability CVE-2014-9222 and CVE-2018-10601 in the respective devices. All such possibilities of attackers acquiring control of the data-captors, IICs, PGS, and the FPS in the example network are shown in Fig. 3.

The performance of the priority-based algorithms are evaluated in synthetic network graphs. The number of attackers and targets are taken as 2. Graphs with 50 nodes and 800 edges are synthesized. As shown in Fig. 4, as the number of attack paths removed increases, the minimum hop-length of the residual paths

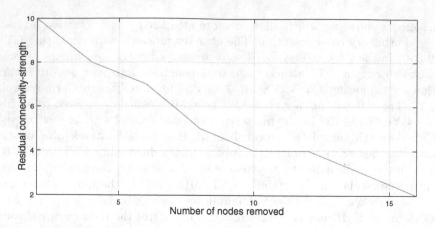

Fig. 5. Effect of removal of nodes on residual connectivity strength

also increases. From Fig. 5, it can be seen that the connectivity strength of the residual nodes decreases, as more number of nodes with higher strength are removed from the graph.

7 Conclusion

In this paper, we have presented a graphical representation to visualize the vulnerability-based attack paths in an IoT integrated healthcare network. The model is helpful for the network security analyst to foresee the attacks leading to critical medical devices in the network and also to take preventive measures. The priority-based strategies proposed in the work can significantly contribute to the security improvement in the network. The techniques discussed in this work can be deployed in tools such as Cygraph, developed for IoT-based industrial networks.

Acknowledgments. This project is sponsored by Dept. of Science and Technology, Govt. of India through WoS-A under sanction order No. SR/WOS-A/ET-97/2016(G).

References

1. Cisco white paper, IoT threat environment, published on 2015. https://www.cisco.com/c/en_in/solutions/security/iot-threat-defense/index.html
2. Huawei technologies, IoT security white paper-evolving security architecture, published on 2018. https://www.huawei.com/minisite/iot/img/iot_security_white_paper_2018_v2_en.pdf
3. FDA, US food and drugs administration, medical device recalls, published on 2018. https://www.fda.gov/MedicalDevices/Safety/ListofRecalls.html
4. Hipaa journal, pacific alliance medical center announces ransomware attack, published on 2017. https://www.hipaajournal.com/pacific-alliance-medical-center-announces-ransomware-attack

5. George, G., Thampi, S.M.: A graph-based security framework for securing industrial IoT networks from vulnerability exploitations. IEEE Access **6**, 43586–43601 (2018)

6. Yu, T., Sekar, V., Seshan, S., Agarwal, Y., Xu, C.: Handling a trillion (unfixable) flaws on a billion devices: rethinking network security for the Internet-of-Things. In: Proceedings of the 14th ACM Workshop on Hot Topics in Networks, p. 5. ACM (2015)

7. Islam, S.R., Kwak, D., Kabir, M.H., Hossain, M., Kwak, K.-S.: The internet of things for health care: a comprehensive survey. IEEE Access **3**, 678–708 (2015)

8. Chiuchisan, I., Costin, H.-N., Geman, O.: Adopting the internet of things technologies in health care systems. In: 2014 International Conference and Exposition on Electrical and Power Engineering (EPE), pp. 532–535. IEEE (2014)

9. Yang, G., et al.: A health-IoT platform based on the integration of intelligent packaging, unobtrusive bio-sensor, and intelligent medicine box. IEEE Trans. Ind. Inform. **10**(4), 2180–2191 (2014)

10. Doukas, C., Maglogiannis, I.: Bringing IoT and cloud computing towards pervasive healthcare. In: 2012 Sixth International Conference on Innovative Mobile and Internet Services in Ubiquitous Computing (IMIS), pp. 922–926. IEEE (2012)

11. Rohokale, V.M., Prasad, N.R., Prasad, R.: A cooperative internet of things (IoT) for rural healthcare monitoring and control. In: 2011 2nd International Conference on Wireless Communication, Vehicular Technology, Information Theory and Aerospace & Electronic Systems Technology (Wireless VITAE), pp. 1–6. IEEE (2011)

12. Catarinucci, L., et al.: An iot-aware architecture for smart healthcare systems. IEEE Internet Things J. **2**(6), 515–526 (2015)

13. Zhang, Y., Sun, L., Song, H., Cao, X.: Ubiquitous wsn for healthcare: recent advances and future prospects. IEEE Internet Things J. **1**(4), 311–318 (2014)

14. Xu, B., Da Xu, L., Cai, H., Xie, C., Hu, J., Bu, F., et al.: Ubiquitous data accessing method in IoT-based information system for emergency medical services. IEEE Trans. Ind. Inform. **10**(2), 1578–1586 (2014)

15. Laplante, P.A., Laplante, N.: The internet of things in healthcare: potential applications and challenges. IT Prof. **3**, 2–4 (2016)

16. Tarouco, L.M.R., et al.: Internet of things in healthcare: Interoperatibility and security issues. In: 2012 IEEE International Conference on Communications (ICC), pp. 6121–6125. IEEE (2012)

17. Gope, P., Hwang, T.: BSN-care: a secure IoT-based modern healthcare system using body sensor network. IEEE Sens. J. **16**(5), 1368–1376 (2016)

18. Anil Chacko, T.H.: Security and privacy issues with IoT in healthcare. EAI Endorsed Trans. Pervasive Health Technol. **4**, e2 (2018)

19. Simpson, A.K., Roesner, F., Kohno, T.: Securing vulnerable home IoT devices with an in-hub security manager. In: 2017 IEEE International Conference on Pervasive Computing and Communications Workshops (PerCom Workshops), pp. 551–556. IEEE (2017)

20. Ge, M., Hong, J.B., Guttmann, W., Kim, D.S.: A framework for automating security analysis of the Internet of Things. J. Netw. Comput. Appl. **83**, 12–27 (2017)

21. George, G., Thampi, S.M.: A graph-based decision support model for vulnerability analysis in IoT networks. In: Thampi, S.M., Madria, S., Wang, G., Rawat, D.B., Alcaraz Calero, J.M. (eds.) SSCC 2018. CCIS, vol. 969, pp. 1–23. Springer, Singapore (2019). https://doi.org/10.1007/978-981-13-5826-5_1

22. Romero-Mariona, J., Hallman, R., Kline, M., San Miguel, J., Major, M., Kerr, L.: Security in the industrial internet of things-the C-SEC approach. In: Proceedings of the International Conference on Internet of Things and Big Data, vol. 1, pp. 421–428 (2016)
23. Jajodia, S., Noel, S., Kalapa, P., Albanese, M., Williams, J.: Cauldron mission-centric cyber situational awareness with defense in depth. In: MILCOM, pp. 1339–1344 (2011)
24. Noel, S., Harley, E., Tam, K., Limiero, M., Share, M.: Cygraph: graph-based analytics and visualization for cybersecurity. In: Handbook of Statistics, vol. 35, pp. 117–167. Elsevier (2016)
25. George, G., Thampi, S.M.: Vulnerability-based risk assessment and mitigation strategies for edge devices in the internet of things. In: Pervasive and Mobile Computing, p. 101068 (2019)
26. Mell, P., Scarfone, K., Romanosky, S.: Common vulnerability scoring system (CVSS) (2011). http://www.first.org/cvss/cvss-guide.html
27. Ammann, P., Wijesekera, D., Kaushik, S.: Scalable, graph-based network vulnerability analysis. In: Proceedings of the 9th ACM Conference on Computer and Communications Security, pp. 217–224. ACM (2002)

ADS-SA: System for Automatically Detecting Sensitive Path of Android Applications Based on Static Analysis

Hong Song[✉], Dandan Lin, Shuang Zhu, Weiping Wang,
and Shigeng Zhang

School of Computer Science and Engineering, Central South University,
Changsha 410083, China
{songhong, danqm, wpwang, sgzhang}@csu.edu.cn,
140159407@qq.com

Abstract. With the booming mobile Internet and Android App market, Android security issues have become increasingly prominent. As the main way for information disclosure in Android Apps, sensitive path has become an important part of Android security research. Aiming at the problem that static analysis cannot verify whether the sensitive path is triggered by reality, this paper proposes a system ADS-SA based on static analysis to automatically detect sensitive path. The system first constructs an Android component conversion diagram through data flow analysis, and then obtains an Android function call graph through control flow analysis. Secondly, the sensitive path backtracking algorithm is designed and used to obtain the sensitive path set. Finally, the automated testing framework, Appium, is used to trigger and verify the authenticity of the sensitive path set. The test results show that the ADS-SA can automatically detect more than 87% of sensitive paths at a low time cost with high reliability and effectiveness.

Keywords: Android security · Static analysis · Sensitive path · Automated trigger · Automated detection

1 Introduction

Recent decades have witnessed the rapid development of mobile terminals. Android system occupies a large share of mobile Internet. National Internet Emergency Center (CNCERT) reports that the number of mobile users is 53% higher than that of PC users in 2018. And Google's Android has become the number one smart phone operating system [1]. Therefore, more attentions should be paid to the security of Android system.

Sensitive path is the primary way of information disclosure in Android Apps. Once an Android App runs vulnerably, it may leak sensitive information in the system through sensitive paths. The existing methods for detecting sensitive paths are mainly based on manual static or dynamic analysis. Their degree of automation is low. It is obviously difficult to adapt to the increasing number of sensitive paths found in Android Apps.

© Springer Nature Singapore Pte Ltd. 2019
G. Wang et al. (Eds.): iSCI 2019, CCIS 1122, pp. 309–322, 2019.
https://doi.org/10.1007/978-981-15-1301-5_25

In order to solve the problem, this paper proposes ADS-SA (Automatic Detection System based on Static Analysis) for automatically detecting sensitive path of Android Apps based on static analysis. The main contributions are as follows:

(1) ADS-SA is used to automatically trigger sensitive paths for detecting Android Apps. It will construct Component Conversion Diagram through data flow analysis and decompilation, as well as Android function call graph through control flow analysis or the function call relationship.

(2) Based on the Android component conversion diagram and the Android function call graph, the sensitive path backtracking algorithm is designed and used to obtain the sensitive path set.

(3) Combined with the automated test framework Appium, ADS-SA triggers each path in the sensitive path set automatically and tests two different sets of sample sets. Experimental results show that ADS-SA can trigger sensitive paths in Android Apps effectively and automatically.

2 Related Work

The increasing usage of Android Apps has boomed in the mobile App market. In order to maintain the stability of the Android App, security detection is necessary. According to the running state of the Android Apps, the security detecting technology for Android App can be divided into three methods, which are static analysis, dynamic analysis, and hybrid analysis [2].

Static analysis gets byte codes or intermediate codes by decompiling Android Apps to obtain the executable path sequence transferred by data flow [3]. In [4] the authors have designed DroidJust for auto-sensing privacy leaks in Android Apps, which trace sensitive information flow from sensitive source to network or SMS-related sink. After detecting 6,000 Android Apps collected from Google stores, DroidJust can find 95.82% of sensitive information. The PScout based on static analysis was proposed in [5] to resolve permissions of Android Apps, while Droid PF in [6] was established a finite state machine to detect vulnerabilities.

Dynamic analysis is different from static analysis. It refers to detect whether the interaction of the Android Apps revealing sensitive information, or the runtime behavior. In [9], Stoat is designed to dynamically generate probability weights for triggering executing events. To improve efficiency and detect more undiscovered system crashes and anomalies, Stoat sets several system events. However, some flash events may be ignored and the random model is incomplete. ANTSdroid in [10] detects malicious Apps by extracting sensitive APIs and privilege-related API call sequences.

Hybrid analysis is a tradeoff between static analysis and dynamic analysis. It can analyzes executable path information by static analysis and monitor executing process by dynamic analysis. In [11], DroidTrace is designed for monitoring malicious behavior and analyzing downloaded executable files based on Android ptrace system call. For revealing some unknown features of malicious Apps, mad4a parses Android Apps information and analyzes privilege-related APIs in [12].

However, most of above researches for detecting secure items of Android Apps ignores automated trigger of sensitive information, and the detecting technologies can't effectively find whether the sensitive paths can be triggered. In order to reduce labor investment, more researches introduce automatically testing technologies, as well as shortening test time and improving efficiency. But few problems are not be solved well. First, static analysis often establishes the relationships of all components, but the relationships can't be triggered directly and automatically. Second, how to construct event trigger conditions is also important, which is the key to automatic detection of sensitive paths.

This paper proposes ADS-SA, Automatic Detection Method based on Static Analysis, for automatically detecting sensitive path. Firstly, ADS-SA uses data flow analysis and control flow analysis to construct Android component relationship and system-call-converting graph respectively. Secondly, a sensitive path backtracking algorithm is used to explore sensitive paths automatically. Finally, ADS-SA uses Appium [13] to trigger each sensitive path and find out the true leakage activities.

3 Overall Architecture and Design of ADS-SA

3.1 Overall Architecture of ADS-SA

Figure 1 shows the overall architecture of the ADS-SA for automatically detecting sensitive path.

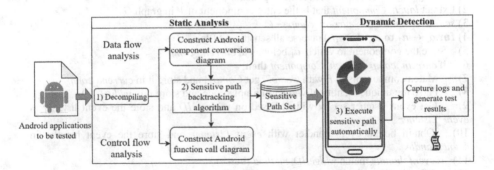

Fig. 1. Overall architecture of ADS-SA.

The method consists of static analysis and dynamic detection, which can be divided into three parts. First, decompiling module extracts information of Android Apps by data flow analysis, and constructs Android component converted diagram. Then it constructs function-call graph by control flow analysis. Second, with the given sensitive API library, the sensitive path backtracking algorithm module obtains sensitive path sets. Third, automated trigger execution module uses Appium to trigger each path in the sensitive path set automatically. Moreover, it captures the log information of the Android Apps at dynamic runtime. Finally, through log analysis, it verifies whether the sensitive path can automatically trigger execution effectively.

Decompiling Module. Obtaining the conversion relationship between components relies on the static analysis framework Soot. Soot converts the Dalvik bytecode into Jimple code for data flow analysis. Similarly, in order to construct the Android function call graph, Dalvik bytecode is converted into Smali code by means of WALA, where WALA is a static analysis framework. Then control flow analysis is carried out. Figure 2 depicts a schematic diagram of the decompiling module.

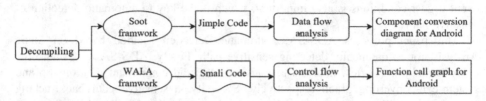

Fig. 2. Schematic diagram of decompiling module for ADS-SA.

Sensitive Path Backtracking Algorithm Module. Algorithm 1 describes sensitive path backtracking algorithm.

Algorithm 1 Sensitive path backtracking algorithm

Input: $A \leftarrow \{a_1, a_2, ..., a_n\}$ // A is a set of sensitive API
  $G \leftarrow \{V, E\}$ //Component conversion diagram of Android Apps
Output: *sensitive_Path* //a set of sensitive paths
1) $TC \leftarrow \{$ trigger conditions between components $\}$
2) Extract *lauch_Component* that is the entry component of V in graph G
3) *sensitive_Path* $\leftarrow \emptyset$, *current_comp* $\leftarrow \emptyset$
4) **for** $a_i \leftarrow a_1$ to a_n **do**   // Traverse all sensitive APIs
5)   Store the component to which a_i belongs in *current_comp*
6)   **if** *current_comp* $\neq$ *lauch_Component* **then**
7)   Match components in E with *Comp2*, get *Comp1*, and store it in *current_comp*
8)   Parse the unique identity of widget in jimple code and store it in *widget_ID*
9)   Get event listener set by widget based on *widget_ID* and store the event listener in *event_Listener*
10)   Obtain bound event handler with *event_Listener* and store the event handler in *event_handle*
11)   **if** *event_handle* match *widgetID_method* **then**
12)   TC $\leftarrow$ *trigger_Cond*
13)   **continue**
14)   **endif**
15)   **else exit**
16)   **endif**
17) Add the path between *launch_Component* and *tmpComp* to *sensitive_Path*
18) output *sensitive_Path*

In the algorithm, the variable TC is a set of trigger conditions between components. The variable *Lauch_Component* represents entry components for extracting Android component conversion diagram G from the table *Components*. Initially, the algorithm sets *sensitive_Path* to $\emptyset$ and *current_comp* to $\emptyset$, where the variable *sensitive_Path* is the set of sensitive paths and the variable *current_comp* is current component. Then it analyzes each element in the set of sensitive APIs one by one. It takes out *tmpCom*, where *tmpCom* is a variable representing the component to which the sensitive API belongs. It backtracks to find out *current_comp*, a variable representing the calling component of the upper level. Combined with *trigger_Cond*, the algorithm adds *current_comp* to *TC*, where the variable *trigger_Cond* is trigger conditions between acquired components. The algorithm goes into a loop until *lauch_Component* is found, where the variable *lauch_Component* is entry components of Android Apps. It constructs a conversion path with *TC* from *lauch_Component* to *tmpComp*. It stores the path in *sensitive_Path*. Then it continues to process the remaining elements in the set of sensitive APIs. Finally it gets *sensitive_Path*.

Automated Trigger Execution Module. In order to execute the set of sensitive paths dynamically, the automated trigger execution module mainly combines two automated trigger test frameworks, Appium and TestNG [20].

(1) Configure test environment

Through annotations provided by Java, TestNG sets up the environment before the test case runs. It loads all attribute values of *Desired capabilities*, including models of test machines, names of the test platform, package names of Android Apps and entry component name, etc. *Desired capabilities* are JSON objects for client session in Appium communication process. TestNG drives the execution of test cases by annotations instead of the Main method in traditional Java programs. It provides test method that automatically loads automated trigger conditions of each sensitive path in the sensitive path set. Moreover, it controls test process from beginning to end and generates report results automatically.

(2) Drive automated execution of sensitive paths

By default, Appium establishes a HTTP connection with test machine using local IP and port 4723. It parses package names of Apps and startups components from the obtained Android component information base. Then it automatically installs and starts Android Apps in the test machine. It extracts sequentially each path in *sensitive_Path*, where the path is a sensitive path from the entry component to the component to which a sensitive API belongs. Appium analyzes all trigger conditions of sensitive paths. Then, it uses the unique identifier ID of the triggering widget as the trigger focus, executes the corresponding trigger method according to the type of the widget. It automatically drives the execution of sensitive paths until all the sensitive paths are executed. At the same time, Appium records and captures log information, such as Android App test path, system state and so on during dynamic runtime. Finally, it generates test results. If it executes successfully, the sensitive path exists and is correct. If fails to execute successfully, the sensitive path is incorrect or there is a false alarm.

3.2 Construction of Conversion Relationship Between Components

In order to analyze the component association information at the code level in a fine-grained way, how to obtain the data flow of conversion between components is the key to mining component relationship. Aiming at this key point, ADS-SA uses static analysis to analyze data flow between components. Considering that component conversion relies on event triggers, ADS-SA performs data flow analysis by customizing functions related to triggering events as tainted objects. It captures the communication-related information of event triggers between components of Android Apps, including the transmission information between components, the corresponding relationship between widgets and binding event listeners. This provides stable and reliable dependencies for triggers between components.

To analyze the data flow transmitted by taints in Android Apps accurately, ADS-SA uses IccTA. IccTA is an open source tool and can detect privacy leaks between components of Android Apps. It traces marked taint propagation paths from *Source* to *Sink*, where *Source* is the defined source function and *Sink* is the sink function.

(1) *Source* and *Sink* Definition

In order to construct the triggering event conversion relationship between components, *Source* and *Sink* are preconditions for taint tracking. ADS-SA defines *findViewById* as *Source*, where *FindViewById* is a function for obtaining triggering widget. Moreover, it defines event listener functions of triggering widgets and methods of starting components as *Sink*, as shown in Table 1. Then combined with the Android event-triggered mechanism, ADS-SA mainly analyzes logical association information among triggering widgets, event listeners of widgets, triggering events, and target components of triggers.

Table 1. Customize *Sink* for taint tracking.

Category	Function name/Method name
Event listener function	setOnClickListener, setOnItemClickListener, onOptionsItemSelected, setOnCheckedChangeListener, onDateChangedListener, setOnKeyListener
Method of starting components	startActivityForReult/starActtivity, startService/bindService, sendBroadcast, contentResolver

(2) Construct conversion relationship between Android components

To construct conversion relationship between Android components, ADS-SA stores the information in the Android component information base. The information is generated by data flow tracking, including names and types of all components, custom class names, information of triggering widgets, event listener functions, privilege descriptions, etc. Table 2 shows the main tables stored in this database.

In order to visualize the conversion relationship between Android components, ADS-SA defines the directed graph structure of the component conversion diagram. The component conversion diagram can be described as $G = \{V, E\}$, where V represents the set of all components of the Android Apps, and E represents the conversion relationship between components.

Table 2. Information of main tables in Android component information base.

Table name	Primary Key (PK)	Details
Classes	Class_id	Store names and types of components
ExitPoints	Exit_id	Store method names of all components
Intents	Intent_id	Store all intent information
Links	Link_id	Store information of Intent filter
Components	Component_id	Store names of Apps and component, etc.
Paths	Path_id	Store information of each path
Stmts	Stmts_id	Store trigger statements, etc.

3.3 Capture of Trigger Condition Between Components

After constructing conversion relationship between Android components, ADS-SA combines details of main tables of the Android component information base, as introduced in Table 2, to capture trigger conditions between components. It uses graph G to describe the information of logical conversion associations between Android components. $G = \{V, E\}$ represents data structure. V is a set of vertexes and includes information of all components in the *Components* table. E is a set of edges and consists of a triple *{Comp1, widgetID_method, Comp2}*. Then ADS-SA analyzes the logic diagram of Android event triggers. Figure 3 shows four elements, including *widget_ID*, *event_Listener*, *event_handle*, and starting target component, where the variable *widget_ID* is the triggering widget, the variable *event_Listener* is the event listener and the variable *event_handle* is event handler. These four elements form a structure of trigger conditions, namely, *trigger_Cond = {Comp1, widget_ID, event_Listener, event_handle, Comp2}*.

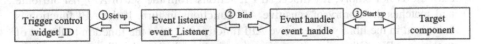

| Trigger control widget_ID | ①Set up | Event listener event_Listener | ②Bind | Event handler event_handle | ③Start up | Target component |

Fig. 3. Android component information base Android event-triggered logic diagram.

3.4 Acquisition of a Sensitive Path Set

ADS-SA can automatically trigger sensitive paths of Android Apps. Acquisition of a set of sensitive paths is the key to realize this technology and mainly includes four steps. First, a function call graph of Android is constructed. Second, a library of sensitive API functions is matched. Third, a set of sensitive APIs in Android Apps is obtained. Fourth, a sensitive path backtracking algorithm is combined.

(1) Construct a function call graph for Android

Considering the API information in function call relationship, ADS-SA analyzes the control flow transmission among functions by static analysis. And it explores the call relationship of logical associations between functions. It resolves class names of the control flow in all Smali codes and obtains required information, including register labels, the list of method call parameters, types of the return value of functions, etc. The *method_name* field stores names of methods executed in components. The *in_list* field stores a list of functions that invoke responding methods in *method_name*. The *out_list* field stores a list of functions invoked by this method. *API_list* field stores functions of system framework layer extracted from *out_list*. The *self_define_list* field stores custom functions that the function in *API_list* invokes. Based on these five fields, ADS-SA forms quaternary logical structure *{method_name, in_list, self_define_list, API_list}* and constructs Android function call graph.

(2) Match a library of sensitive API functions

Triggered events of Android system include user-triggered events and system-triggered events. Based on this truth, ADS-SA obtains a library of sensitive API functions containing more than 10,000 sensitive APIs. Sensitive APIs in Android Apps include user-sensitive APIs and system-sensitive APIs. User-sensitive APIs refer to sensitive APIs triggered by user behavior, such as inputting users' privacy data, dialing phone numbers, sending short messages, etc. System-sensitive APIs refer to system behaviors executed by Android system in the background and dependency functions loaded at runtime, such as starting Service components for background service, obtaining system time, etc.

(3) Obtain a sensitive API set of Android Apps

For obtaining a set of sensitive paths in Android Apps, the key point is to analyze the set of sensitive APIs in function call graphs. Therefore, after completing the first two steps, this method parses *API_list* attribute of each function one by one from Android function call graphs. Then it determines whether *API_list* attribute is empty. If *API_list* attribute is empty, it continues to judge whether Android function call graphs have been read out. In addition, if function call graphs have not been read out, it continues to parse *API_list* attribute of next function. If *API_list* attribute is not empty, it extracts API functions from the set of *API_list* attribute and matches the library of sensitive API functions in turn. If the API function is contained in the library of sensitive API functions, it adds the function to the set of sensitive APIs. Otherwise, it continues to judge whether the library of sensitive API functions has been read out. If not, it reads the API function in the next *API_list* one by one. Then this method matches the API with the library of sensitive API functions. Finally it generates sets of sensitive APIs of Android Apps.

3.5   Automated Trigger of Sensitive Paths

Based on the set of sensitive paths in Android Apps, trigger conditions of each sensitive path are extracted in turn. Then using an API interface provided by Appium and starting from the startup component of Android Apps, triggered widgets in sensitive paths are extracted. Moreover, this method determines whether the triggered widget can trigger the jump of the component. If it can, the execution of corresponding events is triggered automatically and log information of sensitive paths is captured at runtime, by simulating the manual trigger operation. If it cannot, this method continues to extract next sensitive path to be executed from the set of sensitive paths. Repeat the operation of automatic trigger for sensitive paths until all sensitive paths in the set of sensitive paths have been triggered and executed. Finally, a log of the triggered test for sensitive paths is generated.

4 Experiments and Results

4.1 Test Environment

We use Java (JDK 1.8) for experiments and use Appium and TestNG, where Appium and TestNG are automated testing frameworks. In addition, we use several other tools, such as a taint-tracking tool IccTA, a decompiling tool Baksmali, MySQL database and so on. Table 3 shows detailed information of specific experimental tools.

Table 3. Details of experimental tools.

Experimental tool	Function
Appium	Mobile automated open source test framework
Eclipse	Open source Java development integration tool
ADB	Debugging tools for Android development toolkit
IccTA	Static analysis tool for taint
Baksmali	Android decompiling tool
GraphViz	Visual drawing software
TestNG	Annotated-driven automated unit test framework

4.2 Test Sample Set

In order to verify the validity, accuracy and reliability of ADS-SA, two samples sets are prepared, which are the set of self-written samples and the set of samples downloaded from Google App Market, as showed in Tables 4 and 5 shows a set of 53 Android Apps downloaded from Google App Market. The set of self-written samples includes 12 samples of triggering event listener functions and 8 samples of triggering start components. And the other samples set includes six different types, such as image, study, communication, map, system and security.

Table 4. Self-written samples

Type of sensitive paths triggered	Total number of every type
Triggering event listener function	12
Triggering start component	8
Total	20

Table 5. Samples from Google App Market

Samples' type	Total number of every type
Image	8
Study	11
Communication	12
Map	6
System	7
Security	9
Total	53

4.3 Test Results

(1) Result analysis of the number of sensitive paths detected

As shown in Table 6, 45 test samples downloaded from Google stores are triggered automatically by ADS-SA. For further analyzing ADS-SA's reliability and universality, we make a more in-depth analysis of these 45 test cases. We tested Manual analysis, static analysis, Monkey test and ADS-SA respectively. Finally, we make a detailed comparative analysis of the number of sensitive paths detected by four different methods.

Table 6. Experimental results of test samples downloaded from Google stores

Sample type	Num	Num of successful examples	Num of samples without sensitive API	Num of samples that fail to decompile	Tri
Image	8	6	1	1	87.5%
Study	11	10	0	1	90.9%
Communication	12	10	2	0	100%
Map	6	5	0	1	83.33%
System	7	7	0	0	100%
Security	9	7	1	1	88.88%

Figure 4 shows the results of these 45 test samples detected by four detection methods.

We use the number of sensitive paths detected by manual analysis as the reference for other methods. Monkey depends on the time threshold specified in the initial stage. Therefore, we first use static analysis to detect sensitive paths of six types of test samples, and record the specific test time required to detect each sample. The longest time consumed by static analysis for detecting samples is 60 s. So we set the time parameter of Monkey test to 60 s.

From Fig. 4, we can infer four results. The first one is that both static analysis and ADS-SA can detect most of sensitive paths of Android Apps as well as manual analysis. The second is that ADS-SA can trigger a large number of sensitive paths in

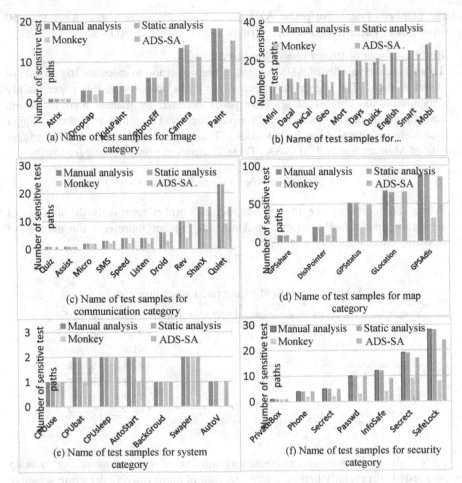

Fig. 4. Comparison of four methods for detecting sensitive paths of six types of test samples.

these six types of test samples automatically and successfully. Compared with the simple static analysis, it can actually verify the accuracy of the existence of sensitive paths. The third, ADS-SA can obtain triggered conditions of sensitive paths through static analysis. Differed from Monkey, ADS-SA can trigger more sensitive paths. In particular, (b) and (c) in Fig. 4 describe detection results of sensitive paths for "learning" and "communication" samples, respectively. By analyzing the number of sensitive paths detected by different methods in (b) and (c), it can be intuitively found that the number of sensitive paths detected by ADS-SA is nearly twice as many as that of Monkey. And the last, some samples just have a few sensitive paths. However, ADS-SA can completely detect all sensitive paths contained in such samples, such as seven "system" samples shown in Fig. 4(e). These results verify the reliability of ADS-SA. Figure 4(d) shows the result of five "map" samples. Through analysis, it is found that three samples (including "GPS status", "GLocation" and "GPS Adis") are contain a large number of sensitive paths. ADS-SA can automatically trigger more than 50 sensitive paths. These results further verifies the versatility of ADS-SA.

(2) Result analysis of trigger rate of sensitive path

To analyze the validity of ADS-SA, we define a method to calculate trigger rate of sensitive paths. The trigger rate of sensitive paths proposed in this paper mainly depends on the number of sensitive paths detected by manual analysis. Then, according to actual number of sensitive paths detected by different methods, trigger rate of sensitive paths can be calculated. This paper mainly compares the trigger rate of Monkey test and ADS-SA. Table 7 shows the result of trigger rate.

$$\text{Tri} = (actual\_number/manual\_number) * 100\% \tag{1}$$

Where Tri represents the trigger rate, actual_number represents the number of sensitive paths actually detected and manual_number represents the number of sensitive paths manually detected.

Table 7. Analysis of trigger rate for sensitive path.

Sample type	Number of samples detected manually	Monkey	ADS-SA
Image	46	47.8%	87%
Study	173	41%	89%
Communication	68	47%	95.6%
Map	237	35.4%	95.7%
System	11	72.7%	100%
Security	79	36.7%	88.6%

Table 7 shows the results of automated-trigger rate of sensitive paths. For those 45 samples tested successfully before, the trigger rate of automatically detecting sensitive paths with ADS-SA reaches over 87%. However, the trigger rate of Monkey test is mostly below 47.8%. This indicates that ADS-SA is more efficient than Monkey test in automated trigger of sensitive paths.

To sum up, we design two sets of test experiments to analyze the rate of success of ADS-SA. Both two sets of experiments achieves high rate of success, proving the versatility of ADS-SA. For the number of sensitive paths detected, combined with manual analysis, static analysis and Monkey test, this paper makes a comparative analysis. The analysis results verify the reliability, accuracy and validity of ADS-SA. However, for samples "Camera" and "Paint" in Fig. 4(a), sensitive paths detected by ADS-SA are three less than that detected by manual analysis. The reason is that for protecting the security of test machine, ADS-SA evades the opening of user-sensitive privileges and cannot invoke API related to privileges. Figure 4(b) shows that sensitive paths detected by static analysis is two more than that detected by manual analysis. In order to find out the reason, we conduct code review and find that there are false alarms when static analysis detects sensitive paths. Static analysis incorrectly regards sensitive APIs that have been commented out in source codes of samples as normal sensitive

APIs. However, sensitive paths containing these sensitive APIs are no longer operational. In addition, samples of "communication" type in Fig. 4(c) needs to interact with a remote server during the test. If the remote server closes abnormally, samples cannot establish the reliable communication link, resulting in reduction of the number of sensitive paths detected. For testing trigger rate of sensitive paths, experimental results show that ADS-SA automatically triggers more sensitive paths than Monkey and achieves a higher trigger rate. This verifies the effectiveness of ADS-SA.

5 Conclusion

This paper proposes a method named ADS-SA for automatically detecting sensitive path of Android Apps based on static analysis. Experimental results on two different sets of test samples show that ADS-SA can realize the automatic trigger detection of sensitive paths in a large number of test samples. Compared with the random test tool, Monkey, it improves the efficiency of detection and achieves high reliability, accuracy and validity.

References

1. CNCERT: Analysis of the proportion of domestic operating systems and browsers in the third quarter of 2018 [EB/OL], 21 November 2018. http://cert.org.cn/publish/main/68/2018/20181121084040286901315/20181121084040286901315_.html. Accessed 16 Mar 2019
2. Rountev, A., Yan, D.: Static reference analysis for GUI objects in Android software. In: Proceedings of Annual IEEE/ACM International Symposium on Code Generation and Optimization, pp. 143–154. ACM (2014)
3. Yang, S., Yan, D., Wu, H., et al.: Static control-flow analysis of user-driven callbacks in Android applications. In: 2015 IEEE/ACM 37th IEEE International Conference on Software Engineering, vol. 1, pp. 89–99. IEEE (2015)
4. Chen, X., Zhu, S.: DroidJust: automated functionality-aware privacy leakage analysis for Android applications. In: Proceedings of the 8th ACM Conference on Security & Privacy in Wireless and Mobile Networks, p. 5. ACM (2015)
5. Au, K.W.Y., Zhou, Y.F., Huang, Z., et al.: PScout: analyzing the Android permission specification. In: Proceedings of the 2012 ACM Conference on Computer and Communications Security, pp. 217–228. ACM (2012)
6. Bai, G., Ye, Q., Wu, Y., et al.: Towards model checking Android applications. IEEE Trans. Softw. Eng. **44**(6), 595–612 (2018)
7. Yang, Z., Yang, M., Zhang, Y., et al.: Appintent: analyzing sensitive data transmission in Android for privacy leakage detection. In: Proceedings of the 2013 ACM SIGSAC Conference on Computer and Communications Security, pp. 1043–1054. ACM (2013)
8. Onwuzurike, L., Almeida, M., Mariconti, E., et al.: A family of droids–Android malware detection via behavioral modeling: static vs dynamic analysis. arXiv preprint arXiv:1803.03448 (2018)
9. Su, T., Meng, G., Chen, Y., et al.: Guided, stochastic model-based GUI testing of Android apps. In: Proceedings of the 2017 11th Joint Meeting on Foundations of Software Engineering, pp. 245–256. ACM (2017)

10. Sun, Y.S., Chen, C.-C., Hsiao, S.-W., Chen, M.C.: ANTSdroid: automatic malware family behaviour generation and analysis for Android apps. In: Susilo, W., Yang, G. (eds.) ACISP 2018. LNCS, vol. 10946, pp. 796–804. Springer, Cham (2018). https://doi.org/10.1007/978-3-319-93638-3_48

11. Zheng, M., Sun, M., Lui, J.C.S.: DroidTrace: a ptrace based Android dynamic analysis system with forward execution capability. In: 2014 International Wireless Communications and Mobile Computing Conference (IWCMC), pp. 128–133. IEEE (2014)

12. Kabakus, A.T., Dogru, I.A.: An in-depth analysis of Android malware using hybrid techniques. Digit. Invest. **24**, 25–33 (2018)

13. Hans, M.: Appium Essentials, pp. 19–29. Packt Publishing Ltd. (2015)

14. Choudhary, S.R., Gorla, A., Orso, A.: Automated test input generation for Android: are we there yet? In: 2015 30th IEEE/ACM International Conference on Automated Software Engineering (ASE), pp. 429–440. IEEE (2015)

15. Zhang, J., Qin, Z., Zhang, K., et al.: Dalvik opcode graph based Android malware variants detection using global topology features. IEEE Access **6**, 51964–51974 (2018)

16. Li, L., Bartel, A., Bissyandé, T.F., et al.: IccTa: detecting inter-component privacy leaks in Android apps. In: Proceedings of the 37th International Conference on Software Engineering, vol. 1, pp. 280–291. IEEE Press (2015)

17. Sun, C., Zhang, H., Qin, S., et al.: DexX: a double layer unpacking framework for Android. IEEE Access **6**, 61267–61276 (2018)

18. Adamo, D., Nurmuradov, D., Piparia, S., et al.: Combinatorial-based event sequence testing of Android applications. Inf. Softw. Technol. **99**, 98–117 (2018)

19. Wei, S., Wu, G., Luo, N., et al.: DroidBet: event-driven automatic detection of network behaviors for Android applications. J. Commun. **38**(5), 84–95 (2017)

20. Garg, S.: Creating automation frameworks using Appium. In: Appium Recipes, pp. 101–127. Apress, Berkeley (2016)

Early Detection of Parkinson Disease Using Wavelet Transform Along with Fourier Transform

Syed Qasim Afser Rizvi, Guojun Wang(✉) ⓘ, and Xiaofei Xing

School of Computer Science, Guangzhou University,
Guangzhou 510006, Guangdong, China
qar1l0@gmail.com, csgjwang@gmail.com,
xingxf@gzhu.edu.cn

Abstract. Parkinson disease (PD) is one of the neurodegenerative diseases caused by numerous factors. The patient is affected by PD grows gradually to the limit that he/she may not be able to perform their daily routine. PD is having two types of major symptoms Motor and Non-motor. Motor symptoms are the major contributor towards the detection of the PD. From the cluster of motor symptoms, Tremor attack is the cause that can depicts the PD by observing the Electroencephalography (EEG). EEG is a rich set of brain signals showing wide variety chronic tasks performed by the brain. The detection of early onset of the PD helps us to investigate that if the patient is having the severe chances of the PD or not. In our propose method we are using the Wavelet Transform along with the Fourier Transform to visualize the EEG signals. Both normal and abnormal EEG's are tested and the result shows that our propose method is good to classify the early tremor attacks.

Keywords: Parkinson disease (PD) · Tremor · Patient · EEG · DWT · FFT

1 Introduction

In the group of neurodegenerative diseases, PD is an increasing threat that affects a lot of daily activities. It is chronic and progressive, means that it initiates with minor efficiency and increases the efficacy as the time passes [1]. It's influence increases so much that patient is not able to move on its own. The batch of neurodegenerative disease contains a lot of disorders [2]. The early detection of PD is more challenging and remarkable for the medical diagnosis [3]. We can assist patients before they caught in diseased stage and provide a proper medication or can aid them in a more prosperous manner [4, 5]. There are a lot of symptoms for diagnosing PD, these symptoms are broadly classified in two groups namely motor and non-motor. The motor symptoms that includes the motor actions, like stiffness in the muscle, freezing of gait (FOG) and Tremors. The tremors are further categorized into action and resting tremors. The resting tremors are mostly known as Parkinsonian Tremors based on the current research.

© Springer Nature Singapore Pte Ltd. 2019
G. Wang et al. (Eds.): iSCI 2019, CCIS 1122, pp. 323–333, 2019.
https://doi.org/10.1007/978-981-15-1301-5_26

Diagnosing the PD is being done in a lot of ways including medical analysis patients background and electronically by using different modalities especially like EEG, EMG and so on. Electroencephalography is process of recording the electrical signals produced by the neurons when performing predefined task. These signals are recorded by placing the electrodes on the scalp of one's head based on the standard 10–20 system. These recordings give us electrical signals ranging from .5 Hz to 50 Hz. Based on the working of the nervous system these signals reflect frequency range for specified task performed by the brain shown in the Fig. 1(a) and (b). These frequency ranges are classified as follows,

1. Delta Waves (0.5–4 Hz): - These waves originate during the sleep. They are usually measure of the depth of the sleep. The stronger is the sleep stronger are the delta waves.
2. Theta Waves (4–7 Hz): - Theta waves usually originate during the processing of cognitive tasks. These waves are common in children's and usually considers as abnormal for normal adults.
3. Alpha Waves (7–12 Hz): - The alpha waves are reflected when a person goes from wakeful state to the relaxing state by closing the eyes. It deepens as far as the relaxing state intensifies and disappears by opening of the eyes.
4. Beta Waves (12–30 Hz): - Beta Waves usually indicates the motor movements of the body. As the brain engages in coordinating the body movements, these waves usually appear.

Apart from the above-mentioned categorization of the EEG waves, there are a lot remains depending upon the morphologic behavior like wicket waves.

A lot of work has been done on EEGs regarding the classification of the waves in various fields. But related to the PD not much work has been done. We have proposed a technique to classify the signals to diagnose the PD just before the patient is being caught by the same. For performing such classification, we are using Discrete Wavelet Transform (DWT) along with the Fast Fourier Transform (FFT). The DWT is used to provide multiresolution analysis of the EEG signals and then classifying through FFT.

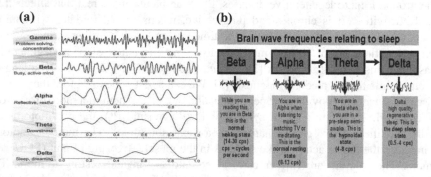

Fig. 1. (a) EEG waves classification, (b) Detail description of EEG waves

2 Methodology

We are using the DWT and FFT for the classification of EEG waves to predict the PD. DWT is being used to provide Multi-resolution analysis which will be then fed to FFT for performing the frequency analysis and feature extraction. The flow of our proposed method is given in the Fig. 2.

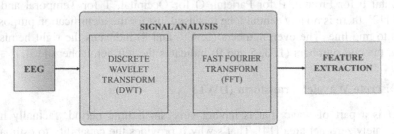

Fig. 2. Flow diagram of the proposed method.

From the Fig. 1, it is depicted that we are using DWT for the EEG signals, the DWT will perform multiresolution decomposing of the signals. This decomposition of signals gives us a real insight of the patient behavior, but because of multiresolution decomposition we need to decode these output DWT signals to draw some flourishing results. After decomposition we applied FFT to perform efficiently frequency analysis. The described feature set is then deduced using feature extraction method. The obtained feature set values provide us the prominent results to decide whether the incoming EEG is deficient of PD or not.

2.1 EEG

Electroencephalography is a technique to record the electrical signals produced by the brain while performing certain task. These signals vary depending upon the nature of task performed by the brain [6]. Any initiation of action is produced by thumping the neurons residing in the brain. These recordings are recorded based on the electrodes placed on the scalp [7]. Each recording is known as the montage. The electrodes are placed on the scalp based on the standard 10–20 system [8].

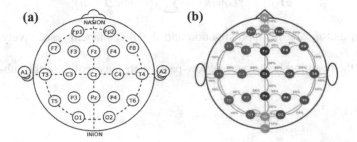

Fig. 3. (a) Brain lobes and electrodes placement, (b) 10–20 system

Our brain is divided into two hemispheres known as left and right hemispheres which is further divide into four lobes namely, Frontal, Parietal, Occipital and Temporal lobe [9, 10]. The standard 10–20 system indicates that the absolute distance between the placed electrodes should be 10% or 20% of the total front-back or right-left distance of the skull [11]. Now the electrode placement is done starting from the "Nasion" the forehead up to the "Inion" the lower back of the head the naming as shown in the Fig. 3, is based on the first alphabetic letter of the lobes expressly, F_p for Pre-Frontal F for Frontal, P for Parietal, O for Occipital, T for Temporal and C as Central [12], there is no any central lobe it is used just for the identification purpose, the z refers to mid-line. The even numbers (2, 4, 6 and 8) indicates the right hemisphere whereas the odd numbers (1, 3, 5 and 9) indicates the left-hemisphere [13].

2.2 Discrete Wavelet Transform (DWT)

Wavelet is a part of wave that is having very small time period, factually having approximately zero net area [14]. That's why it provides the capability to estimate the events obtained from short time intervals. The signal decomposition into diverse scales, is done by the wavelet transform by the dilation of the mother wavelet producing different levels of resolution. The Discrete Wavelet Transform (DWT) uses only sampled wavelet function[15]. The DWT utilizes only subset of scales (a) and positions (b) instead of calculating the values at every point [16]. The wavelet mother $\Psi_{(a, b)}$ (t)

$$\Psi_{(a,b)}(t) = 2^{a/2} \Psi\left(2^{-a/2}(t-b)\right)$$ (1)

the selection of scales and positions varies as power of 2 known as the dyadic positions and scales $[a_j = 2^{-j}; \; b_{j,k} = 2^{-j}k]$ where (J and k are integers).

The DWT decomposes the signal into subsequent frequency bands incorporating scaling and a wavelet function, allying with low-pass and high-pass filters [17], for evaluating the signal. The EEG signal is shaped into discrete time signal x[n]. The first step is to pass the EEG signal along the half-band high-pass filter g(), and a low-pass filter Fig. 4(a). Secondly, the filtering is advanced to the sub-sampling, resulting in the one level of decomposition. The equation of one level of decomposition is shown as:

$$d1(k) = YHigh(k) = \sum x(n) \cdot g(2k-n),$$ (2)

$$a1(k) = YLow(k) = \sum x(n) \cdot h(2k-n),$$ (3)

Here a_1 and d_1 are the approximation and detail coefficient respectively Y_{High} (k) along with Y_{Low}

(k) are the resulting high-pass and low-pass filters succeeding to the sub-sampling [18].

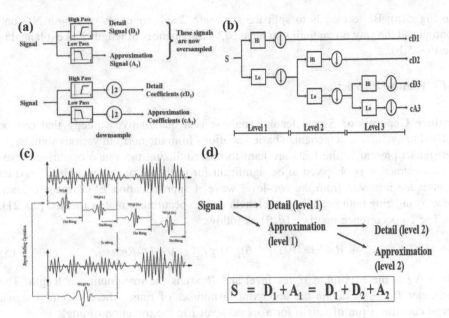

Fig. 4. (a) DWT low-pass and high-pass filtering, (b) DWT decomposition level, (c) DWT scaling and shifting, (d) DWT signal decomposition.

The above stated procedure known as sub-band coding, is reiterated up to the limit of subsampling Fig. 4(b). The output at every level will double the frequency resolution and half the time resolution Fig. 4(d). We are using the Daubechies 4 db4 depicted in the Fig. 4(c) mother wavelet that is proved to be strong candidate for the EEG analysis as compared to others.

2.3   Fast Fourier Transform (FFT)

Fourier analysis is extremely useful for data analysis, as it breaks down a signal into constituent sinusoids of different frequencies as depicted in the Fig. 5(a). For sampled vector data, Fourier analysis is performed using the discrete Fourier transform (DFT). The fast Fourier transform (FFT) is an efficient algorithm for computing the DFT of a sequence; it is not a separate transform. It is particularly used in area such as signal processing, where its uses range from filtering and frequency analysis to power spectrum estimation [19]. Consider the DTFT

$$X[k] = \sum_{n=0}^{N-1} x[n] W^{kn} \tag{4}$$

The approximated N^2 number of complex multiplication and addition need to be applied to for the given equation. Consider $N = 2^{10} = 1024$, then $N^2 = 2^{20} = 10^6$, means very large number of calculations are required. Whereas if we are applying the FFT the calculation is reduced remarkably. The FFT need only 5000 calculations instead significant decline in the time complexity that is reduced to $N/2 \log_2 N$ shown in the Fig. 5(b). Basic idea is to split the sum into 2 subsequences of length N/2 and continue all the way down until you have N/2 subsequences of length 2 as explained in the Fig. 5(b).

2.4 Feature Extraction

Feature Generation: Signal feature analysis is a quantitative strategy that can be utilized to evaluate and recognize basic variations from the norm in various signals. As the signals present in the EEG are hard to order utilizing the shape or surface component extraction is observed to be significant for further arrangement. The 17 spatial features are removed from the two-level wavelet approximation EEG image of each piece by utilizing both prevailing run length and co-occurrence matrix method [20, 21].

The co-occurrence matrix $c\,(d, \emptyset)$ as follow:

$$\emptyset(d, \theta) = [P\,(i, j | d, \theta)], \ 0 < i \leq s, \ 0 < j \leq Rmax \tag{5}$$

where Ng is the maximum signal level and $Rmax$ is the maximum run length. The parameter $P\,(i, j | \theta)$ define the approximate number of runs, where specified signal image contains a run of length for a signal level i in the direction of angle θ.

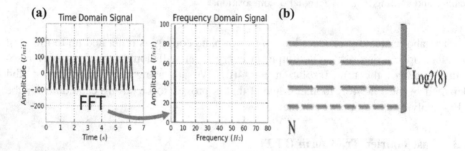

Fig. 5. (a) FFT (b) Subdivision done in FFT

Four prevailing signal-level run length matrices proportionating to $\theta = 0°, 45°, 90°$ *and* $135°$ are enumerate as well the following four prevailing run length signal features such as short-run lowsignal-level emphasis, short-run high-signal-level emphasis, long-run low-signal-level emphasis (LLGE) and long-run high-grey-level emphasis (LHGE) are removed from the two-level wavelet estimation tumor image of each piece's prevailing signal level run length matrix. what's more, take the normal of the considerable number of highlights extricated from four prevailing signal level run length matrix.

The grey-level co-occurrence matrix $c\,(d, \emptyset)$ as follow:

$$\emptyset(d, \theta) = [P\,(i, j | d, \theta)], 0 < i \leq N_s, \ 0 < j \leq N_s \tag{6}$$

where N_s is the maximum signal level. The function $P(i, j|d, \theta)$ is the probability matrix of two signal, which are situated within an inter-sample distance d and direction θ have a signal level i and signal level j.

Four signal-level run length matrices proportionating to $\theta = 0°, 45°, 90°$ *and* $135°$ directions are enumerate with distance $d(= 1, 2)$ and the following 13 textural-based Haralick [reference] features are extricated from the two-level wavelet estimation EEG image of each piece's signal level cooccurrence matrix and take the normal of the considerable number of features separated from four signal level co-event matrices.

Feature Selection: Feature selection is the procedure of decreasing the component of feature vector. Each feature is checked in the process of feature selection. By calculating the mean value of feature in benign patient signals class and malignant patient signal class, Significant features are elected. For illustration, let suppose patient t-test is equipped as a method to separate twain classes. Two-sample patient t-test treated each feature individually. It is feigned that both classes of data values are assigned normally and had akin variance. Test statistics are calculated as follows

$$ t = \left(\frac{X_b - X_m}{\sqrt{\frac{V_{arb}}{n_b} + \frac{V_{arm}}{n_m}}} \right) \tag{7} $$

where, X_b and X_m express mean values from benign and malignant patient classes. V_{arb} and V_{arm} express variances of benign and malignant patients' classes. n_b and n_m be expressed by of numbers of instance in each class. This t value pursue patient t-test with $n_b + n_m - 2$ degree of freedom. The significant P-value is calculated by test statistics and degrees of freedom. The optimal features are selected based on the condition $P < 0.001$ if the P-value of the feature is less than 0.001, then the corresponding feature is selected and used for classification.

We selected the six features given below,

Cluster Tendency (CT): It is the measure of similarity of the signals. As we have considered the normal patient and the Parkinsonian patient and use to predict the pre-tremor attacks [22].

Inverse Difference Movement (IDM): It is used to calculate the signal homogeneity of the normal patient and the parkinsonian patient. Homogeneity of the signals are important to differentiate between the normal patient and the Parkinsonian patient [22].

Maximum Probability (MP): The MP tells us the foremost similarity between the signals.

Energy: Energy tells us the signals uniformity. There are many signals in both type of patient, normal as well as parkinsonian. It is an important feature to measure because sometimes the frequency does not provide the information.

Entropy: Entropy measures the irregularity between the signals.

Correlation: It is used to check the association between the signals.

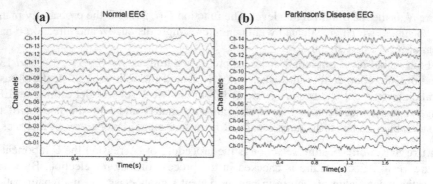

Fig. 6. (a) Normal patient image (b) Parkinsonian patient image.

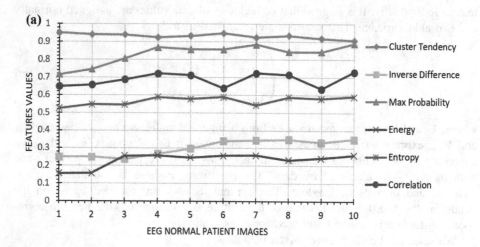

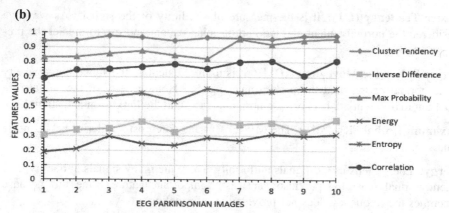

Fig. 7. (a) The comparisons of ten normal patient EEG signals w.r.t the six feature set values, (b) The comparisons of 10 ab-normal patient EEG signals w.r.t the 6 feature set values

3 Analysis and Discussion

For the analysis we have taken the EEG signals of ten control's and ten PD patients, sample is shown as Fig. 6(a) and (b). Feature set contains Cluster Tendency (CT), Inverse Difference Movement (IDM), Maximum Probability (MP), Energy, Entropy and Correlation. The calculated feature set gives us the real insight of the differences between the controls and the patients affected by the PD. The clear differences are depicted by the graph plot, the feature set against the EEG signals of the patients and controls. The detailed could be observed by the Fig. 7(a) and (b). The flow of the graph clearly shows that the plot of the CT declined deflection in the case of the normal patients. As compared to the case of PD patients, a slight inclination is observed proving a little opposite trend for the cluster tendency as in the case of normal patients. Next in order, the Maximum Probability depicted in the graph show much fluctuation in the case of the Normal Patient throughout the graph, on the other hand in the case of PD patients, the deviation is not much more in the beginning but as the graph travels the deviation increases indicating that the signals are quit common but not necessarily. The third qualitative value Correlation the deflection is quite normal in the beginning for both the cases but with the movement towards the end a lot of variation is noted in both the situations normal as well as PD patients. Advancing to the Inverse Difference, the sketch of the graph clearly mentions the difference between the two cases, the normal patient and the abnormal patient. The value lies between 0.25–0.30 in the case of normal patient whereas in the case of PD patients the values lies between 0.30–0.40, can easily be differentiated. The next feature calculated is Energy, same as the IDM, the deviation is quite common can be observed from the plot. The values cached by the normal patients ranges from 0.15–0.26 on the contrary the values for the PD patients ranges form 0.20–0.30. The last quantity undertaken is Entropy, that calculates the degree of randomness between the signals. The values show slight deflection between the signals from the normal patient and PD patients as the values in the case of normal patient floats from 0.52–0.59 and in the case of PD patients the deviation starts from 0.52–0.61.

4 Conclusion

The proposed approach utilizes DWT along with the FFT, the DWT is used due to its advantageous multi-resolution decomposition. The collaborative functionality of FFT to provide frequency analysis and that's too with controlled time complexity.

The DWT has provided the multiresolution decomposition which gives the deep insight of the signals by decomposing the input signal at multiple levels. Some of the signals contains essential information that could be found at finer level. To deduce this cardinal set of properties DWT has been used and refined results has been produced. FFT also provided prominent outcome, this outcome has been processed along with the extracted feature. The output produced illustrated that a lot of deviation have been noticed form the plot between the normal patient and the PD patient in each of the calculated feature. Most of them shows positive deviation while negative deflections have been noticed occasionally.

Acknowledgements. This work was supported in part by the National Natural Science Foundation of China under Grant 61632009, in part by the Guangdong Provincial Natural Science Foundation under Grant 2017A030308006, and in part by the High-Level Talents Program of Higher Education in Guangdong Province under Grant 2016ZJ01.

This work is supported in part by Guangdong Natural Science Foundation of China under Grant No. 2016A030313540, Guangzhou Science and Technology Program under Grant No. 201707010284.

References

1. Bigelow, L.J.: Longitudinal assessment of behaviour and associated biomarkers in a novel progressive model of Parkinson's Disease. University of Prince Edward Island (2018)
2. Zhao, A., et al.: Dual channel LSTM based multi-feature extraction in gait for diagnosis of Neurodegenerative diseases. Knowl.-Based Syst. **145**, 91–97 (2018)
3. Postuma, R.B., Berg, D.: Prodromal Parkinson's disease: the decade past, the decade to come. Mov. Disord. **34**(5), 665–675 (2019)
4. Geman, O., et al.: Ubiquitous healthcare system based on the sensors network and Android internet of things gateway. In: 2018 IEEE SmartWorld, Ubiquitous Intelligence & Computing, Advanced & Trusted Computing, Scalable Computing & Communications, Cloud & Big Data Computing, Internet of People and Smart City Innovation (SmartWorld/SCALCOM/UIC/ATC/CBDCom/IOP/SCI). IEEE (2018)
5. Rizvi, S.Q.A., Wang, G., Chen, J.: A service oriented healthcare architecture (SOHA-CC) based on cloud computing. In: Wang, G., Chen, J., Yang, L.T. (eds.) SpaCCS 2018. LNCS, vol. 11342, pp. 84–97. Springer, Cham (2018). https://doi.org/10.1007/978-3-030-05345-1_7
6. Maria, A.R., Bogdan, H., Sever, P.: Wavelet transform for seizures detection in EEG records. In: 2018 10th International Conference on Electronics, Computers and Artificial Intelligence (ECAI). IEEE (2018)
7. Antony, A.R., et al.: Simultaneous scalp EEG improves seizure lateralization during unilateral intracranial EEG evaluation in temporal lobe epilepsy. Seizure **64**, 8–15 (2019)
8. Barcelon, E.A., et al.: Grand total EEG score can differentiate Parkinson's disease from Parkinson-related disorders. Front. Neurol. **10**, 398 (2019)
9. Muhammad, A., Guojun, W.: Segmentation of calcification and brain hemorrhage with midline detection. In: 2017 IEEE International Symposium on Parallel and Distributed Processing with Applications and 2017 IEEE International Conference on Ubiquitous Computing and Communications (ISPA/IUCC). IEEE (2017)
10. Arif, M., et al.: Maximizing information of multimodality brain image fusion using curvelet transform with genetic algorithm. In: 2014 International Conference on Computer Assisted System in Health. IEEE (2014)
11. Donovan, R., Yu, X.-H.: Motor imagery classification using TSK fuzzy inference neural networks. In: 2018 International Joint Conference on Neural Networks (IJCNN). IEEE (2018)
12. Avidan, M., Sleigh, J.: Introduction to Electroencephalography. Oxford Textbook of Neuroscience and Anaesthesiology (2019)
13. Proverbio, A., Carminati, M.: Finger-counting observation interferes with number processing. Neuropsychologia (2019)
14. Arif, M., Wang, G.: Fast curvelet transform through genetic algorithm for multimodal medical image fusion. Soft Comput. 1–22 (2019)

15. Javaid, Q., et al.: A hybrid technique for de-noising multi-modality medical images by employing cuckoo's search with curvelet transform. Mehran Univ. Res. J. Eng. Technol. **37** (1), 29 (2018)
16. Shaker, M.M.: EEG waves classifier using wavelet transform and Fourier transform. Brain **2**, 3 (2006)
17. Tamersit, K., Djeffal, F.: A computationally efficient hybrid approach based on artificial neural networks and the wavelet transform for quantum simulations of graphene nanoribbon FETs. J. Comput. Electron. 1–13 (2019)
18. Ghorbanian, P., et al.: Discrete wavelet transform EEG features of Alzheimer's disease in activated states. In: 2012 Annual International Conference of the IEEE Engineering in Medicine and Biology Society. IEEE (2012)
19. Kato, K., et al.: Online detection of amplitude modulation of motor-related EEG desynchronization using a lock-in amplifier: Comparison with a fast Fourier transform, a continuous wavelet transform, and an autoregressive algorithm. J. Neurosci. Methods **293**, 289–298 (2018)
20. Arif, M., Alam, K.A., Hussain, M.: Application of data mining using artificial neural network: survey. Int. J. Database Theory Appl. **8**(1), 245–270 (2015)
21. Javaid, Q., et al.: Efficient facial expression detection by using the Adaptive-NeuroFuzzy-Inference-System and the Bezier curve. Sindh Univ. Res. J. SURJ (Sci. Ser.) **48**(3) (2016)
22. Javaid, Q., Arif, M., Talpur, S.: Segmentation and classification of calcification and hemorrhage in the brain using fuzzy C-mean and adaptive neuro-fuzzy inference system. Quaid-e-Awam Univ. Res. J. Eng. Sci. Technol. **15**(1), 50–63 (2016)

Data Sharing and Privacy for Patient IoT Devices Using Blockchain

Gautam Srivastava[1,2]([✉]) [iD], Reza M. Parizi[3] [iD], Ali Dehghantanha[4] [iD],
and Kim-Kwang Raymond Choo[5] [iD]

[1] Department of Mathematics and Computer Science, Brandon University,
Brandon, MB R7A 6A9, Canada
srivastavag@brandonu.ca
[2] Research Center for Interneural Computing, China Medical University,
Taichung 40402, Taiwan, Republic of China
[3] College of Computing and Software Engineering, Kennesaw State University,
Kennesaw, GA 30144, USA
rparizi1@kennesaw.edu
[4] Cyber Science Lab, School of Computer Science, University of Guelph,
Guelph, ON N1G 2W1, Canada
adehghan@uoguelph.ca
[5] Department of Information Systems and Cyber Security,
University of Texas at San Antonio, San Antonio, TX 78249, USA
raymond.choo@fulbrightmail.org

Abstract. Once a fitness fad, wearable and other related Internet of Things (IoT) devices are fast becoming common place in many different smart city applications such as healthcare. However, IoT devices, particularly inexpensive devices, often trade security and privacy for usability. One solution to protect privacy in the healthcare domain which has begun to be explored is blockchain-based technology. However, there are a number of limitations underpinning the use of blockchain, which limits its adoption particularly in applications that require low energy and computational footprints. In this paper, we present a transactional protocol for remote patient monitoring using directed acyclic graphs. We use a newer blockchain protocol called GHOSTDAG in both a public blockchain and a private blockchain. Our novel proposed solution aims to resolve known security issues for healthcare, without affecting scalability (a feature of classic blockchain architecture).

Keywords: Blockchain · Internet of Things · Privacy · Medical device · Smart cities · Healthcare

1 Introduction

We have seen a significant increase in the use of wearable technology in various aspects of life, including in healthcare services. This is not surprising, since with the doctor to patient ratio getting very lopsided, fitting patients with wearable

© Springer Nature Singapore Pte Ltd. 2019
G. Wang et al. (Eds.): iSCI 2019, CCIS 1122, pp. 334–348, 2019.
https://doi.org/10.1007/978-981-15-1301-5_27

technology for monitoring patient activity makes sense. The steep trajectory of Internet of Things (IoT) and access to Internet have contributed to the reality of remote patient monitoring (RPM). Specifically, RPM provides patients with an unconventional yet effective way to monitor their personal health, as shown in Fig. 1. Some known benefits are:

- Allow patients convenience of remote healthcare;
- Stay connected with healthcare providers;
- Reduction of costs (medical); and
- Improve healthcare quality

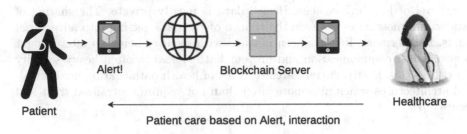

Fig. 1. Remote patient monitoring

RPM devices with respect to personal health are sensor driven electronic devices that are embedded into clothing or attached to a person's body. They are usually user-friendly and connected through a wireless connection, provide accurate feedback, and have some form of notification protocol. We can rely on these devices for accurate vital readings such as blood toxicity, blood pressure and body temperature. Healthcare IoT devices that fall into the RPM general title can be divided as presented in Fig. 2:

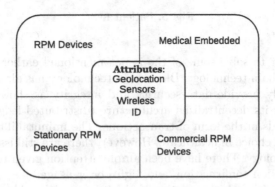

Fig. 2. Healthcare IoT devices

- Stationary RPM Devices - devices are stationary and usually large (e.g., chemotherapy dispensing stations)
- Medical Embedded Devices - are placed inside the body (e.g., pacemakers)
- RPM Devices - wireless devices to monitor some vitals (e.g., blood glucose monitor)
- Commercial RPM Devices - consumer products (e.g., Gear Fit, Apple Watch, etc.)

Internet of Things (IoT) prides itself on its interweaved devices, multi-output machines, sensors, unique identifiers (UIDs) for all involved and data transfer without human involvement as shown in Fig. 3. To accurately and securely share patient health data over multiple locations and/or stakeholders, RPM requires some level of IoT involvement. Health data is mostly private. The sharing of data will in most cases increase the chance of the data getting into adversarial hands. Furthermore, IoT has been plagued with security being an afterthought to ensure fast communication and prevent battery loss to often heavy security algorithms [13]. Lastly, current architectures of health data sharing use centralized architectures which also more often than not require centralized trust and security [7].

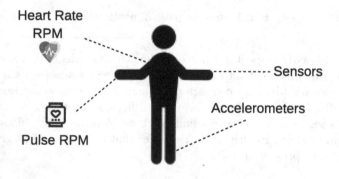

Fig. 3. Patient RPM

In an attempt to solve some of the issues mentioned earlier, we propose to the use of Blockchain technology. Blockchain technology has already shown that it can successfully provide data security and integrity as shown in [24,26]. It is well known for its decentralized architecture (distributed ledger) and also to retain data records in the form of transactions. The immutability of blockchain makes it a logical choice in healthcare. However, there are still issues that plague blockchain technology. There have been ample attention given to its scalability, delays in transaction confirmation, and high power usage.

Since most positive characteristics of blockchain rely on blocks shared to all miners promptly, we can often see delays [1,4]. Delays in propagation are not well suited for healthcare.

In this paper, we introduce a novel and unique blockchain protocol for RPM. This new blockchain protocol makes use of the newly created GHOSTDAG protocol [20], which is well known for both security and throughput. The main noticeable difference in the GHOSTDAG protocol is its use of a directed acyclic graph (DAG), instead of classic long singular blockchains. This directed acyclic graph is known exclusively as blockDAG.

Paper Organization

The rest of this work is organized as follows. In Sect. 2 we present the related work to this research. We then give a brief overview of drawbacks of RPM in Sect. 3. Next, we present our proposed protocol in Sect. 4 and give all technical details is Sect. 5. Lastly, we conclude the paper with Future Work in Sect. 6 and concluding remarks in Sect. 7.

2   Related Work

Mettler was one of the first to look at the possible application of blockchain in healthcare in [15]. He went through an in-depth look at the possible applicable areas of blockchain within healthcare.

Our most recent motivation comes from the Canadian media article entitled "Cybersecurity of medical devices under scrutiny after FDA recalls insulin pumps". It was summarized how the U.S. Food and Drug Administration warned patients as well as healthcare agencies this week regarding a product called Medtronic MiniMed insulin pumps, citing cybersecurity vulnerabilities which could allow someone other than the patient to access the pump and change its settings [25]. With major vulnerabilities still like this present in healthcare, viable options need to be researched, explored, tested and deployed within the near future that not only meet the security needs of patients but also run in an efficient manner.

McGhin et al. surveyed a number of potential research opportunities connecting blockchain and healthcare. They noted that there are strong possibilities using blockchain in healthcare applications through smart contracts [9], detection of fraudulent activity, and verification of ID. However, they still had concerns using classic blockchain technology since it has its own issues that need to be addressed. These issues include many aspects of mining and specific key management issues.

Sullivan et al. dealt with e-Residency using blockchain. Specifically, and how it may take the place of losable objects like passports [23]. They explored the policy and governing related aspects of such a change.

Beninger et al. gave a thorough review of pharmacovigilance. They explored pharmacovigilance with respect to biomedical informatics. Their goal was to provide a discussion starting point for the future of pharmacovigilance as a major field [5].

Azaria *et al.* proposed `MedRec`. `MedRec` is a decentralized system handle Electronic medical records (`EMRs`). They propose the use of classic blockchain technology [2]. Their system gives patients a secure log and quick access to their medical history anywhere. `MedRec` can handle data sharing, authentication, and accountability. They also still had concerns using classic blockchain technology and suggested work on modifications to the classic blockchain protocol.

A recent health startup called `BurstIQ` has explored healthcare and blockchain in detail as shown in Fig. 4. `BurstIQ`'s proprietary blockchain-based big data platform enables a known health provider to securely manage customers's data at scale and perform advanced analytics using the platform's machine learning and collaborative intelligence capabilities. Moreover, this marks the first-time healthcare data and records have been stored and managed on blockchain, making `BurstIQ`'s proprietary blockchain platform the industry's leading Health Insurance Portability and Accountability Act `HIPAA`-compliant secure data platform [19].

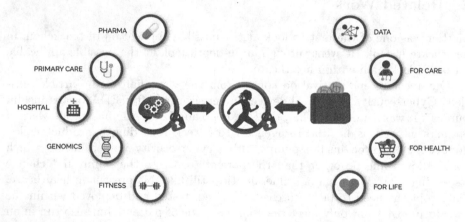

Fig. 4. BurstIQ startup [19]

Finally, in some previous work of ours, we have looked at other applications of blockchain technology as well [9, 17, 18, 21, 22, 26].

3   Drawbacks and Security Issues

RPM systems are mainly concerned with the security of the health data and the efficiency of the transmission of the data. Healthcare data from RPM devices may become a commodity for adversaries. Therefore, being able to secure protected health information has remained a priority of healthcare providers [11, 14]. It was indicated in [3] that a staggering 70% of United States healthcare providers surveyed indicated they had experienced some form of digital data breach in 2018/2019 calendar year. The immutability of information from blocks makes

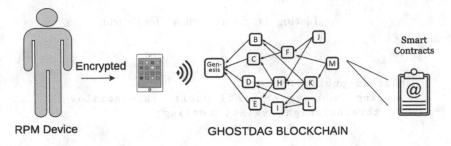

Fig. 5. Health-Data Flow

blockchain technology the best technology for healthcare coupled with its known security strengths makes blockchain worth exploring in this paper. That being said, using classic blockchain from [16] is not viable due to its delays to confirm transactions while also exhibiting high computational needs not suitable for constrained RPM devices. RPMs in the form of wearable devices are often both computationally and energy-consumption wise bounded.

4   Protocol Overview

The patient is affixed with an RPM device. The health-data is sent to their smart device for formatting and aggregation. The aggregated information is then sent on to the blockchain (private) to the respective smart contract. The health data undergoes a full analysis by the smart contract using threshold values. We give an overview of the process in Fig. 5. The desired threshold values as indicated in the smart contract will indicate whether the health-data is in a normal range or not, thus the analysis of health data can be done in real-time. We present a sample smart contract in Listing 41.

If the health reading is normal, no action is taken. However, if abnormal contract will execute the **Alert** function on the public blockchain. The contract will send an alert to the patient's device and authorized health institutions as advised in the contract itself (See Fig. 6). We propose the use of smart contracts like Oracle that can communicate quickly and directly to Oracle enabled smart devices [6].

Listing 41. Smart Contract for Patient

```
1  contract Health {
2      // We can keep most information public in the contract
3
4      address public patient;
5      mapping (address => uint) public thresholdlow,
             thresholdhigh, value, reading;
6
7  //We can create alerts if readings are abnormal
8      event Alert(address fromwho, address towho, uint value);
9
10     // This is the constructor run when contract is created.
11     function Health() public {
12         patient = msg.sender;
13     }
14
15     //This is the main abnormality checker
16     function Send(address receiver, uint value) public {
17         if ((reading[msg.sender] < thresholdhigh) || (
             reading[msg.sender]> thresholdlow)) return;
18
19         emit Alert(msg.sender, receiver, value);
20     }
21 }
```

We note here that no confidential medical information is stored due to HIPAA compliance reasons as mentioned in Sect. 2. The blockchain (public) stores an event when the Alert function executes. The health data gathered by an RPM device will be sent to proper EHR storage units. EHR storage units are most often run by local Medical Health institutions. Ideally as stated in [2], the EHR records could also be stored an a separate secure blockchain that could easily be integrated into our proposed model.

Lastly, treatment details from smart contracts and/or hospitals will be sent to EHR storage units while just the transactional event will be stored on the blockchain (public). The transactions are connected to the EHR system for authentication purposes. Authentication will help with alteration of patient data in the EHR storage units. Nodes on the blockchain will only be permitted to execute smart contracts, not alter them. This will limit visibility of patient data which will in turn assist to reduce data exposure.

5   Proposed Protocol

We break down our protocol into five distinct parts and summarize the protocol flow in Fig. 7

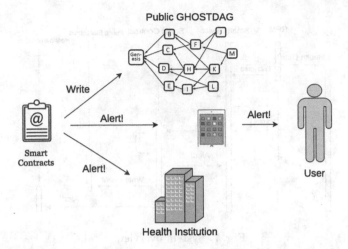

Fig. 6. Smart contracts: alerts for abnormality in readings

- Patient
- Healthcare Institution (Hospital)
- RPM on Patient
- GHOSTDAG blockchain
- Other Authorized Entities

The detail of the proposed protocol are as follows:

1. **Patient**
   All health related data is collected directly from patients [8]. Some examples could be heart-beat, blood glucose levels, thyroid function, bio-markers or even walking distance. The patients own the data. They are independently responsible for data access being granted to any other parties. If the patient is in need of medical treatment, they can share their health data with the desired entity by granting them access. At the end of treatment, patient may choose to deny further access or set specific time periods for granting and revoking access.

2. **Healthcare Institution**
   Healthcare institutions are appointed in some manner by Medical health bodies, other stakeholders, or directly by patients to perform some form of medical action (tests,treatment, etc.). Healthcare institutions can directly request patients to access their data and also medical treatment history if pertinent. Institutions may be able to setup alerts to be able to provide medical treatment once notified from a smart device controlled by the patient.

3. **RPM devices**
   RPM devices are sensor driven devices used to collect the pertinent health data. RPM devices will be streaming data to smart devices like smartphones and raw medical data is transferred promptly. These state of the art devices

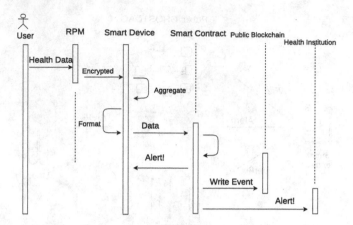

Fig. 7. System overview

will be able to measure many different types of vitals without ever being near a medical treatment facility.

4. `GHOSTDAG` **Blockchain**

   The use of two blockchains is needed, a private blockchain where smart contracts are used to monitor the patient's own healthdata. The smart contracts once setup can effectively issue alerts which can be written to the public blockchain. These transactions that are written to the public blockchain. The private and public blockchains are based on directed acyclic graphs which will be described in detail in Sect. 5.4.

5. **Authorizes Entities**

   A patient may request the sharing of their health data with a myriad of different types of stakeholders. Some examples include family members, insurance companies, medical units or perhaps even just to tender for health insurance.

5.1   Model Details

We use the following terminology for this section:

- Patient: P_i
- Raw Data: D
- RPM wearable device for Patient P: RPM_i
- Smart Device of Patient P: SD_i
- Encrypted Data: ED
- Private Blockchain: PRB
- Smart Contract for Patient P for condition C: SC_i^C
- Public Blockchain: PUB
- Symmetric Key: k_{sym}
- Asymmetric Key Pair: (rk_{priv}, rk_{pub})
- Symmetric Encryption function: $SE(data, k_{sym})$
- Asymmetric Encryption Function: $AE(data, rk_{priv})$

5.2   Technical Details

In this section, we will use an example for Patient P_i suffering from condition C to illustrate the use of the protocol. First, P_i will be equipped with RPM_i to monitor a given condition C. Raw sensor data D generated by patient P_i will be sensed through RPM_i and using a secure symmetrically encrypted path transmitted from RPM_i to SD_i using $SE(D, k_{sym})$ creating ED_1. There may be a processing step at SD_i to format ED for Private blockchain PRB to be used to compare with SC_i^C for a given condition C. Once SD_i sends the data to PRB, a smart contract SC_i^C for the specific condition C will compare reading with a normal range as specified in the contract. At this point, no further action is taken provided the readings are normal. However, if the readings are abnormal, an alert is generated by SC_i^C, sending alerts back to SD_i and authorized entities (Hospital, etc), while also sending a transaction write request to PUB using $AE(D, rk_{priv})$ generating ED_2. Authorized entities can access data ED_2 using there assigned public key rk_{pub}. In Sect. 5.3 we will outline the system requirements that will need to be maintained for security and privacy.

5.3   Requirements

In this section we give details and list some requirements the deployed system must possess. We give comments to requirements our system can achieve and for other we leave as future work.

1. **Strong Authentication**
   A major issue in healthcare is that most devices connect nowadays through a wireless connection. This opens up wireless data being accessed by adversarial users. Strong authentication of users should alleviate such problems, where users will have to prove who they are [10]. We propose using symmetric encryption in the private blockchain and asymmetric encryption in the public blockchain respectively. For accurate timestamps all devices must be logged into an IoT system. Only authorized entities can access health data as instructed by the patient from the public blockchain using their public key rk_{pub} as shared securely by patient to grant access.

2. **Scalability and Security**
   The GHOSTDAG blockchain is leaps ahead of the classic blockchain protocol in both security and speed of use. Its use here will ensure both scalability and security.

3. **Mutual Authentication:**
   In real-time, the user and RPM devices must authenticate one another. This way only trusted channels are used for communication. We propose a symmetric encryption scheme to ensure mutual authentication.

4. **Confidentiality**
   Any health related data can be considered highly sensitive and RPM devices connect only through a wireless connection. Therefore, health related data should stay private from common attacks like eavesdropping. Patient's data

needs to be transmitted only in encrypted form. As seen in Fig. 7 and details in Sect. 5.2, all transmitted data is shared in encrypted form.

5. **Session Key Establishment**
   There should always be a session key between a patient's device(s) and their respective RPM. This way, all communication can take place without fear of being compromised.
6. **Low Communication and Computational Cost**
   RPM devices are resource constrained devices, often created with low energy footprints and small CPUs. Moreover, healthcare application's on smart devices need some flexibility to run in the background not overly draining the device's resources. The protocol must be efficient both in computational, computational, and energy cost. The encryption function at the RPM device level needs to be light in nature. In [13] we propose such a scheme for encryption and decryption that are light in nature suitable for IoT. Moreover, use of a provable efficient blockchain protocol like GHOSTDAG, we ensure that the public and private blockchain will remain low impact [20].
7. **Fresh Data**
   Generally, patient data needs to be monitored at regularly. There must be some form of assurance that the data presented outside of the RPM device is recent. This protects against replay attacks.
8. **Secure Against Popular Attacks**
   Some level of defense should be provided against:
   - replay attacks
   - impersonation attack
   - stolen-verifier attack
   - password guessing attack
   - information-leakage attack

   Our use of symmetric encryption, asymmetric encryption, and secure blockchain protocol in combination provides relief against these types of attacks. We leave testing of this for Future Work as given in Sect. 6.
9. **User-Friendliness**
   Every aspect that involves the patient and other user's must be user-friendly.

5.4   GHOSTDAG Protocol

GHOSTDAG protocol, a variant of another protocol called PHANTOM [20], is a generalization of the original long singular blockchain protocol. The GHOSTDAG blockchain uses a directed acyclic graph (DAG) to structure the blocks. The blocks are placed in a k-cluster as given in Fig. 8. Figure 8 includes coloring of blocks. We see the block red in color as blocks outside the cluster. The blue blocks are inside the cluster. The largest n-cluster of blocks within a given DAG: A, B, C, D, F, G, I, J where $k = 3$ blue in color. Within a cluster, each block has ≤ 3 blue blocks in its anticone. For blocks E, H, and K, red in color have > 3 elements in their anticone respectively. Setting the value of k as 3, the upper limit is set to be 4 blocks that can be created per unit of time. GHOSTDAG finds

GHOSTDAG BLOCKCHAIN

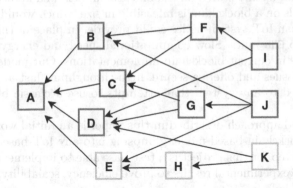

Fig. 8. k-cluster of GHOSTDAG (Color figure online)

a cluster using a greedy algorithm which differs from how PHANTOM does it. The optimization version of the maximum k-cluster problem is NP hard as shown in [12]. This sadly makes the PHANTOM protocol less practical for large blockDAGs. In contrast, finding a k-cluster for $k = 3$ is a feasible problem. This allows the GHOSTDAG protocol using a greedy algorithm more suitable for actual real world implementation.

6   Future Work

As a preliminary model, there is ample room for future work to the novel work presented here. A natural first step would be a simulation environment, to help gauge the performance of the protocol. Furthermore, an in-depth comparative analysis with some existing protocols would show the effectiveness of our scheme. That being said, the work in healthcare blockchain is still in its infancy with limited work presented thus far. To assist to demonstrate specific security goals, performance, limitations, computation complexity, and communication overhead in the IoT-based RPM environment, a simulation environment can help answer some of these questions as a natural next step. In a different direction, a mathematical overview of the schemes beyond what is presented here will also give some provable security guarantees of the protocol.

7   Conclusion

We utilized a GHOSTDAG blockchain that makes use of smart contracts to monitor the health data of patients. Smart contracts are used to trigger alerts when appropriate using patients health data and also record the details of events in blocks in either a private or public blockchain, based on the sensitivity of the actual data that needs to be stored. In a vital HIPAA-compliant manner for actual use, our model successfully delivers health-related notifications. Patient health information is not openly stored on the blockchain. It is well known that placing all health records on a blockchain is infeasible in size, which would require much more storage than IoT system nodes could provide. In place of this health data is transferred to EHR units. Slow computational speed and energy consumption are major issues in current blockchain implementations. Our model attempts to alleviate these issues and offers a secure, high-throughput, fast and reliable RPM system compared to any system that attempts to use a classic blockchain RPM system.

The proposed approach described in this paper is an initial work in progress that offers a blockchain-based model glimpsing into any IoT-based RPM system. The main next step for this project is a test-base able to implement the protocol to provide some experimental results to prove efficiency, scalability, security, and computational load.

References

1. Amiri, W.A., Baza, M., Banawan, K., Mahmoud, M.M.E.A., Alasmary, W., Akkaya, K.: Privacy-preserving smart parking system using blockchain and private information retrieval. CoRR abs/1904.09703 (2019). http://arxiv.org/abs/1904.09703

2. Azaria, A., Ekblaw, A., Vieira, T., Lippman, A.: MedRec: using blockchain for medical data access and permission management. In: 2016 2nd International Conference on Open and Big Data (OBD), pp. 25–30, August 2016. https://doi.org/10.1109/OBD.2016.11

3. Bayern, M.: Why 70% of healthcare orgs have suffered data breaches (2019). https://www.techrepublic.com/article/why-70-of-healthcare-orgs-have-suffered-data-breaches/. Accessed 17 July 2019

4. Baza, M., Lasla, N., Mahmoud, M., Abdallah, M.M.: B-ride: ride sharing with privacy-preservation, trust and fair payment atop public blockchain. CoRR abs/1906.09968 (2019). http://arxiv.org/abs/1906.09968

5. Beninger, P., Ibara, M.A.: Pharmacovigilance and biomedical informatics: a model for future development. Clin. Ther. **38**(12), 2514–2525 (2016)

6. ConsenSys: A visit to the oracle (2016). https://media.consensys.net/a-visit-to-the-oracle-de9097d38b2f

7. Dwivedi, A.D., Malina, L., Dzurenda, P., Srivastava, G.: Optimized blockchain model for internet of things based healthcare applications. In: 42nd International Conference on Telecommunications and Signal Processing, TSP 2019, Budapest, Hungary, 1–3 July 2019, pp. 135–139 (2019). https://doi.org/10.1109/TSP.2019.8769060

8. Dwivedi, A.D., Srivastava, G., Dhar, S., Singh, R.: A decentralized privacy-preserving healthcare blockchain for IoT. Sensors **19**(2), 326 (2019). https://doi.org/10.3390/s19020326

9. Homayoun, S., Dehghantanha, A., Parizi, R.M., Choo, K.R.: A blockchain-based framework for detecting malicious mobile applications in app stores. In: 32nd IEEE Canadian Conference of Electrical and Computer Engineering (IEEE CCECE 2019) (2019)

10. Kumar, P., Lee, S.G., Lee, H.J.: E-sap: efficient-strong authentication protocol for healthcare applications using wireless medical sensor networks. Sensors **12**(2), 1625–1647 (2012). https://doi.org/10.3390/s120201625. https://www.mdpi.com/1424-8220/12/2/1625

11. Liu, V., Musen, M.A., Chou, T.: Data breaches of protected health information in the united states. JAMA **313**(14), 1471–1473 (2015)

12. Mahajan, M., Nimbhorkar, P., Varadarajan, K.: The planar k-means problem is NP-hard. In: Das, S., Uehara, R. (eds.) WALCOM 2009. LNCS, vol. 5431, pp. 274–285. Springer, Heidelberg (2009). https://doi.org/10.1007/978-3-642-00202-1_24

13. Malina, L., Srivastava, G., Dzurenda, P., Hajny, J., Fujdiak, R.: A secure publish/-subscribe protocol for internet of things. IACR Cryptology ePrint Archive 2019, 740 (2019). https://eprint.iacr.org/2019/740

14. Malina, L., Srivastava, G., Dzurenda, P., Hajny, J., Fujdiak, R.: A secure publish/subscribe protocol for internet of things. In: Proceedings of the 14th International Conference on Availability, Reliability and Security, ARES 2019, Canterbury, UK, 26–29 August 2019, pp. 75:1–75:10 (2019). https://doi.org/10.1145/3339252.3340503

15. Mettler, M.: Blockchain technology in healthcare: the revolution starts here. In: 2016 IEEE 18th International Conference on e-Health Networking, Applications and Services (Healthcom), pp. 1–3. IEEE (2016)

16. Nakamoto, S.: Bitcoin: a peer-to-peer electronic cash system (2008)

17. Parizi, R.M., Dehghantanha, A., Choo, K.R., Singh, A.: Empirical vulnerability analysis of automated smart contracts security testing on blockchains. In: Proceedings of the 28th Annual International Conference on Computer Science and Software Engineering, CASCON 2018, Markham, Ontario, Canada, 29–31 October 2018, pp. 103–113 (2018). https://dl.acm.org/citation.cfm?id=3291303

18. Parizi, R.M., Homayoun, S., Yazdinejad, A., Dehghantanha, A., Choo, K.R.: Integrating privacy enhancing techniques into blockchains using sidechains. In: 32nd IEEE Canadian Conference of Electrical and Computer Engineering (IEEE CCECE 2019) (2019)

19. Pennic, F.: Healthcare Blockchain Startup BurstIQ Secures $5M Investment (2018). https://hitconsultant.net/2018/02/23/healthcare-blockchain-startup-burstiq-secures-5m. Accessed 17 July 2019

20. Sompolinsky, Y., Zohar, A.: PHANTOM, GHOSTDAG: two scalable blockDAG protocols. IACR Cryptology ePrint Archive 2018, 104 (2018)

21. Srivastava, G., Dwivedi, A.D., Singh, R.: Crypto-democracy: a decentralized voting scheme using blockchain technology. In: Proceedings of the 15th International Joint Conference on e-Business and Telecommunications, ICETE 2018. SECRYPT, Porto, Portugal, 26–28 July 2018, vol. 2, pp. 674–679 (2018). https://doi.org/10.5220/0006881906740679

22. Srivastava, G., Dwivedi, A.D., Singh, R.: PHANTOM protocol as the new crypto-democracy. In: Computer Information Systems and Industrial Management - Proceedings of the 17th International Conference, CISIM 2018, Olomouc, Czech Republic, 27–29 September 2018, pp. 499–509 (2018). https://doi.org/10.1007/978-3-319-99954-8_41

23. Sullivan, C., Burger, E.: E-residency and blockchain. Comput. Law Secur. Rev. **33**(4), 470–481 (2017)

24. Taylor, P.J., Dargahi, T., Dehghantanha, A., Parizi, R.M., Choo, K.K.R.: A systematic literature review of blockchain cyber security. Digit. Commun. Netw. (2019)

25. Vomiero, J.: Cybersecurity of medical devices under scrutiny after FDA recalls insulin pumps (2019). https://globalnews.ca/news/5446037/insulin-pump-medical-implant-cyber-attack-fda/. Accessed 17 July 2019
26. Yazdinejad, A., Parizi, R.M., Dehghantanha, A., Choo, K.R.: Blockchain-enabled authentication handover with efficient privacy protection in SDN-based 5G networks. IEEE Trans. Netw. Sci. Eng. 1–14 (2019). https://doi.org/10.1109/TNSE.2019.2937481

Light Weight Authentication and Key Establishment Protocol for Smart Vehicles Communication in Smart City

Venkatasamy Sureshkumar[✉], S. Anandhi, R. Madhumathi, and N. Selvarajan

Department of Applied Mathematics and Computational Sciences,
PSG College of Technology, Coimbatore 641004, India
sand.amcs@psgtech.ac.in, san@amc.psgtech.ac.in, madhumathi2698@gmail.com,
eswar.selvarajan@gmail.com

Abstract. The smart vehicular technology in the smart city employs intelligent commitments to the passengers to enhance traffic efficiency and safety with more enjoyable riding in the driving environment. However, the tremendous growth of wireless communication technology makes the smart vehicle communication more vulnerable to potential security attacks. Authentication and key agreement protocol is the basic requirement to establish a secure communication among vehicles in the open network. Though several security schemes have been designed in the literature to establish communication among the smart vehicles, each of them have their own limitations such as requirement of heavy computation, limited to maximum of three entities and so on. In this paper, we design a lightweight four party authentication protocol that employs the strong reinforcement of fog and cloud servers. The formal proof of correctness of the designed protocol has been provided using GNY logic. The protocol is compared with the existing related protocols in the aspects security features, communication cost, computational cost and storage cost. In all these aspects, our protocol outperforms the others' protocol.

Keywords: Smart vehicle · Fog computing · Authentication · GNY logic

1 Introduction

The evolution of smart city paved way to the growth of technology to a great extent. This includes Internet of Things (IoT), Information and Communication Technology (ICT) which are the integral parts of the present and future smart cities [4]. This infrastructure can be a major part of various sectors like transport, healthcare and so on. Also ICT is the driving force behind important innovations in the automotive industry. In recent decades, mobile communication has taken our lifestyle to a higher standard allowing us to exchange information anywhere at any moment [11]. IoT consists of networked physical or virtual objects like devices that are inter-connected with one other for exchanging messages over

© Springer Nature Singapore Pte Ltd. 2019
G. Wang et al. (Eds.): iSCI 2019, CCIS 1122, pp. 349–362, 2019.
https://doi.org/10.1007/978-981-15-1301-5_28

the internet. These objects can be assigned IP address or unique identities, to help them in transmitting and receiving information in network [7]. When this is employed in particular for vehicles they form the Internet of Vehicles (IoV), these vehicles are also called smart vehicles [3]. A Vehicular Ad hoc Network (VANET) is a technology in the smart city that employs moving vehicles as entities and creates a mobile network between them based on the Mobile Ad hoc Network (MANET). The vehicles in VANET are equipped with sensors, On Board Unit (OBU) and Application Unit (AU) for communication between vehicles. These units are also used to exchange messages between vehicles and the Road Side Unit (RSU). There are sensors on vehicles and at certain landmarks to gather information like road damage, blockage, accident, traffic jams and transmit them to other entities of VANET. Intelligent Transport System (ITS) is an efficient way to improve performance of vehicle flow in roads. The goals of ITS includes collecting information of traffic density, updates traffic congestion and report it to vehicles to choose a better path for transport. They also send warning about accidents to avoid further collisions among the vehicles. The communication in this case is wireless and so it is prone to various security issues. Attackers may transmit rumours which may affect the other entities in the network [3,14,18]. Security should be provided to prevent attacks by vehicle dangerously reacting by receiving erroneous messages. The technology of VANET is widely accepted and has received immense attention worldwide. The current work is to make this network secured and privacy preserving for the entities (users). Entities should have mutual authentication for the network of VANET to be more secure, the messages transmitted may also have life critical information. The authentication of vehicles is classified into two classes, Public Key Infrastructure (PKI) and ID based cryptography. PKI require additional communication and cause heavy overheads whereas ID based cryptography reduce the overheads [11,15].

1.1 Architecture Description

The overall architecture that depicts the VANET system is shown in Fig. 1. A VANET with security measures consists of various components like, RSU, Trusted Authority (TA), Vehicles equipped with OBUS, Fog server and a Cloud server. The communication among them takes place at different levels. The communications takes place in various types, Vehicle to Vehicle (V2V), Vehicle to Trusted Authority (V2T), Vehicle to Road Side Units (V2R), Road Side Units to Vehicle (R2V), Vehicle to Fog Server (V2F), Road Side Units to Fog Server (R2F), Fog Server to Cloud Server (F2C). A vehicle has to be registered and get its pseudonyms from the TA and it is referenced with that name in the network. When one vehicle communicates with other, the authentication is based on the pseudonym of the vehicle which is an entity in the network model [17]. An entity can only check the authenticity of another entity and is denied from knowing the personal details like the original identity of the message sender. This preserves privacy of the entity avoiding attacks on the vehicle forwarding the message. The received message in an entity is authenticated with the nearest RSU to know the correctness. RSUs are fixed at certain distance in roads and mainly in junction

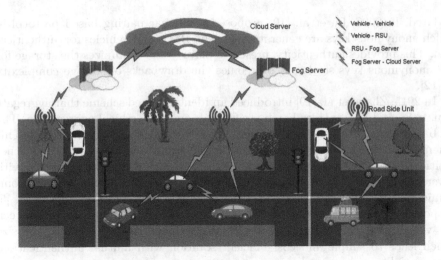

Fig. 1. Architecture of VANET

of roads. Any information sent by an entity is cross checked with RSU and then forwarded to other entities. Any information regarding the entity or around the entity is stored in its OBU, Fog and Cloud Servers for authentication and key management process or for future references [11]. The communications such as V2V, V2R, R2V, V2F, F2C all takes place through internet and so are wireless communications which are vulnerable to attacks. Our aim in this paper is to provide an internet based communication which withstands all such attacks and preserves the privacy, authenticity and integrity of the network components.

1.2 Contribution

In this paper, we have proposed a ECC based lightweight four party authentication and key establishment technique for VANET. The correctness of the proposed protocol has been proven using the formal method GNY logic. The protocol is then compared with the existing related protocol in four aspects.

2 Related Work

As everything is being digitalised the need for security keeps on increasing. This section discusses about the existing protocols and their comparison with our scheme.

In 2007, Raya-Hubaux [12] proposed a scheme for the security of vehicular network in order to establish a secure communication between two vehicles. In this, the scheme require many private keys and anonymous certificates. In addition, corresponding keys to be updated and loaded from time to time. These keys and anonymous certificates are stored in the certification authority for reference. This requires more storage as the key and certificates are being keep on updated. In 2008, Lu et al. [10] proposed a bilinear pairing based protocol in which anonymous keys are generated between RSUs and vehicles for authentication. This provides authenticity, preserves privacy and minimizes the storage for the anonymous keys so that it overcomes the drawbacks of storage complexity in [12].

In 2015, Zhang et al. [19] introduced an identity based scheme that aggregate signatures and also enables batch verification and hierarchical aggregation. The ID based signatures generated by vehicles is verified based on the batch. This scheme reduces the storage and transmission overheads of vehicles and other entities. Also, their scheme possess the provision of verify the messages with lower latency and faster response. Finally, the scheme establishes a secure communication between the vehicle and the road side unit. In 2016, Dua et al. [5] proposed a scheme based on ECC for secure message communication between the vehicle and cluster head. The proposed scheme requires smaller key size which leads to simple and cost efficient solution with mutual authentication, confidentiality and forward secrecy.

Recently Dang et al. [3] proposed ID based authentication and key agreement scheme to build a secure communication between two vehicles. But, their scheme is vulnerable to replay attack, man-in-the-middle attack and also the scheme does not provide vehicle anonymity.

The above mentioned all the schemes [3,10,12,19] are restricted only to two party authentication either vehicle to vehicle or vehicle to RSU. And none of these scheme achieves mutual authentication between vehicle to vehicle via road side unit.

In 2012, Lu et al. [9] has proposed a framework for V2V communication via RSU with privacy preservation for VANETs. They use self-generated pseudonyms instead of their real names for privacy preserving. They use ID based signature (IBS) scheme for authentication between RSUs and vehicles. In 2016, Zhang et al. [20] proposed a protocol which has multiple trusted authority which helps in verifying many messages simultaneously from the vehicle via RSU. This protocol requires tamper-resistance devices in the OBU of the vehicle. In 2017, Wazid et al. [18] proposed a new decentralized lightweight authentication scheme with key agreement for VANETs. This scheme undergoes three types of authentication. First between the vehicles, second between vehicles and their corresponding cluster heads and the last is between vehicles and road side units. In the same year, Liu et al. [8] proposed a protocol for privacy preserving and security through dual authentication for different scenarios. The key management process is comparatively easier in this protocol. Even though [8] supports vehicle to vehicle communication, it requires human assistance for login into the system. It not includes the facility of fog server and it requires the active involvement of trusted authority during authentication. Their scheme is not light weight as it is designed using bilinear pairing function. Dua et al. [4] proposed a scheme based on Elliptic Curve Cryptography (ECC) with two level authentication. The vehicles in the network are clustered and they choose a head for each cluster. Comparatively this scheme has less overhead and latency and high reliability for message exchange.

Table 1. List of notations

Notation	Description
$list$	Consists of V_j, L_j, T_1^j
F_{ID_k}	Identity of kth fog server
r_1, r_2	Pseudo random numbers
CS_{pub}	Public key of the cloud server
s	Private key of the cloud server
Z_q^*	Prime field
v_i	Secret parameter between CS and i^{th} vehicle
f_k	Secret parameter between CS and k^{th} fog server
sk_{fv_i}	Secret key between fog server and i^{th} vehicle
$E_k M$	Symmetric encryption of message M using the key K
$K_{V_i V_j}$	Shared session key between i^{th} vehicle and j^{th} vehicle
T_1, T_2, T_3	Timestamps
V_{ID_i}	Vehicle identity of ith vehicle

The communicated data in the VANET need to be stored for future references. As the number of user is drastically high, the memory needed to store their data is very large. So, cloud computing technology is being used to store those data efficiently. But, the cloud servers are located far away from the vehicles and other components so it requires a high bandwidth for communication among them. To overcome this issue, Fog servers are located at certain distances to communicate with the VANET and the data is sent to cloud from these fog servers.

Recently Ma et al. [11] has designed a new authentication key agreement protocol which doesn't use bilinear pairing. To store data efficiently and effectively they have used cloud computing based fog servers. This overcomes the high bandwidth and latency issue which prevails indirect cloud and entity communication. Wazid et al. [17] introduced a scheme based on authenticated key management protocol on IoVs based on fog-computing called AKM-IoV.

All the above mentioned schemes have their own limitations such as requirement of heavy computation, limited to maximum of three entities and so on. In this paper, we design a lightweight four party authentication protocol that employs the strong reinforcement of fog and cloud servers.

3   Proposed Protocol

The proposed protocol is composed of four phases initial set up phase, vehicle registration phase, fog registration phase and login-authentication phase. The various notations used in the description of the protocol are listed in Table 1. The four phases are detailed as follows.

3.1 Initial Setup Phase

The Cloud Server (CS) holds responsible for the initial set of the secret and public parameters. As the protocol design completely based on the lightweight (bilinear pairing free) ECC, CS constructs an elliptic curve $E(a, b) : y^2 = x^3 + ax^2 + b$ over the prime field Z_q^*. The cloud server also constructs a cyclic additive group G whose points are in $E(a, b)$ with generator P. In addition, the CS selects $s \in Z_q^*$ as its private key and constructs its public key as $CS_{pub} = s \cdot P$. The cloud server publishes the public parameters $\langle E(a, b), Z_q^*, CS_{pub}, h(\cdot) \rangle$ after the selection of the one-way hash function $h : (0, 1)^* \rightarrow Z_q^*$.

3.2 Vehicle Registration Phase

The vehicle V_i selects its identity V_{ID_i} and sends it to CS for the registration. Upon the receipt of the V_{ID_i} from the vehicle, CS computes $v_i = h(V_{ID_i} || s)$ as a secret parameter for the vehicle V_i and sends it to the vehicle through the secure channel so that it can store it in its tamper-resistant module. At the same time, CS stores v_i corresponds to V_{ID_i} in its database.

3.3 Fog Server Registration Phase

Similar to vehicle registration phase, fog server F_k completes its registration with CS before the communication take place. The fog server F_k selects its identity F_{ID_k} and sends it to CS for the registration. Upon the receipt of the F_{ID_k} from the fog, CS computes $f_k = h(F_{ID_k} || s)$ as a secret parameter for the fog server F_k and sends it to the fog through the secure channel. At the same time, CS stores f_k corresponds to F_{ID_k} in its database.

3.4 Login and Authentication

If the vehicle V_i wants to identify and communicate with an arbitrary vehicle V_j which is in a particular location L, V_i contacts the fog server F_k whose range can cover location L. This communication requires the mutual authentication between V_i and F_k and an establishment of a shared secret key sk_{fv_i}. Since the vehicle has been registered at CS and not at fog server, F_k needs to fetch the details about V_i from CS so that F_k authenticates V_i. For which F_k needs to contact CS and therefore the communication also requires the mutual authentication between CS and F_k.

Step V2F: 1 The vehicle V_i selects a random number $r_1 \in Z_q^*$, Computes

$$C_1 = r_1 \cdot P$$
$$C_2 = v_i \cdot P$$
$$C_4 = r_1 \cdot CS_{pub}$$
$$C_3 = V_{ID_i} \oplus C_4$$
$$A_1^i = h(T_1 || C_1 || C_2)$$
$$Auth_V = h(C_2 || V_{ID_i} || T_1)$$

where T_1 is the current timestamp at V_i. The vehicle sends the message $M_1 = \langle C_1, C_3, A_1, Auth_V, T_1 \rangle$ to the fog server F_k through the road side unit at its nearest.

Step F2CS: 2 After receiving M_1 from V_i, the fog server F_k extracts A_1^i, C_1 from M_1 and stores them in its database corresponds to T_1. Further, F_k selects $r_2 \in_R Z_q^*$ and computes

$$C_5 = r_2 \cdot P$$
$$C_6 = f_k \cdot C_5$$
$$Auth_{FS} = h(C_6 \| F_{ID_k} \| T_2)$$

where T_2 is the current timestamp at F_k. Now, the fog server sends the message $M_2 = \langle C_1, C_3, C_5, F_{ID_k}, Auth_V, Auth_{FS}, T_1, T_2 \rangle$. It can be noted that the message M_2 contains the F_{ID_k} as a plaintext, because the fog server does not require anonymity.

Step CS2F: 3 The cloud server extracts f_k corresponds to F_{ID_k} from its database and computes

$$C_6^* = f_k \cdot C_5$$
$$Auth_{FS}^* = h(C_6^* \| F_{ID_k} \| T_2)$$

Now CS checks the correctness of the computed $Auth_{FS}^*$ with the received $Auth_{FS}$. If the check $Auth_{FS}^* \stackrel{?}{=} Auth_{FS}$ is success, CS accepts F_k as an authenticated fog server and rejects otherwise. In addition, to authenticate V_i, CS computes $C_4^* = s \cdot C_1$ and $V_{ID_i}^* = C_3 \oplus C_4^*$. The cloud server extracts v_i corresponds to $V_{ID_i}^*$ from its database and computes

$$C_2^* = v_i \cdot P$$
$$Auth_V^* = h(C_2^* \| V_{ID_i}^* \| T_1)$$

The cloud server checks the correctness of the computed $Auth_V^*$ with the received $Auth_V$. If $Auth_V^* = Auth_V$ does not satisfies then CS rejects V_i and inform the same to F_k otherwise V_i is an authenticated vehicle. Then, CS computes

$$A_2 = f_k \cdot CS_{pub}$$
$$A_3 = A_2 \oplus C_2^*$$
$$Auth_{CS} = h(C_1 \| f_k \| T_3)$$

and sends the message $M_3 = \langle A_3, Auth_{CS}, T_3 \rangle$ to F_k.

Step F2V: 4 After receiving M_3, F_k computes $Auth_{CS}^* = h(C_1 \| f_k \| T_3)$ checks it with the received $Auth_{CS}$. If the check fails, CS is not authenticated, F_k resends the M_2 to CS otherwise F_k computes

$$A_2^* = f_k \cdot CS_{pub}$$
$$C_2^{**} = A_3 \oplus A_2^*$$
$$A_1^* = h(C_1 || C_2^{**} || T_1)$$

The fog server checks $A_1^* \overset{?}{=} A_1$, if not V_i is rejected otherwise F_k computes $A_4 = h(C_1 || C_2^{**} || T_1)$ and sends $M_4 = \langle C_5, A_4, list \rangle$ to V_i. By the same time, F_k computes the shared key $sk_{fv_i} = h(C_2^{**} || C_3 || C_5 || T_1)$. It is to be noted that the message M_4 has the component message $list$ which contains the details of the vehicles V_j, their locations L_j and other details for communication.

Step V2F: 5 After receiving the message M_4, the V_i computes $A_4^* = h(C_1 || C_2 || T_1)$ and checks the correctness of the computed A_4^* with the received A_4. If $A_4^* = A_4$ holds good then the F_k is authenticated and then the vehicle constructs the session key sk_{fv_i}. Now, V_i look into the $list$ obtained from M_4, selects V_j based on L_j, computes $S_1 = E_{sk_{fv_i}}\{V_j, L_j\}$ and sends $M_5 = \langle S_1 \rangle$ to F_k.

Step F2V: 6 Upon the receipt of the message M_5 from V_i, the fog server F_k decrypts the cipher S_1 and gets V_j. As V_j is in connection with F_k, it extracts A_1^j and T_1^j of V_j from its database and computes $S_2 = E_{sk_{fv_j}}\{A_1^i, T_1^i\}$. Finally, F_k sends the message $M_6 = \langle E_{sk_{fv_i}}\{V_j, T_1^j, A_1^j, S_2\} \rangle$ to V_i.

Step V2V: 7 After receiving the message M_6, V_i decrypts, extracts A_1^j, T_1^j and computes $D_1 = h(A_1^i || T_1^i)$. Now V_i sends $M_7 = \langle D_1, S_2 \rangle$ to V_j and at the same time V_i computes the shared key $K_{v_i v_j} = h(A_1^i || A_1^j || T_1^i || T_1^j)$.

Step V2V: 8 The vehicle V_j extracts S_2 from M_7, decrypts it using the shared key sk_{fv_j} and obtains A_1^i, T_1^i. Now, V_j computes $D_1^* = h(A_1^i || T_1^i)$ and checks the correctness of $D_1^* \overset{?}{=} D_1$. If it is not satisfied V_j aborts the connection with V_i otherwise V_j computes the shared key $K_{v_i v_j} = h(A_1^i || A_1^j || T_1^i || T_1^j)$, prepares an acknowledgement Ack and sends the message $M_8 = \langle E_{K_{v_i v_j}}\{Ack\} \rangle$.

4   Analysis

Formal analysis of security protocols discovers many security flaws and results in a better understanding of how to design robust protocols [13,16]. The proposed protocol is verified for mutual authentication among the participating entities vehicles (V_i, V_j), fog server, and cloud server. In this section, the proposed protocol is analyzed using GNY logic [1,2,6]. The protocol messages generated by the parser are as follows.

Table 2. Assumptions

Vehicle V_i	Fog server	Cloud server
$A1 : V_i \ni CS_{pub}$	$A7 : FS \ni r_2$	$A15 : CS \ni f_k$
$A2 : V_i \ni V_{ID_i}$	$A8 : FS \ni P$	$A16 : CS \ni F_{ID_i}$
$A3 : V_i \ni P$	$A9 : FS \ni F_{ID_i}$	$A17 : CS \models \#T_2$
$A4 : V_i \ni r_1$	$A10 : FS \ni f_k$	$A18 : CS \ni P$
$A5 : V_i \ni v_i$	$A11 : FS \ni T_2$	$A19 : CS \ni v_i$
$A6 : V_i \ni T_1$	$A12 : FS \ni CS_{pub}$	$A20 : CS \ni s$
	$A13 : FS \ni sk_{fv_i}$	
	$A13 : FS \ni sk_{fv_j}$	

$$M_1 : FS \triangleleft^* C_1, C_3, A_1, Auth_V, T_1$$

$$M_2 : CS \triangleleft^* C_1, C_3, C_5, F_{ID_k}, Auth_V, Auth_{FS}, T_1, T_2$$

$$M_3 : FS \triangleleft A_3, Auth_{CS}, T_3$$

$$M_4 : V_i \triangleleft C_5, A_4$$

$$M_5 : FS \triangleleft S_1$$

$$M_6 : V_i \triangleleft E_{sk_{fv_i}}\{V_j, T_1^j, A_1^j, S_2\}$$

$$M_7 : V_j \triangleleft D_1, S_2$$

$$M_8 : V_i \triangleleft E_{K_{v_i v_j}}\{Ack\}$$

Table 3. Security correction goals in GNY logic

No.	Goal	Description
G_1	$CS \models Auth_{FS}$	Cloud server authenticates fog server
G_2	$CS \models Auth_v$	Cloud server authenticates vehicle V_i
G_3	$FS \models Auth_{CS}$	Fog server authenticates cloud server
G_4	$FS \models CS \models A_1$	Fog server authenticates V_i
G_5	$V_i \models h(C_1 \parallel C_2 \parallel T_1^i)$	V_i authenticates fog server
G_6	$V_j \models S_2$	V_j authenticates V_i

By using the assumptions $A1-A20$ listed in Table 2, formalized messages M_1-M_8 and the GNY inference rules [6], the goals of the proposed protocol are deduced to prove mutual authentication between the entities. The goals are described in Table 3 and verified in this section. We label the intermediate steps with S followed by a serial number. In GNY logic, it is possible to distinguish what a principal can possess and what it can believe in. The proof of goals G_1-G_6 is shown in Table 4. The GNY Postulates used in this paper (e.g., F1, T1, ..) are referred from [6].

Table 4. Security correctness proof in GNY logic

No.	Derivation	Goal	Reason
S_1	$\dfrac{V_i \ni r_1, V_i \ni P}{V_i \ni (r_1 \cdot P)}$		P_2, A_3, A_4
S_2	$\dfrac{V_i \ni v_i, V_i \ni P}{V_i \ni (v_i \cdot P)}$		P_2, A_4, A_5
S_3	$\dfrac{V_i \ni r_1, V_i \ni CS_{pub}}{V_i \ni (r_1 \cdot CS_{pub})}$		P_2, A_1, A_4
S_4	$\dfrac{V_i \ni VID_i}{V_i \ni VID_i \oplus (r1 \cdot CS_{pub})}$		S_3, P_2, A_2
S_5	$\dfrac{V_i \ni T_1^i}{V_i \ni h(T_1^i \parallel (r_1 \cdot P) \parallel (v_i \cdot P))}$		S_1, S_2, P_4, A_6
S_6	$\dfrac{V_i \ni VID_i, V_i \ni T_1^i}{V_i \ni h((v_i \cdot P) \parallel VID_i \parallel T_1^i)}$		S_2, P_4, A_2, A_6
S_7	$\dfrac{FS \triangleleft *C_1, *A_1^i}{FS \ni C_1, A_1^i}$		M_1, T_1, P_1
S_8	$\dfrac{FS \ni r_2, FS \ni P}{FS \ni (r_2 \cdot P)}$		P_2, A_7, A_8
S_9	$\dfrac{FS \ni f_k}{FS \ni f_k \cdot (r_2 \cdot P)}$		P_2, S_8, A_{10}
S_{10}	$\dfrac{FS \ni F_{ID_k}, FS \ni T_2}{FS \ni h(f_k \cdot r_2 \cdot P) \parallel F_{ID_k} \parallel T_2)}$		S_9, P_4, A_9, A_{11}
S_{11}	$\dfrac{CS \models \phi(f_k), CS \ni C_5}{CS \models (f_k, C_5)}$		R_2, M_2
S_{12}	$\dfrac{CS \ni F_{ID_k}, CS \models T_2}{CS \ni h(C_6 \parallel F_{ID_k} \parallel T_2)}$		P_4, A_9, I_7
S_{13}	$\dfrac{CS \models FS \Rightarrow Auth_{FS}, CS \models FS \models Auth_{FS}}{CS \models Auth_{FS}}$	Goal G1	J_1, M_2, S_{12}
S_{14}	$\dfrac{CS \ni s, CS \models \phi(C_3)}{CS \models \phi(C_3)s^{-1}}$		R_2, A_{20}
S_{15}	$\dfrac{CS \ni v_i, CS \ni P}{CS \ni (v_i \cdot P)}$		P_2, A_{18}, A_{19}
S_{16}	$\dfrac{CS \ni C_2, CS \ni VID_i, CS \ni T_1^i}{CS \ni h(C_2 \parallel VID_i \parallel T_1^i)}$		P_4, S_{15}
S_{17}	$\dfrac{CS \models V_i \Rightarrow Auth_v, CS \models V_i \models Auth_v}{CS \models Auth_v}$	Goal G2	S_{16}, J_1
S_{18}	$\dfrac{FS \triangleleft T_3, Auth_{CS}}{FS \ni T_3, Auth_{CS}}$		P_1, M_3
S_{19}	$\dfrac{FS \ni C_1, FS \ni f_k, FS \ni T_3}{FS \ni h(C_1 \parallel f_k \parallel T_3)}$		P_4, S_{18}
S_{20}	$\dfrac{FS \triangleleft^* Auth_{CS}, FS \ni f_k, FS \models FS \overset{\longleftrightarrow}{f_k} CS}{FS \models CS \mid\sim Auth_{CS}, FS \models CS \ni f_k}$		I_1, S_{18}, S_{19}
S_{21}	$\dfrac{FS \models CS \Rightarrow Auth_{CS}, FS \models CS \models Auth_{CS}}{FS \models Auth_{CS}}$	Goal G3	J_1
S_{22}	$\dfrac{FS \ni f_k, FS \ni CS_{pub}}{FS \ni A_2^*}$		P_2, A_{10}, A_{12}
S_{23}	$\dfrac{FS \triangleleft A_3}{FS \ni A_3}$		T_1, M_3
S_{24}	$\dfrac{FS \ni A_3, FS \ni A_2^*}{FS \ni C_2^{**}}$		P_2, S_{22}, S_{23}
S_{25}	$\dfrac{FS \ni C_1, FS \ni C_2^{**}, FS \ni T_1^i}{FS \ni h(C_1 \parallel C_2^{**} \parallel T_1^i)}$		P_4, S_{24}, S_7
S_{26}	$\dfrac{FS \models CS \Rightarrow A_1 \models *, FS \models CS \mid\sim (A_3 \rightsquigarrow A_1, FS \models A_1}{FS \models CS \models A_1}$	Goal G4	J_2, S_{25}
S_{27}	$\dfrac{V_i \ni C_1, V_i \ni C_2, V_i \ni T_1^i}{V_i \ni h(C_1 \parallel C_2 \parallel T_1^i)}$		P_4, A_6, S_1, S_2
S_{28}	$\dfrac{V_i \ni h(C_1 \parallel C_2 \parallel T_1^i)}{V_i \models \phi(h(C_1 \parallel C_2 \parallel T_1^i))}$		R_6, S_{27}
S_{29}	$\dfrac{V_i \models FS \Rightarrow h(C_1 \parallel C_2 \parallel T_1^i), V_i \models FS \models h(C_1 \parallel C_2 \parallel T_1^i)}{V_i \models h(C_1 \parallel C_2 \parallel T_1^i)}$	Goal G5	J_1, S_{28}, M_4

(*continued*)

Table 4. (*continued*)

No.	Derivation	Goal	Reason
S_{30}	$\dfrac{V_j \lhd D_1, V_j \lhd S_2}{V_j \ni D_1, V_j \ni S_2}$		P_2, M_7
S_{31}	$\dfrac{V_j \mid\equiv \phi(S_2), V_j \ni sk_{fv_j}}{V_j \mid\equiv \phi(S_2)_{sk_{fv_j}}}$		R_2, S_{30}
S_{32}	$\dfrac{V_j \lhd^* (S_2), V_j \ni sk_{fv_j}, V_j \mid\equiv V_j sk_{fv_j} FS, V_j \mid\equiv \phi(S_2), V_j \mid\equiv \#sk_{fv_j}}{V_j \mid\equiv FS \mid\sim S_2, V_j \mid\equiv FS \mid\sim (S_2), V_j \mid\equiv FS \ni sk_{fv_j}}$		I_1, S_{31}, A_4
S_{33}	$\dfrac{V_j \mid\equiv V_i \mid\Rightarrow S_2, V_j \mid\equiv V_i \mid\equiv S_2}{V_j \mid\equiv S_2}$	Goal G6	J_1, S_{32}

Using GNY logic, we are able to prove that the proposed protocol achieves the expected goals that participating entities are confident in the belief that they are communicating to the intended parties.

5 Comparative Analysis

This section details about the comparative study of the proposed scheme with that of the existing related schemes. The comparison is carried out in four aspects security functionalities, computational cost, communication cost and storage cost. Since, so far none of the schemes are designed for four party authentication, we restrict our comparison of computational and communication cost to only three party authentication.

Table 5. Comparison of functionality requirements and security threats

Protocol	SR_1	SR_2	SR_3	SR_4	SR_5	SR_6	SR_7	SR_8	SR_9	SR_{10}	SR_{11}
Liu et al. [8]	✓	✓	✓	✓	✓	×	✓	✓	✓	✓	×
Dang et al. [3]	×	×	×	✓	×	×	×	✓	✓	✓	×
Jia et al. [7]	✓	✓	✓	✓	✓	✓	✓	✓	✓	×	×
Wazid et al. [17]	✓	✓	✓	✓	✓	✓	✓	✓	✓	×	×
Ma et al. [11]	✓	✓	✓	✓	✓	✓	✓	✓	✓	×	×
Proposed	✓	✓	✓	✓	✓	✓	✓	✓	✓	✓	✓

SR_1: Prevents the replay attack, SR_2: Withstands man-in-the-middle attack, SR_3: Robust against vehicle impersonation, SR_4: Overcomes the problem of desynchronization attack, SR_5: Provides mutual authentication between the vehicle and the fog server SR_6: Supports vehicle untraceability, SR_7: Achieves vehicle anonymity, SR_8: Achieves perfect forward secrecy, SR_9: Provides known-key security, SR_{10}: Provides vehicle to vehicle communication, SR_{11}: Supports four party authentication, ✓: Yes, ×: No.

5.1 Security Functionality

In perspective of security protocol, it is required that there must be some essential properties need to be satisfied. Table 5 shows the details of security features supported by various protocols. Except Dang et al. [3] scheme though the other schemes satisfies most of the essential properties, all the schemes fails to support four party authentication. However, the proposed protocol satisfies all the essential security requirements.

5.2 Computational Cost

Table 6 shows the computational cost incur for the proposed scheme and various existing related schemes. With reference to [11], the executing time of bilinear pairing operation, hash value computation and ECC scalar multiplication operation are 32.713, 0.056 and 13.405 ms respectively in the smart phone. Compared to these computational timings, the computation time to execute $\oplus$ is significantly small, hence the computation time of $\oplus$ is omitted. In the proposed protocol at the vehicle side 3 T_H computations and 3 T_{SM} operations are carried out which causes $(0.168 + 40.215 = 40.383\,\text{ms})$, at the fog server side 4 T_H computations and 3 T_{SM} operations that causes $(0.224 + 40.215 = 40.439\,\text{ms})$ and at the cloud server side 3 T_H computations and 4 T_{SM} operations are carried out which causes $(0.168 + 53.62 = 53.788\,\text{ms})$. As a whole, the proposed protocol requires 134.61 ms computation time for the three party login-authentication. This computation time is minimum when compared to the other schemes [7, 8, 11]. Though the scheme by Dang et al. [3] has less computation time compared to all other schemes, their protocol is vulnerable to several security attacks and fails to satisfies the required security properties as indicated in Table 5.

Table 6. Comparison of computational cost

Protocol	Vehicle	RSU\Fog server	Cloud server	Total (in bits)
Liu et al. [8]	$3T_{BP} + 5T_H + 1T_{SM}$	$1T_{BP} + 2T_H + 1T_{SM}$	$3T_H + 1T_{SM}$	171.515
Dang et al. [3]	$1T_H + 4T_{SM}$	–	–	53.676
Jia et al. [7]	$1T_{BP} + 6T_H + 2T_{SM}$	$1T_{BP} + 4T_H + 2T_{SM}$	$3T_{BP} + 5T_H + 1T_{SM}$	231.43
Wazid et al. [17]	$6T_H$	$9T_H + 4T_{SM}$	$6T_H$	54.796
Ma et al. [11]	$4T_H + 3T_{SM}$	$4T_H + 4T_{SM}$	$11T_H + 10T_{SM}$	228.949
Proposed	$3T_H + 3T_{SM}$	$4T_H + 3T_{SM}$	$3T_H + 4T_{SM}$	134.61

T_{BP}: Number of bilinear pairing operations used, T_H: Number of times hash value computed, T_{SM}: Number of times ECC scalar multiplication operations used.

5.3 Communicational Cost

With reference to [11], it is regarded that the bit size of ECC group points from G, field elements from Z_q^* and the timestamp are 1024 bits, 160 bits and 32 bits respectively. Table 7 shows the communication cost for different protocols.

Table 7. Comparison of communicational cost

Protocol	Vehicle	RSU\Fog server	Cloud server	Total (in bits)
Liu et al. [8]	$2|G| + 2|Z_q^*| + |T|$	$5|G| + 10|Z_q^*| + 3|T|$	$2|G| + 3|Z_q^*| + |T|$	11776
Dang et al. [3]	$3|G| + 1|Z_q^*|$	–	–	3104
Jia et al. [7]	$|G| + 4|Z_q^*| + |T|$	$4|G| + 6|Z_q^*| + 3|T|$	$|G| + 4|Z_q^*| + |T|$	8544
Wazid et al. [17]	$3|Z_q^*| + |T|$	$6|Z_q^*| + 2|T|$	$3|Z_q^*| + |T|$	2048
Ma et al. [11]	$|G| + 4|Z_q^*| + |T|$	$6|G| + 6|Z_q^*| + 3|T|$	$3|G| + 4|Z_q^*| + |T|$	12640
Proposed	$2|G| + 2|Z_q^*| + |T|$	$4|G| + 4|Z_q^*| + 2|T|$	$|G| + 2|Z_q^*| + |T|$	8416

$|G|$: Bit size of ECC group points from G, $|Z_q^*|$: Bit size of field elements from Z_q^*, $|T|$: Bit size of timestamp.

Compared to the proposed protocol, the communication cost of the protocols in [7,8,11] is much higher. Though the protocols in [3,17] requires less communication cost than the proposed protocol, their protocol do not support four party authentication.

5.4 Storage Cost

As the vehicle is a smart vehicle OBU in it has less storage capacity. In order to improve the efficiency, it is essential to design the scheme such that it consumes less storage cost. The Table 8 shows the storage cost of various schemes in bits. Compared to others scheme, the proposed protocol requires less computational cost.

Table 8. Storage cost

Protocol	Total (in bits)
Liu et al. [8]	160
Dang et al. [3]	1024
Jia et al. [7]	320
Wazid et al. [17]	320
Ma et al. [11]	1024
Proposed	160

6 Conclusion

In recent days smart vehicular technology is getting much attention from the researchers. In this article, we have proposed a novel four party authentication and key establishment protocol for VANET. The correctness of the proposed protocol is proven using the formal method GNY logic. The protocol is compared with the existing related protocols and comparison shows that our protocol outperforms the others.

References

1. Anandhi, S., Anitha, R., Sureshkumar, V.: An automatic rfid reader-to-reader delegation protocol for scm in cloud computing environment. J. Supercomput. **74**(7), 3148–3167 (2018)
2. Anandhi, S., Anitha, R., Sureshkumar, V.: IoT enabled RFID authentication and secure object tracking system for smart logistics. Wireless Pers. Commun. **104**(2), 543–560 (2019)
3. Dang, L., et al.: Efficient identity-based authenticated key agreement protocol with provable security for vehicular ad hoc networks. Int. J. Distrib. Sens. Netw. **14**(4), 1–16 (2018)

4. Dua, A., Kumar, N., Das, A.K., Susilo, W.: Secure message communication protocol among vehicles in smart city. IEEE Trans. Veh. Technol. **67**(5), 4359–4373 (2017)
5. Dua, A., Kumar, N., Singh, M., Obaidat, M.S., Hsiao, K.F.: Secure message communication among vehicles using elliptic curve cryptography in smart cities. In: International Conference on Computer, Information and Telecommunication Systems (CITS), pp. 1–6. IEEE (2016)
6. Gong, L., Needham, R., Yahalom, R.: Reasoning about belief in cryptographic protocols. In: Computer Society Symposium on Research in Security and Privacy, pp. 234–248. IEEE (1990)
7. Jia, X., He, D., Kumar, N., Choo, K.K.R.: Authenticated key agreement scheme for fog-driven IoT healthcare system. Wirel. Netw. 1–14 (2018)
8. Liu, Y., Wang, Y., Chang, G.: Efficient privacy-preserving dual authentication and key agreement scheme for secure V2V communications in an IoV paradigm. IEEE Trans. Intell. Transp. Syst. **18**(10), 2740–2749 (2017)
9. Lu, H., Li, J., Guizani, M.: A novel ID-based authentication framework with adaptive privacy preservation for VANETs. In: Conference on Computing, Communications and Applications, pp. 345–350. IEEE (2012)
10. Lu, R., Lin, X., Zhu, H., Ho, P.H., Shen, X.: ECPP: efficient conditional privacy preservation protocol for secure vehicular communications. In: IEEE INFOCOM 2008-The 27th Conference on Computer Communications, pp. 1229–1237. IEEE (2008)
11. Ma, M., He, D., Wang, H., Kumar, N., Choo, K.K.R.: An efficient and provably-secure authenticated key agreement protocol for fog-based vehicular ad-hoc networks. IEEE Internet Things J. **6**, 8065–8075 (2019)
12. Raya, M., Hubaux, J.P.: Securing vehicular ad hoc networks. J. Comput. Secur. **15**(1), 39–68 (2007)
13. Sureshkumar, V., Amin, R., Anitha, R.: An enhanced bilinear pairing based authenticated key agreement protocol for multiserver environment. Int. J. Commun. Syst. **30**(17), e3358 (2017)
14. Sureshkumar, V., Amin, R., Anitha, R.: A robust mutual authentication scheme for session initiation protocol with key establishment. Peer-to-Peer Netw. Appl. **11**(5), 900–916 (2018)
15. Sureshkumar, V., Amin, R., Vijaykumar, V., Rajasekar, S.: Robust secure communication protocol for smart healthcare system with FPGA implementation. Future Gener. Comput. Syst. **100**, 938–951 (2019)
16. Sureshkumar, V., Ramalingam, A., Anandhi, S.: Analysis of accountability property in payment systems using strand space model. In: Abawajy, J.H., Mukherjea, S., Thampi, S.M., Ruiz-Martínez, A. (eds.) SSCC 2015. CCIS, vol. 536, pp. 424–437. Springer, Cham (2015). https://doi.org/10.1007/978-3-319-22915-7_39
17. Wazid, M., Bagga, P., Das, A.K., Shetty, S., Rodrigues, J.J., Park, Y.H.: AKM-IoV: authenticated key management protocol in fog computing-based internet of vehicles deployment. IEEE Internet Things J. **6**, 8804–8817 (2019)
18. Wazid, M., et al.: Design of lightweight authentication and key agreement protocol for vehicular ad hoc networks. IEEE Access **5**, 14966–14980 (2017)
19. Zhang, L., Hu, C., Wu, Q., Domingo-Ferrer, J., Qin, B.: Privacy-preserving vehicular communication authentication with hierarchical aggregation and fast response. IEEE Trans. Comput. **65**(8), 2562–2574 (2015)
20. Zhang, L., Wu, Q., Domingo-Ferrer, J., Qin, B., Hu, C.: Distributed aggregate privacy-preserving authentication in vanets. IEEE Trans. Intell. Transp. Syst. **18**(3), 516–526 (2016)

Applications for Smart City Informatization

An Adaptive MAC Layer Energy-Saving Algorithm for ZigBee-Enabled IoT Networks

Yaxuan Zhang[1](✉), Kun Yang[2,3], and Hui Chen[3]

[1] School of Information and Communication Engineering,
University of Electronic Science and Technology of China, Chengdu 611731, China
yasinzhang@std.uestc.edu.cn

[2] School of Computer Science and Electronic Engineering,
University of Essex, Colchester CO43SQ, UK
kunyang@essex.ac.uk

[3] Institute of Zhongshan, University of Electronic Science and Technology of China,
Zhongshan 528400, China
chenhui@zsc.edu.cn

Abstract. Energy conservation has become a major bottleneck for wide deployment of Internet of Things (IoT) technologies. This paper presents energy consumption analysis of ZigBee-enabled IoT networks, and shows the primary energy consumption in a node from a practical aspect. Based on the analysis and experimental measurement, this paper proposes an adaptive MAC layer energy-saving algorithm. This algorithm can adaptively configure the MAC layer in each node based on real-time network traffic conditions. The aim is to minimize the power consumption of each node achieving a longer lifetime and better quality of service. In addition, a software and hardware experimental platform has been built up to verify the reliability and effectiveness of the algorithm. The experimental results show that the adaptive MAC layer energy-saving algorithm is effective and efficient in minimizing node energy consumption.

Keywords: Internet of Things (IoT) · ZigBee · MAC layer · Energy-saving · Adaptive algorithm

1 Introduction

With advances on Internet of Things (IoT) technologies, a growing number of physical objects are being connected to the Internet. From the perspective of private users, the obvious effects of the IoT are visible in both work and home. The applications include domestics, assisted living, e-health and enhanced learning. For business users, the apparent impact will be seen in fields such as, automation and industrial manufacturing, logistics, business/process management, intelligent transportation of people and goods [1]. The IoT communication technologies connect heterogeneous objects together to deliver specific smart services. In

© Springer Nature Singapore Pte Ltd. 2019
G. Wang et al. (Eds.): iSCI 2019, CCIS 1122, pp. 365–378, 2019.
https://doi.org/10.1007/978-981-15-1301-5_29

general, these battery-powered nodes should operate at low power consumption in the presence of loss-and-noise communication links. Examples of wireless communication technologies used for the IoT are ZigBee, Wi-Fi, Bluetooth, IEEE 802.15.4, Z-wave, LTE-Advanced and forthcoming 5G. Some specific communication technologies are also in use like RFID, Near Field Communication (NFC) and ultra-wide bandwidth (UWB) [2]. Among them, ZigBee has many advantages such as high reliability, low power consumption, low cost, high security and large network capacity. These advantages make ZigBee one of the commonly used technologies of IoT networks. The purpose of this paper is to study an effective method to reduce the energy consumption of devices in ZigBee enabled IoT network, which is the most critical and challenging problem in Internet of things network.

There is much work done on energy-saving mechanisms to extend the lifetime of the network. Those works can be typically divided by different working layers. For example, in the physical layer, [3] designs a scheduling mechanism so that the devices can be power by the energy harvested from the environmnet. In [4], the authors do a lot of works on the hardware. The devices can save power by use lower energy to transmit data. However, those works are too complicated for a sensor node. In addition, many works are done in MAC layer. [5,6] discussed various media access protocols, such as periodic terminal initiated polling (PTIP), B-MAC, STEM-T, WiseMAC, S-MAC, or UBMAC. These protocols already target ultra low power operation. [7] designs a composite MAC layer protocol which is compatible with IEEE 802.15.4 standard and can achieve better energy saving effects at different rates. Some research has also been done in the network layer. [8,9] propose clustering algorithms which hand over heavy work to the powered nodes. [10] dynamically promotes a central node by a routing algorithm, avoiding long-term use of a single node, and extending the service life of the overall network. Some literatures evaluate the energy-saving mechanisms in the application layer. For instance, [11] proposes a sleep/wake mechanism for small scale wireless sensor networks. An algorithm for determining the sleep state of terminal nodes through a master node (i.e. coordinator or router) proposed by [12]. However, this method obviously increases the number of control packets. [13,14] realizes the management of dynamic transmission power by detecting the application communication state, thereby realizing the energy saving of the node. In [15], the authors use a redundancy and converged data algorithm to simplify the transmission of data to reduce energy consumption.

Briefly speaking, the energy-saving strategy in physical layer is limited by the prior art. Optimizing the energy-saving mechanism of routing requires exchange of routing information or residual energy data between the nodes, which indirectly increases the traffic of the network and thus extra energy consumption. The energy-saving mechanism of the application layer reduces the transmission of data packets, it also reduces the data exchange of the network, but the data cannot be uploaded in time. The MAC layer can both control the transmission method of the data and the time of a transmission. Therefore, considering the appropriate energy-saving mechanism at the MAC layer is a preferred research direction of this paper.

In this paper we consider a ZigBee enabled IoT network environment where the end devices report data to the gateway/coordinator periodically. Those end devices consume a little energy while it is in the sleep mode [16]. So, reducing the active time of the ZigBee device is a key issue and the focus of this paper. Sect. 2 will present more about the analysis of the active time of a end device.

Furthermore, one common feature of the above-mentioned literature is that none of them has considered the dynamic characteristics of the IoT network. An end device in an IoT would frequently change its state according to the situation. Therefore, an adaptive MAC layer energy-saving algorithm has been proposed in this paper.

In summary, the propose of this paper is to study an adaptive MAC layer energy-saving algorithm for ZigBee-enabled IoT networks. The major contributions lie in the following two aspects. Firstly, the paper analyzes the energy consumption state of the ZigBee nodes, and explains the feasibility of improving the MAC layer protocol in energy saving. Secondly, an adaptive energy-saving algorithm is proposed based on the existing CSMA/CA mechanism. This algorithm is lightweight, and can be easily imported in the nodes. It is also effective, using only information local to the sensor. As a result, it is well suited for resource-constrained sensor nodes, and can meet the reliability request of the IoT network.

The remainder of this paper is organized as follows. Section 2 propose the measurement of the energy consumption of the nodes in ZigBee network. Section 3 propose the adaptive MAC layer energy-saving algorithm for ZigBee-enabled IoT networks. The experiment of the algorithm is given in Sect. 4. Section 5 is the conclusions.

2 Energy Consumption Analysis for an Active ZigBee Node

2.1 The Experimental Model

The ZigBee network topology model used for energy consumption measurement is shown in Fig. 1a. The end devices periodically send data to the gateway. After the report, the end device enters sleep mode for saving energy. In the experimental model of energy consumption analysis, the node periodically reports data to the gateway. To simplify the experiment, the model assumes that the message transmission is reliable, and does not require ACK packet.

In the measurement, the hardware module is CC2530 ZigBee development board, which is shown in Fig. 1b. There are 1 gateway/coordinator and 3 end devices working at 2.4 GHz and equipped with ZigBee protocol. Each node of the network is in the non-beacon mode [16]. All nodes operate at 3.7 V.

Fig. 1. (a) ZigBee network topology model for energy consumption measurement; (b) Hardware model of a node in a ZigBee-enabled IoT network

2.2   Energy Consumption of a Node Sending Message

Figure 2 shows the current consumption of a node while sending message. As shown in the figure, current value changes while a node is in different states. In order to explain the energy consumption of a node, the detail parameters during the node's transmission shows in Table 1. In this table, the node's states is divided by the points marked in the figure.

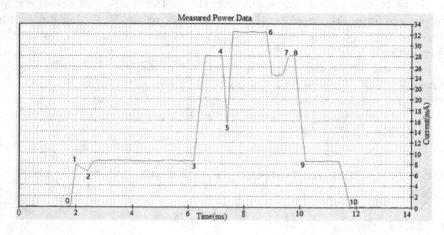

Fig. 2. Current consumption of a node sending message in ZigBee-enabled IoT network

2.3   Lifetime of a Node

According to the above experiment, the energy consumption distribution histogram as shown in Fig. 3 is obtained. From the figure, device idle state, data transmission and reception are the main energy consumption contributors. Table 2 lists the parameters that impact on the node's lifetime.

Assume that there is no packet loss in the communication between the end device and the coordinator. So, the transmission time T_{Trans} and its energy consumption C_{Trans} can be obtained as Eqs. 1 and 2.

Table 1. Energy consumption parameters

Processes	Process description	Voltage (V)	Current (mA)	Time (ms)	Energy consumption (mA * ms)
Before point 0	Sleep mode		0.001		
Point 0–1	Awake MCU	3.70	7.89	0.21	1.66
Point 1–2	MCU working in 16 MHz clock mode	3.70	7.22	0.43	3.10
Point 2–3	MCU working in 32 MHz clock mode	3.70	8.55	3.80	32.49
Point 3–4	CSMA/CA back-off state (receive mode)	3.70	28.05	1.05	29.45
Point 4–5	Switch from receive to transmit	3.70	15.49	0.2	3.09
Point 5–6	Sending MAC packet	3.70	32.50	1.22	39.65
Point 6–7	Switch from transmit to receive	3.70	26.43	0.2	5.29
Point 7–8	Receiving MAC ACK	3.70	28.16	0.35	9.86
Point 8–9	Handling MAC ACK packet	3.70	18.11	0.41	7.42
Point 9–10	Follow-up and shut down MCU	3.70	8.05	1.62	13.04
After point 10	Sleep mode		0.001		
Total				9.49	209.4

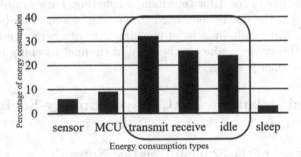

Fig. 3. Energy consumption distribution of an end device in ZigBee network

$$T_{Trans} = T_{Rx,L} + T_{R2T} + T_{Tx,D} + T_{T2R} + T_{Rx,A} + T_{PS} \quad (1)$$

$$C_{Trans} = \frac{\begin{bmatrix} C_{Rx}(T_{Rx,L} + T_{Rx,A}) + C_{R2T}T_{R2T} + \\ C_{Tx}T_{Tx,D} + C_{T2R}T_{T2R} + C_{PS}T_{PS} \end{bmatrix}}{T_{Trans}} \quad (2)$$

Table 2. Energy consumption parameters

Operations		Current consumption	Time
Device startup		C_{UP}	T_{UP}
Transmission	Data request	C_{Tx}	$T_{Tx,Q}$
	Data transmission		$T_{Tx,D}$
	MAC ACK		$T_{Tx,A}$
Switch from receive mode to transmit mode		C_{R2T}	T_{R2T}
Receiving	Listen	C_{Rx}	$T_{Rx,L}$
	Data reception		$T_{Rx,D}$
	MAC ACK		$T_{Rx,A}$
Switch from transmit mode to receive mode		C_{T2R}	T_{T2R}
Preparing to sleep		C_{PS}	T_{PS}
Sleep mode		C_S	C_S

Assume that the battery's power is BC mAh, and the node sends messages every S seconds. The lifetime of a node LT can be calculated as Eq. 3.

$$LT = \frac{(BC - C_{UP}T_{UP})\,S}{(S - T_{Trans})\,C_s + T_{Trans}C_{Trans}} \tag{3}$$

After the ZigBee network is setted up, the energy consumption of each operation is basically fixed except for the channel listening. For example, in the case of a busy network, the device may need to wait for a long time before sending message, which will result in a large consumption of energy and a reduction of the lifetime. Therefore, reducing the time of channel listening is an effective means to achieve energy-saving.

3   Proposed Adaptive MAC Layer Energy-Saving Algorithm

3.1   MAC Layer of the Standard ZigBee Network

ZigBee technology is based on IEEE Std 802.15.4^{TM}-2011 [17], which specifies the MAC layer and PHY layer. IEEE Std 802.15.4^{TM}-2011 [17] use Carrier Sense Multiple Access/Contention Avoidance (CSMA/CA) as channel access protocol. The MAC sublayer of the standard supports two operation modes: beacon-enabled and non beacon-enabled mode. This paper focus on the latter. In this mode, the nodes can send data by using unslotted CSMA/CA [17]. The unslotted CSMA/CA mechanism of the IEEE Std 802.15.4^{TM}-2011 [17] used two variables to schedule the access to the medium:

- NB is the number of times that CSMA/CA algorithm was required to back-off while attempting to access the channel. It is initialized to 0 before each data transmission.

– BE is the back-off exponent, which is related to how many back-off unit periods a node must wait before attempting to perform a Clear Channel Assessment (CCA).

The unslotted version of CSMA/CA can be summarized in the following five steps [17]—initialization of NB and BE, random delay for collision avoidance, clear channel assessment, busy channel processing, idle channel processing.

3.2 CSMA/CA Mechanism Analysis

In the CSMA/CA mechanism, the time of channel listening represents in the form of back-off delay. In order to achieve energy-saving, the analysis of back-off delay is needed. According to the analysis above, it can be seen that BE has a significant influence on the back-off delay. Figure 4 shows the effect of different minBE on network delay. In the figure, the delay time is measured by time slots, a time slot is 1 symbol's transmission time. It can be seen from Fig. 4 that the larger the BE, the greater the probability of the large back-off delay, and the smaller the BE, the smaller the back-off delay. This paper analyzes the impact of CSMA/CA parameters on the network. For the initial value of the BE parameter, minBE, when the minBE of the node is small, the back-off time of the device is small when the device is first retired, and the delay is also small. The large minBE will also bring about a large back-off delay, the resulting network delay is also relatively large.

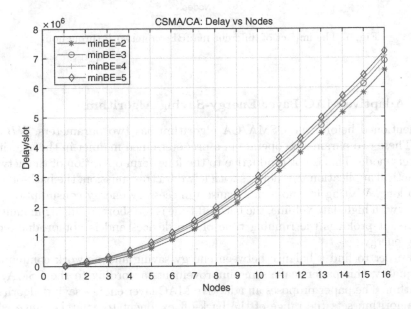

Fig. 4. The impact of different minBE on network delay

As can be seen from the Fig. 4, when minBE increases, the network delay will also increase, which means that the time of back-off delay will increase, which will bring more energy consumption and shorten the network life. For the upper limit of the BE, maxBE, the larger maxBE will bring more net-work throughput, as shown in Fig. 5. So, when the node has a collision with other nodes, the node can maintain network throughput by gradually increase the value of BE.

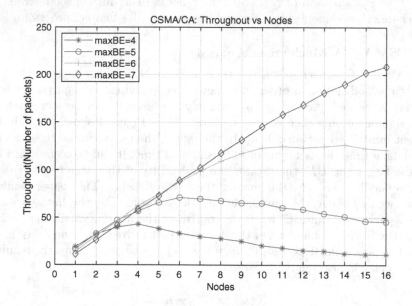

Fig. 5. The impact of different maxBE on network throughout

3.3   Adaptive MAC Layer Energy-Saving Algorithm

As mentioned before, the CSMA/CA algorithm has two parameters, NB and BE. These two parameters operate in a predetermined manner in the algorithm for every node. This is not productive to the long-term operation of the network in practical application. For devices with low data transmission, the back-off time is too long. Waiting for more time cause unnecessary energy consumption. For devices with high data volume, the back-off time is too short, resulting in multiple retreats. It prolongs the running time of the devices and is not productive to saving energy.

In order to find a balance between energy-saving and network communication quality, this paper make some improvements according to the CSMA/CA algorithm. The paper proposes an adaptive MAC layer energy-saving algorithm. The algorithm sets the range of the back-off exponent to a larger range when the node is initialized, sets the minimum value to 2, the maximum value to 6, and the initial value to 4. When the node is with high data volume, the BE gradually increase from the initial value until the maximum, and then remain stable. For the device with small amount of data, the BE gradually decreases from the initial value until it reaches 2. Since the range of the back-off exponent is dynamically variable according to the node's state, the probability of collisions between different nodes is greatly reduced. The node of high data volume increases the range of the back-off period, reduce the collision probability, avoids the energy consumption caused by multiple back-off. The device with little data to transmit adopts a lower back-off period variation range, which reduces the back-off delay and avoiding the energy consumption.

The proposed algorithm divides the nodes in the same time period into two categories: hot node and cold node. Hot node is a node with large amount of data, which has a large amount of data to transfer in a cycle. It can easily collide with other nodes. The cold node has little data to send. Also, the data of cold node is often sent once in a long interval. The algorithm in this paper introduces the interval time, I_i, as the criterion for distinguishing node types. I_i is obtained as the time between the $i - 1^{th}$ message and the ith message sent by the node. The unit of I_i is seconds. For simplicity, this paper assumes a node with I_i greater than 1 as the hot node, and conversely, a cold node. The sending time of the ith message is S_i. So, the interval time I_i can be calculate by Eq. 4.

$$I_i = S_i - S_{i-1} \tag{4}$$

The node type discrimination scheme is described in Algorithm 1.

Algorithm 1. The Node Type Discrimination Algorithm

    Input: S_i, S_{i-1}: Sending Time
    Output: N_T: Node Type
1 $I_i \leftarrow S_i - S_{i-1}$;   // calculate interval time by Eq. 4
2 **if** $I_i < 1$ **then**
3 | // the node is hot node
4 | $N_T \leftarrow$ HOT_NODE_TYPE;
5 **else**
6 | // the node is cold node
7 | $N_T \leftarrow$ COLD_NODE_TYPE;
8 **end**

The proposed algorithm needs the transmission time of the $i - 1^{th}$ message and i^{th} message of the node. At first, this paper calculates the interval time of the ith message I_i. The code from line 2 to 7 shows the main operation of node type discrimination. While I_i is less than 1, then this node is regard as hot node, otherwise, it is a cold node. After classifying the node, this paper adaptively adjusts the MAC layer parameters based on the node type. The adaptive MAC layer energy-saving algorithm is described in Algorithm 2.

The proposed algorithm needs the node type N_T to determine the operation. Line 1–6 show the operation of the hot node. For the hot node, when the channel is detected to be busy when the same packet is sending, BE is reduced until reaches macMinBE. For the cold node, when the channel is busy, BE increased until macMaxBE. After adjusting the parameters, the algorithm enters the step 2 of CSMA/CA mechanism. The algorithm is extremely lightweight, thus well suited for implementation on real sensor nodes. And the change of BE value is bidirectional, thus this algorithm is suited for the nodes in various states.

Algorithm 2. Adaptive MAC Layer Energy-saving Algorithm

Input: BE, NB: MAC Layer Parameters; N_T: Node Type
Output: BE: Back-off Exponent

```
1  if NB < macMaxCSMABackoffs then
2  |   if N_T is HOT_NODE_TYPE then
3  |   |   if BE < macMaxBE then
4  |   |   |   BE + +;
5  |   |   else
6  |   |   |   BE ← macMaxBE
7  |   |   end
8  |   else if N_T is COLD_NODE_TYPE then
9  |   |   if BE > macMinBE then
10 |   |   |   BE − −;
11 |   |   else
12 |   |   |   BE ← macMinBE;
13 |   |   end
14 |   Random delay for collision avoidance based on BE;
15 else
16 |   Transmission failure;
17 end
```

---

4 Experiment and Performance Evaluation

4.1 Experiment Setup

In this experiment, the nodes connect each other by ZigBee protocol. The network topology is shown in Fig. 1a. To ensure the effectiveness and reliability of the experiment, our experiment meets the following points:

- The communication between the nodes is point-to-point.
- End devices report data to the gateway periodically.
- The hardware and software structures of each end device are the same.
- The communication between each end device and gateway is independent.
- The transmission and reception are not controlled by other nodes.
- The distance between each end device and the gateway is the same, to ensure the same transmission power of the nodes.

The hardware platform of the node is CC2530. The CC2530 is a true system-on-chip (SoC) solution for IEEE 802.15.4, Zigbee and RF4CE applications. It enables robust network nodes to be built with very low total bill-of-material costs.

The experiment uses Z-Stack 3.0 of TI as software platform. In order to simulate a standard network communication environment, a periodic data transmission task is set, and a message is sent every 5 s. And every end device has sleep mode.

4.2   Energy Consumption Analysis of a Node

This experiment uses PowerMonitor for node energy analysis. The device can detect the real-time current value of the device and provide a stable voltage for the node. PowerMonitor is controlled by Power Tool software, which can display the current waveform of the node and calculate the power and energy consumption of the node over a period. The software appearance is shown in Fig. 6.

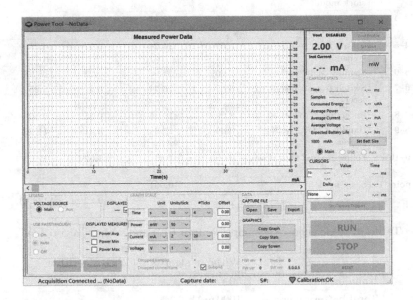

Fig. 6. Power Tool software

In the experiment, the gateway is powered on first. After the network is set up, the end devices are powered on. After searching for the network created by the gateway, the end devices join the network and initiate a periodic message sending task. The current waveform of an end device while sending a message is in Fig. 2.

The point 3 to point 4 in Fig. 2 is the back-off time of the node. Table 3 shows the relevant energy consumption data when the node sends data. It can be seen from Tables 1 and 3, the average time from point 3 to 4 is shortened compared to the node without our algorithm (Table 1). In order to further illustrate the effectiveness of the adaptive MAC layer algorithm, this experiment uses Eqs. 2 and 3 to calculate the lifetime of the nodes. The experiment sets the total energy of the node battery to 1000 mAh. Table 4 compares node energy consumption data with and without algorithms. From this table, the algorithm proposed in this paper extends the lifetime of the node by about 1500 h.

Table 3. Energy consumption analysis when a node sends a message

Processes	Process description	Voltage (V)	Current (mA)	Time (ms)	Energy consumption (mA * ms)
Before point 0	Sleep mode		0.001		
Point 0–1	Awake MCU	3.69	5.23	0.24	1.26
Point 1–2	MCU working in 16 MHz clock mode	3.69	8.39	0.31	2.60
Point 2–3	MCU working in 32 MHz clock mode	3.69	8.32	4.06	33.78
Point 3–4	CSMA/CA back-off state (receive mode)	3.69	19.22	0.71	13.65
Point 4–5	Switch from receive to transmit	3.69	21.26	0.2	4.25
Point 5–6	Sending MAC packet	3.69	31.96	1.22	38.99
Point 6–7	Switch from transmit to receive	3.69	26.74	0.2	5.35
Point 7–8	Receiving MAC ACK	3.69	28.16	0.35	9.86
Point 8–9	Handling MAC ACK packet	3.69	27.34	0.41	11.20
Point 9–10	Follow-up and shut down MCU	3.69	7.46	1.62	12.09
After point 10	Sleep mode		0.001		
Total				9.32	133.03

Table 4. Node energy consumption data with and without algorithms

	Without algorithm	With algorithm
Running time	50 s	
Total battery power	1000 mAh	
T_{Trans}	26.3 mA	24.4 mA
Average current	51.0 μA	47.4 μA
Lifetime of a node (LT)	19607.8 h	21097.0 h

4.3 Network Reliability Analysis

Reliability is also very critical for the IoT network [18]. A point-to-point communication model is designed to test the effective communication distance of nodes, to verify that the equipment using the algorithm still has reliability. The transmit power of the node is fixed at 3 dBm. And the heights of the two node's antennas to the ground is 10 m.

Table 5 shows the experiment results. Compared to the equipments without algorithm, the algorithm doesn't affect the reliability of the network. Although the adaptive MAC layer algorithm reduces the energy consumption of the nodes, it does not have much influence on the network. So, the following conclusions are drawn: the nodes can be energy efficiency and work reliably in a small range.

Table 5. Network reliability analysis experiment results

Antenna height	Node distance	Probability of successful message transmission	
		With algorithm	Without algorithm
10 m	50 m	0.98	0.98
	100 m	0.97	0.98
	150 m	0.91	0.90
	200 m	0.8	0.83
	250 m	0.55	0.54

Therefore, after using the adaptive MAC layer algorithm, the ZigBee network can have reliable network and longer network life in the short-distance communication environment, that is, the common smart home environment or the wireless sensor monitoring network environment.

5 Conclusion

This paper has proposed an effective and light-weight adaptive MAC layer energy-saving algorithm. With the algorithm, nodes can select an appropriate back-off strategy according to its own communication condition, that is, the communication efficiency of the nodes of high data volume is ensured, and the energy-saving effect of the nodes of low data volume is also ensured. At the same time, the node can freely switch between the two states without being affected. The immediate future work is to make certain energy optimization settings to maximize node energy and extend node life based on the node's hardware configuration. On this basis, we will study other aspects of energy conservation, such as network layer and multi-layer cooperation.

Acknowledgments. The work in this paper was partly supported by National Natural Science Foundation of China (NSFC) projects (61572389 and 61620106011), and Zhongshan City Team Project (No. 180809162197874).

References

1. Atzori, L., Iera, A., Morabito, G.: The internet of things: a survey. Comput. Netw. **54**(15), 2787–2805 (2010)
2. Al-Fuqaha, A., Guizani, M., Mohammadi, M., Aledhari, M., Ayyash, M.: Internet of Things: a survey on enabling technologies, protocols, and applications. IEEE Commun. Surv. Tutor. **17**(4), 2347–2376 (2015)
3. Karalis, A., Joannopoulos, J.D., Soljačić, M.: Efficient wireless non-radiative midrange energy transfer. Ann. Phys. **323**(1), 34–48 (2008)
4. Peng, X., Yin, J., Mak, P.I., Yu, W.H., Martins, R.P.: A 2.4-GHZ ZigBee transmitter using a function-reuse class-F DCO-PA and an ADPLL achieving 22.6% (14.5%) system efficiency at 6-dBm (0-dBm) P_{out}. IEEE J. Solid-State Circuits **52**(6), 1495–1508 (2017)

5. El-Hoiydi, A., Decotignie, J.D.: Low power downlink MAC protocols for infrastructure wireless sensor networks. Mob. Netw. Appl. **10**(5), 675–690 (2005)
6. Raghunathan, V., Ganeriwal, S., Srivastava, M.: Emerging techniques for long lived wireless sensor networks. IEEE Commun. Mag. **44**(4), 108–114 (2006)
7. Anchora, L., Capone, A., Mighali, V., Patrono, L., Simone, F.: A novel MAC scheduler to minimize the energy consumption in a wireless sensor network. Ad Hoc Netw. **16**, 88–104 (2014)
8. Alhmiedat, T.: Low-power environmental monitoring system for ZigBee wireless sensor network. KSII Trans. Internet Inf. Syst. **11**(10), 4781–4803 (2017)
9. Pan, M.S., Tseng, Y.C.: Quick convergecast in ZigBee beacon-enabled tree-based wireless sensor networks. Comput. Commun. **31**(5), 999–1011 (2008)
10. Li, S.: Energy consumption optimization method of wireless sensor networks based on ZigBee. Ph.D. thesis, Hunan University (2010)
11. Zhen, C., Liu, W., Liu, Y., Yan, A.: Energy-efficient sleep/wake scheduling for acoustic localization wireless sensor network node. Int. J. Distrib. Sens. Netw. **10**(2), 970524 (2014)
12. Shun, J.: Research on energy consumption mechanism based on ZigBee network. Ph.D. thesis, Beijing University of Posts and Telecommunications (2015)
13. Jiang, B.: Research on MAC layer energy-efficient for ZigBee wireless sensor network. Ph.D. thesis, Shanghai Jiao Tong University (2014)
14. Bai, F.: Research on energy efficiency technology for ZigBee-based wireless sensor network. Ph.D. thesis, National University of Defense Technology (2008)
15. Gharghan, S., Nordin, R., Ismail, M.: Energy-efficient ZigBee-based wireless sensor network for track bicycle performance monitoring. Sensors **14**(8), 15573–15592 (2014)
16. ZigBee Alliance: ZigBee specification (2019). http://www.zigbee.org
17. IEEE: IEEE standard for local and metropolitan area networks-part 15.4: low-rate wireless personal area networks (LR-WPANs). IEEE Std 802.15.4-2011 (Revision of IEEE Std 802.15.4-2006), pp. 1–314, September 2011. https://doi.org/10.1109/IEEESTD.2011.6012487
18. Willig, A.: Recent and emerging topics in wireless industrial communications: a selection. IEEE Trans. Ind. Inform. **4**(2), 102–104 (2008)

Implementing a Lightweight Cloud-Based Process Monitoring Solution for Smart Agriculture

Daniel Clarke, Hussain Al-Aqrabi(✉) ⓘ, Richard Hillⓘ, Pritesh Mistry, and Phil Laneⓘ

School of Computing and Engineering, University of Huddersfield, Huddersfield, UK
{h.al-aqrabi,r.hill,p.mistry,p.lane}@hud.ac.uk

Abstract. In order to meet recent challenges for more efficient and economic industrial manufacturing plants and processes, existing infrastructure is undergoing a digital transformation towards Smart Factories/Industry 4.0. These technologies and approaches also have applications outside of manufacturing, including agriculture. We introduce a fully integrated data analytics infrastructure that can be used to transfer and store relevant agricultural sensor data from microcontrollers. This is applied to a prototype plant monitoring system using a Raspberry Pi for data processing and an IoT Cloud system for Real Time Application. The prototype implementation of the microcontroller integrates a temperature sensor, a humidity sensor, and a capacitive moisture sensor. The design uses a standalone ESP32 micro controller communicating to an MQTT Broker using the publish/subscribe method. Sensor data can be accessed by subscribing to the MQTT topic or by using the Web Application. The ESPlantMonitoring web application is developed for user management to grant access to the MQTT broker and view collected sensor data.

Keywords: Internet of Things · Cloud computing · Distributed systems · Raspberry Pi · Arduino · Smart agriculture

1 Introduction

The Internet of Things (IoT) refers to uniquely identifiable smart devices/objects connected to the internet that can sense data and react with their environment [1,2]. Computing relies on the large amount of data being collected and made available by connecting all objects within an IoT system [4]. The IoT also relies on increasing developments in RFID (radio frequency identification), sensors, communication technologies, and IP [3,5]. The fundamental concept is to have localised intelligent sensors to deliver the upper layers of applications without any ambiguity in human involvement [17].

The horticultural sector has previously depended on stand-alone embedded devices, including weather thermometers and sprinkler systems. Using sensor

© Springer Nature Singapore Pte Ltd. 2019
G. Wang et al. (Eds.): iSCI 2019, CCIS 1122, pp. 379–391, 2019.
https://doi.org/10.1007/978-981-15-1301-5_30

information and other external data, systems that were once stand-alone can be incorporated into larger scale systems and monitored to a higher precision [17]. The internet of things and cloud computing are driving introduction of Artificial Intelligence (AI) and robotics into farming [6]. 'Smart' farming not only targets agriculture on a large commercial scale [23], but can also be used to improve areas such as consumer-level agriculture. There are multiple examples of consumer-focused products such as GreenIQ and the Parrot 'Smart Pot' [7]. Horticulture is a perfect candidate for an IoT smart device solution. The main factors affecting plant growth are easily observable by sensors, which makes monitoring easier to implement accurately.

The internet of things is being used within agriculture to help provide solutions for efficient farming [24]. An expanding worldwide population means that food production volume, and the efficiency of production, both need to increase. Climate change, soil quality and shrinking farmland availability all affect agriculture [21,25]. A Microsoft project called FarmBeat is attempting to find a solution using artificial intelligence and the internet of things for data driven farming. Data is collected from sensors and drones before processing by machine learning algorithms to map the land. This data is used to facilitate precision agriculture, providing information to increase density, quality, and sustainability of the crops grown [8].

Limiting water use within agriculture is also important as it saves money. A real life implementation is SCADAfarm by WaterForce which offers multiple IoT farming solutions. Large scale farms use pivot irrigation systems to water crops. This is installed alongside already active irrigation systems. The sensor data is stored and processed in the cloud [10,18], allowing irrigation control via a web or mobile application.

The sensors permit observation of the soil moisture level and set the watering depth. This is highly customised for different crops and farming layouts making it easier to avoid over-watering and optimising plant growth [9].

Several researchers have worked on automatic water sprinkling or irrigation. To determine the soil condition and water quantity, they opted for different metrics [13–16].

We examined various sensors and microcontrollers. This sophisticated system was a low-power device, with remote control and wireless network sensor technology, that can reduce manual conversion to remote automation [11]. We propose an automatic irrigation system to improve water use for plants in agriculture. A soil moisture sensor has been developed to assess soil water content. The system was tested in a sage crop field. The web application is designed to visualise results [12].

1.1   Motivation

In today's digital world, many farmers still use traditional methods. Digital technology allows farmers and agribusinesses to develop resilience, scale-up and sustainable solutions. Major efforts are being made to improve daily life via the introduction of smart devices and the internet of things. Using smart devices can help in many areas from trivial devices such as smart kettles to security systems. In the area of household horticulture, environmental factors greatly affect the growth of plants. Monitoring these factors can aid plant health and can also be used for home automation. Besides, The implementation of new technology in the field will solve major agricultural challenges.

1.2 Contribution

Our contribution to propose a lightweight cloud monitoring for smart agriculture. The system proposed comprises hardware as well as software. It also provides a platform to transfer and store the sensor data from microcontrollers. The microcontroller integrates a sensor of temperature and humidity as well as a capacitive sensor of moisture. Data is also stored in a SQL database, enabling information to be processed further. The Django framework is developed for user management to grant access to the MQTT broker and view collected sensor data.

Paper Organisation. The remaining part of the paper is organised as follows. In Sect. 2, we discuss the proposed model. Section 3 describes the Raspberry Pi MQTT Broker and SQL Backup Implementation. Section 4, the ESPlantMonitoring web application is developed for user management to grant access to the MQTT broker and view collected sensor data in Sect. 5. Section 5 provides results and subsequent analysis, followed by MOTT Broker testing in Sect. 6. Finally, we conclude with directions for future development in Sect. 7.

2 Description of the Model

The proposed model comprises both hardware and software. The main system, implemented using a Raspberry Pi and microcontroller [19], is shown in the Fig. 1. The proposed IoT cloud for plant monitoring system using a Raspberry Pi comprises of an Internet of Things device (ESP32 microcontroller), Web Application (Django), Database (MYSQL), Web Server and a MQTT broker (Mosquitto) [20]. The Internet of Things device will collect data from multiple sensors. The device will be connected to the Internet via Wi-Fi and will send the sensor data to the MQTT Broker. The database using MQTT publish. An MQTT broker is used to collect information from IoT sensors using MQTT publish, and easily accesses the live data using MQTT Subscribe. The MQTT broker will be running on a Raspberry PI [19,22]. When the data is received via the Raspberry PI, it will be stored into the database by hooking into the publish event, converting to JSON and storing using MYSQL. The web application can be used to see previous sensor data stored and live data, while the Mobile Application is used to view live data from the MQTT Broker. Using the web application the user can register an account, this grants them access to the dashboard, within this dashboard users can add sensors using the unique key stored on the microcontroller. On registering, a new user will be added to the users table, this username/password is also used to access the MQTT server on the mobile application.

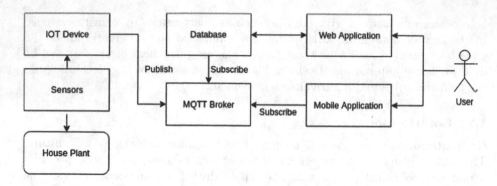

Fig. 1. Proposed model.

3 Raspberry Pi MQTT Broker and SQL Backup Implementation

An MQTT broker is used to manage communication of MQTT messages using the publish-subscribe-based messaging protocol [20]. We chose Eclipse Mosquitto as the MQTT broker. This is a popular choice when configuring a MQTT broker on a Raspberry PI.

Alongside the main function of managing messages, we needed user authentication. This was done using the open-source plugin mosquitto-auth-plug.

Fig. 2. ESPantMonintering Platform.

To set this up we need to compile both the ESPantMonintering Platform (Fig. 2), Mosquitto and the authentication plug-in code from source, using compatible versions. The Mosquitto auth plug-in is compatible with multiple different database back ends; we used MySQL.

- *P*assword Hashing
  The plug-in provides authentication by checking the username and password against the relevant SQL table using a SQL query. The plugin requires the passwords to be stored using PBKDF2 hashing. This was important when developing the Web Application and affected the web development framework chosen to develop the application. Initially we were going to create the application using Laravel, but this would require a long process of modifying the middleware as the default hashing for Laravel is Bcrypt.
- *A*ccess Control List
  Another security of the plug-in is the access control list this is a table within the database that defines which users can access which topic using wildcards. Without this feature users would be able to publish and subscribe to any topic they wanted, which would not be a secure way to manage the MQTT data.
- *M*osquitto Configuration
  The mosquitto config file is used to specify what settings the broker should use when running.
- *S*QL Backup
  A key feature of the platform is the ability to view historical sensor data, Mosquitto does not provide database backup functionality, therefore we chose to write a Python script to store the sensor data. The script uses the Paho MQTT library to connect to the MQTT broker and subscribes to the relevant topic. It then retrieves the messages and deserializes the JSON and places it into an SQL statement. Finally the SQL statement is executed and the data is stored.

4   ESPlantMonitoring Development

The ESPlantMonitoring web application is developed for user management to grant access to the MQTT broker and view collected sensor data. Django is a web framework which follows the Model- View-Template architecture and is based on the Python programming language. Having the a large variety of libraries available, Django is a good choice for Web Applications. Interaction with the website changes depending on whether a user is logged in or not. The homepage/landing page gives a brief overview of what the platform provides and an option to learn more about the platform. Figure 3 The About page gives a more in-depth description of the platform and gives details on how to setup ESP devices to interact with the platform. Figure 4 In order to interact with the website, the user needs to register an account; this is done using the user login/register page. A valid account will have as a username an e-mail with valid syntax, and a unique password which is not similar to other details, and at least 8 characters which cannot be only numeric.

Once a user is logged in, they can access the View Devices and user profile pages through the navigation bar. This page is the dashboard for managing devices, the main feature being to generate new keys. These keys are what links each unique device via the device id. All the users devices are then listed. Selecting the device will take you to the device details/management page. The device details page visualizes the data into a time-series chart for the user and gives the option to delete the device. Doing so will delete all relevant sensor data and remove the device id from their account.

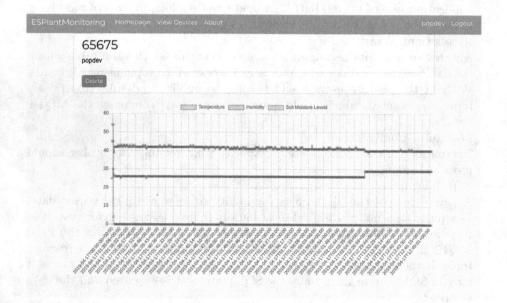

Fig. 3. Creating a new user.

The models define how the data in the database is structured and are used to interact with the data. Django has a built in user model, this creates the auth user table used to store user information. When a user is created they are added to the access control list, and allowed access to the topic sensors/username/. This is a topic that only they can access and use and should be used by all sensors. We then created two models called data and device. The device table stores user devices, linking the device id with the foreign key of user id from the users table. The data table then uses the device id as a foreign key to link devices with data taken from that sensor.

Django also creates multiple tables to structure and provide general admin functionality to the website. An important feature to remember when creating a web application that implements an SQL database is to setup links and restrictions, This prevents users from deleting data that will break the system. SQL creates links and restricions automatically on foreign keys. It is important to use

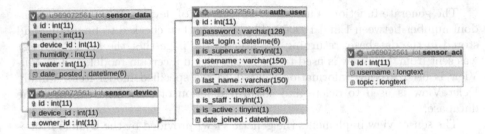

Fig. 4. User authentication.

these links to determine what action is taken if a primary key used as a foreign key in another table is deleted. For example if a user deletes a sensor device, what happens to the linked sensors data. The SQL CASCADE method is used to delete data from child tables meaning that if the user a sensor then all linked data will be deleted also (Fig. 5).

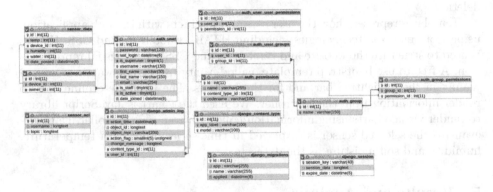

Fig. 5. Full database diagram.

A view function takes a web request and returns a HTTP response. This used for the management of site data and what is presented to the templates on certain pages. Within this work this HTTP response is usually a template alongside context variables. Covering each function within the view would be a large task which is not particularly relevant to the final product, therefore we restrict coverage to the functionality of managing and viewing devices and device data.

The sensor view implements the generic views provided by the Django framework, the views are linked to a selected model. ListView is used to list items within a certain model, Detail View is used to view information of the specified model item. Finally DeleteView is used to delete and confirm deletion of a model item from the database.

The generate function is used for the creation of devices. It generates a random number between 1 and 100000. The value is then checked to be unique and stored in the database, returning the user to the page that the HTTP request was sent from. ListView is used to list items within a certain model, and Detail-View is used to view information related to the specified model item. Finally DeleteView is used to delete and confirm deletion of a model item from the database.

The sensor view implements the generic views provided by the Django framework. These views are linked to a selected model. DateTime Handler is used to convert date time variables from SQL to JSON format. DeviceListView is used on the sensor homepage. Firstly the function retrieves the current logged in user, this makes it so the model items retrieved are user relevant. The DeviceDe-tailView requires context data for charting using the template. A query set is created taking the current user and Device ID selected. It the relevant data from the query set. This data is then converted to JSON format using the json.dumps function and placed into the context to be returned to the template. The DeviceDeleteView is used for the deletion of the selected device, the function check whether the device is owned by the user before confirming the deletion.

Templates represent how the user sees and interacts with the web application, using front-end web technologies including HTML, Bootstrap, and CSS. HTML is used to structure the website and Bootstrap and CSS are for visual representation. A free to use bootstrap template, called Minty from Bootswatch, was used mainly in the navigation bar and for the buttons. The views determine how to render information from the controller. We used the Chart.js JavaScript library to render visual charts using information collected from the controller. Data relevant to the selected sensor is displayed in time-series order with temperature, humidity and soil moisture as the datasets.

5 Results and Analysis

The prototype of the systems has been developed, and is deployed in a garden. The same prototype can also be used for agricultural applications conditioned by which sensor is required. Each sensor with its unique identity can access changes in the environment continuously. The test scenario of the prototype is shown in the figure. We used the serial monitor output to test sensor readings and check for errors. Once the device is switched on it attempts to connect to the WiFi Network specified, once connected to the network it will attempt to connect to the MQTT server and finally it will attempt to connect to the network time server (Fig. 6).

The output shown in the red box is the configuration output, as can be seen all network connections were successful. The device places all relevant sensor information alongside the device ID and DateTime into JSON format, to test if the sensors are functioning correctly the data was printed to the serial monitor, and this is shown in the blue box on the diagram. Each sensor produced a reading

Connecting to WiFi..
2019-04-29 13:19:34
Connected to the WiFi network:
Connecting to MQTT...
connected to MQTT
2019-04-29 13:19:35
2019-04-29 13:19:35
[{"device_id":65675,"temp":27,"humidity":53,"water":12,"date_posted":"2019-04-29 13:19:35"}]

Fig. 6. IoT device is attempting to connect the MQTT server. (Color figure online)

and was placed into the correct JSON format. To test sensor accuracy, we took a reading from the soil moisture sensor in a dry state and then fully submerged it in water to get two readings (Fig. 7).

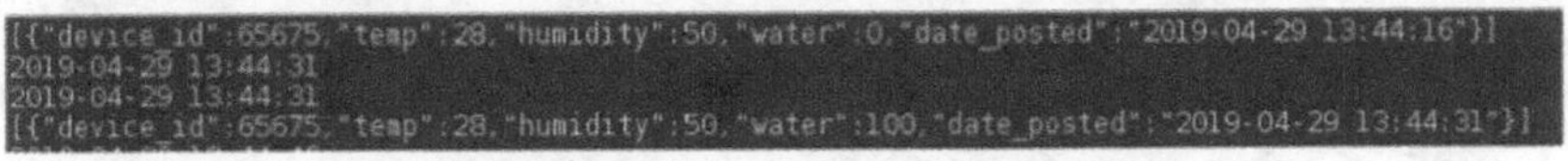

[{"device_id":65675,"temp":28,"humidity":50,"water":0,"date_posted":"2019-04-29 13:44:16"}]
2019-04-29 13:44:31
2019-04-29 13:44:31
[{"device_id":65675,"temp":28,"humidity":50,"water":100,"date_posted":"2019-04-29 13:44:31"}]

Fig. 7. Soil moisture sensor.

The calibration of the soil moisture sensor was correct, with a reading of 0 when dry and 100 when fully submerged. Unfortunately we were unable to verify the accuracy of the temperature and humidity sensor although this has no bearing on the demonstration of the usefulness of the system architecture.

6   MQTT Broker Testing

In order to test basic functionality of the MQTT broker we used a mobile application called MQTTool. This application provides connection testing and basic publish/subscribe functionality. Firstly, we tested if a user which is not specified in the auth user SQL table could connect to the public IP address. We then attempted to connect with an account within the table to the public IP address. The results were as expected and the broker authentication plug-in was working in this aspect.

Having determined the configuration of the ESP32 was correct and authentication worked, We then started the SQL backup script running on the Raspberry PI. We started the script and then powered the ESP32. The script prints the SQL statement derived from the sensor data. Firstly we compared the data from the serial monitor of the ESP32 to the SQL statement and then checked the statement was successfully executed to the database Comparing Figs. 8 to 9 shows that the JSON data was transferred and the correct SQL statement was produced. Figure 10 shows that SQL cursor executed the SQL statement correctly. The device details page is used manage devices, displaying device details and giving the option to delete the device. In order to test this functionality we populated the empty datasets shown in Fig. 8 via the IoT device. Once populated the chart is generated from the updated dataset shown in figure below. This data is shown in that database in figure below. The testing carried out shows the database working for sensor data from the IoT device and for device and user management. Improvements could be made by either changing database type from SQL or by monitoring the database over a period of time to find improvements to the efficiency. The MQTT broker was implemented to a certain extent.

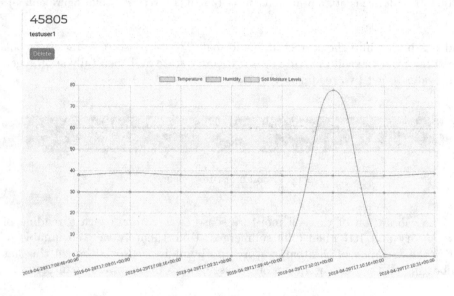

Fig. 8. User1 45805 sensor

In order to test this functionality, we populated the empty datasets via the IoT device. Once populated, the chart is generated from the updated dataset shown in Figs. 8 and 9. This data is shown in that database in Figs. 10 and 11. The testing carried out shows the database working for sensor data from the IoT device and for device and user management. Improvements could be made by either changing database type from SQL or by monitoring the database over a period of time to find improvements to the efficiency. The MQTT broker was implemented to a certain extent, general functionality worked and the SQL authentication was implemented.

The Web Application was fully functional, enabling user account and device managements once logged in. A user can have multiple sensors by using multiple unique device IDs through the device manager. Once devices are setup data is retrieved from the database and visualised in charts, this meets the requirements but with room for improvement, the charts show all data for the specified device, rather than displaying all data a better implementation would be to specify what time frame the data should be within.

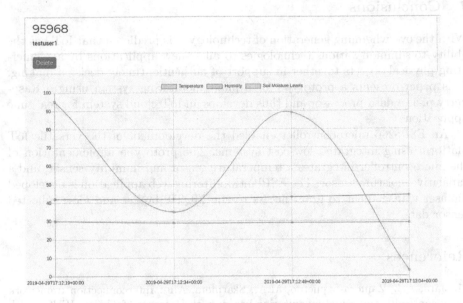

Fig. 9. User1 95969 sensor

id	temp	device_id	humidity	water	date_posted
485	30	95968	42	95	2019-04-29 17:12:19.000000
486	29	95968	42	35	2019-04-29 17:12:34.000000
487	29	95968	43	89	2019-04-29 17:12:49.000000
488	29	95968	44	3	2019-04-29 17:13:04.000000

Fig. 10. 45805 SQL data.

id	temp	device_id	humidity	water	date_posted
485	30	95968	42	95	2019-04-29 17:12:19.000000
486	29	95968	42	35	2019-04-29 17:12:34.000000
487	29	95968	43	89	2019-04-29 17:12:49.000000
488	29	95968	44	3	2019-04-29 17:13:04.000000

Fig. 11. 95969 SQL data.

7   Conclusions

With the overwhelming generation of technology it is predicted that IoT has the ability to summon various technologies to allow new applications by agglomerating physical objects together in support of authentic, timely decision-making. This paper presents a prototype for a plant monitoring system using a Raspberry pi as a data processor and thus develops an IoT cloud system for real time applications.

An ESP8266 microcontroller enabled the development of the versatile IoT platform using integrated low-cost systems. The prototype implementation of the microcontroller integrates a temperature sensor and humidity sensor, and a capacitive moisture sensor. The ESPlantMonitoring web application is developed for user management to grant access to the MQTT broker and view collected sensor data.

References

1. Jara, A.J., Zamora-Izquierdo, M.A., Skarmeta, A.F.: Interconnection framework for mHealth and remote monitoring based on the Internet of Things. IEEE J. Sel. Areas Commun. **31**(9), 47–65 (2013)
2. Ikram, A., et al.: Approaching the Internet of Things (IoT): a modelling, analysis and abstraction framework. Concurr. Comput. Pract. Exp. **27**(8), 1966–1984 (2015)
3. Al-Aqrabi, H., Hill, R.: Dynamic multiparty authentication of data analytics services within cloud environments. In: 2018 IEEE 20th International Conference on High Performance Computing and Communications; IEEE 16th International Conference on Smart City; IEEE 4th International Conference on Data Science and Systems (HPCC/SmartCity/DSS), June 2018, pp. 742–749 (2018)
4. Chui, M., Loffler, M., Roberts, R.: The Internet of Things (2010)
5. Hwang, K., Chen, M.: Big-Data Analytics for Cloud, IoT and Cognitive Computing. Wiley, Hoboken (2017)
6. Wolfert, S., Ge, L., Verdouw, C., Bogaardt, M.-J.: Big data in smart farming - a review. Agric. Syst. **153**, 69–80 (2017)
7. Parrot POT, 29 November 2017. Parrot Official website. https://www.parrot.com/global/connected-garden/parrot-pot. Accessed 27 Aug 2019
8. FarmBeats: AI, Edge & IoT for Agriculture (n.d.). Microsoft Research website. https://www.microsoft.com/en-us/research/project/farmbeats-iotagriculture/. Accessed 27 Apr 2019
9. SCADAfarm - SOLUTIONS (n.d.). https://www.scadafarm.com/solutions. Accessed 27 June 2019
10. Al-Aqrabi, H., Liu, L., Hill, R., Antonopoulos, N.: A multi-layer hierarchical intercloud connectivity model for sequential packet inspection of tenant sessions accessing BI as a service. In: Proceedings of 6th International Symposium on (CSS) and IEEE 11th International Conference on (ESS), France, Paris, 20–22 March 2014, pp. 137–144. IEEE (2014)
11. Gore, T.H., et al.: Crop monitoring analysis and controlling system. J. Adv. Res. Comput. Sci. Softw. Eng. **6**(2), 138–141 (2016)

12. Gutierez, J., et al.: Automated iriigation system using a wireless sensor network and GPRS module. IEEE Trans. Instrum. Measur. **63**(1), 163–176 (2014)
13. Bhawarkar, N.B., et al.: Literature review for automated water supply with monitoring the performance system. Int. J. Curr. Eng. Technol. **4**(5), 3328–3331 (2014)
14. Avatade, S.S., Dhanure, S.P.: Irrigation system using a wireless sensor network and GPRS. Int. J. Adv. Res. Comput. Commun. Eng. **4**(5), 521–524 (2015)
15. Koushik, A., et al.: Automatic drip irrigation system using fuzzy logic and mobile technology. In: 2015 IEEE Technological Innovation in ICT for Agriculture and Rural Development (TIAR). IEEE (2015)
16. Lala, B., et al.: Automatic crop irrigation system. In: 2015 4th International Conference on Reliability, Infocom Technologies and Optimization (ICRITO). IEEE (2015)
17. Ezhilazhahi, A.M., Bhuvaneswari, P.T.V.: IoT enabled plant soil moisture monitoring using wireless sensor networks. In: 2017 Third International Conference on Sensing, Signal Processing and Security (ICSSS), pp. 345–349 (2017)
18. Al-Aqrabi, H., Liu, L., Hill, R., Cui, L., Li, J.: Faceted search in business intelligence on the cloud. In: 2013 IEEE International Conference on Green Computing and Communications and IEEE Internet of Things and IEEE Cyber, Physical and Social Computing. IEEE (2013)
19. ESP8266 vs. ESP32 on Battery Power, 10 December 2018. ESP8266 vs. ESP32 on Battery Power website. https://blog.voneicken.com/2018/lp-wifiesp-comparison/. Accessed 28 June 2019
20. HTTP vs. MQTT: A tale of two IoT protocols (2018). Google Cloud Blog website. https://cloud.google.com/blog/products/iot-devices/http-vsmqtt-a-tale-of-two-iot-protocols/. Accessed 28 Apr 2019
21. Lea, R., Blackstock, M.: Smart cities: an IoT-centric approach. In: ACM International Conference Proceeding Series (2014)
22. Williams, M.G.: A risk assessment on Raspberry PI using NIST standards, December 2012
23. Mohanraj, I., Ashokumarb, K., Naren, J.: Field monitoring and automation using IOT in agriculture domain. In: IJCSNS, no. 6, June 2015
24. Gutiérrez, J., et al.: Automated irrigation system using a wireless sensor network and GPRS module. IEEE Trans. Instrum. Measur. **17**, 166–176 (2017)
25. Liu, C., Ren, W., Zhang, B., Lv, C.: The application of soil temperature measurement by LM35 temperature sensors. In: International Conference on Electronic and Mechanical Engineering and Information Technology, vol. 88, no. 1, pp. 1825–1828 (2011)

Condition Monitoring of Motorised Devices for Smart Infrastructure Capabilities

Pritesh Mistry[✉], Phil Lane, Paul Allen, Hussain Al-Aqrabi, and Richard Hill

School of Computing and Engineering, University of Huddersfield, Huddersfield, UK
{p.mistry,p.lane,p.d.allen,h.al-aqrabi,r.hill}@hud.ac.uk

Abstract. This paper presents a signal processing methodology based on fast Fourier transform for the early fault detection of electrically motorised devices. We used time-stamped, current draw data provided by Network Rail, UK, to develop a methodology that may identify imminent faults in point machine operations. In this paper we describe the data, preprocessing steps and methodology developed that can be used with similar motorised devices as a means of identifying potential fault occurrences. The novelty of our method is that it does not rely on labelled data for fault detection. This method could be integrated into smart city infrastructure and deployed to provide automated asset maintenance management capabilities.

Keywords: Condition monitoring · Fault detection · Point machines · Fast Fourier transform · Smart city

1 Introduction

Smart cities are urban areas that implement electronic sensors and detection devices to collect and process data. These physical devices make up the internet of things (IoT) and aim to provide a means to manage services, assets, and resources within a city [3,7,9]. Cities are complex systems, the idea of a smart city emerged as a means to facilitate the communication between information and communication technologies (ICT), that would be advantageous to serve a city's needs. Indeed a city can only be considered "smart" if it is able to synthesis these data in some intelligent manner.

Harrison et al. [5] described smart cities to have three key components, They must be instrumented, to capture real-world live data through the use of sensors and devices. Interconnected, to allow the integration of collected data into computing platforms, and intelligent, to explore, model, and analyse the data to leverage the information contained within, for the benefit of the city.

A railway infrastructure could be considered smart if it is able to employ smart technology to provide autonomy to its functionalities. One aspect of such autonomy could be the detection of fault occurrences. Such capabilities are

© Springer Nature Singapore Pte Ltd. 2019
G. Wang et al. (Eds.): iSCI 2019, CCIS 1122, pp. 392–403, 2019.
https://doi.org/10.1007/978-981-15-1301-5_31

desirable for many reasons, primarily from a safety perspective [12], but also to streamline servicing and repairs to offer minimal disruption to passengers.

Point machines are a critical part of a railway infrastructure, used for switching and locking railway turnouts. Point machines consist of an electrically driven rotary motor, whose movement is transmitted through gearing to produce linear movement to lock or unlock the rails [11] changing their position from normal (NR) to reverse (RN) and vice versa. The use of an electric motor in point machines makes current based fault identification viable. A point machine will undergo a process of degradation as normal operation tends to complete failure. If the progression or rate of degradation can be identified over time then maintenance can be arranged prior to failure occurrence.

Although guidelines for point machine operation and replacement exist, such as, replacement after a fixed time period or after a number of accumulated actuations, these guidelines do not take into consideration the operational and environmental conditions such as the track load or weather. As such, faults may occur unexpectedly, so more robust fault identification methods are required. When considering fault detections for point machine failures, the early approaches relied on threshold settings, but produced limited success with a high proportion of false alarms [8]. More recent methods used historical data and machine learning techniques [1, 2] to identify anomalies that could signify machine wear and potential imminent failure.

Asada et al. [1] extracted features of point machine electrical power consumption using discrete wavelet transform and trained a support vector machine (SVM) to produce predictive accuracies of 100%. Similarly Bian et al. [2], used self-organising maps (SOM) and SVM to identify degradation states of point machines before classifying the degradation states to 96.97% accuracies. An interesting approach by Garcia et al. [4] used "expected" current signals from historical data and compared these to measured signals. A VARMA (vector auto-regressive moving-average) model and harmonic regression model were used to generate the "expected" signal forms. If the incoming signal produced a trace beyond the "expected" model a fault was deemed to have been detected.

2   Data

The data used for this study were supplied by Network Rail, UK, and covered three regions; London North Eastern (LNE), London North Western (LNWN) and Sussex. The data were collected over the months of April 2018 to June 2018, with each region containing several thousand csv (comma-separated values) files. Each file is a daily log for every actuation of a point machine in a given direction (either NR or RN), recorded in a continuous sequential manner for a given day. Each file is labelled with the point machine name, date of logging, and direction of movement (NR or RN). Within each file, the current draw in amperes (amps or A) is recorded against a millisecond time-stamp for every actuation that occurred on a given day. Table 1 shows the number of files and point machines present in each of the three regions. A total of 45,690 files were initially available in the dataset. All the data available are unlabelled data and therefore no indication of fault occurrences are known.

Table 1. Number of point machine instruments across each region, and files present in the dataset

Region	No. of files	No. of point machines
LNE	15,802	103
LNWN	17,081	129
SUSSEX	12,807	99

An example of a typical file containing current draw time-stamped data is shown in Table 2. The table shows the first five records (Row0-Row4) and the last five records (Row242-Row246) of the first actuation for point machine ALTOFTJT_NOC_P2443B, in the NR direction logged on the 1st June 2018. The table also shows the first five records (Row247-Row251) of the second actuation of the same point machine in the NR direction on the same day. The frequency of data logs during actuation is approximately 10 ms. Once an actuation is complete the data log stops until the next actuation is actioned. An example of this can be seen between Row246 and Row247 of Table 2, which shows the end of one actuation log and the beginning of another. The time-stamp for these records moves from 2018-06-01 02:28:07.977 to 2018-06-01 05:30:57.793, which is a time difference of many minutes, suggesting the two entries cannot be for the same actuation event. It is also worthwhile to note that any given actuation begins with a current reading of 0.00 A (zero amps) and ends with a current reading of 0.00 A, as can be seen for the records at Row0 (start of first actuation) and Row246 (end of first actuation) and again at Row247 (start of second actuation).

2.1 Data Preprocessing

Real-world data is seldom error free and as such an element of preprocessing and data cleansing was required. For this study all the data preprocessing and analysis was performed using the Knime analytics platform [6] and R Statistical package [10]. In the first instance, all 45,690 files (LNE, LNWN and Sussex) were checked for errors. Any files that contained missing records or erroneous values were identified and removed from the data. It also transpired that the data contained files with duplicate names. Unable to ascertain the validity of these files, all duplicates were removed from the data. After this initial preprocessing step the number of remaining files and point machines available for analysis are shown in Table 3. A total of 23,389 files remained. In this study the normal (NR) and reserve (RN) profiles were not considered separately. Rather, the presumption was taken that should a fault occur with the operation of an instrument that is identifiable from the current draw, then this fault would be observable in both the normal (NR) and reverse (RN) direction.

Table 2. Current draw for point machine ALTOFTJT_NOC_P2443B, of direction NR, logged on the 1st June 2018.

Row No	DateTime	ALTOFTJT_NOC_P2443B_NR_current
Row0	2018-06-01 02:28:05.527	0.0
Row1	2018-06-01 02:28:05.537	13.18
Row2	2018-06-01 02:28:05.547	19.43
Row3	2018-06-01 02:28:05.557	18.04
Row4	2018-06-01 02:28:05.567	16.15
⋮	⋮	⋮
Row242	2018-06-01 02:28:07.937	0.82
Row243	2018-06-01 02:28:07.947	0.81
Row244	2018-06-01 02:28:07.957	0.80
Row245	2018-06-01 02:28:07.967	0.76
Row246	2018-06-01 02:28:07.977	0.00
Row247	2018-06-01 05:30:57.793	0.00
Row248	2018-06-01 05:30:57.803	0.81
Row249	2018-06-01 05:30:57.813	16.22
Row250	2018-06-01 05:30:57.823	19.37
Row251	2018-06-01 05:30:57.833	17.55
⋮	⋮	⋮

3 Methodology

For fast Fourier transform (FFT) analysis it was necessary to separate each actuation of every point machine in the data which remained. Since the data is presented in a continuous sequential manner, to separate individual actuations, the time difference between recorded instances was calculated within a file. Where a difference of ≥ 500 ms and a 0.00 A current reading between adjacent records existed, this indicated the beginning of a new actuation event. For example, in Table 2 the time difference between Row246 and Row247 is >500 ms with a 0.00 A current reading, this therefore indicates the beginning of a new actuation event for that point machine. Conversely, the time difference between

Table 3. Number of point machine instruments across each region after preprocessing

Region	No. of files	No. of point machines
LNE	6,533	92
LNWN	9,715	105
SUSSEX	7,141	91

Row247 and Row248 is <500 ms and therefore indicates those records are of the same actuation event. An example of the current draw signal in the normal (NR) and reverse (RN) direction for point machine ALTOFTJT_NOC_P2443B is shown in Fig. 1.

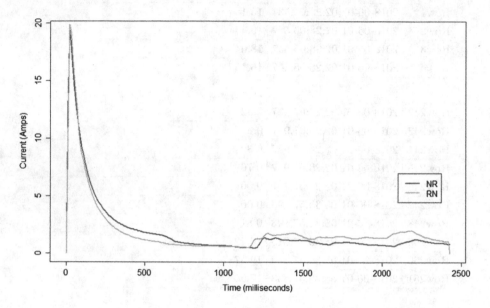

Fig. 1. Current draw profile of point machine ALTOFTJT_NOC_P2443B actuations in the normal (NR) and reverse (RN) directions.

3.1   Fast Fourier Transform (FFT)

The signal produced by each actuation of a point machine is represented by the current (amps) changing over time as shown in Fig. 1. This is commonly referred to as the time domain. A fast Fourier transform can be applied to deconstruct a time domain signal into a frequency domain representation. These frequency domain components are represented as discrete values or bins and used to analyse the different frequencies present in the original signal.

For each point machine, individual actuation profiles were separated as described above. Typically each profile resulted in approximately 250 instances of data. As such, a zero padding was added to the end of each profile that made all profiles up to 512 samples. A sliding window of length 512 and step size of 256 was used for the input signal. To prevent spectral leakage and enhance the ability of an FFT to extract spectral data the Hann windowing function was used. The goal of minimising leakage is to prevent an FFT from producing the wrong frequencies. When an FFT is used to measure the frequency component it assumes a finite data set, or simply, a single period of a periodic signal. When the signal data used is not periodic, windowing helps to reduce the amplitude of the discontinuous data at the boundaries. A frequency domain plot of the data in Table 2 is shown in Fig. 2.

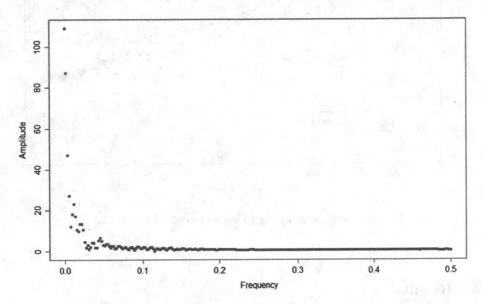

Fig. 2. Frequency domain plot following FFT of the signal data from the actuation of point machine ALTOFTJT_NOC_P2443B in the normal (NR) direction.

3.2   Curve Fitting

To identify anomalies in the processed signal, an attempt was made to fit a curve to the frequency domain data shown in Fig. 2. The goodness of fit achieved from second and third order polynomials were not satisfactory. Therefore it was decided to take the $\log_{10}$ value of both the frequency and amplitude values of the FFT. Using the $\log_{10}$ values resulted in a more linear relationship of the frequency domain and amplitude. A linear curve could then be fitted to the data and the goodness of fit calculated. A plot of the $\log_{10}$ values and fitted curve is shown in Fig. 3. A linear curve was fitted using the R statistical package [10], with the residual standard error obtained for further analysis.

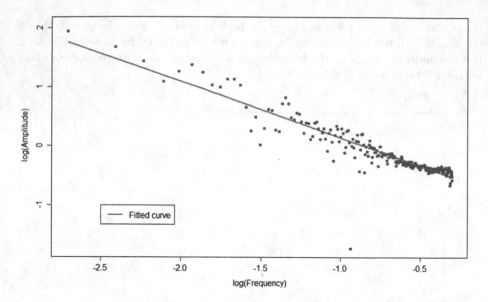

Fig. 3. Linear curve fitting to log values of FFT analysis.

4   Results

The methodology proposed is based on the premise that a poorly functioning point machine can be identified from the signal data it produces. A point machine that produces an irregular unexpected signal is more likely to be showing signs of wear and imminent failure. The process of FFT and curve fitting to ascertain goodness of fit is a novel approach for fault detection. Although the data used in this study is unlabelled, and therefore cannot unequivocally be assigned to a fault, we can gauge how well this methodology works from the residual standard error values produced. For actuations where a fault is not apparent we expect the residual standard error to be comparatively lower.

Figure 4 shows the time domain signal of point machine ALTOFTJT_NOC _P2443A when moving in the reverse direction (RN), whilst Fig. 5 shows a linear curve fitted to the log of the frequency and amplitude upon FFT analysis of the same actuation. From the data processed in this study the signal produced in Fig. 4 seems typical of a point machine in good working order. This is further supported by the residual standard error of the fitted curve shown in Fig. 5 which produced a value of 0.064.

Compare this with the time domain signal of point machine ALTOFTS_TJC3 _P2442A in the reverse direction (RN) as shown in Fig. 6. It is immediately apparent from the signal profile that the period from approximately 500–1500 ms is not as smooth as that of the same period in Fig. 4. Furthermore the log of the frequency and amplitude upon FFT analysis shown in Fig. 7 produces a greater residual standard error value of 0.256.

Using the residual standard error values of every actuation of a given point machine, a profile of the operational characteristics of an instrument can be produced. Plotting the residual standard errors over time quickly shows where an instrument has potentially failed or about to fail. Figure 8 shows a residual standard error plot for all the actuations of point machine APPLYJCT_TJC3_P5109 in the normal (NR) direction. Over 1250 actuations are shown, all of which produce a very consistent baseline residual standard error value of approximately 0.05.

Similarly Fig. 9 shows a residual standard error plot for all the actuations of point machine ALTOFTJT_NOC_P2443A in the normal (NR) direction. On this plot however, the baseline residual standard error value, of approximately 0.10, is higher than for that of point machine APPLYJCT_TJC3_P5109 (Fig. 8). Furthermore there is one actuation event which produces a residual standard error value of >0.30, much higher than the baseline for the instrument, which may suggest operational issues with the instrument. Other actuations along the time line have produced residual standard error values that begin to push beyond the baseline value and may signify the development of a fault.

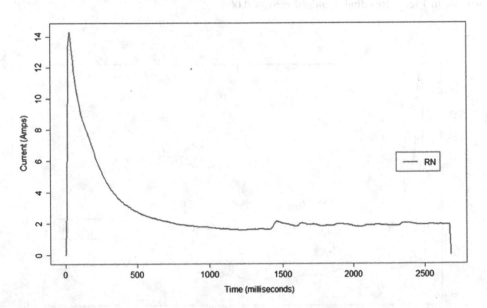

Fig. 4. Time domain signal of point machine ALTOFTJT_NOC_P2443A actuation in the reverse (RN) direction.

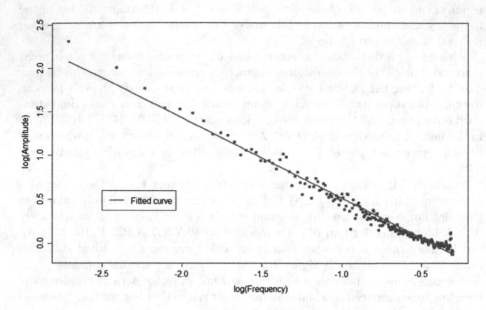

Fig. 5. Curve fitting of the FFT analysis of point machine ALTOFTJT_NOC_P2443A shown in Fig. 4. Residual standard error = 0.064.

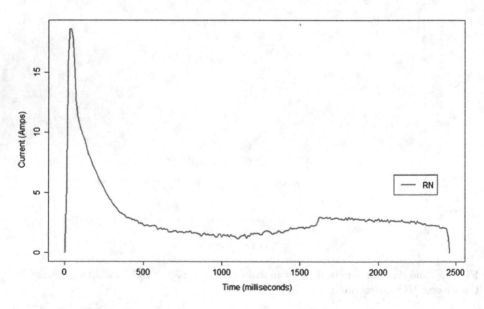

Fig. 6. Time domain signal of point machine ALTOFTS_TJC3_P2442A actuation in the reverse (RN) direction.

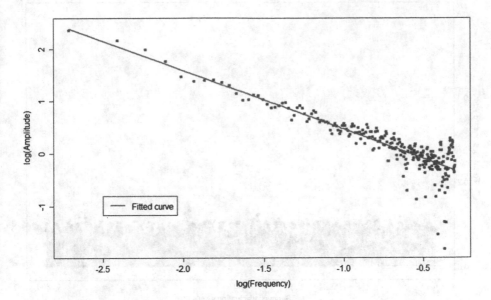

Fig. 7. Curve fitting of the FFT analysis of point machine ALTOFTS_TJC3_P2442A shown in Fig. 6. Residual standard error = 0.256

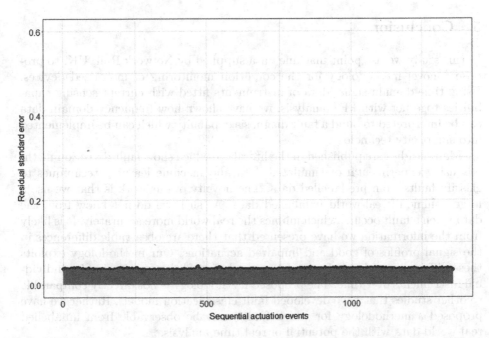

Fig. 8. Residual standard error of sequential actuation events for point machine APPLYJCT_TJC3_P5109 in the NR direction.

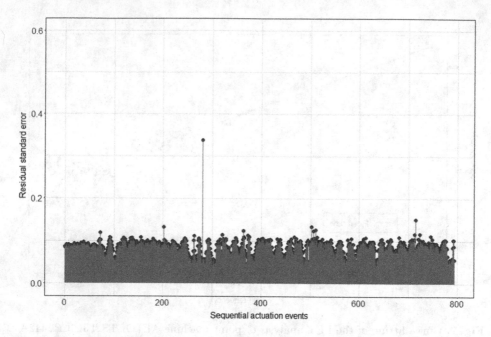

Fig. 9. Residual standard error of sequential actuation events for point machine ALTOFTJT_NOC_P2443A in the NR direction.

5   Conclusion

In this study we use point machine data supplied by Network Rail, UK, to propose a novel methodology for the condition monitoring of motorised devices. Using time domain signal data of instruments fitted with current sensing capabilities together with FFT analysis, we have shown how frequency domain data can be interpreted to build a fault diagnosis capability which can be implemented into smart city technology.

Many studies are published in the literature which show fault detection methods using experimental or simulated data and machine learning techniques to classify faults from pre-labelled data. The novelty of our work is that we use a large volume of real-world unlabelled data. As such we do not know from the data when a fault occurs, which mimics the real world more accurately. It is likely from the information we have presented that there are observable differences in the signal profiles of good and impaired actuations. Our methodology exploits these differences and puts forward a method of condition monitoring for individual instruments over time. The proposed methodology is not directly comparable to other studies that have developed fault classification models. Rather we have proposed a methodology for which faults may be observable from unlabelled real-world data with the potential of real time analysis.

As seen from the evidence presented in our results, the behavioural characteristics of each point machine is unique to that machine. The advantage of this methodology is that it is dynamic to individual instruments and does not rely on a "one size fits all" thresholding approach. Rather it is able to treat each instrument separately and therefore monitor at the individual level.

Our future efforts will focus on using machine learning techniques to establish dynamic levels of residual standard error values for different point machines. It is evident from the data that point machines do not operate at equal baselines. Therefore, developing a system which can establish limits by learning the behaviour unique to each point machine would likely help reduce false positive detections. Furthermore it may be beneficial to separate the normal (NR) and reverse (RN) directions of actuations for improved fault detection.

References

1. Asada, T., Roberts, C., Koseki, T.: An algorithm for improved performance of railway condition monitoring equipment: alternating-current point machine case study. Transp. Res. Part C Emerg. Technol. **30**, 81–92 (2013)
2. Bian, C., et al.: Degradation detection method for railway point machines. arXiv preprint arXiv:1809.02349 (2018)
3. Chen, T.M.: Smart grids, smart cities need better networks [Editor's Note]. IEEE Netw. **24**(2), 2–3 (2010). https://doi.org/10.1109/MNET.2010.5430136. ISSN 0890-8044
4. Garcia, F.P., Pedregal, D.J., Roberts, C.: Time series methods applied to failure prediction and detection. Reliab. Eng. Syst. Saf. **95**(6), 698–703 (2010). ISSN 0951-8320
5. Harrison, C., et al.: Foundations for smarter cities. IBM J. Res. Dev. **54**(4), 1–16 (2010). https://doi.org/10.1147/JRD.2010.2048257. ISSN 0018-8646
6. Knime (2018). https://www.knime.com/. Accessed 2 Aug 2018
7. Barrionuevo, J.M., Berrone, P., Ricart, J.: Smart cities, sustainable progress: opportunities for urban development. IESE Insight 50–57 (2012). https://doi.org/10.15581/002.ART-2152
8. Garcia Marquez, F.P., Roberts, C., Tobias, A.M.: Railway point mechanisms: condition monitoring and fault detection. Proc. Inst. Mech. Eng. Part F J. Rail Rapid Transit **224**(1), 35–44 (2010)
9. Marsal, L., Colomer, J., Melendez, J.: Lessons in urban monitoring taken from sustainable and livable cities to better address the Smart Cities initiative. Technol. Forecast. Soc. Chang. **90**, 611–622 (2014). https://doi.org/10.1016/j.techfore.2014.01.012
10. R (2018). https://www.r-project.org/. Accessed 2 Aug 2018
11. Sa, J., et al.: Replacement condition detection of railway point machines using an electric current sensor. Sensors **17**(2), 263 (2017)
12. Vileiniskis, M., Remenyte-Prescott, R., Rama, D.: A fault detection method for railway point systems. Proc. Inst. Mech. Eng. Part F J. Rail Rapid Transit **230**(3), 852–865 (2016). https://doi.org/10.1177/0954409714567487

A Travel Aid for Visually Impaired: R-Cane

Kanak Manjari(ID), Madhushi Verma(ID), and Gaurav Singal(✉)(ID)

Department of Computer Science Engineering, Bennett University,
Greater Noida 201310, India
{km5723,madhushi.verma}@bennett.edu.in, gauravsingal789@gmail.com

Abstract. An Electronic Travel Aid (ETA) has become a necessity for visually impaired to provide them proper guidance and assistance in their daily routine. As the number of blind persons are gradually increasing, there is a dire need of an effective and low-cost solution for assisting them in their daily tasks. This paper presents a cane called R-Cane which is an ETA for the visually impaired and is capable of detecting obstacles in front direction using sonar sensor and alerts the user by informing whether the obstacle is within the range of one meter. In R-Cane, tensorflow object-detection API has been used for object recognition. It makes the user aware about the nature of objects by providing them voice-based output through bluetooth earphones. Raspberry Pi has been used for processing and Pi camera has been used to capture frames for object recognition. Further, we have implemented four models based on Single Shot Multibox Detector (SSD) for object detection. The experimental analysis shows that out of the four models, the average F1 score for all the classes is highest for SSD_Mobilenet_v1 _Ppn_Coco model.

Keywords: Electronic travel aids · Sensor · Assistive technology · Visually impaired · Ultrasonic sensor · Raspberry Pi

1 Introduction

World is a very beautiful place and we are fortunate enough to be able to see amazing things around us. But a person suffering from vision loss has to face many difficulties in their day-to-day tasks. According to World Health Organization (WHO) [26], 1.3 billion of persons are estimated to be suffering from vision impairment out of which 188.5 million persons have mild vision impairment, 217 million persons have moderate to severe vision impairment, and 36 million are blind [27]. The indoor and outdoor environment contains various obstacles of different shapes and sizes at various locations. Even sighted persons need to be careful sometimes to prevent collision with obstacles, and some of these obstacles can be dangerous for visually impaired (VI) such as descending staircases, conical edges etc. that can cause injuries.

A white cane [25] is the oldest and universal solution which acts like a safe mobility aid for blind persons. This cane is capable of detecting the objects in

G. Wang et al. (Eds.): iSCI 2019, CCIS 1122, pp. 404–417, 2019.
https://doi.org/10.1007/978-981-15-1301-5_32

the front direction at ground level. This cane cannot detect objects in different directions and also cannot perform object recognition. The knowledge of presence of the obstacles and its type is static or dynamic can be a mechanism to offer safety and security to visually impaired persons. Some solutions in the form of cane already exists in market such as: Ultrasonic Cane [1,4], Electronic Cane [2], Smart Cane [3], and HALO [15] etc.

Assistive Technologies (AT) are used to assist blind people which can be wearable or handheld. Wearable devices allow handsfree interaction with minimal use of hands while handheld devices require continuous hand interaction. Wearable devices can be worn on different parts of the body such as: vests and garments [10,11], waist belt [12], devices worn on feet [14], glasses [13], and others [31]. Although, variety of assistive devices are currently available but white cane is the oldest and the most conventional device used by VI. For safe and quick navigation of VI, different developments have been done using different technologies such as Global Positioning System (GPS) [7], Radio Frequency Identification (RFID) [6], Ultrasonic [9], Laser [5] and Global System for Mobile Communication (GSM) [8]. Laser transmits invisible laser beams and produce different audio signals after detecting the obstacle. Ultrasonic is similar to laser technology and follows the same principle that is followed in laser. Based on the distance, different types of tones can be produced through it. GPS is most commonly used for navigation by blind as well as sighted people. It provides voice based output which is followed by users. RFID is also used for navigation, but it requires RFID tags for navigation [6].

The aim of our paper is to build a cost efficient handheld cane to assist VI and make them capable enough to lead a normal life without the help of sighted persons. The device that has been assembled and presented in this paper is built using raspberry pi so that it can gain the benefit of high processing power to make it capable for real time processing. It has a pi-camera attached to raspberry pi which captures the images on which object recognition is performed. Ultrasonic sensor has also been attached to the device to detect the object and determine its range.

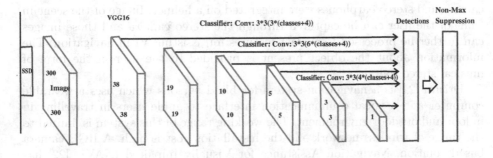

Fig. 1. Multi-scaling in SSD model

Our contribution includes building up of the cane for helping VI using deep learning approach. This cane has an integration of both hardware as well as software components. Raspberry Pi is attached with the cane where object detection model is integrated that performs object detection as well as recognition. Tensorflow framework of deep learning has been used here for serving the purpose of detection. The combination of raspberry pi and Tensorflow object detection API integrated into cane is entirely a different approach than those methods that has been used in the earlier developed canes.

The remaining paper has been organized in following sequence. Related work and methodology has been discussed in Sects. 2 and 3 respectively. In Sect. 4, experimental setup has been described. Finally, Conclusion has been presented in Sect. 5 followed by the resource information.

2   Related Work

A variety of travelling aids have been developed to increase the mobility of visually impaired. Some of the aids relevant to our work has been discussed in this section.

The authors in [1] proposed a small and portable Ultrasonic Cane for blind people with the aim to replace traditional long cane. Ultrasonic cane has few advantages over long cane like longer detection range and the capability to detect the overhanging objects. In [2], the authors have developed a low cost electronic cane for blind people that can perform obstacle detection and recognition using two ultrasonic sensors and one monocular camera. It works well in indoor environment but nothing has been stated about its robustness in urban areas.

Another device introduced in [3] is linked with a GSM-GPS module to locate the VI and to establish a bi-directional communication path in a wireless fashion. It was developed with the aim to guide users who are visually impaired or partially sighted. Another device integrated with cane was developed by authors in [15] which provide haptic alerts during navigation to alert VI of low-hanging obstacles. This device is affordable but somewhat heavier than a traditional cane. A stereo-image processing based system [23] was developed where a stereo camera and stereo earphones were integrated on a helmet. Image of the scene in front of the user can be captured through the stereo camera and those images can further be processed to extract features for assisting VI in navigation. The information about the object present is provided to the user in the form of musical stereo sounds.

Drishti [24] is a navigation system for blind persons which uses a wearable computer and a vocal communication interface to guide users in travelling in indoor and outdoor environment. The working range of this system is limited to the range of wireless network and the installation cost is high. A RGB-camera based solution, Navigation Assistance for Visually Impaired (NAVI) [22] has been developed to assist VI through sound commands. To remove the use of multiple sensors in this device, RGB-camera is used to utilize visual and range information which simplified the process of complex image processing tasks.

Bbeep [20] is another recent aid developed for visually impaired to help them in navigation in crowded environment. It is a suitcase based system that alerts the user as well as nearby persons to prevent collision using sonic feedback through pose estimation. Recently, a path guiding robot [21] was also developed to help VI with the aim to replace guide dogs. It has the capability to move along multiple path as well as retrace them. Thus the path guiding robot, make it easy for blind persons to navigate without the fear of getting lost while traveling.

A very recent development in the form of Text Scanner and Touch Reader [28] for visually impaired was developed to provide them privacy and independence. This system captures the whole scene with text and provide the whole information of environment to user in audio format. Machine learning approach was used here for the purpose of scene description. GuideCall [29], an android application, is a video call assistance for VI that helps them in getting assistance from their relatives and sighted friends through video call when in need. It can also track the location of the user through maps integrated into the application. A Smart Aid [30], which is actually a text to voice converter, helps the VI in knowledge gathering by converting eBooks, audiobooks in voice format. The audio books can be heard in speaker or headphone using Arduino UNO which is a low-cost solution.

Some software based approaches have also been proposed to deal with the problems like object detection. A few of the models which are available in the literature includes Single Shot Multibox Detector (SSD) [18], which is a model for object detection in real time. Faster Region-Based Convolution Neural Network (Faster R-CNN) [16] is also an object detection model which uses Region Proposal Network (RPN) to create bounding boxes and then classify those objects. It has a good accuracy but not suitable for real-time applications. [17] You Only Look Once (YOLO) is another object detection model which is suitable for real-time applications but is not so accurate. It cannot detect small size objects such as a tennis ball. SSD model uses multi-scale features and eliminates the use of RPN which was used in Faster RCNN. This improvement of SSD over Faster RCNN helps it in achieving accuracy using lower resolution images and raises the speed. As shown in Fig. 1, SSD uses base network of VGG-16 which creates feature maps with decreasing sizes. These varying size feature maps are used for scale variance of objects. Detector and classifier are applied to each feature map. Multi-scale features makes it better than YOLO model in terms of accuracy as model gets trained to detect objects at different scale. SSDLite is an extension of SSD model where kernel size is modified and depthwise separable convolution is performed to make it lighter and faster. MobileNetV2 [19] is an extension of MobileNetV1 where a module is introduced with inverted residual structure. Also, the non-linearities that were present in the narrow layers of MobileNetV1 has been removed in MobileNetV2. In the first layer, depthwise convolution is performed where a lightweight filtering is done. In the next layer, a pointwise convolution is performed for detecting the pattern and performing feature extraction. An activation function, ReLU is used because of its robustness while performing low-precision computation.

Despite of the presence of many aids to help visually impaired, there is still a need of having a cost-effective and handy solution for them to make their day to day life easier. The solutions that have been proposed till now are either heavy or costly and therefore, it does not suit the needs of VI.

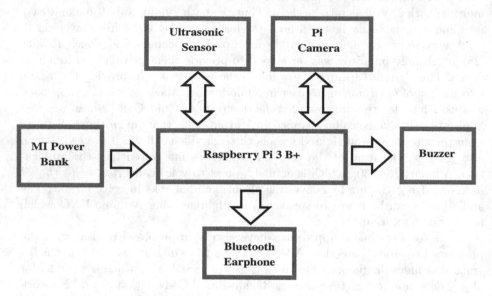

Fig. 2. Block diagram of the proposed system

3   Methodology

In this section, components used for development of this device has been discussed followed by the approach and algorithm that has been implemented in R-Cane.

3.1   Components of R-Cane

The system architecture mainly consists of six parts: raspberry pi 3 B+, ultrasonic sensor, pi camera, vibration motor, MI power bank and bluetooth earphone as shown in Fig. 2. Raspberry Pi is the main controller on which all other components have been attached. Ultrasonic sensor and pi camera provide the captured data to raspberry pi. Vibration motor gets activated when any obstacle is sensed by the ultrasonic sensor and voice-based output is provided through bluetooth earphones to the VI. MI power bank has been used to provide power to raspberry pi which has the capacity of 10000 mAH. This power bank can be used for ~24 h when fully charged but intensive use in not suggested.

Raspberry Pi needs a New Out of the Box Software (NOOBS) which contains Raspbian operating system. Earlier, we attempted working with Arduino, but it did not work out as a good processing power was required to deploy the object detection model on it. Tensorflow library has been used to develop, train and test machine learning models. The TensorFlow object detection API is an open source framework that is built on top of TensorFlow. This makes it easy to construct, train and deploy the object detection models using the API. Open Source Computer Vision Library (OpenCV) has also been used which is an open source computer vision and machine learning software that helps in providing a baseline and infrastructure to computer vision applications and accelerate the use of machine learning in commercial products. Deep Learning is heavy-weight tool which requires a good amount of processing power. Keeping this in mind, a light weight object detection model has been used as a solution which requires lesser processing power.

3.2 Approach

An object detection model is used to detect objects and their location. For example, a model might be trained with images that contain cats and dogs, along with a label that specifies the class of the object they represent (e.g. a cat, or a dog), and data specifying where each object appears in the image. Object detection can perform classification and localization of multiple objects present in an image which is being used in many areas such as crowd management, traffic management, medical imaging, and computer vision. SSD model is trained on COCO dataset which has more than 150 classes. This enlarges the range of object which can be detected when encountered as an obstacle by visually impaired.

Four SSD based models have been deployed in raspberry pi for the purpose of object detection. Although these models are SSD based, but are slightly different from each other in terms of their configuration as stated in Table 1. Batch size, number of steps, regularization and decay are few hyperparameters which can be fine tuned to obtain better accuracy. Batch size varies from 24 to 2048 for these models which defines the number of samples to be worked upon before updating the model's internal parameters. Larger batch size would require more memory space but for larger datasets, using batches makes the process faster. Number of steps for these models varies from 10000 to 200000 which creates an impact on the training time. L2 regularization is used to avoid the risk of overfitting by discouraging the learning of complex model whose value is 0.00004 for these models. Decay rate for these models vary from 0.97 to 0.99997 which controls how quickly or slowly a neural network learns a problem. SSDLite_mobilenet_v2_coco model is the lighter version of SSD with 27ms speed and 22 mAP achieved when trained on coco dataset. SSD_mobilenet_v1_ppn_coco model uses Pooling Pyramid Network (PPN) to make predictions through shared box detector which achieved 26 ms speed and 20 mAP when trained on coco model which does not makes it better than SSDlite. SSD_mobilenet_v1_0.75_depth_coco models uses 0.75 depth multiplier for better detection and achieved 26 ms speed and 18 mAP when trained on the same coco models. Finally, SSD_mobilenet_v1_coco is heavier than other three models but has good detection performance of 21 mAP.

Table 1. Evaluation parameters and its value for all object-detection models

Object detection model	Parameters			
	Batch size	*Num steps*	*Regularizer (l2)*	*Decay*
SSD_mobilenet _v1_0.75_depth_coco (Model1)	2048	10000	0.00004	0.97
SSD_mobilenet _v1_coco (Model2)	24	200000	0.00004	0.99997
SSD_mobilenet _v1_ppn_coco (Model3)	512	50000	0.00004	0.97
SSDlite_mobilenet _v2_coco (Model4)	24	200000	0.00004	0.99997

In Fig. 3, the whole architectural process of convolution and pooling in SSD model has been depicted. An RGB image of size 224*224 having three channel is convolved and ReLU activation function is applied to introduce non-linearity of model. Max pooling is performed to reduce the computational parameters and size is reduced to 112*112. After this process of convolution and pooling, the data is passed to a fully connected layer and then softmax activation function is applied for classification.

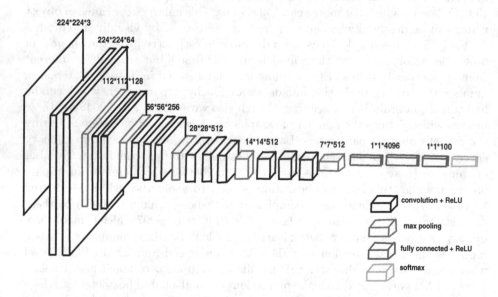

Fig. 3. Architecture of SSD model

3.3 Algorithm

The algorithm used in the developed system has been presented below. It uses a software model for object detection. Initially, frames were captured by pi camera and resized to 224*224. Then, convolution, classification and detection of four classes have been performed using few SSD-based models. If an object is present, then the device provides a voice-based output to the user about the type of object and confidence through the bluetooth earphone.

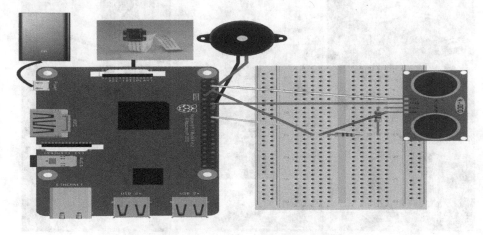

Fig. 4. Inter-connection of components

Algorithm 1. Object Detection & Recognition

Require: Weight & model file for SSD-based models
Ensure: Object name & their range
 1: Frame is captured & resized to (224*224)
 2: Convolution with ReLU, classification using softmax & detection is performed
 3: Object detection performed for four classes
 4: **if** (object==1) **then**
 5:    Ultrasonic sensor activated
 6:    Object name & range is provided through earphone
 7: **else**
 8:    Go back to the beginning of program
 9: **end if**

---

4 Experimental Results

In this section, Experimental Setup and Performance Metrics has been discussed. The whole setup including the circuitry connection of various components has been presented in the first sub-section and the parameters used for the evaluation of performance of the system has been discussed in the second sub-section.

4.1   Experimental Setup

The entire system is organized with different cost-effective components to provide flexibility and comfort to visually impaired or partially sighted people as shown in Fig. 4.

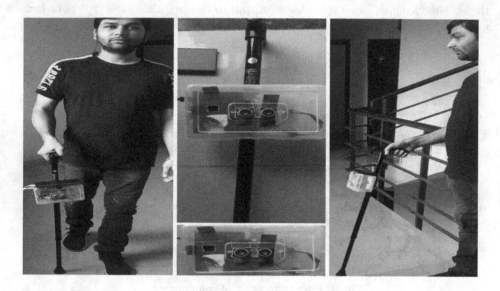

Fig. 5. Model of developed stick (front view, top view, side view)

Raspberry Pi is the main processing board used here which is a cheap, pocket-sized Personal Computer (PC) that fits into a computer screen/TV and utilizes a standard console and mouse. It is a competent little gadget that empowers individuals of any age to explore processing, and to figure out how to program in different languages like Python and Scratch. It can do all that we would anticipate that a computer should do, from perusing the web and playing top notch video, to making spreadsheets, word-handling, and making diversions.

The raspberry pi camera is a high-definition camera module which can capture image as well as video. It is supported by all the versions of raspberry pi and is mainly used in security applications and wildlife camera traps. Ultrasonic sensor can find the distance between user and obstacle to prevent the user from colliding and an alarm is provided to the user in the form of a vibration from vibration motor. The object recognition is done from the image captured through pi camera using deep learning model for object detection and this information about the obstacle is provided to the user through a bluetooth earphone. The system is powered by a power bank to make it more durable. R-Cane along with the integrated components have been presented in Fig. 5 from different viewing angles including front view, top view and side view.

4.2   Performance Metrics

In this section, the results obtained from few SSD based object detection models available in tensorflow has been discussed on the basis of Precision, Recall, F1 score, Frames Per second (FPS) and Confidence of each detected object in a similar scenario. Precision is the measurement of accuracy of prediction. Recall measures how well we find all the positive results. FPS is the frequency of consecutive images called frames that appears on screen. Confidence is the probability of presence of an object in the anchor box.

The experiment presented in this paper considers a video of an indoor scenario with the objects like TV, vase, bottle etc. present in it. Further experiments will be conducted for other classes of objects in both indoor and outdoor to improve performance of the cane in future. Testing was performed on real-time data where videos were captured using raspberry pi and converted into frames with 0.5 frame rate. This actually meant that a frame was captured in every 0.5 s. There were around 250 frames on which performance was evaluated for each model. All the models including SSD_mobilenet _v1_0.75_depth_coco (Model1), SSD_mobilenet _v1_coco (Model2), SSD_mobilenet _v1_ppn_coco (Model3) and SSDlite_mobilenet _v2_coco (Model4) were deployed in the system and for each model FPS and confidence of the above stated objects were noted which has been presented in Table 2. FPS of Model4 was found to be higher than other three models while capturing the same indoor scenario using pi camera as SSDlite is lighter than SSD based models. The confidence of two objects *Vase* and *TV* is higher for Model2 while for the other two objects *Bottle* and *Plant* confidence was found to be higher when Model3 was used.

$$Precision = \frac{TP}{TP + FP} \tag{1}$$

$$Recall = \frac{TP}{TP + FN} \tag{2}$$

Here, TP = True Positive, TN = True Negative, FP = False Positive, FN = False Negative

Using Eqs. (1) and (2), F1 score for each model is calculated which is presented in Table 3.

$$F1\ Score = 2 * \frac{(Precision * Recall)}{(Precision + Recall)} \tag{3}$$

Using Eq. (3), F1 score was compared for all the four classes in each of the four models that were considered and are shown in Table 3. It was observed that Model3 achieves the highest F1 score for two classes *Vase* and *Plant*. For class *TV* and *Bottle*, Model1 and Model4 achieves the highest F1 score than other models. The average value of F1 score of all the classes for each model has also been presented in Table 3 where Model3 achieves the highest score. Using Eqs. (1) and (2), precision and recall has been calculated. In Figs. 6 and 7, the results obtained for Precision and Recall of the four models has

Table 2. Comparative analysis of few object-detection model deployed in this device

Object detection model	Frames per second	Confidence of detected objects			
		Vase	TV	Bottle	Plant
SSD_mobilenet _v1_0.75_depth_coco (Model1)	0.23	49%	64%	40%	47%
SSD_mobilenet _v1_coco (Model2)	0.37	58%	74%	45%	42%
SSD_mobilenet _v1_ppn_coco (Model3)	0.16	54%	72%	50%	51%
SSDlite_mobilenet _v2_coco (Model4)	0.50	50%	42%	40%	61%

Table 3. F1 score of object detection models for four classes

Object detection model	F1 score				Average
	Vase	TV	Bottle	Plant	
SSD_mobilenet _v1_0.75_depth_coco (Model1)	0.48	**0.70**	0.09	0.78	0.51
SSD_mobilenet _v1_coco (Model2)	0.22	0.61	0.25	0.33	0.35
SSD_mobilenet _v1_ppn_coco (Model3)	**0.74**	0.56	0.04	**0.90**	0.56
SSDlite_mobilenet _v2_coco (Model4)	0.29	0.37	**0.33**	0.29	0.32

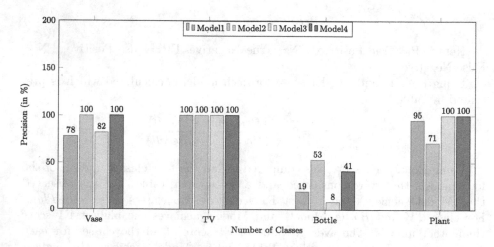

Fig. 6. Precision of models for four classes

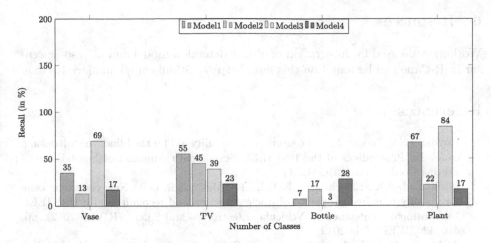

Fig. 7. Recall of models for four classes

been presented where SSD_mobilenet_v1_0.75_depth_coco has been represented as Model1, SSD_mobilenet_v1_coco as Model2, SSD_mobilenet_v1_ppn_coco as Model3 and SSDlite_mobilenet _v2_coco as Model4. Using Model3, the best precision was achieved for the classes *TV* and *Plant* and the best recall was achieved for the classes *Vase* and *Plant*. In Model2, best precision was achieved for classes *Vase* and *TV* whereas best recall was achieved for classes *TV* and *Plant*. For Model1, the best precision and recall was achieved for classes *TV* and *Plant*. Lastly, in Model4, best precision was achieved for classes *Vase*, *TV* and *Plant* whereas the best recall was achieved for classes *TV* and *Bottle*. It was observed that the precision is high for *Vase*, *TV* and *Plant* but low for *Bottle*, probably because of the size of the *Bottle* which is relatively smaller than other objects. This leads to the fluctuation in the detection results from true positive to no detection and false negative.

5 Conclusion

In this paper, we have developed a raspberry pi based cane called R-Cane for guiding visually impaired. In order to provide ease and independence to users, a microcontroller is attached with the cane in which object detection model has been deployed. It can help VI to recognize the obstacles present in front of them and the presence of those object is detected through ultrasonic sensor. Evaluation of the system has been done by attaching the system to the cane. It has been determined through experimental analysis that out of the four models which have been deployed on R-Cane and tested, SSD_mobilenet_v1_ppn_coco model achieves the highest average value of F1 score for all the classes that were considered in the experimentation. In future, we plan to do a comparative study by implementing this work on other gpu-enabled parallel platforms such as Intel Movidius Neural Compute Stick and NVIDIA Jetson Nano.

6   Resource

Working code used for integration of object detection model and ultrasonic sensor in R-Cane can be found on this link: https://github.com/kmanjari/R-cane.

References

1. Hoydal, T.O., Zelano, J.A.: An alternative mobility aid for the blind: the 'ultrasonic cane'. In: Proceedings of the 1991 IEEE Seventeenth Annual Northeast Bioengineering Conference. IEEE (1991)
2. Bouhamed, S.A., Eleuch, J.F., Kallel, I.K., Masmoudi, D.S.: New electronic cane for visually impaired people for obstacle detection and recognition. In: 2012 IEEE International Conference on Vehicular Electronics and Safety (ICVES 2012), pp. 416–420. IEEE, July 2012
3. Alshbatat, N., Ilah, A.: Automated mobility and orientation system for blind or partially sighted people. Int. J. Smart Sens. Intell. Syst. 6(2) (2013)
4. Kumar, K., Champaty, B., Uvanesh, K., Chachan, R., Pal, K., Anis, A.: Development of an ultrasonic cane as a navigation aid for the blind people. In: 2014 International Conference on Control, Instrumentation, Communication and Computational Technologies (ICCICCT), pp. 475–479. IEEE, July 2014
5. Benjamin Jr, J.M., Ali, N.A.: An improved laser cane for the blind. In: Quantitative Imagery in the Biomedical Sciences II, Vol. 40. International Society for Optics and Photonics (1974)
6. Want, R.: An introduction to RFID technology. IEEE Pervasive Comput. 1, 25–33 (2006)
7. Misra, P., Enge, P.: Global Positioning System: Signals, Measurements and Performance, 2nd edn (2006)
8. Mouly, M., Pautet, M.-B., Foreword By-Haug, T.: The GSM System for Mobile Communications. Telecom Publishing (1992)
9. Rozenberg, L. (ed.): Physical Principles of Ultrasonic Technology, vol. 1. Springer, Heidelberg (2013)
10. Bahadir, S.K., Koncar, V., Kalaoglu, F.: Wearable obstacle detection system fully integrated to textile structures for visually impaired people. Sens. Actuators, A 179, 297–311 (2012)
11. Lee, Y.H., Medioni, G.: RGB-D camera based navigation for the visually impaired. In: Proceedings of the RSS (2011)
12. Mahalle, S.: Ultrasonic spectacles & waist-belt for visually impaired & blind person. IOSR J. Eng. 4, 46–49 (2014)
13. Xiang, K., Wang, K., Fei, L., Yang, K.: Store sign text recognition for wearable navigation assistance system. In: Journal of Physics: Conference Series, vol. 1229, no. 1, p. 012070. IOP Publishing, May 2019
14. Patil, K., Jawadwala, Q., Shu, F.C.: Design and construction of electronic aid for visually impaired people. IEEE Trans. Hum.-Mach. Syst. 48(2), 172–182 (2018)
15. Wang, Y., Kuchenbecker, K.J.: HALO: haptic alerts for low-hanging obstacles in white cane navigation. In: 2012 IEEE Haptics Symposium (HAPTICS). IEEE (2012)
16. Girshick, R.: Fast R-CNN. In: Proceedings of the IEEE International Conference on Computer Vision (2015)

17. Redmon, J., Divvala, S., Girshick, R., Farhadi, A.: You only look once: unified, real-time object detection. In: Proceedings of the IEEE Conference on Computer Vision and Pattern Recognition, pp. 779–788 (2016)
18. Hui, J.: SSD object detection: single shot multibox detector for real-time processing (2018). https://medium.com/@jonathan_hui/ssd-object-detection-single-shot-multibox-detector-for-real-time-processing-9bd8deac0e06. Accessed 14 Mar 2018
19. Tsang, S.-H.: Review: MobileNetV2 - light weight model (image classification) (2019). https://towardsdatascience.com/review-mobilenetv2-light-weight-model-image-classification-8febb490e61c. Accessed 19 May 2019
20. Kayukawa, S., et al.: BBeep: a sonic collision avoidance system for blind travellers and nearby pedestrians. In: Proceedings of the 2019 CHI Conference on Human Factors in Computing Systems, p. 52. ACM, April 2019
21. Megalingam, R.K., Vishnu, S., Sasikumar, V., Sreekumar, S.: Autonomous path guiding robot for visually impaired people. In: Mallick, P.K., Balas, V.E., Bhoi, A.K., Zobaa, A.F. (eds.) Cognitive Informatics and Soft Computing. AISC, vol. 768, pp. 257–266. Springer, Singapore (2019). https://doi.org/10.1007/978-981-13-0617-4_25
22. Aladren, A., López-Nicolás, G., Puig, L., Guerrero, J.J.: Navigation assistance for the visually impaired using RGB-D sensor with range expansion. IEEE Syst. J. 10(3), 922–932 (2014)
23. Balakrishnan, G.N.R.Y.S., Sainarayanan, G., Nagarajan, R., Yaacob, S.: A stereo image processing system for visually impaired. Int. J. Sig. Process. 2(3), 136–145 (2006)
24. Ran, L., Helal, S., Moore, S.: Drishti: an integrated indoor/outdoor blind navigation system and service. In: 2004 Proceedings of the Second IEEE Annual Conference on Pervasive Computing and Communications. IEEE (2004)
25. Sjöström, C.: Virtual haptic search tools-the white cane in a haptic computer interface. In: Assistive Technology: Added Value to the Quality of Life, AAATE, vol. 1, pp. 124–128 (2001)
26. World Health Organization, 11 October 2018. https://www.who.int/news-room/fact-sheets/detail/blindness-and-visual-impairment
27. Bourne, R.R., et al.: Magnitude, temporal trends, and projections of the global prevalence of blindness and distance and near vision impairment: a systematic review and meta-analysis. Lancet Glob. Health 5(9), e888–97 (2017)
28. Cui, Z.: Text scanner and touch reader for visually-impaired users (2019)
29. Ravindran, N.M., Cheraghi, S.A.: GuideCall: a remote video call assistance for blind and visually impaired people (2019)
30. Chandrasekaran, R., Dhivya, J.A., Thamizhvani, T.R., Hemalatha, R.J.: Smart aid for the blind. Indian J. Public Health Res. Dev. 10(5), 819–821 (2019)
31. Mcnary, S., Hunter, A.: Wearable device data for criminal investigation. In: Wang, G., Chen, J., Yang, L.T. (eds.) SpaCCS 2018. LNCS, vol. 11342, pp. 60–71. Springer, Cham (2018). https://doi.org/10.1007/978-3-030-05345-1_5

"Think Before You Post": A Cognitive Psychological Approach for Limiting Bullying in Social Media

Sreeshma Mohan[1], Indu Valsaladevi[1,2], and Sabu M. Thampi[1(✉)]

[1] Center for Research and Innovation in Cyber Threat Resilience (CRICTR),
Indian Institute of Information Technology and Management-Kerala (IIITM-K),
Thiruvananthapuram 695581, Kerala, India
{sreeshma.mphilcs06,indu.v,sabu.thampi}@iiitmk.ac.in
[2] University of Kerala, Thiruvananthapuram 695034, India

Abstract. Online social media bullying has become extremely detrimental in recent times with the proliferation of smartphones and the wide popularity of social networks among people. The number of people being victimized as a result of cyberbullying is increasing day-by-day and the researchers are continuously thriving to develop new techniques to detect online social media bullying in order to curb this serious social menace. Current research in this domain focuses on the detection of cyberbullying and only a few works have addressed the problem on how to prevent cyberbullying before it occurs. Considering this aspect, our work mainly concentrates on the prevention of online bullying utilizing the concepts of Cognitive psychology and Intent analysis. We propose a cognitive psychological approach inspired by the Theory of Planned Behavior to understand the psychological factors in a person prompting him/her to perform online bullying and prevent him/her from posting bully comments. Initially, we use sentiment analysis to determine whether the content posted by a user includes bully comments and subsequently Intent analysis is carried out to identify the intention hidden in the text posted by the user and warns him/her about the future consequences if that message contains any negative intention to harm others. The classification of the text data into bully and non-bully comments is employed using different machine learning algorithms of which Naïve Bayes yielded the best result. Later on, cognitive psychology is applied to understand the intention of a user posting or sharing a bully text and thereby diverting his attempt to perform online bullying.

Keywords: Cognitive psychology · Intent analysis · Theory of Planned Behavior · Machine Learning

1 Introduction

The rapid growth of web technologies and the development of the "Internet of Things" have marked a significant role in transforming cities into smart cities.

© Springer Nature Singapore Pte Ltd. 2019
G. Wang et al. (Eds.): iSCI 2019, CCIS 1122, pp. 418–434, 2019.
https://doi.org/10.1007/978-981-15-1301-5_33

The notion of smart cities relies on achieving sustainable development by improving the quality of life and providing a better and safer environment for the residents. Even though the rate of urbanization around the globe is moving at a faster pace, security threats and privacy issues are still a major concern for the people living in all areas especially cities, as city-regions are the most preferred targets of cybercriminals. The increasing availability of data services and the advancement of online media platforms have changed the level of communication and helps in better data management and coordinating the services offered by smart cities [1].

Despite the fact that social media offer greater communication facilities, the ease of access and lack of proper filtering mechanisms in social media have paved way for the tremendous increase in the rate of cyber attacks in recent times. Cyberbullying is one such serious threat experienced by the people due to the pervasive nature of online media platforms and the anonymity enjoyed by social media users. Online bullying can be defined as harassing an individual or group of individuals by means of online social media platforms, smartphones or other electronic media by sending or posting inappropriate textual or multimedia content with the purpose of hurting one's self-esteem and causing embarrassment. The person who performs bullying is termed as 'bully' and the affected one is called as 'victim' [2,3]. Nowadays, women and children usually fall as victims and the aftermath of this serious menace is far beyond what we perceive. Studies have proven that the mental stress caused as a result of online bullying can adversely affect the developing brain in children as indicated in Fig. 1. Victims not only experience heightened stress, but they may also go through depression, trauma, and psychological disorders and may even result in severe health issues such as headaches, sleep deprivation or somatization [4,5].

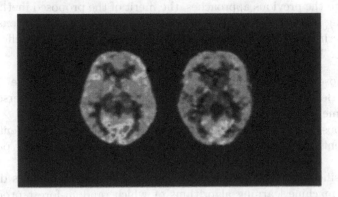

Fig. 1. Corticosterone stimuli caused in brain due to bullying

Several researchers have come up with computationally efficient and other data-driven approaches including text analytics and topic classification to detect online bullying. Facebook Watchdog is one such application developed with the aim of detecting online grooming and bullying activities utilizing the concepts of text, video and social media analytics [6]. Most of the previous research lay focus on the detection of online bullying, understand the scope of this serious issue and its psychological effects on the victims [7]. Only a few works have attempted to investigate the psychological motivation behind this cybercrime which will be more effective in preventing this crime.

Considering this aspect, our research aims at investigating the psychological factors behind the individuals who perform bullying and propose an approach to prevent bullying thereby limiting the rate of bullying through online social media. The underlying factor in social media is that most of the people are unaware of the consequences of what they post or share in their social networking space and how their online activities can be unknowingly converted to bullying activities [8]. Presently, most of the bullying incidents take place due to sudden provocations but the effects of these activities are severe, resulting in physical and mental illness of the sufferer which may even end up in suicides [9].

Existing research on cyberbullying detection in connection with the concepts of social influence and the theory of planned behavior conducted among teenagers supports the role of some factors influencing a person to do this crime. This study implies that, it would be better if we could identify the factors tempting a person to post something negative against a person or a group of people and notify him/her about the after-effects of that activity [10,11]. Based on this, we conducted an online survey among the people above the age group of 20, and our analysis revealed the fact that if a person gets a chance to realize the future impact of the posts they are planning to post or share, it would help them to rethink before posting the content online.

Based on this investigation, we are proposing a psychologically inspired model to divert the attitude of people who are not intentionally performing this crime. In contrast to the previous approaches, the merit of the proposed method is that without going behind the victim, we concentrate on identifying the exact reason behind the crime which will help to alert the user about the after-effects of this serious issue. The major contributions of our work are:

1. We propose a psychologically-inspired model grounded on the Theory of Planned Behavior (TPB) to identify the factors influencing a person to perform online bullying.
2. The proposed approach utilizes sentiment analysis to find the sentiments of the content and intent analysis to find the intention of the user posting the content.
3. The classification of bully comments and non-bully comments is done using different machine learning algorithms of which random-forest produced the best result.
4. The concept of cognitive psychology is utilized and is applied in the form of a survey questionnaire leveraging the concept of cognitive psychology where the user is notified about the impact of posting or sharing bully contents and thereby preventing him/her from posting the bully content.

The rest of the paper is organized as follows: Sect. 2 discusses the existing and ongoing works related to cyberbullying. Section 3 explains the background theory in support of our proposed work. Section 4 describes our proposed methodology and the experimental setup. The results and discussions are discussed in Sect. 5 and finally, the paper concludes in Sect. 6.

2 Related Works

Studies related to cyberbullying had started from early 2000, when Finkelhor, Mitchell and Wolak published a report based on online harassments. They were the first researchers to submit a report based on their investigation done on cyberbullying and their studies supported the fact that online bullying is an extension of traditional bullying. The prominence of the internet and the widespread use of social media are the major factors which drastically increased the rate of online bullying [12]. In 2004, Ybarra et al. studied the role of youth engaging in online harassments and the negative behavioral change exhibited by children and young people due to the overuse of the Internet. The studies were carried out mainly by analyzing the amount of time children, adolescent and young people spend in front of social media and the results proved that the unlimited use of social media has led to an increase in the number of cyberbullying incidents. They also suggested measures to prevent this crime by giving awareness to the students and teachers about the ways on how to effectively use social media [13].

In the following years, the stream of research related to cyberbullying has been focusing on the areas of how online bullying can be defined, measured and its effects on people of different age groups. From the analysis, it was clear that there was a continuous increase in the number of hatred messages appearing online and the people being bullied [14]. Based on the extensive research conducted in [15–17], cyberbullying can occur in 3 different ways: (1) content risk which includes violent and/or pornographic content, (2) conduct risk such as threats, vulgar language, things that can damage your reputation and (3) contact risk like grooming. The line of research related to cyberbullying during the past few years is shown in Fig. 2.

The tremendous growth of social media and the wide use of social networks among common people mainly accounted to the increasing rate of online bullying and people started using social media as one of the main tools for performing cyberbullying. Several techniques based on machine learning, text analytics and intent identification have been developed by the researchers for the detection of online bullying as this serious menace is increasing at an alarming rate. In 2013, Rybniceket et al. developed an application called Facebook Watchdog with the aim of protecting adolescents from bullying and grooming attacks. The work utilized the concept of text/image/video analysis and social media analytics and suggested to include their application as a plug-in for the detection of online bullying activities through Facebook [6]. Later in 2015, Van Hee et al. proposed a method for automatic detection and prevention of cyberbullying using text classification techniques. The authors compiled a Dutch dataset of social

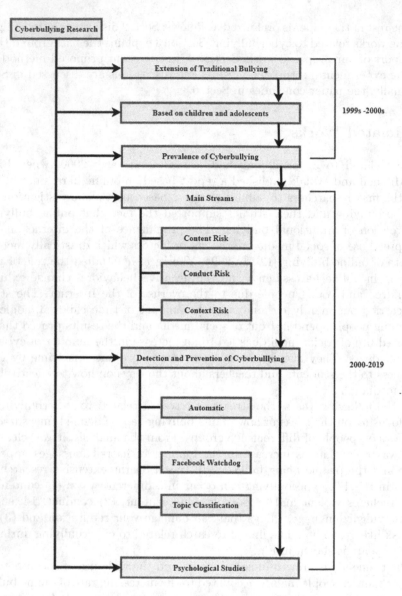

Fig. 2. Research flow of cyberbullying

media messages pertaining to cyberbullying and evaluated their method using it [18]. One of the recent works done on cyberbullying detection mentioned in [2] explored the concepts of soft computing techniques to detect cyberbullying activities across various social media domains and their work proved the scope of applying soft computing techniques for automatic bullying detection for both textual and non-textual data.

Even though several computational approaches were employed for online bullying detection, only a few researchers have focused on the psychological aspects to address this crime. Giving importance to this aspect, in 2017 Jafarkarimi *et al.* conducted a study on cyberbullying among students by applying the Theory of Planned Behavior (TPB). The study attempted to discover the factors influencing an individual's intention to cyberbully others. The research was carried out with the help of a scenario-based questionnaire and data was collected from over 96 students. Based on their research, they put forward three hypotheses as [H1]: The attitude towards cyberbullying has a positive impact on individuals' plan to perform online bullying, [H2]: Social Networks have a positive effect on intention to Cyberbully and [H3]: Perceived Behaviour Control (PBC) has a positive influence on individuals' intention to Cyberbully [19]. In the same year, another study conducted in Taiwan introduced a model called the Attitude Social Influence Efficacy model to determine the factors affecting cyberbullying. The study suggests that the attitude of a person towards cyberbullying is an internal psychology which affects online bullying intention and further that intention influences the cyberbullying behavior [20].

From the literature, it's obvious that studies related to online bullying give more focus to the detection of cyberbullying and research considering the psychological aspects are more centered around victims based on extensive surveys and theoretical study. Considering this, we have proposed a psychologically-inspired computational model that alerts the users to divert their attitude before they do this crime. This work utilizes the concepts of cognitive psychology and intent identification for limiting cyberbullying through social media. Although attitude has proven to be a determinant factor in online bullying in many of the previous studies, our work utilizes this concept with the support of Theory of Planned Behavior in order to avert a person from doing bullying and thereby check the rate of this serious hazard.

3 Background Theory

The main aspect of our work is to explore the psychological factors tempting a person to do cyber harassments and to develop a method to limit the rate of this crime. The studies related to the Theory of Planned Behavior helps discover the factors that can lead a person to perform bullying and the idea of cognitive psychology aids to formulate a new approach to prevent people from doing cyberbullying.

3.1 Theory of Planned Behaviour and Cognitive Psychology

Only a few studies related to cyberbullying has been done utilizing the concept of Theory of Planned Behavior (TPB). The existing studies reveal the fact that the theory of planned behavior has been developed taking inspiration from the theory of reasoned action in which the behavior of a person is influenced by three main factors as Attitude, Subjective norms and Perceived Behavioral Control

(PBC). TPB suggests that the attitude and perceived behavioral control are the most influential factors in predicting the intention of a person which in turn can be used to predict the deliberate behavior exhibited by a person [21]. Nowadays, most of the online bullying issues happen due to sudden provocation from a person's public posts, opinion sharing about some incidents or as a part of making joke of a person's recent activities. In addition, majority of the people are unaware of the legal consequences of bullying a person online and also how this menace affects the mental state of the affected ones. Our proposed approach developed with the supporting factor of TPB is grounded on the fact that the attitude of a person can influence his/her intention and personal behavior since attitude towards cyberbullying is driven by internal psychology. This theory supports the fact that the intention of a person to do online bullying can be reversed by bringing a change in an individual's attitude and thereby we can limit the rate of online bullying to some extent [19].

Another theory utilized in this paper is cognitive psychology which is the study of the mental process. People who bully others display a combination of psychological, cognitive and social characteristics. Thinking or cognition applies to how people perceive, learn, remember and think about information [22]. According to the brain theory, cyberbullying can cause mental and physical stress and it would last for a life time. If a person gets to know about the negative effects of cyber bullying at an early stage, it can positively change the attitude of a person and prevent him/her from the act of online bullying. Here, we apply cognitive psychology in the form of a questionnaire prepared on the basis of an online survey.

4   Proposed Methodology

The proposed approach is developed with the intention of preventing online bullying. The flow diagram of the proposed approach is shown in Fig. 3. Here, we are concentrating only on textual data and the various stages in the methodology are described below:

4.1   Dataset Compilation

The main challenge in this work is the unavailability of a proper dataset. The dataset for the proposed study was obtained by scraping different labeled Twitter data from various Git-hub projects. The collected dataset was re-modified by extracting tweets and their labels. A total of 24,783 tweets were collected from a work of Automated Hate Speech Detection and the Problem of Offensive Language [23].

4.2   Preprocessing

The purpose of pre-processing is to transform the messages into a uniform format that could be understood by the learning algorithm. The Twitter data obtained

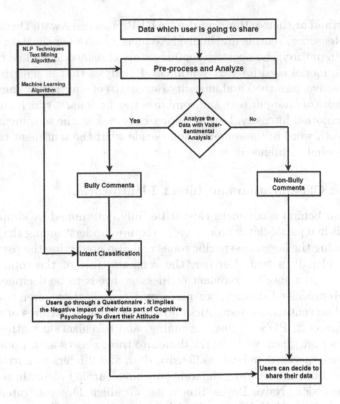

Fig. 3. Flow diagram of proposed methodology

is subjected to tokenization, stemming, POS tagging, stop-word removal, number removal and stripping of whitespaces. For each Tweet in the dataset, automatic spell check and grammar correction are performed. Even though we focused on text-based data, it requires special preparation before analysis. Initially, the text must be parsed to locate word endings, called tokenization. Then the words need to be encoded as integers or floating-point values for using it as proper input for feature extraction (or vectorization).

4.3 Feature Extraction of Each Comment

The scikit-learn library offers easy-to-use tools to perform both tokenization and feature extraction of text data. To calculate word frequencies, we rely on the most popular method called Term Frequency Inverse Document Frequency (TF-IDF), in which weights are assigned to different words for a given textual document.

4.4 Sentimental Analysis

The application of sentimental analysis in social media helps to analyze the social conversations online and determine their context at a deeper level as they apply to a topic, brand or theme. Here, we use VADER (Valence Aware Dictionary and Sentiment Reasoner) sentimental analysis to identify whether the data is positive or negative in nature. The negative comments are classified as bullied comments. VADER is a model used for text sentimental analysis that is sensitive to both polarity (positive/negative) and intensity (strength) of emotion. It calculates the sentiment score of an input text and combines the dictionary, which maps lexical features to emotion intensity. Lexical approaches look at the sentiment category or score of each word in the sentence and decide what the sentiment category or score of the whole sentence is.

4.5   Intent Classification and Intent Identification

The intention behind a comment cannot be fully determined by simply mining the keywords in a particular content. It also requires understanding the sentiment tones, analyzing the language-specific tones and also predicting the psychological intention hidden in a text. Further, the semantic role of the topic - related keywords used in a specific comment or message needs to be deciphered. Here, using the preprocessed dataset, we perform a classification after training our model based on sentiments, semantics and language-based features of a text. We use TF-IDF vector, POS tagging, stemming, and tokenization methods for the feature extraction. Then, we label the data into three classes as 0, 1 and 2, where 0 denotes hate speech, 1 indicates offensive data and 2 refers to normal data.

We trained our model using different machine-learning algorithms including Logistic Regression, Naive Bayes, Stochastic Gradient Descent (often abbreviated SGD), K-Nearest Neighbors, Decision Tree, Random Forest and Support Vector Machine (SVM) and their accuracies are compared. Among the different classifiers used, Random Forest yielded the best result with a training accuracy of 85%. But on testing, Naïve Bayes yielded better result compared to other algorithms and so we chose Naïve Bayes for intent classification.

Followed by intent indent classification, we perform intent identification. Intent identification helps the system to identify the intention behind each message shared by the user. It detects whether the content is related to specific areas such as racial, religious, harassment and so on. The dataset is classified into three bogus utterances such as hate utterances, offensive utterances, and harassment utterances and then we performed the training. Since Naïve Bayes classifier produced better prediction results for intent classification in test data, we chose the same classifier for training the data for intent identification. We tested our model with data obtained from Twitter related to hate speech detection and data related to Terrorist attack and the system successfully identified the intention of a message by matching with the corresponding utterances.

4.6   Cognitive Psychology and Questionnaire Preparation

Cognition or the thinking process in people occurs as the result of some analysis happening in the human brain. Thinking and actions of people are greatly influenced by social media and the unlimited freedom and anonymity enjoyed by people creates a tendency in people to involve in illegal online activities [24,25]. Moreover, majority of the people are unaware of the consequences of what they are sharing through their social networking space. So, in our proposed approach we apply the concept of cognitive psychology in the form of a questionnaire that makes people think before they share something through social media. The questionnaire was prepared on the basis of an online survey conducted among people above the age group of 20. The questionnaire consists of 8 questions which create awareness in people before they share something negative from their profile which can harm others. The questions are listed in Table 1 and through these questions; we analyzed the perceived behavioral control nature in individuals.

Table 1. Online survey questions

What is your response, if anyone lets you know that you are going to do a thing that may adversely affect the society?
Do you agree and change your attitude?
Will you carry out an activity that can create a negative image of your personality?
Will you continue to do an offence even if you are aware that it is against law?
Do you feel stressed when media criticize you very badly?
Are you happy to see bad comments about you in social media?
Do you feel happy in hurting others even if you know about its consequences?
Will you obey if someone advises you to stop sharing unnecessary things in social media?
Are you happy in preventing a problem before it happens?

Based on this online survey, we identified 5 influential factors that can divert a person's attitude from indulging in illegal or dangerous online activities. The five factors are *Awareness, Personality, Alienation, Stress,* and *Law and order* which are indicated in Fig. 4.

On the basis of this analysis, we prepared one more questionnaire with 6 questions related to these identified five factors. Questions were prepared corresponding to each intention identified after intent analysis and these questions focus on the negative consequences if their messages appear online. According to the category of the intention, the corresponding questionnaire will be displayed in front of the user. A sample questionnaire related to the text with the intention of harassment is displayed in Table 2.

- The first question corresponds to the intention hidden behind the comment.
- The second question deals with the user's personality and how he/she will be affected by sharing that content.

- The third question warns the person how he/she will be blamed for posting negative content on social media.
- The fourth question is about how the individual will be isolated from the society as a result of his/her activity and how it can create mental stress and depression.
- The fifth question gives awareness about the legal consequences of online bullying and about the laws and punishments related to cyberbullying.
- The sixth question asks for a final confirmation about whether the person wants to share the offensive content even after knowing its consequences.

The work flow of our proposed method is demonstrated with an example in Fig. 5. When a user tries to enter a message or comment and press the share button, text analysis will be performed with VADER sentiment analysis. The outcome of this analysis is the classification of the comments into bully and

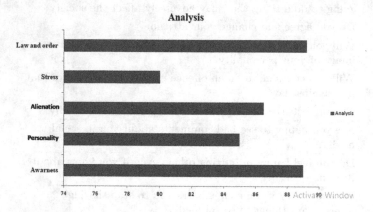

Fig. 4. Analysis the influence of 5 factors in people

Table 2. Questionnaire related to harassment data

This data looks like a negative content which can harass someone; Are you going to share this?
People may react negatively and it can have a negative impact on your personality. Are you going to share this?
People may blame you and your family for sharing this content; Are you sure you want to share?
You will be isolated from the society as a result of your activity and it can create mental stress and depression. Do you want to share this content?
According to Section 295A, you can be punished with imprisonment of either description for a term which may extend up to three years, or with fine, or with both; Do you want to share?
Are you sure about sharing this data ?

non-bully data. If it is a bully comment, then the intention behind that comment is identified and the corresponding questionnaire will be generated to alert the user about the consequences if that message or comment gets shared publicly.

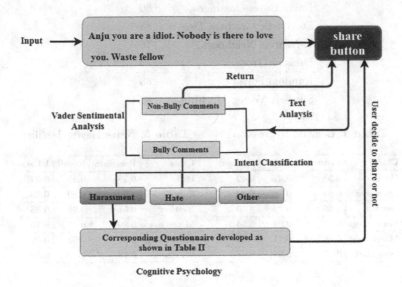

Fig. 5. An example of detecting harassment comment and the subsequent process

4.7 Experimental Setup

The model was developed with the help of a python binding for the TK GUI toolkit. It is the standard Python interface to the GUI toolkit. Tkinter is included with standard Linux, Microsoft Windows and Mac OS X installs of Python.

The code was developed using Python 3 with the help of Jupyter notebook. The Sklearn model was used to import many features required for our methodology. Pandas and NumPy packages were utilized to modify and arrange the data frame and dataset.

5   Results and Discussions

The results obtained for both training data and real-time data are analyzed. The accuracy rate obtained for training using different classifiers such as Logistic Regression, Naive bayes, Stochastic Gradient Descent, K-Nearest Neighbor, Decision tree, Random forest and Support Vector Machine for intent classification are displayed in Table 3. Except K-Nearest Neighbor, all other classifiers show 80% accuracy or more in training.

Table 3. Accuracy obtained using different classifiers

Machine learning classifiers	Accuracy
Logistic Regression	82
Naive Bayes classifier	80
Stochastic Gradient Descent	83
K-Nearest Neighbors	76
Decision Tree	83
Random Forest	85
Support Vector Machine	82

Table 4. Logistic Regression

Class	Precision	Recall	F1 score
Hate	0.38	0.47	0.42
Offensive	0.93	0.88	0.90
Neither	0.68	0.79	0.73
Micro avg	0.84	0.84	0.84
Macro avg	0.66	0.71	0.68
Weighted	0.85	0.84	0.84

Table 5. Naive Bayes classifier

Class	Precision	Recall	F1 score
Hate	0.28	0.43	0.34
Offensive	0.79	0.89	0.89
Neither	0.51	0.68	0.58
Micro avg	0.89	0.75	0.75
Macro avg	0.56	0.63	0.59
Weighted	0.75	0.79	0.80

Table 6. Stochastic Gradient Descent

Class	Precision	Recall	F1 score
Hate	0.50	0.11	0.18
Offensive	0.87	0.93	0.90
Neither	0.65	0.68	0.66
Micro avg	0.83	0.83	0.83
Macro avg	0.67	0.57	0.58
Weighted	0.81	0.83	0.81

Table 7. K-Nearest Neighbor

Class	Precision	Recall	F1 score
Hate	0.21	0.09	0.12
Offensive	0.79	0.96	0.86
Neither	0.56	0.11	0.18
Micro avg	0.76	0.76	0.76
Macro avg	0.52	0.39	0.39
Weighted	0.71	0.76	0.70

Table 8. Decision Tree

Class	Precision	Recall	F1 score
Hate	0.56	0.15	0.24
Offensive	0.87	0.93	0.90
Neither	0.66	0.61	0.63
Micro avg	0.83	0.83	0.83
Macro avg	0.69	0.57	0.59
Weighted	0.81	0.83	0.81

Table 9. Random Forest

Class	Precision	Recall	F1 score
Hate	0.50	0.04	0.08
Offensive	0.87	0.95	0.91
Neither	0.72	0.66	0.69
Micro avg	0.85	0.85	0.85
Macro avg	0.70	0.55	0.56
Weighted	0.82	0.85	0.82

The precision, recall and F1 score obtained during training with each classifier is shown in the Tables 4, 5, 6, 7, 8, 9 and 10.

Table 10. Support Vector Machine

Class	Precision	Recall	F1 score
Hate	0.25	0.25	0.25
Offensive	0.88	0.90	0.89
Neither	0.72	0.65	0.68
Micro avg	0.82	0.82	0.82
Macro avg	0.62	0.60	0.61
Weighted	0.81	0.82	0.81

After training with different classifiers, we tested our model with data obtained from Twitter related to hate speech detection and data related to Terrorist attack. For testing, Naïve Bayes classifier showed better results compared to the other classifiers. The results obtained during testing with different classifiers is shown in Fig. 6.

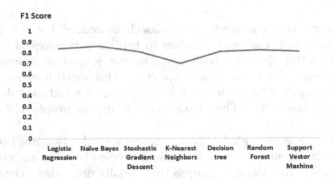

Fig. 6. F1 score obtained during testing with different classifiers

The proposed model has been developed with the idea of limiting the rate of online bullying by diverting the attitude of the people who intend to perform bullying using a cognitive psychological approach. This research aims at bringing a psychological change in the people by creating awareness in them about the negative impact of online bullying. Whenever the user tries to post or share a message, the proposed model analyzes the text to check whether it contains some bullying element or not. If the text contains something that can bully others, the text will be classified as a bully comment and following that the intention hidden behind that comment is identified using Intent analysis. Based on the intention identified from the message posted or shared, the corresponding questionnaire will be displayed in front of the user. Here, cognitive psychology is applied in the form of this questionnaire which was prepared on the basis of an online survey. The questionnaire warns the user on the basis of five factors. An example of intent identification is shown in Fig. 7 where the intent is identified as harassment.

You are an idiot , good for nothing

Fig. 7. Intention identification of a harassment comment

The proposed model suggests an approach to reduce the rate of people involved in this crime. Our research aims to bring a psychological compulsion among people to stop sharing cyberbullying messages. Lack of awareness about the future consequences makes people involve in this social menace. Cognitive psychology was applied in the form of a questionnaire which was designed by conducting an online survey. The questionnaire warns the people relating to five factors.

The questionnaire generated as part of intent identification was prepared on the basis of an online survey conducted among people above the age group of 20. The reason for selecting this age group is that usually users above the age group of 20 are more active users of social media and they are the groups who openly express their views and opinions through their social networking space. There is an existing app called Re-think which has been developed to detect abusive words in the text posted by teenage people. This app was developed with the intention of limiting the posting or sharing of abusive text that can harm others, especially among teenage users [26]. But not only teenagers, people belonging to any age group could be victims of this serious menace. So, in order to understand how people respond and react to these types of negative contents if they see it online, we conducted the online survey on people above the age group of 20 considering different factors. In addition, our model tries to find out the intent behind a negative message posted by a user and generate an appropriate questionnaire related to that particular intent and prevent him/her from posting that message online. Also, our method creates an awareness among people about the negative impact and future consequences of their data posted online if it contains some negative elements.

6 Conclusion and Future Scope

As cities become smarter, it's our duty to come up with technologies that ensure safety for all the residents especially women and children. A safe city is not just a place where women and children can live and travel safely, but it should also be free from any sort of fear of experiencing any violence or harassment even in online social environments. Here comes the relevance of our research so as to limit the rate of bullying through online social media. We have developed a cognitive psychological approach that notifies users if they share or post some negative content through their social network profile. According to the theory of planned behavior, the attitude of a person drives him/her to do the bullying. So if we can bring about a change in the attitude of a person, we can prevent him/her from doing that crime. With this notion, we have applied cognitive psychology in the form of a questionnaire which alerts the users on the negative impacts and consequences of bullying messages if it get shared online. With this approach, we can divert the attitude of people who are not deliberately performing online bullying and it also helps investigation agencies to find out the real culprits who are intentionally involved in this crime. However, it is difficult to prevent this crime entirely from the social media but we can limit its rate to some extent. This work is a small step towards achieving it.

In our current work, we have concentrated only on textual data and the experiments were mainly conducted on the Twitter platform. In future, we can extend this approach to image and video data and apart from Twitter, online bullying detection can be extended to other social media platforms too.

References

1. Poletti, C., Michieli, M.: Smart cities, social media platforms and security: online content regulation as a site of controversy and conflict. City Territory Archit. **5**(1), 20 (2018)
2. Kumar, A., Sachdeva, N.: Cyberbullying detection on social multimedia using soft computing techniques: a meta-analysis. Multimed. Tools Appl. **78**, 23973–24010 (2019)
3. Espelage, D.L., Rao, M.A., Craven, R.G.: Theories of cyberbullying. In: Principles Cyberbullying Research: Definitions, Measures, and Methodology, pp. 49–67 (2012)
4. National Academies of Sciences, Engineering, and Medicine: Preventing bullying through science, policy, and practice. National Academies Press, 14 October 2016
5. Ang, R.P., Goh, D.H.: Cyberbullying among adolescents: the role of affective and cognitive empathy, and gender. Child Psychiatry Hum. Dev. **41**(4), 387–397 (2010)
6. Rybnicek, M., Poisel, R., Tjoa, S.: Facebook watchdog: a research agenda for detecting online grooming and bullying activities. In: IEEE International Conference on Systems, Man, and Cybernetics. IEEE (2013)
7. Dinakar, K., Reichart, R., Lieberman, H.: Modeling the detection of textual cyberbullying. In: Fifth International AAAI Conference on Weblogs and Social Media (2011)
8. Wicker, A.W.: Attitudes versus actions: the relationship of verbal and üvert behavioral responses to attitude objects. J. Soc. Issues **25**, 41–78 (1969)

9. Na, H., Dancy, B.L., Park, C.: College student engaging in cyberbullying victimization: cognitive appraisals, coping strategies, and psychological adjustments. Arch. Psychiatr. Nurs. **29**(3), 155–161 (2015)
10. Hale, J.L., Householder, B.J., Greene, K.L.: The theory of reasoned action. In: Dillard, J.P., Shen, L. (eds.) The Sage Handbook of Persuasion: Developments in Theory and Practice, 2nd edn, pp. 259–286. Thousand Oaks, SAGE (2002)
11. Fishbein, M., Ajzen, I.: Belief, Attitude, Intention and Behavior: An Introduction to Theory and Research. Addison-Wesley, Boston (1975)
12. Völlink, T., et al.: An introduction in cyberbullying research. In: Cyberbullying: From Theory to Intervention. Routledge, New York (2016)
13. Ybarra, M.L., Mitchell, K.J.: Youth engaging in online harassment: Associations with caregiver-child relationships, internet use, and personal characteristics. J. Adolesc. **27**(3), 319–336 (2004)
14. Hasebrink, U.: Children's changing online experiences in a longitudinal perspective (2014)
15. Livingstone, S., et al.: In their own words: what bothers children online? Eur. J. Commun. **29**(3), 271–288 (2014)
16. Bryce, J., Fraser, J.: The role of disclosure of personal information in the evaluation of risk and trust in young peoples' online interactions. Comput. Hum. Behav. **30**, 299–306 (2014)
17. Valkenburg, P.M., Peter, J.: Online communication among adolescents: an integrated model of its attraction, opportunities, and risks. J. Adolesc. Health **48**(2), 121–127 (2011)
18. Van Hee, C., et al.: Automatic detection and prevention of cyberbullying. In: International Conference on Human and Social Analytics (HUSO 2015). IARIA (2015)
19. Jafarkarimi, H., et al.: Cyberbullying among students: an application of theory of planned behavior. In: International Conference on Research and Innovation in Information Systems (ICRIIS) (2017)
20. Lee, Y.C., Wu, W.-L.: Factors in cyber bullying: the attitude-social influence-efficacy model. Anales De Psicología Ann. Psychol. **34**(2), 324–331 (2018)
21. Ajzen, I.: The theory of planned behavior. Organ. Behav. Hum. Decis. Processes **50**(2), 179–211 (1991)
22. Fischer, K.W.: A theory of cognitive development: the control and construction of hierarchies of skills. Psychol. Rev. **87**(6), 477 (1980)
23. Davidson, T., et al.: Automated hate speech detection and the problem of offensive language. In: Eleventh International AAAI Conference on Web and Social Media (2017)
24. Zeitel-Bank, N., Tat, U.: Social media and its effects on individuals and social systems. J. Manag. Knowl. Learn., 1183–1190 (2014, online)
25. Swearer, S.M., et al.: Reducing bullying: application of social cognitive theory. Theory Pract. **53**(4), 271–277 (2014)
26. Prabhu, T.: Rethink: an effective way to prevent cyber bullying (2014)

Hybrid Personalized Music Recommendation Method Based on Feature Increment

Guimei Liu and Wenjun Jiang(✉) (iD)

College of Computer Science and Electronic Engineering,
Hunan University, Changsha 410082, China
{lgm,jiangwenjun}@hnu.edu.cn

Abstract. Over the past few years, the recommender system has been proposed as a critical role to help users choose the preferred product from a massive amount of data. For music recommendation, most recent recommender systems make attempts to associate music with the user's preferences primarily based on emotions in music audio. However, this kind of recommendation mechanism ignores the emotions in lyrics and comment texts and does not consider the followers of the user, which makes the predictions unreliable. To cope with this problem, in this paper, we study the user's listening behavior to discover his or her listening intention. We make three progresses. (1) We analyze the correlation between user preferences and the emotional categories of songs. (2) We analyze the similarity of the emotional categories of songs that users and their followees listen to. (3) We build a classification model based on KMeans and adjust different features(the correlation between the emotional category of song and user preferences, and the similarity between users and their followees) to predict whether the user will listen to the song. The experiment results verify that it is effective to consider the similarity and the correlation, and the similarity takes more effects.

Keywords: Social relationship · Emotion snalysis · Music recommendation

1 Introduction

Over the past few years, the recommender system [19] has been proposed as a critical role to help users choose the preferred product from a massive amount of data. With the continuous development and enrichment of music content in recent years, it is difficult for users to find music suitable for themselves in the huge ocean of music. The purpose of personalized music recommendation is to provide users with tailor-made music services. It is a research topic that benefits users and music platforms.

With the development of natural language processing [17] in recent years, music recommendation based on lyrics has become possible. Emotional description [7,8] is very useful and effective in describing music taxonomy. Since songs

© Springer Nature Singapore Pte Ltd. 2019
G. Wang et al. (Eds.): iSCI 2019, CCIS 1122, pp. 435–446, 2019.
https://doi.org/10.1007/978-981-15-1301-5_34

generally have a certain emotion, we can get the emotions of songs through emotional analysis based on lyrics and comment text. As a pioneering effort to describe human emotions, Russel [9] proposed a rotation model, and each of these emotions is shown in two dimensions. These two dimensions represent unpleasant to pleasure, calmness to excitement. Therefore, each emotional word can be defined as some combination of these two dimensions. Later, Thayer [22] further improved Russel's model. The two main dimensions of the Thayer model are "arousal" and "valence". In this model, in the arousal dimension, emotional terms are described as calm to excitement and are described as negative to positive in the valence dimension. The two-dimensional emotion plane of the Thayer model can be divided into four quadrants, composed of 11 emotions, as Fig. 1 shows.

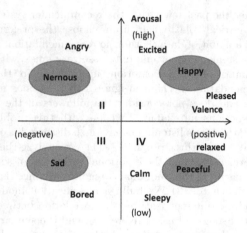

Fig. 1. Thayer's emotion model [22].

There are many types of attributes in music, such as singers, lyrics, audios, etc. More and more researches try to explore the user listening intention based on attributes of the music. Sanchez-Moreno et al. [23]. Use KNN algorithm to find similar users based on singers for music recommendation. Bu et al. [2]. Combines emotional analysis based on music audio with user's social relationships for music recommendation. These works use attributes of the music to construct a music recommendation model. Emotional analysis based on music audio usually analyze the melody, beat and rhythm. It requires a certain music expertise and faces an issue of high cost. Meanwhile, existing work usually ignores the user's social relationship [11,13,14], which makes it difficult to find a song that users may like. In this paper, we combine emotional analysis based on lyrics and comment texts with the user's social relationships to improve music recommendations. To be specific, we aim to (1) find the user's listening interest by analyzing the correlation between the user's preference and the emotional category of songs, and (2) analyze the similarity between the listening behavior of users and their followees to find songs that the user has potential interest.

Our contributions are threefold.

1. We analyze the correlation between user preferences and the emotional categories of songs. We find that the user's listening behavior is related to the emotion of song. At the same time, the user preference is also related to the emotion of song. These analyses can give us an idea of how to identify the user's listening intentions.
2. We analyze the similarity of the emotional categories of songs that users and their followees listen to. We find that the similarity between the listening behavior of users and their followees is different. We can say that the similarity between the listening interest of users and their followees is diversity. Through the above analysis, we find that the user's listening intention can be reflected from their followees.
3. We construct the hybrid personalized music recommendation model. We construct the classification model based on the KMeans and adjust different features (the correlation between the emotional category of a song and user preferences, and the similarity between users and their followees) to predict whether a user will listen to a song. The experiment results show that the importance of the features are different, for different features have different contributions to users' listening intentions.

The method of this paper applies to all music sites because the data types of the datasets used in this paper is common in music websites.

2   Related Work

Since the advent of the music platform, various music recommendation studies have been proposed. There are content-based recommendations [20]. For example, Sanchez-Moreno et al. [23]. Use KNN algorithm to find similar users based on singers for music recommendation. There are model-based recommendations [5,15,18]. For example, Pacula [21]. use matrix decomposition based on user's implicit feedback for music recommendation. There are user-based recommendations [10,16]. For example, Deng et al. [6]. generate music recommendations from listening records of similar users by obtaining the emotion of the user from the blog text. There are recommended methods based on hybrid models [3]. For example, Bu et al. [2] combines content-based recommendations with collaborative filtering to build a hybrid recommendation model.

At present, some music recommendation systems combine music audios and the user's social relationships for mixed recommendations, but they do not consider another important attribute of music, namely lyrics. they only consider the genre of music, but ingore the emotions of music. There are also emotional analysis based on lyrics [1,4,24], but they did not consider the feelings of the user after listening, that is, the emotion in the comment text [12]. The emotions in the comment text can predict the emotions of the music more accurately. The user's social relationship is not considered, which makes it difficult to find the user potential interest songs.

In conclusion, our work differs from others in mainly two aspects. (1) We use emotional analysis based on lyrics and comment texts to get attributes of songs. (2) We consider the user's social relationship to find songs that the target user is potentially interested in.

3   Correlation Analysis of User Listening Behavior in Online Music Platform

In this section, we focus on the user's listening intention as the research object and the analysis of various attributes related to it. We aim to identify the emotions of the song and the user's social relationship how to affects the user's listening behavior. The results of these analyses can help the company to understand the user's listening intentions. Our method is suitable for most music platform websites because we only need the user's listening records, lyrics, comments and the user's followees.

3.1   Raw Data

We use the scrapy crawler framework to crawl data on music website, such as music.163[1]. This dataset contains the user's listening records, lyrics, the comment texts and the user's followees, as the original data. Some user's listening records are shown in Table 1. The score field value has a range of 0 to 100, it indicates how much the user likes the song. The larger the value, the more the user likes the song.

Table 1. Some records of user behavior logs

userId	songId	score
58459	27902876	22
183103	417596830	100
1713095	554367706	86
2881455	417596830	12
3028129	432506809	85

The user's followees information is displayed in Table 2. The first field represents the target user's ID, and the second field indicates her or his followee's ID. For example, if A follows B, B is the followee of A and A is the follower of B. Figure 2 shows some song informations, such as song'ID, lyrics and comments. Songs here are limited to Chinese.

---

[1] https://music.163.com/.

songId	lyric in Chinese	lyric in English	comment in Chinese	comment in English
1569	头脑晕眩 视线模糊	My head spinning around I can't see clear no more	你还在等什么	what are you waiting for?

Fig. 2. Some lyrics and comments information.

Table 2. Followees information of some users

userId	followeeId
58459	319910944
183103	48168
1404462	601070196
2547334	46309613

3.2 Data Preprocessing

According to the statistics of the data, the number of items in the dataset is about 93319, and the number of users is about 1103. Firstly, Chinese songs are filtered from the original data, which gets 16482 items and 1103 users. What's more, ID of songs and users are renumbered, which are represented by 1 to 16482 and 1 to 1103. Then, We remove non-Chinese symbols from lyrics and comment texts to get text containing only Chinese. Finally, we use the tool of THULAC[2] to segment Chinese text.

3.3 Word Embedding

Since the computer cannot directly process Chinese text information, the Chinese text should be constructed as a word vector. We use the emotional value of the emotional words in the text to construct it in this paper. Because not all words in lyrics and comment texts have emotions, some words are only used for connections. Our paper uses the tool of SenticNet[3] to analyze emotion in lyrics and comments. SenticNet contains more emotional words than others (such as NRC, DUTIR). It not only includes the polarity of emotional words, but also includes the emotional value in the four emotional dimensions, which makes the emotional analysis more fine-grained.

We take the first 99 comments and the lyric for each song to make up 100 texts. We match the lyrics and comment texts after the word segmentation with SenNetic to get the emotional value of the emotional word. We use the emotional values in the four sentiment dimensions to construct four matrices E_{dj}, where d is the four emotional dimensions and j is the song's ID. Since the number of

---

[2] http://thulac.thunlp.org/.

[3] https://www.sentic.net/.

emotional words in the lyrics and the comment text is not all the same. For the convenience of processing, we use the maximum number of emotional words in the lyrics and the comment text as the standard. In this paper, it is set to 169. If the number of emotional words is less than 169, we use 0 to fill. The four emotional dimensions in the SenticNet are Pleasantness, Attention, Sensitivity, and Aptitude.

We use the SVD(Singular Value Decomposition) to perform matrix dimension reduction on the emotional matrix E_{dj}, which has a dimension of 100 * 169. Firstly, The matrix is reshaped to obtain a square matrix with a dimension of 130 * 130, and then it is reduced to obtain a matrix e_{dj} with a dimension of 1 * 130. Finally, we combine the emotion matrices in the four emotional dimensions to obtain a matrix with a dimension of 1 * 520 as the word vector of the song.

3.4   Statistical Analysis

From Fig. 3, we can see that the number of listening songs for 1,103 users is mostly between 20 and 40. A few people listen to more than 50 songs. At the same time, a few people listen to less than 10 songs. In Fig. 4, We can see that most songs are listened to by no more than 50 people, and a few songs are listened to by many people, which indicates that the popularity of each song is different.

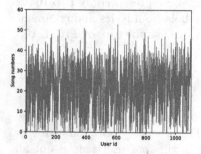
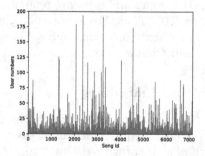

Fig. 3. The number of users listening to songs.

Fig. 4. The number of users whose songs are listened.

Figure 5 displays the distribution of the emotional categories for songs in the dataset. We regard the emotional category to which the song belongs as a classification problem. We train a classifier based on KMeans algorithm. We classify the emotional categories of songs in the dataset into 11 categories. Figure 6 shows the number of samples included in each cluster. We can see that the number of samples contained in each cluster is different. We can say that users have different preferences for songs in different emotional categories.

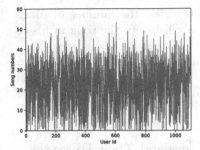

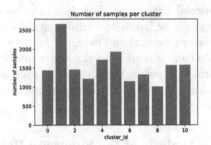

Fig. 5. The emotional clustering map of all songs.

Fig. 6. The number of samples in each cluster.

4 Correlation Analysis

In this section, we analyze the correlation between the emotional category of songs and the user's preferences. We also analyze the similarity between users and their followees. Through analysis, we try to find out the impact of these attributes on the user's listening intentions.

4.1 Correlation Analysis Between Emotional Categories of Songs and User's Preferences

For each user, the emotional category of the song he or she likes may be different. So, when predicting the user's listening intention, we have to consider the different attributes of each user. This section analyzes the correlation between emotional categories of songs and user's preferences to find out the listening interests of different users.

Figure 7 displays the correlation between the emotional category of songs and the user's preference. We find that the user's preference is different in different

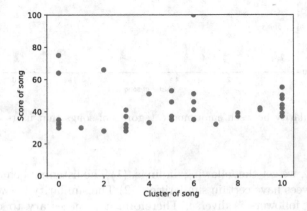

Fig. 7. The relationship between emotional categories of songs and user's preferences.

emotional categories. For different emotional categories, the number of songs that the user listen to is different. The user usually listen to the song in his or her favorite emotional category, and vise Versa.

As can be seen from the above analysis, although the user listens to songs in several categories, the amount in each categories is different. Therefore, we can say that the user's listening preferences are related to the emotional category of songs.

4.2 Analysis of the Similarity Between Users and Their Followees

The emotional categories of songs that different users like are different. Therefore, when looking for similar users, it is also necessary to consider the similarity of their listening interests. We analyze the similarity between the listening records of users and their followees to get the strength of relationship between users and their followees.

Figure 8 displays the distribution of the emotional categories of songs that users and their followees listen to. We can see that the similarity between the target user and the first followee is less than he or she and the second followee. The second followee's listening interest is more similar to the target user. We can say that the similarity between the user and her or his followees is different.

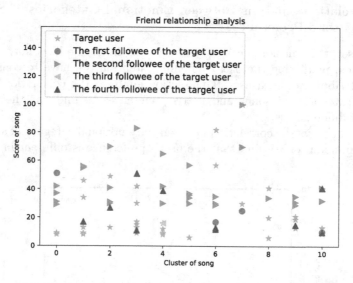

Fig. 8. The similarity between emotional categories of songs that users and their followees listen to.

In summary, we get the following findings. (1) The listening behavior of users and their followees have certain similarities. (2) The similarity between the user and her or his followers is diverse. Therefore, it is necessary to consider the strength of relationship between users and their followees.

5   Recommendation Generation

In this section, we generate candidate items based on the similarity between the user and her or his followers and the followees' preferences for songs. We use the Gaussian function to calculate the similarity between the candidate item and the emotional category of the target user's listening records. We generate recommended items based on the similarity and category weights. We use metrics such as precision and recall to measure recommendations.

5.1   Measuring User's Preferences

We use the trained classification model to get the emotional categories C_{ui} of the target user's listening records R based on the emotion vector e_j of the song. Meanwhile, we calculate the proportion w_{ui} of each category C_{ui}. The formula is as follows:

$$w_{ui} = m_{ui}/M_u \tag{1}$$

where m_{ui} represents the number of samples in the category C_{ui}, M_u represents the total number of samples of all categories of the target user u, and i indicates the category.

5.2   Selecting Candidate Item and Calculating the Similarity

Selecting Candidate Item. We select songs that his or her followees like listening to but the target user does not listen to as candidate items. The song that the followee v likes listening to is judged by its $score_{vj}$. The formula is as follows:

$$\text{score }_{vj} \geq \frac{a}{num} \times \sum_{j=1}^{num} \text{score }_{vj} \tag{2}$$

Where num represents the number of songs that the user v has listened to, and a represents the similarity between the user v and the target user u.

Calculating the Similarity. We use the Gaussian function to calculate the similarity between the candidate item and the emotional category of the target user's listening records. We use the following formular to describe this:

$$S_{h,\text{Cui}} = \frac{1}{\sqrt{2\pi k_g \delta_{\text{Cui}}^2}} \exp\left(-\frac{(e_h - \overline{p_{\text{Cui}}})}{2k_g \delta_{\text{Cui}}^2}\right) \tag{3}$$

Where k_g represents a constant, σ_{Cui}^2 represents the variance of the category C_{ui}, $\overline{p_{\text{Cui}}}$ represents the mean of the category C_{ui}, and e_h represents the emotional vector of the candidate item.

5.3   Generating the Recommendation

We calculate the target user's preference g_{uh} for the candidate item based on the similarity between the candidate item and the emotional category of the target user's listening records, and the weight of each emotional category. The formula is as follows:

$$g_{uh} = \frac{1}{c} \sum_{i=1}^{c} w_{ui} s_{h,Cui} \qquad (4)$$

where c is the number of the emotional categories of the target user listening records, W_{ui} is the weight of emotional category and $s_{h,Cui}$ is the similarity between the candidate item and the emotional category of the target user's listening records.

When the target user's preference g_{uh} for the candidate item h exceeds the threshold t. The candidate item h is added as a recommendation to the recommendation list CL, otherwise, the candidate item h is discarded.

5.4   Result Analysis

We use the sklearn, which is a Python library, as the tool to train the model and get the experimental result. Besides the random baseline, we present three methods to compare the effects of the two features as follows.

1. The Method 1 only uses the similarity of users and their followees, which is described in Sect. 4.2.
2. The Method 2 uses the correlation of user's preference and the emotional categories of songs, which is described in Sect. 4.1.
3. The Method 3 uses the similarity of between users and their followees, combining with the correlation of user's preference and the emotional categories of songs.

The experimental results are shown in Table 3.

Table 3. Experimental results under four different methods.

Methods	Precision	Recall
Random	0.0468	0.1960
Method 1	0.0822	0.5147
Method 2	0.0562	0.2598
Method 3	0.0888	0.6078

The Integrated Effects of Different Features. Comparing with the random baseline, the improvement of Method 1 is 75.64% in precision and 162.60% in recall; that of Method 2 is 20.09% in precision and 32.55% in recall; that of Method 3 is 89.74% in precision and 210.10% in recall. The experiment results verify that it is effective to consider the similarity and the correlation, and the similarity takes more effects.

6   Conclusions

In this paper, we construct the hybrid personalized music recommendation model by combining emotional analysis based on lyrics and comment texts with user social relationships. To be specific, we analyze the correlation between user preferences for songs and emotional categories of songs. Moreover, we analyze the similarity of the emotional categories of songs that users and their followees listen to. We find that the similarities between listening behaviors of users and their followees is different. Our paper constructs the recommendation model by combining the above (correlation and similarly). Our paper test their effects in real data set, and we find that they have different importance. In future work, we are interested in making music recommendation based on English songs and applying our model into more fields.

Acknowledgments. This research was supported by NSFC grant 61632009 and Outstanding Young Talents Training Program in Hunan University 531118040173.

References

1. An, Y., Sun, S., Wang, S.: Naive Bayes classifiers for music emotion classification based on lyrics. In: IEEE ACIS, pp. 635–638 (2017)
2. Bu, J., et al.: Music recommendation by unified hypergraph: combining social media information and music content. In: ACM Multimedia, pp. 391–400 (2010)
3. Chen, X., Tang, T.Y.: Combining content and sentiment analysis on lyrics for a lightweight emotion-aware Chinese song recommendation system. In: ICML pp. 85–89 (2018)
4. Choi, J., Song, J., Kim, Y.: An analysis of music lyrics by measuring the distance of emotion and sentiment. In: IEEE SNPD, pp. 176–181 (2018)
5. De Assuncao, W.G., de Almeida Neris, V.P.: An algorithm for music recommendation based on the user's musical preferences and desired emotions. In: MUM, pp. 205–213 (2018)
6. Deng, S., Wang, D., Li, X., Xu, G.: Exploring user emotion in microblogs for music recommendation. Expert Syst. Appl. **42**(23), 9284–9293 (2015)
7. Feng, Y., Zhuang, Y., Pan, Y.: Music information retrieval by detecting mood via computational media aesthetics. In: Web Intelligence, pp. 235–241 (2003)
8. Feng, Y., Zhuang, Y., Pan, Y.: Popular music retrieval by detecting mood. In: ACM SIGIR, pp. 375–376 (2003)
9. Russell, J.A.: A circumplex model of affect. J. Pers. Soc. Psychol. **39**, 1161–1178 (1980)
10. Jannach, D., Kamehkhosh, I., Lerche, L.: Leveraging multi-dimensional user models for personalized next-track music recommendation. In: ACM SAC, pp. 1635–1642 (2017)
11. Jiang, W., Wang, G., Bhuiyan, Z.A., Wu, J.: Understanding graph-based trust evaluation in online social networks: methodologies and challenges. ACM Comput. Surv. **49**(1), 10 (2016)
12. Jiang, W., Wu, J.: Active opinion-formation in online social networks. In: IEEE INFOCOM, pp. 1–9 (2017)

13. Jiang, W., Wu, J., Wang, G.: On selecting recommenders for trust evaluation in online social networks. ACM Trans. Internet Technol. **15**(4), 14 (2015)
14. Jiang, W., Wu, J., Wang, G., Zheng, H.: Forming opinions via trusted friends: time-evolving rating prediction using fluid dynamics. IEEE Trans. Comput. **65**(4), 1211–1224 (2016)
15. Kelen, D., Berecz, D., Beres, F., Benczur, A.A.: Efficient K-NN for playlist continuation. In: ACM RecSys (2018)
16. Li, M., Jiang, W., Li, K.: When and what music will you listen to? Fine-grained time-aware music recommendation. In: IEEE ISPA, pp. 1091–1098 (2017)
17. Mahedero, J.P.G., Martinez, A., Cano, P., Koppenberger, M., Gouyon, F.: Natural language processing of lyrics. In: ACM Multimedia, pp. 475–478 (2005)
18. Mao, K., Chen, G., Hu, Y., Zhang, L.: Music recommendation using graph based quality model. Sig. Process. **120**, 806–813 (2016)
19. Li, M., Jiang, W., Li, K.: Recommendation systems in real applications: algorithm and parallel architecture. In: Wang, G., Ray, I., Alcaraz Calero, J.M., Thampi, S.M. (eds.) SpaCCS 2016. LNCS, vol. 10066, pp. 45–58. Springer, Cham (2016). https://doi.org/10.1007/978-3-319-49148-6_5
20. Nakamura, K., Fujisawa, T., Kyoudou, T.: Music recommendation system using lyric network. In: IEEE GCCE, pp. 1–2 (2017)
21. Pacula, M.: A matrix factorization algorithm for music recommendation using implicit user feedback (2009)
22. Re, T.: The Biopsychology of Mood and Arousal. Oxford University Press, Oxford (1989)
23. Sanchezmoreno, D., Gonzalez, A.B.G., Vicente, M.D.M., Batista, V.F.L., Garcia, M.N.M.: A collaborative filtering method for music recommendation using playing coefficients for artists and users. Expert Syst. Appl. **66**, 234–244 (2016)
24. Wang, X., Chen, X., Yang, D., Wu, Y.: Music emotion classification of Chinese songs based on lyrics using tf*idf and rhyme. In: ISMIR, pp. 765–770 (2011)

Real-Time Traffic Monitoring Systems Based on Magnetic Sensor Integration

Mohammed Sarrab[1]([✉]), Supriya Pulparambil[1], Naoufel Kraiem[2], and Mohammed Al-Badawi[2]

[1] Communication and Information Research Center, Sultan Qaboos University, Muscat 123, Sultanate of Oman
{sarrab, supriya}@squ.edu.om
[2] Department of Computer Science, Sultan Qaboos University, Muscat 123, Sultanate of Oman
{naoufel, mbadawi}@squ.edu.om

Abstract. Traffic management systems are one of the most significant components of any major city. Ease of use and effective connections are essential for sustainability and growth, impacting citizens, businesses, the environment, and the economy. Nevertheless, these systems represent a major challenge when it comes to digital renovation. This paper proposes a novel intelligent traffic monitoring system for a smart city after considering the research gaps, which are yet to be explored in the current scenario. Our proposed solution presents a system model to broadcast traffic congestion updates through roadside message units. The main objective of this research is to provide real-time traffic updates to users through message units installed at intersections specifically on collector roads to improve the mobility. The proposed system can be further enhanced to provide optimal re-route suggestions to the drivers. This effort is part of a funded research project that investigates Smart Streets: Real-Time Feedback for Adaptive Traffic Signals.

Keywords: Space occupancy · RMU · Vehicle classification · Traffic monitoring · Traffic congestion

1 Introduction

The traffic congestion is a serious problem which adversely affects the daily human life and also the environment through different causes. A significant amount of research has been done in the area of traffic management specifically for predicting, estimating, and managing traffic congestion in the city highways [1] and campuses [2].

To an extent, the traffic congestion problem can be resolved by adopting emerging smart technologies for the efficient use of existing infrastructure [3]. In the new era of smart cities, the Internet of Thing (IoT) paradigm can play a major role in intelligent traffic management systems (ITMS). This can be handled in different dimensions such as real-time warning messages [4, 5] and dynamic traffic light control. The real-time traffic monitoring and management are performed by analyzing the information collected through global positioning (GPS) systems, vehicle to vehicle communication, vehicle to infrastructure communication, probe vehicles, and sensors [6–9].

G. Wang et al. (Eds.): iSCI 2019, CCIS 1122, pp. 447–460, 2019.
https://doi.org/10.1007/978-981-15-1301-5_35

The road traffic in cities like Muscat is drastically increasing and it has been observed as heterogeneous in terms of varying vehicular dimensions. Most of the existing traffic management systems are dedicated to highways/urbanized arterial roads and less emphasis has been given to collector roads or local roads. Real-time traffic updates on these roads are very useful for drivers to save their time on roads. Google Traffic feature in Google Maps [32] is widely used for real-time traffic updates. The traffic updates are based on the locations determined by GPS services. A minimum level of technical knowledge is essential to productively utilize these services. The real-time traffic updates on collector roads also have to be handled along with highway roads to avoid the traffic congestion impact in our daily life.

The automatic vehicle detection and classification is a key component of any traffic management systems. The technologies such as inductive loop detectors [10], feature extraction through camera images [5, 11], and sensors [12] are commonly employed by such systems.

The main objective of this research is to propose a sensor-based system that could: (i) forecast traffic congestions based on road occupancy, (ii) guide drivers to re-route vehicles through early warning traffic messages, and (iii) support authorities to control and broadcast messages on unusual road incidents.

The key contribution of this paper is the proposed system model that provide real-time traffic updates through the digital electronic roadside message units (RMUs) installed at intersections and other identified critical points. This RMUs can also be used to display any kind of early warning messages from governments such as accidents, VIP visits, or any other unexpected road incidents. Another novelty of this paper is that we don't expect any vehicle to vehicle communication or any smart technologies in individual vehicles.

The remainder of this paper is organized as follows: Sect. 2 presents the related work. Section 3 provides the concepts and standards used in this research. Section 4 presents the research steps followed to achieve the research objective. Section 5 discusses the proposed system model and its various components. Section 6 discusses the results of qualitative analysis. Finally, Sect. 7 concludes the discussion with the implementation plan and future works.

2   Related Works

In recent years, many research has been done in the area of ITMS. Different attempts are made to provide real-time traffic information. This section discusses a few related research works.

In 2016, Sodagaran et al., proposed a video detection system to measure traffic congestion based on average vehicle speed. The system broadcasts the messages to identified decision points and displays in three colors green, yellow, and red to indicate the intensity of the traffic [3]. In the same direction, another research has been done by collecting information through GPS [5]. A comparison between the pre-defined traffic capacity of the road and the number of vehicles crossing the intersection is performed to display congestion warning messages.

Mobile-based web applications are also used to update drivers on traffic monitoring messages. Dubey et al. in 2017 and Saikar et al. 2017 proposed real-time traffic-monitoring systems that broadcast traffic updates through mobile applications [6, 9]. This will help drivers to select alternate ways; however, expects a minimum technical knowledge for drivers.

Similarly, the studies [13, 14] focused on dynamic traffic signal management by sensing the demand. In 2014, Kanungo et al. estimated traffic density through video monitoring systems and image processing whereas Atta et al., in 2018 uses sensors and expects RFID tag in every vehicle.

A few studies are published in real-time traffic estimation from connected vehicles through artificial intelligence [7]. The vehicles send information to each other, and the roadside units will collect that information to predict traffic congestion. Similarly, probe vehicles are also used to collect real-time traffic information [15]. The probe vehicles are equipped with wireless communication mechanisms and GPS.

However, to the best of our knowledge, there are very limited studies to assist driver side decision-making process through real-time traffic updates. The existing researches and technologies are mostly to assist highway traffic management systems. This work will focus on providing real-time traffic updates to users through RMUs installed at intersections specifically on collector roads to improve the mobility.

3 Concepts and Standards

This section discusses the basic concepts, standards and the assumptions used.

3.1 Measures of Traffic Congestion

The congestion measures are based on different indicators such as space, time and delay, level of service, speed, and reliability. The traffic congestion measures are expected to be simple and self-describing [16]. The basic parameters are based on the kinematic wave theory defined as Lighthill–Whitham–Richards (LWR) theory [17]. The density, flow, and occupancy are the three microscopic parameters attained by averaging the individual parameters [8]. These parameters are obtained by motion detection through different image recognition techniques.

In this research, we focus on the spatial measure i.e. the road space occupancy by considering the length of the vehicle, safe distance between vehicles, and a buffer length. The safe distance between two vehicles is taken as 2 M, the standard constant [19]. The buffer length is also customizable constant value. The buffer length is assumed to be 2% of the road segment length. This will be added when measuring road space occupancy of local roads.

3.2 Length-Based Vehicle Classification

Each country has its own standards for traffic management specifically to the vehicle dimension limits applicable for different roads. The vehicles are broadly classified as general access vehicles and restricted access vehicles [20]. The US federal highway administration department [21], has classified the vehicles into thirteen groups according to the number of axles. The axle based classification is further mapped to vehicle length for providing a length based vehicle classification. In [21], three different length based classifications are proposed for vehicles namely scheme 1, scheme 2, and scheme 5. Scheme 1 has four vehicle categories, scheme 2 has five vehicle categories, and scheme 5 has six vehicle categories. This research uses the six categories of vehicle classification as per scheme 5 of US federal highway administration guidelines [22]. It is presented in Table 1.

Table 1. Length of vehicles

Vehicle type	Length
Motor Cycles	<6.75 feet (2.05 meter)
Autos	>6.75 <18 feet (2.-5 to 5.48 meter)
Light Trucks	> 18 < 31 (5.48 to 9.45 meter)
Medium	> 31 <47.25 (9.45 to 14.40 meter)
Medium Long	> 47.25 <49 (14 .40 to 15 meter)
Long	> 49 feet (>15 meters)

3.3   Technologies for ITMS

The common technologies used for traffic monitoring are vision-based systems (cameras), RADARs, and different types of sensors. Mostly, the real-time traffic data collected by these devices are sent to the server for further processing. The image recognition techniques [11, 23] are applied to classify vehicles and measure congestion for video/image-based monitoring. In most of the studies, the moving vehicles are identified through the background image subtraction technique [3, 5, 6, 18]. The vehicle identification and their classification in these studies are based on feature extractions from the images.

Similarly, the sensors are used to collect traffic data for detecting and classifying vehicles, estimating vehicle speed and congestion [24, 25]. The sensors in ITMS are either in-vehicle sensors or on-road sensors. The on-road sensors help to collect real-time data to improve current traffic management systems [24]. The on-road traffic sensors are of two types: intrusive and non-intrusive.

The intrusive sensors are expensive and paved on the road. This requires regular maintenance and lane closure [12, 14]. The non-intrusive sensors are installed in different parts of the road and are part of the proposed system. They include video cameras, radar, infrared, ultrasonic, acoustic, and radio frequency identification sensors. Different sensors such as acoustic sensors, magnetic sensors infrared sensors, etc. are used for vehicle classification and length prediction [14, 25–27]. This study focused on magnetic sensors as it is already proven for vehicle classification and cost efficiency [12].

3.4   Magnetic Sensors for Vehicle Classification

Wireless magnetic sensors received wide acceptance among the research community in terms of its low-cost, easy installation, and portability [12, 14, 28, 29]. In any wireless sensor network architecture, many sensor nodes are connected to an access point with powerful computation resources [30] as shown in Fig. 1. Four magnetic sensor nodes are used for vehicle detection in [14]; however, two sensor nodes are used in [12]. These studies claimed that on an average they achieve 99% accuracy in terms of vehicle detection, 97% accuracy in terms of speed estimation, and 97% of accuracy in terms of vehicle classification.

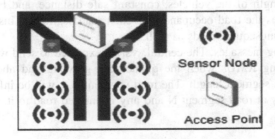

Fig. 1. Wireless sensor networks

In 2018, Balid et al., proposed the hardware design of intelligent vehicle counting and classification sensor based on magnetometer (MAG) sensors [12]. This sensor can be installed on roads or roadsides. However, the corresponding algorithms are required to handle this. The magnetic sensors detect the disturbance in the magnetic field flux lines of the earth caused by the large mass of vehicles made out of ferrous materials [12]. This disturbance is measured as vehicle magnetic length (VML) and use to estimate vehicle physical length.

$$vml = v * T_{oc}$$

$$v = vehicle\,speed\,and\,T_{oc} = sensor\,occupancy\,time$$

The machine learning algorithms such as support vector machines [12, 14], neuron classifiers [28] are applied for vehicle classifications based on magnetic length.

4   Research Methodology

The section provides the research methodology steps to accomplish the research objectives. To achieve the research objective, this research expects to follow the steps:

- Identification of sensors: There are different kinds of sensors available for real-time traffic monitoring. We need to identify cost-efficient sensors to detect traffic situations. Based on an initial analysis of sensors used in traffic management systems, this research has selected magnetic sensors.
- Identification of RMU Location: The objective is to maximize the RMU visibility hence the selection of RMU location is considered as a maximization problem. The positioning of RMUs is critical and very similar to billboard site locations. The key factors that involve in the decision are position, exposure, viewability, and environment [31].
- Identification of length of cars: The real-time traffic data sent to the access points/server and they apply techniques to classify vehicle and identify the vehicle length.
- Identification of growing queues: The queue dynamics are generally estimated using LWR theory [1]. In this research, the space occupancy is estimated by considering the length of the vehicles, constant safe distance, and buffer space. The server calculates the road occupancy for each road segment. This will predict the congestion in subsequent roads as well.
- Display warning messages: The central system expected to send warning messages to corresponding RMUs when the queues are growing and about to reach the maximum road segment length. The road segment N-1 will be informed about the road occupancy at road segment N and any connected road to it.

5 Model of the Proposed System

The proposed system model is given in Fig. 2. The system follows a layered architecture; the bottom layer is real-time traffic data.

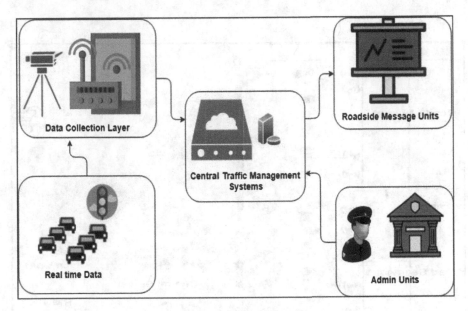

Fig. 2. Proposed system model

The model has three main components: (i) roadside sensor units and access points installed at identified intersections/locations, (ii) a central processing system to process the collected data, and (iii) roadside message units (RMUs) to display traffic warning messages for drivers. The system processes sensor data at the segment level and sends messages to the preceding RMU. In addition, the human monitored admin units can communicate to the central system to broadcast messages for local roads in case of any roadblocks due to VIP visits/emergency works/accidents. The model does not require any embedded devices. The sensors, access points, RMUs, and servers are not embedded on the road. Hence, lane closure or any kind of traffic interruptions is not a requirement to implement the proposed model in real life. The communication between different components of the system model is given in Fig. 3.

As can be seen in Fig. 3 there are sensor nodes placed at each entry and exit points of a road segment to detect and estimate vehicle length. The sensors are placed in a predefined distance (between 6 to 100 m). These sensors communicate with the access point over a wireless network. The ZigBee wireless technologies are widely used for IoT devices [12], which can be used for the communication between sensors and access point nodes. The access points should have a minimum computing power to perform the vehicle classification. Each access point is connected to the central server over a network. The message units are placed between the road segments. The central server/access point can communicate with the message unit over a wireless cellular network. The sensors and RMUs are battery-powered and their health checkups can be performed by access points based on the defined schedules. At this moment the system is modeled for a single lane road because the main focus of this research is local and collector roads.

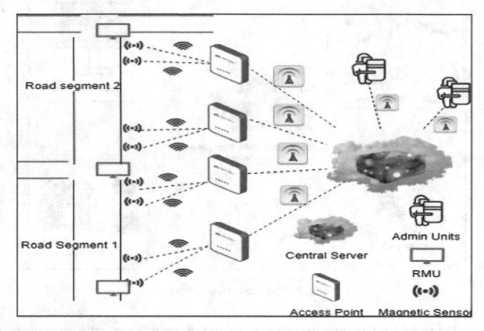

Fig. 3. System communication model

5.1 Data Collection Layer

The data collection layer is to collect real-time traffic data through sensors. The data collection layer of the proposed system consists of sensor nodes and access points installed at different road segments. The sensors and access points can be connected through wireless networks. The access points process the sensor data for vehicle detection and classification. This data will send to the central server system to measure/predict traffic congestion.

5.2 Central Traffic Management System

The sensor access points and RMUs are connected to the central traffic management system. The real-time traffic data collected by sensors are sent to the server through access points. It can be a cloud server in the context of IoT, and the processed data can be stored and accessed real-time. The communication between access points and the server can be over the cellular network. The server analyzes the data from access points and sent messages to the corresponding RMUs on the traffic congestion state. The administration units can also communicate to the server to broadcast messages to a particular road segment in case of any unexpected traffic incidents. In the case of communication failures, the server can retrieve data from access points when the connections are established back.

5.3 Roadside Message Units

RMU is an electronic display board placed at intersections and other identified locations. The RMU displays the traffic status of different road segments in the forthcoming intersections. The local road will be informed about the traffic congestion at another road (located after a certain distance from local road) so that the vehicles from the local road can take alternate option as the message is displayed in the junction. The message units can be permanent or portable. The real-time examples of few messages in the context of Muscat municipality has been given in Fig. 4. It has two scenarios, scenario A indicates traffic messages based on real-time monitoring. Scenario B indicates a broadcast by traffic admin units.

Fig. 4. Traffic messages

5.4 Algorithm

The pseudo-code to update the message units are presented in this section. The algorithm presents the logic for calculating the road occupancy and message unit display. The runtime is infinite for the algorithm as it is an infinite loop. As the vehicle enters a particular road segment the vehicle length is added to the occupancy measure. Similarly, when the vehicle exits from the particular road segment the occupancy measure is decreased by vehicle length. When the occupancy measure of a specific road segment reaches the threshold, the display message will be sent to corresponding roadside units.

Besides, this study requires efficient algorithms for RMU location identification and vehicle detection and classification.

Input: Vehicle data from access points ($S_i = i^{th}$ segment, $V_j = j^{th}$ vehicle)
Output: RMU Message
S: Safe distance between vehicles
B: Buffer length added to check if the road is full
T: Timer to keep the message ON at RMU
While (1)
    S_i.Vcnt: Vehicle count at i^{th} road segment
    S_i.length: Length of ith road segment
    V_j.length: Length of jth vehicle
    S_i.Occupancy: Space occupancy at i^{th} road segment

    If (S_i.Vcnt ++)
        S_i.Occupancy = S_i.Occupancy + S_i.V_j.length
    If (S_i.Vcnt --)
        S_i.Occupancy = S_i.Occupancy - S_i.V_j.length
    If (S_i.Vcnt * S + B + S_i.Occupancy > S_i.length)
    MT_i = Current Time (the time message send to i-1)
        Send 'FULL' message to RMU_{i-1}
    If (S_i.Occupancy < S_i.length &&
        Current Time > MT_i + T)
        Turnoff $RMUi_1$
END

6   Qualitative Analysis Results

The existing system models that use magnetic sensors for vehicle classification are analyzed in terms of few system design objectives such as portability, scalability, real-time monitoring, server storage, and real-time visibility. The portability indicates whether the entire system model can be implemented for temporary traffic studies and the setup is intrusive or non-intrusive. The scalability indicates any additional sensors or system components can be integrated. The real-time monitoring indicates whether the system performs real-time traffic monitoring through real-time vehicle detection and classification. The server storage indicates whether the processed data are stored in central servers. The real-time visibility indicates the public delivery of traffic updates through any mechanisms. The four models compared are iVCCS [12], SMOTE [33], portable roadside sensor (PRS) model [14], low-speed congested traffic (LCT) model [35]. All these models use 3 axis magnetic sensors except iVCCS which uses a 6 axis MAG. As per the analysis, it is clear that the proposed model offers an additional functionality of real-time traffic updates through message units. The analysis summary is given in Table 2. The proposed model only considers real-time delivery of traffic updates to the public.

Table 2. Qualitative analysis of system models

Model	Portability	Scalability	Real-time monitoring	Server storage	Real-time public visibility
SMOTE	Yes	Yes	Yes	No	No
iVCCS	Yes	Yes	Yes	Yes	No
PRS	Yes	Yes	Yes	No	No
LCT	Yes	Yes	Yes	No	No
Proposed model	Yes	Yes	Yes	Yes	Yes

For instance, consider the traffic complexity of a closed community such as a university or hospital. The road occupancy rate will be very high during peak hours. Such gated community normally has more than one entry/exit points and collector road segments of different length. To provide the real-time traffic updates for such a campus, different message units can be displayed at main intersection points so that users can go with alternate options. To maximize the visibility for message units, the system will take the campus map as input and identify the key junction points to keep the message units. The road occupancy rate will be calculated in real-time based on vehicle length detected by magnetic sensors placed at different road segments. The sensors will send data to access points at real-time, the access points will do vehicle classification and send the information to the central server. The central server updates the message units with appropriate messages, which help in the decision-making process.

7   Conclusion

Several kinds of research have been carried out on intelligent traffic monitoring system, but a secure and efficient solution for traffic congestion is yet to discuss.

This study has proposed a system model to provide real-time traffic congestion updates through roadside message units. The RMUs are placed in intersections to assist the decision-making process. The magnetic sensors are selected for vehicle detection and length estimation. The central system calculates the road space occupancy of each road segment and broadcast messages to the corresponding RMUs in case of any segments are full. The road occupancy is calculated based on individual vehicle length.

The proposed model not only provides real-time traffic congestion updates through roadside message units but also can deliver emergency messages with several priorities. The expected outcome from this investigation:

- System model to broadcast traffic congestion updates through roadside message units
- Real-time traffic updates to users through installed roadside message units
- Implementation prototype.

For future directions, our initial finding is encouraging as the proposed system could provide further opportunities such as prevent false warnings from malicious entities. Also, our system will eliminate the time delay in medical assistance for accident victims, transporting critical patients and medicines.

The main issue with IoT is that the security of the entire system has to be concentrated on and not a particular IoT layer, device or software. Hence, integrating the entire traffic management system with multiple layer security for various data generated from various sources can be another subject of future scope.

Acknowledgments. This article is based on the research work funded by The Research Council (TRC) of the Sultanate of Oman, under Grant No: RC/SR-SC/CIRC/19/01, (www.trc.gov.om).

References

1. Geroliminis, N., Skabardonis, A.: Identification and analysis of queue spillovers in city street networks. IEEE Trans. Intell. Transp. Syst. **12**(4), 1107–1115 (2011). https://doi.org/10.1109/TITS.2011.2141991
2. Yu, X., Xiong, S., He, Y., Wong, W.E., Zhao, Y.: Research on campus traffic congestion detection using BP neural network and Markov model. J. Inf. Secur. Appl. **31**, 54–60 (2016)
3. Sodagaran, A., Zarei, N., Azimifar, Z.: Intelligent traffic information system a real-time traffic information system on the Shiraz bypass. In: MATEC Web of Conferences, vol. 81, p. 04003 (2016). https://doi.org/10.1051/matecconf/20168104003
4. Makino, H., Tamada, K., Sakai, K., Kamijo, S.: Solutions for urban traffic issues by ITS technologies. IATSS Res. **42**(2), 49–60 (2018). https://doi.org/10.1016/j.iatssr.2018.05.003
5. Simdiankin, A., Uspensky, I., Belyu, L., Ratnikov, K.: A method to assess congestion in various traffic directions. Transp. Res. Procedia **36**, 725–731 (2018). https://doi.org/10.1016/j.trpro.2018.12.099
6. Dubey, A., Akshdeep, Rane, S.: Implementation of an intelligent traffic control system and real time traffic statistics broadcasting. In: Proceedings of the International Conference on Electronics, Communication and Aerospace Technology, ICECA 2017, pp. 33–37 (2017). https://doi.org/10.1109/ICECA.2017.8212827
7. Kanungo, A., Sharma, A., Singla, C.: Smart traffic lights switching and traffic density calculation using video processing. In: 2014 Recent Advances in Engineering and Computational Sciences, RAECS, pp. 1–6 (2014)
8. Khan, S.M., Dey, K.C., Chowdhury, M.: Real-time traffic state estimation with connected vehicles. IEEE Trans. Intell. Transp. Syst. **18**(7), 1687–1699 (2017). https://doi.org/10.1109/TITS.2017.2658664
9. Saikar, A., Parulekar, M., Badve, A., Thakkar, S., Deshmukh, A.: TrafficIntel: smart traffic management for smart cities. In: 2017 International Conference on Emerging Trends and Innovation in ICT, ICEI 2017, pp. 46–50 (2017). https://doi.org/10.1109/ETIICT.2017.7977008
10. Bhaskar, L., Sahai, A., Sinha, D., Varshney, G., Jain, T.: Intelligent traffic light controller using inductive loops for vehicle detection. In: Proceedings on 2015 1st International Conference on Next Generation Computing Technologies, NGCT 2015, pp. 518–522, September 2016. https://doi.org/10.1109/NGCT.2015.7375173
11. Aqel, S., Hmimid, A., Sabri, M.A., Aarab, A.: Road traffic: vehicle detection and classification. In: 2017 Intelligent Systems and Computer Vision, ISCV 2017 (2017). https://doi.org/10.1109/ISACV.2017.8054969

12. Balid, W., Tafish, H., Refai, H.H.: Intelligent vehicle counting and classification sensor for real-time traffic surveillance. IEEE Trans. Intell. Transp. Syst. **19**(6), 1784–1794 (2018). https://doi.org/10.1109/TITS.2017.2741507

13. Atta, A., Abbas, S., Khan, M.A., Ahmed, G., Farooq, U.: An adaptive approach: smart traffic congestion control system. J. King Saud Univ.-Comput. Inf. Sci. (2018). https://doi.org/10.1016/j.jksuci.2018.10.011

14. Taghvaeeyan, S., Rajamani, R.: Portable roadside sensors for vehicle counting, classification, and speed measurement. IEEE Trans. Intell. Transp. Syst. **15**(1), 73–83 (2014). https://doi.org/10.1109/TITS.2013.2273876

15. Comert, G., Cetin, M.: Analytical evaluation of the error in queue length estimation at traffic signals from probe vehicle data. IEEE Trans. Intell. Transp. Syst. **12**(2), 563–573 (2011). https://doi.org/10.1109/TITS.2011.2113375

16. Mohan Rao, A., Ramachandra Rao, K.: Measuring urban traffic congestion – a review. Int. J. Traffic Transp. Eng. **2**(4), 286–305 (2012). https://doi.org/10.7708/ijtte.2012.2(4).01

17. Whitham, G.B.: On kinematic waves I. Flood movement in long rivers. Proc. R. Soc. London. Ser. A Math. Phys. Sci. **229**(1178), 281–316 (2006). https://doi.org/10.1098/rspa.1955.0088

18. Asmaa, O., Mokhtar, K., Abdelaziz, O.: Road traffic density estimation using microscopic and macroscopic parameters. Image Vis. Comput. **31**(11), 887–894 (2013). https://doi.org/10.1016/j.imavis.2013.09.006

19. Arasan, V.T., Dhivya, G.: Measuring heterogeneous traffic density. World Academy Sci., Eng. Technol. **46**(10), 342–346 (2008)

20. Nsw, T.: Vehicle standards information. **27**(4), 1–16 (2014)

21. Minge, E., et al.: Loop- and Length-Based Vehicle Classification, Federal Highway Administration – Pooled Fund Program [TPF-5(192)], 5(November), 106p. (2012). http://www.dot.state.mn.us/research/TS/2012/2012-33.pdf. http://www.lrrb.org/media/reports/201233.pdf. https://trid.trb.org/view/1298660

22. FHWA: Simplified highway capacity calculation method for the highway performance monitoring system (2017). https://www.lrrb.org/media/reports/201233.pdf

23. Avery, R.P., Wang, Y., Scott Rutherford, G.: Length-based vehicle classification using images from uncalibrated video cameras, pp. 737–742 (2005). https://doi.org/10.1109/itsc.2004.1398994

24. Guerrero-Ibáñez, J., Zeadally, S., Contreras-Castillo, J.: Sensor technologies for intelligent transportation systems. Sensors (Switzerland) **18**(4), 1–24 (2018). https://doi.org/10.3390/s18041212

25. Odat, E., Shamma, J.S., Claudel, C.: Vehicle classification and speed estimation using combined passive infrared/ultrasonic sensors. IEEE Trans. Intell. Transp. Syst. **19**(5), 1593–1606 (2018). https://doi.org/10.1109/TITS.2017.2727224

26. Assy, N., Chan, N.N., Gaaloul, W.: An automated approach for assisting the design of configurable process models. IEEE Trans. Serv. Comput. **8**(6), 874–888 (2015). https://doi.org/10.1109/TSC.2015.2477815

27. Ntalampiras, S.: Moving vehicle classification using wireless acoustic sensor networks. IEEE Trans. Emerg. Top. Comput. Intell. **2**(2), 129–138 (2018). https://doi.org/10.1109/tetci.2017.2783340

28. Yang, B., Lei, Y.: Vehicle detection and classification for low-speed congested traffic with anisotropic magnetoresistive sensor. IEEE Sens. J. **15**(2), 1132–1138 (2014). https://doi.org/10.1109/jsen.2014.2359014

29. Cheung, S., Coleri, S., Dundar, B., Ganesh, S., Tan, C.-W., Varaiya, P.: Traffic measurement and vehicle classification with single magnetic sensor. Transp. Res. Rec.: J. Transp. Res. Board **1917**(January), 173–181 (2005). https://doi.org/10.3141/1917-19

30. Cheung, S., Varaiya, P.: Traffic surveillance by wireless sensor networks : final report. California Path Program Institute of Transportation Studies University of California, Berkeley, pp. 1–161, January 2007
31. DeVito, A.: Four key factors in billboard site selection four key factors in billboard site selection putting your message in a big, outdoor context can grab attention (2016). http://butlertill.com/wp-content/uploads/2016/11/4701-BillboardSelection-eGuide1.pdf
32. Google: Roads API. https://developers.google.com/maps/documentation/roads/intro
33. Xu, C., Wang, Y., Bao, X., Li, F.: Vehicle classification using an imbalanced dataset based on a single magnetic sensor. Sensors (Switzerland) **18**(6), 1–16 (2018)

Identification of Functional Modules in Dynamic Weighted PPI Networks by a Novel Clustering Algorithm

Yimin Mao[✉], Xin Yu, and Haiwan Zhu

School of Information Engineering, Jiangxi University of Science
and Technology, Ganzhou 341000, Jiangxi, China
mymlyc@163.com

Abstract. The Density-Based Spatial Clustering of Application with Noise algorithm (DBSCAN) suffers the limitations of selecting global parameters and having the low accuracy in recognizing overlapping protein complexes. In order to overcome the disadvantage of slow convergence and being vulnerable to trap in local optima in Artificial Bee Colony algorithm (ABC), we designed a method with novel weights and distance calculated which is suitable for network topology and the interaction between proteins. Furthermore, a truncation-championship selection mechanism (TCSM) was proposed to avoid local optimum when onlooker bees search nectar source. Meanwhile, we present the adaptive step strategy (ASS) to improve the clustering speed in ABC algorithm. Finally, in order to overcome the shortcoming which is unable to identify protein complexes in the DBSCAN algorithm, a strategy is proposed to optimize the clustering result. The experimental results on superior precision and recall parameters demonstrate that our method has competitive performance for identifying protein complexes.

Keywords: DBSCAN · ABC · Dynamic weighted PPI network · TCSM · Adaptive step strategy · Protein complexes

1 Introduction

Large-scale experiments are producing huge data sets of protein-protein interactions making it increasingly difficult to visualize and analyze the information contained in these data [1]. Being able to apply computational methods can alleviate a lot of problems in this regard. Therefore, a general trend is to represent the interactions as a network/graph and to apply suitable graph algorithms to extract necessary information. In the post-genomic era, one of the most important issues is to find protein complexes from the protein-protein interaction (PPI) networks. Protein complexes can help us to predict the functions of proteins [2], and they are also useful to understand and explain certain biological processes [3].

In recent years, several algorithms based on graph clustering, dense region finding or clique finding have been developed to discover protein complexes from PPI networks, including Clustering-based Maximal Cliques (CMC) [4] and Core-attachment Based Method (COACH) [5]. Although the above methods were shown to effectively

G. Wang et al. (Eds.): iSCI 2019, CCIS 1122, pp. 461–472, 2019.
https://doi.org/10.1007/978-981-15-1301-5_36

identify protein complexes, their results are sensitive to noisy data, which is still a challenge we have to face [6]. Density-Based Spatial Clustering of Applications with Noise [7] proposed by Ester implemented the density-based strategy with the considerations of noises in network data. It can efficiently discover the clusters with arbitrary size, shape and number in a large dataset. It is noise tolerant and independent of ordering of data objects. However, it needs two input parameters, ε—the radius of neighborhood and *Minpts*-the density threshold, which are domain specific and thus hard to be determined [8]. For density-based methods, it is difficult to decide the input parameters that the algorithm is sensitive to, hence detecting global parameters of DBSCAN for the best clustering result has become an essential and challenging research problem.

Swarm intelligence optimization algorithms are commonly used to solve optimization problems by simulating the collective behavior of social insects. Thus, swarm intelligence has also attracted the interest of many research scientists of related fields. Such as in 2014, Lei et al. proposed F-MCL clustering model [9, 10] which automatically adjusts the parameters of Markov clustering method by using Firefly algorithm. Ding et al. proposed a method named P-DBSCAN [11] which combines DBSCAN and Pigeon-Inspired Optimization Algorithm (PIO) algorithm, for addressing the shortcoming of DBSCAN such as the difficulties of determining the parameters and the unreasonable strategy of using a set of global static parameters for a large varying dense database. The performance of above methods based on swarm intelligence optimization is better than existing clustering algorithms. Artificial Bee Colony (ABC) algorithm [12–14] is one of the swarm-based algorithms. Experiments show that the performance of the ABC is better than or similar to those of other population-based algorithms with the advantage of employing fewer control parameters. However, the results of DBSCAN are sensitive to global parameters, cannot identify protein complexes which are still challenges we have to face.

In order to address the aforementioned challenge, in this paper, a novel algorithm (IABC-DBSCAN) is proposed. The main contributions of this paper are summarized as follows:

(1) The originally weighted strategy and foot distance method (FD) were proposed.
(2) The performance of ABC algorithm is improved through adaptive step size strategy (ASS) and truncation-champion selection mechanism (TCSM).
(3) The parameters of the improved ABC are served as the input values in DBSCAN algorithm.
(4) The tentative strategy (TS) is designed for overcoming the defect in DBSCAN algorithm, which cannot identify protein complexes.

2 Methods

2.1 Artificial Bee Colony Optimization Algorithm

The ABC algorithm is inspired from intelligent foraging behavior of honey bee swarm searching for food [15, 16]. In bee colony algorithm, position of each nectar source corresponds to a possible solution for the optimization problem and the amount of nectar source depicts the fitness value of the associated solution. The total bees in colony can be categorized into three groups: employed, onlooker, and scout. The number of employed and onlooker corresponds to the number of solutions in population.

Employed and onlooker bees search neighborhoods by Eq. (1):

$$new\_x_{ij} = x_{ij} + r_{ij}(x_{ij} - x_{kj}) \tag{1}$$

where $k(k \in \{1, 2, ..., N\})$ and $j(j \in \{1, 2, ..., d\})$ are random numbers and $k \neq i$, r_{ij} is a random number from 0 to 1.

Onlooker bees select nectar source according to the probability P_i, which is calculated as follows:

$$p_i = \frac{fval(i)}{\sum\limits_{j=1}^{N} fval(j)} \tag{2}$$

If a nectar source has not been updated after $limit$ times searching, we should abandon it and make scouts search novel nectar source as follows:

$$new\_pop(i) = (upbond - lbond) \bullet rand + lbond \tag{3}$$

where $upbond$ and $lbond$ are the upper and lower bound of the neighborhood, respectively.

2.2 DBSCAN Algorithm

Density Based Spatial Clustering of Applications with Noise (DBSCAN) is the precursor of density-based clustering method which can detect clusters of arbitrary shape and also handles noise or outliers effectively. DBSCAN algorithm has a quadratic time complexity with dataset size. The algorithm can be extended to large datasets by reducing its time complexity using spatial index structures like R-trees for finding neighbors of a pattern.

2.3 Module Similarity

The similarity of two modules is defined as the interaction degree of nodes, it is calculated as follows:

$$Sim(I_i, I_j) = \frac{\sum\limits_{x \in I_i, y \in I_j} c(x, y)}{max(|I_i|, |I_j|)} \tag{4}$$

where $C(x, y)$ is:

$$c(x, y) = \begin{cases} 1 & \text{if} \quad x = y \\ w(x, y) & \text{if} \quad x \neq y, \text{ and } <x, y> \ \in E \\ 0 & \text{otherwise} \end{cases} \tag{5}$$

2.4   Highest K-Core

The highest k-core of a graph is the one with the maximal k value among all the k-cores and is denoted as $hkc(G)$ [17]. It is the central most densely connected sub-graph. The highest k-core of G can be found in the following way: suppose the lowest degree of nodes in G is d, delete all nodes with degree d, if all remaining nodes have a least degree $d_1(d_1 < 1)$, we will get the d_1-core of G; if some of the remaining nodes have degree lower than or equals to d, continue delete all nodes with the least degree until all remaining nodes have a degree higher than d, or until all nodes have been deleted. In this way we can find all k-cores and the one with the maximal k value is the highest k-core

3   Dynamic Network

3.1   Construction of Dynamic Network

The construction of dynamic networks is a process of continuously adding, filtering out and adjusting protein interactions based on static PPI networks and gene expression profile [17, 18]. The dynamic information of proteins can be obtained from the gene expression profile, which contains the gene expression values of each protein in three cycles. In this paper, the average of gene expression values of the three cycles at a timestamp is used as the final gene expression value at the time point. Subsequently, we construct the dynamic PPI network based on the static PPI network and dynamic characteristic of the proteins.

3.2   Weighted Dynamic Network

Based on the dynamic model described, we obtain the dynamic PPI network which contains 12 static PPI sub-networks at each time point. However, there are a lot of false positives and false negatives in high throughput protein interaction, and some inter-action relationships are unreliable. Therefore, a novel strategy is presented to optimize the network. In this strategy, the edge weight is evaluated by combining the GO annotations with the co-neighbor numbers of protein.

4 IABC-DBSCAN Algorithm

There are several defects in the process of mining protein complexes by DBSCAN. For example, the setting and selection of global parameters are difficult. In addition, the interaction of proteins cannot be measured by distance measure methods and overlapping function modules cannot be identified. In this paper, for the above problems, we propose IABC-DBSCAN algorithm based on dynamic weighted PPI network. We first construct TCSM and ASS method for avoiding premature convergence and improving the global detection capability of ABC algorithm. Then, we use improved ABC algorithm to optimize the parameters of DBSCAN. Finally, we present the hypothetical strategy to overcome the problem of overlapping complexes which cannot be identified in DBSCAN.

4.1 Improved Artificial Bee Colony Algorithm

TCSM. In the ABC algorithm, onlookers merely adopt the roulette selection mechanism (RSM) [19] to search nectar sources, and a major issue of RSM is that the entire solution space cannot be searched effectively, in addition, the RSM is weak to detect the fittest nectar source. In consequence, individuals with higher fitness value are eliminated with randomness, which affects the result of ABC algorithm. Therefore, in this paper, RSM is replaced by the truncation selection mechanism (TSM) [20], whose selection capability is stronger. In TSM, individuals first are in descending order of fitness value, and then, top $t\%$ individuals are selected to produce next generation. The TSM is defined as:

$$P_k = \begin{cases} 1 & k \leq M \times t\% \\ 0 & k > M \times t\% \end{cases} \tag{6}$$

where P_i denotes the probability of next generation that individual i produces, M is population size, and $t\%$ is truncation threshold, which controls the parameters of selecting strength. In order to improve the diversity of population, an adaptive truncation selection mechanism is constructed, which employs different truncation thresholds in different phase. In the preliminary phase of iteration, we set a greater threshold to ensure that the poor nectar source can be searched. While in the later phase, the threshold is set a lower value to avoid the result falling into local optimum. The truncation threshold $t\%$ is defined by the following equation:

$$t = t_{min} + \frac{(t_{max} - t_{min})(cyc - 1)}{Maxiter - 1} \tag{7}$$

where t_{max} and t_{min} are the maximal and minimal truncation threshold, respectively. In addition, cyc is the remaining detection times by employed and onlooker bees and *Maxiter* is the maximal detection times by them. The diversity of population still declines by using TSM. Therefore, we combine champion selection mechanism with TSM for keeping the diversity of population. The specific implementation steps are as follows:

Step 1: Firstly, the individuals are in descending order of fitness value and k individuals are selected randomly from the population for constructing a group. And then select individual i with the optimal fitness value, which is calculated according to the TSM. If the fitness value of i is greater than $M \times t\%$, then onlookers search the neighborhoods of i and produce next generation, else implement Step.1.

Step 2: Step 1 is implemented for m times to produce next population.

ASS Method. The efficiency of finding locally optimal nectar source by the searching method in ABC algorithm is not satisfied. Therefore, inspired by the ASS method in the drosophila optimization algorithm [21], the method of onlookers searching nectar source is dynamically adjusted for improving the global searching capability of onlookers. The updated strategy is as follows:

$$x_{ij} = x_{ij} + step_{ij} r_{ij}(x_{ij} - x_{kj}) \tag{8}$$

$$step_{ij} = h_{min} + (h_{max} - h_{min}) \times \frac{\|f_i - f_{best}\|}{f_{max}} + \sigma \times randn() \tag{9}$$

where $step_{ij}$ is adaptive step size, r_{ij} denotes a random number from 0 to 1, h_{max} and h_{min} are the maximal and minimal step size, respectively. $|f_i - f_{best}|$ is the difference in fitness value between nectar source i and globally optimal nectar source, f_{max} is the maximal fitness value of globally optimal nectar source, σ is the difference between $step_{ij}$ and the expectation of $step_{ij}$. $randn()$ is a normally distributed random number. Onlookers find the locally optimal nectar source based on the globally optimal solution, which will reduce searching times and blindness.

4.2 Improved DBSCAN Algorithm

FD Method. In the PPI network, the Euclidean Distance and Hamming Distance are not suitable to calculate the degree of interaction between nodes, because the interaction between nodes is uncertain. Therefore, in this paper, $1 - W$ is used as the equation of distance measured, furthermore, the ε-neighborhood and core nodes are redefined. The equation of FD is defined as follows:

$$FD(u, v) = 1 - W(u, v) \tag{10}$$

For making the DBSCAN algorithm can be applied to the PPI network, the core node and ε-neighborhood are redefined according to the topological structure of PPI network. Some definitions are described firstly.

Definition 1 (ε-neighborhood). For a point $x \in D$, the ε-neighborhood denotes the points whose distance from x is less than ε and interaction with x.

Definition 2 (core point). For a point $x \in D$, at least M nodes whose distance from x is less than 0.65 and score k is greater than or equal to 2 in the ε-neighborhood of x.

TS. As the function module of protein complexes cannot be identified by the DBSCAN algorithm, we propose the TS strategy to search it by defining fuzzy nodes after clustering.

Definition 3 (fuzzy node). The protein node is in the function module I_i and it interacts with proteins which are in other function modules.

The elaborate of TS strategy is as follows: if protein v is in the function module I_i and it interacts with proteins which are in the function module I_j, then we calculate the fitness value of protein v which is in the function module I_i and I_j, simultaneously. If the fitness value is higher than before, indicating protein v is in I_i and I_j at same time, otherwise end the process.

4.3 Search of Optimal Parameters by IABC

For DBSCAN algorithm, the global parameter is set unreasonable and selected difficultly. Therefore, we propose the IABC algorithm to search the optimal parameter in every dynamic sub-network. In the IABC algorithm, we first set the optimal range of parameter ε, and then initialize k nectar sources, which positions are the value of parameter ε and fitness values are identical with the fitness values in DBSCAN algorithm. Secondly, onlookers select nectar source based on TCSM method and search nectar source in local by ASS method.

4.4 Implementation Steps of IABC-DBSCAN Algorithm

The specific implementation steps are as follows:

Step 1: Produce n dynamic weighted sub-networks $i(i = 1)$ through dynamic weighted model, which is based on expressive data of gene and static PPI data.
Step 2: Set parameters in sub-network i: M and $limit$ represent the number of bees and parameter of solution, respectively. What's more, $maxiter$ is the maximal iteration times. Initialize a group of nectar sources $(v1, v2, \ldots v_k)$, which is the position of nectar sources. Subsequently, the fitness value is calculated based on Eq. (5) and ordered in descending. The bees at corresponding position of nectar source in top $M/2$ of fitness value are used as employed bees, and the other half are onlookers.
Step 3: Go into the loop and set the loop time $iter = 1$.
Step 4: By Eq. (1), employed bees search the neighborhoods and obtain the new solution, then calculate the fitness value of new solution. If $new - fval(i) > fval(i)$, update the position of nectar source.
Step 5: The onlookers select nectar source by TCMS and search the neighborhoods by ASS method. Subsequently, calculate the fitness value of new solution. If $new - fval(i) > fval(i)$, update the position of nectar source.
Step 6: Record the currently optimal solution.
Step 7: If the fitness value of the i-th nectar source is constant, then $s(i) = s(i) + 1$.
Step 8: If $s(i) \geq limit$, scouts search global by Eq. (3) for updating solution, additionally, set $s(i) = 0$, else implement step 10.

Step 9: If iteration time achieves maximum value, output the optimal solution, else $iter = iter + 1$.

Step 10: The position of optimal nectar source is used as the input value of DBSCAN. In addition, the *i-th* dynamic sub-network is processed by the clustering algorithm in DBSCAN. Protein complexes are searched by TS strategy for optimizing the clustering result. Subsequently, put the clustering function module in total function module.

Step 11: If ($ni < n$ is the number of dynamic sub-network), go back to Step.2, else output the function modules of protein at every time point.

5   Experiments and Discussion

5.1   Material

An experimental computer is configured with the windows 7 ultimate operating system, an Intel i5 dual-core processor, 2.5-GHz frequency and 6.0 GB of memory. The algorithm is programmed in python.

We download dynamic gene expression data set GSE3431 about the yeast metabolic cycle from GEO dataset. This dataset includes 6777 genes that cover 95% protein in the static DIP network. By using the methods for construction, we get the DPIN of DIP which contains 12 static PPI sub-networks at 12 time points. Different sub-network has different scales, shown in Table 1.

Table 1. The number of active proteins and interactions in dynamic PPI networks

Time point	1	2	3	4	5	6
The number of active proteins	1638	1742	1659	1444	1368	1211
The number of interaction	7574	8497	8262	6697	6250	5264
Time point	7	8	9	10	11	12
The number of active proteins	1221	1444	1756	1285	1410	1249
The number of interaction	5438	7109	8698	5999	6598	5306

Benchmark complex sets which are respectively derived from CYC2008, which contains 408 standard compounds, the maximum and minimum size of the cluster are 81 and 2, respectively.

5.2   Effect of IABC-DBSCAN Algorithm

To evaluate the clustering effect of IABC-DBSCAN, the algorithm was tested on every sub-networks generated from DIP dataset. We picked the average of running result for ten times. Table 2 shows the comparative results of two algorithms over 12 different time points in terms of *f-measure*. It is clear that the optimal parameter and clustering performance is different in the different sub-networks of IABC-DBSCAN. The results demonstrate that PPI network can be divided to numbers of dynamic sub-network based on genic data, which will improve the clustering performance of every sub-network.

Table 2. Optimal parameters and clustering performance in the 12 dynamic sub-networks

Time point	1	2	3	4	5	6
ε	0.578	0.625	0.697	0.524	0.663	0.586
MinPts	3	3	3	3	3	3
precision	0.6795	0.7735	0.8675	0.6859	0.5644	0.7139
recall	0.4755	0.5887	0.4891	0.7023	0.5091	0.7354
f − measure	0.5595	0.6685	0.6255	0.6940	0.5353	0.7244
Time point	7	8	9	10	11	12
ε	0.575	0.487	0.653	0.559	0.514	0.601
MinPts	3	3	3	3	3	3
precision	0.8012	0.6715	0.7523	0.7267	0.6218	0.7428
recall	0.6745	0.5841	0.6754	0.6021	0.6179	0.6453
f − measure	0.7324	0.6247	0.7117	0.6585	0.6198	0.7428

In order to compare IABC-DBSCAN with traditional clustering method MCODE [3], CMC [4], MCL [10], COACH [5], DBSCAN [7] and OPTICS [8], and clustering algorithm based on swarm intelligence optimization F-MCL [9] and P-DBSCAN [11]. All those algorithms are compared with each other on dynamic PPI dynamic weighted network using the CYC2008 gold standard. The performances of all clustering algorithms are reported in Fig. 1, which contains the precision, recall and *f-measure*. For the value of *f-measure*, P-DBSCAN and F-MCL is 15.34% and 75.195% higher than

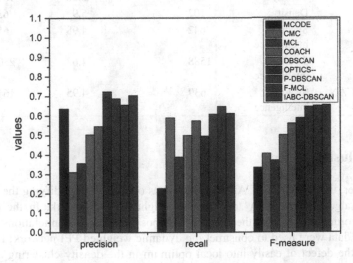

Fig. 1. The performance of clustering algorithms

DBSCAN and MCL. The IABC-DBSCAN algorithm has the highest values in *F-measure*, which is 95.92%, 61.117%, 76.158%, 30.46%, 16.925%, 11.34%, 1.374% and 0.549% higher than MCODE, CMC, MCL, COACH, DBSCAN, OPTICS, P-DBSCAN and F-MCL algorithm, respectively.

To test further the performance of algorithm, Table 3 provides the basic information of the detection results for nine algorithms. For each algorithm, we have listed the number of clustering, the average size of protein complexes and the coverage ratio. From the Table 3, it can be seen that the number of clustering of IABC-DBSCAN is only lower than DBSCAN and P-DBSCAN, but the average size of function module in IABC-DBSCAN is much more close to the average size of gold standard. In addition, the reliability is measured based on the degree of nodes in DBSCAN, and the negative impact of false positives and false negatives on clustering result is not considered in P-DBSCAN. However, IABC-DBSCAN use the dynamic weighted network, TCSM method and ASS method to optimize the clustering process, which makes the interaction between proteins more reliable and the identified function module closer to gold standard. Therefore, it has much better clustering performance than the other algorithms.

Table 3. The clustering performance of algorithms

Algorithm	Type	The number of clustering	Average size	Coverage ratio
Standard clustering	–	408	4.71	1628
MCODE	Density	63	19	1032
CMC	Density	1263	4.39	2048
MCL	Stream	623	6.57	4096
COACH	Core-attachment	903	3.89	2133
DBSCAN	Density	492	6.26	1817
OPTICS	Density	107	5.9	630
P-DBSCAN	Swarm intelligence	642	4.98	1652
F-MCL	Swarm intelligence	1588	4.62	2808
ABC-DBSCAN	Swarm intelligence	639	4.95	1645

6   Conclusion

In this paper, the IABC-DBSCAN algorithm was obtained by modifying the ABC and DBSCAN algorithm to apply to dynamic weighted PPI network. In the clustering process, in order to overcome the effect of false positives, the GO annotations and genic expression data were used to construct the dynamic weighted PPI network; In order to overcome the defect of easily into local optimum in the density clustering algorithm, the clustering algorithm was modified using TCSM method to search the optimal parameter; Furthermore, in order to improve the searching efficiency of optimal parameter, ASS method was used to solve the problem that the efficiency of searching optimal nectar source is not satisfied; Finally, the FD and TS strategy were used to optimize the performance of clustering result in the DBSCAN algorithm. The comparative results show that the IABC-DBSCAN algorithm for mining protein complexes is superior in terms of *precision, recall* and *f-measure*. In the future, we will keep trying to improve the accuracy of protein function module recognition and solve the problem of parameter setting in the DBSCAN algorithm completely.

References

1. Ji, J., Zhang, A., Liu, C., et al.: Survey: functional module detection from protein-protein interaction networks. IEEE Trans. Knowl. Data Eng. **26**(2), 261–277 (2014)
2. Zhao, B., Wang, J., Li, M., et al.: A new method for predicting protein functions from dynamic weighted interactome networks. IEEE Trans. Nanobiosci. **15**(2), 131–139 (2016)
3. Bader, C., Hogue, C.: An automated method for finding molecular complexes in large protein interaction networks. BMC Bioinform. **4**(1), 2 (2003)
4. Liu, G., Wong, L., Chua, H.N.: Complex discovery from weighted PPI networks. Bioinformatics **25**(15), 1891–1897 (2009)
5. Leung, H.C., Xiang, Q., Yiu, S.M., et al.: Predicting protein complexes from PPI data: a core-attachment approach. J. Comput. Biol. **16**(2), 133–144 (2009)
6. Kessler, J., Andrushchenko, V., Kapitan, J., et al.: Insight into vibrational circular dichroism of proteins by density functional modeling. Phys. Chem. Chem. Phys. **20**(7), 4926–4935 (2018)
7. Ester, M., Kriegel, H.P., Xu, X.: A density-based algorithm for discovering clusters a density-based algorithm for discovering clusters in large spatial databases with noise. In: International Conference on Knowledge Discovery and Data Mining, pp. 226–231. AAAI Press (1996)
8. Ankerst, M., Breunig, M.M., Kriegel, H.P.: OPTICS: ordering points to identify the clustering structure. ACM Sigmod Rec. **28**(2), 49–60 (1999)
9. Lei, X., Wang, F., Wu, F.X., et al.: Protein complex identification through Markov clustering with firefly algorithm on dynamic protein–protein interaction networks. Inf. Sci. **329**(6), 303–316 (2016)
10. Lei, X., Ying, C., Wu, F.X., et al.: Clustering PPI data by combining FA and SHC method. BMC Genom. **16**(S3), S3 (2015)
11. Lei, X., Ding, Y., Wu, F.X.: Detecting protein complexes from DPINs by density based clustering with pigeon-inspired optimization algorithm. Sci. China Inf. Sci. **59**(7), 070103 (2016)
12. Singh, K., Sundar, S.: Artifical bee colony algorithm using problem-specific neighborhood strategies for the tree t-spanner problem. Appl. Soft Comput. **62**, 110–118 (2018)
13. Lei, X., Tian, J.: The information flow clustering model and algorithm based on the artificial bee colony mechanism of PPI network. Chin. J. Comput. **35**(1), 134–145 (2012)
14. Tian, J.F., Lei, X.J.: PPI network clustering based or artificial bee colony and breadth first traverse algorithm. PR&AI **25**(3), 481–490 (2012)

15. Wu, S., Lei, X., Tian, J.: An improved bacteria foraging optimization algorithm based on intuition fuzzy set for clustering PPI network. In: The 3rd International Conference on Quantitative Logic and Soft Computing, Xi'an, vol. 5, pp. 362–369, 12–15 May 2012

16. Karaboga, D., Akay, B.: A comparative study of artificial bee colony algorithm. Appl. Math. Comput. **214**(1), 108–132 (2009)

17. Amaya, A.F.F.: Protein Interaction Network. Springer, New York (2013)

18. Hu, S., Xiong, H., Zhao, B.: Construction of dynamic-weighted protein interactome network and its application. Acta Autom. Sinica. **41**(11), 1893–1900 (2015)

19. Letovsky, S., Kasif, S.: Predicting protein function from protein-protein interaction data: a probabilistic approach. Bioinformatics **19**(6), 197–204 (2003)

20. Li, P.: Artificial plant optimization algorithm with different selection strategy. Taiyuan University of Science and Technology (2014)

21. Lei, X., Ding, Y., Fujita, H., et al.: Identification of dynamic protein complexes based on fruit fly optimization algorithm. Knowl. Based Syst. **105**(C), 270–277 (2016)

22. Wang, J., Peng, X., Li, M., et al.: Construction and application of dynamic protein interaction network based on time course gene expression data. Proteomics **13**(2), 301–312 (2013)

23. Bihai, Z., Jianxin, W., Min, L., et al.: Prediction of essential proteins based on overlapping essential modules. IEEE Trans. Nanobiosci. **13**(4), 415–424 (2014)

24. Tu, B.P., Mcknight, S.L.: Logic of the yeast metabolic cycle: temporal compartmentalization of cellular processes. Science **310**(5751), 1152–1158 (2005)

25. Junzhong, J., Zhijun, L., Hongxin, L., et al.: An overview of research on functional module detection for protein-protein interaction networks. Acta Autom. Sinica **40**(4), 577–593 (2014)

26. Bihai, Z., Jianxin, W., Min, L., et al.: Detecting protein complexes based on uncertain graph model. IEEE/ACM Trans. Comput. Biol. Bioinform. **11**(3), 486–497 (2014)

27. Ester, M.: A density-based algorithm for discovering clusters in large spatial databases with noise, pp. 226–231 (1996)

28. Enright, A.J., Dongen, S.V., Ouzounis, C.A.: An efficient algorithm for large-scale detection of protein families. Nucleic Acids Res. **30**(7), 1575–1584 (2002)

Recommending Costume Matching with User Preference and Expert's Suggestion

Yuanyuan Hu and Wenjun Jiang[✉] [iD]

College of Computer Science and Electronic Engineering,
Hunan University, Changsha 410082, China
{huyuanyuan,jiangwenjun}@hnu.edu.cn

Abstract. With the continuous development of e-commerce, clothing products have been greatly expanded in terms of types, styles, colors, etc., and the quantity of clothing products is increasing. How to choose your favorite clothing from a large number of products and carry out the right and appropriate dressing has become a problem that people need to consider in their daily life. Therefore, the emergence of user-oriented recommendation system comes into being, which solves the problem of information overload. However, existing work usually focuses on forming collocation recommendations from image features and related textual descriptions, which are primarily subject to low accuracy and non-personalized issues. In this paper, we consider the clothing mix purchase forecast from the users' point of view. Specifically, we first analyze each user's clothing preference category from the user's historical purchase behaviors, which is used to measure each user's preference style. Next, we select the candicated products that match with his purchased clothing according to the experts' suggestion. Then, we calculate the similarity score between the clothing products in users' preference and experts' suggestion. Finally, we sort clothing items in descending order of the similarity scores, so as to generate the final recommendation list.

Keywords: Consumer behaviors · Personality · Clothing match · Recommendation

1 Introduction

With the rapid development of the Internet and e-commerce [14], a series of popular e-commerce shopping platforms such as Taobao and Jingdong have emerged. At the same time, various commodities are increasingly diversified. Recently, clothing matching recommendation becomes a very important content in the apparel shopping guide. It mainly provides users with personalized dressing and matching suggestions. And it has gradually applied to the big data marketing strategy of major e-commerce platforms. In real online shopping, due to the huge number of clothing and numerous matching methods, many users

© Springer Nature Singapore Pte Ltd. 2019
G. Wang et al. (Eds.): iSCI 2019, CCIS 1122, pp. 473–485, 2019.
https://doi.org/10.1007/978-981-15-1301-5_37

also have problems with clothing matching. In response to the above requirements, we need to propose a clothing matching recommendation algorithm to give a user some personalized dressing instructions. When making predictions about clothing matching recommendations, the sparseness of the data leads to problems of low accuracy and non-personalized (Fig. 1).

Fig. 1. Some examples of outfit composition

At present, most of the existing research work mainly focuses on clothing retrieval [2,13,27], clothing analysis [16,25], and clothing prediction [15,19,28]. Some researchers manually annotate the clothing features and occasion categories in the dataset, and propose a recommendation model based on potential support vector machine (SVM). The model can achieve clothing and its matching recommendation of the occasions by combining the clothing attributes and occasion characteristics [17]. Some researchers have proposed a scalable decomposition model that directly integrates visual perception information into recommendation systems, with implicit feedback to achieve a more accurate personalized ranking method [5,21]. Some researchers have proposed a DeepStyle method. It learns the style features of the project and the perceived preferences of the user, mainly subtracts the potential representation of the corresponding category from the clothing visual feature vector. The vector is generated by CNN to obtain the style characteristics of the project. Then use the BPR framework to integrate style features for personalized recommendations [20]. There are other researchers who have proposed new methods in the field of fashion clothing matching, such as Andreas Veit et al. [23] propose a framework for learning semantic information about visual styles to generate outfits of clothes, and Song et al. [22] propose a method of modeling compatibility between two fashion apparels by a content-based neural network, etc.

These clothing recommendation methods are helpful for improving the accuracy of clothing recommendation. However, since the clothing matching dataset comes from the expert matching dataset rather than the user individual, simply recommending clothes according to the expert matching dataset may make the user's low acceptance of the clothes. At the same time, due to the lack of full consideration of the user's real needs and the lack of exploration of the user's clothing style, it will make clothing matching recommendations less personalized.

Many methods only consider the visual compatibility of the clothing goods on the image, but ignore the text description information of the goods themselves, and do not use the semantic attributes. This may make the clothing matching incompatible. In addition, most clothing matching recommendations are too singular. But in fact, the types, styles and etc. of existing clothing are diverse in various aspects, so that the clothing matching recommendation methods should also be more diverse. In view of the above problems, we try to analyze the user's historical behaviors [3] to predict the clothing matching recommendation. In generally speaking, The goals of this paper are: (1) According to the user's historical purchase information and products' attributes, analyze the user's preferred clothing category. (2) According to the matching suggestions in the data set and the user historical purchase behavior data, predict the clothes which can be matched with the user's purchased costumes.

Our contributions are mainly the following: (1) We analyze the users' historical behaviors in Taobao clothing matching dataset, and find that different users have different purchasing behaviors for clothing goods, which may reflect their preference of clothing styles. A user can purchase different products, and there may be a match between these products. At the same time, a user may have repeated purchase behaviors, which also reflects the user's preference. These analysis of the users' historical behaviors can help us make predictions about the user's purchases. (2) We explore the information characteristics of goods, and analyze these characteristics play a very important role in the recommendation of clothing matching. Each item has its own category and title description, and the analysis results indicate that the item's category and title description may affect the clothing matching methods. (3) We use the TFIDF algorithm to calculate the similarity between the clothing of the user's preference category and the matching clothing. Then we sort the clothing items in descending order by the similarity scores, so that we can recommend clothing products with high scores to users.

2   Related Work

2.1   User Preference

At present, there have been some studies on user personalized preferences. Wan et al. [24] observe that users are more inclined to purchase products that match their preferences. He et al. [7] consider long-term user preferences and short-term dynamics to predict personalized sequential behavior, and he [6] also proposes to build an extensible model based on product images and user feedback for a deeper understanding of user preferences. Xu et al. [26] propose ranking of user preferences based on phrase-level sentiment analysis of multiple categories, and then by combining this technique with Collaborative Filtering (CF) method to boost the performance of recommendation.

At the same time, there have been some studies on users' visual features, including visual feature modeling [8] and visual recommendation [6]. Julian McAuley et al. [18] study the individualized matching of clothing products based on visual features. Similarly, Kang et al. [12] attempt to construct a system of comprehensive image retrieval recommendation and generation based on the Siamese CNN framework for users' preference prediction, while using the GAN generative confrontation network for fashion image generation. Some researchers also explore user's preferences based on user's reviews [9,11]. However, most of these tasks are based on users' visual characteristics for preference prediction, they do not analyze users' historical behaviors, and they also do not consider the issue of clothing collocation.

2.2 Costume Matching Recommendation

In the field of fashion apparel, more and more researchers are paying attention to clothing recommendation, and also put their own opinions on clothing matching from multiple dimensions of clothing. Song et al. [22] analyze the image features and text descriptions of clothing goods, they propose a content-based neural network scheme for compatibility matching modeling of clothing matching, mainly using dual automatic encoder networks to learn potential compatibility space. Then, the Bayesian personalized rankings are used to jointly model the coherence between visual and contextual modalities and the implicit preferences between two clothing items. Similarly, Han et al. [4] suggest jointly training Bi-LSTM model and visual semantic embeddings for fashion compatibility learning. Chao et al. [1] propose a system of fashion recommendation, mainly using intelligent visual recognition technology for real-time clothing recommendation. But most of these methods are only recommended for clothing or its collocation, and did not take into account the users' personalized preferences. This may result in the user's low acceptance of the recommended clothing.

In conclusion, our work focuses on combining the user's personalized preferences with the clothing matching recommendations. By analyzing the different users' preference categories for clothing products, we can find the products that are consistent with the user's personalized style to achieve the purpose of recommending clothes which suits the user's style.

3   Problem Definition

In this section, we need to formulate the issues we solve and define some initial concepts. Our goal is to recommend the matched clothing of users' preference, based on users' historical purchase records and experts' suggestions. Next we give the details of the problem.

First, we describe the preliminary concepts that we use in the paper. We define a set of users as $U = \{u_1, u_2, ..., u_n\}$, which refers to the people have historical purchased records. And a set of categories can be regarded as $C = \{c_1, c_2, ..., c_n\}$, which represents the products' categories. We can also define a user as u_i. Then we define a set of clothing items as $D = \{d_1, d_2, ..., d_n\}$, which refers to the clothing that purchased by the user u_i. Next we define a set of clothing as $M = \{m_1, m_2, ..., m_n\}$, refers to the clothing products that can be matched with u_i' purchased clothing by experts' suggestions.

Definition(Preferred category): For each targeted user u_i, he has his own category preference. We need to denote a category c_i of clothing that the user purchases the most. A set of clothing items $T_i = \{t_1, t_2, ..., t_n\}$, that characterize the user's most purchased clothing.

Definition(Matched clothing): According to the experts' suggestions, we need to define the clothing $M_i = \{m_1, m_2, ..., m_n\}$, that matched with the clothing $t_i, t_i \in T_i$.

Definition(Candidate clothing): A set of clothing $P_i = \{p_1, p_2, ..., p_n\}$, denoted as the clothing that belong to the user's preferred category c_i.

Definition(Clothing similarity): C_{sim} represents the similarity between p_i and $m_i, p_i \in P_i, m_i \in M_i$. Preferentially recommend k clothing products with high similarity scores to the targeted user.

4   Data Analysis

In this section, we mainly analyze the different purchase behaviors of users and their purchase intentions. From these analyses, we can study the impact of the user's preferred clothing categories on their purchase intents, and the results can help improve the accuracy of the user's personalized clothing matching recommendation.

4.1   Raw Data

In this paper, the data set[1] mainly includes three parts: the basic product information data, the users' historical behaviors data and the experts' matching data. The first part is the basic information of the product, mainly including the item_id, the category_id of the product, and the terms of the product title segmentation. The second part is the users' history behavior records, there are mainly user_id, item_id and the purchase date. The time span of the dataset is from 2014 to 2015. The third part is the recommendations of the matching suggestions given by the experts, mainly about the two item_ids of products that can be matched. The statistics of this dataset are shown in Table 1. In Table 2, some records of items are shown.

4.2   Analysis of the User Behavior

We analyze users' history purchase records and perform statistics on each clothing category. The results are shown in Fig. 2. In Fig. 2, we can find that in the users' history purchase records, there are 280 categories of clothing products. In

---

[1] https://tianchi.aliyun.com/competition/entrance/231575/information/.

Table 1. Statistics of the dataset

Item	Statistics
Users	1,103,702
Clothes	499,983
Category	280
Fashion match sets	204,319
Purchased time	2014–2015

Table 2. Some records of items

item_id	cat_id	The results of products' title segmentation
109	461	122071, 35420, 123950, 27207, 116593, 24893, 31897, 190554, 196564, 120213, 200685, 163272
414	368	8640, 20864, 20819, 48909, 53517, 116593, 148988, 127004, 5026, 195998, 204385, 20819, 154365
1019	111	123950, 58561, 116593, 146780, 172413, 7275, 104575, 56917, 93927, 22837, 176333, 136242, 177816, 30097
16084	48	191108, 96020, 122020, 87617, 191824, 131272, 212581, 147893, 61580
21139	516	212881, 138048, 187719, 25144, 102256, 127692, 212881, 197924, 98773, 106068, 123294

these categories, the cat_id of the most popular clothing which are bought by users is 368, the cat_id of the second number of clothing which are bought is 52, and the cat_id of the third ranked is 461. It indicates that these three categories of clothing are the most popular in users, so most people may have higher acceptance of these categories than other categories. If the user does not specifically prefer a certain clothing category, then we can recommend these categories of clothing to users.

We also analyze the purchase quantity of each user based on the users' history purchase records. The result is shown in Fig. 3. In Fig. 3, we can see that the number of clothing items which are purchased by each user is different. The number of users who purchase the most clothing items has purchased 4,807 pieces, but the number of clothing which are purchased by most users is less than 500. This is in line with the purchase behaviors of most users. In the Fig. 3, the x-axis is the user_id, and the y-axis is the statistical clothing purchase quantity of each user.

We select four types of users to analyze their historical purchase information, mainly to illustrate that different users have different purchase behaviors and

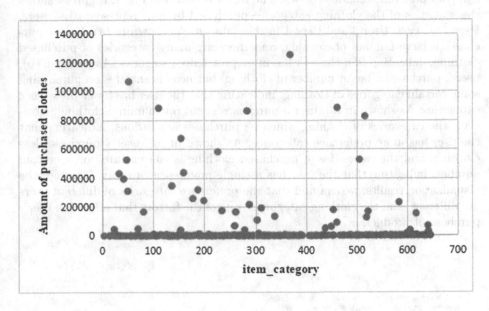

Fig. 2. The total number of purchases for each clothing category.

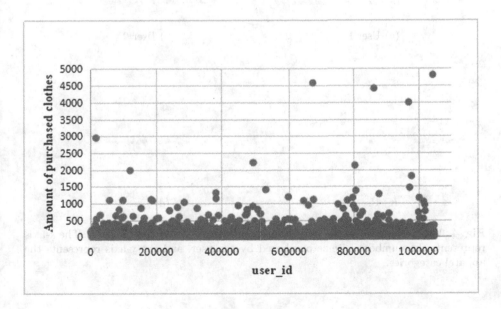

Fig. 3. The total number of clothing purchased by each user.

category preference characteristics. The result is shown in Fig. 4. Figures 4 shows
the statistics of the clothing categories purchased by four representative users,
User 1, User 2, User 3 and User 4 in the data set. As shown in (a), User 1 purchases a large number of clothing, and there are many categories of purchased
clothing, indicating that the user has more preference categories; As shown in (b),
user 2 purchases a larger number of clothing, but he concentrates on purchasing
some certain categories of clothing, indicating that the user has fewer preference
categories; As shown in (c), user 3 purchases about one hundred clothing. However, the categories of clothing which he purchases are various, indicating that
the user has more preference categories; As shown in (d), user 4 purchases less
clothing, and the categories of purchased clothing is concentrated on a certain
number, indicating that the user has a single preference category. Through the
visualization results, we can find that the preference categories of different users
are different, and the clothing category is one of the factors that affect the user's
purchase of products.

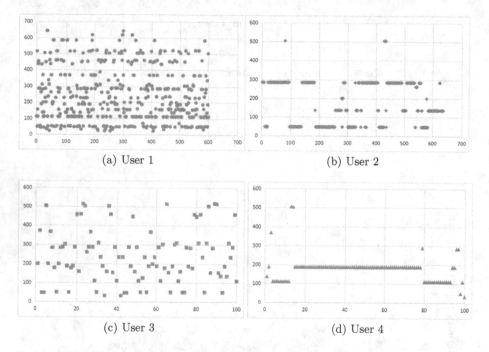

(a) User 1   (b) User 2

(c) User 3   (d) User 4

Fig. 4. The clothing categories and quantity purchases of four specific users. The x-axis
represents the number of items purchased by the user, and the y-axis represents the
apparel categories.

5 Recommendation with User Preference and Experts' Suggestion

In this section, we need to give the details of the method that used in this paper. There are two main steps. The first is to analyze the clothing categories which are preferred by the users, and the second is to calculate the similarity by the TFIDF algorithm. Figure 5 shows the overview of our solution.

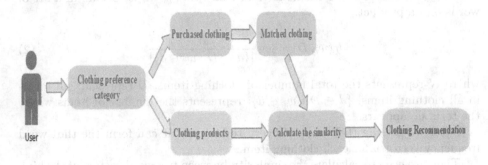

Fig. 5. Overview of the method

5.1 User Preference

We try to find the preferred category c_t of a targeted user u_t. From the user's historical purchased records, we need to calculate the total number of each clothing category. Then select the largest number of category c_t as u_t's preferred category. At the same time, filter the clothing t_t that belong to the category c_t from u_t's purchased clothes.

5.2 Experts' Suggestion

In the provided experts' collocation data set, there are many clothing matching suggestions. What we need to do is that find the matched clothing with the product t_t. We regard these clothing as a product set M_t.

5.3 Calculate the Similarity

In the all clothes, we need to select the clothing items $P_t = \{p_1, p_2, ..., p_n\}$ of the user u_t's preferred category c_t as the candidate products which may be recommended to u_t. Then we demand to obtain the similarity between p_i and $m_i, p_i \in P_t, m_i \in M_t$.

For each product d, it has a set of words $W_t = \{w_1, w_2, ..., w_n\}$, which are the term results after the product title segmentation. In order to vectorize the title description of the item, we need to use TFIDF method to calculate the tfidf weight matrix of each clothing item. First, we calculate the tfidf value of every title segmentation in product d_t.

$$tfidf(w_i) = tf(w_i, d) \times idf(w_i, D) \tag{1}$$

where $tf(w_i, d)$ represents the number of times that term w_i occurs in a set of words d of a product.

$$idf(w_i, D) = \log \frac{N}{|\{d \in D : w_i \in d\}|} \tag{2}$$

where N represents the total number of clothing items. D represents all terms in all clothing items. $\{d \in D : w_i \in d\}$: represents the number of items where the term w_i appears.

After we get the tfidf value of every term in d_t, it can form the tfidf word frequency vector v for each clothing item.

Then, we need to calculate the similarity between two word vectors of clothing items p_i, m_i. After we obtain the tfidf weight matrix vi of these two products, we calculate the cosine similarity between two clothing items. The formula is as follows:

$$similarity(v_1, v_2) = \frac{\sum_{i=1}^{n}(v_{1i} \times v_{2i})}{\sqrt{\sum_{i=1}^{n}(v_{1i})^2} \times \sqrt{\sum_{i=1}^{n}(v_{2i})^2}} \tag{3}$$

5.4   Case Study

In this experiment, we analyze the user's historical purchase behaviors, get the clothing category that the user prefers, and obtain the clothing items that matches with the clothing of preferred category which was purchased by the user from the expert matching data set. Then we filter out the clothing of user's preferred category and regard them as the candidate clothing product set. We need to calculate the similarity between the goods in the candidate clothing product set and the matched clothing goods. In the search for a similar product, we need to find the top 10 items which have a higher similarity with the target clothing product, and make a top10 recommendation. The results are shown in Table 3. In Table 3, we enumerate the particular user and analyze his clothing category preferences, finding out the clothing product t_i that the user purchased which belongs to his preferred category. From the expert matching data set, we select the clothing products m_i which can be matched with the product t_i, then calculate the similarity scores between the product m_i and the clothing products p_i of the user's preferred category, and sort by descending order.

Table 3. Similarity scores of a user

user_id	cat_id	purchase_id	cloth_match_id	item_id	score
90780	188	1943005	2674666	3227847	0.1388
				1722583	0.1276
				410023	0.1252
				498010	0.1102
				2306435	0.1079
				1955656	0.1071
				777675	0.0982
				693828	0.0969
				1456253	0.0918
				2725828	0.0842
1695542	368	3089061	310333	1259105	0.1895
				304351	0.1615
				99171	0.1570
				1850942	0.1515
				1444075	0.1375
				1308804	0.1372
				423181	0.1274
				883073	0.1269
				1226785	0.1255
				530873	0.1247
...	...	...	...	...	...

6   Conclusion

In this paper, we study the users' historical purchase behaviors, and conduct an in-depth analysis of the users' historical purchase of clothing data set. Considering that each user's purchase behavior is different and they all have their own unique clothing category preferences, the styles of clothing that each user prefers are also different. In addition, we analyze the attributes of each apparel item and generate several useful discoveries for exploring clothing categories. We explore clothing and its collocation recommendations based on each user's preferred clothing category. This method should consider the similarity of clothing when making clothing matching recommendation. The clothing that has a higher similarity score can be recommended to the user. It can help the user make a purchase decision for personalized clothing wear. Our method has a certain effect. In the future work, we need to find as many matching schemes as possible between different clothing products. We cannot only recommend matching with the schemes based on the experts' dataset, but also explore more matching schemes. At the same time, we can also analyze the users' purchase behaviors that evolve over time [10], and find the users' changes in clothing category preferences to achieve better recommendation.

Acknowledgements. This research was supported by NSFC grant 61632009 and Outstanding Young Talents Training Program in Hunan University 531118040173.

References

1. Chao, X., Huiskes, M.J., Gritti, T., Ciuhu, C.: A framework for robust feature selection for real-time fashion style recommendation. In: International Workshop on Interactive Multimedia for Consumer Electronics (2009)
2. Di, W., Wah, C., Bhardwaj, A., Piramuthu, R., Sundaresan, N.: Style finder: fine-grained clothing style detection and retrieval. In: IEEE Conference on Computer Vision & Pattern Recognition Workshops (2013)
3. Dong, Y., Jiang, W.: Brand purchase prediction based on time-evolving user behaviors in e-commerce. Concurrency Comput.: Pract. Experience **31**(1) (2019). https://doi.org/10.1002/cpe.4882
4. Han, X., Wu, Z., Jiang, Y.G., Davis, L.S.: Learning fashion compatibility with bidirectional LSTMs (2017)
5. He, R., Mcauley, J.: VBPR: visual bayesian personalized ranking from implicit feedback (2015)
6. He, R., Mcauley, J.: Ups and downs: modeling the visual evolution of fashion trends with one-class collaborative filtering (2016)
7. He, R., Mcauley, J.: Fusing similarity models with markov chains for sparse sequential recommendation. In: IEEE International Conference on Data Mining (2017)
8. Hu, Y., Yi, X., S. Davis, L.: Collaborative fashion recommendation: a functional tensor factorization approach, pp. 129–138, October 2015. https://doi.org/10.1145/2733373.2806239
9. Jiang, W., Jie, W., Wang, G., Zheng, H.: Forming opinions via trusted friends: Time-evolving rating prediction using fluid dynamics. IEEE Trans. Comput. **65**(4), 1211–1224 (2016)
10. Jiang, W., Jie, W., Wang, G., Zheng, H.: Fluidrating: A time-evolving rating scheme in trust-based recommendation systems using fluid dynamics. In: Infocom. IEEE (2014)
11. Jiang, W., Wu, J.: Active opinion-formation in online social networks, pp. 1–9, May 2017. https://doi.org/10.1109/INFOCOM.2017.8057103
12. Kang, W.C., Fang, C., Wang, Z., Mcauley, J.: Visually-aware fashion recommendation and design with generative image models (2017)
13. Kiapour, M.H., Han, X., Lazebnik, S., Berg, A.C., Berg, T.L.: Where to buy it: matching street clothing photos in online shops. In: IEEE International Conference on Computer Vision (2015)
14. Li, M., Jiang, W., Li, K.: Recommendation systems in real applications: algorithm and parallel architecture. In: Wang, G., Ray, I., Alcaraz Calero, J.M., Thampi, S.M. (eds.) SpaCCS 2016. LNCS, vol. 10066, pp. 45–58. Springer, Cham (2016). https://doi.org/10.1007/978-3-319-49148-6_5
15. Li, Y., Cao, L.L., Jiang, Z., Luo, J.: Mining fashion outfit composition using an end-to-end deep learning approach on set data. IEEE Trans. Multimed. **PP**(99), 1 (2016)

16. Liang, X., Liang, L., Wei, Y., Ping, L., Huang, J., Yan, S.: Clothes co-parsing via joint image segmentation and labeling with application to clothing retrieval. IEEE Trans. Multimed. **18**(6), 1175–1186 (2016)

17. Liu, S., Nguyen, T.V., Feng, J., Wang, M., Yan, S.: Hi, magic closet, tell me what to wear! In: ACM International Conference on Multimedia (2012)

18. Mcauley, J., Targett, C., Shi, Q., Hengel, A.V.D.: Image-based recommendations on styles and substitutes. In: International ACM SIGIR Conference on Research & Development in Information Retrieval (2015)

19. O'Cass, A.: An assessment of consumers product, purchase decision, advertising and consumption involvement in fashion clothing. J. Econ. Psychol. **21**(5), 545–576 (2000)

20. Qiang, L., Shu, W., Liang, W.: Deepstyle: learning user preferences for visual recommendation. In: International ACM SIGIR Conference (2017)

21. Rendle, S., Freudenthaler, C., Gantner, Z., Schmidt-Thieme, L.: BPR: bayesian personalized ranking from implicit feedback. In: Conference on Uncertainty in Artificial Intelligence (2009)

22. Song, X., Feng, F., Liu, J., Li, Z., Nie, L., Ma, J.: Neurostylist: neural compatibility modeling for clothing matching, pp. 753–761, October 2017. https://doi.org/10.1145/3123266.3123314

23. Veit, A., Kovacs, B., Bell, S., Mcauley, J., Bala, K., Belongie, S.: Learning visual clothing style with heterogeneous dyadic co-occurrences. In: IEEE International Conference on Computer Vision (2015)

24. Wan, M., Wang, D., Liu, J., Bennett, P., McAuley, J.: Representing and recommending shopping baskets with complementarity, compatibility and loyalty, pp. 1133–1142, October 2018. https://doi.org/10.1145/3269206.3271786

25. Wei, Y., Ping, L., Liang, L.: Clothing co-parsing by joint image segmentation and labeling (2015)

26. Xu, C., Zheng, Q., Zhang, Y., Tao, X.: Learning to rank features for recommendation over multiple categories (2016)

27. Yan, S.: Street-to-shop: cross-scenario clothing retrieval via parts alignment and auxiliary set. In: Computer Vision & Pattern Recognition (2012)

28. Young Kim, E., Kim, Y.K.: Predicting online purchase intentions for clothing products. Eur. J. Mark. **38**, 883–897 (2004). https://doi.org/10.1108/03090560410539302

Software Tamper Resistance Based on White-Box SMS4 Implementation

Tingting Lin[1,3(✉)], Yixin Zhong[1], Xuejia Lai[1,2], and Weidong Qiu[3]

[1] School of Electrical and Information Engineering,
Shanghai Jiao Tong University, Shanghai 200240, China
lintingting00@163.com
[2] Westone Cryptologic Research Center, State Key Laboratory of Cryptology,
P. O. Box 5159, Beijing 100878, China
[3] School of Cyber Security, Shanghai Jiao Tong University,
Shanghai 200240, China

Abstract. In software protection, we've always faced the problem that an attacker is assumed to have full control over the target software and its execution. This is similar to the attack model in white-box cryptography, which aims to provide robust and secure implementations of cryptographic schemes against white-box attacks. In this paper, we propose our tamper-resistance technique, Siren, that uses white-box implementation to make software tamper resistant. We interpret the binary of software code as lookup table and incorporate these tables into the underlying white-box SMS4 implementation. In addition, we prove that Siren has good performance in security, and show the lower space complexity and higher efficiency. Finally, we present CBC-Siren, a white-box encryption scheme using CBC mode, which can provide protection to code with flexible size.

Keywords: White-box cryptograpyh · Software · Tamper resistance · SMS4 · CBC

1 Introduction

Compare to hardware, software is more flexible and lower-cost. However, with the need of software grows, the security of software becomes a big issue. For example, a host is potentially attacked by a malicious downloaded applet or a virus-infested installed application. How to develope techniques to protect software is increasingly important. Three conventional countermeasures for software protection are obfuscation [1,2], watermarking [3–5] and tamper resistance [6,7]. Obfuscation is used to protect a software program against reverse engineering by modifying a software program so that it is no longer useful to a hacker but remains fully functional. Watermarking allows people to prove ownership where a structure (the watermark) is embedded into a program such that the mathematical property of the structure can be used to argue its presence in the program

© Springer Nature Singapore Pte Ltd. 2019
G. Wang et al. (Eds.): iSCI 2019, CCIS 1122, pp. 486–495, 2019.
https://doi.org/10.1007/978-981-15-1301-5_38

is a result of deliberate actions. Tamper resistance can protect a software by detecting any modification and cause the software to fail when tampering is evident. The most common way to use these countermeasures is to combine them together; For example, obfuscation and watermarking. In this paper we present a solution with no need to combine with other methods to make software tamper resistant.

Meanwhile, software protection is facing a more severe challenge, white-box attack environment. Instead of traditional "black-box attack" environment, in which attackers can only access to the input and output values, a white-box attacker could have full control over internal details during the execution. It is urgent to deal with white-box attack environment because the communication end-points are no longer trusted and an adversary is easy to launch attack from inside of a device. For example, the adversary is typically a malicious program that has installed by accident on the device. Hence the traditional cryptographic schemes which have been used in conventional software protection can no longer ensure their functionalities such as integrity, authentication etc.

White-box cryptography is designed to providing robust and secure implementations of cryptographic schemes even against white-box attacks and constructing functional cryptographic schemes with encryption/decryption and authentication abilities in white-box environment. In 2002, Chow et al. first put forward the conception of white-box environment and designed white-box DES and AES implementation [8,9], both implemented by look-up tables. The main method is to embed a fixed key into the non-linear part (e.g. S-box) of a block cipher, and then break the cipher into several parts, which are wraped by randomly chosen encodings and come out with lookup tables. The whole cipher was implemented by a serial of lookup tables. The table-based method was enlightening and taken by many subsequent white-box implementations, such as Xiao-Lai white-box SMS4 implementation [10], white-box AES with dual ciphers [11], ASASA-based white-box implementation [12], lightweight white-box symmetric encryption algorithm [13], and masked white-Box AES implementation [14].

In other respect, tamper resistance is an important issue in software protection, and applied to prevent attackers from maliciously manipulation on software to fulfill illegal functionality. Countermeasures such as code obfuscation and cryptographic hashing are common methods against the problem, incurred execution-time penalty though. In 2007, Michiels et al. [15] proposed a new technique, aka. Medusa, which use white-box AES implementation to make software tamper resistant. The basic idea is to embed the binary of a software into lookup tables of a white-box implementation, and verify the integrity of the software by checking if the white-box implementation is operated correctly.

Since Xiao-Lai's white-box SMS4 implementation is efficient and easy to be constructed with multiple modes of operation, we apply it to protect the integrity of software in this paper. In detail, we propose our tamper-resistance technique, aka. Siren, with underlying white-box SMS4 implementation and give proof on its security. Also, by using CBC mode or increase the rounds of the SMS4 implementation, we can provide protection to code with flexible size. In short, Siren makes use of a different underlying model and proposed a new method (CBC mode/increase rounds) to change the size of the protected code. Comparing with Medusa, Siren has less lookup tables and good performance in the security and efficiency because of the underlying white-box SMS4 implementation. Meanwhile, Siren can remedy Medusas limitations and enlarge application range because of the flexibility of the code size.

This paper is organized as follows. First, we introduce in Sect. 2 the SMS4 and its white-box implementation. In Sect. 3 we introduce our tamper resistance technique "Siren" as well as the security analysis. We make a conclusion in Sect. 4.

2   SMS4 and White-Box Implementation

2.1   SMS4

The SMS4 algorithm is a block cipher with 128-bit key and 128-bit input block. Both encryption and decryption take 32 rounds of nonlinear substitutions with same structure but different round key schedule.

Let the input plaintext be $X = (X_0, X_1, X_2, X_3)$, where $X_i \in GF(2^{32})$ and the round key be $rk_i \in GF(2^{32}, i = 0, 1, 2, \ldots, 31)$. Figure 1 depicts round function of SMS4. There are 3 steps:

1. Input plaintext X
2. Calculate $X_{i+4} = X_i \oplus T(X_{i+1} \oplus X_{i+2} \oplus X_{i+3} \oplus rk_i)$ where $i = 0, 1, 2, \ldots, 31$
3. Output ciphertext $Y = (Y_0, Y_1, Y_2, Y_3) = (X_{35}, X_{34}, X_{33}, X_{32})$

In detail,

- T is a reversible transformation from $GF(2^{32})$ to $GF(2^{32})$, consists of a linear transformation L and a non-linear transformation τ

$$T(\cdot) = L(\tau(\cdot))$$

- L is a linear transformation,

$$L(B) = B \oplus (B \ll 2) \oplus (B \ll 10) \oplus (B \ll 18) \oplus (B \ll 24)$$

where $\ll i$ means circular shift of a 32-bit word with i bits shifted left
- τ is a non-linear transformation using 4 8×8 S-boxes in parallel,

$$\tau(A) = (Sbox(a_0), Sbox(a_1), Sbox(a_2), Sbox(a_3))$$

where $A = (a_0, a_1, a_2, a_3) \in (GF(2^8)^4)$

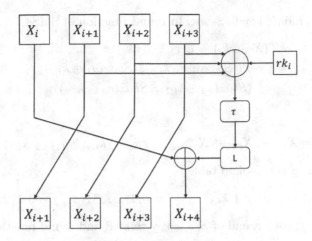

Fig. 1. One round of SMS4

2.2 Xiao-Lai's White-Box SMS4

We apply Xiao-Lai's white-box SMS4 implementation [10] as the underlying white-box scheme in Siren. The basic idea of Xiao-Lai's implementation is to hide key in S-box and use lookup table with input and output obfuscation in round function. Each round needs 4 lookup table operation and 5 affine transformations. The space consuming is 150KB. There are mainly 3 steps shown as Fig. 2.

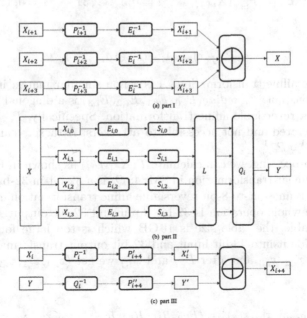

Fig. 2. A basic round implementation of white-box SMS4

First of all, hiding key in S-box. In round function of SMS4,

$$T(X \oplus rk_i) = L(\tau(X \oplus rk_i))$$
$$= L((Sbox(a_0 \oplus k_{i,0}), (Sbox(a_1 \oplus k_{i,1}),$$
$$(Sbox(a_2 \oplus k_{i,2}), (Sbox(a_3 \oplus k_{i,3})))$$

Where

$$X = X_{i+1} \oplus X_{i+2} \oplus X_{i+3}, \qquad rk_i = (k_{i,0}, k_{i,1}, k_{i,2}, k_{i,3})$$

Thus, we define a new lookup table $S_{i,j}$,

$$S_{i,j}(x) = Sbox(x \oplus k_{i,j}), \qquad i = 0, 1, \dots, 31 \qquad j = 0, 1, 2, 3$$

Correspondingly, each round of $S_{i,j}$ is key related and round function becomes

$$L((S_{i,0}(a_0 \oplus k_{i,0}), (S_{i,1}(a_1 \oplus k_{i,1}), (S_{i,2}(a_2 \oplus k_{i,2}), (S_{i,3}(a_3 \oplus k_{i,3}))) \tag{1}$$

Since S-box of SMS4 is public to everybody, attackers can retrieve key information from $S_{i,j}$ easily. We need to apply obfuscation encoding for $S_{i,j}$ to protect key.

The second step is to calculate $T(X_{i+1} \oplus X_{i+2} \oplus X_{i+3})$, as shown in Fig. 2 part I. Since all intermediate results contain output encoding, we have to eliminate such encoding before next computation via an input encoding. The pre-processing of $X_{i+1}X_{i+2}X_{i+3}$ should be

$$X'_{i+j} = E_i^{-1} \circ P_{i+j}^{-1}(X_{i+j}), \qquad i = 0, 1, \dots, 31 \qquad j = 0, 1, 2, 3$$

where

$$P_{i+j}(x) = A_{i+j}(x) \oplus a_{i+j}$$

is a reversiable affine transformation. A is a non-singular matrix in $GF(2)$ and a is a 32-bit constant. $E_i = diag(E_{i,0}, E_{i,1}, E_{i,2}, E_{i,3})$ is a diagonal block matrix where $E_{i,j}$ is a reversible affine transformation. Specifically, P_{i+j} and E_i are randomly generated and not accessible to attackers. Attackers can only access to $M_{i+j}^i = E_i^{-1} \circ P_{i+j}^{-1}$.

After pre-processing, we can calculate $T(X \oplus rk_i)$ as shown in Fig. 2 part II. Here L is the linear transformation in SMS4; Q_i is a 32-bit-in-32-bit-out output encoding; $E_{i,j}$ is an 8-bit-to-8-bit reversible affine transformation using as input encoding. The whole operation is 32-bit input and 32-bit output. If we take it as a lookup table, the table size is $16\,\mathrm{GB}$ which is too large for calculation. Hence, we divide it into 48-bit input and 32-bit output transformation. Denote $X = x_{i,0}, x_{i,1}, x_{i,2}, x_{i,3}$ and after $E_{i,j}$ and $S_{i,j}$ we get $(z_{i,0}, z_{i,1}, z_{i,2}, z_{i,3})$. Then $Q_i \cdot L$ can be

$$(Q_i \cdot L) \cdot (z_{i,0}, z_{i,1}, z_{i,2}, z_{i,3})^T = (R_{i,0}, R_{i,1}, R_{i,2}, R_{i,3}) \cdot (z_{i,0}, z_{i,1}, z_{i,2}, z_{i,3})^T \oplus r_i$$
$$= (R_{i,0} \cdot z_{i,0}) \oplus (R_{i,1} \cdot z_{i,1}) \oplus (R_{i,2} \cdot z_{i,2}) \oplus (R_{i,3} \cdot z_{i,3}) = v_{i,0} \oplus v_{i,1} \oplus v_{i,2} \oplus v_{i,3}$$

where $R_{i,j}$ is a 32×8 matrix and r_i is a 32×1 constant vector. So far we've obtained 4 $x_{i,j} \rightarrow z_{i,j}$ lookup table with 8-bit input and 32-bit output. We define such lookup tables as $T_{i,j}, i = 0, 1, 2, \ldots, 31, j = 0, 1, 2, 3$.

The third step is to calculate X_{i+4}. $X_{i+4} = X_i \oplus T(X_{i+1} \oplus X_{i+2} \oplus X_{i+3})$, where $T(X_{i+1} \oplus X_{i+2} \oplus X_{i+3})$ is already done by the second step. As shown in Fig. 2 part III, to eliminate obfuscation encoding is also necessary. Here

$$P'_{i+4}(x) = P_{i+4}(x) \oplus a'_{i+4}, \qquad P''_{i+4}(x) = P_{i+4}(x) \oplus a''_{i+4}$$

Each round of white-box SMS4 should go through the iteration of all three steps. The final output $(X_{35}, X_{34}, X_{33}, X_{32})$ is the ciphertext. Each round needs 4 lookup tables with 8-bit input and 32-bit output and 5 32-bit-to-32-bit affine transformation. So the space consuming is $148.625\,\mathrm{KB}$. In total, there're 128 lookup table operations and 160 affine transformations.

3 Siren

3.1 Basic Implementation of Siren

Since Xiao-Lai's white-box SMS4 implementation is efficient and easy to be constructed with multiple modes of operation, we apply it as the underlying algorithm of our tamper-resistant technique. The basic idea of Siren is to interpret the binary of software code as lookup table and incorporate these tables into the second part of white-box SMS4 implementation. The program will be tamper resistant because any change in the program code will imply unintentional changes in the key. In other word, the tamper resistance of a software is equivalent to the well-functionality of white-box implementation.

Let $C_{i,j}$ be a lookup table that defines a 1024-byte code fragment $\widehat{C}_{i,j}$, which includes 256 rows and each rows contains 4 bytes. Thus, same to $T_{i,j}$, $C_{i,j}$ is a lookup table with 8-bit input and 32-bit output. Next, we define lookup table

$$W_{i,j}(x) = T_{i,j}(x) \oplus C_{i,j}(x), \qquad i = 0, 1, 2, \ldots, 31 \qquad j = 0, 1, 2, 3$$

Then loopup table $T_{i,j}$ can be the XOR value of $W_{i,j}(\cdot)$ and $C_{i,j}(\cdot)$.

In white-box implementation, each intermediate value is obfuscated with encodings. Samely, we need to apply obfuscation to $W_{i,j}(\cdot)$ and $C_{i,j}(\cdot)$. Specifically, obfuscation to $W_{i,j}(\cdot)$ and $C_{i,j}(\cdot)$ should be different otherwise the obfuscation is of no effect.

- The input and output encoding of $W_{i,j}$ is the same as $S_{i,j}$ and affine transformation L in Fig. 2 part II, which is

$$W_{i,j} \Rightarrow Q_i \circ W_{i,j} \circ E_{i,j}$$

- The input and output encoding of $C_{i,j}$ is different. Without affine transformation Q_i, we combine affine transformation in Fig. 2 part II and part III together, which is

$$C_{i,j} \Rightarrow E_{i,j} \circ C_{i,j} \circ P''_{i+4}$$

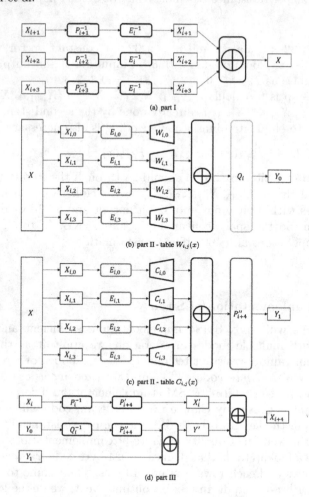

Fig. 3. The implementation of Siren

The whole implementation of Siren is shown as Fig. 3. The first part is the calculation of $X = X_{i+1} \oplus X_{i+2} \oplus X_{i+3}$. In the second part, input X goes through the encoded version of $W_{i,j}(\cdot)$ and $C_{i,j}(\cdot)$ separately and the result Y_0 and Y_1 is the input of the third part. The third part leads to the final result of round function X_{i+4}.

3.2   Feasibility of Siren

Compare to Xiao-Lai's white-box implementation, each round of Siren has four more lookup tables, which is 128 lookup tables in total. And code size that each encryption or decryption of Siren can protect is the same as the size of 128 lookup tables, 128 KB. Therefore, in Siren, all additional lookup tables can be used to protect code while in Medusa, only half additional lookup tables can be used to protect code.

Moreover, we proposed two options to protect code of arbitrary size.

- CBC mode of white-box SMS4 implementation, shown as Fig. 4. In this scheme, we first apply the block cipher mode of operation onto the white-box SMS4 implementation, i.e. the block cipher is replaced by a white-box implementation; then white-box implementation is replaced by Siren. The length of plaintext depends on the protected code size.
- More rounds of SMS4 encryption. Since the protected code size of each round of Siren is constant, adding more rounds can protect larger size of code.

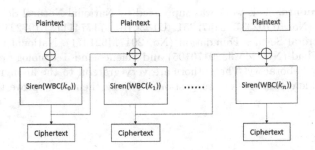

Fig. 4. An implementation of SMS4 based on CBC mode

Basically, both of the two options will cause the linear growth of the number of lookup tables, as well as the space consuming.

3.3 Security of Siren

We assume that the goal of attackers is to modify the software protected by Siren without losing the ability of encryption or decryption functionality. Changing the software to a non-sense bitstring is not considered as a successful attack. We give the following theorem:

Theorem 1. *Suppose that an attacker plans to XOR a row of $\widehat{C}_{i,j}$ with a value Δ. Then the invalidated key can be repaired by XORing a 32-bit value $Q_i(\Delta)$ to the corresponding row in the obfuscated version of lookup table $W_{i,j}$, where Q_i is the output encoding in Sect. 3.1.*

Proof. Since $C_{i,j}$ is generated by $\widehat{C}_{i,j}$, the modification of $\widehat{C}_{i,j}$ affects $C_{i,j}$ in the same way. To make the invalidated key functional, the attacker needs to XOR Δ to the corresponding row of $W_{i,j}$. However, the attacker can only access to the obfuscated version of $W_{i,j}$. Therefore the attacker should XOR $Q_i\Delta$ to the obfuscated lookup table.

Since Q_i is randomly generated and unknown to attacker, there's no way to compute the value of $Q_i\Delta$ effectively. Thus the only attack is exhaustively search all 32-bit value. The complexity is 2^{32}, which is the same as Medusa.

4   Conclusion

Applying white-box cryptogrpahy on software protection adds new values for white-box cryptography as well as provides fresh idea to software protection. In this paper, we provided a practical technique, Siren, which the binary of a software into lookup tables of Xiao-Lai's white-box SMS4 implementation. Under this protection, the code is tamper resistant because any changes in the code result invalidations of the white-box implementation. Our technique has the same security, consumes less additional space and protects software code more effectively. Moreover, we provided CBC-Siren scheme to solve the problem of how to protect programs of arbitrary size.

Acknowledgments. This work was supported by National Natural Science Foundation of China (No. 61702331, 61472251, U1536101, 71774111, 61972249, 61972248), China Postdoctoral Science Foundation (No. 2017M621471). National Cryptography Development Fund (NO. MMJJ20170105) and Science and Technology on Communication Security Laboratory. The authors are very grateful to the anonymous referees for their valuable comments and suggestions, helping them to improve the quality of this paper.

References

1. Collberg, C., Low, D., Thomborson, C.: Breaking abstractions and unstructuring data structures. In: Proceedings of the 1998 International Conference on Computer Languages (Cat. No. 98CB36225), pp. 28–38. IEEE (1998)
2. Lynn, B., Prabhakaran, M., Sahai, A.: Positive results and techniques for obfuscation. In: Cachin, C., Camenisch, J.L. (eds.) EUROCRYPT 2004. LNCS, vol. 3027, pp. 20–39. Springer, Heidelberg (2004). https://doi.org/10.1007/978-3-540-24676-3_2
3. Lach, J., Mangione-Smith, W.H., Kahng, A.B.: Watermarking techniques for intellectual property protection. In: Proceedings of the 35th annual Design Automation Conference, pp. 776–781. ACM (1998)
4. Ma, H., Lu, K.: Software watermarking using return-oriented programming. In: Proceedings of the 10th ACM Symposium on Information, Computer and Communications Security, pp. 369–380. ACM (2015)
5. Dalla, P.M., Preda, M.: Software watermarking: a semantics-based approach. Electron. Notes Theor. Comput. Sci. **331**, 71–85 (2017)
6. Kannan, S., Blum, M.: Designing programs that check their work. J. ACM (JACM) **42**(1), 269–291 (1995)
7. Blum, M., Wasserman, H.: Software reliability via run-time result-checking. J. ACM (JACM) **44**(6), 826–849 (1997)
8. Chow, S., Eisen, P., Johnson, H., van Oorschot, P.C.: A white-box DES implementation for DRM applications. In: Feigenbaum, J. (ed.) DRM 2002. LNCS, vol. 2696, pp. 1–15. Springer, Heidelberg (2003). https://doi.org/10.1007/978-3-540-44993-5_1
9. Chow, S., Eisen, P., Johnson, H., Van Oorschot, P.C.: White-box cryptography and an AES implementation. In: Nyberg, K., Heys, H. (eds.) SAC 2002. LNCS, vol. 2595, pp. 250–270. Springer, Heidelberg (2003). https://doi.org/10.1007/3-540-36492-7_17

10. Xiao, Y., Lai, X.: White-box cryptography and implementations of SMS4. In: Proceedings of the 2009 CACR Annual Meeting, vol. 34. Science Press, Beijing (2009)
11. Karroumi, M.: Protecting white-box AES with dual ciphers. In: Rhee, K.-H., Nyang, D.H. (eds.) ICISC 2010. LNCS, vol. 6829, pp. 278–291. Springer, Heidelberg (2011). https://doi.org/10.1007/978-3-642-24209-0_19
12. Biryukov, A., Bouillaguet, C., Khovratovich, D.: Cryptographic schemes based on the ASASA structure: black-box, white-box, and public-key (extended abstract). In: Sarkar, P., Iwata, T. (eds.) ASIACRYPT 2014. LNCS, vol. 8873, pp. 63–84. Springer, Heidelberg (2014). https://doi.org/10.1007/978-3-662-45611-8_4
13. Shi, Y., Wei, W., He, Z.: A lightweight white-box symmetric encryption algorithm against node capture for wsns. Sensors 15(5), 11928–11952 (2015)
14. Kang, Y.A., Lee, S., Kim, T.: A masked white-box cryptographic implementation for protecting against differential computation analysis. IEEE Trans. Inf. Forensics Secur. 13(10), 2602–2615 (2018)
15. Michiels, W., Gorissen, P.: Mechanism for software tamper resistance: an application of white-box cryptography. In: Proceedings of the 2007 ACM Workshop on Digital Rights Management, pp. 82–89. ACM (2007)

Competitiveness Indicator in Colombia Through of Multivariable Statistics

Elcira Solano Benavides[1]([⊠]), Nelson Alandete Brochero[1],
and Amelec Viloria[2]

[1] Universidad del Atlántico, Barranquilla, Colombia
elcirasolano@hotmail.com, alandete@outlook.es
[2] Universidad de la Costa, Barranquilla, Colombia
aviloria7@cuc.edu.co

Abstract. The objective of this research is to estimate a competitiveness indicator in Colombia through a factorial methodology of principal components. A competitiveness indicator was estimated presenting significant correlations between chosen variables and according to Kaiser-Mayer-Olkin test, the indicator presents a high degree of usefulness, in terms of correlation, standing out in hierarchical order with the science and technology factors with 0.80; economic affluence with 0.77, geographical condition with 0.75, logistic structure with 0.73, human capital with 0.68, institutional factor with 0.67 and economic dispersion with 0.65. On the other hand, it was found that competitiveness in Colombia is determined by the influx factor of economic activity in the main urban centers of Cundinamarca/Bogotá, Antioquia, Valle and Santander.

Keywords: Competitiveness · Principal Component Analysis ·
Economic affluence, geographic condition, human capital · Institutions

1 Introduction

Regional competitiveness is a process of generating skills that depends on the ability to create an environment that favors sustained growth in productivity and the standard of living of the population, considering the capabilities offered by the territory to facilitate development and economic activity [1, 3].

The Principal Component Analysis is one of the statistical tools that allows the analysis of competitiveness in relation to a number of quantitative variables that make up the factors and transforms them into a reduced number of variables called components. For this reason, this is one of the most used method in competitiveness studies, because it allows to extract from a set of variables the factors that determine competitiveness in the territories [5, 7].

The study is organized as follows: the first part presents the state of the art. In the second part, the methodology, in the third part, competitiveness indicators are estimated and analyzed, and finally, the conclusions.

© Springer Nature Singapore Pte Ltd. 2019
G. Wang et al. (Eds.): iSCI 2019, CCIS 1122, pp. 496–505, 2019.
https://doi.org/10.1007/978-981-15-1301-5_39

2 State of the Art

The factor analysis with Principal Component Analysis method was developed by Pearson and Spearman in the early 20th century. By analyzing correlations between variables and identifying basic data structures, this method can extract abstract factors to reveal most of the information from the original data. It is a useful solution for reducing dimensions when variables are correlated [7]. According to Vyas and Kumaranayake [13], Principal Component Analysis (PCA) is a multivariate statistical technique used to reduce the number of variables in a dataset in a smaller number of dimensions. In mathematical terms, from an initial set of n correlated variables, PCA creates non-correlated indices or components, where each component is a linear weighted combination of the initial variables. For example, from a set of variables X_1 to X_n,

$$
\begin{aligned}
PC_1 &= a_{11}X_1 + a_{12}X_2 + \ldots + a_{1n}X_n \\
PC_2 &= a_{21}X_1 + a_{22}X_2 + \ldots + a_{2n}X_n \\
&\vdots \\
PC_m &= a_{m1}X_1 + a_{m2}X_2 + \ldots + a_{mn}X_n
\end{aligned}
\tag{1}
$$

Where a_{mn} represents the weight of the m-th major component and the n-th variable. The uncorrelated property of the components is highlighted by the fact that they are perpendicular, i.e. at right angles to each other, which means that the indices measure different dimensions in the data.

The weights for each principal component are given by the vectors of the correlation matrix, or if the original data were standardized, the covariance matrix. The variance (λ) for each principal component is given by the own value of the corresponding own vector. The components are ordered in such a way that the first component (PC1) explains the greatest possible amount of variation in the original data; this first component is the one chosen in the empirical works of competitiveness as the indicator, because it fulfills the condition of high correlation and explanation of competitiveness [9, 12]. Since the sum of own values is equal to the number of variables in the initial data set, the proportion of the total variation in the original data set accounted for by each major component is given by λ_i/n. The second component (PC$_2$) is not fully correlated with the first component, and explains additional variations, but less than the first component, subject to the same constraint.

3 Method

A factorial model of principal component analysis (ACP) we used as a multivariate method whose objective is to convert a problem of statistical information with many variables of quantitative type in another almost equivalent model with few variables, without significant loss of information [10]. By this method, seven indexes were estimated, which were conformed by 26 variables chosen according to their significance with the real GDP per capita and obtained from secondary data for the years 2013–2016. The analysis was carried out through the SPSS software.

According to Lin, He, and Hao [7], in order to perform the component analysis, the following steps must be followed: first, the model must pass the following tests: Bartlett's sphericity, which verifies if the data are adequate for analysis, and the Kaiser-Mayer-Olkin (KMO) test, which determines if the original variables have a strong correlation, and requires that the value of the KMO statistics be higher than 0.50. Likewise, the extracted factor is rotated by the maximum variance method with Kaiser standardization. The own value of each extracted factor must be greater than one. The rotation of factors facilitates the identification of factors and makes the extracted factors have a significant data value. Finally, the results are normalized and standardized to make the indicators.

4   Regional Competitiveness in Colombia

The indicator proposed in this paper is composed of seven determining factors for departmental competitiveness in Colombia, which are: Economic influx, centrifugal forces, logistic structure, geographical condition, institutional condition, human capital, and science and technology. For the analysis, the Bartlett and KMO tests will be taken into account, as well as the factorial load, which represents the degree of representativeness of the variables in the index. Finally, the results obtained will be divided into three levels; high from 100 to 70, medium from 69 to 30, and low from 29 to 0 [14, 15].

4.1   Economic Affluence Factor

The economic affluence factor is constituted by the participation variables of the departmental GDP in the national (DepGDP), participation of the departmental industry in the national (Inddep), participation of the departmental services in the national services (Serdep) and employed population (Ocup), for the years 2013 and 2016.

$$\text{Economic Affluence Factor} = f(\text{GDPdep; Inddep, Serdep, Ocup}) \qquad (2)$$

According to Bartlett's test, the correlation between the variables in both years was significant. Likewise, the KMO statistic is 0.80 and 0.73, i.e. there is a strong correlation between the variables. The result of the estimated factor presents the participation variable of the GDP with the highest factorial load on average with 0.996, followed by the participation of the service GDP with 0.993, employed population with 0.992 and participation of the industrial GDP with 0.973, that is to say, all the variables show a great representation in the index. By levels, only one department is at the high level: Cundinamarca/Bogotá. In the middle level are Antioquia and Valle del Cauca. The rest 90%, are at the low level.

4.2   Economic Dispersion Factor

The economic dispersion factor is made up of the following variables: departmental mining GDP (Pibmin), departmental agricultural GDP (Pibagro) and the global irradiation of solar energy in the department (Solar), for the years 2013 and 2016.

$$\textbf{Economic Dispersion Factor} = f(\text{Pibmin, Pibagro and Solar}) \qquad (3)$$

According to Bartlett's test in both years, the correlation between the variables is significant. Likewise, the KMO statistic is 0.62 and 0.63, i.e. there is a strong correlation between the variables. The result of the estimated factor, has the mining GDP variable with the highest average factorial load with 0.811, followed by the agricultural GDP with 0.775 and solar energy irradiation with 0.701, that is, the production of immobile factors has a great representation in the index. By levels, the leading departments are Meta and Antioquia, and the increase to third and fourth position of Cesar and Guajira for the increase in mining production in 2016 stands out. In the middle level, 40% of the departments are found and in the low level, 50%.

4.3   Logistic Structure Factor

The logistic structure factor is constituted by the variables of investment in transportation (Transp), investment in communication (Comun), investment in mines and energy (Mines), and density in secondary roads (viassecun), for the years 2013 and 2016.

$$\textbf{Logistic Structure Factor} = f(\text{Transp; Comun; Mines and viassecun}) \qquad (4)$$

According to Bartlett's test, in both years, the correlation between the variables is significant. Likewise, the KMO statistic is 0.76 and 0.70, i.e. there is a strong correlation between the variables. The result of the estimated factor has the variable investment in communications with the highest average factorial load of 0.925, followed by investment in mines and energy with 0.920, investment in transport with 0.892 and secondary road density with 0.454. That is to say, the investments in logistic structure and public services have a great representation in the index. By level, the leading departments are Cundinamarca/Bogotá and Antioquia. In the middle level, on average about 30% of the departments are found and in the lower level 66% are concentrated.

4.4   Geographical Condition Factor

The geographical condition factor is made up of the variables of cost of land transportation to ports (Costpuer), cost of land transportation to internal market (Costint), distance to seaports (Distpuer), area covered by forest (Bosque), protected areas (Areasprot), for the years 2013 and 2016.

$$\textbf{Geographical condition factor} = f(\text{Costpuer; Costint; Distpuer; Bosque; Areasprot}) \qquad (5)$$

According to Bartlett's test, in both years, the correlation between the variables is significant. Likewise, the KMO statistic is 0.72 and 0.78, i.e. there is a strong correlation between the variables. The result of the estimated factor, presents the variable distance to ports with the highest average factorial load of 0.920, followed by the area covered by forest with 0.89, land costs, ports with 0.875, protected areas with 0.875, and transportation costs to internal markets with 0.620. The variable distance to ports with the highest average factorial load of 0.920, followed by the area covered by forest with 0.89, land costs, ports with 0.875, protected areas with 0.875 and transportation costs to internal markets with 0.620. In other words, protected areas, transportation costs and international trade are highly representative in the index. By levels, the departments in the first positions belong to the region. At the high level, the group of departments goes from 47% in 2013 to 70% in 2016. In the middle level, it goes from 44% in 2013 to 13% in 2015. At the lower level are 13% of the country.

4.5   Institutional Factor

The institutional factor is made up of the integral performance index (Idi), fiscal performance index (Idf) and open government index (Iga) variables for 2013 and 2016.

$$\textbf{Institutional Factor} = f(\text{Idi}; \text{Idf}; \text{Iga}) \tag{6}$$

According to Bartlett's test, in both years, the correlation between the variables is significant. Likewise, the KMO statistic is 0.673 and 0.677, i.e. there is a strong correlation between the variables. The result of the estimated factor (Table 1) presents

Table 1. Statistical tests, factor loads and institutional factor scores, 2013 and 2016.

Statistical tests				Institutional factor scores					
	2013	2016		Departments	position	2013	Departments	position	2016
KMO Test	0,673	0,677		Quindío	1	85,5	Cund/bogota	1	99,5
Bartlett Sphericity test	0,000	0,000		Meta	2	84,9	Risaralda	2	91,5
Factor Loads				Boyacá	3	79,3	Antioquia	3	88,8
Variables	2013	2016		Santander	4	77,3	Quindío	4	86,7
Iga	0,821	0,925		Nariño	5	76,7	Meta	5	86,2
Idi	0,795	0,881		Cund/bogota	6	76,4	Nariño	6	84,5
Idf	0,776	0,823		Antioquia	7	75,1	Huila	7	83
				Casanare	8	74,1	Atlántico	8	81,5
				Risaralda	9	69,3	Valle	9	79,9
				Huila	10	68,2	Casanare	10	77,9
				Atlántico	11	68	Santander	11	76,8
				Valle	12	67,8	Boyacá	12	75,9
				N. de Santander	13	66,5	Sucre	13	75,1
				Tolima	14	66,3	N. de Santander	14	73,8
				Cauca	15	65,4	Caldas	15	73,7
				Sucre	16	61,8	Caquetá	16	72,2
				Caldas	17	60,6	Cauca	17	70,8
				Cesar	18	58,9	Magdalena	18	68,7
				Córdoba	19	58,9	Arauca	19	66,7
				Arauca	20	57,7	Cesar	20	63,8
				Caquetá	21	55,6	Tolima	21	63
				Magdalena	22	53,9	Bolívar	22	60,9
				Bolívar	23	53,1	Córdoba	23	58,2
				La Guajira	24	48,8	Vichada	24	56,7
				Guainía	25	38,6	Guaviare	25	56,7
				Guaviare	26	35,9	Vaupés	26	52,5
				Chocó	27	31,9	San Andrés	27	41,7
				Vichada	28	30	La Guajira	28	41,5
				Putumayo	29	28,7	Putumayo	29	41,3
				San Andrés	30	27,9	Amazonas	30	34,6
				Vaupés	31	26,8	Chocó	31	33,4
				Amazonas	32	14	Guainía	32	20,6

the open government index variable with the highest average factorial load of 0.873, followed by the integral performance index with 0.838 and the fiscal performance index. That is to say, those that transparency and the fight against corruption show a great representativity in the index. By levels, the high level represents 41%, in the middle level, 39% of the departments are in average, and in the low level, 20%.

4.6 Human Capital Factor

The human capital factor is made up of the variables: university labor demand by department (Demlabor), gross secondary education coverage (Cobersecun), gross secondary education coverage (Cobermedia), saber 11 test score (saber11), for the years 2013 and 2016.

$$\textbf{Human Capital} = (\text{Demlabor; Cobersecun; Cobermedia; saber11}) \qquad (7)$$

According to Bartlett's test, in both years the correlation between the variables is significant. Likewise, the KMO statistic is 0.691 and 0.688, i.e. there is a strong correlation between the variables. The result of the estimated factor (Table 2) presents

Table 2. Statistical tests, factor loads, and human capital factor scores, 2013 and 2016.

Statistical tests			Human capital fator score, 2013 y 2016					
	2013	2016	Departments	Position	2013	Departments	Position	2016
KMO test	0,691	0,688	Cund/bogota	1	98,3	Cund/bogota	1	98,3
Bartlett Sphericity test	0	0	Santander	2	72,6	Santander	2	72,6
Factor loads			Boyacá	3	68,6	Boyacá	3	68,4
Variables	2013	2016	Antioquia	4	66,1	Quindío	4	66,2
Cobermedia	0,948	0,947	Quindío	5	66	Antioquia	5	65,8
Cobersecun	0,921	0,921	Atlántico	6	64	Atlántico	6	64
saber11	0,872	0,873	Valle	7	62,7	Casanare	7	62,4
Demlabor	0,674	0,663	Casanare	8	62,2	Risaralda	8	62,2
			Risaralda	9	62	Valle	9	61,5
			Caldas	10	60,5	Caldas	10	60,5
			Meta	11	59	Meta	11	59
			Huila	12	57	Huila	12	56,9
			Tolima	13	54,2	Tolima	13	54,5
			N. de Santander	14	53,2	N. de Santander	14	52,9
			Sucre	15	50,6	Sucre	15	50,6
			Córdoba	16	50,4	Córdoba	16	49,9
			Bolívar	17	47,6	Bolívar	17	47,4
			Cesar	18	47,3	Cesar	18	47,2
			San Andrés	19	46,9	San Andrés	19	47,1
			Nariño	20	44,4	Nariño	20	44,5
			Cauca	21	40,2	Cauca	21	40,2
			Arauca	22	39,5	Arauca	22	39,6
			Putumayo	23	39,3	Putumayo	23	39,5
			Magdalena	24	37,9	Magdalena	24	37,7
			Caquetá	25	34,3	Caquetá	25	34,4
			Guaviare	26	24,8	Guaviare	26	24,9
			Amazonas	27	23,1	Amazonas	27	23,2
			La Guajira	28	21,7	La Guajira	28	21,7
			Guainía	29	17,2	Guainía	29	17,2
			Vichada	30	14,7	Vichada	30	14,7
			Chocó	31	12,9	Chocó	31	12,8
			Vaupés	32	5,1	Vaupés	32	5,2

the middle education coverage variable with the highest factorial load on average of 0.947, followed by secondary education coverage with 0.921, saber 11 score with 0.872 and university demand with 0.668. In other words, the quality of secondary and secondary education is highly representative of the index. By level, the leading departments are Bogotá/Cundinamarca and Santander. In the middle level, they are found in 71% of the departments and in the lower level, 23% are concentrated.

4.7 Science and Technology Factor

The science and technology factor is made up of the variables Investment in research project (Invproy), doctoral scholarships (Becdoc), master's degree scholarships (Becmaes) and patent applications (Patente); for the years 2013 and 2016.

$$\text{Science and Technology} = f(\text{Invproy; Becdoc; Becmaes and Patent}) \qquad (8)$$

According to Bartlett's test, in both years, the correlation between the variables is significant. Likewise, the KMO statistic is 0.778 and 0.826, i.e. there is a strong correlation between the variables. The result of the estimate (Table 3) presents the variable doctoral scholarships with the highest average factorial load of 0.979, followed

Table 3. Statistical tests, factor loads, and science and technology factor scores, 2013 and 2016.

Statistical Tests				Science and technology factor scores, 2013 and 2016					
	2013	2016		Dep	Position	2013	Dep	Position	2016
KMO tests	0,778	0,826		Cund/bogota	1	92,9	Cund/bogota	1	83,6
Bartlett sphericity test	0,000	0,000		Antioquia	2	51,5	Antioquia	2	37,5
Factor loads				Valle	3	19,5	Valle	3	35,6
Variables	2013	2016		Santander	4	18,2	Santander	4	18,4
Becdoc	0,994	0,964		Atlántico	5	10,5	N. de Santander	5	12,4
Patente	0,991	0,973		Caldas	6	4,9	Atlántico	6	10,3
Becmaes	0,976	0,964		Boyacá	7	4,1	Tolima	7	8,3
Invproy	0,919	0,773		Cauca	8	3,2	Nariño	8	6,4
				Nariño	9	3,2	Caldas	9	6,2
				Tolima	10	3,1	Boyacá	10	5,5
				Risaralda	11	2,9	Risaralda	11	4,3
				Bolívar	12	2,5	Quindío	12	4,2
				Quindío	13	2,2	Bolívar	13	4,2
				Huila	14	1,6	Putumayo	14	3,5
				N. de Santander	15	1,4	Huila	15	2,8
				Amazonas	16	1,2	Cauca	16	1,5
				Córdoba	17	1,1	Córdoba	17	1,5
				Meta	18	1	Meta	18	1,5
				Chocó	19	0,9	Magdalena	19	1,3
				Cesar	20	0,7	Cesar	20	1,3
				Caquetá	21	0,6	Sucre	21	1,2
				Magdalena	22	0,6	Caquetá	22	0,6
				La Guajira	23	0,4	La Guajira	23	0,6
				Putumayo	24	0,3	Guainía	24	0,2
				Sucre	25	0,3	Casanare	25	0,2
				Guaviare	26	0,3	San Andrés	26	0,1
				Casanare	27	0,2	Arauca	27	0,1
				Arauca	28	0,1	Amazonas	28	0
				San Andrés	29	0,1	Chocó	29	0
				Guainía	30	0	Guaviare	30	0
				Vaupés	31	0	Vaupés	31	0
				Vichada	32	0	Vichada	32	0

by patent applications with 0.982, master's scholarships with 0.970 and project amount with 0.846. That is to say, innovation and human capital formation have a great representation in the index. By levels, the leading department is Bogota/Cundinamarca, in the middle level is Antioquia and in the lower level is 93% of the country.

4.8 Competitiveness Indicator in Colombia, 2013–2016

The Competitiveness Indicator in Colombia collects, in an aggregate manner, the seven factors of economic affluence (Afluecon), economic dispersion (Disper), logistic structure (Estruclog), geographic condition (Condigeo), institutional condition (Inst), human capital (Caphum) and science and technology (Science), for the years 2013 and 2016.

$$\text{Competitiveness indicator} = f(\text{Afluecon, Disper, Estruclog, Condigeo, Inst, Caphum, Science})$$
(9)

Table 4. Statistical tests, factor loads, and competitiveness indicator scores in Colombia, 2013 and 2016.

Statistical tests			Competitiveness Indicator scores in Colombia, 2013 and 2016					
	2013	2016	Departments	Position	2013	Departments	Position	2016
KMO test	0,789	0,768	Cund/bogota	1	78,9	Cund/bogota	1	83,4
Bartlett sphericity test	0	0	Antioquia	2	57,3	Antioquia	2	55,5
Factor loads			Santander	3	43,6	Valle	3	48,7
Variables	2013	2016	Meta	4	38	Santander	4	42,6
Afluecon	0,899	0,927	Atlántico	5	37,3	Atlántico	5	38,4
Estruclog	0,923	0,901	Boyacá	6	37	Boyacá	6	37,2
Caphum	0,888	0,877	Valle	7	36,7	Meta	7	36,6
Ciencia	0,87	0,913	Tolima	8	32,7	Cesar	8	33,3
Disper	0,838	0,798	Bolívar	9	31,4	Nariño	9	32,6
Inst	0,784	0,745	Nariño	10	30,6	Tolima	10	31,8
Condigeo	0,496	0,4	Cesar	11	30,5	Bolívar	11	31,3
			Córdoba	12	29,6	Huila	12	30,5
			Huila	13	29,4	Magdalena	13	29,7
			Casanare	14	29,3	Risaralda	14	29,7
			Quindío	15	29,3	Casanare	15	29,3
			Magdalena	16	27,5	N. de Santander	16	28,9
			Caldas	17	27,4	Quindío	17	28,8
			N. de Santander	18	26,7	Córdoba	18	28
			Cauca	19	26,6	Caldas	19	27,9
			Sucre	20	26,1	Cauca	20	26,4
			Risaralda	21	25,6	Sucre	21	26,3
			San Andrés	22	22	San Andrés	22	22,9
			La Guajira	23	21,9	Arauca	23	22,1
			Arauca	24	21,2	La Guajira	24	20,5
			Caquetá	25	16,7	Caquetá	25	20,3
			Putumayo	26	11,8	Putumayo	26	15,4
			Chocó	27	10,8	Vichada	27	14,4
			Guaviare	28	8,5	Guaviare	28	14,3
			Guainía	29	7,9	Chocó	29	12
			Vichada	30	5,2	Amazonas	30	11
			Vaupés	31	5	Vaupés	31	9,8
			Amazonas	32	2,3	Guainía	32	9,2

According to Bartlett's test, in both years, the correlation between the variables is significant. Likewise, the KMO statistic is 0.789 and 0.901, i.e. there is a strong correlation between the variables. The result of the estimated indicator (Table 4), presents the economic affluence factor with the highest factorial load in average of 0.913, followed by logistic structure with 0.912, science and technology with 0.892, human capital with 0.882, institutional with 0.764 and geographical condition with 0.444. In other words, the factors related to the affluence of the economic activity are the main determinants of competitiveness in the country. By level, every year, it is Bogotá/Cundinamarca. In the middle level, they are: Antioquia, Valle, Santander and Atlántico, and at the low level, 87% of the departments.

5 Conclusions

The regional competitiveness indicator, estimated by principal component, presents an innovation in methodological terms. The variables and factors were chosen taking into account their level of significance with the GDP per capita, so that the indices provide information on the economic reality of the country for territorial public policy decision-making. In addition, according to Bartlett's test, the correlation of the variables that make up the competitiveness indices are statistically significant. In the same way, all indices present high statistics in the KMO test, showing the degree of usefulness, in terms of correlation of the indices, standing out the following: science and technology with 0.80, economic affluence with 0.77, geographical condition with 0.75, logistic structure with 0.73, human capital with 0.68, institutional with 0.67, and economic dispersion with 0.65. In the same way, the general indicator of competitiveness, the factors that present greater representation, are associated with the factors of economic affluence with 0.913, logistic structure with 0.912, and science and technology with 0.892.

With respect to levels, it is evident that Cundinamarca/Bogotá is the largest urban center in Colombia and presents the greatest inequality in terms of economic activities, investment in logistic structure and science and technology. In contrast, the factor of geographical condition, institutional and human capital present less degrees of inequality between departments, due to the fact that the physical characteristics and public management of the regions are highlighted. In conclusion, it is inferred that competitiveness in Colombia is determined by the influx of economic activity.

References

1. Abdel, G., Romo, D.: Sobre el concepto de competitividad. Comercio exterior **55**(3), 200–214 (2004)
2. Alarcón, O.A., González, H.E.: El desarrollo económico local y las teorías de localización. Revisión teórica. Revista Espacios **39**(51) (2018)
3. Begg, I.: "Urban Competitiveness", Policies for Dynamic Cities, p. 248. The Policy Press, Great Britain (2002)

4. Fu, Y., He, W., Hao, R.: Comparative analysis of financial industry competitiveness of regions in China (2019)
5. Fujita, M., Krugman, P.: The new economic geography: past, present and the future. In: Florax, R.J.G.M., Plane, D.A. (eds.) Fifty Years of Regional Science. ADVSPATIAL, pp. 139–164. Springer, Heidelberg (2004). https://doi.org/10.1007/978-3-662-07223-3_6
6. Fujita, M., Krugman, P., Venables, A.: The Spatial Economy: Cities, Regions and International Trade. The MIT Press, Cambridge (1999)
7. Lin, Z., He, W., Hao, R.: Analysis of regional competitiveness in the high-tech industry. Curr. Sci. (00113891) 114(4), 854–860 (2018)
8. Newman, P.V., Ángel, M.P.: Estado del arte sobre la corrupción en Colombia. Fedesarrollo (2017)
9. Ramírez, J.C., de Aguas, J.M.: Escalafón de la competitividad de los departamentos en Colombia. CEPAL, Bogotá (2017)
10. Romer, P.M.: Increasing returns and long-run growth. J. Polit. Econ. 94(5), 1002–1037 (1986)
11. Salinas, H., Albornoz, J., Reyes, A., Erazo, M., Ide, R.: Análisis de componentes principales aplicado a variables respecto a la mujer gestante en la región de las américas. Revista chilena de obstetricia y ginecología 71(1), 17–25 (2006)
12. Ochoa, J.J.G., Lara, J.D.D.L., De la Parra, J.P.N.: Propuesta de un modelo de medición de la competitividad mediante análisis factorial. Contaduría y administración 62(3), 775–791 (2017)
13. Vyas, S., Kumaranayake, L.: Constructing socio-economic status indices: how to use principal components analysis. Health Policy Plann. 21(6), 459–468 (2006)
14. Amelec, V.: Increased efficiency in a company of development of technological solutions in the areas commercial and of consultancy. Adv. Sci. Lett. 21(5), 1406–1408 (2015)
15. Viloria, A.: Commercial strategies providers pharmaceutical chains for logistics cost reduction. Indian J. Sci. Technol. 8(1), 1–6 (2016)

Assistive Engineering and Information Technology

Network Intrusion Detection Based on Hidden Markov Model and Conditional Entropy

Linying Xiao[✉] and Huaibin Wang

Tianjin University of Technology, Tianjin 300384, China
864995510@qq.com

Abstract. Nowadays, more and more machine learning algorithms are introduced into intrusion detection. Some researchers improved existing algorithms, while others combined a variety of methods. Each method have their benefits but limitations are inevitable. In this paper, we proposed a novel model of network intrusion detection based on anomaly traffic. And hidden Markov model (HMM) is utilized into this field, which effectively combines statistics and traffic classification. Based on network, some extracted traffic features based PCA are used as the input value of HMM. Eventually, the types of the traffic are judged by the probability value of output. If the traffic type is abnormal, the network is already under attack. Conversely, it's under security. During model training, we creatively use conditional entropy to optimize the Baum-Welch algorithm, and the performance evaluation results indicate HMM achieve better precision and lower computational cost compared with others.

Keywords: Network security · Intrusion detection · Conditional entropy · Hidden Markov model (HMM) · Baum-Welch algorithm

1 Introduction

The 21st century is an era of computer and Internet. The network is ubiquitous in our life and people have become gradually inseparable from the network. We are experiencing the "information revolution" in human history. Along with the development of the technology and society, the Internet plays an increasingly vital role in people's life. In order to promote the progress of the Internet, China has put forward and implemented the "Internet+" action plan. With the rapid growth of Internet, the network security has also became an essential research direction in computer network. At present, the network attack become more and more frequent and personal privacy needs to be protected securely. However, there are some inevitable loopholes in traditional security protection products. Intrusion detection, as a critical protection means of information security, make up for the lack of firewall. It provides effective network anomaly detection approaches and protects security of the network.

Intrusion detection aims at finding abnormal or unexpected sequences. It has drawn strong attention in recent decade. However, there are many problems in the traditional intrusion detection system. Therefore, in order to tackle these problems, a most accurate means of anomaly detection should be taken to guarantee the security of the network environment.

© Springer Nature Singapore Pte Ltd. 2019
G. Wang et al. (Eds.): iSCI 2019, CCIS 1122, pp. 509–519, 2019.
https://doi.org/10.1007/978-981-15-1301-5_40

Security researchers have provided various techniques and models for detecting intrusions into a software system. Recently, researchers have applied data mining and machine learning techniques to intrusion detection system [1–3]. They attempt to create intelligent models to detect dangerous behavior patterns. Whereas most existing researches only focus on the accuracy rate of anomaly detection, relatively less studies have been devoted to problems of precious rate and efficiency.

Hidden Markov model (HMM), being regarded as one of the most commonly used statistical models, can model the dynamic behavior of time series with a simple. This model has been successfully applied to a wide range of fields such as credit ratings [4], fault diagnosis [5, 6] and others [7, 8].

Based on the characteristics and limitations of the network intrusion detection technology, in this paper, the traditional intrusion detection technology has been improved and innovated. Meanwhile, hidden Markov model is applied to the network intrusion detection. In order to improve the efficiency of detection, we creatively use conditional entropy to optimize the Baum-Welch algorithm in the stage of model training, thus reducing computation of the training time as well as improving detection accuracy.

The rest of this paper is organized as follows. In Sect. 2, related work is presented. A brief summary of Conditional Entropy and HMM is introduced in Sect. 3. The proposed intrusion detection model is discussed in Sect. 4. Section 5 is focused on experimental results and discussion. Finally, in Sect. 6, we draw a conclusion and make future work.

2 Related Work

A large number of research work have been reported on this topic over the last few years. Many researchers combine machine learning with intrusion detection methods to realize intelligent detection of network attacks, which boost the efficiency of intrusion detection and reduce the false alarm rate.

A real-time detection method was proposed in the literature [9]. This method, using packet sniffer, sniffs network packets every two seconds and classifies network data with decision tree algorithm. It will output three results: denial of service, thorough investigation and normal. The accuracy rate of algorithm is up to 97.5%, but the model cannot detect unknown attacks.

Fung proposed a collaborative intrusion detection network [10], which allows distributed intrusion detection systems to collaborate and share their perceptions and perspectives on intrusion. This method enhances the overall accuracy of intrusion detection and the ability to detect new intrusion classifications. In this process, each intrusion detection system evaluates the detection accuracy and error rate of the neighbor detection system through the Bayesian learning method and aggregates these results.

Thanks to the maximum entropy model is good at dealing with discrete symbolic features, so the paper [11] proposes to utilize the maximum entropy model, which has been satisfactorily applied to network security field, to handle the network traffic classification problem with a large number of continuous features. Though the maximum entropy model has great advantages in classification performance and stability, it consumes lots of training time and has low classification efficiency in parameter estimation.

3 Theoretical Preparation for the Proposed Method

3.1 Conditional Entropy

If $H(Y|X = x)$ is the entropy of the discrete random variable Y conditioned on the discrete random variable X taking a certain value x, then $H(Y|X)$ is the result of averaging $H(Y|X = x)$ over all possible values x that X may take [12].

$$
\begin{aligned}
H(Y|X) &\equiv \sum_{x \in X} p(x) H(Y|X = x) \\
&= -\sum_{x \in X} p(x) \sum_{y \in Y} p(y|x) \log p(y|x)
\end{aligned}
\tag{1}
$$

While $\sum_{y \in Y} p(y|x) \log p(y|x)$ is the information entropy of $p(y|x)$.

3.2 Hidden Markov Model

Hmm is a double stochastic process that satisfies Markov hypothesis. It consists of two parts: Markov chain and General stochastic process. Among them, Markov chain utilizes transfer probability to describe the transfer of state. The general stochastic process uses the observation probability to describe the relationship between the state and the observation sequence. An illustrative example of HMM is shown in Fig. 1.

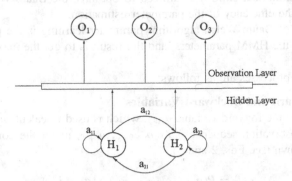

Fig. 1. Illustrative example of HMM

HMM can be described by a five-tuple (X, Y, A, B, Π) consisting of two state sets and three probability matrices. You can also use a simple three-tuple $\lambda = (A, B, \Pi)$ to describe:

$$X = (x_1, x_2, \ldots, x_{nX})$$
$$Y = (y_1, y_2, \ldots, y_{nY})$$
$$A = (a_{ij}); a_{ij} = P(q_{t+1} = y_j | q_t = y_i)$$
$$B = (b_j(o_t)); b_j(o_t) = P(o_t = xt | q_t = y_j)$$
$$\Pi = (\pi_i); \pi_i = P(q_1 = y_i)$$

Where X is the observation set, the corresponding observation sequence $O = o_1 o_2 \ldots o_T$ is a general stochastic process. The observation value that represents the t moment is $o_t = x_t$;

Y is an implicit state set and the corresponding implicit state sequence.

$H = h_1 h_2 \ldots h_T$ is a Markov process. $h_t = y_i$ indicates that the implicit state of the t moment is y_i;

A is a transfer probability matrix of implicit state. a_{ij} indicates a probability from state y_i move to state y_j;

B is a transfer probability matrix of observation state. $b_j(o_t)$ represents the probability that the observed value o_t appears under implicit state y_j;

Π is a probability matrix of initial state, which represents the probability matrix of the implicit state at the initial moment.

3.3   Optimization of Baum-Welch Algorithm

The Baum-Welch algorithm is proposed to solve the problem of parameter estimation in HMM, that is to solve the problem of unknown parameter estimation of HMM's observation state sequence. Specifically, when the observation sequence $O = o_1 o_2 \ldots o_T$ and parameters of the estimable model $\lambda = (A, B, \Pi)$ are known, the Baum-Welch algorithm can calculate the maximum probability of the observation sequence. In this paper, conditional entropy is utilized to optimize the Baum-Welch algorithm, which enhance the efficiency of the parameter estimation.

The process of Baum-Welch algorithm parameter learning is the process of constantly updating the HMM parameters, and the result is to get the maximum value of $P(O|\lambda)$.

The specific processes are as follows:

Calculate Forward and Backward Variables

Firstly, we define the forward variable $\alpha_t(i)$, which is used to calculate the probability of the partial observation sequence $o_{t+1}, o_{t+2}, \ldots o_{t+T}$, under the condition that the current h_i is known (see Eqs. 2 and 3).

$$\alpha_t(i) = P(o_{t+1}, o_{t+2}, \ldots o_{t+T} \mid q_t = i, \lambda) \tag{2}$$

Effective calculation by iterative algorithm:

$$\alpha_t(i) = \sum_{j=1}^{N} \alpha_{t+1}(i) a_{ij} b_{jk}, \ 1 \leq i \leq N, \ 1 \leq t \leq T \tag{3}$$

Similarly, we define the backward variable $\beta_t(i)$, which is used to calculate the probability of the partial observation sequence $o_{t+1}, o_{t+2}, \ldots o_{t+T}$, under the condition that the current hi is known (see Eqs. 4 and 5).

$$\beta_t(i) = P(o_{t+1}, o_{t+2}, \ldots o_{t+T} \mid q_t = i, \lambda) \tag{4}$$

Further,

$$\beta_t(i) = \sum_{j=1}^{N} \beta_{t+1}(i) a_{ij} b_{jk}, \ 1 \le i \le N, \ 1 \le t \le T \tag{5}$$

Calculate Two Auxiliary Variables

The first variable is the probability of state i at time t along with the probability of state j at time t + 1 (see Eq. 6).

$$\zeta_t(i,j) = P(S_t = i, S_{t+1} = j \mid O, \lambda) \tag{6}$$

Which is comparable to the definition in Eq. 7.

$$\zeta_t(i,j) = \frac{P(S_t = i, S_{t+1} = j \mid O, \lambda)}{P(O \mid \lambda)} \tag{7}$$

Using the Forward and Backward variables, we can define Eq. 8.

$$\zeta_t(i,j) = \frac{\alpha_t(i) p_{ij} \beta_{t+1}(j) b_j(O_{t+1})}{\sum_{i=1}^{N} \sum_{j=1}^{N} \alpha_t(i) p_{ij} \beta_{t+1}(j) b_j(O_{t+1})} \tag{8}$$

The second variable (Eq. 9) depicts the Backward probability of state i, given a sequence of observation and the HMM.

$$\gamma_t(i) = P(S_t = i \mid O, \lambda) \tag{9}$$

The variable in Eq. 9 can be defined using the Forward and Backward variables as can be seen in Eq. 10.

$$\gamma_t(i) = \left[\frac{\alpha_t(i) \beta_t(i)}{\sum_{i=1}^{N} \alpha_t(i) \beta_t(i)} \right] \tag{10}$$

The relationship between formula 6 and 9 can be expressed using Eq. 11.

$$\gamma_t(i) = \sum_{i=1}^{N} \zeta_t(i,j), \ 1 \le i \le N, \ 1 \le t \le M \tag{11}$$

Update Model Parameters

In the next step, the model parameters are updated according to the estimation formulas 12, 13, and 14.

$$\hat{\pi}_i = \gamma_1(i), \ 1 \le i \le N \tag{12}$$

$$\hat{p}_{ij} = \frac{\sum_{t=1}^{T-1} \zeta_t(i,j)}{\sum_{t=1}^{T-1} \gamma_t(i)}, \ 1 \le i \le N, \ 1 \le j \le N \tag{13}$$

$$\hat{b}_j(k) = \frac{\sum_{\substack{t=1 \\ ot=ok}}^{T} \gamma_t(i)}{\sum_{t=1}^{T} \gamma_t(j)}, \ 1 \le j \le N, \ 1 \le k \le M \tag{14}$$

In this paper, conditional entropy is utilized to calculate the probability of observed value Y under implicit state X, which can effectively raise the efficiency of parameter estimation to a certain extent. Where,

$$\begin{aligned} \hat{b}_j(k) &= H(Y|X) \equiv \sum_{x \in X} p(x) H(Y|X = x) \\ &= -\sum_{x \in X} p(x) \sum_{y \in Y} p(y|x) \log p(y|x) \end{aligned} \tag{15}$$

Probability of Observation Sequence

$$P(O|\lambda) = \sum_{i=1}^{N} P(O, q_t = i|\lambda) = \sum_{i=1}^{N} \alpha_t(i)\beta_t(i), \ 1 \le i \le N, \ 1 \le t \le T \tag{16}$$

4 Application of Proposed Model on Network Intrusion Detection

4.1 Model of Network Intrusion Detection

To detect anomaly network, researchers have come up with many effective methods. Many real-time or non-real-time intrusion detection models have been proposed. In this paper, the hidden Markov model is applied to the network intrusion detection. The process of intrusion detection system is shown in Fig. 2.

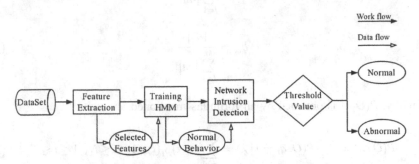

Fig. 2. The process of network intrusion detection

As shown in the figure above, the process comprises of three sections: feature extraction, model training and network intrusion detection. In the step of feature extraction, parameter selection techniques for cutting the input dimension are utilized, the primary parameters are confirmed for creating the anomaly detection model. The process of Hidden Markov model training will be described in detail in Sect. 4.2. This training model is used as the behavior model of the system. Once we have a behavior model of the system, we can use it to detect the type of current network state, which is the process of network intrusion detection.

4.2   Training Process of Hidden Markov Model

The training process of hidden Markov model is the process of constantly updating parameters $\lambda = (A, B, \Pi)$. In this paper, there are two hidden states in HMM, which correspond to normal and abnormal state. Thereby, the initial vector Π, state transition matrix A and emission matrix B are expressed as follows.

$$\Pi = [\, \pi_1(normal) \quad \pi_2(abnormal) \,] \tag{17}$$

$$A = \begin{bmatrix} a_{11}(normal \rightarrow normal) & a_{12}(normal \rightarrow abnormal) \\ a_{21}(abnormal \rightarrow normal) & a_{22}(abnormal \rightarrow abnormal) \end{bmatrix} \tag{18}$$

$$B = \begin{bmatrix} b_{11} & \cdots & b_{1M} \\ b_{11} & \cdots & b_{2M} \end{bmatrix} \tag{19}$$

Further, initializing parameters with the following formulas.

$$\pi_i = \frac{|q_i|}{\sum q} \tag{20}$$

$$a_{ij} = \frac{|q_{ij}|}{\sum\limits_{j=1}^{N} |q_{ij}|} \tag{21}$$

$$b_{ik} = \frac{|o_{il}|}{\sum\limits_{l=1}^{M} |o_{il}|} \tag{22}$$

Finally, $P(O|\lambda)$ is obtained by all formulas mentioned above.

$$P(O \mid \lambda) = \sum_{i=1}^{N} P(O, q_t = i \mid \lambda) = \sum_{i=1}^{N} \alpha_t(i)\beta_t(i), \ 1 \leq i \leq N, \ 1 \leq t \leq T \tag{23}$$

5 Experimental Result and Analysis

The simulation environment that we used is Matlab. The proposed method is applied to network intrusion detection. In this section, we firstly introduce the data set used in our experiment and the data preprocessing is also described briefly. What's more, performance metrics are utilized to evaluate the proposed method. Finally, many performance metrics are considered to compare different approaches of network intrusion detection.

5.1 Data Set and Data Preprocessing

In this experiments, a new data set called Kyoto 2006+ obtained from diverse types of honeypots [13] is utilized to evaluate the network intrusion detection. Although the KDD Cup 1999 data set has existed for a long time but cannot reflect the current network situation. By comparison, the Kyoto 2006+ data set is relatively new. The data set contains the period between 2006 and 2009 of real flow data. Each record has 24 different features consisting of 14 statistical features and 10 additional features.

Data preprocessing contains three main stages: data transferring, data normalization and feature extraction. The trained classifier requires that each input record should be expressed as a vector of real number. Therefore, features in the data set must be converted into a numeric value firstly. Data normalization is to remove unit limits for data and normalizes each record into the same range of [0–1]. In order to obtain the most informative features of traffic data and achieve higher performance, feature extraction is considered. This paper usages the same method proposed in paper [14] to make a decision of the optimal number of required features (Table 1).

5.2 Performance Evaluation

To quantify the performance and usefulness of the proposed network intrusion detection model, a plenty of experiments are carried out. Meanwhile, four performance

Table 1. Extracted features of Kyoto 2006+ data set.

No.	Feature	No.	Feature
1	Duration	7	Flag
2	Source bytes	8	Source_IP_Address
3	Destination bytes	9	Source_Port_Number
4	Count	10	Destination_IP_Address
5	Des host count	11	Destination_Port_Number
6	Des host srv count	12	Start_time

metrics are applied, which are recall (RR), precision rate (PR), accuracy (ACC) and F1-measure [15]. These metrics are defined in Table 2.

Table 2. Performance metrics.

Metric	Defined
Recall rate (RR)	$RR = \frac{TP}{TP+FN}$
Precision rate (PR)	$PR = \frac{TP}{TP+FP}$
Accuracy (ACC)	$ACC = \frac{TP+TN}{TP+TN+FP+FN}$
F1-measure	$F1 = \frac{2(PR \times \text{Re}call)}{PR + \text{Re}call}$

Where TP, FP, TN, FN are four measurement factors of confusion matrix.

(1) True Positive: TP shows the number of attack records correctly anticipated as attacks.
(2) False Positive: FP shows the number of normal records correctly anticipated as normal.
(3) True Negative: TN shows the number of normal records incorrectly anticipated as normal attacks.
(4) False Negative: FN shows the number of attack records incorrectly anticipated as normal.

5.3   Results and Discussion

In this section, experiment results are presented in Table 3 and three performance metrics are considered to compare different systems of network intrusion detection. The details of the comparison has been showed in Table 4.

Table 3. Performance metrics of traffic classification.

Class	PR	ACC	Recall
Normal	0.999	0.994	0.942
Abnormal	0.961	0.984	0.984
Overall	0.983	0.991	0.951

Table 4. Comparison results in terms of three metrics.

Model	PR	Recall	F1-measure
Proposed	0.983	0.951	0.996
SVM [16]	0.971	0.929	0.950
Bayesian Net [17]	0.948	0.930	0.940
Neural Tree [18]	0.981	0.923	0.951

The results that described clearly in these tables strongly point out the proposed detection model in this paper enjoys the highest recall rate and relatively high precision rate in comparison with other models. Moreover, the value of F1-measure demonstrates that this system shows promising results compared with others. In particular, it can boost the efficiency of the intrusion detection in anomaly traffic, as show in Fig. 3.

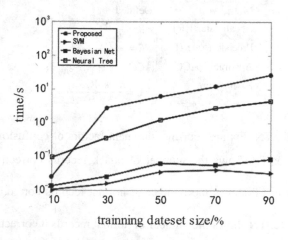

Fig. 3. Comparison of proposed model and other methods in training time

6   Conclusion and Future Work

This paper proposed a novel model of network intrusion detection based on anomaly traffic. Meanwhile, conditional entropy is creatively used to optimize the Baum-Welch algorithm. A series of experiments are completed. And performance metrics that are showed in Table 4 demonstrate the performance of the proposed network intrusion detection model is better than other models in terms of accuracy, precision and efficiency.

In the future, another worth investigating is to, with hidden Markov model, classify anomaly traffic into more categories like DOS, U2L, R2L and so on, which will makes network intrusion detection more accurate.

References

1. Potluri, S., Diedrich, C.: Accelerated deep neural networks for enhanced Intrusion Detection System. In: IEEE International Conference on Emerging Technologies & Factory Automation. IEEE (2016)
2. Bhuvaneswari, G., Manikandan, G.: A novel machine learning framework for diagnosing the type 2 diabetics using temporal fuzzy ant miner decision tree classifier with temporal weighted genetic algorithm. Computing **100**, 759–772 (2018)
3. Boukhris, I., Elouedi, Z., Ajabi, M.: Toward intrusion detection using belief decision trees for big data. Knowl. Inf. Syst. **53**, 671–698 (2017)
4. Elliott, R.J., Siu, T.K., Fung, E.S.: A Double HMM approach to Altman Z-scores and credit ratings. Expert Syst. Appl. **41**(4), 1553–1560 (2014)
5. Li, Z., Fang, H., Huang, M.: Diversified learning for continuous hidden Markov models with application to fault diagnosis. Expert Syst. Appl. **42**(23), 9165–9173 (2015)
6. Ying, J., Kirubarajan, T., Pattipati, K.R., et al.: A hidden Markov model-based algorithm for fault diagnosis with partial and imperfect tests. IEEE Trans. Syst. Man Cybern. Part C (Appl. Rev.) **30**(4), 463–473 (2000)
7. Cao, Y., Li, Y., Coleman, S., et al.: Adaptive hidden Markov model with anomaly states for price manipulation detection. IEEE Trans. Neural Netw. Learn. Syst. **26**(2), 318–330 (2015)
8. Soualhi, A., Clerc, G., Razik, H., et al.: Hidden Markov models for the prediction of impending faults. IEEE Trans. Industr. Electron. **63**(5), 3271–3281 (2016)
9. Komviriyavut, T., Sangkatsanee, P., Wattanapongsakorn, N., et al.: Network intrusion detection and classification with Decision Tree and rule based approaches. In: International Conference on Communications & Information Technologies. IEEE Press (2009)
10. Fung, C.J., Zhang, J., Boutaba, R.: Effective acquaintance management based on Bayesian learning for distributed intrusion detection networks. IEEE Trans. Netw. Serv. Manag. **9**(3), 320–332 (2012)
11. Saha, S.K., Sarkar, S., Mitra, P.: Feature selection techniques for maximum entropy based biomedical named entity recognition. J. Biomed. Inform. **42**(5), 905–911 (2009)
12. Kyoto 2006+ dataset Homepage. https://en.wikipedia.org/wiki/Conditional_entropy
13. Song, J., Takakura, H., Okabe, Y., et al.: Statistical analysis of honeypot data and building of Kyoto 2006+ dataset for NIDS evaluation. In: Workshop on Building Analysis Datasets & Gathering Experience Returns for Security (2011)
14. Callegari, C., Gazzarrini, L., Giordano, S., et al.: Improving PCA-based anomaly detection by using multiple time scale analysis and Kullback–Leibler divergence. Int. J. Commun. Syst. **27**(10), 1731–1751 (2015)
15. Almseidin, M., Alzubi, M., Kovacs, S., et al.: Evaluation of machine learning algorithms for intrusion detection system (2018)
16. Salama, M.A., Eid, H.F., Ramadan, R.A., Darwish, A., Hassanien, A.E.: Hybrid intelligent intrusion detection scheme. In: Gaspar-Cunha, A., Takahashi, R., Schaefer, G., Costa, L. (eds.) Soft Computing in Industrial Applications. AINSC, vol. 96, pp. 293–303. Springer, Heidelberg (2011). https://doi.org/10.1007/978-3-642-20505-7_26
17. Chebrolu, S., Abraham, A., Thomas, J.P.: Feature deduction and ensemble design of intrusion detection systems. Comput. Secur. **24**(4), 295–307 (2005)
18. Chen, Y., Abraham, A., Yang, B.: Feature selection and classification using flexible neural tree. Neurocomputing **70**(1–3), 305–313 (2006)

Superior Prosthetic Member Based on Assistive Technologies

Sorin Curea[1], Oana Geman[1(✉)], Iuliana Chiuchisan[1],
Valentina Balas[2], Guojun Wang[3], and Muhammad Arif[3]

[1] Stefan cel Mare University, 720229 Suceava, Romania
oana.geman@usm.ro
[2] Aurel Vlaicu University, 310130 Arad, Romania
[3] Guangzhou University, Guangzhou 510006, China

Abstract. Assistive Technology (AT) is a concept that refers to devices and services that can offset the functional limitations of people with disabilities and can facilitate their independent lives. Assistive Technology refers to products and services for those needs that are specific to people with disabilities, elderly and those with chronic diseases. AT allows these people to more in daily life and supports their independent life. In this paper, we propose the theoretical and practical approach to the use of AT instruments for a patient with the arm prosthesis. From communication to mobility, without forgetting devices that help the patient in daily activities, AT is a field of opportunities based on assistive equipment as solutions for social inclusion, health monitoring, and the life quality of the patients. Some of the objectives of this paper are: miniaturization of a bionic prosthesis, characteristic of the specific needs of the patient; the inclusion of sensors assigned to the prosthesis, by which the motion control is made, according to the interpretations the analysis of the sensors and the adaptation of prosthesis through the use of the assistive technologies.

Keywords: Disabilities · Prosthetic hand · Assistive Technologies

1 Introduction

Assistive Technologies (AT) are designed to make daily activities accessible to as many as possible people with disabilities through the most appropriate information/access set technologies. AT devices are tools used for the independent functioning of people with physical limitations or cognitive dysfunctions. Assistive technology, also known as access technology, represents all the mechanical, optical, electronic and computer solutions that provide greater autonomy to the people with sensory impairments, allowing them to perform tasks that are otherwise impossible to achieve or with major difficulties by improving or changing the mode of interaction with the technology needed to accomplish that task [1–4].

It is necessary to implement measures to ensure the distribution and efficient use of assistive technologies, in order to encourage future assistive technologies by maximizing the value of these technologies. These measures may include encouraging the involvement of people with disabilities in the developmental phases of future assistance

© Springer Nature Singapore Pte Ltd. 2019
G. Wang et al. (Eds.): iSCI 2019, CCIS 1122, pp. 520–530, 2019.
https://doi.org/10.1007/978-981-15-1301-5_41

technologies. Another measure that could be implemented in this direction is the promotion and development of new sectors of activity and occupational profiles dedicated to assistive technologies [5–8].

Nowadays, the specialists have intended to print human cells in various ways through rapid prototyping, on silicon models, cells that can also act as sensors. The new technology field develops devices and applications that promise to ease the lives of people with disabilities. The possibility of personalizing 3D prints can easily be customized at the digital model stage and respond to more and more problems at the same time.

The hand is one of the most complicated segments of the human body, due to its structural and functional adaptation to the complexity of human activities. Severe hand trauma creates a major handicap. The human hand is a masterpiece of mechanical complexity capable to perform both fine and powerful motor manipulations. The design of prosthesis for human hand that is close to its natural movements requires a great complexity of anatomical details to be modeled and simulated [8–12]. The movement of the hand prosthesis must be controlled by the muscular contraction created by the artificial muscles. It is desirable to develop a hybrid model to convert the values given by the actual contraction of the muscles to the action of the phalanges. Artificial muscles directly control bone rotation based on anatomical data and mechanical laws, and can deform artificial tissue with a spring system. The prosthesis will have to perform the correct movements from the anatomically and physically perspectives.

Some of the objectives of this paper are: miniaturization of a bionic prosthesis, characteristic of the specific needs of the patient; the inclusion of sensors assigned to the prosthesis, by which the motion control is made, according to the interpretations the analysis of the sensors and the adaptation of prosthesis through the use of the assistive technologies.

2 Related Work

In previous studies [13–19] we have proposed the use of intelligent sensors in various biomedical applications for support of elderly patients or for the people with various neurodegenerative disorders. The use of Ambient Assisted Living (AAT) or specific tools with Internet of Things (IoT) and Assisted Technologies (AT) contributes to increasing the quality of life of patients with special needs.

Nowadays, from the medicine perspective, prosthesis means any artificial device that replaces a part of the body, a part that is missing due to certain causes, generated by traumas, diseases, cognitive impairment or tumors. Each bionic prosthesis is individualized according to the individual profile of the whom it is intended to be attributed. In the design and assembly process of the prosthesis, the decision factors are provided by the analysis of the individual's appearance and needs [20].

With advances in biomedical sciences, some experimental prostheses have been integrated with body tissues, including the nervous system. These advanced devices can respond to commands in the central nervous system, getting closer to normal movement and use.

The prosthetic system is made up of all types of prostheses that come into its composition, among them: cosmetic, mechanical, electrical, pneumatic, and mioelectrical prostheses. Passive prostheses are usually designed to look like a natural arm, hand, and fingers. These prostheses are lightweight and, while not active, can improve a person's function by providing a surface for stabilizing or wearing objects. Passive prostheses can be covered with high-definition silicone that is custom-painted to resemble a person's arm, hand, and fingers, or with a basic manufacturing glove. Multiposition joints are sometimes combined with a passive prosthesis to provide the ability to position the shoulder, elbow, wrist, or finger joints to improve the function of a person [21].

Prostheses for a human organ are operated by a system of cables, harnesses, and sometimes-manual control. The movements of the upper body (arm, shoulder, and chest) are caught by a ham and a cable system and are used to control the prosthesis. As users become accustomed to the variable tension sensation on the cable, they can feel an improved look the position of the limbs and the degree of opening on the terminal device. People who are involved in manual labor may favor the durability and basic function of body-operated prostheses.

An electrically powered prosthesis includes motors and batteries that provide movement and strength of the prosthesis. The electrical components vary depending on the level of limb loss. There may be sensors or various inputs that detect muscle movement in the residual limb or upper body. These sensors or inputs then signal the motors in the prosthesis to provide the desired movements. Many electric prostheses have the option of being covered with a cosmetic glove. Cosmetic gloves are available in a wide range of color tones and can even be customized to fit the original hand [22].

Hybrid prostheses combine both body-powered and electrical components with a single prosthesis. In some cases, this combination may provide a better functional result. Hybrid prostheses are often useful for people with higher limb loss levels that require more than one moving component. A hybrid may have an increased variation in functions that can widen use in the workplace and other activities. Activity-specific prostheses are designed for an activity where a residual member without prostheses or with passive prostheses with body or electrical could be damaged or simply will not work as needed for specific activities. The active artificial prosthesis needs: an energy source, a resultant force transmission system, a control or action system, and a clamping device [23].

Prostheses are classified taking into account two important aspects, if they are active or passive. Cosmetic prostheses are passive prostheses because they cover only the aesthetic appearance, hence their name. Three materials can be used for cosmetic prostheses: rigid or flexible PVC, latex or silicone. These materials are light, maintenance-free because they have fewer moving parts than other prostheses. Latex is the most commonly used material for cosmetic restorations, usually a thin fabric, which comes in predetermined sizes called gloves to fit over the prosthetic hands.

The myoelectric prostheses are electrophoresis controlled by exothermic myoelectric sources. These prostheses are today the type of artificial member with the highest degree of rehabilitation. They have the best aesthetic appearance, high strength, adhesion and speed and can be found in many possible combinations. Myoelectric control is probably the most common. It is based on the concept that whenever a muscle contracts, it generates a small electrical signal of the chemical interaction that takes place in the body.

This signal is very small from 5 to 20 μV. This signal is one million times smaller than the electricity required to power a bulb. The use of sensors called electrodes that come into contact with the surface of the skin allows the recording of the electromyographic signal (EMG), once recorded, this signal being amplified and transmitted to the prosthesis [24–26].

The principle of prosthesis is the use of artificial parts (prostheses) to improve the vital function and lifestyle of people with motor deficiencies and beyond. In the case of the amputated arm from the shoulder, the new prosthesis control mode identifies all the nerve fibers that control the muscles of the affected member. They are individually implanted in the pectoral muscles, each nerve controlling a distinct muscular fiber [26]. When the patient wishes to close the fist, his brain transmits the remaining nerves and re-implants the command to the designated pectoral fibers, contracting them.

The prosthesis reads this muscular activity through an electromyogram (an investigation recording the electrical signals from the brain to the muscles), detecting what nerve has been attributed to that area of the pectoral, thus realizing the desired action.

3 The Proposed System

In this section, the system developed for a bionic prosthesis for an arm is presented. The proposed integrated system consists of two components: an assembly for the patient with the arm prosthesis and one for caretaker. The proposed system is used at the patient's home. The patient assembly includes motion and position sensors, a complex system for real-time monitoring of vital parameters (systolic and diastolic blood pressure, pulse, ECG, oxygen saturation in the blood, respiratory signal, EEG), an audio signaling system/or video and a radio transmitter. The caretaker or caregiver has a radio receiver system with a loudspeaker. The bionic prosthesis is characterized by the fact that, through the sensors, the signals transmitted by the brain acquired and transformed into the movements of the bionic arm. The components used for the prosthesis are:

- 3D printed elements;
- MyoWare sensors;
- FEETECH FT90R actuators;
- Nylon wire 0.5 mm;
- 9 V alkaline battery;
- ELEGOO MEGA 2560 Processing platform;
- Conductors;
- ECG electrodes.

The printing of the elements was performed with a 3D printer, Bitmi 2+ brand, using 1.75 mm PLA filament. The 3D printed elements are presented in Fig. 1.

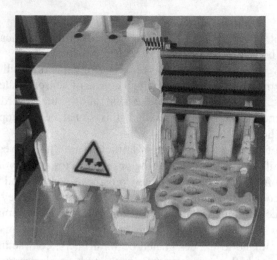

Fig. 1. The 3D printed elements.

In the developing process of the bionic prosthesis, MyoWare sensors were used to detect the nervous stimuli transmitted by the brain through which the actual limb movement is performed (see Fig. 2).

MyoWare muscular sensors are the latest review of traditional sensors, being improved by a design that allows the biometric sensor to be attached directly to the board itself, the need for cables attributed to the sensors being greatly reduced.

Among the new features that have been added to these sensors are the single power supply between 3.1–5 V, the RAW EMG output port, polarity-protected power terminals, LEDs, and finally a start/stop switch. Lately, several shields have been developed that can be attached to the sensors in order to increase the versatility and functionality.

Measuring muscle activity by detecting electrical potential, referring to EMG, has been used in medical research. However, immediately after emerging microprocessors and increasingly integrated and powerful circuits, EMG circuits and sensors have been integrated into all kinds of control systems.

The FT90R is a small-sized digital servomotor, produced by FEETECH (formerly known as Fitec), especially for continuous rotations. Powered by a 6 V voltage, it has a maximum rotation speed of about 135 RPM (without load) and can produce a torque of up to 21 oz-in (1.5 kg-cm).

The servomotor can be controlled through a direct connection to an I/O line of the microcontroller without any additional electronics, making it an excellent miniature actuator for robotic projects.

Fig. 2. MyoWare senzor.

ELEGOO MEGA 2560 presented in Fig. 3 is a development kit based on the Atmega2560 microcontroller. It has 54 digital inputs/outputs, of which 15 can be used as PWM outputs. The development kit contains 16 analog inputs, 4 hardware serial ports, 16 MHz crystal oscillator. The kit includes a USB port that provides PC connection, a power jack, and a reset button. The kit has everything it need to support the microcontroller.

It is powered by connecting to a computer via a USB cable, with an AC-DC adapter or a battery. The ELEGOO MEGA 2560 is compatible with the most shields made for Arduino Uno or past editions of the Duemilanove or Diecimila kits. Thus, the Mega2560 is a version that has been improved by bringing new features and functions to the Arduino Mega kit, which is replaced by it.

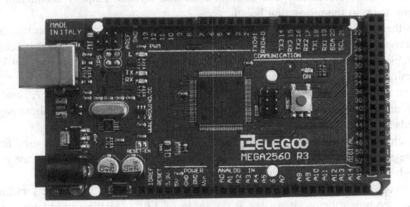

Fig. 3. ELEGOO MEGA 2560 development kit.

The operation principle of this prosthesis consists in acquiring the electromyographic signals specific to each finger movement using the EMG (electromyographic) sensors. After acquiring the signals, they are interpreted by the processing board, which transmit command to the actuator specific to each finger of the prosthesis. The control system of the prosthesis is shown in Fig. 4.

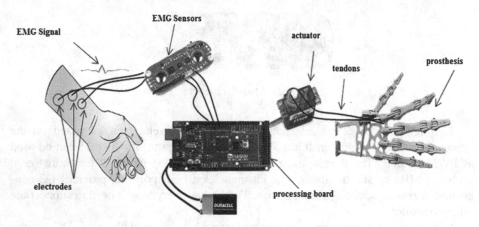

Fig. 4. The control system of the prosthesis.

In order to acquire the electromyographic signals, a series of electrodes are used, which are glued to the forearm in precise areas. These signals are acquired by the EMG sensors through electrodes. The sensors filter the signals, amplify them, and then transmit them to the processing board.

In the case of muscle relaxation, the sensor following the state of contraction of the respective muscle sends a signal of amplitude between 60–100 mV to the processing board, as is shown in Fig. 5. Otherwise, a signal with an amplitude between 2.5–3 V is transmitted, as is shown in Fig. 5.

The signals are acquired by the processing board via analogue ports A0 and A1. These are analyzed by the processing board. When the amplitude of these signals exceeds 2 V, the rotary control is transmitted to the servomotor.

Each finger of the prosthesis is controlled by two-nylon wire; a wire is used for the closure movement, and the other for the opening movement. These wires are routed through individual paths to servomotors.

Servomotors are mounted at the bottom of the prosthesis. When the servomotor receives co-turn rotation, it rotates at an angle of 170°. On the servomotor shaft is mounted a lever that holds the nylon wires at the ends at one finger. After turning the actuator, finger movement is performed.

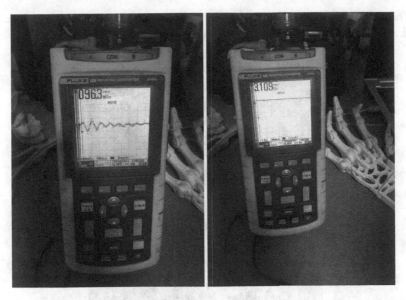

Fig. 5. Amplitude between 60–100 mV in the left and amplitude between 2.5–3 V in the right.

The first successful situation is where the prosthesis identified the signals by which the flip-open command was given. This is illustrated by the Figs. 6, 7, and 8, which show the beneficial result obtained. The second situation concerns the opening and closing of a finger. It is to be noted that these commands are performed independently by one finger, the other being in a state of rest. The result obtained is shown in Fig. 6.

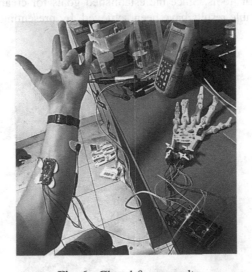

Fig. 6. Closed finger result.

When one finger is closed, the sensors responsible for this action are those positioned above the forearm, as can be seen in Fig. 6.

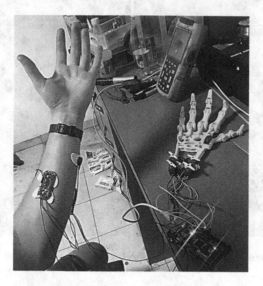

Fig. 7. Open - fist result.

If the amplitude of the signals is less than 2 V, then the primary servomotor is commanded to remain in the 10° position. The power card is powered by two Duracell 9 V batteries. The design and development of the processing platforms was performed with the Arduino IDE tools. Since the established goals for creating prosthesis have been fulfilled, favorable results have been achieved, by presenting the ways in which protease operates.

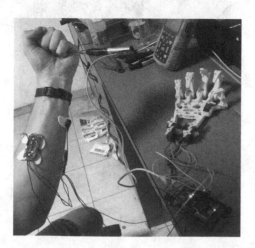

Fig. 8. Closed - fist result.

As shown in Figs. 7 and 8, the goal of closing opening the first was a challenge. The sensors responsible for identifying the signals are the positioned on the back of the forearm as shown in Figs. 7 and 8. The advantages of the prosthesis presented in this paper can be the following: low costs, low energy consumption, accessibility for all categories of individuals, simple, pleasant design, easy to adapt, according to the needs of each person, easy to attach.

4 Conclusions

Due to the social and technical regulatory tendencies of identified assistance technologies, they play a very important role in the lives of people with disabilities, supporting their integration into society, education and employment.

The advantages of the hand prosthesis presented in this paper can be the following: low costs, low energy consumption, accessibility for all categories of individuals, simple, attractive design, easy to adapt, according to the needs of each person, easy to attach.

In other words, the prosthesis obtained has all the features of an accessible neuroprosthesis, form both functionally and financially perspective.

Acknowledgement. This work was supported from the project GUSV – "Intelligent Techniques for Medical Applications using Sensor Networks", Project No. 10BM/2018, financed by UEFISCDI, Romania under the PNIII framework.

References

1. Arif, M., et al.: Maximizing information of multimodality brain image fusion using curvelet transform with genetic algorithm. In: 2014 International Conference on Computer Assisted System in Health (2014)
2. Arif, M., Wang, G.: Segmentation of calcification and brain hemorrhage with midline detection. In: 2017 IEEE International Symposium on Parallel and Distributed Processing with Applications and 2017 IEEE International Conference on Ubiquitous Computing and Communications (2017)
3. Qaisar, J., et al.: A hybrid technique for de-noising multi-modality medical images by employing cuckoo's search with curvelet transform. Mehran Univ. Res. J. Eng. Technol. **37**(1), 29–48 (2018)
4. Arif, M., Wang, G.: Fast curvelet transform through genetic algorithm for multimodal medical image fusion. Soft Comput. 1–22 (2019)
5. Scott, R.N.: Feedback in myoelectric prostheses. Clin. Orthop. Relat. Res. **256**, 58–63 (1990)
6. Scott, R.N.: Myoelectric control systems research at the Bio-Engineering Institute, University of New Brunswick. Med. Prog. Technol. **16**, 5–10 (1990)
7. Kelly, M.F., Parker, P.A., Scott, R.N.: The application of neural networks to myoelectric signal analysis: a preliminary study. IEEE Trans. Biomed. Eng. **37**, 221–230 (1990)
8. Lake, C., Miguelez, J.: Comparative analysis of microprocessors in upper-extremity prosthetics. J. Prosthet. Orthot. **15**, 48–65 (2003)

9. Michael, J.W., Gailey, R.S., Bowker, J.H.: New developments in recreational prostheses and adaptive devices for the amputee. Clin. Orthop. Relat. Res. **256**, 64–75 (1990)
10. Meeks, D., LeBlanc, M.: Preliminary assessment of three new designs of prosthetic prehensors for upper limb amputees. Prosthet. Orthot. Int. **12**, 41–45 (2001)
11. Kruit, J., Cool, J.C.: Body-powered hand prosthesis with low operating power for children. J. Med. Eng. Technol. **13**, 129–133 (1989)
12. Sensky, T.E.: A simple and versatile driving appliance for upper-limb amputees. Prosthet. Orthot. Int. **4**, 47–49 (2002)
13. Geman, O., Hagan, M., Chiuchisan, I.: A novel device for peripheral neuropathy assessment and rehabilitation. In: 2016 International Conference and Exposition on Electrical and Power Engineering (EPE), pp. 309–312 (2016)
14. Barleanu, A., Hagan, M., Geman, O., Chiuchisan, I.: Wearable ballistocardiography system for heartbeat detection. In: 2016 International Conference and Exposition on Electrical and Power Engineering (EPE), pp. 294–298 (2016)
15. Chiuchisan, I., Geman, O., Prelipceanu, M., Costin, H.-N.: Healthcare system for monitoring older adults in a "green" environment using organic photovoltaic devices. Environ. Eng. Manag. J. (EEMJ) **15**, 2595–2604 (2016)
16. Geman, O., Chiuchisan, I., Ungurean, I., Hagan, M., Arif, M.: Ubiquitous healthcare system based on the sensors network and Android Internet of Things gateway. In: 2018 IEEE SmartWorld, Ubiquitous Intelligence Computing, Advanced Trusted Computing, Scalable Computing Communications, Cloud & Big Data Computing, Internet of People and Smart City Innovation (SmartWorld/SCALCOM/UIC/ATC/CBDCom/IOP/SCI), pp. 1390–1395 (2018)
17. Chiuchisan, I., Geman, O., Postolache, O.: Future trends in exergaming using MS Kinect for medical rehabilitation. In: 2018 International Conference and Exposition on Electrical and Power Engineering (EPE), pp. 0683–0687 (2018)
18. Geman, O., Chiuchisan, I., Hagan, M.: Body sensor networks and Internet of Things for management and screening of patients with diabetic neuropathy. In: 2018 International Conference and Exposition on Electrical and Power Engineering (EPE), pp. 0688–0692 (2018)
19. Geman, O., Postolache, O.A., Chiuchisan, I., Prelipceanu, M., Hemanth, D.J.: An intelligent assistive tool using exergaming and response surface methodology for patients with brain disorders. IEEE Access **7**, 21502–21513 (2019)
20. Chappell, P.H., Kyberd, P.J.: Prehensile control of a hand prosthesis by a microcontroller. J. Biomed. Eng. **13**, 363–369 (1991)
21. Bergman, K., Ornholmer, L., Zackrisson, K., Thyberg, M.: Functional benefit of an adaptive myoelectric prosthetic hand compared to a conventional myoelectric hand. Prosthet. Orthot. Int. **16**, 32–37 (1997)
22. Almstrom, C., Herberts, P., Körner, L.: Experience with Swedish multifunctional prosthetic hands controlled by pattern recognition of multiple myoelectric signals. Int. Orthop. **5**, 15–21 (1981)
23. Bender, L.F.: Upper-extremity prosthetics. In: Handbook of Physical Medicine and Rehabilitation, 4th ed. WB Saunders, Philadelphia (1990)
24. Miguelez, J., Lake, C., Conyers, D., Zenie, J.: The transradial anatomically contoured (TRAC) interface: design principles and methodology. J. Prosthet. Orthot. **15**, 148–157 (2003)
25. Andrews, J.T.: Principles of prosthetics. In: Atlas of Limb Prosthetics, 2nd edn, pp. 255–265. Mosby-Year Book, Inc., St Louis (2002)
26. Lipschutz, R.D., Kuiken, T.A., Miller, L.A., Dumanian, G.A., Stubblefield, K.A.: Shoulder disarticulation externally powered prosthetic fitting following targeted muscle innervation for improved myoelectric prosthesis control. J. Prosthet. Orthot. **18**, 28–34 (2006)

Rehabilitation System by Interest Induction with VR and MR

Xingrun Shen[1(✉)], Kazuyoshi Yoshino[2], and Shanjun Zhang[1]

[1] Kanagawa University, Yokohama, Kanagawa 259-1293, Japan
Machiko1993@gmail.com
[2] Kanagawa Institute of Technology, Atsugi, Kanagawa 243-0292, Japan

Abstract. This study is to use VR and MR technology to intelligently help user get physical and psychology rehabilitation train. System can enter a recovery training plan based on recovery to the position of the disorder, and the purpose is to build a rehab system that promotes pleasure without a supervisor. For this purpose, we will create an experimental VR game that can guide the user's movement, record healthy university students as samples of health, collect sample images, and build a reference model of health. Then, each category of VR games of interest induction including animation characters is produced. Psychology rehabilitation train can provide special scenes to effect user with visual impact. Finally, field experiments are conducted to examine the function and user experience of the rehabilitation system by interest induction.

Keywords: Rehabilitation · User experience · VR MR · Game · Intelligently diagnose · Animation character

1 Introduction

In recent years, research on rehabilitation systems using VR technology has been developed. Among them, rehabilitation support is developed for patients who are in need of movement disorder, but the guidance doctor has to teach by side from disability symptom judgment to recovery training, that is, the patient's will need a supervisor who will grasp your health status and lead you into your recovery plan. There are many cases that same screen and operation occur in the recovery training process. And progressing under the instruction of the instructor leads. The patients recognized that the training is not a game but a medical practice. It will weaken the patient's interest and subjective awareness. Furthermore, the recovery training plan provided by the attending physician is expensive with human resources, and there is also the problem that only nursing homes and medical institutions can provide only a few services. Therefore, we need a kind of VR game which can guiding the user's movement, while making diagnosis by intelligently analyzes the image of point movements and proceed to the next recovery training by the diagnosis result which does not need a supervisor. It will emphasize the user's interest induction with the rehearsal system too.

The cause of using the VR game is the VR technology that cannot see user's own body is relies heavily on sense of vision, so that the painful feeling will be suppressed [1]. Therefore, it can be used that discomfort and tension are largely suppressed during

© Springer Nature Singapore Pte Ltd. 2019
G. Wang et al. (Eds.): iSCI 2019, CCIS 1122, pp. 531–541, 2019.
https://doi.org/10.1007/978-981-15-1301-5_42

training. And entertainment recognition depends on many evaluation factors. Since this research focuses on interest induction and rehabilitation, the installation of VR games is classified into "motion judgment games", "curiosity training games", "tension feeling training games" and "achievement feeling training games". Furthermore, as KDDI research showed, virtual YouTuber viewers created by motion tracking technology can feel a sense of security, empathy and self-affirmation [2], and in the VR game, animation characters express user's movements in real time, this point is to provide service of nursing homes and rehabilitation institution with sense of fulfillment and happiness.

VR technology is a technology that captures people and conveys them to people and is considered highly applicable to medical welfare [3]. In order to realize pleasant rehabilitation, VR related simulator technology is advanced to the field of medical welfare. Train efficiently using limited resources, which requires accuracy and real-time capability [4]. Not only in patients but also in studies involving the elderly, they argue that the elderly should actively adopt muscle training [5]. The VR rehabilitation system acts as a physical therapist and can provide effective coaching to users. The process of performing physical therapy must grasp the subject's mental state and training procedure and needs a sense of achievement of the goal during training [6].

Communication is the essence of human life, and it is connected with huge invisible lines in the current network age. The connection between humans and computers has been discussed in the field of information sociology, and various research results have attracted attention. There are individual differences in attitudes towards the character, and cuteness is related to interaction and sensibility [7]. The reaction to the user is an important reputation. The fun of computer games is related to intrinsic motives, and includes "challenge," "curiosity," "competition," etc., and classifications of "fun of sensorimotor skills", "fun of visual excitement", and "fun of challenge" [8].

2 VR Games

A. Create the VR game
The experimental environment of this study, one PC for VR runs with software on Windows 10. The hardware using VR game environment development is HTC Vive Pro HMD, and the game engine is Unity 3D (v2016.2). The game images were produced with Photoshop and 3dsMAX. Image analysis uses OpenCV for unity. Use Kinect for Windows to work with Unity3D to simultaneously express user movements in a 3D model.

B. Operation judgment game
Firstly, the core of the action judgment game is the ability to observe the entire body. Create an inspection game which can analyze user body completely in order to understand the user's health condition. To express the user's movement in real time,

the animation character is given the coordinates of the user's bones through the Kinect, using the official "Kinect for Windows SDK" from Microsoft. As shown in Fig. 1, since the user's presence is recognized, the coordinates of bone marrow can be seen.

Begin the movement of anime characters. A movement target is set in a certain safety activity space. The guidance target object moves by a prescribed rule. In order to reach the goal, the user's actions can proceed to a prescribed rule. The guidance target object is placed at a distance that both hands can deliver from the character, and guides from the lower right to the upper left to the lower left so that the entire body can be moved.

Using this game to diagnose health conditions, motion data is taken from one health university student, and this data is used as a basic sample to construct a basic model for experiments.

Fig. 1. Class: getbonestransform

The movement of the user is compared with the model in real time, and the part that does not match is indicated by the "GUI.Box" as the failure position. Then, it is set to enter the next VR game (next recovery training) based on the judgment of the failure position.

Here, the meaning of using the animation character is that the animation character existing in the virtual space is expressed the action of the user in front of the eyes through the VR, it looks like the user's movement clearly and sympathizes like a mirror. Therefore, users can imagine cute characters in their own bodies. Under the influence, the user enters the virtual world from the lonely reality and reduce psychological pain. Furthermore, user can imagine the awareness of being young and healthy, project that positive awareness to the reality of myself, and hope to improve the rehabilitation effect.

C. Curiosity Training Game

Secondly, the core of the curiosity training game is to draw out the user's curiosity and to explore spontaneously. Here we make a puzzle recovery training game that can be guided to a sense of problem solving. Since the puzzle game does not have a time limit, users can achieve their goals slowly, and have time to get used to their bodies, and proceed with a search as Fig. 2.

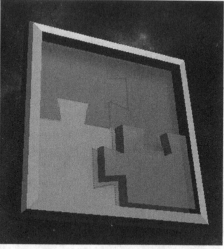

Fig. 2. Puzzle game

The same action is happily duplicated for training. Depending on the judgment of the obstacle position, the place where the puzzle target board appears differs. The number of pieces can control the number of repetitions, and the position of the puzzle board can adjust the distance between the trainable body part and the distance. It is to decide by the purpose of use.

D. Tension Training Game

Thirdly, the core of the tension training game is that it gives user a sense of tension and can carry out high-intensity training. Here, create enemies that randomly fall on users who are given pressure.

The user has to destroy the falling ones in a limited amount of time, the points decrease if they fall to the ground. The tension that results from this pressure can gather concentration, reduce pain and suffering, and perform difficult training. As shown in Fig. 3.

If the target is pierced before falling, it disappears, and the target falls from a new position at random within the range of ±5.0 f. The number of enemies falling and the sense of distance to the user are variables that give pressure to the user.

With the previous fault diagnosis, a large number of enemies are set up from a long distance from the specified direction of training needs and fly toward the user. The user

Fig. 3. Tense game

has a sword in the hand and cutting an enemy within the 'reach' is a success, and 'inability' is a failure. In order to ensure safety and accuracy, this game prohibits all user position movement in the real space. The image analysis system also analyzes the Kinect captured image with OpenCV and diagnoses the user's condition. The time to enter the image analysis system is only the "moment to cut".

E. Sense of Achievement Training Game

Fourthly, the core of the sense of accomplishment training game is to go through a difficult and painful process until user achieve a certain goal. Here we create an "irritated stick" game. The user holds a bar and advances to the prescribed rudder, it is judged to be a failure when hitting the pathway wall, and it is a game that starts over from the beginning. Focusing on the spirit so that it does not hit the 'Rood wall', overcoming the pain caused by movement and reaching the end point, user can feel a strong sense of accomplishment.

It works as a training which usually be easy to give up. As shown in Fig. 4, when the hand-held iron wheel comes in contact with the pathway, it returns to the beginning. pathway is not a smooth flat surface, and there are particularly difficult parts. It will turn blue if it can arrive to the end with care. Here, the complexity of the pathway also allows control of concentration and sense of accomplishment.

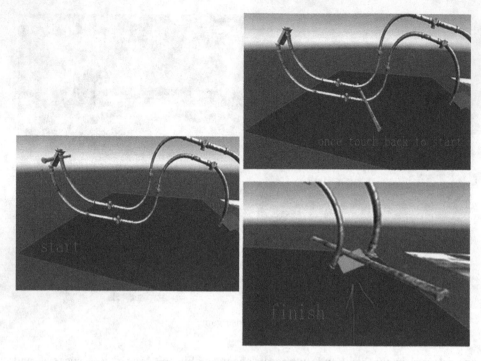

Fig. 4. Achievement feeling game

The previous diagnosis provides a pathway that points to the obstacles in need of training. The hardest part is that user need control the muscles carefully where need to be training with bear suffering and pain. And the sense of accomplishment given at the end suppresses painful memories. This micro control can also be the basis for complete recovery.

3 Game System and Experience

The theme system structure is classified into three courses of "experimental", "training enhancement" and "health exercise" as shown in Fig. 5.

Since the experimental course is started, it enters an easy-to-understand action judgment game, and user can easily experience the form and relevance of the game. Doctors can observe the analysis results of the examination and the setting of recovery training and understand the sense of the user who contacts the VR game for the first time. In the game of curiosity, user can slowly learn how to operate the environment and steering wheel of the virtual world and explore in the game.

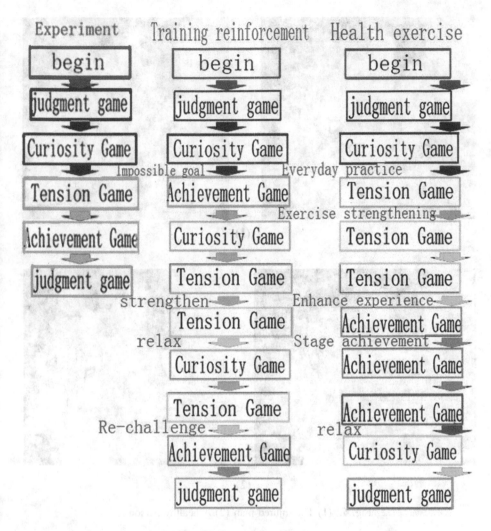

Fig. 5. Course classification

At the beginning, the screen looks clear with simple puzzles, so the possibility of VR sickness is low. After getting used to operations related to VR, the movement gets intensely tense. If user can move your body sufficiently, they will progress to a micro control achievement feeling game and perform intensive training intensively. Finally, it is the structure that it enters an inspection game again and verifies the training effect.

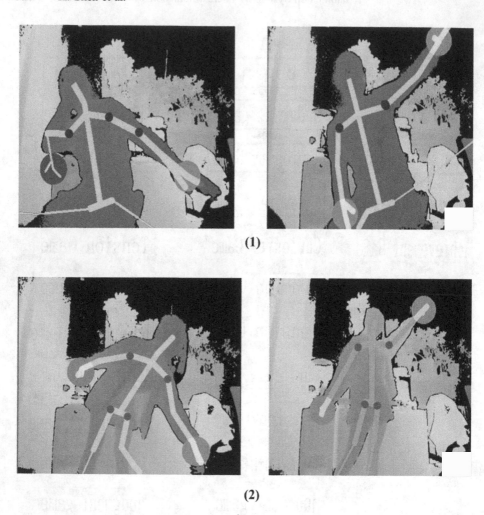

Fig. 6. (1) The injured man (2) A healthy person

The puzzle game is a simple puzzle game experience experiment in order to guide the user's movement and to validate the effect. Normal college students with a patient who right shoulder muscles are damaged are experience the puzzle game.

As Fig. 6(1) and (2) show. During the course of achieving the goal of the game, the patient voluntarily raises his right shoulder and receives training, expressing that there is no refusal such as pain.

4   MR Experience

The MR experience game for psychology rehabilitation train without human experiment is about PTSD rehabilitation and overcome phobia.

People are vulnerable and the mind needs careful nursing. After a fire, survivors sometimes experience intense fear and powerlessness. It's very difficult for patients to overcome the discomfort barrier if they want to recover from the trauma, it takes a long time, the higher the cost.

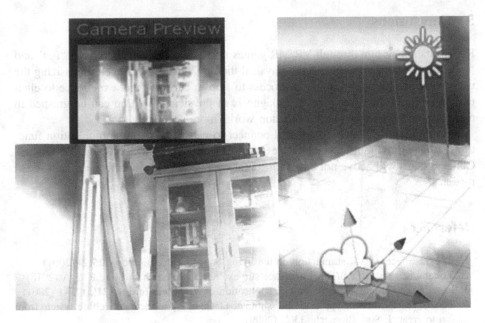

Fig. 7. Fire scene

If use VR as usual, it can take scenes that are difficult to reproduce in reality and build them with digital models. Give the patient the necessary stimulation. Use the scene corresponding to the disorder for psychotherapy. Specific virtual space can not only build materials, but also expect more exciting effects than the real scene. By influencing their thoughts and bringing them back to the place of fear, they can help. As a result, time and costs tend to fall.

However, the created scenes and objects must be created one by one, and the same screen stimulation effect cannot be expected. The connection with reality is deeply related to the patient's image ability, and the stimulus effect depends on the screen effect and the sense of presence.

Therefore, we are thinking of a solution that uses mixed reality to connect the real world and the virtual space in real life. Mixed reality can change what is visible in front of you in real time.

For example as Fig. 7, a fire simulate, you can "burn" things in the space where the user is in real time and experience a real fire scene. In mixed reality, you can directly simulate disaster scenes in the real world right before your eyes.

There is almost no lack of presence, especially in the daily life of the place simulated fire, the stimulation effect will be greatly improved. In addition, the steps of constructing virtual space are reduced. By utilizing the space recognition function of the composite reality device "HoloLens", the object recognition and "burning" can be calculated in real time and the picture can be constructed. The time and cost can be greatly reduced.

5 Conclusions

Rehabilitation system through VR/MR games and anime characters conveys "fun" and "fulfillment" to users, with execute physical therapy efficiently. Since emphasizing the user experience, it is an important process to step in curiosity and experience to elicit user interest. At the same time, the diagnosis of physical condition can be grasped in real time, and the rehabilitation function works more accurately.

In the future, I believe that it will connect to networks, add communication functions. It may draw out the social issues and competitiveness with VR and MR games. Game systems will active not only in medical welfare but also in kinematics and social media.

References

1. Ino, S.: Effects of VR stimulation on the living body. J. Soc. Biomech. **25**(2) (2001)
2. Yokota, K.: Virtual YouTuber audience survey. KDDI Research Institute R & A (2018)
3. Kuroda, T.: Current status of welfare application of VR. Med. Inform. **21**(5), 341 (2001)
4. Terada, H.: Toward the application of simulator technology to medical welfare system from fun to great. J. Soc. Biomech. **33**(2) (2009)
5. Asakawa, Y.: Strength and strength training for the elderly. Phys. Ther. Sci. **18**(1), 25–40 (2003)
6. Nara, I., Nagashima, F.: Coaching theory for physiotherapists. Mov. Physiol. **9**, 157–162 (1994)
7. Hisao, S.: On the cuteness and interactivity of characters. Kogakuin University Research Report No. 112 (2013)
8. Yamashita, T.: Analysis of characteristics and enjoyment of computer games. J. Jpn. Soc. Educ. Technol. **28**(4), 349–355 (2004)
9. Rose, T., Nam, C.S., Chen, K.B.: Immersion of virtual reality for rehabilitation – review. Appl. Ergon. **69**, 153–161 (2018)
10. Ma, S.: EMG biofeedback based VR system for hand rotation and grasping rehabilitation. In: 14th International Conference on Information Visualisation, IV 2010, London, UK, 26–29 July 2010. IEEE (2010)
11. Beemster, T.T., van Velzen, J.M., van Bennekom, C.A.M.: Test-retest reliability, agreement and responsiveness of productivity loss (iPCQ-VR) and healthcare utilization (TiCP-VR) questionnaires for sick workers with chronic musculoskeletal pain. J. Occup. Rehabil. **29**(1), 91–103 (2019)
12. Wang, Z., Lubetzky, A., Gospodarek, M.: Virtual environments for rehabilitation of postural control dysfunction (2019)
13. Sorrento, G., Archambault, P.S., Fung, J.: Adaptation and post-adaptation effects of haptic forces on locomotion in healthy young adults. J. Neuroeng. Rehabil. **15**(1), 20 (2018)

14. Dhiman, A., Solanki, D., Bhasin, A.: An intelligent, adaptive, performance-sensitive, and virtual reality-based gaming platform for the upper limb. Comput. Animat. Virtual Worlds **29**(2), e1800 (2018)
15. Hussain, N., Alt Murphy, M., Sunnerhagen, K.S.: Upper limb kinematics in stroke and healthy controls using target-to-target task in virtual reality. Front. Neurol. **9**, 300 (2018)
16. Wout, M., Spofford, C.M., Unger, W.S.: Skin conductance reactivity to standardized virtual reality combat scenes in veterans with PTSD. Appl. Psychophysiol. Biofeedback **42**(1), 1–13 (2017)
17. Rizzo, A.S., Shilling, R.: Clinical virtual reality tools to advance the prevention, assessment, and treatment of PTSD. Eur. J. Psychotraumatology **8**(5), 1414560 (2017)
18. Gavhane, A., Kokkula, G., Shinde, S.: Virtual reality: a possible technology to subdue disorder and disability. In: International Conference on Global Trends in Signal Processing. IEEE (2017)
19. Taylor, S.: Comparative efficacy, speed, and adverse effects of three PTSD treatments: exposure therapy, EMDR, and relaxation training. J. Consult. Clin. Psychol. **71**(2), 330–338 (2003)
20. Brady, K.T.: Exposure therapy in the treatment of PTSD among cocaine-dependent individuals: preliminary findings. J. Subst. Abus. Treat. **21**(1), 35–45 (2001)
21. Stanley, I.: Posttraumatic stress disorder symptoms and mindfulness facets in relation to suicide risk among firefighters. J. Clin. Psychol. **75**(4), 696–709 (2019)
22. Dias, P.: Using virtual reality to increase motivation in poststroke rehabilitation. IEEE Comput. Graph. Appl. **39**(1), 64–70 (2019)
23. Rast, J., Roux, A.M., Shattuck, P.T.: Use of vocational rehabilitation supports for postsecondary education among transition-age youth on the autism spectrum. J. Autism Dev. Disord. (2019)
24. Geman, O., Postolache, O.A., Chiuchisan, I.: An intelligent assistive tool using exergaming and response surface methodology for patients with brain disorders. IEEE Access **7**, 21502–21513 (2019)
25. Rangelova, S., Flutura, S., Huber, T., Motus, D., André, E.: Exploration of physiological signals using different locomotion techniques in a VR adventure game. In: Antona, M., Stephanidis, C. (eds.) HCII 2019. LNCS, vol. 11572, pp. 601–616. Springer, Cham (2019). https://doi.org/10.1007/978-3-030-23560-4_44
26. Delaney, E.: Predicting firearms performance based on psychiatric symptoms and medication usage. Prof. Psychol. Res. Pract. **49**(3), 227–233 (2018)
27. Tarrant, J.M., Viczko, J., Cope, H.: Virtual reality for anxiety reduction demonstrated by quantitative EEG: a pilot study. Front. Psychol. **9**, 1280 (2018)
28. Guillén, V., Baños, R.M., Botella, C.: Users' opinion about a virtual reality system as an adjunct to psychological treatment for stress-related disorders: a quantitative and qualitative mixed-methods study. Front. Psychol. **9**, 1038 (2018)

Bone-Conduction Audio Interface to Guide People with Visual Impairments

Jacobus C. Lock[1]([✉]), Iain D. Gilchrist[2], Grzegorz Cielniak[1], and Nicola Bellotto[1]

[1] University of Lincoln, Lincoln LN6 7TS, UK
{jlock,gcielniak,nbellotto}@lincoln.ac.uk
[2] University of Bristol, Bristol BS8 1TH, UK
i.d.gilchrist@bristol.ac.uk

Abstract. The ActiVis project's aim is to build a mobile guidance aid to help people with limited vision find objects in an unknown environment. This system uses bone-conduction headphones to transmit audio signals to the user and requires an effective non-visual interface. To this end, we propose a new audio-based interface that uses a spatialised signal to convey a target's position on the horizontal plane. The vertical position on the median plan is given by adjusting the tone's pitch to overcome the audio localisation limitations of bone-conduction headphones. This interface is validated through a set of experiments with blindfolded and visually impaired participants.

Keywords: Human-machine interface · Vision impairment · Spatialised sound · Varying pitch · Bone-conduction

1 Introduction

In recent years, governments have spearheaded numerous initiatives to support people with disabilities and enable them to play a more active role in modern society. The UK's Royal National Institute of Blind People (RNIB) for example has prioritised improving access to everyday services and products, such as public transport and mobile apps [26]. Improvements in modern computing have made it possible for new and innovative solutions to these problems to come to the fore. In particular, researchers in the active vision field have made much progress in enabling machines to autonomously manipulate cameras to gather information about an environment for mapping and object finding tasks [2,21]. There is, however, a significant research question about whether techniques from active machine vision can be applied to humans, i.e. can a machine identify a point of interest in a scene and direct a human, instead of an electronic servo, to focus on that point? If this can be done, it would be beneficial to people with visual impairments and will augment their ability to search for an arbitrary point or object of interest and identify an unknown scene.

© Springer Nature Singapore Pte Ltd. 2019
G. Wang et al. (Eds.): iSCI 2019, CCIS 1122, pp. 542–553, 2019.
https://doi.org/10.1007/978-981-15-1301-5_43

The ActiVis[1] project aims to deliver a mobile guidance system that will ultimately be able to guide a user with vision impairments on the last leg of their journey, i.e. the so-called 'last 10-yard problem'. The prototype platform is based on a Google Project Tango[2] device, pictured in Fig. 1a and b, that embeds a colour camera and provides access to powerful real-time localisation (through IMU measurements and landmark tracking) and image-processing facilities. It also provides access to Android's full range of interface tools and I/O options. Furthermore, a set of bone-conduction headphones (pictured in Fig. 1b), which are placed on a user's cheekbones instead of their ears and do not interfere with normal hearing, are used to transmit the audio signals to the user.

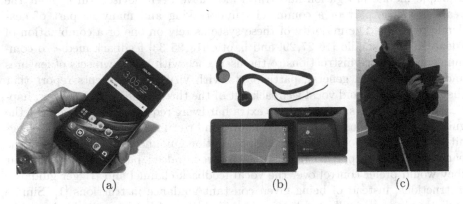

(a)   (b)   (c)

Fig. 1. Pictures of the latest Tango mobile phone (left), the former Tango tablet and the bone-conduction headphones used in this work (centre), and a participant with visual impairments during an experiment (right).

Humans are able to determine the 3D position of a sound source and by exploiting this natural ability, the real-time guidance instructions can easily be interpreted without posing a significant cognitive load. A sound source can be spatialised by adjusting a tone's spectral make-up (elevation angle), time delay and level difference (pan angle), and intensity (distance). In our case, only the pan and elevation positions are transmitted to the user to point the camera towards a target object or visual feature. However, since bone-conduction headphones bypass the outer ear structure, their spectral signature cannot properly be interpreted and we therefore convey the target's elevation angle by adjusting the tone's pitch. A similar approach was used in [8], but the study did not focus on or investigate the interface's efficacy. Indeed, the work presented in this paper serves as an initial study into an interface that can effectively communicate the pan and elevation angles of a target location through a set of bone-conduction headphones using standard audio libraries and audio manip-

---

[1] https://lcas.github.io/ActiVis/.
[2] https://en.wikipedia.org/wiki/Tango_(platform).

ulations. Furthermore, we demonstrate this approach's effectiveness through a simple experiment.

The rest of the paper starts by discussing previous relevant works and research in Sect. 2, followed by a discussion on the design and implementation of our interface in Sect. 3. This is followed by a description of the experiments that were conducted and a discussion of their results in Sect. 4. Finally, the paper concludes with a summary and a short discussion on future research prospects in Sect. 5.

2 Previous Work

Multiple mobile navigation and travel aids have been devised throughout the years, some as part of a commercial undertaking and many as part of academic research. The majority of these systems rely on one or a combination of vocal [7,14,23], audio [16,27,29] and haptic [18,25,33] feedback media to communicate guidance instructions to the user, each with their own sets of features and limitations. In general, participants with visual impairments report that they prefer haptic and vocal feedback out of the three options [1]. However, haptic feedback systems typically have extra hardware requirements to transmit the guidance instructions. Furthermore, haptic and vocal feedback can become a cognitive burden, particularly where high resolution guidance, which can exceed the bandwidth of these particular senses, is required. Indeed, participants report that they would prefer control over the vocal feedback channel and trigger guidance instructions, instead of being given constant guidance instructions [1]. Simple audio tones are less affected by these bandwidth and hardware limitations, but they can potentially fatigue the user's senses if too unpleasant.

Researchers have investigated using audio signals that are spatialised with a head-related transfer function (HRTF), simulating a sound source located at some arbitrary 3D position [6,11,16,32]. The authors generally report favourable results for this guidance approach when used with standard over-ear headphones or speakers. However, other authors have found that the choice of audio transmission medium can have a significant effect on performance. Cheaper headphones and bone-conduction headphones generally report unfavourable results when compared to over-ear or more expensive alternatives [22,28,31]. This seems to be limited to the elevation dimension, however, and can be improved with HRTFs adjusted for the bone-conduction pathway [31]. In [8], they transmit a target's elevation angle by adjusting the signal's pitch and report favourable results. However, these studies focussed on their system's total effectiveness, rather than the effectiveness of the pitch adjustment mechanism alone. In the next sections we want to investigate this more closely.

3 Interface Description

3.1 Hardware Selection

Electronic navigation aids and guidance systems for people with vision impairments often have acceptability and usability problems due to limitations in academic research and prototypes, such as prohibitive costs, unfriendly user interfaces and significant hardware requirements (e.g. head-mounted cameras and GPS antennae) [1,12,34]. Indeed, the traditional walking cane remains the standard tool for navigation and obstacle avoidance. With the ActiVis system, we aim to tackle the issue of cost, user-acceptance and usability by using only off-the-shelf devices and hardware, as far as possible, and avoiding any special requirements. Following this design principle, we adopted a hand-held mobile device and a discreet headset to avoid the person standing out in public places while using the system. The ActiVis system is based on a concept proposed in [20,21] that uses a Google Tango device that is able to localise itself in real-time and has the benefit of a compact, familiar form-factor, which will help to overcome the hurdle of user-acceptance and usability.

A set of bone-conduction headphones is used as the audio transmission medium. These headphones sit on a user's cheekbones and conduct the audio signals through the skull into the inner ear, instead of through the outer part like typical over-ear headphones. This has the benefit of allowing the user access to ambient sounds and noise, so a person with limited vision can still relies on sound to detect, for example, oncoming vehicles and people [19]. Alternative solutions, such as open-back headphones, were also considered. These allow ambient noise through, but they still filter the incoming sound. The AfterShockz headphones (Fig. 1b) were ultimately selected since they do not interfere on other sounds and are also more discreet than the larger over-ear headphones.

3.2 Human Audio Localisation

Humans localise a sound source in 3 dimensions by considering cues recorded in one ear (monaural cues) and comparing cues received at both ears (binaural cues) [4,5]. The binaural cues include inter-aural time and level differences (ITD and ILD respectively) that help to determine a source's location on the horizontal plane. Monaural cues are taken from the interaction of the sound with the human anatomy, e.g. head, shoulders, outer ear, before it enters the ear canal. When the modified audio signal enters the inner ear canal, the human brain is able to analyse the frequency response and accurately determine the position of the sound source on the median plane. The distance to the source is simply derived as the intensity, or volume, of the source, i.e. a louder sound would appear closer to the user than a softer one.

When an audio signal is transmitted via a set of speakers or headphones, it can be transformed with an HRTF to mimic the characteristics of a natural sound source before it is transmitted, tricking the brain into believing a sound is located at some arbitrary position. An HRTF is a mathematical function that simulates the response signal of a human head and is derived by capturing key characteristics that affect the monaural and binaural responses, such as the user's hearing levels and head size. Since hearing responses are unique amongst different users, the best results would be observed if each user had their own customised HRTF. However, given the complicated process involved to capture the required user characteristics, making unique HRTFs is often an untenable solution and using average values (e.g. head measurements, height, etc.) have shown to produce acceptable results [10].

3.3   Interface Design

The guidance information is presented to the user in terms of pan and elevation angles, indicating the angular adjustments required to point the device camera at the target location, as shown in Fig. 2a. Spatialised audio signals are well-suited to the task, displaying similar levels of performance to vocal feedback, but with less cognitive load and higher resolution [17]. However, given the previously discussed limitations of bone-conduction and spatialised audio, we propose a simple linear adjustment to the signal's pitch as a function of the elevation angle. The pan angle, instead, can be conveyed by transforming the audio signal with an HRTF, and indeed it has been found that this dimension is unaffected by using bone-conduction headphones [22, 28, 31].

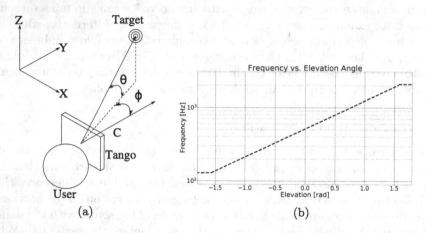

(a)   (b)

Fig. 2. The reference system used by the guidance interface showing the camera vector and pan and elevation angles (left) and the pitch gain function used to convey the target's elevation angle (right). Note the logarithmic scale of the frequency axis.

Pan. The human audition system uses binaural comparison cues, such as ITD and ILD, to localise a sound source on the horizontal plane [5]. The ITD is the perceived time delay between the signal reaching both ears, while the ILD is the perceived volume difference in the signal. For example, a sound that comes from the individual's right will hit the right ear first with a slightly higher volume.

In this work, a pure sinusoidal wave was used. People typically have trouble localising a pure tone without a sufficiently rich spectral signature. However, the ITD and ILD are independent of the tone's spectral make-up, while the elevation angle is given through a different mechanism. Therefore, a pure sine wave is suitable to convey the target's pan angle. To transform and spatialise the audio signal, we used OpenAL's default HRTF, based on the MIT's KEMAR dataset [13], which uses the person and targets' positions as input, and outputs a transformed audio signal.

Elevation. A generic HRTF implementation with bone-conduction headphones is not very effective in conveying the elevation angle of a sound source [22,28]. To compensate for this, we communicate the target's elevation angle by adjusting the tone's pitch (i.e. the sine wave's frequency) as a function of the elevation. When the camera vector is at the correct elevation, the tone pitch is set to neutral. When the target is above or below the camera vector, the pitch is increased or decreased, respectively. This high/low association scheme is motivated by humans' natural association of high-pitched sounds with elevated sound sources, and low-pitched sounds with source's below the individual's earline [4,24]. An octave- and semitone-based function is used to adjust the tone's pitch to ensure perceptible changes, while keeping the timbre roughly constant [30]. The pitch is updated at a rate of 10 Hz and changes as the user moves the device.

The pitch is changed as a linear function of the elevation angle and the gradient is determined by setting the angle and pitch limits. For this work, we only consider a 180° field of view in front of the user and limit the elevation angle to a range of $\pm 90°$, or $[-\frac{\pi}{2}, \frac{\pi}{2}]$. The pitch limits are set at some integer number of octaves above and below the neutral, on-elevation pitch. After practical tests with the interface, we set the neutral pitch to 512 Hz, which is comfortably audible and allows for a large number of suitable octave limits to be selected. We set the pitch limits to 2 octaves away from the neutral pitch, giving frequency limits of [128 Hz, 2048 Hz]. The linear function is visualised in Fig. 2b.

3.4 Implementation

A diagram of the experimental system pipeline is shown in Fig. 3, where the arrows indicate the direction of the information flow. When the user taps the Tango's screen, a new virtual target is generated and its coordinates are sent to the audio generation module, along with the device's current position and orientation. The audio generator then produces a tone based on the difference between the device and the target's positions. The tone is sent to the audio output channel, which plays it back to the user. A WiFi recording module is constantly monitoring the different values of the device's parameters and of the target's position, as well as the system's output, recording everything to a remotely stored datafile.

4   Experiments and Results

4.1   Procedure

To test the interface's effectiveness at guiding the user in a pointing task, a set of experiments were conducted to capture the difference between the targets' actual direction and the directions the participants' perceived them to be. The

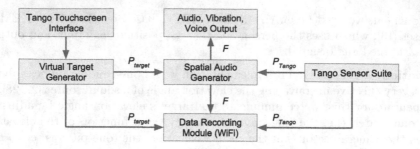

Fig. 3. A diagram of the individual system components and their communication pipelines. F indicates a feedback signal and P a pose signal.

participants are given a Tango device running an app written for the experiment that generates a set of virtual targets and presents them to each participants, one at a time. The targets are generated at a constant distance from the participant and their pan and elevation angles are uniformly generated across the four quadrants of the pan-elevation plane to avoid clustering. Each target's angular position is communicated to the participant through the audio interface, the output of which is adjusted in real-time as the participant points the device around. When a participant was confident that the device was on-target, i.e. hearing the audio front-on at 512 Hz, they tapped the screen, marking the location and generating the next target. The targets' positions are all set relative to the device's coordinate system, which is tracked using the Tango hardware and localisation API. A total of 28 targets were generated per participant.

Two groups of participants were recruited for the experiments. Group $G1$ consisted of 10 young adults with normal eyesight who were blindfolded for the experiments, and group $G2$ contained 4 people with severe visual impairments. Both groups were given some time before the experiments to familiarise with the system, the audio signal's behaviour and the 512 Hz on-level tone. To minimise the speed/accuracy biases in the results, we asked the participants to focus on finding the targets, without worrying about the time it took.

4.2   Results

The data collected during the experiment were clustered together by participant groups and analysed. Similar to the results from [22,28], we use the absolute mean errors for each dimension, which allows us to compare our results to the aforementioned works'. These results are presented in the boxplots in Fig. 4 and summarised in Table 1.

The average pan error from group $G1$ falls well within the ranges observed in [22,28] of [0.16, 0.38] radians and [0.17, 0.26] radians respectively. Indeed, the majority of samples fall even within the latter, more conservative range. However, the participants with visual impairments in group $G2$ demonstrate a wider spread in error data and higher average error than $G1$ (0.23 vs. 0.45 rad, Kruskal-Wallis test $p < 0.001$). The results in [15,35] reported a similar trend, although

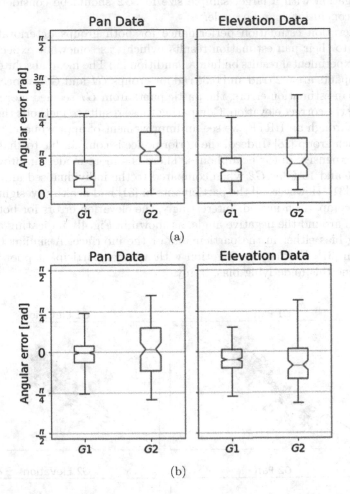

Fig. 4. Boxplots of the absolute (top) and signed (bottom) angular errors collected during the pointing experiment.

Table 1. A summary of the results collected from the experiment.

		Mean absolute error [rad]	Spearman correlation score
G1	Pan	0.23 ± 0.24	$0.88\ (p < 0.001)$
	Elevation	0.25 ± 0.28	$0.64\ (p < 0.001)$
G2	Pan	0.45 ± 0.21	$0.41\ (p < 0.001)$
	Elevation	0.36 ± 0.32	$0.61\ (p < 0.001)$

an investigation with a larger sample size for *G2* should be considered before definitive conclusions can be made.

The elevation estimation performance for both groups deteriorated when compared to their pan estimation results, which was somewhat expected given previous experimental results on human audition [3]. The mean absolute errors of the participants are 0.25 rad and 0.36 rad for groups *G1* and *G2*, respectively. As with the pan estimation errors, the participants from *G1* seemed more adept at estimating the correct elevation. Comparing these results to methods that convey elevation through an HRTF, we see an improvement of approximately 63% and 47% for each group [28]. Indeed, the performance is comparable to that of open-back and expensive in-ear headphones. There is a more modest improvement of 43% in *G1* and 16% for *G2* when compared to the individualised and adjusted HRTFs in [31]. However, all the participants in [31] had healthy eyesight, making the latter comparison invalid. Interestingly, the elevation errors for both groups are centred around the negative angle, as shown in Fig. 4b, indicating a possible underlying bias either in the participants or the interface. A similar trend was observed in [31]. Further investigation with a larger participant pool is needed to determine this underlying bias, if any.

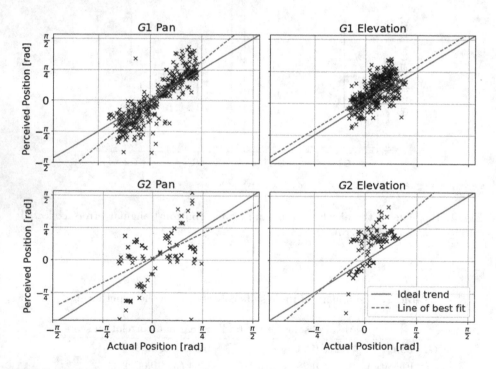

Fig. 5. Scatter plots that show the targets' actual positions and the participants' guesses, as well as the line of best fit showing the relationship between the data.

The error data was used to generate scatter plots that show the correlation between the target's direction presented by the guidance system to the participants and the one they thought the targets were. These plots are given in Figure 5 and show a reasonably positive correlation between the guidance and the selected targets, indicating that the participants correctly interpreted the interface's output in most of the cases. The Spearman correlation scores for each dataset, listed in Table 1, confirm this, as well as the negative angle bias in the elevation dimensions.

5   Conclusion

In this work, we proposed a new audio interface that conveys a target's pan and elevation angles through a spatialised audio tone. The tone's pitch is adjusted to convey the elevation and compensate for the shortcomings of bone-conduction headsets in transmitting the elevation component of a spatialised signal. The results obtained from a simple pointing experiment are encouraging as they show improved performance over purely spatialised signals transmitted via bone-conduction headphones. Furthermore, the limitations of the latter were largely overcome by communicating the target's elevation with the tone's pitch, achieving pan and elevation errors comparable to that of normal over-ear headphones.

Future work should consider a more in-depth investigation with a larger participant pool and a more detailed statistical analysis. Interesting questions include whether adjusting the gradient of the elevation function would make it easier for the user to guess the actual target's elevation, and to what degree the performance of participants with limited and healthy eyesight differs. Furthermore, experiments with a large group of people with visual impairments would provide an opportunity to gauge their opinion on the interface and identify possible avenues of improvements. Finally, it would be interesting to incorporate a co-adaptation mechanism between human and assistive device, as suggested in [9], to improve its usability and performance over time.

Acknowledgements. This research is partly supported by a Google Faculty Research Award. We would like to thank the Voluntary Centre Services UK for their help in facilitating the experiments with people with limited vision.

References

1. Arditi, A., Tian, Y.: User interface preferences in the design if a camera-based navigation and wayfinding aid. J. Vis. Impair. Blind. **107**(2), 118–129 (2013)
2. Bajcsy, R., Aloimonos, Y., Tsotsos, J.K.: Revisiting active perception. Auton. Robot. **42**(2), 177–196 (2018)
3. Barfield, W., Cohen, M., Rosenberg, C.: Visual and auditory localization as a function of azimuth and elevation. Int. J. Aviat. Psychol. **7**(2), 123–138 (1997)
4. Blauert, J.: Spatial Hearing: The Psychophysics of Human Sound Localization. MIT Press, Cambridge (1997)

5. Blauert, J.: Sound localization in the median plane. Acta Acustica United Acustica **22**(4), 205–213 (1969)

6. Blum, J.R., Bouchard, M., Cooperstock, J.R.: Spatialized audio environmental awareness for blind users with a smartphone. Mob. Netw. Appl. **18**(3), 295–309 (2013)

7. Chessa, M., Noceti, N., Odone, F., Solari, F., Sosa-García, J., Zini, L.: An integrated artificial vision framework for assisting visually impaired users. Comput. Vis. Image Underst. **149**, 209–228 (2016)

8. Durette, B., Louveton, N., Alleysson, D., Hérault, J.: Visuo-auditory sensory substitution for mobility assistance: testing TheVIBE. In: Workshop on Computer Vision Applications for the Visually Impaired (2008)

9. Gallina, P., Bellotto, N., Luca, M.D., Di Luca, M.: Progressive co-adaptation in human-machine interaction. In: International Conference on Informatics in Control, Automation and Robotics, vol. 2, pp. 362–368 (2015)

10. Gardner, W.G., Martin, K.D.: HRTF measurements of a KEMAR. J. Acoust. Soc. Am. **97**(6), 3907–3908 (1995)

11. Geronazzo, M., Bedin, A., Brayda, L., Campus, C., Avanzini, F.: Interactive spatial sonification for non-visual exploration of virtual maps. Int. J. Hum. Comput. Stud. **85**, 4–15 (2016)

12. Golledge, R.G., Marston, J.R., Loomis, J.M., Klatzky, R.L.: Stated preferences for components of a personal guidance system for nonvisual navigation. J. Vis. Impair. Blind. **98**(3), 135–147 (2004)

13. Hiebert, G.: OpenAL 1.1 Specification and Reference (2005)

14. Kanwal, N., Bostanci, E., Currie, K., Clark, A.F.: A navigation system for the visually impaired: a fusion of vision and depth sensor. Appl. Bionics Biomech. (2015). https://www.hindawi.com/journals/abb/2015/479857/cta/

15. Katz, B.F.G., Picinali, L.: Spatial audio applied to research with the blind. In: Advances in Sound Localization, pp. 225–250 (2011)

16. Katz, B.F.G., Truillet, P., Thorpe, S.J., Jouffrais, C.: NAVIG: navigation assisted by artificial vision and GNSS. In: Workshop on Multimodal Location Based Techniques for Extreme Navigation, vol. 1, pp. 1–4 (2010)

17. Klatzky, R.L., Marston, J.R., Giudice, N.A., Golledge, R.G., Loomis, J.M.: Cognitive load of navigating without vision when guided by virtual sound versus spatial language. J. Exp. Psychol.: Appl. **12**(4), 223–232 (2006)

18. Lee, Y., Medioni, G.: RGB-D camera based wearable navigation system for the visually impaired. Comput. Vis. Image Underst. **149**, 3–20 (2015)

19. Lichenstein, R., Smith, D.C., Ambrose, J.L., Moody, L.A.: Headphone use and pedestrian injury and death in the united states: 2004–2011. Inj. Prev. **18**(5), 287–290 (2012)

20. Lock, J.C., Cielniak, G., Bellotto, N.: Portable navigations system with adaptive multimodal interface for the blind. In: AAAI Spring Symposium - Designing the User Experience of Machine Learning Systems (2017)

21. Lock, J.C., Cielniak, G., Bellotto, N.: Active object search with a mobile device for people with visual impairments. In: International Conference on Computer Vision Theory and Applications, pp. 476–485 (2019)

22. MacDonald, J.A., Henry, P.P., Letowski, T.R.: Spatial audio through a bone conduction interface. Int. J. Audiol. **45**(10), 595–599 (2006)

23. Mocanu, B., Tapu, R., Zaharia, T.: When ultrasonic sensors and computer vision join forces for efficient obstacle detection and recognition. Sensors **16**(11), 1807 (2016)

24. Pratt, C.: The spatial character of high and low tones. J. Exp. Psychol. **13**(3), 278 (1930)
25. Rivera-Rubio, J., Arulkumaran, K., Rishi, H., Alexiou, I., Bharath, A.A.: An assistive haptic interface for appearance-based indoor navigation. Comput. Vis. Image Underst. **149**, 126–145 (2015)
26. RNIB: UK vision strategy. Technical report, RNIB (2016). Accessed 19 July 2016
27. Rodríguez, A., Bergasa, L.M., Alcantarilla, P.F., Yebes, J., Cela, A.: Obstacle avoidance system for assisting visually impaired people. In: Intelligent Vehicles Symposium Workshops, pp. 1–6 (2012)
28. Schonstein, D., Ferré, L., Katz, B.F.: Comparison of headphones and equalization for virtual auditory source localization. J. Acoust. Soc. Am. **5**, 3724–3724 (2008)
29. Schwarze, T., Lauer, M., Schwaab, M., Romanovas, M., Bohm, S., Jurgensohn, T.: An intuitive mobility aid for visually impaired people based on stereo vision. In: International Conference on Computer Vision Workshops, pp. 17–25 (2015)
30. Shepard, R.: Circularity in judgments of relative pitch. J. Acoust. Soc. Am. **36**(12), 2346–2353 (1964)
31. Stanley, R.M., Walker, B.N.: Lateralization of sounds using bone-conduction headsets. In: Proceedings of the Human Factors and Ergonomics Society Annual Meeting, vol. 50, pp. 1571–1575. SAGE Publications, Los Angeles (2006)
32. Wilson, J., Walker, B.N., Lindsay, J., Cambias, C., Dellaert, F.: SWAN: system for wearable audio navigation. In: International Symposium on Wearable Computers, pp. 91–98 (2007)
33. Xiao, J., Joseph, S.L., Zhang, X., Li, B., Li, X., Zhang, J.: An assistive navigation framework for the visually impaired. IEEE Trans. Hum.-Mach. Syst. **45**(5), 635–640 (2015)
34. Yusif, S., Soar, J., Hafeez-Baig, A.: Older people, assistive technologies, and the barriers to adoption: a systematic review. Int. J. Med. Informatics **94**, 112–116 (2016)
35. Zwiers, M.P., Van Opstal, A.J., Cruysberg, J.R.M., Opstal, A.J.V., Cruysberg, J.R.M.: A spatial hearing deficit in early-blind humans. J. Neurosci. **21**(1529–2401), RC142–RC145 (2001)

Cyberspace Security

Mining Weighted Protein Complexes Based on Fuzzy Ant Colony Clustering Algorithm

Yimin Mao[✉], Qianhu Deng, and Yinping Liu

School of Information Engineering,
Jiangxi University of Science and Technology, Ganzhou 341000, Jiangxi, China
mymlyc@163.com

Abstract. Aiming at the defect that the accuracy of the protein complexes based on fuzzy ant colony clustering is not high, the time performance and recall are low, a novel algorithm named FAC-PC (mining weighted protein complexes based on fuzzy ant colony clustering algorithm) is proposed. The weighted protein network is established by the integration of both edge aggregation coefficient and gene expression data to eliminate the effect of false positives, and the selection of essential protein by using a new function EPS (essential protein selection). Then, this paper proposes that PFC (protein fitness calculation) and SI (similarity improvement) overcome the problems of massive merger, repeated picking and dropping operations in ant colony clustering algorithm. Furthermore, a new FCM (fuzzy C-means) objective function which takes a balance between inter-clustering and intra-clustering variation is proposed for protein complexes. The experimental results show that the superiority of the FAC-PC algorithm in terms of accuracy and computational time.

Keywords: Protein-protein interaction (PPI) network · Protein complex · Ant colony clustering algorithm · FCM · Fitness

1 Introduction

Since analysis of the underlying relationships in protein data can potentially yield and considerably expand useful insights into roles of proteins in biological processes, it is greatly significant to study the mechanism of human disease and discover new therapeutic interventions. In particular, Protein–Protein Interactions (PPI) provide us with a good opportunity to systematically analyze the structure of a large living system and also allow us to use them to understand essential principles [1, 2]. Identifying protein complexes is important in understanding the functional mechanisms and cellular organizations, therefore, the mining algorithm for protein complexes becomes a crucial issue in academic research [3].

Over the past decade, the prediction and identifying of protein complexes have been performed by biological experimental procedures [4, 5]. However, these techniques require a large investment of resources and time. Considering these experimental constraints, a variety of computational approaches have been proposed, which become a useful supplement to identify protein complexes [6]. According to the advantages of having good accuracy and efficiency in the fuzzy C-means (FCM)

© Springer Nature Singapore Pte Ltd. 2019
G. Wang et al. (Eds.): iSCI 2019, CCIS 1122, pp. 557–569, 2019.
https://doi.org/10.1007/978-981-15-1301-5_44

clustering algorithm, an interesting line of researches has focused on clustering of protein complexes based on FCM clustering algorithm [7]. In particular, Trivodaliev et al. [8] propose a new algorithm for mining the protein modules by combining FCM with spectral clustering, which use fuzzy membership to divide data into different classes, but experimental results are sensitive to the initial clustering center and clustering numbers. Recently, many swarm intelligence optimization algorithms are used to detect protein complex by simulating the collective behavior of social insects [9]. Based on ant colony clustering, Ji et al. [10] propose ACC-FMD algorithm to detect the PPI network module. In another work, Zhao et al. [11] propose ACC-DPC (Ant colony algorithm based on function continue feature for identifying dynamic protein complexes) algorithm to identify protein complexes by integrating temporal function continue feature with ant colony clustering on dynamic PPI networks. However, the processes of these algorithms have massive merger, filter, repeated picking and dropping operations, the efficiency and precision of clustering are slow. The FCM clustering algorithm is sensitive to the initial clustering center and the number of clusters, therefore, a novel clustering model for identifying protein complexes is proposed by Lei et al. [12], which combines the optimization mechanism of artificial bee colony (ABC) with the fuzzy membership matrix.

Most protein complexes mining methods based on unweighted graphs, the correlation of neighbor nodes is neglected in these methods, which present a challenge for modules mining from PPI data. In order to assess the reliability of high-throughput protein interactions, some studies have been proposed to improve the reliability of PPI networks. Using a weighted graph model to dispose such PPI networks is more reasonable than the existing graph model [13]. Recently, a great deal of attention has been concentrated on clustering issues for protein complexes based on the weighted graph model. Similarly, Dimitrakopoulos et al. [14] propose gradually expanding neighborhoods with adjustment (GENA), a novel algorithm to predict overlapping protein complexes from weighted protein interaction graphs, which accepts weighted PPI graphs by using a weighted evaluation function for each cluster. Kouhsar et al. [15] propose WCOACH (improved COACH algorithm in weighted PPI network) algorithm for predicting protein complexes in the weighted PPI network. Moreover, IMHRC (Inter-Module Hub Removal Clustering) algorithm proposed by Ama et al. [16] based on inter-module hub removal in the weighted PPI network, which effectively improves the performance to identify the overlapping complexes. Even for these methods overcome the influence of false positives on the experimental results, the sensitivity and accuracy of clustering results are low. Furthermore, these methods are not sufficient to deduce satisfactory conclusions when a large amount of protein interaction data appears.

Though the detection of protein complexes in weighted PPI networks has attracted widespread attention over the past few years, how to design effective and correct detection methods for protein complexes is still a challenging and important scientific problem in computational biology. In this paper, we take into account the reliability of PPI and construct a weighted PPI network. In order to detect the effectiveness of the weighted PPI network, a new prediction method for protein complexes named FAC-PC (algorithm for identifying weighted protein complexes based on fuzzy ant colony clustering) is proposed. The remainder of this paper is organized as follows. In Sect. 2, general methods are described. In Sect. 3, the weighted protein network is structured by combing the gene expression data with edge aggregation coefficient. EPS (essential protein selection) and PFC (protein fitness calculation) are proposed to obtain the essential group proteins. To optimize the probability of picking and dropping operations, the SI (similarity improvement) measure is designed based on the ant colony algorithm. Furthermore, a novel FCM (fuzzy C-means) objective function is proposed for protein complexes. Experimental results are analyzed and shown in Sect. 4. In Sect. 5, conclusions and directions for future research are given.

2 Methods

2.1 FCM Clustering Algorithm

Let $X = \{X_1, X_2, X_3, \ldots, X_n\}$ be a sample of N observations in D-dimensional Euclidean space $(x_i \in R^p)$. Clustering is a process which separates this data set into C subsets. Fuzzy c-means clustering algorithm tries to minimize the following objective function which is the generalized form of the least-squared errors function [17]:

$$F = \sum_{i=1}^{N} \sum_{j=1}^{C} u_{ij}^m E(x_i, c_j) \tag{1}$$

where m is fuzzy weighted index, K is the number of classes, $E(x_i, c_j)$ is the Euclidean distance between x_i and c_j.

Fuzzy partitioning is carried out through an iterative optimization of the objective function shown above, with the update of membership u_{ij} and the cluster centers c_j by Eqs. (2) and (3):

$$u_{ij} = \left[\sum_{k=1}^{C} \left(\frac{d(x_i, c_j)}{d(x_i, c_k)} \right)^{\frac{1}{m-1}} \right]^{-1} \quad i = 1, 2, \ldots, N; j = 1, 2, \ldots, K \tag{2}$$

$$c_j = \frac{\sum_{i=1}^{N} u_{ij}^m \cdot x_i}{\sum_{i=1}^{N} u_{ij}^m}, j = 1, 2, \ldots, K \tag{3}$$

2.2 Ant Clustering Algorithm

This paper describes the process of ant colony clustering by using the idea of ACC-FMD algorithm [10]. A PPI network is usually regarded as an undirected graph $G = (V, E)$, where $V = \{v_1, v_2, \ldots, v_n\}$ is a set of proteins, $E = \{e_1, e_2, \ldots, e_m\}$ is a set of interactions. The main processes are summarized as follows:

(1) Seed selection: Compute the clustering coefficient for each node and select nodes to compose the set of seed proteins. The clustering coefficient of i is represented as:

$$\phi_i = \frac{2n_i}{|Neigh(i)|(|Neigh(i) - 1|)} \tag{4}$$

where $Neigh(i)$ is the direct neighbor set of node i, n_i is the number of links which connect the $|Neigh(i)|$ of node i to neighbors.

(2) Ants clustering: The clustering process of ants is evolving in discrete time steps. At the initial time, each ant is in the unloaded state. An ant randomly selects a seed node as a starting point and begins to specifically search and assign proteins located in its neighborhood. The probability of picking and dropping the protein is defined as follows:

$$P_p(j) = \left[\frac{k_p}{k_p + s(i,j)}\right]^2 \tag{5}$$

$$P_d(j) = \begin{cases} 2s(i,j) & s(i,j) < k_d \\ 1 & otherwise \end{cases} \tag{6}$$

where k_p is a picking constant, k_d is a dropping constant, $s(i,j)$ is the similarity between the protein j and the current seed protein i, their structural similarity is described as follows:

$$s(i,j) = \frac{|\tau(i) \cap \tau(j)|}{\sqrt{|\tau(i)||\tau(j)|}} \tag{7}$$

where $\tau(i)$ is a set of node i and its direct neighbors, $\tau(j)$ is a set of node j and its direct neighbors.

(3) Information transmission mechanism: Select the highest value D in the iteration as optimum clustering result, update the similarity function in term of the assignment membership of the optimum solution.

(4) Post-processing: Select the optimum solution with the largest value in all iterations, merge and filter the clustering result, and the similarity is defined as follows:

$$S(M_x, M_y) = \frac{\sum\limits_{i \in M_x, j \in M_y} s(i,j)}{\min(|M_x|, |M_y|)} \tag{8}$$

Where

$$s(i,j) = \begin{cases} 1 & i = j \\ \frac{|g^i \cap g^j|}{|g^i \cup g^j|} & i \neq j, (i,j) \in E \\ 0 & otherwise \end{cases} \tag{9}$$

3   FAC-PC Algorithm

3.1   Construction of Weighted PPI Network

The protein-protein interaction (PPI) network and other biological data generally bear complexity attributed to noise,incompleteness and inaccuracy in practice, and the PPI data contains false positive and false negative rates, which impact the correctness of predicting protein complexes. The importance of edges in biological protein networks is different, and protein complexes appear in clusters and tend to be co-expressed. In order to improve the prediction accuracy, the PPI network is modeled as a weighted graph, in which each protein-protein interaction is endowed with a measure using edge clustering coefficient.

As an important topological property of protein interaction network, edge clustering coefficient can be used to describe the reliability of protein interaction and measure the probability of protein belonging to a clustering. Therefore, edge clustering coefficient can identify accurately essential protein. The edge clustering coefficient $ECC(u, v)$ between node u and v can be defined as follows:

$$ECC = \frac{|N(u) \cap N(v)|}{\min(N_u - 1, N_v - 1)} \tag{10}$$

where $|N(u) \cap N(v)|$ is the number of common neighbor nodes between node u and v. N_u is the number of degrees of node u, N_v is the number of degrees of node v.

An illustrative example of the weighted PPI network construction described in Fig. 1. From Fig. 1(a), we construct a static PPI network based on high-throughput PPI data, which contains 8 proteins and 18 interactions. In Fig. 1(b), to construct the weighted PPI network, we use edge clustering coefficient to calculate the weight of each interaction in the weighted PPI network.

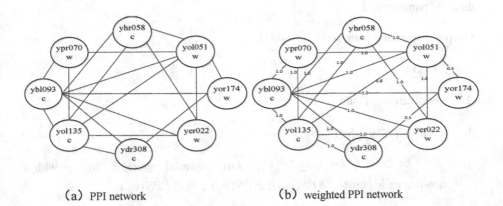

(a) PPI network   (b) weighted PPI network

Fig. 1. Weighted network construction graph

3.2   Improved Ant Colony Algorithm

3.2.1   Selecting Essential Proteins

For the ant colony clustering algorithm, the seed nodes are selected based on PPI data, the accuracy of identification relies on a reliable network. However, the experimental result is susceptible to false positives. In order to reduce the influence of false positives and improve the accuracy of clustering, in the weighted PPI network, the similarity measure named EPS is proposed by combining edge clustering coefficient and Pearson correlation coefficient [18].

(EPS measure) gives a weighted PPI network $G = (V, E, P)$, where $ECC(u, v)$ represents the edge clustering coefficient between node u and v, $PCC(u, v)$ represents the Pearson correlation coefficient between nodes. The weight of essential nodes in the PPI network can be defined as follows:

$$EPS(u) = \delta + \sum_{(u,v) \in E} \frac{P(u, v) - \min P(u, v)}{\max P(u, v) - \min P(u, v)} \quad (11)$$

$EPS(u)$ takes into account clustering degree of topological characteristics of nodes u and v in PPI networks, and the degree of gene co-expression is designed to measure the possibility of clustering between nodes, and $EPS(u)$ considers the difference of data between gene expression and PPI networks. Therefore, it is effective to evaluate the criticality of protein. The nodes above the critical threshold are selected by Eq. (5), which reduces the influence of false positives and false negatives. Furthermore, it effectively improves the performance of selecting essential protein. In this paper, we set $\delta = 0.01$. The EPS method can be summarized as follows:

Algorithm 1. selecting essential proteins

Input: the weighted network $G(V, E, P)$, critical threshold θ, gene expression data and parameter δ

Output: essential protein set $\{v_1, v_2, \ldots, v_k\}$

1. $L = \varnothing$

2.   For each $v_i \in V$ do

3.   If $EPS(v_i) > \theta$ do

4. $L = L \cup v_i$, $L = \{v_1, v_2, \ldots, v_k\}$, sort essential proteins in L with non-decreasing order, $EPS(v_1) \geq EPS(v_2) \geq \ldots \geq EPS(v_k)$

5.   End if

6. End for

3.2.2 Obtaining Essential Group Protein

In the ant colony clustering algorithm, seed nodes are used to expand and form protein complexes. The two protein complexes formed by clustering are similar when the similarity between the two seed nodes is high. In the post-processing process, the merge operation of two modules causes high computational consumption. Therefore, the time performance of the ant colony clustering algorithm is low. In order to deal with this problem, the PFC measure is proposed based on the weighted PPI network, which formats essential group protein by using node fitness to traverse the neighbors of essential nodes. The PFC measure select the value of node fitness before picking and dropping operations, which reduces the times of picking and dropping operations and improves the calculation efficiency.

3.2.3 SI Measures for Similarity Improvement

For the ant colony algorithm, it is necessary to repeatedly calculate the number of nodes and normalize the common neighbor nodes, the efficiency and precision of clustering is low. In order to solve this problem, in the weighted PPI network, the SI similarity measure named SI is proposed to calculate the probability of picking and dropping operations, and use the model to complete clustering.

3.3 Improved FCM Algorithm

3.3.1 Improved Strategy of Membership Update

In order to reduce the invalid update, we design an accelerated membership update strategy, which can change the update rate according to the attribute of the membership value. First, a more reliable membership value is obtained by optimizing the initial clustering center. Based on competitive learning, the maximum membership degree u_{ti} of the data point x_i becomes the winner. According to the dissimilarity degree between u_{ti} and the residual membership degree in the same line, its update speed and the update speed of other nodes are increased and inhibited in different degrees, respectively. The update formula is defined as follows:

$$u'_{ti} = u_{ti} + \eta u_{si} \tag{12}$$

$$u'_{si} = (1 - \eta)u_{si} \tag{13}$$

where η represents inhibition of parameter.

It can be seen from the definition of η, when the membership degree is updated, the attribute is fully taken into consideration in this paper. If the difference between membership degrees is little, the value of η obtained will be smaller, which results in a slower membership update rate obtained from the formulas (6) and (7). On the contrary, if the difference between membership degrees is large, at this time, the value of η also becomes big. In this paper, we set $\eta = 0.6$.

3.3.2 Improved Method of Selecting Objective Function

The objective function of FCM algorithm does not consider inter-clustering, which uses the gradient method to resolve the extremum. However, the experiment result is easy to fall into the local optimum, the accuracy of the complex mining is low. In order to solve this problem, we fully take into account intra-clustering and inter-clustering, and excavate high cohesive and low-coupling complexes. Furthermore, a novel FCM objective function which takes a balance between intra-clustering and inter-clustering variation is proposed for protein complexes.

The intra-clustering $W(u, c, k)$ and inter-clustering $A(u, c, k)$ are defined as follows:

$$W(u, c, k) = \sum_{i=1}^{N} \sum_{j=1}^{K} u_{ij}^m d(x_i, c_j) \tag{14}$$

$$A(u, c, k) = n \times \min_{j \neq k} ||c_j - c_k||^2 \tag{15}$$

The improved objective function of FCM algorithm is defined as follow:

$$J(u, c, k) = \frac{W(u, c, k)}{kA(u, c, k)} = \frac{\sum\limits_{i=1}^{N} \sum\limits_{j=1}^{K} u_{ij}^m d(x_i, c_j)}{kn \min\limits_{j \neq k} ||c_j - c_k||^2} \tag{16}$$

3.4   Clustering Process of FAC-PC Algorithm

The specific steps of FAC-PC algorithm are shown as follows:

Step 1: initialize parameter.
Step 2: calculate the probability between each group of interactions by using edge clustering coefficient and then construct a weighted PPI network.
Step 3: calculate the weight of node.
Step 4: calculate the fitness of node.
Step 5: calculate the fitness between the node and *Set*.
Step 6: repeat step 5, and obtain the clustering number M based on improved ant colony algorithm.
Step 7: obtain initial clustering center c and clustering number M based on the FCM algorithm, update the membership matrix and clustering center.
Step 8: calculate the objective function. If objective function is less than ε, then stop, otherwise, repeat step 7.

4   Experimental Results and Analysis

4.1   Experiment Environment

An experimental computer is configured with the windows 7 ultimate operating system, an Intel i5 dual-core processor, 2.5 GHz frequency and 6.0 GB of memory. The algorithm is programmed in python.

4.2   Datasets

In order to investigate the performance of our algorithm, the relatively complete and reliable network yeast PPI network is selected as the experimental data. The specific experimental data are shown as follows:

(1) The yeast PPI network data is derived from the DIP database [19], removing self-interactions and repeated ones, which consists of 21554 interactions among 4995 proteins.
(2) To evaluate the protein complexes predicted by our method, a benchmark set is derived from CYC2008 [20], which consists of 408 protein complexes.

4.3   Evaluation Index

4.3.1   Specificity (Sp), Sensitivity (Sn) and *F-Measure*

To assess the quality of the produced protein complexes, for any predicted complex pc_n and known complex bc_m, the overlap score NA is defined as: $NA(pc_n, bc_m) = |pc_n \cap bc_m|^2/(|pc_n||bc_m|)$. The overlap threshold F is set as 0.2 [21]. They are perfectly matched when $NA(pc_i, bc_j) = 1$.

Specificity (Sp) and sensitivity (Sn) are commonly used to evaluate the performance of protein complex prediction methods. Specificity is the fraction of predicted complexes that are true complexes while sensitivity is the fraction of benchmark complexes that are retrieved.

Given the predicted protein complex set $PC = \{pc_1, pc_2, pc_3, \ldots, pc_n\}$ and the benchmark complexes set $BC = \{bc_1, bc_2, \ldots bc_m\}$.

$$TP = |\{pc_i \in PC | \exists bc_j \in BC, NA(pc_i, bc_j) \geq F\}|$$

$$FP = |\{pc_i \in PC | \forall bc_j \in BC, NA(pc_i, bc_j) < F\}|$$

$$FN = |\{bc_i \in BC | \forall pc_j \in PC, NA(pc_i, bc_j) < F\}|$$

where TP is the number of correctly predicted complexes, FP is the number of incorrectly predicted complexes, TN is the number of predicted benchmark complexes and FN is the number of unpredicted benchmark complexes.

$$Sp = \frac{TP}{TP + FP}, \qquad Sn = \frac{TP}{TP + FN}$$

F-measure is a harmonic mean of specificity and sensitivity, so it can be used to evaluate the overall performance. It is defined as:

$$F-measure = \frac{2 \times Sn \times Sp}{Sn + Sp}$$

4.3.2 *P-value* Measure

In the PPI network, protein modules can be statistically evaluated using *P-value* from the hypergeometric distribution [22], which is defined as:

$$P\text{-}value = 1 - \sum_{i=0}^{k-1} \frac{\dbinom{|F|}{i}\dbinom{|V|-|F|}{|C|-i}}{\dbinom{|V|}{|C|}}$$

where $|V|$ is the total number of proteins, F is a known protein complex, the size is $|V|$, C is a predicted protein complex, $|V|$ denotes the size of the complex, and l is the size of the intersection of protein complex C and F.

4.4 Performance Comparison

(1) Comparative Analysis of *Sp*, *Sn* and *F-measure*

In order to verify the performance of the algorithm in this paper, 20 experiments are performed on the DIP data sets. The average results are shown in Table 1 and Fig. 2:

Table 1. Basic information of protein complexes by various algorithms

Algorithms	PM	Full	TP
ACC-FMD	283	9.5	150
ACC-DPC	273	7.8	137
GENA	290	5.6	136
WCOACH	354	10.3	147
IMHRC	366	12.7	210
FAC-PC	369	13.5	233

As can be seen from Table 1, *PM* is the total number of predicted protein complexes, while *Full* is the number of protein complexes perfectly matching the known protein complexes. From Table 1, it can be seen that the *Full* and *TP* of FAC-PC algorithm achieves the highest *value* of 13.5 and 233, respectively.

The basic performance comparison about predicted protein complexes by various algorithms running on DIP data is presented in Fig. 2, including *Sn, Sp* and *F-measure*.

From Fig. 2, it can be seen that FAC-PC algorithm achieves the largest value of *F-measure*, *Sp* and *Sn*. The *F-measure* of FAC-PC algorithm is 63.14%, 19.13%, 34.64%, 52.06% and 10.05% higher than ACC-FMD, ACC-PDC, GENA, WCOACH and IMHRC. Experimental results indicate that FAC-PC algorithm performs significantly better than the state-of-the-art methods. The reason is that ACC-FMD and ACC-PDC algorithms identified complexes from the PPI networks based on the ant colony clustering, the protein complexes overlapping to a very high extent are predicted. In the clustering process of the GENA algorithm, the cluster assignment is initialized randomly, which results that the performance and stability of the algorithm are low. In WCOACH and IMHRC algorithm, the clustering is predicted only based on gene features, some important topology information in the weighted PPI network may be lost, which results that the performance of the algorithms is low. However, in the entire clustering process of the FAC-PC algorithm, the weighted PPI network is constructed to overcome the effect of false positives using edge aggregation coefficient. At the same time, the ant colony clustering algorithm with EPS measure is designed to preprocess the weighted PPI network, which can reduce the dimension of the data. Furthermore, in the ant colony algorithm, the essential group proteins are selected by PFC method, and the picking and dropping operations are optimized by the SI metric. In return, based on ant colony clustering and FCM algorithm, no matter what sample space structure it is, there are fewer iterations, faster convergence and higher clustering accuracy for the FAC-PC algorithm. Therefore, our method achieves state-of-the-art performance for protein complexes identification.

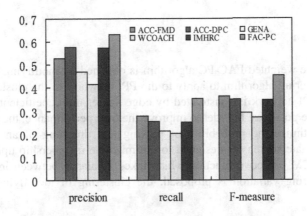

Fig. 2. Performance comparison of different algorithms

(2) Comparative Analysis of GO Terms

A low P-value of complexes indicates that those proteins in the complex do not happen merely by chance, so the complex has high statistical significance. Generally,a module is considered to be significant with corrected *P-values* < 0.01, and the proportion of significant complexes overall predicted ones can be used to evaluate the overall performance of various algorithms. The comparison results of various algorithms on the DIP data listed in Table 2.

Table 2. Statistical significance of predicted protein complexes mined by various algorithms

Algorithms	PM	SC	Proportion
ACC-FMD	283	141	49.82%
ACC-DPC	237	160	67.51%
GENA	290	135	46.55%
WCOACH	354	263	74.29%
IMHRC	366	180	49.18%
FAC-PC	369	305	82.66%

In Table 2, *PM* is the number of predicted complexes, and *SC* is the number of significant complexes. From Table 2, we can see that our method achieves the largest value of proportion, and the value of the proportion of our complex is 82.66%, 49.82%, 67.51%, 46.55%, 74.29% and 49.18% higher than ACC-FMD [10], ACC-DPC [11], GENA [14], WCOACH [15] and IMHRC [16], respectively. The experimental results show that our FAC-PC approach outperforms these algorithms in terms of statistical significance.

5   Conclusion

In this paper, the weighted FAC-PC algorithm is obtained by modifying the FCM and ant colony clustering algorithm to apply to the PPI network. In the clustering process, the weighted PPI network is constructed by edge aggregation coefficient to overcome the effect of false positives. In order to improve the time performance, the SI measure is designed to optimize the probability of picking and dropping of ant colony. The membership update strategy is designed to optimize the membership update. Furthermore, a new FCM objective function which takes a balance between intra-clustering and inter-clustering variation is proposed, the clustering of identifying complex is completed.

References

1. Ji, J.Z., Gao, G.X.: Detecting functional module method based on cultural algorithm in protein-protein interaction networks. J. Beijing Univ. Technol. **43**(1), 0013–0021 (2017)
2. Zheng, W.P., Li, J.Y., Wang, J.: Protein complex recognition algorithm based on genetic algorithm. J. Front. Comput. Sci. Technol. **12**(5), 794–803 (2018)
3. Cai, L.X., Chen, R., Lv, Q.: Selecting the best of the predictions of compound structures for protein docking by spectral clustering. J. Chin. Comput. Syst. **36**(10), 2365–2368 (2015)
4. Li, M., Wang, J.X., Liu, B.B.: An algorithm for identifying protein complexes based on maximal clique extension. J. Cent. South Univ. **41**(2), 560–565 (2010)
5. Kessler, J., Andrushchenko, V., Kapitan, J., et al.: Insight into vibrational circular dichroism of proteins by density functional modeling. Phys. Chem. Chem. Phys. **20**(7), 4926–4935 (2018)

6. Aldeco, R., Marin, I.: Jerarca: efficient analysis of complex networks using hierarchical clustering. PLoS ONE **5**(7), 11585–11591 (2010)
7. Lei, X.J., Gao, Y., Guo, L.: Mining protein complexes based on topology potential weight in dynamic protein-protein interaction networks. Acta Electron. Sin. **46**(1), 145–151 (2018)
8. Yao, X.H., Yan, J.W., Liu, K.F., et al.: Tissue-specific network-based genome wide study of amygdala imaging phenotypes to identify functional interaction modules. Bioinformatics **33** (20), 3250–3257 (2017)
9. Ji, J.Z., Yang, M.H., Yang, C.C.: Fast ant colony clustering for functional module detection algorithm in PPI networks. J. Beijing Univ. Technol. **42**(8), 1182–1192 (2016)
10. Ji, J.Z., Liu Hong, X., Zhang, A.D., et al.: ACC-FMD: ant colony clustering for functional module detection in protein-protein interaction networks. Int. J. Data Min. Bioinform. **11**(3), 331–363 (2015)
11. Zhao, X.W., Cheng, X.D., Lv, J.W.: Identify protein complexes by integrating temporal function continue feature and ant colony clustering on dynamic PPI networks. J. Chin. Comput. Syst. **38**(6), 1311–1316 (2017)
12. Lei, X.J., Wu, F.X., Tian, J.F., et al.: ABC and IFC: modules detection method for PPI network. Biomed. Res. Int. **8**(1), 968173–968183 (2014)
13. Zhang, Y., Jia, K.B., Zhang, A.D.: Consistent protein functional module detection from multi-view of biological data. Acta Electron. Sin. **42**(12), 2337–2344 (2014)
14. Dimitrakopoulos, C., Theofilatos, K., Pegkas, A., et al.: Predicting overlapping protein complexes from weighted protein interaction graphs by gradually expanding dense neighborhoods. Artif. Intell. Med. **71**(C), 62–69 (2016)
15. Kouhsar, M., Zaremirakabad, F., Jamali, Y.: WCOACH: protein complex prediction in weighted PPI networks. Genes Genet. Syst. **91**(1), 47 (2016)
16. Ama, M., Eslahchi, C.: Discovering overlapped protein complexes from weighted PPI networks by removing inter-module hubs. Sci. Rep. **7**(1), 3247–3260 (2017)
17. Kesemen, O., Tezel, O., Ozkul, E.: Fuzzy c-means clustering algorithm for directional data (FCM4DD). Expert Syst. Appl. **58**(C), 76–82 (2016)
18. Ni, W.Y., Wang, J.X., Xiong, H.J.: Research of detecting functional modules based on uncertainty data. Sichuan Daxue Xuebao (Gongcheng Kexue Ban)/J. Sichuan Univ. (Eng. Sci. Ed.) **45**(5), 0080–0087 (2013)
19. Li, X.L., Wu, M., Kwoh, C.K., et al.: Computational approaches for detecting protein complexes from protein interaction networks: a survey. BMC Genom. **11**(Suppl 1), 1–19 (2010)
20. Pu, S., Wong, J., Turner, B., et al.: Up-to-date catalogues of yeast protein complexes. Nucl.C Acids Res. **37**(3), 825–831 (2009)
21. Zhang, Y.J., Lin, H.F., Yang, Z.H., et al.: A method for predicting protein complex in dynamic PPI networks. BMC Bioinform. **17**(Suppl 7), 229–239 (2016)
22. Lei, X.J., Wu, S., Liang, G., et al.: Clustering and overlapping modules detection in PPI network based on IBFO. Proteomics **13**(2), 278–290 (2013)

Mixing Property Tester: A General Framework for Evaluating the Mixing Properties of Initialization of Stream Ciphers

Lin Ding[1,2]([⊠]), Dawu Gu[1], and Lei Wang[1,3]

[1] Department of Computer Science and Engineering, Shanghai Jiao Tong University,
Shanghai 200240, China
dinglin_cipher@163.com
[2] PLA SSF Information Engneering University, Zhengzhou 450001, China
[3] Westone Cryptologic Research Center, Beijing 100000, China

Abstract. In this paper, a general framework for evaluating the mixing properties of initialization of stream ciphers, called **Mixing Property Tester-MPT**, is exploited and formalized. Based on this general framework, we propose a concrete and efficient algorithm, which can compute the maximum number of initialization rounds of a given stream cipher such that any internal state bit or generated keystream bit does not achieve full mixing properties. Our algorithm has linear time complexity and needs a negligible amount of memory. As illustrations, we apply our algorithm to ZUC-128, ZUC-256 and Trivium stream ciphers. The results show that though ZUC-256 has a much larger initial input size than ZUC-128, its mixing properties are almost as good as ZUC-128. As for Trivium, the tap positions of keystream output function are not chosen optimally with respect to this tester and we provide some better selections of tap positions. As a general cryptanalytic tool, **MPT** can help to give the designers more insights to choose the initialization functions and the required number of initialization rounds.

Keywords: Stream cipher · Initialization · Mixing property ·
ZUC-128 · ZUC-256 · Trivium

1 Introduction

Almost any cryptographic scheme contains both secret variables (e.g., key bits) and public variables (e.g., plaintext bits in block ciphers or IV bits in stream ciphers). In general, the key and IV bits are mapped to the internal state of the stream cipher by an initialization function, and then produces the keystream bits using update functions G and an output function f. The internal state is updated by the update functions G, while the output bit is generated by the output function f after an initialization of a sufficient number of rounds. The

© Springer Nature Singapore Pte Ltd. 2019
G. Wang et al. (Eds.): iSCI 2019, CCIS 1122, pp. 570–582, 2019.
https://doi.org/10.1007/978-981-15-1301-5_45

security of the initialization function relies on its mixing properties: each key and IV bit should affect each internal state bit and keystream bit in a complex way. Good mixing can be achieved with a round-based approach, where the number of initialization rounds is well-chosen and some nonlinear operations are used in each round. However, if mixing is not perfect, the initialization function may be distinguished from a uniformly random Boolean function.

How many initialization rounds are needed to make the mixing properties enough? This is a question that every stream cipher designer has been faced with, but we have not yet seen any satisfactory answer to this question. The mixing properties of initialization are closely related to the security of stream cipher, and then evaluating the mixing properties of initialization can help to give the designers more insights to choose the initialization functions and the required number of initialization rounds.

ZUC-128 [1] is a word-oriented stream cipher, which is the core of the 3GPP confidentiality and integrity algorithms 128-EEA3 and 128-EIA3. In September 2011, ZUC-128 was approved as the LTE international standard cipher for 3GPP at the 53rd 3GPP Meeting for System Architecture Group held at Fukuoka, Japan. It can resist many cryptanalytic attacks such as chosen-IV attack [2], guess-and-determine attack [3], and algebraic attacks [4]. ZUC-256 stream cipher [5] is a successor of ZUC-128 stream cipher, and offers 256-bit security for the upcoming applications in 5G. With the development of the communication and computing technology, there is an emerging need for the new core stream cipher in the upcoming 5G applications which offers 256-bit security. As far as we know, no attacks on ZUC-256 have been published so far.

The Trivium stream cipher [6] is one of the seven finalists by eSTREAM project and has been accepted as ISO standard. Trivium has a simple structure, with only bit operations, so that it can be applicable to source restricted applications such as RFID. It has been studied extensively and shows good resistance to cryptanalysis, even after more than a decade of effort by cryptanalysts [7–12].

Related Works. In [13,14], a framework for chosen IV statistical analysis of stream ciphers is suggested to investigate the structure of the initialization. This framework works with the concept of probabilistic neutral key bits, i.e. key bits which have no influence on the value of a coefficient with some (high) probability. Compared to these attacks, the cube attack proposed by Dinur and Shamir at EUROCRYPT 2009 [15] is much more general. Cube attack treats a cryptosystem as a black-box polynomial. An attacker computes the sum of the keystream output polynomial with a fixed key over a subset of IV bits, called a *cube*, hoping to find a linear coefficient of the term with maximum degree over the cube, referred to as a *superpoly*. This is achieved via probabilistic linearity tests, to check that a superpoly is linear, and to identify which key bits it contains. Cube tester, dynamic cube attack, conditional cube attack and correlation cube attack were put forward in [16–19] respectively as four variants of cube attack. As a whole, the cube-attack-like cryptanalysis aims at analyzing the initialization of stream ciphers to construct distinguishing attacks or key recovery attacks by statistical methods. Unlike cube-attack-like cryptanalysis,

MPT is deterministic rather than statistical, and aims at evaluating the mixing properties of initialization of stream ciphers to help the stream cipher designers.

Our Contributions. In this paper, a general framework for evaluating the mixing properties of initialization of stream ciphers, called **Mixing Property Tester-MPT**, is exploited and formalized. We hope **MPT** can be considered as a general cryptanalytic tool like NIST Statistical Toolkit, to help the stream cipher designers to choose the initialization functions and the required number of initialization rounds. As illustrations, we apply our framework to ZUC-128, ZUC-256 and Trivium stream ciphers. The results show that though ZUC-256 has a much larger initial input size than ZUC-128, its mixing properties are almost as good as ZUC-128. As for Trivium, the tap positions of keystream output function are not chosen optimally with respect to this tester and we provide some better selections of tap positions.

This paper is organized as follows. A general framework for evaluating the mixing properties of initialization of stream ciphers is exploited and formalized in Sect. 2. In Sects. 3 and 4, applications to ZUC-128, ZUC-256 and Trivium stream ciphers are given to prove the effectiveness of our framework. The paper is concluded in Sect. 5.

2   Mixing Property Tester

In this section, we will propose a general idea for iteratively evaluating the mixing properties of initialization of stream ciphers, called **Mixing Property Tester-MPT**.

For a given stream cipher, let the set Ω_{Key} be made up of all key bits, and the set Ψ_{IV} be made up of all IV bits. As is well known, any internal state bit or keystream bit can be described by a multivariate master polynomial over some key bits and IV bits,

$$x_i = h(\Omega_i, \Psi_i)$$

where the set Ω_i is made up of all possible key bits in the expression of x_i, and the set Ψ_i is made up of all possible IV bits in the expression of x_i.

When evaluating the mixing properties of initialization using **MPT**, we do not need to know the algebraic normal form of function h, but just concern the two sets Ω_i and Ψ_i. For simplicity, $x_i = h(\Omega_i, \Psi_i)$ is denoted as $x_i \doteq (\Omega_i, \Psi_i)$ in this paper.

Certainly,

$$\Omega_i \subseteq \Omega_{Key} \text{ and } \Psi_i \subseteq \Psi_{IV}.$$

If the mixing is not enough, $\Omega_i \subset \Omega_{Key}$ or $\Psi_i \subset \Psi_{IV}$ probably holds, and then differential trail with probability 1 can be easily constructed. Let us investigate different scenarios:

1. If the key mixing of internal state bit $s_i^{(t)}$ at t-th clock is not enough, that is, $\Omega_i^{(t)} \subset \Omega_{Key}$, then differential trail with probability 1 in the related key

setting can be constructed for any key bit k_j satisfying $k_j \in \{\Omega_{Key} - \Omega_i^{(t)}\}$, since it has

$$\bigoplus_{k_j=\{0,1\}} s_i^{(t)} = 0.$$

2. If the IV mixing of internal state bit $s_i^{(t)}$ at t-th clock is not enough, that is, $\Psi_i^{(t)} \subset \Psi_{IV}$, then differential trail with probability 1 in the chosen IV setting can be constructed for any IV bit iv_j satisfying $iv_j \in \{\Psi_{IV} - \Psi_i^{(t)}\}$, since it has

$$\bigoplus_{iv_j=\{0,1\}} s_i^{(t)} = 0.$$

3. If the key mixing of keystream bit $z^{(t)}$ at t-th clock is not enough, that is, $\Omega^{(t)} \subset \Omega_{Key}$, then related key distinguisher with probability 1 can be constructed for any key bit k_j satisfying $k_j \in \{\Omega_{Key} - \Omega^{(t)}\}$, since it has

$$\bigoplus_{k_j=\{0,1\}} z^{(t)} = 0.$$

4. If the IV mixing of keystream bit $z^{(t)}$ at t-th clock is not enough, that is, $\Psi^{(t)} \subset \Psi_{IV}$, then chosen IV distinguisher with probability 1 can be constructed for any IV bit iv_j satisfying $iv_j \in \{\Psi_{IV} - \Psi^{(t)}\}$, since it has

$$\bigoplus_{iv_j=\{0,1\}} z^{(t)} = 0.$$

To iteratively evaluate the mixing properties of initialization of stream ciphers, we first present a basic fact on the mixing properties of initialization, and then utilize it to evaluate the mixing properties of the internal state bits and keystream bits.

Let $s_i \doteq (\Omega_i, \Psi_i)$ and $s_j \doteq (\Omega_j, \Psi_j)$ be two internal state bits, then it certainly has

$$s_i \oplus s_j \doteq (\Omega_i \cup \Omega_j, \Psi_i \cup \Psi_j)$$
$$s_i \cdot s_j \doteq (\Omega_i \cup \Omega_j, \Psi_i \cup \Psi_j)$$

As shown above, when using **MPT** to evaluate the mixing properties of initialization, we do not need to compute the algebraic normal forms of bits s_i and s_j, but just make simple set operations. To demonstrate our basic idea, a simple example is presented as follows.

Example 1. Given a toy stream cipher with the key set $\Omega_{Key} = \{k_1, k_2, k_3, k_4\}$ and the IV set $\Psi_{IV} = \{iv_1, iv_2, iv_3, iv_4\}$. Supposing that two initial state bits are loaded as $s_0 = k_2 \cdot iv_1 \oplus k_1 \cdot iv_2$ and $s_1 = k_3 \cdot iv_2 \oplus k_4 \cdot iv_3$ respectively, and the internal state bits and keystream bit are calculated as

$$s_2 = s_0 \oplus s_1$$
$$s_3 = s_0 \cdot s_1$$
$$z_0 = s_2 \oplus s_3$$

By **MPT**, we have $s_0 \doteq (\{1,2\}, \{1,2\})$ and $s_1 \doteq (\{3,4\}, \{2,3\})$, and then

$$s_2 \doteq (\{1,2\} \cup \{3,4\}, \{1,2\} \cup \{2,3\}) \doteq (\{1,2,3,4\}, \{1,2,3\})$$
$$s_3 \doteq (\{1,2\} \cup \{3,4\}, \{1,2\} \cup \{2,3\}) \doteq (\{1,2,3,4\}, \{1,2,3\})$$

$$z_0 \doteq (\{1,2,3,4\} \cup \{1,2,3,4\}, \{1,2,3\} \cup \{1,2,3\}) \doteq (\{1,2,3,4\}, \{1,2,3\})$$

Thus,

$$\bigoplus_{iv_4=\{0,1\}} z_0 = 0$$

This fact implies that we can iteratively compute the two sets of any internal state bit or keystream bit by **MPT**, without computations of the algebraic normal forms. Now we present an algorithm for iteratively computing the two sets of any internal state bit or keystream bit by **MPT**, to evaluate the mixing properties of initialization of stream ciphers, as depicted in Algorithm 1.

Algorithm 1. MPT: Evaluation on the Mixing Properties of Initialization of Stream Ciphers

---

Require: Given the ANFs of the initial state $S^{(0)} = \left(s_1^{(0)}, s_2^{(0)}, \cdots, s_L^{(0)}\right)$, the ANFs of the update functions G and output function f, and the key set $\Omega_{Key} = \{k_1, k_2, \cdots, k_n\}$ and the IV set $\Psi_{IV} = \{iv_1, iv_2, \cdots, iv_m\}$.

1: For all $1 \leq i \leq L$, set $(\Omega_i^{(0)}, \Psi_i^{(0)})$ using $s_i^{(0)}$;
2: For t from 1 to N do:
3:    For all $1 \leq i \leq L$, compute $(\Omega_i^{(t)}, \Psi_i^{(t)})$ using G and $(\Omega_i^{(t-1)}, \Psi_i^{(t-1)})$;
4: Compute (Ω_f, Ψ_f) using f and $(\Omega_i^{(N)}, \Psi_i^{(N)})(1 \leq i \leq L)$;
5: Return (Ω_f, Ψ_f).

In Algorithm 1, $S^{(t)} = \left(s_1^{(t)}, s_2^{(t)}, \cdots, s_L^{(t)}\right)$ denotes the internal state at time t with size L. The update functions $G = (g_1, g_2, \cdots, g_L)$ is written as vectorial Boolean functions from $\mathbb{F}_2^L$ to $\mathbb{F}_2^L$. The algorithm gives two sets Ω_f and Ψ_f as outputs, which are the key set and IV set of the keystream bit after N rounds respectively.

Complexity of Algorithm 1. Since the sizes of the ANFs of the update functions $G = (g_1, g_2, \cdots, g_L)$ and the output function f are constant and thus $(\Omega_i^{(t)}, \Psi_i^{(t)})(1 \leq i \leq L)$ can be calculated in constant time, the time complexity of Algorithm 1 mainly depends on the value of N. Therefore, Algorithm 1 has a linear time complexity of $\mathcal{O}(N)$. In the algorithm, it requires to store $(\Omega_i^{(t)}, \Psi_i^{(t)})(1 \leq i \leq L)$ for $t = 1, 2, \cdots, N$, which leads to a negligible memory complexity of $\mathcal{O}(N)$.

To describe the mixing property in keystream, a notion is introduced as follows.

Definition 1. The keystream bit z_t at t-th clock is called **full mixing in keystream**, if its key set Ω_{z_t} and IV set Ψ_{z_t} satisfies $\Omega_{z_t} = \Omega_{Key}$ and $\Psi_{z_t} = \Psi_{IV}$ simultaneously.

Similarly, we can define another notion to describe the mixing property in internal state as follows.

Definition 2. The internal state $S^{(t)}$ at t-th clock is called **full mixing in internal state**, if for each internal state bit $s_i^{(t)}$ the corresponding key set $\Omega_{s_i^{(t)}}$ and IV set $\Psi_{s_i^{(t)}}$ satisfies $\Omega_{s_i^{(t)}} = \Omega_{Key}$ and $\Psi_{s_i^{(t)}} = \Psi_{IV}$ simultaneously.

3 Applications to ZUC-128 and ZUC-256 Stream Ciphers

In this section, we will apply **MPT** to evaluate the mixing properties of initializations of ZUC-128 and ZUC-256 stream ciphers. We first give a brief description of these two ciphers, for more details, we refer to [1] and [5] for full specifications.

3.1 A Brief Description of ZUC-128 and ZUC-256

As depicted in Fig. 1, the stream cipher ZUC-128 is made up of three parts, i.e., a 496-bit linear feedback shift register (LFSR) defined over the field $GF(2^{31}-1)$ which consists of 16 31-bit integers $(s_{15}, s_{14}, \cdots, s_0)$ defined over the set $\{1, 2, \cdots, 2^{31} - 1\}$, a bit reorganization layer (BR) which extracts the content of the LFSR to form 4 32-bit words (X_0, X_1, X_2, X_3), a finite state machine (FSM) which takes (X_0, X_1, X_2, X_3) as inputs and 2 32-bit words R_1 and R_2 as memory cells.

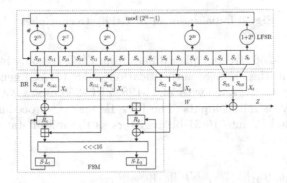

Fig. 1. Keystream generation of ZUC-128 stream cipher

The Key/IV loading procedure will expand the 128-bit initial key and the 128-bit IV into 16 31-bit registers as the initial state of the LFSR, described as follows.

For $0 \le i \le 15$, let $s_i = k_i || d_i || iv_i$.

Where k_i and iv_i, $0 \le i \le 15$, are all 8-bit bytes, and $D = d_0||d_1||\cdots||d_{15}$ is a 240-bit long constant string composed of 16 substrings of 15 bits, $||$ denotes the bit string concatenation.

During the initialization stage, as depicted in Fig. 2, the cipher executes the key/IV loading procedure, set the 32-bit memory cells R_1 and R_2 to be all 0 and then runs the following operations $32 + 1 = 33$ times.

1. Load the key, IV, and constants into the LFSR.
2. Let $R1 = R2 = 0$.
3. for $i = 0$ to 31 do
   – Bitreorganization( )
   – $W = F(X_0, X_1, X_2)$
   – LFSRWithInitializationMode($W >> 1$)
4. Bitreorganization( )
   $W = F(X_0, X_1, X_2)$ and discard W
   LFSRWithworkMode()

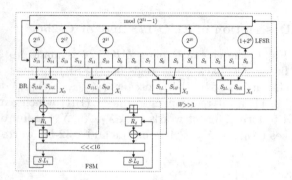

Fig. 2. Initialization of ZUC-128 stream cipher

The new ZUC-256 stream cipher differs from ZUC-128 only in the initialization phase and in the message authentication codes (MAC) generation phase, other aspects are all the same with ZUC-128. ZUC-256 uses a 256-bit secret key and a 184-bit IV as initial inputs. The Key/IV loading procedure will expand the initial key and IV into 16 31-bit registers as the initial state of the LFSR, described as follows.

$$s_0 = k_0||d_0||k_{21}||k_{16}, s_1 = k_1||d_1||k_{22}||k_{17}$$
$$s_2 = k_2||d_2||k_{23}||k_{18}, s_3 = k_3||d_3||k_{24}||k_{19}$$
$$s_4 = k_4||d_4||k_{25}||k_{20}, s_5 = iv_0||(d_5|iv_{17})||k_5||k_{26}$$
$$s_6 = iv_1||(d_6|iv_{18})||k_6||k_{27}, s_7 = iv_{10}||(d_7|iv_{19})||k_7||iv_2$$
$$s_8 = k_8||(d_8|iv_{20})||iv_3||iv_{11}, s_9 = k_9||(d_9|iv_{21})||iv_{12}||iv_4$$
$$s_{10} = iv_5||(d_{10}|iv_{22})||k_{10}||k_{28}, s_{11} = k_{11}||(d_{11}|iv_{23})||iv_6||iv_{13}$$
$$s_{12} = k_{12}||(d_{12}|iv_{24})||iv_7||iv_{14}, s_{13} = k_{13}||d_{13}||iv_{15}||iv_8$$
$$s_{14} = k_{14}||(d_{14}|(k_{31})_H^4)||iv_{16}||iv_9, s_{15} = k_{15}||(d_{15}|(k_{31})_L^4)||k_{30}||k_{29}$$

Where k_i for $0 \leq i \leq 31$ and iv_i for $0 \leq i \leq 16$ are all 8-bit bytes, $(k_{31})_H^4$ is the high 4 bits of the byte k_{31}, $(k_{31})_L^4$ is the low 4 bits of k_{31}, iv_i for $17 \leq i \leq 24$ are 6-bit string occupying the 6 least significant bits of a byte, d_i for $0 \leq i \leq 15$ are the 7-bit constants used in the ZUC-256 stream cipher, and | denotes the bitwise logic OR.

3.2 Evaluation on the Mixing Properties of Initializations of ZUC-128 and ZUC-256 Stream Ciphers

In this subsection, the mixing properties of initializations of ZUC-128 and ZUC-256 stream ciphers are evaluated by **MPT**.

When Will Full Mixing in Keystream Be Achieved? By **MPT**, we can iteratively compute the two sets of any keystream bit, without computations of the algebraic normal forms. We apply Algorithm 1 to initializations of ZUC-128 and ZUC-256 stream ciphers, and then their mixing properties in keystream are obtained, as depicted in Table 1.

Table 1. The maximum numbers of rounds of not achieving full mixing in keystream for ZUC-128 and ZUC-256

Stream cipher	ZUC-128	ZUC-256
# Rounds with respect to all key bits	4	4
# Rounds with respect to all IV bits	4	3

As shown in Table 1, related key distinguisher and also chosen IV distinguisher with probability 1 on 4-round ZUC-128 can be constructed. Similarly, related key distinguisher with probability 1 on 4-round ZUC-256, and chosen IV distinguisher with probability 1 on 3-round ZUC-256 can be constructed.

When Will Full Mixing in Internal State Be Achieved? By **MPT**, we can iteratively compute the two sets of any internal state bit, without computations of the algebraic normal forms. We apply Algorithm 1 to initializations of ZUC-128 and ZUC-256 stream ciphers, and then their mixing properties in internal state are obtained, as depicted in Table 2.

Table 2. The maximum numbers of rounds of not achieving full mixing in internal state for ZUC-128 and ZUC-256

Stream cipher	ZUC-128	ZUC-256
# Rounds with respect to all key bits	19	19
# Rounds with respect to all IV bits	18	19

As shown in Table 2, related key differential trail with probability 1 on 19-round ZUC-128, and chosen IV differential trail with probability 1 on 18-round ZUC-128 can be constructed. Similarly, related key differential trail and also chosen IV differential trail with probability 1 on 19-round ZUC-256 can be constructed.

The results above imply that the initializations of ZUC-128 and ZUC-256 stream ciphers both have enough security margin towards this tester, since both of them have 33 rounds in the initialization phase. Simultaneously, though ZUC-256 has a much larger initial input size than ZUC-128, its mixing properties are almost as good as ZUC-128, as showed by our results.

4   Application to Trivium Stream Cipher

In this section, we will apply **MPT** to evaluate the mixing properties of initialization of Trivium stream cipher. We first give a brief description of this cipher, for more details, we refer to [6] for full specification.

4.1   A Brief Description of Trivium Stream Cipher

Trivium consists of 288 internal state bits, denoted by $s_1, s_2, \cdots, s_{288}$, stored in three NFSRs of different lengths 93, 84 and 111. The keystream generation process is given as follows.

For $i = 1$ to N do
$$z_i \leftarrow s_{66} \oplus s_{93} \oplus s_{162} \oplus s_{177} \oplus s_{243} \oplus s_{288}$$
$$t_1 \leftarrow s_{66} \oplus s_{91} \cdot s_{92} \oplus s_{93} \oplus s_{171}$$
$$t_2 \leftarrow s_{162} \oplus s_{175} \cdot s_{176} \oplus s_{177} \oplus s_{264}$$
$$t_3 \leftarrow s_{243} \oplus s_{286} \cdot s_{287} \oplus s_{288} \oplus s_{69}$$
$$(s_1, s_2, \cdots, s_{93}) \leftarrow (t_3, s_1, \cdots, s_{92})$$
$$(s_{94}, s_{95}, \cdots, s_{177}) \leftarrow (t_1, s_{94}, \cdots, s_{176})$$
$$(s_{178}, s_{179}, \cdots, s_{288}) \leftarrow (t_2, s_{178}, \cdots, s_{287})$$
End for

In the initialization, the 80-bit key and 80-bit IV are loaded into the initial state, and all the remaining bits, except three bits, are set to 0. Before generating the keyscream bit z_i, the internal state is updated $4 \times 288 = 1152$ times.

$$(s_1, s_2, \cdots, s_{93}) \leftarrow (k_1, k_2, \cdots, k_{80}, 0, \cdots, 0)$$
$$(s_{94}, s_{95}, \cdots, s_{177}) \leftarrow (iv_1, iv_2, \cdots, iv_{80}, 0, 0, 0, 0)$$
$$(s_{178}, s_{179}, \cdots, s_{288}) \leftarrow (0, \cdots, 0, 1, 1, 1)$$

In [20], Turan and Kara proposed a new method for initialization of Trivium which is very similar to the original. In this modified Trivium, the only difference is related to the initial assignment of state bits, and only 22 of the internal state variables are set to constants.

4.2 Evaluation on the Mixing Properties of Initialization of Trivium Stream Cipher

In this subsection, the mixing properties of initializations of Trivium and modified Trivium stream ciphers are evaluated by **MPT**.

When Will Full Mixing in Keystream and Internal State Be Achieved Respectively? By **MPT**, we can iteratively compute the two sets of any keystream bit or internal state bit, without computations of the algebraic normal forms. We apply Algorithm 1 to initializations of Trivium and modified Trivium stream ciphers, and then their mixing properties in keystream and internal state are obtained, as depicted in Table 3.

Table 3. The maximum numbers of rounds of not achieving full mixing in keystream and internal state for Trivium and modified Trivium

Trivium \ modified Trivium	Full mixing in keystream	Full mixing in internal state
# Rounds with respect to all key bits	343 \ 280	555 \ 426
# Rounds with respect to all IV bits	333 \ 288	546 \ 405

As shown in Table 3, the results imply that the initializations of Trivium and modified Trivium stream ciphers both have enough security margin towards this tester, since both of them have 1152 rounds in the initialization phase. It is also implied that modified Trivium has better mixing properties than original Trivium. In [20], Turan and Kara claimed that full mixing in internal state is achieved after 525 rounds for Trivium, while 484 rounds are enough for modified Trivium. However, our results show that 525 rounds are not enough to achieve full mixing in internal state for Trivium, and 426 rounds are enough for modified Trivium. It implies and confirms the effectiveness and accuracy of our general framework.

Whether the Tap Positions of Keystream Output Function Be Well-chosen? Trivium uses a simple linear keystream output function, which selects two variables from each of three NFSRs as inputs and outputs a keystream bit. Thus, different tap positions of keystream output function imply different mixing properties. Now, we formalize the linear keystream output function of Trivium as follows.

$$z_i \leftarrow s_a \oplus s_{n_A} \oplus s_b \oplus s_{n_B} \oplus s_c \oplus s_{n_C}$$

Where the tap positions satisfy $1 \leq a < n_A = 93, 94 \leq b < n_B = 177, 178 \leq c < n_C = 288$.

We have exhausted all the possible tap positions of keystream output function within one second on a common PC. The amount of such possible tap positions

Table 4. Some better tap positions of keystream output function of Trivium

Tap positions $a = 0, b = 99, c = 206$	Full mixing in keystream
# Rounds with respect to all key bits	263
# Rounds with respect to all IV bits	274
Tap positions $a = 5, b = 95, c = 220$	Full mixing in keystream
# Rounds with respect to all key bits	273
# Rounds with respect to all IV bits	267
Tap positions $a = 6, b = 96, c = 195$	Full mixing in keystream
# Rounds with respect to all key bits	274
# Rounds with respect to all IV bits	259
Tap positions $a = 7, b = 98, c = 212$	Full mixing in keystream
# Rounds with respect to all key bits	269
# Rounds with respect to all IV bits	270

is $92 \times 83 \times 110 = 839960$. For each possible (a, b, c), Algorithm 1 is executed. As results, some better tap positions are obtained, as depicted in Table 4.

5　Conclusions

A general framework for evaluating the mixing properties of initialization of stream ciphers, called **Mixing Property Tester-MPT**, is exploited and formalized in this paper. Based on this general framework we propose a concrete and efficient algorithm, which can compute the maximum number of initialization rounds of a given stream cipher such that any internal state bit or generated keystream bit does not achieve full mixing properties. Our algorithm has linear time complexity and needs a negligible amount of memory. As illustrations, we apply our algorithm to ZUC-128, ZUC-256 and Trivium stream ciphers. We hope **MPT** can be considered as a general cryptanalytic tool like NIST Statistical Toolkit, to help stream cipher designers to choose the initialization functions and the required number of initialization rounds.

Acknowledgments. The authors would like to thank the anonymous reviewers for their valuable comments and suggestions. This work was supported by the National Natural Science Foundation of China under Grant 61602514, 61802437, 61272488, 61202491, 61572516, 61272041, 61772547, National Cryptography Development Fund under Grant MMJJ20170125 and National Postdoctoral Program for Innovative Talents under Grant BX201700153.

References

1. ETSI/SAGE: Specification of the 3GPP Confidentiality and Integrity Algorithms 128-EEA3 & 128-EIA3, Document 2: ZUC Specification, Version 1.6, 28 June 2011. http://gsmworld.com/documents/EEA3_EIA3_ZUC_v1_6.pdf

2. Zhou, C., Feng, X., Lin, D.: The initialization stage analysis of ZUC v1.5. In: Lin, D., Tsudik, G., Wang, X. (eds.) CANS 2011. LNCS, vol. 7092, pp. 40–53. Springer, Heidelberg (2011). https://doi.org/10.1007/978-3-642-25513-7_5

3. Guan, J., Ding, L., Liu, S.: Guess and determine attack on SNOW3G and ZUC. J. Softw. **24**(6), 1324–1333 (2013). (in Chinese)

4. Lafitte, F., Markowitch, O., Heule, D.V.: SAT based analysis of LTE stream cipher ZUC. J. Inf. Secur. Appl. **22**, 54–65 (2015)

5. Design Team: ZUC-256 stream cipher. J. Cryptologic Res. **5**(2), 167–179 (2018)

6. De Cannière, C., Preneel, B.: Trivium. In: Robshaw, M., Billet, O. (eds.) New Stream Cipher Designs. LNCS, vol. 4986, pp. 244–266. Springer, Heidelberg (2008). https://doi.org/10.1007/978-3-540-68351-3_18

7. Maximov, A., Biryukov, A.: Two trivial attacks on TRIVIUM. In: Adams, C., Miri, A., Wiener, M. (eds.) SAC 2007. LNCS, vol. 4876, pp. 36–55. Springer, Heidelberg (2007). https://doi.org/10.1007/978-3-540-77360-3_3

8. Fouque, P.-A., Vannet, T.: Improving key recovery to 784 and 799 rounds of trivium using optimized cube attacks. In: Moriai, S. (ed.) FSE 2013. LNCS, vol. 8424, pp. 502–517. Springer, Heidelberg (2014). https://doi.org/10.1007/978-3-662-43933-3_26

9. Liu, M., Lin, D., Wang, W.: Searching cubes for testing Boolean functions and its application to Trivium. In: IEEE International Symposium on Information Theory (ISIT 2015), Hong Kong, China, 14–19 June 2015, pp. 496–500. IEEE (2015)

10. Liu, M.: Degree evaluation of NFSR-based cryptosystems. In: Katz, J., Shacham, H. (eds.) CRYPTO 2017. LNCS, vol. 10403, pp. 227–249. Springer, Cham (2017). https://doi.org/10.1007/978-3-319-63697-9_8

11. Todo, Y., Isobe, T., Hao, Y., Meier, W.: Cube attacks on non-blackbox polynomials based on division property. In: Katz, J., Shacham, H. (eds.) CRYPTO 2017. LNCS, vol. 10403, pp. 250–279. Springer, Cham (2017). https://doi.org/10.1007/978-3-319-63697-9_9

12. Wang, Q., Hao, Y., Todo, Y., Li, C., Isobe, T., Meier, W.: Improved division property based cube attacks exploiting algebraic properties of superpoly. In: Shacham, H., Boldyreva, A. (eds.) CRYPTO 2018. LNCS, vol. 10991, pp. 275–305. Springer, Cham (2018). https://doi.org/10.1007/978-3-319-96884-1_10

13. Englund, H., Johansson, T., Sönmez Turan, M.: A framework for chosen IV statistical analysis of stream ciphers. In: Srinathan, K., Rangan, C.P., Yung, M. (eds.) INDOCRYPT 2007. LNCS, vol. 4859, pp. 268–281. Springer, Heidelberg (2007). https://doi.org/10.1007/978-3-540-77026-8_20

14. Fischer, S., Khazaei, S., Meier, W.: Chosen IV statistical analysis for key recovery attacks on stream ciphers. In: Vaudenay, S. (ed.) AFRICACRYPT 2008. LNCS, vol. 5023, pp. 236–245. Springer, Heidelberg (2008). https://doi.org/10.1007/978-3-540-68164-9_16

15. Dinur, I., Shamir, A.: Cube attacks on tweakable black box polynomials. In: Joux, A. (ed.) EUROCRYPT 2009. LNCS, vol. 5479, pp. 278–299. Springer, Heidelberg (2009). https://doi.org/10.1007/978-3-642-01001-9_16

16. Aumasson, J.-P., Dinur, I., Meier, W., Shamir, A.: Cube testers and key recovery attacks on reduced-round MD6 and Trivium. In: Dunkelman, O. (ed.) FSE 2009. LNCS, vol. 5665, pp. 1–22. Springer, Heidelberg (2009). https://doi.org/10.1007/978-3-642-03317-9_1

17. Dinur, I., Shamir, A.: Breaking Grain-128 with dynamic cube attacks. In: Joux, A. (ed.) FSE 2011. LNCS, vol. 6733, pp. 167–187. Springer, Heidelberg (2011). https://doi.org/10.1007/978-3-642-21702-9_10

18. Huang, S., Wang, X., Xu, G., Wang, M., Zhao, J.: Conditional cube attack on reduced-round keccak sponge function. In: Coron, J.-S., Nielsen, J.B. (eds.) EURO-CRYPT 2017. LNCS, vol. 10211, pp. 259–288. Springer, Cham (2017). https://doi.org/10.1007/978-3-319-56614-6_9

19. Liu, M., Yang, J., Wang, W., Lin, D.: Correlation cube attacks: from weak-key distinguisher to key recovery. In: Nielsen, J.B., Rijmen, V. (eds.) EUROCRYPT 2018. LNCS, vol. 10821, pp. 715–744. Springer, Cham (2018). https://doi.org/10.1007/978-3-319-78375-8_23

20. Sönmez Turan, M., Kara, O.: Linear approximations for 2-round trivium. In: Proceedings of First International Conference on Security of Information and Networks (SIN 2007), Gazimagusa (TRNC), North Cyprus, 8–10 May 2007, pp. 96–105. Trafford Publishing (2007)

Blockchain Based Data Transmission Control for Tactical Data Link

Wei Feng[1], Yafeng Li[2], Xuetao Yang[1], Zheng Yan[1,3]($\boxtimes$) (iD), and Liang Chen[2]

[1] State Key Laboratory of Integrated Services Networks, Xidian University,
Xi'an 710071, China
weifeng.imk@gmail.com, bsyangxt@foxmail.com, zyan@xidian.edu.cn
[2] The 20th Research Institute of China Electronics Technology Group Corporation,
Xi'an 710061, China
xxddxdd@yeah.net, 772029466@qq.com
[3] Department of Communications and Networking, Aalto University,
02150 Espoo, Finland

Abstract. Tactical Data Link (TDL) is a communication system that utilizes a certain message format and a protocol to transmit data via wireless channels in an instant, automatic, and secure way. So far, TDL has shown special importance in military applications. Current TDL adopts a distributed architecture to enhance anti-destruction capacity. However, TDL faces the problem of data inconsistency and thus cannot well support cooperation across multiple militarily domains. To tackle this problem, we propose to leverage blockchain to build an automatic and adaptive data transmission control mechanism for TDL. It achieves automatic data transmission and realizes information consensus among TDL consensus nodes. Besides, smart contracts based on blockchain further enable adjusting data transmission policies automatically. The experimental results illustrate effectiveness and efficiency of our proposed blockchain based data transmission control for TDL.

Keywords: Blockchain · Tactical Data Link · Consensus · Data transmission control

1 Introduction

Tactical Data Link (TDL) is a communication system that utilizes a certain message format and a common protocol to transmit data via wireless channels in an instant, automatic, and secure way [10]. It aims to reduce the time of Observing, Orientating, Deciding, and Acting (OODA) loop so that the reaction time of military units is greatly shortened. Therefore, TDL is significant in terms of military capacity improvement, and thus has attracted considerable attention [9,11].

Existing TDL systems are able to achieve high throughput, low latency, and high anti-destruction capacity, which makes a great difference in battlefields.

© Springer Nature Singapore Pte Ltd. 2019
G. Wang et al. (Eds.): iSCI 2019, CCIS 1122, pp. 583–595, 2019.
https://doi.org/10.1007/978-981-15-1301-5_46

Currently, TDLs are widely applied in different military scenarios and various dedicated TDLs have been developed [3]. Different from original TDLs, nowadays, TDLs usually adopt a distributed architecture rather than a point-to-point or centralized architecture. In this way, it achieves strong anti-destruction capacity. However, the emergence of various types of TDLs also leads to a severe problem, i.e., how to support cooperation across multiple military domains in an automatic and adaptive way, especially in inter-military-domain scenarios. In modern battlefields, it is unavoidable that combat units from different military domains cooperate with each other. A battlefield event usually requires the cooperative reaction of multiple military domains. To achieve this goal, it is necessary to build a practical data transmission control system so that each domain is well aware of the events, status, and decisions of a battle.

It is challenging to control data transmission in inter-domain cooperation in a trustworthy way. Past work about trust management cannot solve this issue [14–16]. First, current TDLs cannot guarantee data consistency among different domains. Second, data transmission in TDL is dynamic. The data should be transmitted to different parties based on the status of a battlefield. Third, modern military request high autonomy, and the military information and messages should be transmitted automatically rather than artificially in order to reduce transmission delay. However, these issues have rarely been explored.

On the other hand, the emergence of blockchain provides an effective tool to achieve automatic data transmission in a TDL system. Blockchain, which is first applied in a decentralized cryptocurrency system, has attracted considerable attention. It provides a way of data storage with immunity, trust and traceability in a decentralized manner. The development of Ethereum that employs blockchain as a platform for smart contract expands the application of blockchain from cryptocurrency or decentralized ledger to Internet of Things (IoT) [4], smart cities [13], etc. Ethereum supports trustworthy execution of codes called smart automatically in a decentralized method. Therefore, applying blockchain into TDL could overcome the mentioned three challenges.

There are three types of blockchain: public blockchain, private blockchain, and consortium blockchain. Among them, public blockchain is an open system. Obviously, it is not suitable for TDLs since the openness provides enemies more opportunities to compromise the system. Private blockchain involves a centralized party for management and thereby faces single point of failure problem. Therefore, we consider the utilization of consortium blockchain for data transmission control in TDLs since in consortium blockchain, only authenticated entity can work as consensus nodes and it well supports decentralization. A typical consortium blockchain is based on Practical Byzantine Fault Tolerance (PBFT) algorithm [2]. However, employing PBFT based blockchain to build a practical data transmission control system for TDL confronts several problems. PBFT suffers from high communication overhead. Besides, it treats all consensus nodes equally, which may not be reasonable in TDL, since military consensus nodes differ in terms of importance and authority. Furthermore, how to achieve autonomy, adaptivity, and flexibility in blockchain based data transmission control for

TDL is seldom investigated. In our opinion, PBFT is not proper to be applied into TDL for data transmission control based on blockchain.

In this paper, we employ a consortium blockchain based on a newly proposed weighted PBFT algorithm to build automatic and adaptive data transmission control in TDL with smart contract as a support. Our work is different from existing works because we aim to solve the cooperation problem among various tactical parties in an autonomic and trustworthy way by employing blockchain. Concretely, we deploy blockchain to control data transmission among various combat centres rather than end devices [12]. As far as we know, this is the first work that builds a consistent and automatic data transmission mechanism for TDL based on blockchain. The main contributions of this paper can be summarized as follows:

1. We propose a weighted PBFT algorithm, which considers the variety of resistance capacities to attacks.
2. Based on the weighted PBFT algorithm and the properties of TDL, we design a consortium blockchain for controlling data transmission across multiple domains of TDL.
3. The proposed blockchain based data transmission control system enables military entities to obtain data transmission strategies automatically and solves the data asymmetry problem in TDL.

The rest of the paper is organized is follows. In Sect. 2, we describe the research background as well as related works. We present our problem statement of our research in Sect. 3, and detail the design of the automatic and adaptive data transmission control mechanism in Sect. 4. We evaluate the performance of our mechanism in Sect. 5. Finally, we conclude our paper in Sect. 6.

2   Background and Related Work

In this section, we introduce the development and application of TDL, as well as the recent advance of blockchain.

2.1   Tactical Data Link

The first TDL system was developed and deployed in America in 1950s [10]. The original TDL system, called Link-4, greatly reduces the time of OODA loop and helps quick military reaction. However, Link-4 itself faces several problems. First, Link-4 adopts point-to-point communication for data transmission, thus cannot effectively achieve data broadcast or multi-cast. Second, it transmits data in plaintext, thus cannot resist eavesdropping. To tackle these problems, Link-11 introduces encryption in TDL for achieving data confidentiality.

To improve the performance of TDL in cooperation, anti-destruction, and throughput, Link-16 and Link-22 were developed [10]. The two TDL systems well improve throughput. Especially, they adopt a distributed architecture, which helps enhancing anti-destruction ability. However, they still cannot support the cooperation of different armed forces. Apart from Link-16 and Link22, TDLs for dedicated applications were also developed and explored, such as command and control system for coast guard shipboard [7], imagery transmission issue in Link-16 [5], and IP address translation method for tactical networks [8], etc. However, the automatic data transmission among various data links still remains open.

2.2 Blockchain and Its Applications

Blockchain, the fundamental technology of Bitcoin [6], is composed of a number of data blocks that are linked through applying a one-way hash function. A blockchain system is decentralized and its security relies on a consensus mechanism, rather than a fully trusted centralized party. Owing to its advantage of decentralization, immunity, and consistency, blockchain has attracted impressive attention. Currently, the application of blockchain have expanded from cryptocurrency to various fields, like data management [17], Internet of Things (IoT) [4], etc. Therefore, it is an effective tool to build a decentralized and robust data transmission control mechanism for TDL. Among the various blockchain, public blockchain is not suitable for TDLs due to its openness and low efficiency. Therefore, we consider to apply consortium blockchain in TDL.

However, blockchain's application in TDL has seldom been investigated. Different from the public blockchain, the consortium blockchain usually leverages a consensus mechanism like Practical Byzantine Fault Tolerance (PBFT) Algorithm [1], etc., rather than Proof of Work (PoW) [6]. Among the consensus mechanisms, PBFT algorithm outperforms others because of its excellent performance in Byzantine fault tolerance. However, it also faces some problems, e.g., high communication overhead. In addition, It attaches equal importance to each consensus node, which cannot reflect the situation of TDL. Therefore, PBFT algorithm seems not proper to be applied in TDL directly.

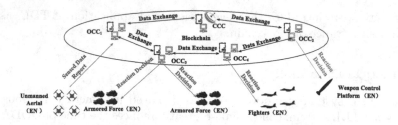

Fig. 1. System model

3   Problem Statement

This section presents the system model and security model of TDL and specifies the research problems and design goals of our work.

3.1   System and Security Model

In this subsection, we present a system model of TDL and specify the security model as well.

System Model: The TDL system is composed of a Chief Command Center (CCC), multiple Operation Command Centers (OCC) for different regions, and various types of execution nodes (EN), as depicted in Fig. 1. Generally, there is a unique CCC in the whole system and a number of OCCs for different regions or armies that send commands to relative ENs. ENs can be armies, combat platforms, and sensors deployed in battlefield. They are responsible for collecting data, submitting data to corresponding OCC, and reacting based on the commands received. For easy presentation, we suppose there are totally N consensus nodes in blockchain network including one unique CCC and $N-1$ OCCs. We denote the set of all consensus nodes as $CN = \{cn_i\}_{0 \leq i \leq N-1}$, where cn_0 represents the CCC and $cn_i(1 \leq i \leq N-1)$ represents OCC.

The CCC and the OCCs work as consensus nodes to cooperatively maintain a blockchain network. The blockchain stores key information for data transmission control, i.e., code of smart contracts for data transmission control and data transmission history. When an EN senses battlefield data, it sends the data to corresponding OCC. The OCC, when receiving the collected data, loads the smart contract stored in the blockchain to obtain the data transmission strategy of and then transmits the data to data receivers. All consensus nodes publish a notification message on the blockchain when receiving the data so that others can notice whether the data has been received by others to ensure data consistency.

Security Model: In our scheme, the CCC is the most powerful entity among all TDL entities, and it has strong ability to resist outer attackers. Besides, for the CCC and OCCs, they may be compromised or ruined, although the probability is low. We assume the adversary can only compromise a limited number of them. We also assume that the probability that a consensus node is ruined or compromised is different from each other. Compared with OCCs and CCC, ENs may be ruined by adversary, so we assume that they cannot be fully trusted.

In our security model, we measure the resistance capacities of the CCC and OCCs with the cost required by the attackers to compromise them. Denote the set of cost to compromise CCC or OCCs as $C = \{c_i\}_{0 \leq i \leq N-1}$, where c_i represents the cost to compromise cn_i. Obviously, a larger c_i means more powerful resistance capacity to attacks. Since cn_0 has more powerful resistance capacity than the others, $\forall c_i$, we have $c_0 \geq c_i$. Without loss of generality, we assume that $c_0 \geq c_1 \geq \ldots \geq c_{N-1}$.

3.2   Research Problems and Design Goals

Herein, we specify the research problems we aim to solve and present our design goals. As aforementioned, the PBFT algorithm is not proper for TDL because it incurs high communication overhead and treats all consensus nodes equal, while in TDL, different entities have different probability of being ruined or compromised. Besides, how to achieve autonomy, adaptivity, and flexibility in blockchain based data transmission control for TDL has not yet been explored. We aim to employ a consortium blockchain to build an automatic and trustful data transmission control mechanism for TDL. To be specific, our design goals are summarized as below:

1. Improve the PBFT algorithm to make it suitable for TDL.
2. Design a flexible and efficient blockchain system for TDL based on the proposed PBFT algorithm.
3. Build an automatic and trustworthy data transmission control mechanism based on the designed blockchain and smart contacts.

4 Mechanism Design

In this section, we introduce the weighted PBFT based on node capability, the blockchain based on the weighted PBFT, and the blockchain-based data transmission control mechanism.

4.1 Overview

The whole system operates as follows. First, ENs sense battlefield data and send the data to corresponding OCCs. When an OCC receives data sent by an EN, it first checks whether the data is from an authorized EN. If not, the OCC will ignore the data. If the data pass the verification, the OCC will take the data attributes, like content, type, location, etc., as input, invoke the smart contract in blockchain, and output the related data transmission strategy. Then, the OCC sends the data to the receivers according to the transmission strategy obtained through smart contract via a pre-established secure channel. Besides, it will also generate a notification, which includes the attributes and the digest of the data, and transmit the data to the CCC. When the number of notification received by the CCC reaches the predefined threshold, the CCC generates a block and delivers the block to all OCCs in network. The CCC and all OCCs will employ weighted PBFT algorithm to achieve consensus on the block.

4.2 Weighted Practical Byzantine Fault Tolerance

In this subsection, we present the details of the weighted PBFT algorithm based on node capacity, which is derived from the PBFT algorithm. Considering the variety in the ability of resisting military strikes and network attacks, the weight of each consensus node should be determined by their resistance capacities to attacks. Inspired by this idea, we herein propose the weighted PBFT algorithm. The details of weighted PBFT are described as follows:

1. **SystemSetup:** The system establishes a series of security parameters for all system consensus nodes. First, cn_0 generates its own public/private key pairs

(PK_{cn_0}, SK_{cn_0}). Based on the importance and capacity, we attach a weight to each cn_i in CN denoted as ω_i. The sum of the weight of all consensus nodes is 1. Besides, the system consists of a leader, and at the beginning of the system setup, cn_0 acts as the leader.

2. **Request:** When the leader needs the system to reach consensus on a message m, it will generate $PrePrepare$ involving m, signs it, and broadcasts the message to all consensus nodes.

3. **Preprepare:** In this process, each cn_i that receives the $PrePrepare$ message will check its validity by verifying its signature and the content of the message.

4. **Prepare:** If the validity check on the message holds in the node cn_i, cn_i will generate a $Prepare$ message, signs it, and broadcasts it to the other $N - 1$ nodes. Then cn_i waits for $Prepare$ message sent by others. Once cn_i receives sufficient $Prepare$ messages, it starts the next procedure. The requirement to judge whether to start the next procedure is presented as below:

   Suppose $CN_{Prepare}$ is the set of nodes whose $Prepare$ message has been received by cn_i (including cn_i), then cn_i enters the next procedure if and only if the equation $\sum_{cn_j \in CN_{Prepare}} \omega_j > \frac{2}{3}$ holds.

5. **Commit:** When a node cn_i starts the $Commit$ procedure, it generates a $Commit$ message and broadcasts it to all other nodes in the System. The number of the $Commit$ messages received by cn_i indicates whether the system has reached consensus. Suppose CN_{Commit} is the set of nodes whose $Commit$ message has been received by cn_i (including cn_i), then cn_i considers the procedure of $Commit$ ends and the system has reached the consensus, if and only if $\sum_{cn_j \in CN_{Commit}} \omega_j > \frac{2}{3}$.

Weight Setting: In TDL, different cn_i has different resistance capacities to attacks, which is measured with the cost needed by attackers to compromise it. Generally, attackers will minimize their cost to compromise the system. PBFT attaches equal importance to each consensus node, which enables attackers to compromise the whole system with little cost by selecting consensus nodes that have low resistance capacities. Informally, given $c_t = \sum_{1 \leq j \leq N} c_i$, attackers may be able to compromise the blockchain with cost less than $\frac{1}{3}c_t$ by selecting $N/3$ nodes with the lowest cost in CN. To tackle issue, we proposed weighted PBFT, and the weight of each consensus node is related to the cost needed by attackers to compromise it. We aim at that the total cost to compromise the system is at least $\frac{1}{3}c_t$ regardless of the strategies of attackers.

To achieve this goal, in our scheme, a consensus node cn_i has higher weight if the corresponding c_i is higher. To be specific, suppose that the weight of the consensus node cn_i in TDL is denoted as ω_i, then $\omega_i = \frac{c_i}{\sum_{1 \leq j \leq N} c_j}$. We consider the method reasonable since it guarantees that the total weight of compromised consensus nodes is linear to the cost of attackers. As a result, the attackers has no way to gain more weight with less cost. While in PBFT, the attackers can compromise the consensus nodes with weaker abilities to reduce the total cost, which illustrates the superiority of our scheme.

Leader Change: The cn_i with the highest resistance capacity acts as the leader. At the beginning of the system setup, the cn_0 acts as leader. However, it is possible that cn_0 is compromised or ruined. In this case, the cn_i except the cn_0 with highest resistance capacity will be selected as the next leader for block creation. Specifically, if the next leader detects that current leader is ruined or compromised, it generates a signal and broadcasts the signal to all cn_i. If the system reaches consensus on the signal, current leader will be excluded from the system, and the next leader begin working.

4.3   Blockchain Based on Weighted PBFT

Based on the weighted PBFT algorithm proposed in Sect. 4.2, we further build a blockchain system for TDL. For each block, it contains the ID of its previous block, i.e., the hash of the previous block; the block number, which indicates the location of the block in the blockchain; smart contracts for data transmission control, with which TDL entities can obtain the data transmission strategies in a trustworthy way; the signature on the block content generated by CCC.

The leader is responsible for block creation. When the leader collects a certain number of notifications from other consensus nodes, it will create a block and leverage the weighted PBFT algorithm to reach the consensus on the block content. However, in reality, especially in military scenarios, there will certainly be some urgent messages that have to be sent to other consensus nodes without any delay. When there is an urgent message but the number of messages has not reached the predefined threshold, it will cause serious risks and loss. To tackle this problem, we attach a priority to each type of message, and propose three criteria for block generation listed as follows:

1. The number of messages received exceeds the predefined threshold Thr_{Num};
2. There is a message with a priority higher than a threshold Thr_{Pri};
3. The leader has waited for a period longer than the threshold Thr_{Time}.

4.4   Blockchain Based Data Transmission Control

Based on the proposed blockchain, we design a data transmission control mechanism for TDL.

Autonomous Data Transmission: The TDL requests automatic control on data transmission. Specifically, all OCCs, when receiving data from ENs, will obtain a data transmission strategy indicating to whom the message should be sent. In this way, the data collected can be automatically transmitted to expected receivers. Besides, the OCCs will also send a notification that indicates data transmission history. The whole process is described below:

1. The leader sets up a smart contract of data transmission control, which takes as input data type, data content, etc., and outputs a data transmission strategy indicating the receiver, priority, etc. Then, the leader generates a new

block by inserting the smart contract into it, and then broadcasts the block to all consensus nodes, which load the weighted PBFT algorithm to reach the consensus on the block. Once a consensus node convince that the block has been accepted by most of network consensus nodes, it will consider the smart contract recorded in the block to be valid.

2. When an OCC receives a data report from the ENs, it will first check the validity of the data packet. If it passes the verification, the OCC will load the smart contract recorded in the blockchain and obtain the transmission strategy for the data. Then, it generates a data report, involving the data content, transmission strategy, and its signature on the report, and transmits the data report to the receivers obtained by the contract. It will also send a notification message to the leader, which only differs from data report in that the data content is replaced by a data digest.

3. All OCCs receiving the data report will check its validity by verifying the strategy involved in the data report is correctly calculated through smart contract. If the data report is valid, it will accept the data report and as well send a notification to the leader indicating that it has received the report.

4. The leader checks whether the requirement to generate a new block is fulfilled each time it receives a new notification. If there exist enough notifications or an urgent notification, the leader will package all notifications and generate a new block. All consensus nodes will reach consensus via the weighted PBFT algorithm. In this way, all consensus nodes are aware of whether the data has reached the corresponding OCC.

5   Performance Evaluation

In this section, we conduct a series of experiments to test the performance of the weighted PBFT. To demonstrate its superiority, we compare our mechanism with PBFT in terms of the above evaluation metrics.

5.1   Communication Analysis

In this subsection, we analyzed the communication complexity to evaluate the communication overhead of our scheme. To be specific, the communication overhead is mainly resulted by the consensus algorithm. Our weighted PBFT has almost the same communication complexity as PBFT, i.e., $\mathcal{O}(N^2)$. If we take into account the number of messages m, the total communication complexity is $\mathcal{O}(mN^2)$. However, our scheme allows the consensus node to batch multiple messages into a block and then communicate with each other to reach consensus on the block rather than each message. In this way, the communication complexity is reduced to $\mathcal{O}(\frac{mN^2}{N_{thr}})$, where N_{thr} the threshold for block generation.

5.2   Experiment Setting

We conduct our experiments with JAVA language on a laptop running Windows 10 with 1.7 GHz Intel Core I5 CPU and 8 GB DDR3 RAM. We simulated the weighted PBFT based blockchain system with 50 consensus nodes. In our implementation, the average size of each transaction is 600 bytes. The size of each block is determined by the threshold for block creation. When the threshold is 100, the block size is around 60 KB. We tested the performance under different message generation rates and different thresholds for block generation. Our evaluation does not use the metrics such as network bandwidth since our scheme is designed for combat centres rather than execution nodes. Therefore, we evaluated the proposed weighted PBFT with three criteria: block generation latency, and message confirmation latency, and throughput, which are defined as follows:

1. **Block Generation Latency:** The block generation latency is measured as the average generation time of a single block.
2. **Message Confirmation Latency:** The transaction confirmation latency is the response time per transaction, which is measured as the length of the time duration from when the message is submitted to blockchain to the system reaches consistency on the block containing the message.
3. **Throughput:** The throughput is measured as the maximum number of messages successfully recorded in blockchain per second without incurring long message confirmation delay.

5.3   Block Generation Latency

We conducted experiments to test the block generation latency with regard to the message rate and compared the block generation latency of the weighted PBFT based blockchain with that of PBFT based blockchain. The experimental results are summarized in Fig. 2(a). From the Fig. 2(a), we can see that the block generation latency decreases with the increase of message generation rate at first, and then it keeps unchanged. This is because a higher a message generation rate makes it faster to meet the threshold for block generation. However, it takes a certain time for a block to reach consistency among consensus nodes. In this case, the increase of message generation rate does not cause the consensus time of a block reducing because the leader does not create a new block until the previous block reaches consistency. Therefore, when the message generation rate is high enough, the block generation latency almost remains unchanged.

We could also see that the block generation latency of weighted PBFT based blockchain is shorter than PBFT based blockchain. This is because in PBFT, the number of honest consensus nodes involved is at least $2f + 1$ ($> \frac{2}{3}N$), where the total number of consensus nodes is $N = 3f + 1$. While our scheme requires that the total weight the involved honest consensus nodes exceeds $\frac{2}{3}$ to reach consensus on one block. Since some consensus nodes has higher weight, the number of honest consensus nodes required is smaller than $\frac{2}{3}N$. As a result, our scheme does not need to wait for as many messages received as that in PBFT. Therefore, the consensus time of weighted PBFT based blockchain is shorter than PBFT based blockchain.

5.4   Message Confirmation Latency

We further tested the message confirmation latency. Figure 2(b) plots the message confirmation latency with regard to message generation rate. We can see that the confirmation latency first decreases with the increase of message generation rate and then remain unchanged. The reason is that the message confirmation latency is related to block generation latency, and a high message generation rate reduces block generation latency when the message generation rate is low. When the message generation rate is high enough, message generation rate does not influence the block generation latency. Figure 2(c) plots the message confirmation latency with regard to the threshold to generate a new block, from which we can see that the increase of threshold also increases the message confirmation latency. The reason is that a higher threshold increases the block generation latency, which leads to the increase of message confirmation latency. Besides, we can also see that when the confirmation latency of the weighted PBFT based blockchain is as low as 1.1s, the proposed system is quite efficient. Our scheme also achieves shorter message confirmation latency than PBFT based blockchain. The main reason for this is that our scheme achieves shorter block generation latency, which is related to message confirmation latency.

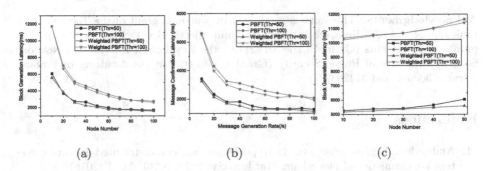

(a)   (b)   (c)

Fig. 2. Experimental results

5.5   Throughput

In this part, we discuss the throughput of the weighted PBFT based blockchain. Throughput refers to the maximum number of messages the blockchain can process, and meanwhile does not incur high confirmation delay. Suppose the blockchain generation latency is T_{Gen} and the threshold for block generation is Thr. When the message generation rate is high enough, the throughput TP can be calculated as $TP = \frac{Thr}{\min T_{Gen}}$. From Fig. 2(b) we could see the minimum length of block generation latency when the threshold is 100 is around 1.5 s. Based on this formula, we calculate the throughput of the proposed blockchain system (67 messages/s) when the threshold is 100.

A main reason constraining the throughput is the computational capacity of computers. OCCs and the CCC would have much more powerful computing capacities than the computer used in our experiments, which will greatly improve the throughput. To achieve efficient message confirmation when the message generation rate is low, we set a time threshold for block generation, as described in Sect. 4. In practice, the time should be set around the minimum length of block generation latency, so that it can achieve low message confirmation delay even there is a low message generation rate.

6 Conclusion

In this paper, we investigated automatic and adaptive data transmission control issue in TDL and proposed a blockchain based data transmission system for TDL. We proposed the weighted PBFT, which has better anti-destruction capacity than PBFT and outperforms PBFT in terms of block generation and message confirmation. We further employed the proposed weighted PBFT algorithm to design an automatic and adaptive data transmission control system based on blockchain. The experimental results demonstrate its effectiveness and efficiency.

Acknowledgments. This work is sponsored by the open grant of the Tactical Data Link Lab of the 20th Research Institute of China Electronics Technology Group Corporation, P.R. China (Grant CLDL-20182119), the Key Lab of Information Network Security, Ministry of Public Security (Grant C18614), and the Academy of Finland (Grants 308087 and 314203).

References

1. Androulaki, E., Barger, A., et al.: Hyperledger fabric: a distributed operating system for permissioned blockchains. In: EuroSys 2018, p. 30. ACM (2018)
2. Castro, M., Liskov, B.: Practical Byzantine fault tolerance. In: OSDI, vol. 99, pp. 173–186 (1999)
3. Dinc, M.: Design considerations for military data link architecture in enabling integration of intelligent unmanned air vehicles (UAVs) with navy units. In: NATO SCI Conference, Germany, June 2009
4. Huh, S., Cho, S., Kim, S.: Managing IoT devices using blockchain platform. In: ICACT 2019, pp. 464–467. IEEE (2017)
5. Martinez-Ruiz, M., Artés-Rodríguez, A., Diaz-Rico, J.A., Fuentes, J.B.: New initiatives for imagery transmission over a tactical data link. a case study: JPEG2000 compressed images transmitted in a Link-16 network. Method and results. In: MILCOM 2010, pp. 1163–1168, October 2010
6. Nakamoto, S.: Bitcoin: A peer-to-peer electronic cash system (2008). http://bitcoin.org/bitcoin.pdf
7. Raber, M.E.: The coast guard shipboard command and control system and its role in future joint military operations. Technical report, NAVAL WAR COLL NEWPORT RI (1996)

8. Schrecke, G.S., Davidson, S., Kahn, M.A., Wang, M.C., Henry, M.W.: IP address translation for tactical networks, US Patent App. 14/499,835, 15 December 2016
9. Sorroche, J., Byers, R., Barrett, N.: Tactical digital information link-technical advice and lexicon for enabling simulation II: Link 11/11B. Technical report, ASRC Communication Ltd. Kirtland AFB NM Distributed Mission Operations Center (2006)
10. Stoica, A., Militaru, D., Moldoveanu, D., Popa, A.: Tactical data link - from link-1 to link-22. Sci. Bull. Mircea cel Batran Naval Acad. **19**(2), 346 (2016)
11. Sturdy, J.T.: Military data link integration application. Technical report, Honeywell Inc. Albuquerque NM Defense Avionics Systems Div (2004)
12. T.J., W.: On blockchain technology and its potential application in tactical networks. https://info.publicintelligence.net/CA-DRDC-TacticalBlockchain.pdf. Accessed April 2018
13. Wood, G.: Ethereum: a secure decentralised generalised transaction ledger. Ethereum Project Yellow Paper, vol. 151, pp. 1–32 (2014)
14. Yan, Z.: Trust modeling and management in digital environments: from social concept to system development. Information Science Reference (2010)
15. Yan, Z., Chen, Y., Shen, Y.: PerContRep: a practical reputation system for pervasive content services. J. Supercomput. **70**(3), 1051–1074 (2014)
16. Yan, Z., Cofta, P.: A mechanism for trust sustainability among trusted computing platforms. In: Katsikas, S., Lopez, J., Pernul, G. (eds.) TrustBus 2004. LNCS, vol. 3184, pp. 11–19. Springer, Heidelberg (2004). https://doi.org/10.1007/978-3-540-30079-3_2
17. Zyskind, G., Nathan, O., et al.: Decentralizing privacy: using blockchain to protect personal data. In: 2015 IEEE S&P Workshops, pp. 180–184. IEEE (2015)

A Cyberspace Ontology Model Under Non-cooperative Conditions

Jinkui Yao$^{(\boxtimes)}$ (iD) and Yulong Zhao

Jiangnan Institute of Computing Technology, Wuxi 214000, China
pelops.yao@gmail.com, zhaoyl04@163.com

Abstract. The activities of cyberspace are not always cooperative, and confrontational behavior under non-cooperative conditions has even occurred at the beginning of the Internet and will persist. To describe the non-cooperative situation, we construct an ontology model to depict the entities and relations in the cyberspace. We divide the cyberspace into physical, logical, and social domains, and then build a conceptual model. According to the ontology modeling method, the upper layer, the domain and the application ontology are hierarchically constructed. Based on the Semantic Web Rule Language (SWRL), a reasoning framework is initially constructed to implement basic logical reasoning. We map the structured data in the data source to the model according to the predefined rules file, and extract the unstructured data to obtain the structured data. In order to verify the validity of the model, we designed a prototype system to integrate multi-source heterogeneous data and to achieve efficient query and reasoning.

Keywords: Cyberspace model · Ontology · Ontology modeling · Non-cooperative conditions · Ontology reasoning

1 Introduction

Cyberspace, an extension of physical space, is a indispensable virtual reality for all countries. In the virtual world, parties of confrontation and related environments constitute a non-cooperative cyberspace. The data sources of the cyberspace are complex, and the data coexists in a structured and unstructured form. Competitors use a variety of methods to collect and acquire data, and to understand and organize data according to tasks and purposes, resulting in data multi-source and heterogeneity, which leads to knowledge understanding and reuse barriers. Therefore, constructing an ontology-based non-cooperative network space model is conducive to knowledge reuse, integrating existing data to form a large-scale knowledge base, and on this basis, conducting automated reasoning analysis to improve the effectiveness of cyberspace confrontation. Based on the real data and the hierarchical structure and characteristic attributes of non-cooperative cyberspace, this paper builds a model extracted the related elements of cyberspace in physical domain, logical domain and social domain,

G. Wang et al. (Eds.): iSCI 2019, CCIS 1122, pp. 596–609, 2019.
https://doi.org/10.1007/978-981-15-1301-5_47

abstracted ontology related concepts such as entities, attributes and relationships. The conceptual diagram of the model we designed is shown in the Fig. 1. The model covers the macro description of non-cooperative cyberspace, framework of domain ontology, vocabulary classification and definition of basic concept, and supports machine reasoning to achieve information query and other capabilities.

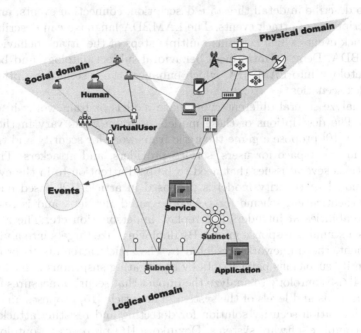

Fig. 1. Cyberspace conceptual model figure under non-cooperation conditions.

In the remainder of the paper, we discuss its connections with related methods in Sect. 2. We describe design and construction of our model in Sects. 3 and 4. We finally conclude by summarizing our model in Sect. 5.

2 Related Works

The ontology concept has long existed and was originally used in the field of philosophy. After the introduction of computer science, it is often used as a conceptual design model. The development of description logic solves the problem of machine readability of ontology. Based on Attributive concept description Language with Complements (ALC) [1], SHIQ [2] was proposed by Horrocks as the mathematics basis of (OWL). OWL is designated by the W3C as the standard language for ontology description. Ontology language OWL2, as the successor to OWL, has a complete mathematical language based on description logic

SROIQ [3], which provides a theoretical basis for ontology reasoning. Ontology reasoning methods include Tableaux algorithm, logical programming rewriting, first-order query rewriting and production rules, and so on. Among them, the Tableaux algorithms are the most widely used, such as FaCT [4], DRAGO [5], FaCT++ [6] and HermiT [7]. The ontology automatic reasoning tools alleviate the combined explosion problem of logical reasoning to some extent. LAMBDA [8] is a formal description language for network attack modeling. It has the ability to describe in detail the state description, connection events, and transition descriptions of attack events. The LAMBDA language can describe a complete attack event, which contains multiple steps of the attack behavior. Based on LAMBDA, Deng [9] introduces behavioral subject ontology and behavioral object ontology into LAMBDA, which enhances the system description ability in complex scenarios.

We analyze several different cyberspace models or frameworks in other literatures. The descriptions of these models or frameworks vary in their focus. The article [10] propose a game theoretic framework for security and trust relationship in cyberspace for users, service providers, and attackers. The article [11] mentions several issues that need to be paid attention to in the cyberspace defense model. A security model is proposed in article [12] based on Identity Based authentication scheme for UAV-integrated HetNets, and is resistant to the vulnerabilities of intruders like replay, impersonation etc. The article [13] describes a stimulus-response model. By deploying fake targets into a virtualized environment, the framework presented by the article attempts to probabilistically identify suspicious participants by aggregating suspicious behavior. Intel's Vishik [14] uses ontology to analyze the impact that security measures may have on various areas and levels of the system. The article [15] proposes an ontology-driven information security solution for detecting and resisting attacks on distributed complex software systems. Doynikova [16] proposes an ontology-based network overall security state measurement model, which obtains a measure of security state through relation calculation.

3   Design of Non-cooperative Cyberspace Ontology Model

The cyberspace domain under non-cooperative conditions should consider the total of physical, information, and human elements in physical space and cyberspace, and is a multi-level stereo domain including physical domain, logical domain, and social domain. The elements of cyberspace are dynamic and continually changing. There are many influencing factors in cyberspace domain, causing the situation to change over time. This paper builds a cyberspace confrontation model hierarchically. The hierarchic makes the model hierarchy clear and easy to understand and enhance the scalability of the model. Many influencing factors interact together, similar to a mesh structure and iterative changes over time. This section will elaborate the conceptual design and modeling methodology of the non-cooperative cyberspace model.

3.1   Conceptual Design of the Description Framework

This subsection designs a conceptual model based on the elements involved in the physical, logical, and social domains of non-cooperative cyberspace. Each domain contains several entities and relations, and there are partial cross-domain relations. In addition, event entities are time-dependent (see Fig. 1).

Physical Domain. The physical domain entities are the basis of the cyberspace conceptual model consisted of hardware and the physical platform, and describe the device entity, wired and wireless communication connection, transmission media attributes, and geospatial attributes of hardware and physical platforms. The physical domain entity plays a supporting role in the model, and the physical connection relationships have physical connections and channel communication. Non-cooperative confrontation in the physical domain includes physical entity destruction damage and channel interference blocking.

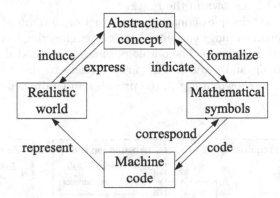

Fig. 2. Model abstraction process diagram.

Logical Domain. Entities in the logical domain are the core of the cyberspace conceptual model, including subnets, nodes, and carried services. In this paper, the logical network of cyberspace is defined as a large virtual network, and various networks are subnets thereof, for example, the Internet is also a subnet of the cyberspace. Nodes are abstract entities that undertake computation, storage, and information transmission functions in a logical domain, including compute nodes or transport nodes. Operations are an information processing abstract entities including programs, services and processes. The confrontation of non-cooperative cyberspace mainly revolves around the operation of information processing and circulation. Blocking subnets, controlling nodes, and obtaining privilege are aimed at obtaining the control ability.

Social Domain. Entities in the social domain are portray agents based on human will and their attributes, behaviors, activities, organizations, and so on. Society refers to human society based on physical world activities and virtual society based on cyberspace activities.

3.2 Modeling Methods

For entities of non-cooperative cyberspace, our understanding is mostly figurative and fragmented, such as a satellite communication receiving equipment, an authorized account of a application system, and so on. Model should organize realistic knowledge according to certain regulations and design reasonable rules to establish a relationship. The construction of the model is the process of abstract extraction. The entities abstract the concept through induction and generalization, then represent the abstract concepts to mathematical symbol, and then digitizes it into the coding expression that the machine can understand, and finally it can be calculated and stored by the machine. The abstract process of the model is shown in the Fig. 2.

According to the principle of ontology construction, our model describes hierarchically the domain ontology concept. Ontology engineering has a strong correlation with domain knowledge. The ontology building method should be chosen based on the domain and project. This article refers to the classic seven-step modeling method, as shown in Fig. 3, the process can be divided into the following steps.

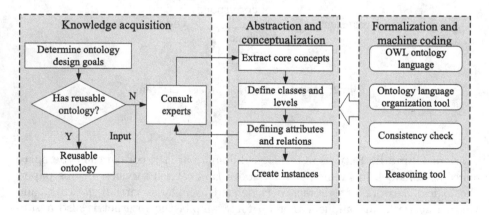

Fig. 3. Modeling step diagram.

In order to ensure the quality of ontology development, the participation of domain experts is particularly important. The whole process of ontology development almost requires the support of domain experts. The task of the developers is only the formalization and coding of knowledge, since they lack the depth and breadth of understanding of domain knowledge relative to domain experts.

The extraction and definition of core concepts, classes and attributes can be carried out in multiple rounds until the abstraction and conceptualization of the model meets the following requirements, (1) completeness, model has complete ability to represent knowledge in the domain; (2) consistency, model has clear and consistent semantic expression ability; (3) clarity, model has semantic comprehensibility and reasonable granularity of concept division; (4) practicality, model in line with the real world, convenient for knowledge abstraction; (5) rationality, model has reasonable structure and is easy to maintain, expand and management.

4   Construction of Non-cooperative Cyberspace Ontology Model

The model mainly covers the objects and their constraints and specifications. Classes can use to describe objects, and are constrained by properties. The properties are the qualifications, constraints, and complements of classes, and are the basis of the relationship of the class. Class properties include object properties and data properties, which are qualitatively and quantitatively restricted to the corresponding class. Reasonable class and attribute design can improve the efficiency of ontology query, reasoning and calculation.

4.1   Ontology Model Hierarchically Construction

This paper constructs hierarchically ontology model. As shown in Fig. 4, the model is divided into three levels from top to bottom, which are respectively top-level ontology, domain ontology (or task ontology), and application ontology.

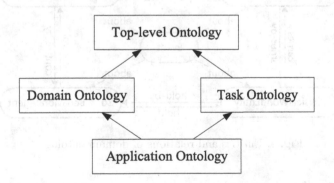

Fig. 4. Ontology hierarchical diagram.

Top-level ontology is represented by a seven-tuple, and the definition of the top-level ontology *Cyberspace_Onto* is given below.

Definition 1. *Cyberspace_Onto* :: $\{C, H, R, A, A^R, A^C, I\}$ *Where: C is classes set, which is an abstract description of the entities; H is the hierarchical semantic relation of classes; R is relation set;A represents properties set that restrict, constraint and accomplish classes, including object properties and data properties; A^R represents the properties set of the specified relations, limits the range of the properties; A^C represents the properties set of the specified class, the define domain of the properties; I represents the instance set or individual set with instantiations of classes as elements.*

Domain ontology describes the core concepts in the domain and the relationship between them, which is a high-level abstraction of the ontology model. The set of classes of domain ontology contains five entities which are PhysicalWorldEntity, CyberWorldEntity, CyberBehavioralAgent, SocialBehavioralAgent and Event, as shown in Fig. 5. PhysicalWorldEntity and CyberWorldEntity are respectively the root entities of physical domain and logical domain. Social domain has two root entities which are and SocialBehavioralAgent. The Event describes a class of entity associated with a time series, and its subclasses have timestamp properties. Lines with arrow indicate the relations of classes, *carries* indicates that the PhysicalWorldEntity carries the CyberWorldEntity, *permited* indicates that the CyberBehavioralAgent has been *permited* to operate the CyberWorldEntity, *control* indicates that the SocialBehavioralAgent has control over the CyberBehavioralAgent, and *hold* means that the SocialBehavioralAgent holds the PhysicalWorldEntity. Obviously, *carries-by, permited-by, control-by* and *hold-by* are the inverse of the above relations. In addition, *about* is the association of events with other entities.

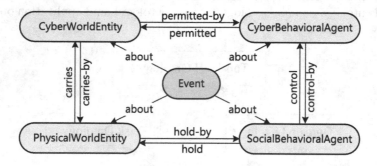

Fig. 5. Entities and relations of domain ontology.

Application ontology is a subclass of domain ontology and is a further refinement description of domain ontology. In order to facilitate the classification of concepts, the application ontology has multiple levels.

The physical world subdomain application ontology describes various entities that affect the physical and objective existence of cyberspace, including two core subclasses of hardware and platform, as shown in Fig. 6. The hardware entity

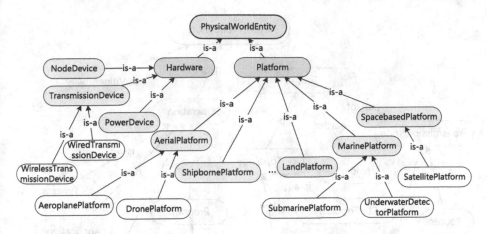

Fig. 6. Entity hierarchy of physical domain.

focuses on the information processing device and the running support device, including the node device, the transmission device, and the power device and so on. These devices are indispensable for the processing and transmission of information. A node device should have computing or storage resources, and the transmission device can transfer data from one node to another, and the power device provides the necessary energy support. The node device is represented by description logic in Eq. 1, and the constraint in the expression is a hardware device containing computing or storage capabilities. The platform subclass focuses on physical entities that integrate multiple devices. Generally, according to platform activity area in physical space, it can be divided into AerialPlatform, ShipbornePlatform, LandPlatform, MarinePlatform, SpacebasedPlatform and so on. More fine-grained classification can refer to the classification method in the engineering field.

$$NodeDevice \sqsubseteq \forall hasProcessUnit.Hardware \sqcap \geqslant 0 \quad hasProcessUnit$$
$$\sqcap \forall hasStorageUnit.Hardware \sqcap \geqslant 0 \quad hasStorageUnit \quad (1)$$
$$\sqcap \forall hasUnit.Hardware \sqcap \geqslant 1 \quad hasUnit$$

The cyberspace subdomain is the core of the cyberspace model, including subnets, services, and vulnerability subclasses, as shown in Fig. 7. The subnet class is a division of cyberspace logical networks or virtual networks. All networks can be classified as subnets and organized hierarchically according to certain affiliations. The operations run on the nodes in the form of software, services, and processes. The ultimate goal of the most important behavior in a non-cooperative cyberspace is to exert influence on operations. In other words, non-cooperative behaviors affect the information of operations transmitted or stored in cyberspace. Vulnerabilities are weakness in the hardwares, softwares or protocols that can be utilized by opponents in cyberspace. An attacker exploits the vulnerability as an entry point for the attack, thereby obtains or tampers information and even destroys the hardware and software system. Figure 8 depicts a

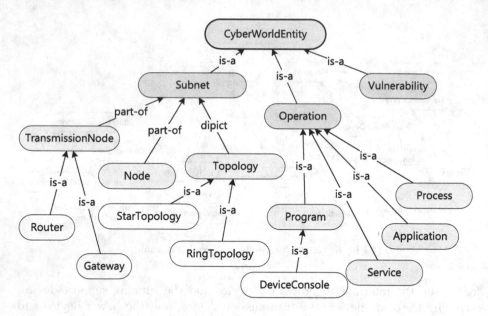

Fig. 7. Entity hierarchy of cyber domain.

simplified model where the Operation runs at Node, the Node are connected by a TransmissionNode, and the Node and TransmissionNode form a Subnet. The Vulnerability exists in Operation, Node and TransmissionNode. For example, Eq. 3 uses description logic to express a router on the ring network.

$$Router_{Ring} \sqsubseteq Router \sqcap \forall part-of.Subnet(Subnet)$$
$$\sqcap \forall hasTopology.Topology(RingToplogy) \tag{2}$$

The CyberBehavioralAgent includes the virtual object of the network such as email address, social network account, system administrator account, phone number and so on, and has two important subclasses, VirtualUser and VirtualOrganization, respectively. The VirtualUser is the authorized object of the cyberspace entity. In this paper, the VirtualUsers are divided into authorized users and guest users. The VirtualOrganization is a group of VirtualUsers organized according to certain rules, as shown in Fig. 9. The SocialBehavioralAgent are human or organizations that have an influence on cyberspace, as shown in Fig. 10. Social organizations are composed of human, including countries, companies, and so on. The quantitative relation between them is many-to-many. For example, Eq. 3 uses description logic to express that soldier is a member of the army.

$$Soldier \sqsubseteq Human \sqcap \forall jointToOrgnization.SocialOrgnization(Army) \tag{3}$$

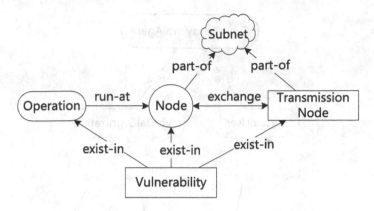

Fig. 8. Relations in the cyber world.

4.2   Reasoning Framework of Non-cooperative Cyberspace Model

According to the ontology model above, this paper constructs a reasoning framework based on description logic. Description logic is the mathematical theoretical basis for the most widely used ontology reasoning. Based on the open world hypothesis, non-true assertions are not necessarily false or unknowable. Semantic inference based on description logic infers semantic results from a set of asserted facts or axioms. A priori assertions are explicitly defined or reasoned, and then implicitly correlated to obtain implicit correlation results.

Semantic Web Rule Language (SWRL) recommended by W3C introduces the rule language of unary and binary datalog into the OWL specification. OWL axioms can be expressed logically using the similar Horn rule to enhance the description ability of the OWL knowledge base. Each SWRL rule is divided into two parts: the rule body and the rule header. The rule body and the rule header are composed of atomic predicate statements (which can be empty). Under the condition that the rule body is established, the rule header is also established. The empty rule body means that the rule header is true, and the rule header is empty means that the rule body is false.

This paper designs a set of reasoning rules, which are expressed in the SWRL and stored in the knowledge base. SWRL rules are represented by concepts such as classes, properties, instances, and constants.

The following is an example of an reasoning rule to find reachable connections between two nodes. Node x and node y both link to the same subnet n, then there is a reachable connection between x and y. Table 1 shows some predicate statements (used to define rules) and their meanings. Describe logical expression shows in Eq. 4.

$$Node(?x) \wedge Node(?y) \wedge Subnet(?n) \wedge connectIn(?x;?n) \wedge connectIn(?y;?n)$$
$$\rightarrow hasConnection(?x;?y)$$

$$(4)$$

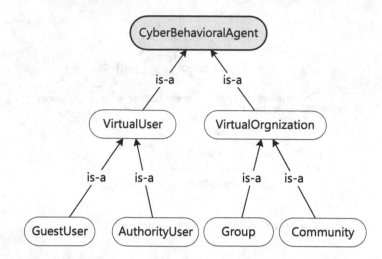

Fig. 9. Subclass hierarchy of cyber behavior agent.

Table 1. Predicate sentences and descriptions.

Predicate sentence	Description
Node(?x)	Determine if variable x is a node instance
Subnet(?n)	Determine if variable n is a subnet instance
connectIn(?x;?n)	Determine if node instance x is connected to the subnet n instance
hasConnection(?x;?y)	Determine if node instance x and node y have a connection

4.3 Prototype System and Model Verification

To validate our model, we designed a prototype system. There are three subsystems of the prototype system, namely the data input subsystem, the data processing subsystem and the visualization subsystem. The data input subsystem is compatible with both structured and unstructured data, as shown in Fig. 11. The structured data is semantically mapped according to preset semantic conversion rules, and then the mapped triple data is stored in the knowledge base. The old ontology base can be merged into the new ontology base after the ontology alignment to achieve ontology reuse. Several sensors are deployed to capture the data which is submitted to the event generator after deduplication and cleaning. The sensors are the collective term for data collection software and hardware in the network. In order to deal with the lack of data, we designed several simulators in the prototype system to generate data according to predetermined rules. The data processing subsystem implements knowledge processing and storage, provides interfaces of data read and write, implements data query functions, and parses the SWRL language. The subsystem perform format verification, type conversion, data cleaning and deduplication before the data is stored in the database, and implement ontology alignment and collision

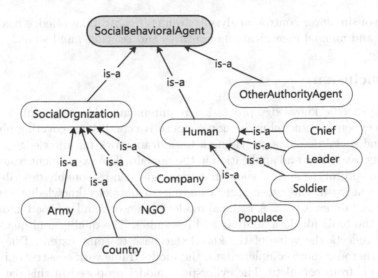

Fig. 10. Subclass hierarchy of social behavior agent.

detection when the ontology reuse. The rules required by the event generator generated by the subsystem and updated according to changes in knowledge. In addition, the subsystem realizes data expansion through functions such as entity representation and relationship prediction based on knowledge representation, and data completion. The visualization subsystem provides a human-machine

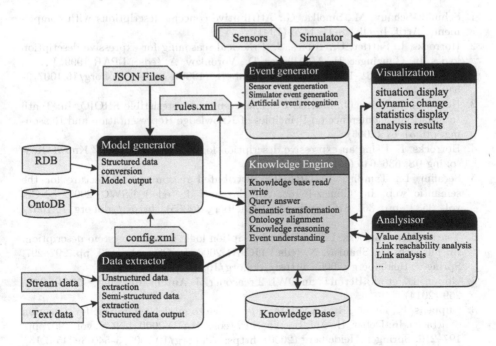

Fig. 11. Prototype system architecture diagram.

interface of simulator control, analyzer parameter control, knowledge base management and manual identification of entities and relations, and so on.

5   Conclusion

From the specific knowledge processing requirements, this paper initially constructs a cyberspace model under non-cooperative conditions, covering physical, logical and social domains, providing a basic framework for knowledge storage, processing, reasoning and application in the domain. The experiment results verified in the prototype system show that the model can reasonably describe most of the scenarios in the cyberspace. Building an ontology knowledge base is a complex and difficult task. A rational model framework and a broad knowledge base are the basis for data analysis and reasoning. The quality and quantity of the data reflects the value of the knowledge base to some extent. Due to the lack of richer and more complete data, the model framework constructed in this paper is far from complete. The cyberspace model proposed in this paper is a meaningful exploration. As the knowledge base of cyberspace situational awareness system, our model improves the level and ability of information processing, obtains more valuable knowledge from the data, and gains greater advantages in non-cooperation cyberspace confrontation.

References

1. Schmidt-Schauß, M., Smolka, G.: Attributive concept descriptions with complements. Artif. Intell. **48**(1), 1–26 (1991)
2. Horrocks, I., Sattler, U., Tobies, S.: Practical reasoning for expressive description logics. In: Ganzinger, H., McAllester, D., Voronkov, A. (eds.) LPAR 1999. LNCS, vol. 1705, pp. 161–180. Springer, Heidelberg (1999). https://doi.org/10.1007/3-540-48242-3_11
3. Horrocks, I., Kutz, O., Sattler, U.: The even more irresistible SROIQ. In: Tenth International Conference on Principles of Knowledge Representation and Reasoning, pp. 57–67 (2006)
4. Horrocks, I.: Using an expressive description logic: FaCT or fiction? Knowl. Reasoning **98**, 636–645 (1998)
5. Serafini, L., Tamilin, A.: DRAGO: distributed reasoning architecture for the semantic web. In: Gómez-Pérez, A., Euzenat, J. (eds.) ESWC 2005. LNCS, vol. 3532, pp. 361–376. Springer, Heidelberg (2005). https://doi.org/10.1007/11431053_25
6. Tsarkov, D., Horrocks, I.: FaCT++ description logic reasoner: system description. In: Furbach, U., Shankar, N. (eds.) IJCAR 2006. LNCS, vol. 4130, pp. 292–297. Springer, Heidelberg (2006). https://doi.org/10.1007/11814771_26
7. Glimm, B., et al.: HermiT: an OWL 2 reasoner. J. Autom. Reasoning **53**(3), 245–269 (2014)
8. Cuppens, F., Ortalo, R.: LAMBDA: a language to model a database for detection of attacks. In: Debar, H., Mé, L., Wu, S.F. (eds.) RAID 2000. LNCS, vol. 1907, pp. 197–216. Springer, Heidelberg (2000). https://doi.org/10.1007/3-540-39945-3_13

9. Deng, Z., et al.: An extensible description model of cyber war system. J. Natl. Univ. Defense Technol. **36**(01), 184–190 (2014)
10. Njilla, L.Y., et al.: Game theoretic modeling of security and trust relationship in cyberspace. Int. J. Commun Syst **29**(9), 1500–1512 (2016)
11. Barford, P., et al.: Cyber SA: situational awareness for cyber defense. In: Jajodia, S., Liu, P., Swarup, V., Wang, C. (eds.) Cyber Situational Awareness. ADIS, vol. 46, pp. 3–13. Springer, Boston (2010). https://doi.org/10.1007/978-1-4419-0140-8_1
12. Rashid, A., Sharma, D., Lone, T.A., Gupta, S., Gupta, S.K.: Secure communication in UAV assisted HetNets: a proposed model. In: Wang, G., Feng, J., Bhuiyan, M.Z.A., Lu, R. (eds.) SpaCCS 2019. LNCS, vol. 11611, pp. 427–440. Springer, Cham (2019). https://doi.org/10.1007/978-3-030-24907-6_32
13. Bilar, D., Saltaformaggio, B.: Using a novel behavioral stimuli-response framework to defend against adversarial cyberspace participants. In: 2011 3rd International Conference on Cyber Conflict, pp. 1–16. IEEE (2011)
14. Vishik, C., Balduccini, M.: Making sense of future cybersecurity technologies: using ontologies for multidisciplinary domain analysis. In: Reimer, H., Pohlmann, N., Schneider, W. (eds.) ISSE 2015, pp. 135–145. Springer, Wiesbaden (2015). https://doi.org/10.1007/978-3-658-10934-9_12
15. Vorobiev, A., Bekmamedova, N.: An ontology-driven approach applied to information security. J. Res. Pract. Inf. Technol. **42**(1), 61–76 (2010)
16. Doynikova, E., et al.: Ontology of metrics for cyber security assessment. In: Proceedings of the 14th International Conference on Availability, Reliability and Security, p. 52. ACM (2019)

Blockchain and Its Applications

Research on Decentralized Music Sharing Model Based on Consortium Blockchain

Wentao Gao and Guiyun Zhang[✉]

College of Computer and Information Engineering, Tianjin Normal University,
Tianjin 300387, China
dyxy1999@126.com

Abstract. To solve the problem of low transparency of digital copyright and insufficient data storage in current traditional music industry, we propose a decentralized music sharing model based on blockchain technology and InterPlanetary File System (IPFS). Blockchain technology has the characteristics of decentralization, non-tampering and traceability, thus we build the Ethereum consortium blockchain in the application environment of digital music copyright. Compared to the PoW algorithm, we use the PoA consensus algorithm suitable for the Ethereum consortium blockchain scenario to avoid hashrate mining and reduce the consensus time of the whole network. IPFS is combined to realize distributed and reliable storage of massive music data. In the paper, the business process of decentralized music sharing model is proposed, and personalized access control strategy is designed to set access permission, and smart contracts is used to ensure the reliability and transparency of transactions between users. The experimental analysis and testing of blockchain transaction processing efficiency is also conducted. The results show that when out-of-block time is 100 s, the throughput of system reaches 324 pens per second which is far higher than PoW algorithm, and has high operating efficiency.

Keywords: Consortium blockchain · IPFS · Smart contracts · Access control policy · Music sharing

1 Introduction

Blockchain technology [1], with its features of decentralization, non-tampering and distributed storage, has been widely used in the fields of finance and internet, and has gradually penetrated into the music industry. However, the traditional music industry is currently facing a major problem, that is, the copyright management of digital music content. With the development of blockchain technology, a new blockchain music solution is provided for digital content copyright protection.

Many scholars in China have conducted research on digital copyright issues. Yang et al. [2] proposed a framework which uses digital watermarking technology to embed copyright information in data sharing, and adopts blockchain to store

© Springer Nature Singapore Pte Ltd. 2019
G. Wang et al. (Eds.): iSCI 2019, CCIS 1122, pp. 613–624, 2019.
https://doi.org/10.1007/978-981-15-1301-5_48

data sharing records and watermarking. The author in [3] proposed a digital copyright registration data interaction and storage model based on blockchain technology by using the digital certificate access mechanism. Li et al. [4] proposed a digital copyright identifier control model of digital works without trusted third party to guarantee the copyright information not be tampered. However, the limitations of directly storing large text, audio, and other contents on blockchain are not specifically mentioned in the above papers.

The research on blockchain of music industry in China is still in the preliminary stage. Chen et al. [5] proposed a new path based on blockchain technology from three aspects through analyzing the problems of unclear ownership and uneven distribution in music copyright protection. This paper provides an innovative business model for Chinese music copyright protection. However, the massive music data stored in the blockchain will generate a large amount of block data, affecting the performance and storage capacity of blockchain. It is undoubtedly a big challenge for blockchain technology. There is no reasonable solutions have been given in the paper.

Some music service providers in the world also begin to use the model of "blockchain + music" to solve the low transparency of digital music copyrights. There are many music media platforms based on blockchain technology, such as BitTunes, Ujo Music, Peertracks, *etc.* However, most platforms only implement copyright management or file sharing in combination with blockchain technology. The storage defects of the blockchain itself are still not considered, and it's difficult to realize distributed storage and wide sharing for massive music data with the poor user experience.

InterPlanetary File System (IPFS) is a point-to-point distributed file system and provides permanent and distributed storage of data [6], which can be combined with blockchain to both maintain the query and storage of music data.

In this paper, combining blockchain technology and IPFS, we propose a decentralized music sharing model based on the Ethereum consortium blockchain. The model uses IPFS to provide data storage for blockchain, and realizes transaction functions between users through smart contracts, thereby ensuring transaction reliability and transparency. The main contributions are as follows:

- We propose a decentralized music sharing model based on the Ethereum consortium blockchain and IPFS to ensure that each transaction between the creator and other users is completely recorded in the blockchain. Each one can be queried, and cannot be tampered.
- We design the business process flow of the music sharing model, and realize the uploading, querying, traceability and sharing of music data. The transaction process is completed through the smart contracts to ensure the data can be tamper-proof and traceable. We also formulate user access control policy to set the access permission.
- We realize the development of the data access layer and the application layer, test the effectiveness of the smart contracts, and we also analyze the block transaction processing efficiency, as well as the security of the model. The results show that the model has higher operating efficiency.

2 Blockchain

Blockchain is derived from the underlying technology of Bitcoin. In order to ensure the tamper-proof feature of data, blockchain introduces a chain data structure which is composed of blocks as units and connected in time sequence. Each block is composed of block header and block body, in which block header is used to link to the previous block and ensure the integrity of historical data through the timestamp, while block body stores all the transaction information generated after the verified previous block [7]. The blockchain structure is shown in Fig. 1.

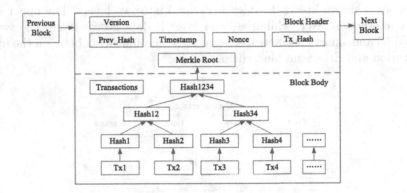

Fig. 1. Blockchain structure.

Ethereum is a decentralized platform based on the public blockchain. It ensures the system operation through the consensus mechanism and the participation of various nodes, and supports smart contracts. It also can execute Turing's complete scripting language [8].

The consensus algorithm is devoted to the issue of how all nodes in a decentralized and distributed network agree with each other [9]. The Ethereum consensus algorithm is divided into Proof of Work (PoW) and Proof of Authority (PoA) [10]. Different from PoW, PoA is responsible for the generation of new blocks and block verification by a set of authoring nodes (signers). Although the degree of decentralization of PoA is weak, it is more suitable for the application scenario of the consortium blockchain for its reliable authoritative node authentication mechanism and efficient consensus efficiency.

Smart contracts is a piece of computer program running on a blockchain that extends its functionality, but contracts cannot run directly on blockchain nodes [11]. Ethereum has customized Turing's complete scripting language such as Solidity to develop smart contracts. Decentralized application (DApp) needs to call smart contracts, executes transactions and accesses status data.

Blockchain can establish a direct link between the creator and the consumer, avoiding the intermediate links of the third party, thus ensuring that the creator can better collect royalties paid by the consumer. With the introduction of smart contracts in blockchain of music, it can help the creator's work to be used more fairly and reasonably, and also allow consumers to prove their legal use rights to a certain musical piece through the ledger, and the copyright of the work will be more executable.

3 System Design

3.1 System Architecture Design

The architecture of the decentralized music sharing model system designed in this paper is shown in Fig. 2, which is divided into two layers. The upper layer is user interaction layer, while the lower layer is data access layer. The system uses Web3 and smart contracts to realize the communication between the upper application and Ethereum blockchain.

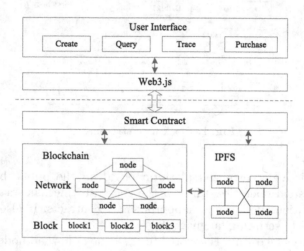

Fig. 2. The architecture of decentralized music sharing model system.

The user interaction layer provides the user with a visual operation interface, which is a bridge for the user to interact with the system, including the basic functional modules of the system. It also can convert the user's operation request data into virtual assets and transactions and send them to the underlying Ethereum blockchain to save permanently.

The data access layer is implemented by a distributed Ethereum P2P network and an IPFS network. Each node in the Ethereum network forms a consortium, which uses Clique algorithm of PoA to reach an agreement and provides decentralized data storage services for the system. The data stored in the blockchain is managed by all nodes in the chain, ensuring that data cannot be tampered with. Due to decentralization and content-based addressing, IPFS can be used to store large text, audio, *etc.*, and the hash value of the file content is stored in the Ethereum blockchain.

The public blockchain architecture design requires a large number of public nodes to participate in ensuring system operation [12], while in the application environment of music digital copyright, large-scale node participate is not required. It is not suitable for this environment, which is easy to cause waste of resources. Therefore, the consortium blockchain is used to build a secure, reliable, and decentralized music sharing model.

3.2 System Process Design

Figure 3 shows the workflow of the decentralized music sharing model in this paper. The working steps of the model are as follows:

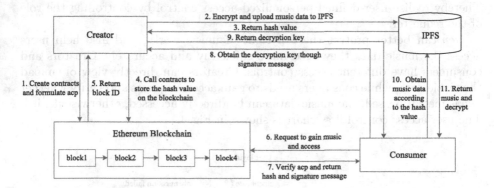

Fig. 3. The flowchart of decentralized music sharing model system.

(1) The creator is the copyright owner of music digital content, creates smart contract and formulates the user access control policy (*acp*). After the identity verification, the music file is encrypted into a ciphertext and uploaded to IPFS.
(2) IPFS calculates a unique hash value based on the music content and returns it to the creator to achieve distributed and reliable storage of music. Then the creator calls the smart contract to store the hash value and other music attribute information on the Ethereum in the form of transactions.
(3) The creator can verify the copyright based on the hash value see if the music contents have been tampered with, and allow other users to access the music data.
(4) In order to obtain music data, consumer users need to send a request to Ethereum blockchain to get the hash value stored in the chain first. While in keep with the *acp* formulated by the data owner, they have the right to obtain the key though signature message sent by the node of blockchain. Then they can gain music content from IPFS according to the unique hash value and use the key to decrypt it.

The music files are encrypted and stored in IPFS to realize distributed shared storage of files. Smart contracts are used to generate transactions between creators and other users, which reduce the intermediate links, enabling the transparency and automation of the transaction process. The transaction information is written into the blockchain after the broadcasting verification of the whole network nodes, which ensures the traceability of digital content and the tamper resistance of transaction information.

3.3　Access Control Policy Design

$acp = (<U, seq>, R, P)$ can be understood as a tuple, where U represents a set of data owner users, R is a set of roles (i.e. a set of identity attributes of user in the system), seq represents the data serial number allowed to request access, and P is the user attribute permission that the data owner allows to access seq. Thereby realize user-defined personalized access control by controlling the role of the requester.

acp can better protect the copyright of music works, and also help users access the music data they need more efficiently and accurately. Creators and consumers have different access controls. Creators can directly view or upload the music data, while consumers needs to gain access requests and verify whether acp is met. If passed, the music data can be directly accessed, otherwise denied. The user access control flow chart is shown in Fig. 4.

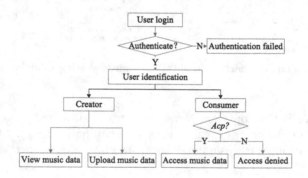

Fig. 4. The flowchart of access control model.

Access control policies are stored in the blockchain, and the policy information is verifiable, traceable and non-tamperable to anyone, improving the robustness and credibility of the system effectively. In addition, the decision result of the access control policy is implemented in the form of smart contracts, which avoids the participation of third-party central institutions.

3.4　Smart Contract Design

Smart contract is the core component of the music sharing model and implements the business logic of the platform. As part of the Ethereum, it can convert user operations into transactions in the blockchain, which are fully documented in the Ethereum network and are not controlled by third-party agencies. The smart contract in this paper is based on Truffle framework, and uses Solidity language to design and implement the music sharing model between creators and consumers. Truffle is the most popular framework in Ethereum, which can implement the entire process from smart contract compilation, deployment to release.

Access Control Contract. Access control policies are stored in the blockchain in the form of transactions, and there may be one or more access control policies in each transaction. The decision results of access control are divided into two types, namely, allowing access and denying access. For access requests sent by users (UAR), if the request attribute information satisfies the user attribute permission (P) in the access control policy (ACP), the request is permitted (seq) or denied (seq) according to the policy description. The contract algorithm for the access control is shown in Table 1.

Table 1. Contract algorithm of access control.

Algorithm 1: ACP
Input: UAR, ACP_SET
Output: Policy Decision Result
1: FOR i=1 to ACP_SET.length DO
2:     IF UAR == ACP_SET[i].P THEN
3:         IF ACP_SET[i].seq THEN
4:             return permit;
5:         ELSE return deny;
6:         END IF
7:     END IF
8: END FOR

User Purchase Contract. The function of user purchasing music is one of the functions of the smart contract has to implement in music sharing model. The prerequisites for user purchasing are: (1) account.ethBalance > music.price, where ethBalance is the Ethereum balance held by the current account, price is the price of the music; (2) the account is not the creator himself.

After the consumer queries the music piece, if the purchase condition is met and the payment is selected, a transaction is completed, and then a block is added correspondingly to the blockchain. If the current account balance is not enough to pay for the music price, the purchase fails. The contract algorithm for the purchase process is shown in Table 2.

Table 2. Contract algorithm of user purchasing.

Algorithm 2: payforMusic
Input: Music ID
Output: Purchase Result
1: IF msg.value < music.price THEN
2:    break;
3: ELSE IF msg.value > music.price THEN
4:      IF music.users[msg.sender].addr == 0 THEN
5:          music.users.addr = msg.sender;
6:          restBalance = msg.value - music.price;
7:          music.user[msg.sender].purchased=true;
8:          return restBalance;
9:      END IF
10:    END IF
11: END IF

Music Traceability Contract. Users can trace the copyright according to the hash value of the music work, and view the owner of the work and other related information. The traceability process has no transaction data and therefore does not consume transaction costs. The contract algorithm for the traceability process is shown in Table 3.

Table 3. Contract algorithm of music tracing.

Algorithm 3: tracebackMusic
Input: Music ID, Audio Hash
Output: Traceback Result
1: IF music.artist.addr == msg.sender THEN
2:    display music information;
3: ELSE IF music.audioHash != audio hash THEN
4:      break;
5:    ELSE display music information;
6:      return true;
7:    END IF
8: END IF

4   Experimental Analysis

Based on the related theories of Ethereum and IPFS, this paper builds a six-node Ethereum consortium blockchain and an IPFS private cluster, tests and verifies the proposed decentralized music sharing model. The experimental test environment is: the operating system uses Ubuntu14.04 LTS, the CPU is AMD Opteron Processor 6234, the main frequency is 2.4 GHz, and the memory is 10G.

Geth is used as an Ethereum client to create, mine, and deploy smart contracts. The local IPFS private cluster is built using the go-ipfs client. The Geth nodes synchronize and verify the block information to form an Ethereum network to ensure the stability of the system.

4.1 Security Analysis

The solution is based on the Ethereum consortium blockchain and IPFS technology to ensure the security of user data. Music files are stored in IPFS in encrypted form, and can only be decrypted by obtaining the key. The user wants to get the key, provided that the accounting node verifies the access control policy, thus realizing the ciphertext sharing of data.

The main security risk faced by the blockchain comes from the attacker's attack on the consensus mechanism, in order to achieve the target of modifying the block data. The model adopts the P2P network structure to avoid single-point attacks, and is maintained by all nodes that can guarantee the stability of the system. The Ethereum consortium blockchain uses the PoA consensus algorithm to generate blocks through trusted signers, and it also has strong tamper resistance.

4.2 Algorithm Performance Analysis

This paper uses manually generated data as test data to conduct experiments and simulate the actual application environment.

Throughput is a measure of the ability of a system to process requests per unit of time, and is also one of the important indicators for measuring the performance of a system [3]. This paper uses transactions per second (TPS) to represent throughput, as shown in Eq. (1):

$$TPS = \frac{Transactions}{\Delta t} \tag{1}$$

Where Δt represents the consensus interval, that is, the out-of-block time, and Transactions represents the amount of transaction data contained in the block within the interval.

In this paper, a six-node consortium blockchain environment is set up, which takes 4 different time intervals, such as 10 s, 20 s, 40 s and 100 s. The algorithm performs 10 non-differential throughput experiments continuously. The transactions within the different Δt is shown in Fig. 5(a)–(d).

Figure 6 shows the TPS changes under the different Δt. It can be seen from the experimental results that the throughput of the PoA algorithm is relatively stable and far exceeds the PoW consensus algorithm, which can meet the system requirements. Taking the average value of 10 experiments as the TPS value of different Δt, the relationship between TPS and out-of-block time is shown in Fig. 7. When the number of transactions processed in the system is increasing, the consensus efficiency of the algorithm will decrease, and the throughput will also decrease as the network communication and time overhead between nodes.

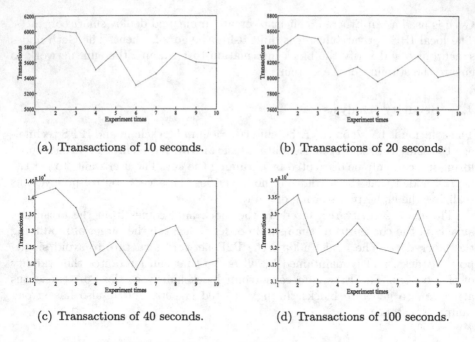

(a) Transactions of 10 seconds.

(b) Transactions of 20 seconds.

(c) Transactions of 40 seconds.

(d) Transactions of 100 seconds.

Fig. 5. Transactions of different seconds.

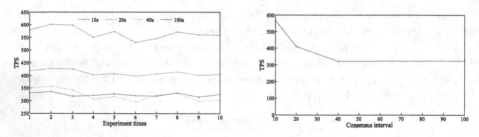

Fig. 6. Line chart of system throughput.

Fig. 7. Line chart of TPS and consensus interval.

4.3 Blockchain Transaction Efficiency Analysis

Under the condition that the network bandwidth is 20 Mbps, the relationship between the number of different transactions and the processing time of the system is as shown in Fig. 8. As can be seen from the figure, as the number of transactions increases, the system processing time will also increase. Figure 9 shows the time variation graph of the system processing 1000 transactions under different network bandwidth conditions. As the network bandwidth increases, the system processing time will be shortened accordingly.

Figure 10 is a comparison of block processing time under different network bandwidths. It can be seen that under the same number of transactions, the processing time decreases correspondingly with the increase of band-

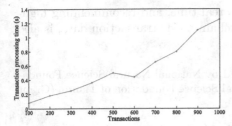

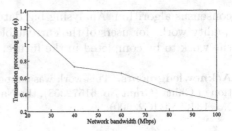

Fig. 8. Line chart of processing time and transactions.

Fig. 9. Line chart of processing time and network bandwidth.

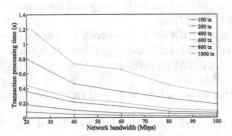

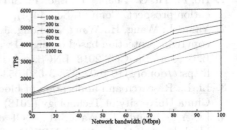

Fig. 10. Comparison of processing time under different network bandwidths.

Fig. 11. Comparison of TPS under different network bandwidths.

width. Figure 11 shows the comparison of the data transaction efficiency of the Ethereum blockchain with the increase of network bandwidth under different transaction numbers. It can be seen that the transaction efficiency is significantly improved when the network bandwidth allows. While the number of transactions in the network exceeds a certain amount, the efficiency of data transaction in the blockchain is slowly increasing.

5 Conclusion

As a kind of blockchain technology application, the music blockchain has significant advantages in achieving digital content copyright protection and traceability. It is an important development direction in the application research of blockchain technology. This paper builds the consortium blockchain and IPFS private cluster respectively to implement the system model, and adopts the PoA consensus mechanism of Ethereum to make the whole network reach a consensus, as well as verifies the validity of smart contracts. The proposed model realizes the distributed sharing, storage and query of music data, and present a new solution for current digital music copyright and low transparency. The TPS of this model is relatively stable, and guarantees the irreparable modification, integrity and security of the data under the premise of satisfying the basic functions. However, there are also some shortcomings, and the next step is to improve the consensus algorithm. Analysing big data in real time, and recommending high-quality works for users of the current blockchain music transaction data, is also the work to be completed in the future.

Acknowledgments. This work was supported by National Natural Science Foundation of China (Grant No. 61572358), the Natural Science Foundation of Tianjin (Grant No. 16JC YBJC23600).

References

1. He, P., Yu, G., Zhang, Y., Bao, Y.: Survey on blockchain technology and its application prospect. Comput. Sci. **44**(4), 1–7+15 (2017)
2. Yang, J., Wang, H., Wang, Z., Long, J., Du, B.: BDCP: a framework for big data copyright protection based on digital watermarking. In: Wang, G., Chen, J., Yang, L.T. (eds.) SpaCCS 2018. LNCS, vol. 11342, pp. 351–360. Springer, Cham (2018). https://doi.org/10.1007/978-3-030-05345-1_30
3. Li, L.: Research and application of block chain technology in digital rights. North China University of Technology (2018)
4. Li, Y., Huang, J., Wang, R.: DCI control model of digital works based on blockchain. J. Comput. Appl. **37**(11), 3281–3287 (2017)
5. Chen, L., Guan, S., Du, R.: Study on copyright protection path of music from the perspective of blockchain technology. In: 6th International Conference on Management Science and Management, Innovation Advances in Economics, Business and Management Research (2019)
6. Nizamuddin, N., Hasan, H.R., Salah, K.: IPFS-blockchain-based authenticity of online publications. In: Chen, S., Wang, H., Zhang, L.-J. (eds.) ICBC 2018. LNCS, vol. 10974, pp. 199–212. Springer, Cham (2018). https://doi.org/10.1007/978-3-319-94478-4_14
7. Shao, Q., Jin, C., Zhang, Z., Qian, W., Zhou, A.: Blockchain: architecture and research progress. Chin. J. Comput. **41**(5), 969–988 (2017)
8. Yan, Y., Zheng, K., Guo, Z.: Detailed Technical Explanation and Practical Warfare of Ethereum Technology. China Machine Press, Beijing (2018)
9. Yuan, Y., Ni, X., Zeng, S., Wang, F.: Blockchain consensus algorithms: the state of the art and future trends. Acta Automatica Sinica **44**(11), 2011 (2018)
10. Proof-of-Authority Chains - Wiki. https://wiki.parity.io/Proof-of-Authority-Chains. Accessed 30 May 2019
11. Buterin, V.: A next-generation smart contract and decentralized application platform. White Paper (2014)
12. Ra, G.-J., Seo, D., Bhuiyan, M.Z.A., Lee, I.-Y.: An anonymous protocol for member privacy in a consortium blockchain. In: Wang, G., Feng, J., Bhuiyan, M.Z.A., Lu, R. (eds.) SpaCCS 2019. LNCS, vol. 11611, pp. 456–464. Springer, Cham (2019). https://doi.org/10.1007/978-3-030-24907-6_34

A Distributed Storage System Based on Blockchain and Pipelined Code

Xuewei Li[1(✉)], Yue Chen[1], Yang Ba[1], Shuai Li[1], and Huaiyu Zhu[2]

[1] PLA Information Engineering University, Zhengzhou 450001, China
lxwyujin@qq.com
[2] 95937 Unit of PLA, Fuxin 123004, Liaoning, China

Abstract. To achieve data reliability and security in distributed storage systems, different coding schemes have been proposed. Encoded data would be stored in different nodes which are called hosts. However, the knowledge of hosts is learned by each other, and all of it must be known by the central server that stores meta-data, so that users and hosts cannot keep anonymity which reduces the difficulty of eavesdropping attack. The central server is a bottleneck due to single point of failure or low performance. These problems reduce the stability and the security of the storage system. To address these problems, we proposed a decentralized secure distributed storage system based on pipelined code and blockchain. In our scheme, we use blockchain to realize decentralization to solve the single point of failure problem and anonymity to data breach. An explicit pipelined code process combined with blockchain is presented to construct the storage function basis. Furthermore, a time-based replica storage mechanism is used in our scheme to achieve better trade-off between storage overhead and decode computation overhead.

Keywords: Security · Anonymity · Decentralized storage · Blockchain · Pipelined code

1 Introduction

In the big data era, distributed storage system (DSS) is used to meet large-scale data storage demand [1]. Commercial DSSs make a great role in people's daily life, such as Google file system (GFS) [2], Amazon S3 [25] or Hadoop file-system (HDFS) [26]. In these DSSs, replica mechanisms are used to strengthen reliability and availability of data and erasure code schemes are used to deduce storage overhead. Storage schemes that combine replica mechanism and erasure code schemes are usually introduced to achieve better trade-off between storage overhead and computation overhead [3, 4] in DSSs. Meanwhile, the security problems of DSS draw widespread concern due to the DSSs' nature. On the one hand, DSS runs in an open environment which leads its components to be attacked by adversaries easily. On the other hand, DSS data hosts storing the user data and the central server storing the meta-data are the main targets of adversaries. Furthermore, DSS data hosts need to learn the knowledge of each other in the process of encoding or decoding. That is, the data hosts cannot keep anonymity. The open environment and non-anonymity can be used by eavesdropping attack and

G. Wang et al. (Eds.): iSCI 2019, CCIS 1122, pp. 625–638, 2019.
https://doi.org/10.1007/978-981-15-1301-5_49

collusion attack and lead to data breach. In addition, the central server needs to undertake all route and computation work in the process of encoding and decoding. If the server is compromised by adversaries or has poor performance, it becomes a bottleneck of the DSS.

In the past 10 years, the security of DSS has been well studied by researchers. First, to solve the problem of eavesdropping attack, a lot of coding schemes [5–7] have been proposed, such as regenerating code schemes, cryptography-based code scheme [12]. Sensible coding schemes increase the difficulty of data breach through eavesdropping attack. Second, to solve the problem of single point of failure (SPoF), server replica scheme and decentralized system [12–14] have been widely studied. Server replica or decentralized technology migrate the central server work to different nodes to deduce system crash rate comes from SPoF. With the development of blockchain technology [15, 27], a new way which uses blockchain to realize decentralized DSS has attracted a lot of attention due to the blockchain's good performance in decentralization. It is easy to achieve anonymity and solve the SPoF problem with the anonymity and decentralization characteristics of blockchain in DSS.

The overarching goal of our study is to establish a secure DSS, in which users and data hosts can keep anonymity and the system does not suffer from the problem of SPoF. In this paper, we propose a decentralized secure distributed storage scheme, a pipelined code scheme based on blockchain, and a time-based replica storage mechanism. Specifically, we mainly focus on the following questions: (a) how to keep anonymity between users and each data host? (b) how to construct a coding scheme based on blockchain? (c) how to enhance the robustness of the system? The main contributions of this paper are three-fold.

- We introduce the framework of our decentralized DSS which is constructed by a two-layer blockchain and pipelined code.
- We provide a generic code construction that present the explicit process of pipelined code combined with blockchain.
- We show a time-based replica storage mechanism which achieves better trade-off between storage overhead and decode computation overhead.

The rest of the paper is organized as follows. We discuss related work in Sect. 2. In Sect. 3, we describe our main work from three aspects. And in Sect. 4, we discuss the security of our proposed scheme. Section 5 is the conclusion.

2   Related Work

When the personal data is outsourced in the DSS, a system running in an open environment, lots of security problems need to be concerned. The high value data and open environment make the data breach and SPoF be the main problems we need to address. Researchers have proposed many methods, such coding schemes, replica mechanism and blockchain-based DSS. The following Table 1 gives a summary that related work's performance in different aspects.

Table 1. Related work and their performance in different aspects.

	Sample	Anonymity	Anti-SPoF	Robust	Communication bandwidth	Computation overhead	Storage overhead
Coding schemes	[5–11, 14]	Weak	Weak	Strong	High	High	Low
Replica mechanism	[12, 14, 23]	Weak	Strong	Weak	Low	Low	High
Blockchain-based DSS	[15–19]	Strong	Strong	Strong	High	High	High

2.1 Coding Schemes

Data breach is a common problem in DSS due to its nature. To address it, lots of coding schemes have been proposed. Coding schemes used in DSS aim to provide a storage-efficient alternative to replication [14] in the beginning. In the same time, they play an important role when it comes to the data breach problem of DSS. Ankit et al. proposed a secure coding scheme and first investigated security in the presence of colluding eavesdroppers [5], and achieved the upper bounds on the secure file size and establish the secrecy capacity for any (l_1, l_2)-eavesdropper with $l_2 \leq 2$. In the same time, they employed cooperative regenerating codes to face multiple simultaneous node failures and eliminated the information leakage to the eavesdropper [6]. Shah et al. [7] provided constructions of regenerating codes that achieve information-theoretic secrecy capacity in the sitting where an eavesdropper may gain access to the data stored in a subset of the storage nodes and possibly to the data downloaded during repair of some nodes. To realize better trade-off between secrecy and system reliability, paper [8] provided explicit code constructions against eavesdropping attack and adversarial attacks in repair dynamics setting. Ravi et al. [9–11] investigated two types of wiretapping scenarios is DSS: (a) Type-I (node) adversary which can wiretap the data stored on any $l < k$ nodes; and (b) Type-II (repair data) adversary which can wiretap the contents of the repair data that is used to repair a set of l failed nodes over time. And they realized the optimal characterization of the secure storage-vs-exact-repair-bandwidth trade-off region of a (n, k, d)-DSS, with $n \leq 4$ and any $l < k$ in the presence of both Type-I and Type-II adversaries.

Coding scheme can solve the eavesdropping problem to some extent. But its shortcoming is obvious that it greatly increases computation overhead and communication bandwidth. And it is weak when it comes to collusion in DSS. It is expensive and weak to block data breach just through coding scheme in DSS.

2.2 Replica Mechanism

In [12], Lin et al. addressed the privacy issue of DSS with secure decentralized networked erasure code combined a threshold public key encryption scheme. This system is fully decentralized which introduces a new way to address another problem of DSS,

SPoF. SPoF may show up in the meta-data server when we encode or decode data. To some extent, the low performance of a server would lead to system crash. And the meta-data server is the important target of adversaries due to its high value, which may leak to adversaries more information when it is compromised. Cassandra [13] is a decentralized DSS which provides scalability, high performance, and wide applicability. Paper [14] proposed a decentralized erasure coding process that achieves the migration in a network-efficient manner in contrast to the traditional coding process.

Replica mechanism is a good method to address the SPoF problem. But it cannot achieve a good balance between SPoF problem and data breach. If decentralization cannot be implemented in the proper way, it increases the risk of data breach in the contrary.

2.3   Blockchain-Based DSS

With the development of blockchain technology [15], a new way to realize secure and decentralized DSS has drawn a lot of attention [18, 19]. Metadisk [16] is a new model in which a blockchain can serve as the backbone for a distributed application. It allows integration with existing open-source projects in a modular fashion to simplify the development of a decentralized storage network. In addition, Metadisk can use its own cryptocurrency as a means to pay for and exchange storage space and bandwidth in a peer to peer network, which may harness the powerful free-market force of self-interest to drive the networks growth and efficiency. Blockstack [17] is a decentralized DSS which combines blockchain and cloud storage. In this system, blockchain serves as a manager to guarantee system stability and security in the control plane with a two-layer blockchain (Blockchain Layer and Virtualchain Layer).

Considering to the advantages of blockchain-based DSS, we construct a decentralized secure DSS based on pipelined code and blockchain. With the anonymity characteristic of blockchain, we realize anonymity between users and hosts to against data breach. And with the decentralization characteristic of blockchain, we realize decentralization in our system to against the SPoF problem.

3   Proposed Secure DSS

In this section, we describe the proposed secure DSS. We present the system framework at first. Then we describe the explicit process of pipelined code scheme and replica placement mechanism based on the system framework.

3.1   System Framework

Our DSS framework is a three-layer architecture as shown in Fig. 1.

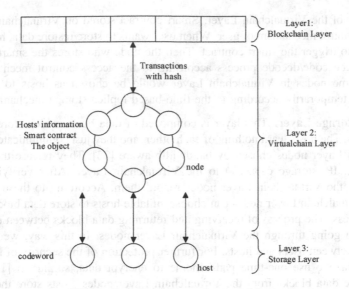

Fig. 1. Overview of our scheme architecture

The top two layers, Blockchain Layer and Virtualchain Layer, are in the control plane. The bottom layer, Storage Layer, is in the data plane. Users store or restore data in Storage Layer through Virtualchain Layer. Virtualchain Layer storages its own hash value in Blockchain Layer to protect its integrity. The characteristics of different layers are described as below.

Layer 1: Blockchain Layer. The Blockchain Layer is the security cornerstone of our system. It protects the security of Virtualchain Layer through storing the Virtualchain Layer's hash value as a transaction data. We take public chain, like Bitcoin's blockchain, as the underlying blockchain to maintain the Blockchain Layer. Public chain has lots of excellent characters, such as anonymity, tamper resistance and full historical record, that are useful for a secure DSS. In this paper, we use Bitcoin's blockchain as the underlying blockchain to construct our DSS. The reason is that Bitcoin's blockchain uses proof-of-work (PoW) as its consensus mechanism, which is known as the safest consensus. Another reason why we use Bitcoin's blockchain is that it is the safest public blockchain so far. It has been running for several years safely and steadily.

Layer 2: Virtualchain Layer. The Virtualchain Layer is the core functional module of our system. It realizes most main functions of our DSS, such as restoring hosts' information and smart contract, encoding and decoding user data and relaying on anonymous communication between users and hosts. It's a permissioned blockchain and uses fast consensus (e.g., Conflux [21]) to get high throughput. With fast consensus, even just a leader election algorithm [22], the Virtualchain can generate blocks to form ledger as fast as we need. So that it can record the information of hosts, meta-data and user's operation history log in transactions as fast as we need. The SHA-1 hash of Virtualchain would be sent to Blockchain Layer periodically as a transaction. The Blockchain Layer stores the SHA-1 hash permanently in order that we can check the integrity of the Virtualchain Layer. Smart contract stored on Virtualchain records the access control mechanism of user. When user wants to store/restore data, he sends a transaction to trigger the smart contract. Then the node who stores the smart contract carries out the code/decode process according to the access control mechanism. In addition, some nodes in Virtualchain Layer would be chosen as hosts to store the replica data temporarily according to the time-based replica storage mechanism.

Layer 3: Storage Layer. This layer is composed of data hosts, which store the true data of users. The hosts learn nothing of each other, and they just communicate with the Virtualchain Layer nodes chosen by bandwidth-aware [23]. They release their information (e.g., IP, storage capacity) to the Virtualchain Layer. After verifying these information, the Virtualchain Layer nodes record them. According to these information, the Virtualchain Layer nodes can choose suitable hosts to store data blocks in the encode process. The process of receiving and returning data blocks between users and hosts is also going through the Virtualchain Layer nodes. In this way, we keep the anonymity between users and hosts. For further protection of the security of hosts and the user data, we use one-time pad scheme to encrypt data, similar to [18]. After receiving the data blocks from the Virtualchain Layer nodes, hosts store them in its own storage system without any change.

3.2 Pipelined Code

Our pipelined code scheme is inspired by the RapidRAID [20], which is a pipelined erasure code used in DSS for fast data archival. We combine it with blockchain to realize an anonymous blockchain-based code scheme to construct the storage function basis. We depict an example of our code scheme using the code parameters (8, 4) in Fig. 2. An object $O = (o_1, o_2, o_3, o_4)$ is encoded into an 8-dimensional codeword $C = (c_1, \ldots, c_8) = (O, c_5, \ldots, c_8)$ using a classical systematic (8, 4) erasure code, that is, each o_i is a string of l bits. Every operation is performed using finite field arithmetic in the simulations of our scheme, and we use $\mathbb{F}_{2^8}$ as the finite field to deduce the computational complexity. But we do not insist on the code being systematic in the pipelined encode process. The host i (denoted by h_i on the figure) stores a replica of the raw data block $c_i = o_i$, $i = 1, \ldots, 4$. And hosts 5 to 8 store a second replica of the same object as well. The pipelined encoding process proceeds as follows. The host h_i sends o_i to node n_i, $i = 1, \ldots, 8$. Then the first node n_1 sends a multiple of o_1 to the second node n_2. The node 2 computes a linear combination of this multiple of o_1 with o_2, which h_2 sends to n_2, and forwards the result to n_3. The node 3 has now data o_3 from h_3, and again computes a linear combination of o_3 with which it received from n_2. The process is iteratively repeated from n_i to n_{i+1}, $i = 1, \ldots, 7$. And we get the final linear combination of all codewords from n_8 with which users can get the raw data.

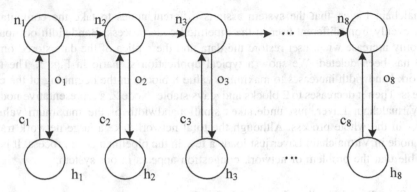

Fig. 2. An example of pipelined code process

At the same time, every node also generates a redundancy block c_i, based on what it receives, and forwards c_i back to h_i to update the codeword, $i = 1, \ldots, 8$. The generated blocks $C = (c_1, \ldots, c_8)$ constitute the final codeword. A formal description of this pipelined encode process is provided in Algorithm 1. Note that we use $x_{i,i+1}$ for the data which is forwarded from node i to node $i+1$, and $\psi_i, \xi_i \in \mathbb{F}_{2^l}, i = 1, \ldots, 8$ are predetermined values (Table 2).

Table 2. The pipelined code process with codeword generated by the $(8, 4)$ erasure code.

Algorithm 1. Pipelined code process	
1: **for** $i = 1, \ldots, 8$ **do**	// hosts send codeword to nodes
2: (h_i sends o_i to n_i)	
3: **end for**	
4: $x_{1,2} \leftarrow o_1 \cdot \psi_1$	//nodes do pipelined code and forward it to successor
5: **for** $i = 2, \ldots, 7$ **do**	
6: $x_{i,i+1} \leftarrow x_{i-1,i} + o_i \cdot \psi_i$	
7: (n_i sends $x_{i,i+1}$ to n_{i+1})	
8: **end for**	
9: $c_1 \leftarrow o_1 \cdot \xi_1$	//nodes calculate codeword and return it back to hosts
10: **for** $i = 2, \ldots, 8$ **do**	
11: $c_i \leftarrow x_{i-1,i} + o_i \cdot \xi_i$	
12: (n_i sends c_i to h_i)	
13: **end for**	

The decode of object O can use linear coding notation $G \cdot O^T = C^T$, where G is composed by the predetermined values, ψ_i and ξ_i.

In our scheme, the pipelined code process requires little computation resources of every node. Because the process has fundamental difference with the normal datacenter operations and the system's computation overhead is shared by many nodes in the

Virtualchain Layer, that the system assigns different nodes to take the computation work evenly from different user in the pipelined code process. Bandwidth occupancy will only increase when user restore the data and the replica of the data stored on the node has been deleted. We show a typical application scenario in Fig. 3. The total network bandwidth increases to maximum value 8 blocks in the beginning of the code process. Then it decreases to 2 blocks and stays stable. Node 2, a representative node in the Virtualchain Layer, just undertakes small bandwidth of the maximum value 2 blocks in the whole process. Although the total network take a large network traffic, each node in Virtualchain Layer just loads a few in the pipelined code process. It is not possible that the problem of network congestion appears in our system.

3.3   Time-Based Replica Storage Mechanism

Erasure code scheme and replica mechanism are coexist to get better trade-off between storage overhead and computation overhead in most DSS. For the same purpose, we propose a time-based replica storage mechanism in company with pipelined code scheme in our DSS.

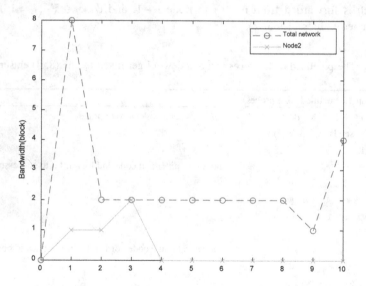

Fig. 3. Bandwidth Occupancy in the pipelined code process

We store the object' replica in a Virtualchain Layer node when the first time the user uploads the object or user reads the object. We take the object as hot data which the user may read it again within a short time. And for the hot data, we store its replica to reduce the computation overhead when user reads it the next time. A clock t and a threshold T are set and stored in the node along with the replica. The parameter value of the clock t is zero at beginning and it increases along with time. If user reads the object once again when $t < T$, he could get the object from the Virtualchain Layer node directly and the parameter value of t will be reset to zero in the same time. The computation overhead is reduced to zero and the storage overhead is increased by four blocks. Through this way, we deduce the computation overhead at the cost of storage overhead. The replica stored in the node would be deleted when $t \geq T$, and the storage space is released. That is if user has not read the object for a time which is longer than T, we take the object as a cold data which the user would not read it in a long time. And for the cold data, we delete its replica to release the storage space.

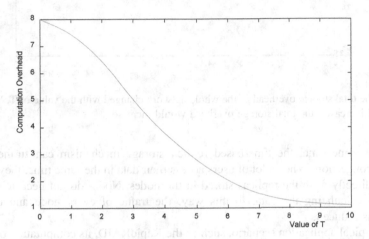

Fig. 4. The total computation overhead of the whole network changed with the value of T. When the value of T is big enough, the computation overhead decrease to very low.

The value of T is depended on the time interval t between user accesses the data tow times and the source value of the network. We need to keep a value C for the available computing resources of the network and a value S for the available storage resources of the node that storages the replica. We update the value of T when user accesses the replica:

$$T_{new} = \frac{t + T_{old}}{2} \cdot \frac{\alpha C_{new} + \beta S_{new}}{\alpha C_{old} + \beta S_{old}} \cdot \lambda \tag{1}$$

where $\alpha, \beta \in [0, 1], \alpha + \beta = 1, \lambda \in (0, +\infty)$, α and β denote the weights of computing resources and storage resources for network. If we want to reduce computation overhead, we can set $\lambda > 1$ to get a bigger value of T, that we can store the replica of the object for longer time. If user accesses the object during $T_{old} < t < T_{new}$, he can get it from its replica without computation. If we want to reduce storage overhead, we can set $0 < \lambda < 1$ to get a smaller value of T, that we store the replica of the object for shorter time. As shown in Fig. 4.

If the object has not been accessed until $t \geq T_{new}$, its replica stored in the node would be deleted, instead of $t \geq T_{old} \geq T_{new}$. In this way, we can get a better trade-off between storage overhead and computation overhead. As shown in Fig. 5.

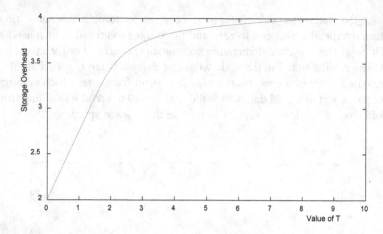

Fig. 5. The total storage overhead of the whole network changed with the value of T. When the value of T increases, the total storage overhead would increase.

In the same time, the time-based replica storage mechanism can further avoid network congestion. When a lot of users access their data in the same time, they can get the data directly from the replicas stored in the nodes. Nodes do not need to transmit blocks to calculating the data. In this way, the traffic of every node and the total network is reduced.

In a typical application scenario, such as the RapidRAID, its computation overhead and storage overhead remain at a fixed value respectively. Without the time-based replica storage mechanism, network congestion appears frequently in the RapidRAID when many users access their data in the same time. Compared with it, our system has a better performance to face the challenge that lots of users access their data in the same time.

4   Security Evaluation

In this section, we evaluate the security of our DSS. We focus on three aspects of the system security. The first is the data breach caused by adversaries attack, including eavesdropping attack and collusion attack. The second is the anonymity between users and hosts. The third is the SPoF problem.

4.1   Data Breach

Our system is running in an open environment that any computer can access the system and choose to be a user or a host if it wants. Adversaries can take advantage of this to pretend as trusted users or hosts. Then, they can implement eavesdropping attacks, one type of passive attack, to get user data in the pipelined code process. In our system, however, it is very hard for adversaries to detect the target hosts who store the codeword. Because the storage hosts that store the codeword are selected randomly. And it is impossible to find target hosts through traversal search. In addition, the one-time pad scheme will make the replay attack meaningless to adversaries. Thus adversaries can not get user data even they can access our system as a user or host.

Collusion is one type of active attack which is prone to appear in DSS. There are three types of collusion in our system, hosts collusion, nodes collusion and collusion between nodes and hosts. First, as to hosts collusion, hosts in Storage Layer just communicate with nodes in Virtualchain Layer and they learn nothing of other hosts' knowledge. Therefore a host cannot communicate with another host and make collusion attack. Then, in our system, the message transformed between nodes and hosts and the message between different nodes will be formed a transaction and be written in the Virtualchain. Then the SHA-1 hash value of the Virtualchain will be sent to Blockchain Layer and recorded. The message will be permanently recorded as a tamper-resilience log due to the characteristic of blockchain. We can detect timely when nodes collusion and the collusion between nodes and hosts take place. And we can find out the malicious nodes or hosts at the same time. Thus collusion attack can not be implemented successfully.

From these above discussions, we can learn that adversary attack and collusion attack can be detected timely and blocked. It is very difficult for adversaries to steal the user data in our system.

4.2 Anonymity

In our system, the connection model between users and hosts is shown in Fig. 6. When the user wants to outsource his data to the system, the Virtualchain Layer plays a security-mediator role between users and hosts as the server does in [24]. The user encrypts the data with one-time pad key to keep the data's security before he sends it to the nodes and hosts. Then he sends the data O and smart contract SC, (O, SC), to the Virtualchain Layer nodes. On receiving the tuple, the Virtualchain Layer nodes encode O to $C = (c_1, \ldots, c_8)$ according to SC. Next, the system selects nodes from the Virtualchain Layer to store (O, t, T) and selects eight hosts from the Storage Layer to store C according to SC. When the user wants to restore the data form hosts, he needs to send a transaction to trigger the SC stored on the Virtualchain Layer. And then the node would decode C to O and return it to user.

We can know that users communicate with hosts anonymously and indirectly in the store and restore process, that the messages are relayed by the Virtualchain Layer nodes. So that the user anonymity is preserved. There is no message transmission between different hosts in the pipelined code process or decode process. And a host learns nothing of other hosts' knowledge. A host does not know other hosts' information even the existence of them. So that the host anonymity is preserved too.

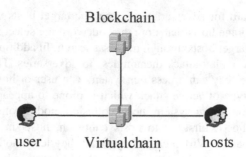

Fig. 6. The connection between user and hosts

4.3 SPoF

In our DSS, we take the Virtualchain Layer as a security-mediator to take the place of a central server. So the workload undertaken by the central server is shifted to the nodes in the Virtualchain Layer. When one user is outsourcing data through one node, another user can fulfil his own requirements through other nodes in the Virtualchain Layer. The computation overhead and communication overhead can be evenly shared by all Virtualchain Layer nodes. So that we do not need to worry about the poor performance of the central server.

Let us consider the situation that one node in the Virtualchain Layer is compromised by adversaries or permanently offline. In this situation, the codeword stored on it can be reconstructed through erasure code scheme and the replica stored on it can be stored on another node in the next time the user restores the object. Meanwhile, the bad node would be found and excluded from the Virtualchain Layer. The workload done by the bad node would be naturally shifted to other nodes. So that the problem comes form compromised central server does not exist in our DSS.

In a word, there is no SPoF in our DSS. The Virtualchain Layer can perform well in the place of a central server.

5 Conclusion

In this paper, we combine pipelined code and blockchain to form a decentralized secure distributed storage system. The proposed scheme employs double-chain structure, encryption and pipelined code in order to outsource the user data securely. In the proposed scheme, we present an explicit process of pipelined code scheme combined with blockchain, which could realize anonymity between hosts. And the blockchain is used to take the place of a central server, which can better solve the SPoF problem and realize the anonymity between user and host. In terms of performance, our system is robust and realize great trade-off between computation overhead and storage overhead.

In the future we will continue developing and evaluating other schemes that combine erasure codes and blockchain to form blockchain-based DSS.

Acknowledgements. This work is supported by the Key Technologies R & D Program of Henan Province (172102210017).

References

1. You, P., Huang, Z., Peng, Y., et al.: Towards a delivery scheme for speedup of data backup in distributed storage systems using erasure codes. J. Supercomput. **75**(1), 50–64 (2019)
2. Ghemawat, S., Gobioff, H., Leung, S.T.: The Google file system. In: Proceedings of the ACM Symposium on Operating Systems Principles (SOSP) (2003)
3. Li, J., Li, B., Li, B.: Mist: efficient dissemination of erasure-coded data in data centers. IEEE Trans. Emerg. Top. Comput. **7**, 468–480 (2018)
4. Hou, H., Shum, K.W., Chen, M., et al.: BASIC codes: low-complexity regenerating codes for distributed storage systems. IEEE Trans. Inf. Theory **62**(6), 3053–3069 (2016)
5. Rawat, A.S., Koyluoglu, O.O., Silberstein, N., et al.: Optimal locally repairable and secure codes for distributed storage systems. IEEE Trans. Inf. Theory **60**(1), 212–236 (2013)
6. Koyluoglu, O.O., Rawat, A.S., Vishwanath, S.: Secure cooperative regenerating codes for distributed storage systems. IEEE Trans. Inf. Theory **60**(9), 5228–5244 (2014)
7. Shah, N.B., Rashmi, K.V., Kumar, P.V.: Information-theoretically secure regenerating codes for distributed storage. In: 2011 IEEE Global Telecommunications Conference-GLOBECOM 2011, pp. 1–5. IEEE (2011)
8. Pawar, S., El Rouayheb, S., Ramchandran, K.: Securing dynamic distributed storage systems against eavesdropping and adversarial attacks. IEEE Trans. Inf. Theory **57**(10), 6734–6753 (2011)
9. Tandon, R., Amuru, S.D., Clancy, T.C., et al.: On secure distributed storage systems with exact repair. In: 2014 IEEE International Conference on Communications (ICC), pp. 3908–3912. IEEE (2014)
10. Tandon, R., Amuru, S.D., Clancy, T.C., et al.: Distributed storage systems with secure and exact repair—new results. In: 2014 Information Theory and Applications Workshop (ITA), pp. 1–6. IEEE (2014)
11. Tandon, R., Amuru, S.D., Clancy, T.C., et al.: Toward optimal secure distributed storage systems with exact repair. IEEE Trans. Inf. Theory **62**(6), 3477–3492 (2016)
12. Lin, H.Y., Tzeng, W.G.: A secure decentralized erasure code for distributed networked storage. IEEE Trans. Parallel Distrib. Syst. **21**(11), 1586–1594 (2010)
13. Lakshman, A., Malik, P.: Cassandra: a decentralized structured storage system. ACM SIGOPS Oper. Syst. Rev. **44**(2), 35–40 (2010)
14. Pamies-Juarez, L., Oggier, F., Datta, A.: Decentralized erasure coding for efficient data archival in distributed storage systems. In: Frey, D., Raynal, M., Sarkar, S., Shyamasundar, Rudrapatna K., Sinha, P. (eds.) ICDCN 2013. LNCS, vol. 7730, pp. 42–56. Springer, Heidelberg (2013). https://doi.org/10.1007/978-3-642-35668-1_4
15. Crosby, M., Pattanayak, P., Verma, S., et al.: Blockchain technology: beyond bitcoin. Appl. Innov. **2**(6–10), 71 (2016)
16. Wilkinson, S., Lowry, J., Boshevski, T.: Metadisk a blockchain-based decentralized file storage application. Technical report, hal, pp. 1–11, Storj Labs Inc. (2014)
17. Ali, M., Nelson, J., Shea, R., et al.: Blockstack: a global naming and storage system secured by blockchains. In: 2016 USENIX Annual Technical Conference (USENIX ATC 2016), pp. 181–194 (2016)

18. Fukumitsu, M., Hasegawa, S., Iwazaki, J., et al.: A proposal of a secure P2P-type storage scheme by using the secret sharing and the blockchain. In: 2017 IEEE 31st International Conference on Advanced Information Networking and Applications (AINA), pp. 803–810. IEEE (2017)

19. Chen, Y., Li, H., Li, K., et al.: An improved P2P file system scheme based on IPFS and Blockchain. In: 2017 IEEE International Conference on Big Data (Big Data), pp. 2652–2657. IEEE (2017)

20. Pamies-Juarez, L., Datta, A., Oggier, F.: RapidRAID: pipelined erasure codes for fast data archival in distributed storage systems. In: 2013 Proceedings IEEE INFOCOM, pp. 1294–1302. IEEE (2013)

21. Li, C., Li, P., Xu, W., et al.: Scaling Nakamoto consensus to thousands of transactions per second. arXiv preprint arXiv:1805.03870 (2018)

22. Aniello, L., Baldoni, R., Gaetani, E., et al.: A prototype evaluation of a tamper-resistant high performance blockchain-based transaction log for a distributed database. In: 2017 13th European Dependable Computing Conference (EDCC), pp. 151–154. IEEE (2017)

23. Shen, J., Gu, J., Zhou, Y., et al.: Bandwidth-aware delayed repair in distributed storage systems. In: 2016 IEEE/ACM 24th International Symposium on Quality of Service (IWQoS), pp. 1–10. IEEE (2016)

24. Chen, F., Xiang, T., Yang, Y., et al.: Secure cloud storage meets with secure network coding. IEEE Trans. Comput. **65**(6), 1936–1948 (2015)

25. Amazon.com, "Amazon S3". http://aws.amazon.com/s3

26. Apache.org, "HDFS". http://hadoop.apache.org/hdfs

27. Nakamoto, S.: Bitcoin: a peer-to-peer electronic cash system (2008). https://bitcoin.org/bitcoin.pdf

Concept Timestamping on Blockchain and Decentralization of Patents

Kar Seng Loke$^{(\boxtimes)}$

Data Smart PLT, Kuala Lumpur, Malaysia
Loke.ks@gmail.com

Abstract. We describe a system for registering new inventions and design based on conceptual graphs and the blockchain. Instead of describing the innovation in text as in patent claims, the claims are documented using conceptual graphs as a structured graphical method for capturing concepts and their relationship. Conceptual graphs as a structured graphical method allows easier automatic semantic comparisons. It obviates the need from extracting semantic concepts from text using natural language processing techniques. The graphs then can be hashed and submitted to the blockchain for timestamping to claim the innovation.

Keywords: Blockchain · Patents · Timestamping · Conceptual graphs · Concept timestamping · Decentralized systems

1 Introduction

Intellectual property (IP) refers to creations of the mind that includes inventions, literary and artistic works according to World Intellectual Property Organization (WIPO). Protection to the creators for these intellectual goods are provided by IP laws so that economic benefits may accrue to them while at the same time taking into consideration the wider public interest so that innovation can flourish as well. IP protection includes patents, copyrights and trademarks. Patents, a dominant system for IP, encourage research and development (R & D) and at the same time allow diffusion of knowledge. It is intended to solve the issue of economic incentives and knowledge diffusion. A patent gives the inventor the right to decide who can use his invention. In exchange for this right, the inventor has to disclose the technical information for it.

Patent assessment is a key component in the patent system. Patents are awarded based on novelty and the non-obviousness of the invention. The increase in the number of patent application creates additional demands on the patent examiners because of the difficulty of keeping pace with the increase in workload and increasing technological complexity [1]. This creates difficulty in determining if a claimed invention is really novel and non-obvious. Good quality patents are said to promote innovation and economic benefits. Dubious and low-quality patents are those that have a lower threshold of non-obviousness or novelty. They can result from improper examinations and assessments. This can lead to stifling of innovation and greater uncertainty that may lead to disputes that has be determined by legal means.

© Springer Nature Singapore Pte Ltd. 2019
G. Wang et al. (Eds.): iSCI 2019, CCIS 1122, pp. 639–648, 2019.
https://doi.org/10.1007/978-981-15-1301-5_50

One suggestion to improve the quality of patents is to expand the number of independent reviewers [2, 3] and by crowdsourcing. Another approach may be to employ computational methods to aid in determine prior art and non-obviousness of the invention.

Patent claims are semi-structured text [4]. The description section is divided into claims, diagrams and description of invention. Computational patent text improvement approaches can be classified into 3 general approaches:

1. Perform structural analysis of text and highlighting important section of texts using natural language [5–7].
2. Improving searching, indexing and retrieval mechanism [8]. This could also involve the creation of structured databases so that comparisons can be performed easier.
3. Use of automatic classification and mining [4] for patterns within text. Vector space methods have been used to classify texts, and by using machine learning techniques such as Latent Semantic Analysis (LSA), the semantic difference (distance) between patent text can be determined.

There are still challenges remaining for making patents more accessible. We would like to make a preliminary proposal to use a supplementary system for recording innovation and novel inventions that may ameliorate some of the shortcomings of the patent system in relation to the ability to compare inventions and prior art. We propose the use conceptual graphs (CG) to describe the invention and using CG for determining prior art and novelty automatically through graph matching algorithms. The blockchain is used for decentralized timestamping the invention after it has been determined to be sufficiently novel. The entire process again can be automated without a central authority.

2 Related Works - Conceptual Graphs

A conceptual graph (CG) [9] is a graph-based method for representing structural and semantic relationships between concepts. CG is based on the ideas of semantic networks [10] and existential graphs [11]. The concept nodes can represent entities, events, actions, states, attributes, etc. A CG consist of a network of concept nodes linked by relation nodes. Mineau et al. [12] have argued that CG through its simplicity and graphical constructs, it is simple to use and yet sufficiently expressive. Graphs such as CG have non-linear structures that are make easy to identify similarities and differences.

For example, in the example below Stock and 10 are concepts and quantity (Qty) relationship links them up. The rectangular box represents concepts and circular shape gives the relationship (rel) between the concepts. The CG can be read as: the quantity (qty) of the stock is 10 (Fig. 1).

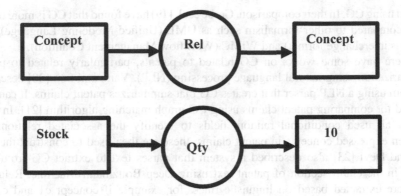

Fig. 1. Example of Concept Graph (CG)

For example, the sentence: "John is going to Boston by bus" can be represented in a conceptual graph (CG) as:

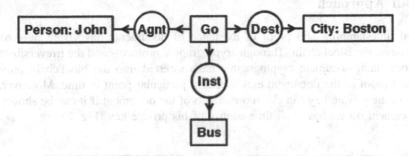

Fig. 2. Example of CG.

In Fig. 2 two of the concepts have names which represents the referent John or Boston. The type of relations is agent (Agnt), destination (Dest), or instrument (Inst). The CG has the following meaning: John is the agent of the concept Go which has destination City that is Boston, and a bus is the instrument.

CG have been used in a variety of domains for knowledge representation, query processing and automated extraction of knowledge. In the medical domain, Croitoru et al. [13] have described CG representation and querying system to improve tumor classification. SNOMED [14] also uses a manual input CG system for describing patient-description (e.g. headache, cough, chest pain) with modifiers (severity, duration, location, etc.). Another CG input system [15] are able to generate text description based on CG input. Image retrieving based on CG have also been described [16, 17]. CG have also been used in assisting of writing software requirements. Ryan and Mathews [18] described a CG system for documenting software requirements using a domain language. The tool developed allowed previous requirement definitions to be retrieved so that it can be reused. They described a CG comparison tool to identify likely CG for re-use. It recognizes that a similar problem has been solved before. However, it is a text-based tool using the textual form to write or input CG. Business processes documentation has also been applied using CG. In their comparison, Gerbé et al. [19] have found that CG is more useful when compared to other formalism such as UML (Unified Modeling Language), PIF (Process interchange format) and WfMC (Workflow Management Coalition).

There have some works on CG related to patents, particularly related to patent summarization using natural language processing (NLP). Yang and Soo [20] described a system using a NLP parser that creates CG that summarizes patent claims. It can also be used for comparing patent claims using CG graph matching algorithm [21]. In [22], Rao et al. used conditional random fields to identify the associated relationships between expressed concepts in patent claims, these are then used to construct the CG. Rao and Devi [23] also described a system that parses text to extract CG from sentences in the claim section of patent text using Deep Boltzmann Machine. Relationships are extracted based on linguistic rules, for example if concept c1 and c2 are connected by "is", then the relationship is a "sub-type" or "isa" relationship. The issue with extracting CG from text is that it tends to follow the sentential form rather closely and may obscure the conceptual form.

3 Our Approach

Trusted timestamping and proof of existence of documents have been numerously proposed on the Blockchain. Through cryptographic protocols and the irreversibility of the blockchain, document cryptographic hash inserted into the blockchain provides sufficient proof of the document existence at a particular point in time. Moreover, the holder of the private key can claim ownership of the document if it can be shown that the document owner has at all time control of his private key (Fig. 3).

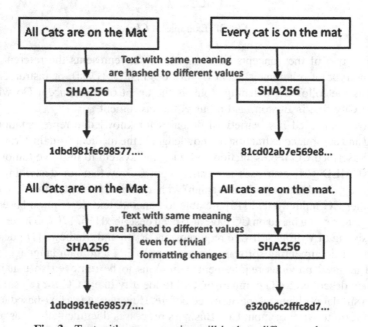

Fig. 3. Text with same meaning will hash to different values

However, documents do not equal content. Two documents with same semantical content except that one has an extra space tagged at the end, will produce a different cryptographic hash. A cryptographic hash is also useless in the case of images as a series of the same photos of different scales (size) will produce different hash value. We can't determine from the hash that they are the same photo but off different sizes. Similarly, a textual document with variations in formatting, capitalization, etc. but of the same semantical content will produce a different hash. We therefore cannot use the hash to determine similarity of content but of document. A hash value only provides proof of a particular document and does not rule out the existence another version of similar content (Fig. 4).

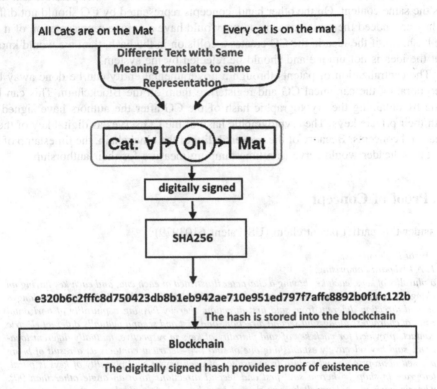

Fig. 4. Concept timestamping and registration

Language (and text) itself is very expressive and can express the same semantical contents with an infinite variety of ways. We seek an approach that is less flexible and more economical in its expression so that different concept will have different expressions, but similar concept should not differ in their expression. Once we have this expression, we can obtain its cryptographical hash to represent the concepts. This hash will then be embedded into the blockchain and claims of its existence of the concept at a particular time can be made.

Languages and formalism for expressing concepts have been developed in the area knowledge representation under cognitive science and artificial intelligence. Various suitable formalism includes First order Logic, Description Logic [24] and Conceptual Graphs [9]. Ideas and concepts then can be expressed in natural language and converted automatically to Conceptual Graphs structure. These structures would be more concise. Yang and Soo [20] have worked on extracted CG from patent text. We propose to work the other way, that is, the patentable concepts are themselves written in text and translated to CG. These CG are then held as canonical representation of those concepts. There are advantages in using the hash of the CG instead of text. As mentioned earlier various text can represent exact same semantical content and will generate different hashes. So, the existence of a hash for a document does not rule other possible text that has the same content. On the other hand, concepts represented by CG should not differ if they are indeed the same concept, so we would have a unique representation of it as the hash. So, if the idea in the CG creates a collision in the hash, then we would know that the idea is not unique and should be rejected by the system.

The centralization of patents through a governmental entity can be done away by incorporating the canonical CG and registering them on the Blockchain. This can be done by obtaining the cryptographic hash of the CG after the authors have signed it with their private keys. The cryptographic hash of the CG serves as digital key of their ideas and concepts. Because of the irreversibility of the blockchain, the timestamp of in the block header would serve as a timestamping measure for their authorship.

4 Proof of Concept

Consider this partial patent claim (US Patent 6103979):

"What is claimed is:
1. A keyboard comprising:
a plurality of keys, each key having a character illustrated at each end, and each key having an elongated shape elongated in a first direction, said plurality of keys being aligned along a second direction different from said first direction, thereby forming a plurality of horizontal rows of characters along said second direction; and first and second mutually different electric contacts provided for each key of said plurality of keys in respective, mutually different locations, said key selectively establishing one of said two electrical contacts as a result of being pressed appropriately, wherein a front surface of each key of said plurality of keys is parallelogram in shape, wherein said first and second directions form an angle other than 90°, wherein each of said parallelogram-shaped keys has a longitudinal axis thereof extending along said first direction, said first and second mutually different electric contacts being located beneath two respective ends of each said key along said longitudinal axis thereof."

We can create a partial CG in the figure below using the CharGer software [25]:

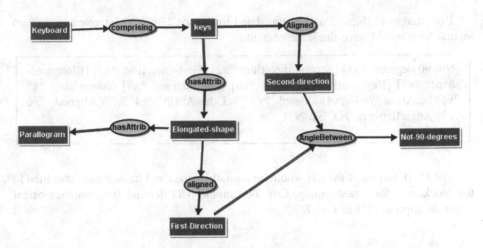

Fig. 5. Partial CG for the patent claim US Patent 6103979

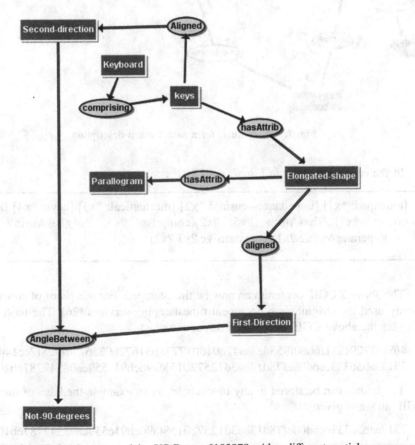

Fig. 6. Partial CG for the patent claim US Patent 6103979 with a different spatial arrangement

Both diagrams (Figs. 5 and 6) translated to linear CGIF (CG interchange format) textual form would have the same content:

[Not-90-degrees: *x1] [Second-direction: *x2] [First-Direction: *x3] [Elongated-shape: *x4] [Keyboard: *x5] [keys: *x6] [Parallogram: *x7] (comprising ?x5 ?x6)(hasAttrib ?x6 ?x4)(aligned ?x4 ?x3)(hasAttrib ?x4 ?x7)(Aligned ?x6 ?x2)(AngleBetween ?x3 ?x2 ?x1)

The CGIF format of the CG would be digitally signed and hashed and submitted to the blockchain for timestamping. Consider another CG derived from another patent claim description [22] in Fig. 7.

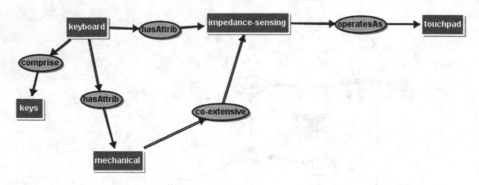

Fig. 7. CG (partial) for a patent claim description

In the case for the CG in Fig. 7, the CGIF is:

[touchpad: *x1] [impedance-sensing: *x2] [mechanical: *x3] [keys: *x4] [key-board: *x5] (hasAttrib ?x5 ?x2)(comprise ?x5 ?x4)(hasAttrib ?x5 ?x3)(operatesAs ?x2 ?x1)(co-extensive ?x3 ?x2)

The above 2 CGIF contents can now be timestamped. For this proof of concept, we simply used the OriginStamp document timestamping services [26]. The hash (SHA-256) for the above CGIF is obtained respectively as:

- 4f6145729e381f6680f953de3aa47b01d017778b51672b0336774f928f2cc144
- 7217aab5e333cc6d00ef78d13ba3d125720158fa96cb91c559ca08547787eb10

The hashes can be stored in any blockchain, as an example the hash of one of the CGIF above is given as:

- 7217aab5e333cc6d00ef78d13ba3d125720158fa96cb91c559ca08547787eb10

It is stored as an Ethereum Smart Contract with the following address:

- 0xa66a943be0c956ae90eae98b9703b98a7bbd4309

The entire system would, however, require an off-chain database for storing the original CGIF files. This would be elaborated in further research.

5   Conclusion

In summary we propose the use of CG as a representation of ideas and concepts for the purpose of making a claim of priority. Secondly, we have proposed a low-cost, universal, borderless and decentralized system for filing priority that obviates the use of any centralization through the use of the Blockchain. In addition, the uniqueness of the idea can be checked automatically using semantic graph matching algorithms.

References

1. Levin, R.: A patent system for the 21st century. Issues Sci. Technol. **4**(20), 49–54 (2004)
2. Whalen, R.: Complex innovation and the patent office. Chicago-Kent J. Intellect. Property **17** (1), 226–278 (2018)
3. Wagner, R.P.: Understanding patent quality mechanisms. Univ. Pennsylvania Law Rev. **157**, 2135 (2009)
4. Zhang, L., Li, L., Li, T.: Patent mining: a survey. ACM SIGKDD Explor. Newsl. **16**, 1–19 (2014)
5. Wang, J., Lu, W.F., Loh, H.T.: A two-level parser for patent claim parsing. Adv. Eng. Inform. **29**, 431–439 (2015)
6. Sheremetyeva, S.: Automatic text simplification for handling intellectual property. In: Proceedings of the Workshop on Automatic Text Simplification: Methods and Applications in the Multilingual Society, Dublin, Ireland (2014)
7. Shinmori, A., Okumura, M., Marukawa, Y., Iwayama, M.: Patent claim processing for readability: structure analysis and term explanation. In: Proceedings of the ACL-2003 Workshop on Patent Corpus Processing, Sapporo, Japan (2003)
8. Lupu, M., Hanbury, A.: Patent retrieval. Found. Trends Inf. Retrieval **7**(1), 1–97 (2013)
9. Sowa, J.: Conceptual graphs. In: van Harmelen, F., Lifschitz, V., Porter, B. (eds.) Handbook of Knowledge Representation, pp. 213–237. Elsevier (2008)
10. Woods, W.: What's in a link: foundations for semantic networks. In: Bobrow, D., Collins, A. (eds.) Representation and Understanding, pp. 35–82. Academic Press, New York (1975)
11. Peirce, C.S.: Manuscripts on existential graphs. In: Collected Papers of Charles Sanders Peirce, vol. 4, pp. 320–410. Harvard University Press, Cambridge (1906)
12. Mineau, G., Missaoui, R., Godinx, R.: Conceptual modelling for data and knowledge management. Data Knowl. Eng. **33**(2), 137–168 (2000)
13. Croitoru, M., et al.: Conceptual graphs based information retrieval in HealthAgents. In: Twentieth IEEE International Symposium on Computer-Based Medical Systems, Maribor, Slovenia (2007)
14. Campbell, K.E., Musen, M.A.: Representation of clinical data using SNOMED III and conceptual graphs. In: Proceedings of the Annual Symposium Computer Applications in Medical Care (1992)

15. Bernauer, J.: Conceptual graphs as an operational model for descriptive findings. In: Proceedings of the Annual Symposium on Computer Application in Medical Care (1991)
16. Ounis, I., Pa©ca, M.: Modeling, indexing and retrieving images using conceptual graphs. In: Quirchmayr, G., Schweighofer, E., Bench-Capon, T.J.M. (eds.) DEXA 1998. LNCS, vol. 1460, pp. 226–239. Springer, Heidelberg (1998). https://doi.org/10.1007/BFb0054484
17. Mulhem, P., Leow, W.K., Lee, Y.K.: Fuzzy conceptual graphs for matching images of natural scenes. In: Proceedings of the 17th International Joint Conference on Artificial Intelligence, Seattle, WA (2001)
18. Ryan, K., Mathews, B.: Matching conceptual graphs as an aid to requirements re-use. In: Proceedings of the IEEE International Symposium on Requirements Engineering, San Diego (1993)
19. Gerbé, O., Keller, R.K., Mineau, G.W.: Conceptual graphs for representing business processes in corporate memories. In: Mugnier, M.-L., Chein, M. (eds.) ICCS-ConceptStruct 1998. LNCS, vol. 1453, pp. 401–415. Springer, Heidelberg (1998). https://doi.org/10.1007/BFb0054931
20. Yang, S., Soo, V.W.: Extract conceptual graphs from plain text in patent claims. Eng. Appl. Artif. Intell. 25(4), 874–887 (2012)
21. Zhong, J., Zhu, H., Li, J., Yu, Y.: Conceptual graph matching for semantic search. In: Priss, U., Corbett, D., Angelova, G. (eds.) ICCS-ConceptStruct 2002. LNCS, vol. 2393, pp. 92–106. Springer, Heidelberg (2002). https://doi.org/10.1007/3-540-45483-7_8
22. Rao, P., Devi, S.L., Rosso, P.: Automatic identification of concepts and conceptual relations from patents using machine learning methods. In: Proceedings of the 10th International Conference on Natural Language Processing ICON-2013 (2013)
23. Rao, P., Devi, S.L.: Automatic identification of conceptual structures using deep Boltzmann machines. In: Proceedings of the 7th Forum for Information Retrieval Evaluation, FIRE 2015, Gandhinagar, India (2015)
24. Levesque, H., Brachman, R.: Knowledge Representation and Reasoning. Elsevier/Morgan Kaufmann, Amsterdam (2004)
25. Delugach, H.S.: Implementation and visualization of conceptual graphs in CharGer. Int. J. Conceptual Struct. Smart Appl. 2(2), 1–19 (2014)
26. Gipp, B., Meuschke, N., Gernandt, A.: Decentralized trusted timestamping using the crypto currency bitcoin. In: Proceedings of the iConference 2015, Newport Beach, California (2015)

Smart Wallets on Blockchain—Attacks and Their Costs

Akshay Pillai, Vishal Saraswat(✉) ⓘ, and Arunkumar V. R.

Robert Bosch Engineering and Business Solutions Pvt. Ltd., Bangalore, India
{Akshay.Pillai,Vishal.Saraswat,Arunkumar.VR}@in.bosch.com

Abstract. Smart wallets are the future of e-payments and digital payments but to utilize them to their full potential, we need to secure them from malicious actors who have already started exploiting various vulnerabilities in the existing wallets. In this work, we study the existing attacks and vulnerabilities and present possible hypothetical attack scenarios which may get executed in future by these particular vulnerabilities. We have surveyed on different attacks with comparison of attack cost and benefits of the attacker and comparison of mitigation cost and damage cost of each attack. We focus on the different attacks and usecases on the blockchain smart wallets which would help developers to secure the smart wallets. We describe each attack with its mechanism, usecase, benefits and requirements of attacker for successful attack with the possible damage scenarios and consequences, comparison of attack cost and benefits, comparison of mitigation cost and damage cost, possible mitigation and some security measures for each attack.

Keywords: Blockchain · Smart wallets · Security · Attacks · Costs

1 Introduction

As the popularity of the smartphones, laptops, tablets, etc. increases, the rate of using digitization and digital payments/e-payment also increases. Digital payment is provided by the bank providers to transfer the currency from one to another in an online gateway. As this technology emerges, the demand of securing the digital/e-payment also increases. There are number of bank providers which provide security of e-payment through user-id and password, OTP (One-Time Password), passphrases, etc. Blockchain is the decentralized way of data storage which mitigates single point of failure and plays a vital role in providing integrity to digital payments by enhancing those to smart wallets.

1.1 Our Contribution

Smart wallets will play a major role in digital payment/e-payment in future so the blockchain wallet security is needed for utilizing more advantages of the blockchain smart wallets. In this paper, we focus on the different attacks and

© Springer Nature Singapore Pte Ltd. 2019
G. Wang et al. (Eds.): iSCI 2019, CCIS 1122, pp. 649–660, 2019.
https://doi.org/10.1007/978-981-15-1301-5_51

usecases on the blockchain smart wallets, which will help the smart wallet developers to develop the secure smart wallets. We survey the existing and possible attacks and also provide some attack usecases also created which may be executable if particular precautions are not taken. We describe each attack with its mechanism, usecase, benefits and requirements of attacker for successful attack with the possible damage scenarios and consequences, comparison of attack cost and benefits, comparison of mitigation cost and damage cost, possible mitigation and security measures for each attack.

2   Malware and Trojans

Malware and trojans play vital role in offline wallet's private key theft. Offline based wallets store their private key in user's system (computer or laptop). To steal private key or seed file from the victim's system, attacker use malwares and use trojans to remotely transfer cryptocurrencies from victim's account to attacker's account.

Mechanism: 1. Attacker will detect flaws on user's system (that is, a system with free anti-virus or without anti-virus system) for installing malware software on that particular system.
2. After installation of malware, attacker will hijack the system to find the location of the private key.
3. If private key is encrypted then attacker will try to find the seed in same system or he/she will destroy the private key in that system. On the other hand if private key is not encrypted then attacker will steal key for accessing user account and steal sensitive information.

Usecases: Cryptocurrencies stolen from Exodus wallet by using bots and malwares [7].

Requirements: Attacker needs a full fledged application/software developer to develop malwares. On the hand, attacker should have good knowledge on social engineering for the execution of successful attack.

Goal: The goal of the attacker is to steal the private key or seed file from victim's computer.

Benefits: After stealing private key, attacker can gain access to victim's wallet account and transfer cryptocurrency from victim to attacker account.

Attack Cost vs Benefits: Attacker may or may not require a team for execution of this attack and benefits will depend on how much cryptocurrencies victim is stored in his wallets.

Damage Scenario: All of victim's cryptocurrency saving can get stolen.

Damage Consequence: Victim may suffer huge money loss which he/she invested in that cryptocurrency.

Mitigation: If user realize that his/her system contains some virus, then change passcode immediately and backup the private key.

Mitigation cost vs Damage cost: Mitigation requires immediate action otherwise it will be a successful attack. Damage depends on victim's investment in that particular wallet.

Recommendations: 1. Use paid or trusted anti-virus avoid free version.

2. Never store seed passphrase in any text files, writing seed phrase in paper will be better solution.

3. Avoid surfing insecure websites to avoid downloading any phishing bots or trojans and always clear cache and cookies for safe side.

3   Windows Clipboard Hijacking

Clipboard hijacking is the attack in which attacker takes control of the victim's system clipboard and replaces its content with the malicious content which can be a link of malicious website. In terms of blockchain wallets, clipboard hijacking is used to steal the seed phrase of the wallet's private key.

Mechanism: 1. First, attacker will find the details of the victim who have smart-wallets installed their system.

2. Attacker will inject malicious software using social engineering or phishing bots to the victim's system.

3. Malware or trojan will hijack clipboard and steals all the contents of the clipboard. If victim copied seed phrase then attacker will get seed phrase and execute next stage of attack.

Usecases: 1. In Google Play, several android apps have found impersonating Metamask for stealing seed phrase from mobile clipboard storage [9].

2. Clipboard hijackers monitored 2.3 million addresses, as public addresses are long and difficult to remember wallet users copy-paste the public address to transfer cryptocurrency [20].

Requirements: Attacker should be application/software developer to develop malwares or trojans suitable for clipboard hijacking. Attacker should also have good knowledge on social engineering and phishing attack to increase the success rate of this attack.

Goal: Attacker wants the seed phrase of victim's wallet private key which may be stored in clipboard database.

Benefits: Compromising seed phrase results in gaining complete access of the victim's wallet to attacker or any malicious user. Benefits depends on victim's investment.

Attack Cost vs Benefits: Attacker may or may not require a team for execution of attack, so a team of two will also make this attack successful and benefit will be very low as compared to web phishing and networks. This attack depends on particular user so benefits will vary on cryptocurrency investment by victim.

Damage Scenario, Consequence and Mitigation: Same as malware and trojan attack.

Recommendations: 1. Avoid copy-pasting of the seed phrase in computers.

2. Never store seed phrase in computers, writing seed phrase in paper will be better option.

3. Use paid anti-virus and beware of insecure websites which contains phishing bots.

4   Web Phishing and Browser Hijacking

In web phishing attacker can alter the address bar of the website by placing a picture of legitimate URL over address using JavaScript commands. These attacks are executed due to flaws in web page scripts [24].

Cryptojacking is also similar to web phishing in which an attacker hijacks a user's browser to mine cryptocurrencies in blockchain. In cryptojacking, attacker uses JavaScript code and malicious link to hijack other user browser [15].

Mechanism: 1. Attacker need to detect the flaw in the website to execute attack against victim.
2. Attacker use their own scripts also known as cross-site scripting [10] to make the phishing website.
3. To execute the attack without sending any mails or links to victim, attacker can do network attacks(BGP hijacking [8]) for better results.

Usecase: Attacker can apparently send mails or links related to the respective professions of the victim about expiration of account or deactivation of cards. On the other hand attacker can use BGP hijacking to set their phishing site in the legitimate server [12]. Recently MyEtherWallet got attacked by DNS attack, BGP hijacking and phishing attack [24]. The attack was not identity based but same kind of attack can also get executed for identity for both user-id and password based and public-private key based DApps.

Requirements: 1. Attacker need a team to find the vulnerabilities in different websites.
2. Attacker should have a very knowledge of designing websites and JavaScript.

Goal: The goal of the attacker is to steal the login credentials or to steal the private key from the decentralized application.

Benefits: With the compromised credentials and private keys attacker can steal sensitive data from the particular organization. Profit will be based on organization.

Attack Cost vs Benefits: For successful attack, attacker needs a team who have good knowledge on websites and networking whereas benefits will depend on the organization whose credentials got compromised. Hence, *bigger the organization, bigger the benefits.*

Damage Scenario and Consequence: Same as broad based and spear phishing attack.

Mitigation: If DApp is user-id and password based then for recovery contact organization immediately and if it is public-private key based then always keep a backup of your private key and contact organization. If private key is not backed up then user will not be able to access their account.

Mitigation cost vs Damage cost: If DApp is public-private key based and user took a backup of the private key then mitigation cost will be lower than userid-password based DApp. Damage depends on the respective organization and user.

Recommendations: 1. Avoid using HTTP for website server.

2. For public-private key based DApp, keep good anti-virus in the system and also take a backup of private key every-time after each transactions.

3. Use two-factor authentication for both userid-password based and public-private key based DApps.

5 Trickbot Trojan

Trickbot is the banking trojan which targets windows machine to steal banking credentials via webinjects. Trickbot can also steal cryptocurrencies from blockchain wallets [14]. There are two techniques, static and dynamic injection, to trick the victim to giveaway their credentials.

Static injection is similar to phishing attack in which attacker replaces bank site legitimate login page with a fake one which looks exact same. Dynamic injection redirects the web browser to attacker's server whenever user enters the targeted bank website URL [6].

Mechanism: 1. For static injection, attacker can make a fake email and website and broadcast across users. Those emails may be located in spam messages.

2. For dynamic injection, attacker will detect flaws on network using wireshark or other networking tool to intercept victim's hostname, port or proxy settings and exploit that flaw to execute the attack [25].

3. After exploitation, trojan captures the credential and then attacker will execute next stage of attack.

Usecases: Trickbot targets coinbase as one of its attack vectors. Once trojan gets infected in victim's system, the malware injects a fake login page so that whenever victim visits that particular wallet site, the attacker will get the credentials of the victim [15].

Requirements: 1. Attacker will require a team, who should have expertise in using networking tools, social engineering, website development and application development.

2. Attackers should make the malicious links of targeted bank in a legitimate way so victim will give away their credentials.

Goal: The goal of the attacker is to steal the credentials of the wallet account.

Benefits: As trickbot trojan is specifically designed for banking system, so a successful attack will give very huge benefits to the attackers and an approximate damage can range from $100 Million to $10 Billion (depending on the banks).

Attack Cost vs Benefits: Attacker need a team of full fledged network and application engineer for successful attack and benefits will be huge because if bank server gets compromised then attacker can steal the money or cryptocurrency from the targeted bank or wallet company.

Damage Scenario: Cryptocurrency theft from targeted wallet company.

Damage Consequence: Users and organization will suffer huge money loss and it may result in closure of that wallet company.

Mitigation: If user realizes that his/her contains the trojan then cash-in the cryptocurrency and report the wallet organization.

Mitigation cost vs Damage cost: Mitigation cost will increase if organization have to change their network architecture whereas successful attack gives huge profit to attackers.

Recommendations: 1. Avoid using free anti-virus, always use trusted or paid anti-virus.

2. Wallet company should use HTTPS server.

3. Use trusted or secure browsers to avoid session hijacking.

6   JSON-RPC Bug

JSON-RPC is a protocol which allows data to be exchanged between clients and servers. Electrum and exodus use JSON-RPC protocol in their wallet [26]. JSON-RPC listens the localhost that can be exploited as CSRF (Cross Site Request Forgery) [23].

Mechanism: 1. First victim has to login to a legitimate site where attacker will use JavaScript which makes GET request to the JSON server which returns sensitive information.

2. After that if victim goes to new browser and type website URL, it will get redirected to the malicious login page. On the other hand if JSON does not send response then attacker will use Array constructor (JavaScript allows to redefine Array constructor) to access the data in array and send it to malicious website [11].

Usecases: Electrum and Exodus are vulnerable to this attack as electrum is daemon running so attacker can use virtual host on the web server that can easily give access to victim's wallet via Local RPC port [5].

Requirements: Attacker should have the good knowledge on client-server protocol, network ports and JavaScript. Attacker may need team of five members for successful execution of this attack.

Goal: The goal of the attacker is to steal login credentials from victim's computer using Cross Site Request Forgery (CSRF).

Benefits: Successful attack depends on router which the organization is using. If attack gets successful then attacker can steal cryptocurrencies from all the customers of that organization.

Attack Cost vs Benefits: Attack will get waste if JSON-RPC API is authenticated, if it is not authenticated then it will result in success. Benefits will be huge but possibility of attack occurrence is very low unless you have insecure router or unauthenticated JSON-RPC API.

Damage Scenario: Customer credential theft and wallet theft.

Damage Consequence: Organization will suffer huge money loss as well as their customer's money loss.

Mitigation: Make sure that JSON services should always return its response as non-array JSON object [11].

Recommendations: 1. The token should require authentication on each request.

2. The token must reset on every authentication/authorization request to prevent CSRF or replay attacks and token should have a sufficient length to avoid hash collisions.

7   BGP Hijacking

BGP is a de-facto routing protocol and regulates how IP packets are forwarded to their destination. To intercept the network traffic of blockchain. Attackers either leverage or manipulate BGP routing. BGP hijacking typically requires the control of network operators, which could potentially be exploited to delay network messages. Attackers conduct BGP hijacking to intercept bitcoin miner's connections to a mining pool server [13].

Mechanism: 1. First, attackers will find the target in the small ISP which peered at different connected exchange points, which give them access to the number of ISPs.

2. After getting access the targeted ISP data centre was a fake DNS server which selectively responds queries for targeted Wallet organization. In addition, all other requests silently get discarded and for that particular amount of time attacker will hijack the wallet server and executes next stage of attack [17].

Usecases: In web phishing we discussed about BGP hijacking through which attackers stole more than $150k of ethers from MyEtherWallet using DNS spoofing and phishing attack. In terms of network attacks in blockchain, this attack happened recently [16].

Requirements: Attacker need a team who are full-fledged network engineer. They require in different expertise in networking such as network tracing, network scanning (wireshark) and DNS spoofing, etc. They may also require website developer to make phishing website to increase the success rate of this attack.

Goal: The goal of the attacker is to gain access to a small ISP which are connected to different exchange points and also it will give access to number of ISPs which are peered to connected exchange point.

Benefits: Attackers can hijack the organization server for a short amount of time, so that attackers can inject their phishing website to the server. Attacker requires multiple attacks to make this attack successful and earn huge profit.

Attack Cost vs Benefits: Attacker needs professional network engineer and website developer for successful and benefits will be high due to compromise of the wallet company server. If attack will not get successful then for attacker it will be a huge loss.

Damage Scenario: Organization server hijack, customer credential and wallet theft.

Damage Consequence: Users of that particular organization will suffer money loss and organization will suffer reputation loss.

Mitigation: It is difficult to prevent without acceptance of techniques like Route Origin Authorizations (ROAs) but they can be detected and resolve quickly using monitoring services [17].

Mitigation cost vs Damage cost: If detection of attack is monitored quickly then only BGP hijacking can be prevented otherwise in short amount of time attacker will steal cryptocurrencies from many users.

Recommendations: 1. Announce only owned prefixes.

2. Limit maximum number of prefixes.

3. Filter and accept only prefixes with length /24 and less [21].

8   Crypto Dusting

Crypto Dusting is an attack on cryptocurrency wallets in which attacker distributes illegal funds from unknown source to legitimate cryptocurrency holders which in turn affects the wallet's company reputation draws attention of law enforcement [2].

Mechanism: 1. Attacker will collect illegal funds from either from corrupted employee or businessman.

2. After collecting funds, attacker will anonymously distribute the funds to innocent public address of wallet holders.

Usecases: Bitcoin users began to get BTC anonymously from BestMixer.io [3].

Requirements: Depending how attacker is collecting illegal funds (spear phishing, malwares or network attacks) requirements may vary.

Goal: The goal of the attacker either will harm the reputation of the particular wallet company or distribution of illegal funds to normal cryptocurrency holders.

Benefits: Crypto dusting is harmless to normal users but if attacker have any grudge towards wallet company, he/she can do this attack for attacker's personal satisfaction.

Attack Cost vs Benefits: In terms of attacker's point of view there is no benefit for attacker for executing this attack, so in this scenario, attack cost will be more than benefits depending on how illegal funds has been collected.

Attack Scenario: Micro-transaction on adding cryptocurrencies to multiple address.

Attack Consequence: Organization may suffer reputation loss because *law of enforcement* keeps an eye on some organization and this attack will give attention.

9   Distributed Denial of Service (DDoS) Attack

This attack will get executed when attacker will send excessive data to a node and make it so busy that it cannot process normal transactions. In terms of blockchain, spamming of transactions will also create a huge load on network which results in DDoS [1].

Mechanism: 1. Attacker will do malicious attempt to jam normal traffic with excessive packets or data.

2. Overwhelming the target server with packet/data flood and use the compromised server.

Usecases: In 2018, IOTA users lost their funds by unknown attacker. The user used iotaseed.io for generating seed, maybe iotaseed.io server got compromised and attacker stole cryptocurrencies. In addition attacker executes DDoS attack so users were not able to recover their funds [4].

Requirements: Attacker needs to know the use of attack tools like *Slowloris* to execute the DDoS attack after compromise of that particular server.

Goal: The goal of the attacker is to slow down the network so that victim will not be able to recover its cryptocurrencies.

Benefits: Particularly DDoS attack will not give much benefits, attacker have to use DDoS attack in combination with other attacks for benefits.

Attack Cost vs Benefits: In terms of DDoS, much effort is not required from attacker and benefits will be very low if the solo attack is executed. In combination, benefits will increase.

Damage Scenario: Server will get down and delaying services to customers.

Damage Consequence: Due to delay services, organization reputation will affect.

Mitigation: Route traffic across multiple data centres and detect the fingerprint of the attack. After that drop malicious traffic at network edge and analyse attack pattern.

Mitigation cost vs Damage cost: Mitigation of DDoS is little bit complicated and lot of time to recover the network. If DDoS attack is not in combination with other attack then damage will be low.

Recommendations: 1. Secure the network infrastructure and practice basic network security.

2. If network architecture is strong then one server can handle extra network traffic.

3. Cloud based service providers offers many advantages which may help to fight DDoS attack. If user see lack of performance, network slowdown, website shutdown then it results in DDoS attack and organization should act.

10   Man-in-the-Middle Attack

A MitM attack is executed on an organization or user that can result in credentials compromise if executed correctly. An attacker can intercept the network connection by session hijacking that compromises web sessions by stealing session tokens. In terms of blockchain, attacker can steal session tokens from decentralized applications (DApps) [22].

Mechanism: 1. Attacker intercepts an insecure network connection that the user's device unknowingly connects. For example, evil twin attack.

2. If data is encrypted then attacker will install malicious certificate by tricking the user for data decryption.
3. Then the attacker steals the session token to authenticate user's account and execute data breach.

Usecases: Attackers alters the address secretly and user will send funds to the wrong address [19].

Requirements: 1. Attackers needs the strong knowledge on networking and cryptography to intercept or eavesdrop the keys between users.
   2. Attackers needs a team knowledgeable in wireshark for detecting weak or vulnerable networks.

Goal: The goal of the attacker is to intercept or eavesdrop keys in weak network to steal sensitive data from decentralized applications.

Benefits: Attacker can use the sensitive information from DApp data breach to blackmail normal user or employee from organization for money.

Attack Cost vs Benefits: Attacker needs a well experienced network engineer and good knowledgeable cryptographer for executing attack whereas benefits depend on the DApp and web security of that particular organization. If popular organization has low network properties in DApp then benefits will huge otherwise it will be low.

Damage Scenario: Leakage of sensitive communication between high profiles of that organization or financial information from DApp.

Damage Consequence: Organization will suffer financial loss and reputation loss which may result in shut down of particular organization.

Mitigation: If user realizes that someone is intercepting or eavesdropping their communication or stealing session key then drop the communication immediately and contact the organization or bank.

Mitigation cost vs Damage cost: In terms of communication eavesdropping of sensitive information, the damage rate will high because attacker already have that particular sensitive information. In terms of session key hijacking there is the chance of recovery if organization is contacted immediately after attack.

Recommendations: 1. Use HTTPs server in DApp or website server.
   2. Use end-to-end encryption for secure communication to avoid eavesdropping.
   3. Use multi factor authentication to avoid compromise of login credentials.

11 Insider Attack

An insider may be an employee or people within the organization who have inside information of organization's security and sensitive information. An insider is a malicious threat to a company or organization. As some of the hot wallets stores private key and seed files in the organization server, insider can steal the files from organization server and can take access of all the customer's account.

Usecases: Insiders can steal private keys of the users stored in the server of an online wallets [18].

Requirements: Attacker needs to be an employee or associate in an organization to execute attack from inside.

Goal: The Goal of the attacker is to steal organization's or customers sensitive information to use for its own benefits.

Benefits: By selling organization sensitive information to the rival company, insider will get huge amount of money from that information as well as insider can misuse customers information to gain more money.

Attack Cost vs Benefits: This attack contains big risk of getting caught as attacker is an associate there is more chance of getting caught due to less suspects. So attacker will try to most the information which will make the extreme profit for insider.

Damage Scenario: High sensitive information theft from organization and stealing of financial data of high level clients.

Damage Consequence: Organization and customers related to that organization suffers money loss and reputation loss, also results in shutting down of organization.

Recommendations: 1. Avoid storing customer's private key in organization server.

2. The organization should keep access control of their employees to avoid this attack.

References

1. Aitzhan, N.Z., Svetinovic, D.: Security and privacy in decentralized energy trading through multi-signatures, blockchain and anonymous messaging streams. IEEE Trans. Dependable Secure Comput. **15**(5), 840–852 (2016)
2. BTCManager: Crypto dusting attack sends illegally obtained bitcoin to random cryptocurrency wallets, January 2019. https://btcmanager.com/crypto-dusting-attack-sends-illegally-obtained-bitcoin-to-random-cryptocurrency-wallets/
3. CipherTrace: Alert: Crypto dusting is a new type of blockchain spam that corrodes reputations and impacts cryptocurrency AML, December 2018. https://ciphertrace.com/crypto_dusting/
4. CryptoVest: $4m iota stolen from wallets which used online seed generation websites, January 2018. https://cryptovest.com/news/4m-iota-stolen-from-wallets-which-used-online-seed-generation-websites/
5. Electrum: Password protect the JSONRPC interface, November 2017. https://github.com/spesmilo/electrum/issues/3374
6. F-Secure: Trojan:W32/Trickbot (2019). https://www.f-secure.com/v-descs/trojan_w32_trickbot.shtml
7. Forum, B.B.: All crypto assets stolen from Exodus, March 2018. https://bitcointalk.org/index.php?topic=3203818.0
8. Gavrichenkov, A.: Breaking HTTPS with BGP hijacking. In: Black Hat USA Briefings (2015)
9. GBHackers: Metamask - first copy-and-paste hijacking crypto malware found in Google Play, February 2019. https://gbhackers.com/clipper-hijacking-malware/
10. Grossman, J.: XSS Attacks: Cross-site Scripting Exploits and Defense. Syngress Media, Syngress (2007). https://books.google.co.in/books?id=dPhqDe0WHZ8C

11. Haacked: Anatomy of a subtle JSON vulnerability, November 2008. https://haacked.com/archive/2008/11/20/anatomy-of-a-subtle-json-vulnerability.aspx/
12. Holub, A., O'Connor, J.: COINHOARDER: tracking a Ukrainian bitcoin phishing ring DNS style. In: 2018 APWG Symposium on Electronic Crime Research (eCrime), pp. 1–5. IEEE (2018)
13. Li, X., Jiang, P., Chen, T., Luo, X., Wen, Q.: A survey on the security of blockchain systems. Fut. Gener. Computer Syst. (2017)
14. MalwareBytes: Trojan. TrickBot (2019). https://blog.malwarebytes.com/detections/trojan-trickbot/
15. McAfee: Cryptojacking. In: Blockchain Threat Report, August 2018. https://www.mcafee.com/enterprise/en-us/assets/reports/rp-blockchain-security-risks.pdf
16. MyEtherWallet: Official statement regarding dns spoofing of myetherwallet domain, April 2018. https://www.reddit.com/r/MyEtherWallet/comments/8eloo9/official_statement_regarding_dns_spoofing_of/
17. Naik, A.: Anatomy of a BGP hijack on amazon's route 53 DNS service, April 2018. https://blog.thousandeyes.com/amazon-route-53-dns-and-bgp-hijack/
18. News18: Bitcoins worth rs 19 crore stolen from india's coinsecure, company claims insider job, April 2018. https://www.news18.com/news/business/bitcoins-worth-rs-19-crore-stolen-from-indias-coinsecure-company-claims-insider-job-1717457.html
19. NewsBTC: Ethereum user reports loss of 7182 eth through mist wallet, May 2016. https://www.newsbtc.com/2016/05/13/ethereum-user-reports-loss-7182-eth-mist-wallet/
20. NewsBTC: New clipboard hijacker malware monitoring 2.3 million crypto addresses, July 2018. https://www.newsbtc.com/2018/07/02/new-clipboard-hijacker-malware-monitoring-2-3-million-crypto-addresses/
21. Noction: Bgp hijacking overview, April 2018. https://www.noction.com/blog/bgp-hijacking
22. Okta: 5 identity attacks that exploit your broken authentication (2018). https://www.okta.com/resources/whitepaper/5-identity-attacks-that-exploit-your-broken-authentication/
23. Project, T.O.W.A.S.: Cross-site request forgery (CSRF), June 2018. https://www.owasp.org/index.php/Cross-Site_Request_Forgery_(CSRF)
24. Ramzan, Z.: Phishing attacks and countermeasures. In: Stavroulakis, P., Stamp, M. (eds.) Handbook of Information and Communication Security. Springer, Heidelberg (2010). https://doi.org/10.1007/978-3-642-04117-4_23
25. ThreatPost: Trickbot malware goes after remote desktop credentials, February 2019. https://threatpost.com/trickbot-remote-desktop/141879/
26. Vice: Electrum bitcoin wallets were vulnerable to hackers for two years, January 2018. https://www.vice.com/en_us/article/ev55na/electrum-bitcoin-wallets-were-vulnerable-to-hackers-for-two-years-json-rpc

Libra Critique Towards Global Decentralized Financial System

Saqib Ali[1,2] (iD), Guojun Wang[1](✉)(iD), Bebo White[3](iD), and Komal Fatima[2](iD)

[1] School of Computer Science, Guangzhou University,
Guangzhou 510006, China
{saqibali,csgjwang}@gzhu.edu.cn
[2] Department of Computer Science, University of Agriculture,
Faisalabad 38000, Pakistan
{saqib,2014ag5719}@uaf.edu.pk
[3] Stanford Linear Accelerator Center,
P.O. Box 4349, Menlo Park, CA 94309, USA
bebo@slac.stanford.edu

Abstract. The advent of the Bitcoin blockchain as a peer-to-peer, open, and decentralized financial system has empowered millions of people globally to make transactions without any trusted third parties. This realization leads to the birth of more than 2300 cryptocurrencies in the last decade. Despite this evolvement, the Bitcoin and other cryptocurrencies are facing many challenges right now. Facebook's Libra is a new kind of cryptocurrency built on the foundation of blockchain technology conceived by Libra Association - twenty-eight high-profile governing members that will work together to create a more inclusive financial system using consortium blockchain technology. The goal of the Libra is to serve as a solid foundation for a highly scalable, frictionless, and traceable global financial systems with extremely high transactions rate. However, the proposed Libra cryptocurrency has yet to face many issues. In this paper, we critically analyzed the status of the Libra, its underlying concept, and the challenges faced by it once launched as a global decentralized financial system. Currently, the proposed Libra is very ambiguous with uncertain goals and intentions. In particular, we explored the placement technology of Libra, which is not very much well define in comparison with Bitcoin and other public blockchains which are fully decentralized, transparent, borderless and fully open for transparency. Also, we explore the security and privacy features of Libra concerning around three-billion user base of Facebook social media ecosystem (i.e., Messenger, WhatsApp, Instagram, and Facebook).

Keywords: Cryptocurrency · Blockchain · Libra · Facebook · Decentralized finance · Open finance

1 Introduction

Bitcoin is a popular and widely used cryptocurrency that has no central controlling authority. Bitcoin is also distributed, open, and peer-to-peer payment

© Springer Nature Singapore Pte Ltd. 2019
G. Wang et al. (Eds.): iSCI 2019, CCIS 1122, pp. 661–672, 2019.
https://doi.org/10.1007/978-981-15-1301-5_52

network that records all transactions with the use of blockchain technology [37]. The transaction logs are distributed across the peer-to-peer network which provide transparency and security [23]. Beside these magnetized features, Bitcoin is facing many issues in terms of scalability, limited programming ecosystems, identity management, usability, and interoperability [18]. Therefore, there is a need to keep developing emerging cryptocurrency technologies that can balance between centralized and distributed systems. Also, the question arises where we are and what is coming next in the billion-dollar economy as revolution [34].

Facebook is planning to launch a global financial system called Libra managed by a central Libra Association (twenty-eight high-profile governing members) and probably will launch in 2020 [4]. The basic concept of Libra is to empower the economy by providing billions of people a global cryptocurrency. In Libra framework, it is mentioned that it is scalable, fast, stable, secure, and accessible to everyone through smartphones. Libra is based on a decentralized blockchain system which is programmable and provides a high level of efficiency in exchanging currency worldwide. No matter what people do, how much money they earn and where they live, Libra aim is to move money around the world at a cheaper rate via text messages [31,32].

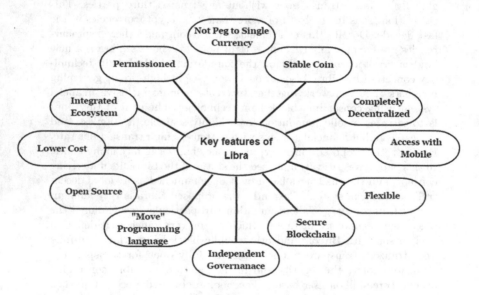

Fig. 1. Key features of Libra

In the white paper of Libra, it is clear that Libra framework is permissioned, decentralized, scalable, secure, open-source, and flexible [4]. Moreover, it is powered with blockchain technology, high-capacity storage system, high-transaction throughput, a powerful ecosystem of applications, single data structure, mixed network structure, and diverse governance with independent members [10]. There is no doubt Libra vision is very clear in terms of its key features as summarized in Fig. 1. However, these are only suggestions. Before its complete implementation, we cannot say that Libra will prove itself as a revolution in the global financial market. At present, it is struggling with its proposed technology. Not only Libra proposed framework have technical loopholes; also, it is not seeing accepted at world level. In particular, the world's finance ministers are very unsure because of its blurry proposal. Therefore, it is very hard to say that it will be the game-changer in the world financial system [16].

In this paper, we thoroughly analyze the key features of Libra and its strategic underlying technology, which are essential for its realization. Libra is planning to adopt a consortium blockchain infrastructure comprising of twenty-eight high-profile founding members named as Libra Association. It includes Facebook, VISA, MasterCard, PayPal, etc. However, there are many ambiguities in their governance and implementation strategies. Therefore, a critical comparison between Bitcoin and Libra is carried out to reveal the real imperfections of Libra financial system. It shows that the Libra and Bitcoin cryptocurrencies have some similarities, but their focus is quite different. We also figure out the technical issues related to governance, strategy, technology, and deployment of the Libra, which give a clear vision of its future perspective. This reveals the potentials of Libra to affect the global financial system of the world. Finally, we discuss the security and privacy aspects of the Libra concerning three-billion user base of Facebook social media ecosystem (i.e., Messenger, WhatsApp, Instagram, and Facebook).

The main contributions of this paper are summarized as follows.

- First of all, we summarized the key features of cryptocurrencies along with the vision of Libra and its key underlying blockchain technology.
- Secondly, we investigate the key differences between the Libra and Bitcoin blockchain technology.
- Thirdly, we analyze the technical issues in detail to show that what Libra is showing and how things are happening in the cryptocurrency industry.
- Finally, we demonstrate the global financial system perspective of Libra considering its security and privacy issues.

The remaining of the paper is organized as follows. Section 2 describes the related work. Section 3 summarized the key features of the cryptocurrencies. Section 4 gives a brief description of the vision and design philosophy of Libra. Section 5 depicts the comparative view of Libra and Bitcoin. Section 6 comprises of Libra critique towards global decentralized financial system. Finally, Sect. 7 concludes the paper.

2   Related Work

The blockchain - distributed ledger in a peer-to-peer network is definitely an innovative invention. In a blockchain, transaction records are grouped in the form of blocks and are linked and secured using a cryptographic function [25]. By design, blockchain is a simple and an easy way of managing transaction history in a peer-to-peer network without the need of the trusted third parties. Besides crypto finance, blockchain technology has vital applications in IoT, supply chain, governance, identity management, voting system, and health care industry [1, 40].

At first glance, understanding the blockchain architecture may seem complicated as it has cryptographically secured linked data record called blocks. A typical blockchain architecture has five components, i.e. transactions & blocks, cryptography, smart contracts, consensus algorithms, and peer-to-peer network. These five components are the essence of blockchain technology [36]. The transactions & block component hold the verified, ordered and grouped blocks of data records [2]. The cryptography component has an encrypted hash that provides the security and immutability to the linked blocks. The smart contracts are autonomous agents used to automate and track transactions in the network [14]. The consensus algorithm governs the blockchain and ensures that the same copy of the data is available to all the peers of a distributed environment. Finally, the peer-to-peer network provides the processing and storage capacity to the system [11].

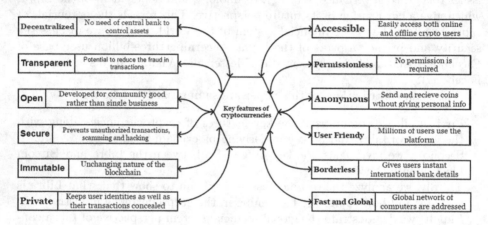

Fig. 2. Key features of cryptocurrencies

3   Key Feature of Cryptocurrencies

The most popular cryptocurrencies in circulation include Bitcoin, Ethereum, Ripple, Litecoin, Neo, etc. They share a common set of features with slightly different priorities which make them unique in the crypto industry. This contains decentralize, open, permissionless, interoperable, borderless, transparent, irreversible & immutable, fast, global, secure, private, ease of access, greater user freedom, and anonymous/pseudo-anonymous. These features are summarized in Fig. 2. Among these features, the most common and unique one is that these cryptocurrencies have no central authority to control and govern it i.e., by default they are decentralized in nature [8].

In regard to above-mentioned key features of the successful cryptocurrencies, recently announced Facebook Libra is lacking in many key features particularly regarding its governance framework [9]. Therefore, there is a need to understand the key differences between Libra and leading industry icons in the crypto market. It will help to conceive the vision, future and success of the Libra in the global financial system of the world.

4   Vision and Design Philosophy of Libra

The vision of Libra is to provide a stable, global, digitally native, reserve-backed cryptocurrency built on a secure network. The key features of Libra include permissioned blockchain protocols, decentralized in nature, secure & reliable transactions, and open-source platform. However, it will be governed by an independent organization called Libra Association - twenty-eight high-profile governing members like Facebook, VISA, Mastercard, PayPal, Stripe, etc. The aim of Libra is to provide low-cost money transactions, by adding value for money and having global access to everyone just with the help of smartphones [4].

4.1   Design Philosophy of Libra

The design philosophy of Libra is to provide a global financial ecosystem enabling billions of people to access monetary services at extremely low cost with high security, scalability, and reliability. Technically, the Libra ecosystem consists of Libra Blockchain, Move – a programming language, and LibraBFT - robust and efficient state machine replication system. Each of these components is explained as follows.

i. **Libra blockchain:** The Libra blockchain is decentralized, initially permissioned, and highly programmable database which is going to be designed, managed, and governed by a group of validators (set of Founding members). The blockchain provides a platform for secure and reliable transactions for billions of people using smart phones [39]. At present, the Libra blockchain is permissioned, however, the Libra's mission is to move towards a permissionless blockchain. However, the detailed migration mechanism is not clearly outlined by the association [29].

ii. **Move programming language:** Libra introduces an executable bytecode programming language to execute custom transactions and implement smart contracts. Also, it is used to create custom resources which can never be copied or implicitly discarded. Thus, making customer resources including Libra coin and smart contracts to transact only between the entities in a secure and a reliable manner [27].

iii. **LibraBFT protocol:** The heart of the Libra ecosystem is LibraBFT - a consensus protocol based on HotStaff which is a leader-based Byzantine fault-tolerant replication protocol [38]. The aim of the protocol is to provide low latency to billions of users in a global network of the nodes. Moreover, it keeps high reliability even with the small number of nodes in a distributed network. Initially, the protocol decentralized the trust only among the validators of the network to facilitate high transaction throughput suitable for a global financial system [20].

The initial deployment of Libra protocol can be examined at Libra Testnet [3].

Table 1. Comparison between Libra and Bitcoin blockchain

Features	Bitcoin	Libra
Technology	Bitcoin blockchain	Libra blockchain
Centralization	Decentralized	Not fully decentralized
Blockchain type	Permissionless	Permissioned
Consensus algorithm	Proof of Work	Proof of Stake
Programming language	Scripting language	Move
Smart contracts	Limited support	Full support
Trust	No trust issues	Yes it has trust issues
Coins	Limited	Unlimited
Wallet	No built-in wallet	Native wallet (Calibra)
Volatility	High	Low
Censorship resistance	Yes	No
Asset value	Not tied to any financial institutions	Tied to key financial institutions

5   Comparison: Libra vs Bitcoin Blockchain

Bitcoin is a pioneer cryptocurrency. Thus, majority of the existing cryptocurrencies are based on it [34]. Facebook's Libra is also a cryptocurrency however, both of them differ in many ways. From a technology perspective, the Bitcoin blockchain is completely decentralized and permissionless. It has a vast number of nodes in the world operating without any central authority. On the other hand, Libra is a permissioned blockchain which is managed and governed by a central authority known as Libra Association [30, 35]. In terms of volatility, Bitcoin value fluctuates quite frequently against fiat currencies. This is because it does not tie to any financial institution of the world. Thus, geopolitical events and the statements issued by governments' agencies about its regulation policy have a direct effect on the value of the Bitcoin [12]. In contrast, Libra is tied to the strategic monetary institutions of the world which make it a stable currency in the future. Similarly, Bitcoin does not have a native wallet application whereas Facebook proposed a Calibra - a wallet for Libra ecosystem accessible via WhatsApp and Messenger. Other key differences between Libra and Bitcoin blockchain are summarized in Table 1.

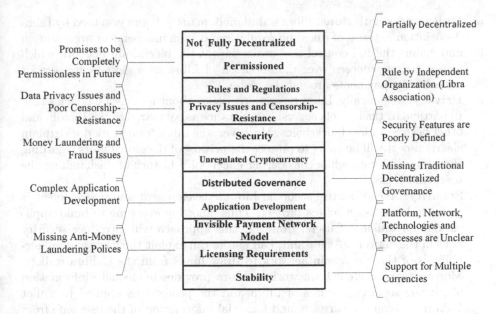

Fig. 3. Technical issues of Libra

6   Libra Critique Towards Global Decentralized Financial System

Libra aims to reinvent money by providing a global currency and a financial ecosystem which is cheap, fast, secure, scalable, and reliable and can empower billions of people using smartphones. This extraordinary aim raises many technical and global issues for the proposed open decentralized financial system of the Libra blockchain [24]. Therefore, in this section, we critically discussed and analyzed these issues in terms of a technical issues and global perspective of a decentralized financial system.

6.1   Technical Issues

The list of technical issues of Libra are summarized in Fig. 3.

i. **Decentralized:** In contrast to Bitcoin blockchain, Libra is not fully decentralized. It is designed, managed, and governed by the group of validators (founding members of Libra), thus raises serious concerns over the full control or ownership of the financial network when it already has 2.7 billion users worldwide [17].

ii. **Permissioned:** Libra is going to be a permissioned blockchain i.e., not fully open like Bitcoin and Ethereum. It means that ledger updates are only managed and govern by pre-approved member organizations (Libra Association) which may discriminate against participants based on the circulation of the funds [19].

iii. **Rules and regulations:** Libra is designed, managed, and governed by Libra Association in terms of rules and regulation. It is an independent organization and claims the full control and ownership of the blockchain network which causes serious concern over the adoption of Libra as a global currency for cross-border payments around the globe [22].

iv. **Privacy:** Technically, Libra has serious issues about its privacy policies [24]. In particular, the lack of censorship-resistance as compared to the Bitcoin and other permissionless blockchains. Moreover, the Libra framework does explain clearly how it will be going to protect the privacy of the global users regarding their financial data while considering Facebook's history of mishandling the users' data. [28].

v. **Security:** According to Facebook, Libra's development and management is going to be an open-source project. Thus, allowing everyone to build applications for billions of users. However, this approach will introduce security risks in the network. As a result, bad actors can exploit the flaws and vulnerabilities of the blockchain network to draw funds from the Calibra wallets. Moreover, the current framework of Libra provides inadequate information about the security features of Libra and the protections applied to wallet Calibra to keep the currency and financial information of the user safe from the hackers [28].

vi. **Unregulated cryptocurrency & Invisible payments:** Like other cryptocurrencies, Libra is also an unregulated and untested digital currency. Thus, possess a risk of destabilizing the international financial system. Moreover, Libra does not provide any rules and regulations to curb illegal activities like invisible payments, money laundering, ransomware payments, and terrorist financing [5, 15, 19].

vii. **Distributed governance:** Many critiques believe that Libra is not based on a real blockchain as it is dropping the key principle of the technology i.e., distributed governance, which is a vital part of the most of the public blockchains. As a result, it is more likely a distributed database with a single data structure managed by an organization [28].

viii. **Libra App development:** Since the release of the Libra code and Testnet available on GitHub, blockchain developers around the world are making progress to develop actual products over the network. The development includes the design of anti-money laundering solutions, quick translation of stable fiat currencies & other financial assets into Libra coins, and secure wallets that can hold the cryptocurrency safely. However, these developments are facing key technical challenges regarding the diverse rules and regulations of the international financial system [7].

ix. **Licensing requirements:** One of the key objectives of the Libra is to empower around 1.7 billion unbanked people leaving in the developing countries of the world. However, Facebook underwent temporary bans in such countries during recent years. Moreover, in many parts of the world, the financial regulatory authorities are hostile towards the use of cryptocurrencies. Therefore, it is quite challenging for Facebook to achieve its objectives in the global market. Moreover, it needs to develop a strategy to comply with the multiple licensing requirements i.e., Know Your Customer (KYC), Anti-Fraud (AF), Anti-Money Laundering (AML), and many others for every country of its destination [28].

x. **Stability:** Libra is seeming to be more stable coin than many other cryptocurrencies like Bitcoin or Ethereum which are highly volatile in the market. This is because its value is pegged to several fiat currencies and other real assets of the existing financial system [21]. However, the current documentation of Libra does not mention the mechanism to resolve the exchange rates between Libra coin and other fiat currencies of the world.

It is very important to embrace new technologies and emerging cryptocurrencies. However, their acceptance in the global market requires a lot of regulations and stabilities. Therefore, Libra ecosystem needs to adhere to the key technical and regulatory frameworks of the current financial systems to work even better as an open decentralized global financial system.

6.2 Global Perspective

Besides above-mentioned technical issues, Libra is facing many political issues around the world [13,26]. These issues highlight the major concerns of the countries regarding the implementation of the Libra cryptocurrency. On the top is Facebook's worst reputation for privacy (like recent privacy scandal that involved data harvesting of over 50 million Facebook profiles i.e., Cambridge Analytica). Therefore, US Congress, House of Financial Services Committee, Senate Banking Committee, and other Federal financial institutions are examining the Libra project in terms of user data privacy and its potential financial risks to the international monetary system of the world [6,33].

7 Conclusion

In this paper, we analyze the key features of successful cryptocurrencies along with Libra to give a clear picture concerning the vision and goals of the Libra Association towards a global decentralized financial system. The critical comparison between Bitcoin and Libra leads towards their key differences in terms of governance, technology, and deployment policy. We summarized the technical perspective of Libra as a decentralized financial institution for global transaction system and conclude that it is pretty different from the Bitcoin. At present, Libra is a consortium blockchain comprising of twenty-eight validating partners, which will increase to a hundred with an equal share of voting rights (i.e., 1%). Libra's governance strategy and deployment technology are ambiguous. As a result, it is facing criticism from cryptocurrency developers and investors, opposition from central financial authorities, and concerns of governments. Moreover, it does not highlight the security and privacy-preserving mechanism of the transaction history of the Libra account holders.

Acknowledgments. This work was supported in part by the National Natural Science Foundation of China under Grant 61632009, in part by the Guangdong Provincial Natural Science Foundation under Grant 2017A030308006, and in part by the High-Level Talents Program of Higher Education in Guangdong Province under Grant 2016ZJ01.

References

1. Ali, S., Wang, G., Bhuiyan, M.Z.A., Jiang, H.: Secure data provenance in cloud-centric internet of things via blockchain smart contracts. In: 2018 IEEE SmartWorld, Ubiquitous Intelligence Computing, Advanced Trusted Computing, Scalable Computing Communications, Cloud Big Data Computing, Internet of People and Smart City Innovation (SmartWorld/SCALCOM/UIC/ATC/CBDCom/IOP/SCI), Guangzhou, China, pp. 991–998, October 2018. https://doi.org/10.1109/SmartWorld.2018.00175
2. Ali, S., Wang, G., White, B., Cottrell, R.L.: A blockchain-based decentralized data storage and access framework for PingER. In: 2018 17th IEEE International Conference on Trust, Security and Privacy in Computing and Communications/12th IEEE International Conference on Big Data Science and Engineering (TrustCom/BigDataSE), Guangzhou, China, pp. 1303–1308, August 2018. https://doi.org/10.1109/TrustCom/BigDataSE.2018.00179
3. L'Association: Libra Testnet (2019). https://libra.org/en-US/white-paper/#the-libra-blockchain. Accessed August 2019
4. L'Association: Libra white paper (2019). https://libra.org/en-US/white-paper/
5. Baraniuk, C.: Libra: Could Facebooks new currency be stopped in its tracks? (2019). https://www.bbc.com/news/business-49090753. Accessed August 2019
6. Bartz, D.: U.S. lawmakers take jabs at Amazon, big tech in antitrust hearing (2019). https://www.reuters.com/article/us-congress-tech-antitrust/u-s-lawmakers-take-jabs-at-amazon-big-tech-in-antitrust-hearing-idUSKCN1UB108. Accessed August 2019
7. Castillo, M.: Facebook Libra app development already exploding despite lawmakers concerns (2019). https://www.forbes.com/sites/michaeldelcastillo/2019/07/18/facebook-libra-app-development-already-exploding-despite-lawmakers-concerns/#4c587e32776c. Accessed August 2019
8. Chen, X., et al.: Characteristics of bitcoin transactions on cryptomarkets. In: Wang, G., Feng, J., Bhuiyan, M.Z.A., Lu, R. (eds.) SpaCCS 2019. LNCS, vol. 11611, pp. 261–276. Springer, Cham (2019). https://doi.org/10.1007/978-3-030-24907-6_20
9. Crypto Confidential: Coinmarketcaps fake data; problem Facebooks Libra scams (2019). https://www.forbes.com/sites/cryptoconfidential/2019/07/27/coinmarketcaps-fake-data-problem-facebooks-libra-scams/#7ed7a1bb1e9e. Accessed August 2019
10. Cottis, P.: Facebook coin good news or bad news ? (2019). https://medium.com/swlh/facebook-coin-good-news-or-bad-news-6137745a591e. Accessed August 2019
11. Dinh, T.T.A., Liu, R., Zhang, M., Chen, G., Ooi, B.C., Wang, J.: Untangling blockchain: a data processing view of blockchain systems. IEEE Trans. Knowl. Data Eng. **30**(7), 1366–1385 (2018). https://doi.org/10.1109/TKDE.2017.2781227
12. Dwyer, G.P.: The economics of bitcoin and similar private digital currencies. J. Financ. Stab. **17**, 81–91 (2015). https://doi.org/10.1016/j.jfs.2014.11.006

13. Fanusie, Y.: Will crypto rogues threaten the geopolitical order? (2019). https://www.forbes.com/sites/yayafanusie/2019/07/23/will-crypto-rogues-threaten-the-geopolitical-order/#6ae9f4354155. Accessed August 2019

14. Fotiou, N., Siris, V.A., Polyzos, G.C.: Interacting with the internet of things using smart contracts and blockchain technologies. In: Wang, G., Chen, J., Yang, L.T. (eds.) SpaCCS 2018. LNCS, vol. 11342, pp. 443–452. Springer, Cham (2018). https://doi.org/10.1007/978-3-030-05345-1_38

15. Harper, J.: Facebooḱs libra puts unregulated cryptocurrencies into focus (2019). https://www.dw.com/en/facebooks-libra-puts-unregulated-cryptocurrencies-into-focus/a-49647123. Accessed August 2019

16. Hussain, Z.: Facebooḱs Libra is not a real cryptocurrency (2019). https://medium.com/swlh/facebooks-libra-is-not-a-real-cryptocurrency-a622b8f3567b. Accessed August 2019

17. Khalid, A.: Facebooḱs Libra in regulatory chains - decentralize or control for acceptance (2019). https://blockpublisher.com/facebooks-libra-in-regulatory-chains-decentralize-or-control-for-acceptance/. Accessed August 2019

18. Kus Khalilov, M.C., Levi, A.: A survey on anonymity and privacy in bitcoin-like digital cash systems. IEEE Commun. Surv. Tutor. **20**(3), 2543–2585 (2018). https://doi.org/10.1109/COMST.2018.2818623

19. Lee, T.B.: Thereś a big problem with Facebooḱs Libra cryptocurrency (2019). https://arstechnica.com/tech-policy/2019/07/facebooks-half-baked-cryptocurrency-libra-explained/. Accessed August 2019

20. Mathieu, B., Avery, C., Alberto, S.: State machine replication in the Libra blockchain, pp. 1–44, August 2019. https://developers.libra.org/docs/state-machine-replication-paper

21. Mauldin, J.: Libra is nothing more than a nice idea (2019). https://www.forbes.com/sites/johnmauldin/2019/08/05/libra-is-nothing-more-than-a-nice-idea/#467e8cf95a9a. Accessed August 2019

22. Maurer, B., Ticsher, D.: Facebooḱs Libra itś not the crypto thatś the issue, itś the organisation behind it (2019). https://theconversation.com/facebooks-libra-its-not-the-crypto-thats-the-issue-its-the-organisation-behind-it-121223. Accessed August 2019

23. Nakamoto, S., et al.: Bitcoin: a peer-to-peer electronic cash system (2008)

24. Paul, K.: Breathtaking arrogance: senators grill Facebook in combative hearing over Libra currency (2019). https://www.theguardian.com/technology/2019/jul/15/big-tech-behemoths-face-grilling-from-us-lawmakers-as-hearings-kick-off. Accessed August 2019

25. Pierro, M.D.: What is the blockchain? Comput. Sci. Eng. **19**(5), 92–95 (2017). https://doi.org/10.1109/MCSE.2017.3421554

26. Ravi, R.D.: Analyst: Walmartś cryptocurrency may create less political cryptocurrency prices friction than Facebook Libra a cryptocurrency similar to rechargeable gift cards. https://all-stocks.net/analyst-walmarts-cryptocurrency-may-create-less-political-friction-than-facebook-libra/. Accessed August 2019

27. Sam, B., Evan, C., Runtian, Z.: Move: a language with programmable resources, pp. 1–26, July 2019. https://developers.libra.org/docs/move-paper

28. Shawdagor, J.: Top-6 issues experts/entities have with Libra (2019). https://cointelegraph.com/news/top-6-issues-experts-entities-have-with-libra. Accessed August 2019

29. Shehar, B., Christian, C., Nils, W.: Moving toward permissionless consensus, pp. 1–4, August 2019. https://libra.org/en-US/permissionless-blockchain

30. Sontakke, M.: Walmart coin: A bigger deal than FBś Libra and Bitcoin? (2019). https://marketrealist.com/2019/08/walmart-coin-bigger-than-libra/.   Accessed August 2019
31. Taskinsoy, J.: Facebook's project Libra: Will Libra sputter out or spur central banks to introduce their own unique cryptocurrency projects? Available at SSRN 3423453 (2019). https://doi.org/10.2139/ssrn.3423453
32. Taskinsoy, J.: This time is different: Facebookś Libra can improve both financial inclusion and global financial stability as a viable alternative currency to the U.S. Dollar. Available at SSRN 3434493 (2019). https://doi.org/10.2139/ssrn.3434493
33. Telford, T.: Why governments around the world are afraid of Libra, Facebookś cryptocurrency   (2019).   https://www.washingtonpost.com/business/2019/07/12/why-governments-around-world-are-afraid-libra-facebooks-cryptocurrency/?noredirect=on. Accessed August 2019
34. Tschorsch, F., Scheuermann, B.: Bitcoin and beyond: a technical survey on decentralized digital currencies. IEEE Commun. Surv. Tutor. **18**(3), 2084–2123 (2016). https://doi.org/10.1109/COMST.2016.2535718
35. Underwood, S.: Blockchain beyond bitcoin. Commun. ACM **59**(11), 15–17 (2016). https://doi.org/10.1145/2994581
36. Vukolić, M.: Rethinking permissioned blockchains. In: Proceedings of the ACM Workshop on Blockchain, Cryptocurrencies and Contracts, BCC 2017, pp. 3–7. ACM, New York (2017). https://doi.org/10.1145/3055518.3055526
37. Yang, R., Yu, F.R., Si, P., Yang, Z., Zhang, Y.: Integrated blockchain and edge computing systems: a survey, some research issues and challenges. IEEE Commun. Surv. Tutor. **21**(2), 1508–1532 (2019). https://doi.org/10.1109/COMST.2019.2894727
38. Yin, M., Malkhi, D., Reiter, M.K., Gueta, G.G., Abraham, I.: HotStuff: BFT consensus with linearity and responsiveness. In: Proceedings of the 2019 ACM Symposium on Principles of Distributed Computing, PODC 2019, pp. 347–356. ACM, New York (2019). https://doi.org/10.1145/3293611.3331591
39. Zachary, A., Ramnik, A., Runtian, Z.: The Libra Blockchain, July 2019. https://developers.libra.org/docs/the-libra-blockchain-paper
40. Ølnes, S., Ubacht, J., Janssen, M.: Blockchain in government: benefits and implications of distributed ledger technology for information sharing. Gov. Inf. Q. **34**(3), 355–364 (2017). https://doi.org/10.1016/j.giq.2017.09.007. http://www.sciencedirect.com/science/article/pii/S0740624X17303155

Author Index

Printed in the United States
By Bookmasters